# ENVIRON

*Cases and Materials*

**REVISED THIRD EDITION**

**Philip Weinberg**

**University Press of America,® Inc.**
**Lanham · Boulder · New York · Toronto · Oxford**

4501 Forbes Boulevard
Suite 200
Lanham, Maryland 20706
UPA Acquisitions Department (301) 459-3366

PO Box 317
Oxford
OX2 9RU, UK


Printed in the United States of America
British Library Cataloging in Publication Information Available

Library of Congress Control Number: 2005932226
ISBN 0-7618-3294-7 (paperback : alk. ppr.)

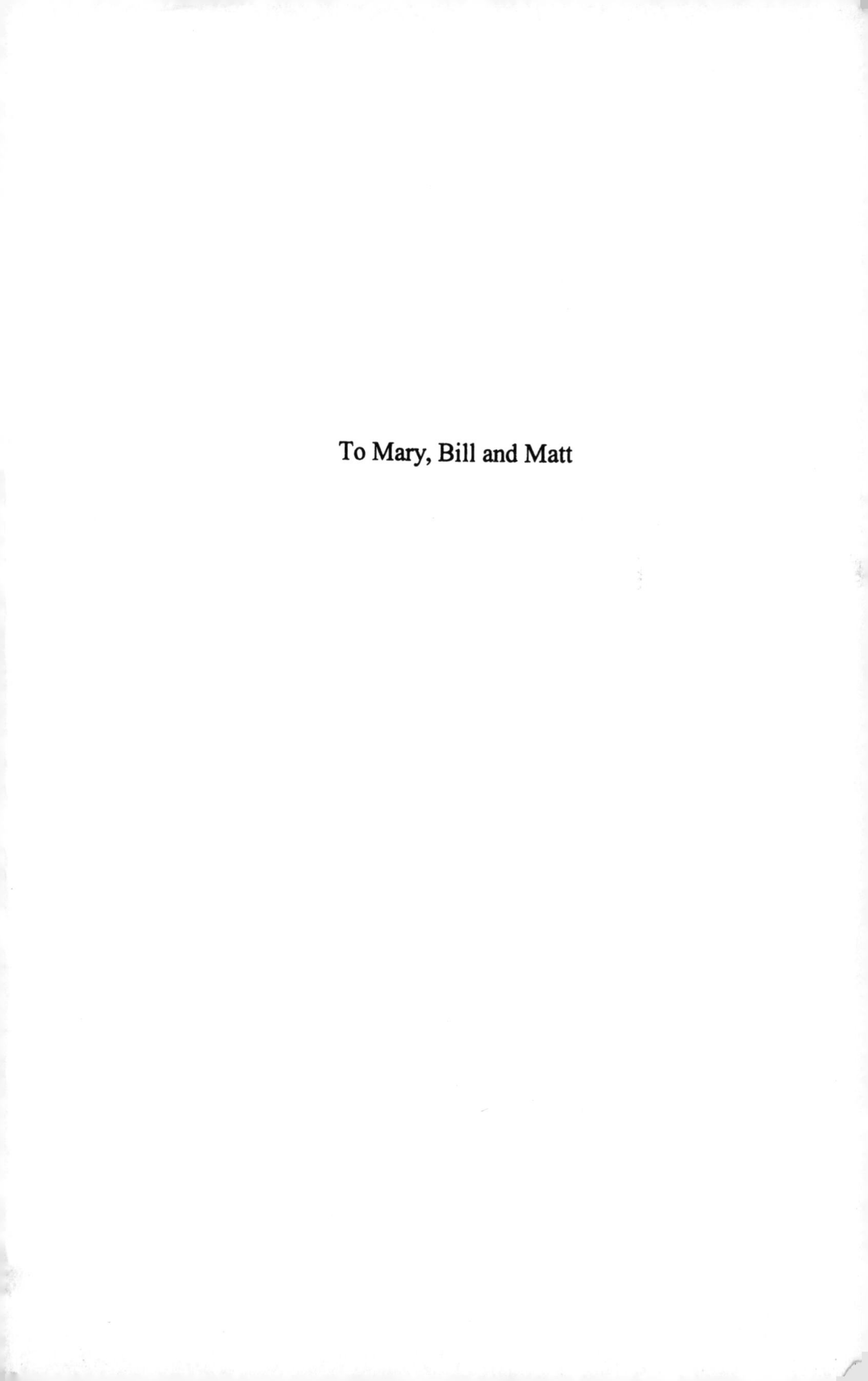

To Mary, Bill and Matt

SUMMARY OF CONTENTS

# DETAILED TABLE OF CONTENTS

ACKNOWLEDGEMENTS

I acknowledge the courtesy of the following authors and publishers for allowing me to reprint with permission excerpts from their materials:

William H. Rodgers, Jr., Environmental Law (West Publishing Co.).

The Public Trust in Tidal Areas: A Sometimes Submerged Legal Doctrine, The Yale Law Journal and Fred B. Rothman & Co., 79 Yale Law Journal 762.

Philip Weinberg, Coastal Area Legislation, 6 Seton Hall Legis. Journal 317 (1983).

Paul S. Weiland, Amending the National Environmental Policy Act: Federal Environmental Protection in the 21st. Century, 12 Fla. State J. of Land Use and Environmental Law 275.

Philip Weinberg, Power Plant Siting in New York: High Tension Issue, 25 N.Y. Law School Law Review 569.

Edith Brown Weiss, International Environmental Law: Contemporary Issues and the Emergence of a New World Order, 81 Geo.L.J. 675.

Geoffrey Palmer, New Ways to Make International Environmental Law, 86 Am.J. International L. 259.

Philippe Sands, The "Greening" of International Law: Emerging Principles and Rules, 1 Ind.J.Global Legal Stud. 293.

June Starr and Kenneth C. Hardy, Not by Seeds Alone: The Biodiversity Treaty and the Role for Native Agriculture, 12 Stan.Envtl.L.J. 85.

Daniel B. Botkin, Global Warming: What It Is, What Is Controversial About It, and What We Might Do In Response To It, 9 U.C.L.A. J. of Envtl. L. & Policy 119.

David D. Caron, Protecton of the Stratospheric Ozone Layer and the Structure of International Environmental Law Making, 14 Hastings Int'l and Comp. L. Rev. 755.

# Introduction to Third Revised Edition

This environmental law casebook is designed to reflect the vital and symbiotic connection between land-use regulation and the more traditional scope of environmental law. In addition it recognizes the importance of administrative agency decision-making in environmental law.

The book therefore commences with a look at judicial review of agency decisions and important issues such as standing. It then examines the common-law remedy of nuisance, the matrix of so much of environmental law and still a significant cause of action, and goes on to look at land-use controls, with particular emphasis on critical areas--landmarks, wetlands, coastal resources--and the de facto taking issue, before turning to air and water quality, waste, toxics and the other areas of comprehensive statutory control. It ends by examining the National Environmental Policy Act, electric generation, and the increasingly important area of international environmental law.

Since the Third Edition was published three years ago, much has occurred in this fast-shifting field. Several important decisions have dealt with takings and air and water quality, and international issues like global warming have expanded. The Third Revised Edition reflects these recent events.

The author gratefully acknowledges the diligent and patient assistance of Rose Di Martino (St. John's 1982), Susan Schneider (St. John's 1981), Marie Corrado (St. John's 1982), and Charles Ordine (St. John's 1982), in the preparation of this volume; and Heidi Luna (St. John's 1999) in helping with the Second, Darren Mogil (St. John's 2001) with the Third, and Alissa Picardi (St. John's 2006) with the Third Revised Edition.

Philip Weinberg
Professor of Law

St. John's University School of Law
Jamaica, New York 11439
November 2004

# 1. THE ENVIRONMENT AND THE COURTS

## A. THE SCOPE OF JUDICIAL POWER

### Introductory Note

Environmental law has its origin in the law of nuisance, riparian rights and other common law remedies enforceable in the courts like any other action. The increasing public awareness of the need to protect the earth's limited resources led to the enactment of laws to require permits to discharge pollutants into the air, water and land, such as the Clean Air Act and Clean Water Act and their state counterparts. In addition, the enactment in 1969 of the National Environmental Policy Act (NEPA), described in Chapter 10, requires all federal government agencies to consider environmental concerns before acting (or permitting or funding action by others).

At the same time the existing statutes requiring permits or other administrative approval for highways, power plants and other activities with impact on the environment began in the 1960s, as a result of augmented environmental concern, to be interpreted by the courts so as to reflect that concern. The "hard look" given administrative decisions since the *Overton Park* case and the *Scenic Hudson* decision requiring the Federal Power Commission to weigh environmental considerations furnish two vivid examples of this judicial renaissance which led to environmental law as a separate field of interest.

CITIZENS TO PRESERVE OVERTON PARK v. VOLPE, Supreme Court of the United States, 1971. 401 U.S. 402, 91 S.Ct. 814, 28 L.Ed.2d 136.

Marshall, J.: We are concerned in this case with Section 4(f) of the Department of Transportation Act of 1966, as amended, and § 18(a) of the Federal-Aid Highway Act of 1968, 23 USC § 138, which prohibit the Secretary of Transportation from authorizing the use of federal funds to finance the construction of highways through public parks if a "feasible and prudent" alternative route exists. If no such route is available, the statutes allow him to approve construction through parks only if there has been "all possible planning to minimize harm" to the park.

Petitioners, private citizens as well as local and national conservation organizations, contend that the Secretary has violated these statutes by authorizing the expenditure of federal funds for the construction of a six-lane interstate highway through a public park in Memphis, Tennessee. Their claim was rejected by the District Court, which granted the Secretary's motion for summary judgment, and the Court of Appeals for the Sixth Circuit affirmed.* * *

We now reverse the judgment below and remand for further proceedings in the District Court.

Overton Park is a 342-acre city park located near the center of Memphis. The park contains a zoo, a nine-hole municipal golf course, and outdoor theater, nature trails, a bridle path, an art academy, picnic areas, and 170 acres of forest. The proposed highway, which is to be a six-lane, high-speed, expressway, will [isolate] the zoo from the rest of the park. Although the roadway will be depressed below ground level except where it crosses a small creek, 26 acres of the park will be destroyed. The highway is to be a segment of Interstate Highway I-40, part of the National System. [It] will allow easier access to downtown Memphis from the residential areas on the eastern edge of the city.

Although the route through the park was approved by the Bureau of Public Roads in 1956 and by the Federal Highway Administrator in 1966, the enactment of § 4(f) of the Department of Transportation Act prevented distribution of federal funds for the section of the highway designated to go through Overton Park until the Secretary of Transportation determined whether the requirements of § 4(f) had been met.* * * In April 1968, the Secretary announced that he concurred in the judgment of local officials that I-40 should be built through the park.* * *

Neither announcement approving the route and design of I-40 was accompanied by a statement of the Secretary's factual findings. He did not indicate why he believed there were no feasible and prudent alternative routes or why design changes could not be made to reduce the harm to the park.

Petitioners contend that the Secretary's action is invalid without such formal findings and that the Secretary did not make an independent determination but merely relied on the judgment of the Memphis City Council. They also contend that it would be "feasible and prudent" to route I-40 around Overton Park either to the north or to the south.* * * Respondents argue that it was unnecessary for the Secretary to make formal findings, and that he did, in fact, exercise his own independent judgment which was supported by the facts. In the District Court, respondents introduced affidavits, prepared specifically for this litigation, which indicated that the Secretary had made the decision and that the decision was supportable. These affidavits were contradicted by affidavits introduced by petitioners, who also sought to take the deposition of a former Federal Highway Administrator who had participated in the decision to route I-40 through Overton Park.

The District Court and the Court of Appeals found that formal findings by the Secretary were not necessary and refused to order the deposition of the former Federal Highway Administrator because those courts believed that probing of the mental processes of an administrative decisionmaker was prohibited. And, believing that the Secretary's authority was wide and reviewing courts' authority narrow in the approval of highway routes, the lower courts held that the affidavits contained no basis for a determination that the Secretary had exceeded his authority.

We agree that formal findings were not required. But we do not believe that in this case judicial review based solely on litigation affidavits was adequate.* * *

A threshold question,whether petitioners are entitled to any judicial review,is easily answered. Section 701 of the Administrative Procedure Act, 5 USC § 701

(1964 ed, Supp V), provides that the action of "each authority of the Government of the United States," which includes the Department of Transportation, is subject to judicial review except where there is a statutory prohibition on review or where "agency action is committed to agency discretion by law." In this case, there is no indication that Congress sought to prohibit judicial review and there is most certainly no "showing of 'clear and convincing evidence' of a . . . legislative intent" to restrict access to judicial review.

Similarly, the Secretary's decision here does not fall within the exception for action "committed to agency discretion." This is a very narrow exception.* * * The legislative history of the Administrative Procedure Act indicates that it is applicable in those rare instances where "statutes are drawn in such broad terms that in a given case there is no law to apply."* * *

Section 4(f) of the Department of Transportation Act and § 138 of the Federal-Aid Highway Act are clear and specific directives. Both provide that the Secretary "shall not approve any program or project" that requires the use of any public parkland "unless (1) there is no feasible and prudent alternative to the use of such land, and (2) such program includes all possible planning to minimize harm to such park * * *." This language is a plain and explicit bar to the use of federal funds for construction of highways through parks,only the most unusual situations are exempted.

Despite the clarity of the statutory language, respondents argue that the Secretary has wide discretion. They recognize that the requirement that there be no "feasible" alternative route admits of little administrative discretion. For this exemption to apply the Secretary must find that as a matter of sound engineering it would not be feasible to build the highway along any other route. Respondents argue, however, that the requirement that there be no other "prudent" route requires the Secretary to engage in a wide-ranging balancing of competing interests. They contend that the Secretary should weigh the detriment resulting from the destruction of parkland against the cost of other routes, safety considerations, and other factors, and determine on the basis of the importance that he attaches to these other factors whether, on balance, alternative feasible routes would be "prudent."

But no such wide-ranging endeavor was intended. It is obvious that in most cases considerations of cost, directness of route, and community disruption will indicate that parkland should be used for highway construction whenever possible.

[T]here will always be a smaller outlay required from the public purse when parkland is used since the public already owns the land and there will be no need to pay for right-of-way. And since people do not live or work in parks, if a highway is built on parkland no one will have to leave his home or give up his business. Such factors are common to substantially all highway construction. Thus, if Congress intended these factors to be on an equal footing with preservation of parkland there would have been no need for the statutes.

Congress clearly did not intend that cost and disruption of the community were to be ignored by the Secretary. But the very existence of the statutes indicates that protection of parkland was to be given paramount importance. The few green havens that are public parks were not to be lost unless there were truly unusual factors present[.] If the statutes are to have any meaning, the Secretary cannot approve the destruction of parkland unless he finds that alternative routes present unique problems.* * *

Plainly, there is "law to apply" and thus the exemption for action "committed to agency discretion" is inapplicable. But the existence of judicial review is only the start: the standard for review must also be determined. For that we must look to § 706 of the Administrative Procedure Act, which provides that a "reviewing court shall . . . hold unlawful and set aside agency action, [if] arbitrary, capricious, an abuse of discretion, or otherwise not in accordance with law" or if the action failed to meet statutory, procedural, or constitutional requirements.* * * In certain narrow, specifically limited situations, the agency action is to be set aside if the action was not supported by "substantial evidence." And in other equally narrow circumstances the reviewing court is to engage in a de novo review of the action and set it aside if it was "unwarranted by the facts."* * *

Petitioners argue that the Secretary's approval of the construction of I-40 through Overton Park is subject to one or the other of these latter two standards of limited applicability. First, they contend that the "substantial evidence" standard of § 706(2)(E) must be applied. In the alternative, they claim that § 706(2)(F) applies and that there must be a de novo review to determine if the Secretary's action was "unwarranted by the facts." Neither of these standards is, however, applicable.

Review under the substantial-evidence test is authorized only when the agency action is taken pursuant to a rulemaking provision of the Administrative Procedure Act itself, 5 USC § 553, or when the agency action is based on a public adjudicatory hearing. See 5 USC §§ 556, 557. The Secretary's decision to allow the expenditure of federal funds to build I-40 through Overton Park was plainly not an exercise of a rule-making function.* * * And the only hearing [required,] a public hearing conducted by local officials for the purpose of informing the community about the proposed project and eliciting community views on the design and route * * * is nonadjudicatory, quasi-legislative in nature. It is not designed to produce a record that is to be the basis of agency action,the basic requirement for substantial-evidence review.* * *

Even though * * * the Secretary's approval of the route of I-40 does not have ultimately to meet the substantial-evidence test, the generally applicable standards of § 706 require the reviewing court to engage in a substantial inquiry. Certainly, the Secretary's decision is entitled to a presumption of regularity. But that presumption is not to shield his action from a thorough, probing, in-depth review.

The court is first required to decide whether the Secretary acted within the scope of his authority. [However,] scrutiny of the facts does not end [there]. Section 706(2(A) requires a finding that the actual choice made was not "arbitrary, capricious, an abuse of discretion, or otherwise not in accordance with law." 5 USC § 706(2)(A). To make this finding the court must consider whether the decision was based on a consideration of the relevant factors and whether there has been a clear error of judgment.* * * Although this inquiry into the facts is to be searching and careful, the ultimate standard of review is a narrow one. The court is not empowered to substitute its judgment for that of the agency.

The final inquiry is whether the Secretary's action followed the necessary procedural requirements. Here the only procedural error alleged is the failure of the Secretary to make formal findings and state his reason for allowing the highway to be built through the park.

Undoubtedly, review of the Secretary's action is hampered by his failure to make such findings, but the absence of formal findings does not necessarily require that the case be remanded to the Secretary. Neither the Department of Transportation Act nor the Federal-Aid Highway Act requires such formal findings. Moreover, the Administrative Procedure Act requirements that there be formal findings in certain rule-making and adjudicatory proceedings do not apply here.* * *

Petitioners contend that although there may not be a statutory requirement that the Secretary make formal findings and even though this may not be a case for the reviewing court to impose a requirement that findings be made, Department of Transportation regulations require them. This argument is based on DOT Order 5610.1, which requires the Secretary to make formal findings when he approves the use of parkland for highway construction but which was issued after the route for I-40 was approved. Petitioners argue that even though the order was not in effect at the time approval was given * * * and even though the order was not intended to have retrospective effect the order represents the law at the time of this court's decision and should be applied to this case. [T]he general rule is "that an appellate court must apply the law in effect at the time it renders its decision."* * * While we do not question that DOT Order 5610.1 constitutes the law in effect at the time of our decision, we do not believe that [the general rule] compels us to remand for the Secretary to make formal findings. Here, there has been a change in circumstances,[right-of-way] has been purchased by the State. Moreover, there is an administrative record that allows the full, prompt review of the Secretary's action that is sought without additional delay which would result from having a remand to the Secretary.

That administrative record is not, however, before us. The lower courts based their review on the litigation affidavits that were presented. These affidavits were merely "post hoc" rationalizations, * * * which have traditionally been found to be an inadequate basis for review.* * * And they clearly do not constitute the "whole record" compiled by the agency: the basis for review required by § 706 of the Administrative Procedure Act.* * * Thus it is necessary to remand this case to the District Court for plenary review of the Secretary's decision. That review is to be based on the full administrative record that was before the Secretary at the time he made his decision. But since the bare record may not disclose the factors that were considered or the Secretary's construction of the evidence [t]he court may require the administrative officials who participated in the decision to give testimony explaining their action. Of course, such inquiry into the mental processes of administrative decision-makers is usually to be avoided. United States v. Morgan,

313 US 409, 422, 85 L.Ed. 1429, 1435, 61 S. Ct. 999 (1941). And where there are administrative findings that were made at the same time as the decision, as was the case in Morgan, there must be a strong showing of bad faith or improper behavior before such inquiry may be made. But here there are no such formal findings and it may be that the only way there can be effective judicial review is by examining the decision-makers themselves.

The District Court is not, however, required to make such an inquiry. It may be that the Secretary can prepare formal findings including the information required by DOT Order 5610.1 that will provide an adequate explanation for his action. Such an explanation will, to some extent, be a "post hoc rationalization" and thus must be viewed critically. If the District Court decides that additional explanation is necessary, that court should consider which method will prove the most expeditious so that full review may be had as soon as possible.

Reversed and remanded.

Mr. Justice Douglas took no part in the consideration or decision of this case.

Separate opinion of Mr. Justice Black, with whom Mr. Justice Brennan joins.

I agree with the court that the judgment of the Court of Appeals is wrong and that its action should be reversed. I do not agree that the whole matter should be remanded to the District Court. I think the case should be sent back to the Secretary of Transportation. It is apparent from the Court's opinion today that the Secretary of Transportation completely failed to comply with the duty imposed upon him by Congress not to permit a federally financed public highway to run through a public park "unless (1) there is no feasible and prudent alternative to the use of such land, and (2) such program includes all possible planning to minimize harm to such park."* * * That congressional command should not be taken lightly by the Secretary or by this Court. It represents a solemn determination of the highest law-making body of this Nation that the beauty and health-giving facilities of our parks are not to be taken away for public roads without hearings, factfindings, and policy determinations under the supervision of a Cabinet officer,the Secretary of Transportation.* * * It is our duty, I believe, to remand this whole matter back to the Secretary of Transportation for him to give this matter the hearing it deserves in full good-faith obedience to the Act of Congress.* * * I dissent from the Court's failure to send the case back to the Secretary, whose duty has not yet been performed.

## Notes

In *Overton Park*, the Court took an extremely narrow reading of the Administrative Procedure Act exception that precludes judicial review where "agency action is committed to agency discretion by law." Agency action will be unreviewable, the Court held, only where there is no law to apply. will this interfere with the flexibility a federal administrative official, such as the Secretary of Transportation, should have in order to function effectively? Or are the decisions about highway location, like war, too important to be left to the generals?

Does the "hard look" doctrine imposed by the Court allow the courts to substitute their judgment for that of the agency--a role they traditionally decline to play? What are the advantages of the doctrine? Does it create more opportunity for delay?

On remand, the District Court directed a hearing, then sent the case back to Secretary of Transportation Volpe to review the record, 335 F. Supp. 873 (W.D. Tenn. 1972). This time he rejected the road through the park, finding a feasible and prudent alternative existed. The Court of Appeals, 494 F.2d 1212 (6th Cir. 1974), cert. den. 421 U.S. 991 (1975), upheld that determination as against a challenge by the state highway department, which insisted on the original route. Overton Park was saved. In 1980 the park was listed in the National Register of Historic Places, protecting it from alteration by the federal government or any federally-funded program such as an Interstate highway.

Is the "substantial inquiry" or hard look doctrine particularly apt in reviewing decisions of administrative agencies in the environmental field, where the public policy considerations are often powerful? See Oakes, *The Judicial Role in Environmental Law,* 52 N.Y.U.L. Rev. 498 (1977).

Are there countervailing considerations justifying giving great weight to an agency's findings where it must predict whether a substance to which numerous people will be exposed is hazardous to health? In *Ethyl Corp. v. Environmental Prot. Agency,* 541 F.2d 1 (D.C. Cir. 1976), cert. den. 426 U.S. 941, the EPA found lead was an additive to gasoline which, in the language of the Clean Air Act, "will endanger the public health or welfare." It adopted regulations requiring annual reductions in the lead content of leaded gasoline. In upholding the regulations as not arbitrary or capricious, the Court, sitting *en banc,* held, in an eloquent opinion by Skelly Wright, J.:

Regulations such as the Administrator's must be accorded flexibility, a flexibility that recognizes the special judicial interest in favor of protection of the health and welfare of the people, even in areas where certainty does not exist. *Environmental Defense Fund, Inc., v. Ruckelshaus,* 142 U.S. App. D.C. 74, 88, 439 F.2d 584, 598 (1971).

Questions involving the environment are particularly prone to uncertainty. Technological man has altered his world in ways never before experienced or anticipated. The health effects of such alternations are often unknown, sometimes unknowable. While a concerned Congress has passed legislation providing for protection of the pubic health against gross environmental modifications, [Clean Air Act, 42 U.S.C. §§ 7401-7671q], the regulators entrusted with the enforcement of such laws have not thereby been endowed with a prescience that removes all doubt from their decision-making. Rather, speculation, conflicts in evidence, and theoretical extrapolation typify their every action. How else can they act, given a mandate to protect the public health but only a slight or nonexistent data base upon which to draw? Never before have massive quantities of asbestiform tailings been spewed into the water we drink. Never before have our industrial workers been occupationally exposed to vinyl chloride or to asbestos dust. Never before has the food we eat been permeated with DDT or the pesticides aldrin and dieldrin. And never before have hundreds of thousands of tons of lead emissions been disgorged annually into the air we breathe. Sometimes, of course, relatively certain proof of danger or harm from such modifications can be readily found. But, more commonly, "reasonable medical concerns" and theory long precede certainty. Yet the statutes,and common sense,demand regulatory action to prevent harm, even if the regulator is less than certain that harm is otherwise inevitable.

Undoubtedly, certainty is the scientific ideal, to the extent that even science can be certain of its truth.* * * But certainty in the complexities of environmental medicine may be achievable only after the fact, when scientists have the opportunity for leisurely and isolated scrutiny of an entire mechanism. Awaiting certainty will often allow for only reactive, not preventive, regulation. Petitioners suggest that anything less than certainty, that any speculation, is irresponsible. But when statutes seek to avoid environmental catastrophe, can preventive, albeit uncertain, decisions legitimately be so labeled?* * *

Our review of the evidence is governed by Section 10(e)(2)(A) [of the Administrative Procedure Act], which requires us to strike "agency action, findings, and conclusions" that we find to be "arbitrary, capricious, an abuse of discretion, or otherwise not in accordance with law * * *." 5 U.S.C. § 706(2)(A). This standard of review is a highly deferential one. It presumes agency action to be valid. *Overton Park.* Moreover, it forbids the court's substituting its judgment for that of the agency, *Overton Park,* and requires affirmance if a rational basis exists for the agency's decision.

This is not to say, however, that we must rubber-stamp the agency decision as correct. To do so would render the appellate process a superfluous (although time-consuming) ritual. Rather, the reviewing court must assure itself that the agency decision was "based on a consideration of the relevant factors * * *." Moreover it must engage in a "substantial inquiry" into the facts, one that is searching and careful." *Overton Park.* This is particularly true in highly technical cases such as this one. A court does not depart from its proper function when it [studies] the record * * * even as to the evidence on technical and specialize matters, for this enables the court to [examine] the underlying decisions of the agency, to satisfy itself that the agency has exercised reasoned discretion, with reasons that do not deviate from or ignore the ascertainable legislative intent.

There is no inconsistency between the deferential standard of review and the requirement that the reviewing court involve itself in even the more complex evidentiary matters; rather, the two indicia of arbitrary and capricious review stand in careful balance. The close scrutiny of the evidence is intended to educate the court.* * * The more technical the case, the more intensive must be the court's effort to understand the evidence, for without an appropriate understanding of the case before it the court cannot properly perform its appellate function. But that function may be performed with conscientious awareness of its limited nature. The forced education into the intricacies of the problem before the agency is not designed to enable the court to become a superagency that can supplant the agency's expert decision-maker. To the contrary, court must give due deference to the agency's ability to rely on its own developed expertise.

Thus, after our careful study of the record, we must take a step back from the agency decision. We must look at the decision not as the chemist, biologist or statistician that we are qualified neither by training nor experience to be, but as a reviewing court exercising our narrowly defined duty of holding agencies to certain minimal standards of rationality.* * *

Notes

See *Dow Chemical Co. v. Blum,* Chapter 9, Part C, using the *Ethyl Corp.* test, and quoting from that decision in upholding an EPA determination to ban a pesticide found to cause spontaneous abortions.

Does this sort of deference hamper attempts by courts to *promote* environmental interests when agencies act against them? Has the same deferential rhetoric accompanied both types of decisions?

SCENIC HUDSON PRESERVATION CONFERENCE v. FEDERAL POWER COMMISSION, United States Court of Appeals, Second Circuit, 1965. 354 F.2d 608, *cert. denied,* 384 U.S. 941 (1966).

Hays, Circuit Judge:

In this proceeding the petitioners are the Scenic Hudson Preservation Conference, an unincorporated association consisting of a number of non-profit, conservationist organization and the Towns of Cortlandt, Putnam Valley and Yorktown. Petitioners ask us, pursuant to § 313(b) of the Federal Power Act, 16 U.S.C. § 8251(b), to set aside three orders of the respondent, the Federal Power Commission:

(a) An order of March 9, 1965 granting a license to the intervenor, the Consolidated Edison Company of New York, Inc., to construct a pumped storage hydroelectric project on the west side of the Hudson River at Storm King Mountain in Cornwall, New York;

(b) An order of May 6, 1965 denying petitioners' application for a rehearing of the March 9 order, and for the reopening of the proceeding to permit the introduction of additional evidence;

(c) An order of May 6, 1965 denying joint motions filed by the petitioners to expand the scope of supplemental hearings to include consideration of the practicality and cost of underground transmission lines and of the feasibility of any type of fish protection device.

A pumped storage plant generates electric energy for use during peak load periods[.]

The contemplated Storm King project would be the largest of its kind in the world. Consolidated Edison has estimated its cost, including transmission facilities, at $162,000,000. The project would consist of three major components, a storage reservoir, a powerhouse, and transmission lines. The storage reservoir, located over a thousand feet above the powerhouse, is to be connected to the powerhouse, located on the river front, by a tunnel 40 feet in diameter. The powerhouse, which is both a pumping and generating station, would be 800 feet long and contain eight pump generators.

Transmission lines would run under the Hudson to the east bank and then underground for 1.6 miles to a switching station which Consolidated Edison would build at Nelsonville in the Town of Philipstown. Thereafter, overhead transmission lines would be placed on towers 100 to 150 feet high and these would require a path up to 125 feet wide through Westchester and Putnam Counties for a distance of some 25 miles until they reached Consolidated Edison's main connections with New York City.

During slack periods Consolidated Edison's conventional steam plants in New York City would provide electric power for the pumps at Storm King to force water up the mountain, through the tunnel, and into the upper reservoir. In peak periods water would be released to rush down the mountain and power the generators. Three kilowatts of power generated in New York City would be necessary to obtain two kilowatts from the Cornwall installation. When pumping the powerhouse would draw approximately 1,080,000 cubic feet of water per minute from the Hudson, and when generating would discharge up to 1,620,000 cubic feet of water per minute into the river. The installation would have a capacity of 2,000,000 kilowatts, but would be so constructed as to be capable of enlargement to a total of 3,000,000 kilowatts. The water in the upper reservoir may be regarded as the equivalent of stored electric energy; in effect, Consolidated Edison wishes to create a huge storage battery at Cornwall.* * *

To be licensed by the Commission a prospective project must meet the statutory test of being "best adapted to a comprehensive plan for improving or developing a waterway," Federal Power Act § 10(a), 16 U.S.C. § 803(a).* * * If the Commission is properly to discharge its duty in this regard, the record on which it bases its determination must be complete. The petitioners and the public at large have a right to demand this completeness. It is our view, and we find, that the

Commission has failed to compile a record which is sufficient to support its decision. The Commission has ignored certain relevant factors and failed to make a thorough study of possible alternatives to the Storm King Project. While the courts have no authority to concern themselves with the policies of the Commission, it is their duty to see to it that the Commission's decisions receive that careful consideration which the statute contemplates.

The Storm King project is to be located in an area of unique beauty and major historical significance. The highlands and gorge of the Hudson offer one of the finest pieces of river scenery in the world. The great German traveler Baedeker called it "finer than the Rhine." Petitioners' contention that the Commission must take these factors into consideration in evaluating the Storm King project is justified by the history of the Federal Power Act.

The Federal Water Power Act of 1920, (now Federal Power Act, 16 U.S.C. § 791a et seq.), was the outgrowth of a widely supported effort on the part of conservationists to secure the enactment of a complete scheme of national regulation which would promote the comprehensive development of the nation's water resources.* * *

It "was passed for the purpose of developing and preserving to the people the water power resources of the country." United States ex rel. Chapman v. Federal Power Comm., 191 F.2d 796, 800 (4th Cir. 1951), aff'd, 345 U.S. 153, 73 S. Ct. 609, 97 L.Ed. 918 (1953).

Congress gave the Federal Power Commission sweeping authority and a specific planning responsibility.* * *

Section 10(a) of the Federal Power Act, 16 U.S.C. § 803(a), reads:

"§ 803. Conditions of license generally.

All licenses issued under sections 792, 793, 795-818, and 820-823 of this title shall be on the following conditions:

> (a) That the project adopted* * * shall be such as in the judgment of the Commission *will be best adapted to a comprehensive plan for improving or developing a waterway or waterways for the use or benefit of interstate or foreign commerce, for the improvement and utilization of water-power development, and for other beneficial public uses, including recreational purposes;* and if necessary in order to secure such plan the Commission shall, have authority to require the modification of any project and of the plans and specifications of the project works before approval." (Emphasis added.)

"Recreational purposes" are expressly included among the beneficial public uses to which the statute refers. The phrase undoubtedly encompasses the conservation of natural resources, the maintenance of natural beauty, and the preservation of historic sites. See Namekagon Hydro Co. v. Federal Power Comm., 216 F.2d 509, 511-512 (7th Cir. 1954). All of these "beneficial uses," the Supreme Court has observed, "while unregulated, might well be contradictory rather than harmonious." Federal Power Comm. v. Union Electric Co., 381 U.S. 90, 98, 85 S. Ct. 1253, 1258 (1965). In licensing a project, it is the duty of the Federal Power Commission properly to weigh each factor.

In recent years the Commission has placed increasing emphasis on the right of the public to "out-door recreational resources." 1964 F.P.C. Report 69. Regulations issued in 1963, for the first time, required the inclusion of a recreation plan as part of a license application.* * * The Commission has recognized generally that members of the public have rights in our recreational, historic and scenic resources under the Federal Power Act [and that "the] public interest must be considered and it cannot be evaluated adequately only in dollars and cents." In affirming Namekagon the Seventh Circuit upheld the Commission's denial of a license, to an otherwise economically feasible project, because fishing, canoeing and the scenic attraction of a "beautiful stretch of water" were threatened. Namekagon Hydro Co.v. Federal Power Comm., 216 F.2d 509, 511-512 (7th Cir. 1954).

Commissioner Ross said in his dissent in the present case: "[I]t appears obvious that had this area of the 'Hudson Highlands' been declared a State or National park, that is, had the people in the area already spoken, we probably would have listened and might well have refused to license it."

Respondent argues that "petitioners do not have standing to obtain a review" because they "make no claim of any personal economic injury resulting from the Commission's action."

Section 313(b) of the Federal Power Act, 16 U.S.C. § 825(b), reads:

> "(b) Any party to a proceeding under this chapter aggrieved by an order issued by the Commission in such proceeding may obtain a review of such order in the United States Court of Appeals for any circuit wherein the licensee or public utility to which the order relates is located * * *."

The Commission takes a narrow view of the meaning of "aggrieved party" under the Act. Although a "case" or "controversy" which is otherwise lacking cannot be created by statute, a statute may create new interests or rights and thus give standing to one who would otherwise be barred by the lack of a "case" or "controversy." The "case" or "controversy" requirement of Article III, § 2 of the Constitution does not require that an "aggrieved" or "adversely affected" party have a personal economic interest. * * *

Even in cases involving original standing to sue, the Supreme Court has not made economic injury a prerequisite where the plaintiffs have shown a direct personal interest. See, e.g., School District of Abington Township v. Schempp, 374 U.S. 203, 83 S. Ct. 1560, 10 L.Ed.2d 844 (1963); Engel v. Vitale, 370 U.S. 421, 82

S. Ct. 1261, 8 L.Ed.2d 601 (1962); Zorach v. Clauson, 343 U.S. 306, 72 S. Ct. 679, 96 L.Ed. 954 (1952).

In State of Washington Dept. of Game v. Federal Power Comm., 207 F.2d 391, 395 n.11 (9th Cir. 1953), cert. denied, 347 U.S. 936, 74 S. Ct. 626 (1954), the Washington State Sportsmen's Council, Inc., a non-profit organization of residents, the State of Washington, Department of Game, and the State of Washington, Department of Fisheries, opposed the construction of a dam because it threatened to destroy fish.

[T]he court upheld their standing, noting:

> "All are 'parties aggrieved' since they claim that the Cowlitz Project will destroy fish in [sic] which they, among others, are interested in protecting."

The Federal Power Act seeks to protect non-economic as well as economic interests. Indeed, the Commission recognized this in framing the issue in this very case:

> The project is to be physically located in a general area of our nation steeped in the history of the American Revolution and of the colonial period. It is also a general area of great scenic beauty. The principal issue which must be decided is whether the project's effect[s] on the scenic, historical and recreational values of the area are such that we should deny the application.

In order to insure that the Federal Power Commission will adequately protect the public interest in the esthetic, conservational, and recreational aspects of power development, those who by their activities and conduct have exhibited a special interest in such areas, must be held to be included in the class of "aggrieved" parties under § 313(b). We hold that the Federal Power Act gives petitioners a legal right to protect their special interests.* * *

Moreover, petitioners have sufficient economic interest to establish their standing. The New York-New Jersey Trail Conference, one of the two conservation groups that organized Scenic Hudson, has some seventeen miles of trailways in the area of Storm King Mountain. Portions of these trails would be inundated by the construction of the project's reservoir.

The primary transmission lines are an integral part of the Storm King project.* * * The towns that are co-petitioners with Scenic Hudson have standing because the transmission lines would cause a decrease in the proprietary value of publicly held land, reduce tax revenues collected from privately held land, and significantly interfere with long-range community planning.* * * Yorktown, for example, fears that the transmission lines would run over municipal land selected for a school site, greatly decreasing its value and interfering with school construction. Putnam Valley faces similar interference with local planning and a substantial decrease in land tax revenues.

We see no justification for the Commission's fear that our determination will encourage "literally thousands" to intervene and seek review in future proceedings.* * * Our experience with public actions confirms the view that the expense and vexation of legal proceedings is not lightly undertaken.

In any case, the Federal Power Act creates no absolute right of intervention. Since the right to seek review under § 313(a) and (b) is limited to a "party" to the Commission proceeding, the Commission has ample authority reasonably to limit those eligible to intervene or to seek review.* * * Representation of common interests by an organization such as Scenic Hudson serves to limit the number of those who might otherwise apply for intervention and serves to expedite the administrative process.

The Federal Power Act § 313(b), 16 U.S.C. § 825 (b), reads in part:

> (b) If any party shall apply to the court for leave to adduce additional evidence, and shall show to the satisfaction of the court that such additional evidence is material and that there were reasonable grounds for failure to adduce such evidence in the proceedings before the Commission, the court may order such additional evidence to be taken before the Commission and to be adduced upon the hearing in such manner and upon such terms and conditions as to the court may seem proper.

The Commission in its opinion recognized that in connection with granting a license to Consolidated Edison it "must compare the Cornwall project with any alternatives that are available." There is no doubt that the Commission is under a statutory duty to give full consideration to alternative plans.* * * On January 7, 1965 the testimony of Mr. Alexander Lurkis, as to the feasibility of an alternative to the project, the use of gas turbines, was offered to the Commission. [I]it was rejected because it represented "at best" a "disagreement between experts." On the other hand, we have found in the record no meaningful evidence which contradicts the proffered testimony supporting the gas turbine alternative.

Mr. Lurkis is a consulting engineer of thirty-nine years experience. He has served as Chief Engineer of the New York City Bureau of Gas and Electric, in charge of a staff of 400, and as Senior Engineer of the New York City Transit Authority, where he supervised the design and construction of power plants. The New York Joint Legislative Committee on Natural Resources, after holding hearings on the Storm King project on November 19 and 20, 1964, summarized Mr. Lurkis's testimony as

> meeting the alleged peak power needs and saving money for the ratepayer, [by giving] the company greater flexibility in meeting the power needs of its service area.* * * Small installations can be added as needed to meet demand. This, in contrast to a single, giant, permanent installation such as Con Ed proposes at Storm King

> Mountain, which would tie the technology and investment of one company to a method of power production that might be obsolete in a few years.* * *
>
> This would not only avoid the desecration of the Hudson Gorge and Highlands, but, also, would eliminate the great swath of destruction down through Putnam and Westchester Counties and their beautiful suburban communities. Preliminary Report at 6.

* * *Mr. Lurkis's analysis was based on an intensive study of the Consolidated Edison system, and of its peaking needs projected year by year over a fifteen year period. He was prepared to make an economic comparison of a gas turbine system (including capital and fuel operating costs) and the Storm King pumped storage plant. Moreover, he was prepared to answer Consolidated Edison's objections to gas turbines[.]

Aside from self-serving general statements by officials of Consolidated Edison, the only testimony in the record bearing on the gas turbine alternative * * * occupied less than ten pages of the record [and] was too scanty to meet the requirement of a full consideration of alternatives. Indeed, under the circumstances, we must conclude that there was no significant attempt to develop evidence as to the gas turbine alternative; at least, there is no such evidence in the record.

* * *It is not our present function to evaluate this evidence. Our focus is upon the action of the Commission.* * *

Especially in a case of this type, where public interest and concern is so great, the Commission's refusal to receive the Lurkis testimony, as well as proffered information on fish protection devices and underground transmission facilities, exhibits a disregard of the statute and of judicial mandates instructing the Commission to probe all feasible alternatives.* * *

The Federal Power Commission argues that having intervened "petitioners cannot impose an affirmative burden on the Commission." But, as we have pointed out, Congress gave the Federal Power Commission a specific planning responsibility. See Federal Power Act § 10(a), 16 U.S.C. § 803(a). The totality of a project's immediate and long-range effects, and not merely the engineering and navigation aspects, are to be considered in a licensing proceeding.

[T]he Commission has claimed to be the representative of the public interest. This role does not permit it to act as an umpire blandly calling balls and strikes for adversaries appearing before it; the right of the public must receive active and affirmative protection at the hands of the Commission.

This court cannot and should not attempt to substitute its judgment for that of the Commission. But we must decide whether the Commission has correctly discharged of its planning function in deciding that the "licensing of the project would be in the overall public interest." The Commission must see to it that the record is complete. The Commission has an affirmative duty to inquire into and consider all relevant facts.* * *

In addition[,] [t]he Commission neither investigated the use of interconnected power as a possible alternative to the Storm King project, nor required Consolidated Edison to supply such information. The record sets forth Consolidated Edison's interconnection with a vast network of other utilities, but the Commission dismissed this alternative by noting that "Con Edison is relying fully upon such inter-connections in estimating its future available capacity." [Yet] in its October 4, 1965 order, the Commission in explaining how Consolidated Edison would be able to send "substantial amounts" of Storm King power to upstate New York and New England power companies, each December, said:

> ample spinning reserve would be available during the winter from the interconnected companies in New Jersey and Pennsylvania, * * *. Thus, even at times of the greater diversion of Cornwall power, Con Edison would have other power sources immediately available to it for its peak requirements.

If interconnecting power can replace the Storm King project in December, why was it not considered as a permanent alternative?

There is no evidence in the record to indicate that either the Commission or Consolidated Edison ever seriously considered this alternative.* * * The failure of the Commission to inform itself of these alternatives cannot be reconciled with its planning responsibility under the Federal Power Act.

In its March 9 opinion the Commission postponed a decision on the transmission route to be chosen until the May 1965 hearings were completed. Inquiry into the cost of putting lines underground was precluded because the May hearings were limited to the question of overhead transmission routes. The petitioners' April 26, 1965 motion to enlarge the scope of the May hearing was denied. The Commission insisted that the question of underground costs had been "extensively considered." We find almost nothing in the record to support this statement.

Consolidated Edison estimated the cost of underground transmission at seven to twelve times that of overhead lines. These estimates were questioned by the Commission's own staff, which pointed out that Consolidated Edison's estimates incorrectly assumed that the underground route would be the same as the overhead; in fact, an underground route along the New York Central [railroad] right-of-way would be clearly less costly than the estimate, since there are no large differences of elevation requiring special pumping facilities and no new cross-country right-of-way would be necessary. Moreover, the staff noted that the estimates were based on Consolidated Edison's experience in New York, where excavation and other costs are higher. The Examiner noted the staff's reservations in his opinion, but since no alternative figures had been presented, he accepted those submitted by Consolidated Edison, as did the Commission.

Consolidated Edison witnesses testified that the Storm King project would result in annual savings of $12,000,000 over a steam plant of equivalent capacity.

Given these savings, the Commission should at least have inquired into the capital and annual cost of running segments of the transmission line underground in those areas where the overhead structures would cause the most serious scenic damage. We find no indication that the Commission seriously weighed the esthetic advantages of underground transmission lines against the economic disadvantages.

At the time of its original hearings, there was sufficient evidence before the Commission concerning the danger to fish to warrant further inquiry. The evidence included a letter from Kenneth Holum, Assistant Secretary of the Department of the Interior, and a statement made for the record by Robert A. Cook, on behalf of the New York State Water Resources Commission in which Mr. Cook said: "[T]he possibility still exists that extensive losses of eggs and/or young of valuable species might occur after installation of the proposed screening devices."

Just after the Commission closed its proceedings in November the hearings held by the New York State Legislative Committee on Natural Resources alerted many fisherman groups to the threat posed by the Storm King project. On December 24 and 30, January 8, and February 3 each of four groups, concerned with fishing, petitioned for the right to intervene and present evidence. They wished to show that the major spawning grounds for the distinct race of Hudson River striped bass was in the immediate vicinity of the Storm King project and not "much farther upstream" as inferred by Dr. Perlmutter, the one expert witness called by Consolidated Edison; to attempt to prove that, contrary to the impression given by Dr. Perlmutter, bass eggs and larvae float in the water, at the mercy of currents; that due to the location of the spawning ground and the Hudson's tidal flow, the eggs and larvae would be directly subject to the influence of the plant and would be threatened with destruction; that "no screening device presently feasible would adequately protect these early stages of fish life" and that their loss would ultimately destroy the economically valuable fisheries. Their evidence also indicated that in the case of shad, the young migrate from their spawning grounds, down past Cornwall, and being smaller than the meshes of the contemplated fish screens, would be subject to the hazards already described. The commission rejected all these petitions as "untimely," and seemingly placing great reliance on the testimony of Dr. Perlmutter, concluded:

> The project will not adversely affect the fish resources of the Hudson River provided adequate protective facilities are installed.

Although an opportunity was made available at the May hearings for petitioners to submit evidence on protective designs, the question of the adequacy of any protective design was inexplicably excluded by the Commission.

Recent events illustrate other deficiencies in the Commission's record. In hearing before the House Subcommittee on Fisheries and Wildlife Studying the Hudson River Spawning Grounds, 89th Cong. 1st Sess. May 10, 11, 1965, Mr. James McBroom, representing the Department of the Interior, stated:

> Practical screening methods are known which could prevent young-of-the-year striped bass and shad from being caught up on the [Storm King] project's pumps, but practical means of protection of eggs and larvae stages have yet to be devised. Furthermore the location of the proposed plant appears from available evidence to be at or very near the crucial spot as to potential for harm to the overall production of eggs and larvae of the Hudson River striped bass. The cumulative effect of unmitigated loss of eggs and larvae of striped bass by this power project could have a serious effect on the Hudson River striped bass fishery and the defendant fisheries around Long Island and offshore.* * *

On remand, the Commission should take the whole fisheries question into consideration before deciding whether the Storm King project is to be licensed.

The Commission should reexamine all questions on which we have found the record insufficient and all related matters. The Commission's renewed proceedings must include as a basic concern the preservation of natural beauty and of national historic shrines, keeping in mind that, in our affluent society, the cost of a project is only one of several factors to be considered. The record as it comes to us fails markedly to make out a case for the Storm King project on, among other matters, costs, public convenience and necessity, and absence of reasonable alternatives. Of course, the Commission should make every effort to expedite the new proceedings.

Petitioners' application, pursuant to Federal Power Act § 313(b), 16 U.S.C. § 825(b), to adduce additional evidence concerning alternatives to the Storm King project and the cost and practicality of underground transmission facilities is granted.

The licensing order of March 9 and the two orders of May 6 are set aside, and the case remanded for further proceedings.

## Notes

Is the court reviewing the Commission's determination here substantively, deciding whether it was supported by substantial evidence in the record, or is it imposing an added element of fairness on the part of the administrative agency? Is the burden of proof being shifted to the agency to justify its findings?

What is the Federal Power Act did not refer to recreation as one of the elements to be weighed? Would the result have been different? Or would the court have found a way to impose the same conditions on the agency, using some other handle?

How did the petitioners show their standing to bring this proceeding?

On remand, the Commission considered the elements the court had directed it to consider, and again granted the license. The court upheld that decision by a 2-1 vote, 453 F.2d 463 (2d Cir. 1971), cert. den. 407 U.S. 926 (1972). Then additional evidence of the danger to the Hudson River fishery, which the Commission refused to hear, led to a third review by the Court of Appeals, this one reported at 498 F.2d 822. The court once again directed further hearings.

In a settlement in December 1980, Con Edison withdrew its application to build the plant in return for an agreement by conservation agencies and groups not to require cooling towers at the company's nuclear power plants at Indian Point in New York's Westchester county, a few miles down the Hudson. Con Edison also agreed, together with four other power companies, to build a fish hatchery and to stock the river. See Chapter 11.

## B. STANDING AND JURISDICTION

SIERRA CLUB v. MORTON,
Supreme Court of the United States, 1972. 405 U.S. 727, 92 S. Ct. 1361, 31 L.Ed.2d 636.

Mr. Justice Stewart delivered the opinion of the Court.

The Mineral King Valley is an area of great natural beauty in the Sierra Nevada Mountains in Tulare County, California, adjacent to Sequoia National Park. It has been part of the Sequoia National Forest since 1926, and is designated as a national game refuge by special Act of Congress. Though once the site of extensive mining activity, Mineral King is now used almost exclusively for recreational purposes. Its relative inaccessibility and lack of development have limited the number of visitors each year, and at the same time have preserved the valley's quality as a quasi-wilderness area largely uncluttered by the products of civilization.

The United States Forest Service, which is entrusted with the maintenance and administration of national forests, began in the late 1940's to give consideration to Mineral King as a potential site for recreational development. Prodded by a rapidly increasing demand for skiing facilities, the Forest Service published a prospectus in 1965, inviting bids from private developers for the construction and operation of a ski resort that would also serve as a summer recreation area. The proposal of Walt Disney Enterprises, Inc., was chosen[.]

The final Disney plan, approved by the Forest Service in January 1969, outlines a $35 million complex of motels, restaurants, swimming pools, parking lots, and other structures designed to accommodate 14,000 visitors daily. This complex is to be constructed on 80 acres of the valley floor under a 30-year use permit from the Forest Service. Other facilities, including ski lifts, ski trails, a cog-assisted railway, and utility installations, are to be constructed on the mountain slopes and in other parts of the valley under a revocable special-use permit. To provide access to the resort, the State of California proposes to construct a highway 20 miles in length. A section of this road would traverse Sequoia National Park, as would a proposed high-voltage power line needed to provide electricity for the resort. Both the highway and the power line require the approval of the Department of the Interior, which is entrusted with the preservation and maintenance of the national parks.

Representatives of the Sierra Club, who favor maintaining Mineral King largely in its present state, unsuccessfully sought a public hearing on the proposed development in 1965, and in subsequent correspondence with officials of the Forest Service and the Department of the Interior, they expressed the Club's objections to Disney's plan as a whole and to particular features included in it. In June 1969 the Club filed the present suit in the United States District Court for the Northern District of California, seeking a declaratory judgment that various aspects of the proposed development contravene federal laws and regulations governing the preservation of national parks, forests, and game refuges, and also seeking preliminary and permanent injunctions restraining the federal officials involved from granting their approval or issuing permits in connection with the Mineral King project. The petitioner Sierra Club sued as a membership corporation with "a special interest in the conservation and the sound maintenance of the national parks, game refuges and forests of the country," and invoked the judicial-review provisions of the Administrative Procedure Act, 5 U.S.C. § 701 et seq.* * *

The first question presented is whether the Sierra Club has * * * standing to sue. Where the party does not rely on any specific statute authorizing invocation of the judicial process, the question of standing depends upon whether the party has alleged such a "personal stake in the outcome of the controversy" * * * to ensure that "the dispute sought to be adjudicated will be presented in an adversary context and in a form historically viewed as capable of judicial resolution." Flast v. Cohen, 392 U.S. 83, 101, 20 L.Ed.2d 947, 962, 88 S. Ct. 1942. Where, however, Congress has authorized public officials to perform certain functions according to law, and has provided by statute for judicial review of those actions under certain circumstances, the inquiry as to standing must begin with a determination of whether the statute in question authorizes review at the behest of the plaintiff.

The Sierra Club relies upon § 10 of the Administrative Procedure Act (APA), 5 U.S.C. § 702[:]

> "A person suffering legal wrong because of agency action, or adversely affected or aggrieved by agency action within the meaning of a relevant statute, is entitled to judicial review thereof."

[I]n Data Processing Service v. Camp, 397 U.S. 150, 25 L.Ed.2d 184, 90 S. Ct. 827, * * * we held that persons had standing to obtain judicial review of federal agency action under § 10 of the A.P.A. where they had alleged that the challenged action had caused them "injury in fact," and where the alleged injury was to an interest "arguably within the zone of interests to be protected or regulated" by the statutes that the agencies were claimed to have violated.

[E]conomic injuries have long been recognized as sufficient to lay the basis for standing with or without a specific statutory provision for judicial review. [But Data Processing did not address] what must be alleged by persons who claim injury of a noneconomic nature to interests that are widely shared. That question is presented in this case.* * *

The injury alleged by the Sierra Club will be incurred entirely by reason of the change in the uses to which Mineral King will be put, and the attendant change in the esthetics and ecology of the area. Thus, in referring to the road to be built through Sequoia National Park, the complaint alleged that the development "would destroy or otherwise adversely affect the scenery, natural and historic objects and wildlife of the park and would impair the enjoyment of the park for future generations." We do not question that this type of harm may amount to an "injury in fact" sufficient to lay the basis for standing under § 10 of the A.P.A. Esthetic and environmental well-being, like economic well-being, are important ingredients of the quality of life in our society, and the fact that particular environmental interests are shared by the many rather than the few does not make them less deserving of legal protection through the judicial process. But the "injury in fact" test requires more than an injury to a cognizable interest. It requires that the party seeking review be himself among the injured.

The impact of the proposed changes in the environment of Mineral King will not fall indiscriminately upon every citizen. The alleged injury will be felt directly only by those who use Mineral King and Sequoia National Park, and for whom the esthetic and recreational values of the area will be lessened by the highway and ski resort. The Sierra Club failed to allege that it or its members would be affected in any of their activities or pastimes by the Disney development. Nowhere in the pleadings or affidavits did the Club state that its members use Mineral King for any purpose, much less that they use it in any way that would be significantly affected by the proposed actions of the respondents.[8]

The Club apparently regarded any allegations of individualized injury as superfluous, on the theory that this was a "public" action involving questions as to the use of natural resources, and that the Club's long-standing concern with and expertise in such matters were sufficient to give it standing as a "representative of the public."[9] This theory reflects a misunderstanding of our cases involving so-

---

[8] The only reference in the pleadings to the Sierra Club's interest in the dispute is contained in paragraph 3 of the complaint, * * *. "For many years the Sierra Club by its activities and conduct has exhibited a special interest in the conservation and the sound maintenance of the national parks, game refuges, and forests of the country, regularly serving as a responsible representative of persons similarly interested. One of the principal purposes of the Sierra Club is to protect and conserve the national resources of the Sierra Nevada Mountains. Its interests would be vitally affected by the acts hereinafter described and would be aggrieved by those acts of the defendants as hereinafter more fully appears." * * * Our decision does not, of course, bar the Sierra Club from seeking in the District Court to amend its complaint by a motion under Rule 15, Federal Rules of Civil Procedure.

[9] This approach to the question of standing was adopted by the Court of Appeals for the Second Circuit in Citizens Committee for the Hudson Valley v. Volpe, 425 F.2d 97, 105:

> "We hold, therefore, that the public interest in environmental resources--an interest created by statutes affecting the issuance of this permit--is a legally protected interest affording these plaintiffs, as responsible representatives of the public, standing to obtain judicial review of agency action alleged to be in contravention of that public interest."

called "public actions" in the area of administrative law.* * * *Scripps-Howard Radio v. F.C.C.*, 316 U.S. 4, 86 L.Ed. 1229, 62 S. Ct. 875 [and] *F.C.C. v. Sanders Bros. Radio Station*, 309 U.S. 470, 477, 84 L.Ed. 869, 875, 60 S. Ct. 693 [establish that] the fact of economic injury is what gives a person standing to seek judicial review under the statute, but once review is properly involved, that person may argue the public interest in support of his claim that the agency has failed to comply with its statutory mandate. It is in a similar sense that we have used the phrase "private attorney general" to describe the function performed by persons upon whom Congress has conferred the right to seek judicial review of agency action. See Data Processing, *supra*, at 154, 25 L.Ed. 2d at 188.

The trend of cases arising under the APA and other statutes authorizing judicial review of federal agency action has been toward recognizing that injuries other than economic harm are sufficient to bring a person within the meaning of the statutory language, and toward discarding the notion that an injury that is widely shared is ipso facto not an injury sufficient to provide the basis for judicial review. We noted this development with approval in Data Processing, 397 U.S., at 154, 35 L.Ed.2d at 188, in saying that the interest alleged to have been injured "may reflect 'esthetic, conservational, and recreational' as well as economic values." But broadening the categories of injury that may be alleged in support of standing is a different matter from abandoning the requirement that the party seeking review must himself have suffered an injury.

Some courts have indicated a willingness to take this latter step by conferring standing upon organizations that have demonstrated "an organizational interest in the problem" of environmental or consumer protection. Environmental Defense Fund v. Hardin, 138 U.S. App. D.C. 391, 428 F.2d 1093, 1097.[14] It is clear that an organization whose members are injured may represent those members in a proceeding for judicial review. *See, e.g.*, *NAACP v. Button*, 371 U.S. 415, 428, 9 L.Ed.2d 405, 415, 83 S. Ct. 328. But a mere "interest in a problem," no matter how longstanding the interest and no matter how qualified the organization is in evaluating the problem, is not sufficient by itself to render the organization "adversely affected" or "aggrieved" within the meaning of the A.P.A. The Sierra Club is a large and long-established organization, with a historic commitment to the cause of protecting our Nation's natural heritage from man's depredations. But if a "special interest" in this subject were enough to entitle the Sierra Club to commence this litigation, there would appear to be no objective basis upon which to disallow a suit by any other bona fide "special interest" organization, however small or short-

---

[14] See Citizens Committee for the Hudson Valley v. Volpe, n. 9, supra; * * *. See also Scenic Hudson Preservation Conf. v. FPC, supra * * *:

> "In order to insure that the Federal Power Commission will adequately protect the public interest in the esthetic, conservational, and recreational aspects of power development, those who by their activities and conduct have exhibited a special interest in such areas, must be held to be included in the class of 'aggrieved' parties under § 313(b) [of the Federal Power Act]."

In most, if not all, of these cases, at least one party to the proceeding did assert an individualized injury either to himself or, in the case of an organization, to its members.

lived. And if any group with a bona fide "special interest" could initiate such litigation, it is difficult to perceive why any individual citizen with the same bona fide special interest would not also be entitled to do so.

The requirement that a party seeking review must allege facts showing that he is himself adversely affected does not insulate executive action from judicial review, nor does it prevent any public interests from being protected through the judicial process. It does serve as at least an * * * attempt to put the decision as to whether review will be sought in the hands of those who have a direct stake in the outcome. That goal would be undermined were we to construe the A.P.A. to authorize judicial review at the behest of organizations or individuals who seek to do no more than vindicate their own value preferences through the judicial process. The principle that the Sierra Club would have us establish in this case would do just that. As we conclude that the Court of Appeals was correct in its holding that the Sierra Club lacked standing to maintain this action, we do not reach any other questions presented in the petition, and we intimate no view on the merits of the complaint. The judgment is

Affirmed.

Mr. Justice Powell and Mr. Justice Rehnquist took no part in the consideration or decision of this case.

Mr. Justice Douglas, dissenting.

I share the views of my Brother Blackmun and would reverse the judgment below.

The critical question of "standing" would be simplified and also put neatly in focus if we fashioned a federal rule that allowed environmental issues to be litigated before federal agencies or federal courts in the name of the inanimate object about to be despoiled, defaced, or invaded by roads and bulldozers and where injury is the subject of public outrage. Contemporary public concern for protecting nature's ecological equilibrium should lead to the conferral of standing upon environmental objects to sue for their own preservation. See Stone, Should Trees Have Standing?--Toward Legal Rights for Natural Objects, 45 S. Cal. L. Rev. 450 (1972). This suit would therefore be more properly labeled as Mineral King v Morton.

Inanimate objects are sometimes parties in litigation. A ship has a legal personality, a fiction found useful for maritime purposes. the corporation sole--a creature of ecclesiastical law--is an acceptable adversary and large fortunes ride on its cases. The ordinary corporation is a "person" for purposes of the adjudicatory processes, whether it represents proprietary, spiritual, esthetic, or charitable causes.

So it should be as respects valleys, alpine meadows, rivers, lakes, estuaries, beaches, ridges, groves of trees, swampland, or even air that feels the destructive pressures of modern technology and modern life. The river, for example, is the living symbol of all the life it sustains or nourishes--fish, aquatic insects, water ouzels, otter, fisher, deer, elk, bear, and all other animals, including man, who are dependent on it or who enjoy it for its sight, its sound, or its life. The river as plaintiff speaks for the ecological unit of life that is part of it. Those people who have a meaningful relation to that body of water--whether it be a fisherman, a canoeist, a zoologist, or a logger--must be able to speak for the values which the river represents and which are threatened with destruction.* * *

Mineral King[5] is doubtless like other wonders of the Sierra Nevada * * *. Those who hike it, fish it, hunt it, camp in it, frequent it, or visit it merely to sit in solitude and wonderment are legitimate spokesmen for it, whether they may be few or many. Those who have that intimate relations with the inanimate object about to be injured, polluted, or otherwise despoiled are its legitimate spokesmen.

The Solicitor General takes a wholly different approach. He considers the problem in terms of "government by the Judiciary." With all respect, the problem is to make certain that the inanimate objects, which are the very core of America's beauty, have spokesmen before they are destroyed. It is, of course, true that most of them are under the control of a federal or state agency. The standards given those agencies are usually expressed in terms of the "public interest." Yet "public interest" has so many differing shades of meaning as to be quite meaningless on the environmental front. Congress accordingly has adopted ecological standards in the National Environmental Policy Act of 1969[.] [See chapter 10.]

Yet the pressures on agencies for favorable action one way or the other are enormous. The suggestion that Congress can stop action which is undesirable is true in theory; yet even Congress is too remote to give meaningful direction and its machinery is too ponderous to use very often. The federal agencies of which I speak are not venal or corrupt. But they are notoriously under the control of powerful interests who manipulate them through advisory committees, or friendly working relations, or who have that natural affinity with the agency which in time develop between the regulator and the regulated.

---

[5] Although in the past Mineral King Valley has annually supplied about 70,000 visitor-days of simpler and more rustic forms of recreation--hiking, camping, and skiing (without lifts)--the Forest Service in 1949 and again in 1965 invited developers to submit proposals to "improve" the Valley for resort use. Walt Disney Productions won the competition and transformed the Service's idea into a mammoth project 10 times its originally proposed dimensions. For example, while the Forest Service prospectus called for an investment of at least $3 million and a sleeping capacity of at least 100, Disney will spend $35.3 million and will bed down 3,300 persons by 1978. Disney also plans a nine-level parking structure with two supplemental lots for automobiles, 10 restaurants and 20 ski lifts. The Service's annual license revenue is hitched to Disney's profits. Under Disney's projections, the Valley will be forced to accommodate a tourist population twice as dense as that in Yosemite Valley on a busy day. And, although Disney has bought up much of the private land near the project, another commercial firm plans to transform an adjoining 160-acre parcel into a "piggy-back" resort complex, further adding to the volume of human activity the Valley must endure.

* * * Michael Frome cautions that the national forests are "fragile" and "deteriorate rapidly with excessive recreation use" because "[t]he trampling effect alone eliminates vegetative growth, creating erosion and water runoff problems. The concentration of people, particularly in horse parties, on excessively steep slopes that follow old Indian or cattle routes, has torn up the landscape of the High Sierras in California and sent tons of wilderness soil washing downstream each year." M. Frome, The Forest Service 69 (1971).

[One] court of appeals [has] observed, "the recurring question which has plagued public regulation of industry [is] whether the regulatory agency is unduly oriented toward the interest of the industry it is designed to regulate, rather than the public interest it is designed to protect." *Moss v. CAB*, 139 U.S. App. D.C. 150, 152, 430 F.2d 891, 893. The Forest Service--one of the federal agencies behind the scheme to despoil Mineral King--has been notorious for its alignment with lumber companies, although its mandate from Congress directs it to consider the various aspects of multiple use in its supervision of the national forests.[7]

The voice of the inanimate object, therefore, should not be stilled. That does not mean that the judiciary takes over the managerial functions from the federal agency. It merely means that before these priceless bits of Americana (such as a valley, an alpine meadow, a river, or a lake) are forever lost or are so transformed as to be reduced to the eventual rubble or our urban environment, the voice of the existing beneficiaries of these environmental wonders should be heard.* * *

Those who hike the Appalachian Trail into Sunfish Pond, New Jersey, and camp or sleep there, or run the Allagash in Maine, or climb the Guadalupes in West Texas, or who canoe and portage the Quetico Superior in Minnesota, certainly should have standing to defend those natural wonders before courts or agencies, though they live 3,000 miles away.[8] Those who merely are caught up in environmental news or propaganda and flock to defend these waters or areas may be treated differently. That is why these environmental issues should be tendered by the inanimate object itself. Then there will be assurances that all of the forms of life which it represents will stand before the court--the pileated woodpecker as well as the coyote and bear, the lemmings as well as the trout in the streams. Those inarticulate members of the ecological group cannot speak. But those people who have so frequented the place as to know its values and wonders will be able to speak for the entire ecological community.

---

[7] [T]he Multiple-Use Sustained-Yield Act of 1960, 74 Stat 215, 16 USCA §§ 528-531 * * * provides that competing considerations should include outdoor recreation, range, timber, watershed, wildlife, and fish purposes. The Forest Service, influenced by powerful logging interests, has, however, paid only lip service to its multiple-use mandate and has auctioned away millions of timberland areas without considering environmental or conservational interests. * * * [And] despite much criticism, the Forest Service had adhered to a policy of permitting logging companies to "clearcut" tracts of auctioned acreage. "Clearcutting," somewhat analogous to strip mining, is the indiscriminate and complete shaving from the earth of all trees--regardless of size or age--often across hundreds of contiguous acres.

Of clearcutting, Senator Gale McGee, a leading antagonist of Forest Service policy, complains: "The Forest Service's management policies are wreaking havoc with the environment. Soil is eroding, reforestation is neglected if not ignored, streams are silting, and clearcutting remains a basic practice." N.Y. Times, Nov. 14, 1971, p. 60, col. 2. He adds: "In Wyoming . . . the Forest Service is very much . . . nursemaid . . . to the lumber industry . . . ." * * *

[8] Permitting a court to appoint a representative of an inanimate object would not be significantly different from customary judicial appointments of guardians ad litem, executors, conservators, receivers, or counsel for indigents.

Ecology reflects the land ethic; and Aldo Leopold wrote in A Sand County Almanac 204 (1949), "The land ethic simply enlarges the boundaries of the community to include soils, waters, plants, and animals, or collectively: the land."

That, as I see it, is the issue of "standing" in the present case and controversy.

Mr. Justice Brennan, dissenting.

I agree that the Sierra Club has standing for the reasons stated by my Brother Blackmun in Alternative No. 2 of his dissent.

Mr. Justice Blackmun, dissenting.

* * *If this were an ordinary case, I would join the opinion and the Court's judgment and be quite content.

But this is not ordinary, run-of-the-mill litigation. The case poses--if only we choose to acknowledge and reach them--significant aspects of a wide * * * problem, that is, the Nation's and the world's deteriorating environment with its resulting ecological disturbances. Must our law be so rigid and our procedural concepts so inflexible that we render ourselves helpless when the existing methods and the traditional concepts do not quite fit and do not probe to be entirely adequate for new issues?* * * Rather than pursue the course the Court has chosen to take by its affirmance of the judgment of the Court of Appeals, I would adopt one of two alternatives:

1. I would reverse that judgment and, instead, approve the judgment of the District Court which recognized standing in the Sierra Club and granted preliminary relief. I would be willing to do this on condition that the Sierra Club forthwith amend its complaint to meet the specifications the Court prescribes for standing. If Sierra Club fails or refuses to take that step, so be it; the case will then collapse. But if it does amend, the merits will be before the trial court once again. As the Court, ante, so clearly reveals, the issues on the merits are substantial and deserve resolution. They assay new ground. They are crucial to the future of Mineral King. They raise important ramifications for the quality of the country's public land management.* * *

2. Alternatively, I would permit an imaginative expansion of our traditional concepts of standing in order to enable an organization such as the Sierra Club, possessed, as it is, of pertinent, bona fide, and well-recognized attributes and purposes in the area of environment, to litigate environmental issues. This incursion upon tradition need not be very extensive. Certainly, it should be no cause for alarm. It is no more progressive than was the decision in Data Processing itself. It need only recognize the interest of one who has a provable, sincere, dedicated, and established status. We need not fear that Pandora's box will be opened or that there will be no limit in environmental litigation. The courts will exercise appropriate restraints just as they have exercises the in the past. Who would have suspected 20 years ago that the concepts of standing enunciated in Data Processing and Barlow would be the measure for today? And Mr. Justice Douglas, in his eloquent opinion,

has imaginatively suggested another means and one, in its own way, with obvious, appropriate, and self-imposed limitations as to standing. As I read what he has written, he makes only one addition to the customary criteria (the existence of a genuine dispute; the assurance of adversariness; and a conviction that the party whose standing is challenged will adequately represent the interests he asserts), that is, that the litigant be one who speaks knowingly for the environmental values he asserts.

## Notes

Does the Court's decision in *Sierra Club* encourage imagination in pleadings in order to be assured of standing? Should these exercises be encouraged? Will citizens at large be able to litigate under the injury in fact language of the Court? Does this toss the ball back to Congress? How did the standing of Sierra Club in this case differ from that of the petitioners in *Scenic Hudson?* Did this decision overrule or modify *Scenic Hudson*?

Who are the "users" with a "personal stake" in a natural resource such as a river or wilderness area? Might not various users have widely conflicting interests--lumber companies, hikers, developers, campground operators? How may the courts decide which "user" has standing? Might all have it? Does Justice Douglas's standing for inanimate objects solve this problem?

Why did the Sierra Club not assert an individualized interest? On remand, it amended its complaint to assert the requisite injury specific to it. A motion to dismiss that complaint was denied. 348 F.Supp. 219 (1972). Later the Department of the Interior changed its mind about the Mineral King Development. It became a national park in 1978.

A year after *Sierra Club v. Morton* the Supreme Court held, in *United States v. SCRAP*, 412 U.S. 669, 93 S.Ct. 2405, 37 L.Ed.2d 254' (1973), that a group of law students using "SCRAP' as an acronym had standing to challenge an Interstate Commerce Commission decision allowing higher railroad freight rates for scrap than for original metal and thus encouraging the fabrication of new steel and aluminum rather than recycling. The plaintiffs' allegation of standing was that they used the parks and forests of the Washington, D.C. area and that "these uses have been adversely affected by the increased freight rates" that presumably led to greater discarding of beer cans and the like. They also alleged the disparity in rates caused air pollution and higher taxes. The Supreme Court upheld the students' standing in an opinion by Stewart, J., who had written the Court's opinion in *Sierra Club v. Morton*. Three justices dissented.

Despite the seeming impact of SCRAP, two years later in *Warth v. Seldin*, 422 U.S. 490, 95 S.Ct. 2197, 45 L.Ed.2d 343 (1975), the Supreme Court found a wide assortment of plaintiffs lacked standing in a land-use case, holding a plaintiff must allege a "distinct and palpable injury to himself, even if it is an injury shared by a large class of other possible litigants." 422 U.S. at 501.

In *Warth v. Seldin* various citizen groups and builders, along with individuals, challenged a zoning ordinance as excluding low- and moderate-income persons and as racially discriminatory by excluding these income levels. All the plaintiffs were denied standing for various reasons. Individuals asserting standing as persons of low or moderate income and as members of minority racial groups were found not to have been personally injured. None had ever lived in Penfield (the town whose zoning was being challenged) and none said they had specifically been denied housing. Their claim rested on the general unavailability of low income housing in Penfield. The Court held this was an insufficient basis for standing since they could not show they would be able to obtain housing if the zoning ordinance were invalidated.

Taxpayers from a neighboring large city, Rochester, were denied standing to raise their claim that Penfield's zoning practices compel Rochester residents to provide more public housing at a higher cost to taxpayers. The Court found this claim was mere conjecture and could not be traced to Penfield's zoning specifically. The Court also noted that there is no statutory or constitutional right not to have neighboring communities adversely affect your taxes.

Three builders' associations were also denied standing. They claimed lost profits for their members since they could not build low- and moderate-income housing in Penfield. Here the Court looked to the pleadings and the relief sought. The associations were seeking damages yet no member alleged specific monetary injury to itself. The injunctive relief they sought was rejected on the grounds that no builder had not been denied any specific project. The builders did not allege denial of permits or variances nor did they assert any specific plan to rebuild in Penfield.

Two years later, in *Village of Arlington Heights* v. *Metropolitan Housing Development Corp*., 429 U.S. 252, 97 S.Ct. 555, 50 L.Ed 2d 450 (1977), the Supreme Court, citing *Warth v. Seldin* with approval, changed its tack and allowed the plaintiff organization to challenge a zoning ordinance, which it asserted to be an absolute barrier to its building plans. Here the builders had acquired a specific site and had plans for low- and moderate-income housing to be built there. The Court distinguished the position of the builders in Arlington Heights from those in *Warth v. Seldin* on this basis.

The Court also found an individual plaintiff, Ransom, had standing to challenge the zoning as discriminatory. Ransom, who was black, worked in Arlington Heights yet alleged he could not obtain housing there. He claimed he would qualify for the specific housing sought to be built and would probably move there if it was built. His was found not to be a generalized grievance since it focused on a particular project. Here, unlike the individual plaintiffs in *Warth*, Ransom asserted that it was the zoning which prevented him from obtaining housing in Penfield.

How do these cases affect *SCRAP?* Are they distinguishable? Does it matter that the issues in *SCRAP* involved nation-wide freight rates while those in the two exclusionary zoning cases were more local and site-specific, though with national overtones?

State courts have generally lagged behind the federal courts in granting standing to environmental and other citizen groups. Until the late 1970s New York's courts insisted on a showing of financial injury (*St. Clair* v. *Yonkers Raceway*, 13 N.Y.2d 72, 192 N.E.2d 15, 242 N.Y.S.2d 43 [1963], cert. denied 375 U.S. 970), which the federal courts had long abandoned. In the past few years New York has accepted a standing rule close to the federal courts'. See *Boryszewski v. Brydges*, 37 N.Y.2d 361, 334 N.E.2d 579, 372 N.Y.S.2d 623 (1975); *Douglaston Civic Ass'n* v. *Galvin*, 36 N.Y.2d 1, 324 N.E.2d 317, 364 N.Y.S. 2d 830 (1974).

Some environmental statutes provide automatic standing through citizen-suit provisions. See Clean Air Act § 304 (42 USCA § 7604); Clean Water Act § 505 (33 USCA § 1365). Do these provide a basis for challenging all acts which degrade air or water quality? The provisions require 60 days' notice to the EPA before bringing suit. Is this a prerequisite to the court's taking jurisdiction? See *Natural Resources Defense Council v. Callaway*, Chapter 7, Part B, where the court ruled the 60-day notice provision "not an absolute bar to earlier suits [since] jurisdiction * * * can exist under either the general federal question statute, 28 U.S.C. § 1331, or the Administrative Procedure Act, 5 U.S.C. §§ 701-06."

In 1990 the Supreme Court reminded environmental plaintiffs that the concerns it voiced in *Sierra Club* v. *Morton* are still alive. In *Lujan* v. *National Wildlife Federation*, 497 U.S. 871, 110 S.Ct. 3177, 111 L.Ed.2d 695 (1990), it held a respected nationwide conservation group lacked standing to challenge the reclassification of lands by the Bureau of Land Management, an agency within the Interior Department. The plaintiff failed to show it was aggrieved since, in the Court's view, its members' affidavits related to large tracts of land, not just to those to be reclassified. Further, the Court held, the Federation could not challenge the agency's "land withdrawal review program," by which it reviewed classifications of government lands, since that amounted to "seek[ing] *wholesale* improvement of the program by court decree." (Emphasis in original.)

The Court shrugged off the broader standing allowed in *SCRAP*, noting that the decision's "expansive expression of what would suffice for [Administrative Procedure Act] review . . . has never since been emulated by this Court . . ."

A 1992 Supreme Court decision, *Lujan* v. *Defenders of Wildlife*, 504 U.S. 555, 112 S.Ct. 2130, 119 L.Ed.2d 351 (1992), limits standing even more dramatically than *National Wildlife Federation*, and despite the presence of a citizen suit provision designed, one might think, to obviate standing concerns. *Defenders of Wildlife* was a suit challenging an Interior Department rule limiting to actions within the United States the Endangered Species Act requirement that federal agencies consult with Interior to ensure that their actions not injure the critical habitat of endangered species. (See Chapter 4 for a discussion of this provision.)

The Supreme Court held that the plaintiff organization and its members lacked standing. Affidavits of members that they visited the habitats of endangered species in Egypt and Sri Lanka that were jeopardized by United States-funded projects were rejected because the members failed to assert imminent injury. Their statements of intent to return to those countries without specifying when were held to lack specificity. So was their claim that the impact of the federal action on these foreign ecosystems would be reflected in this country.

To cap it off, the Court (Scalia, J.) held the Act's citizen suit section could not be used, without assertions of actual injury, to enforce the merely procedural right that the federal agencies funding the projects consult with Interior:

> To permit Congress to convert the undifferentiated public interest in executive officers' compliance with the law into an "individual right" vindicable in the courts is to permit Congress to transfer from the President to the courts the Chief Executive's most important constitutional duty, to "take care that the Laws be faithfully executed," Art. II, §3.* * * As we said in *Sierra Club*, "[Statutorily] broadening the categories of injury that may be [asserted] in support of standing is a different matter from abandoning the requirement that the party seeking review must himself have suffered an injury."

Soon after, in *Bennett v. Spear*, 520 U.S. 154, 117 S.Ct. 1154, 137 L.Ed.2d 281 (1997), the Supreme Court swung back toward broader standing. It held the citizen-suit provision of the Endangered Species Act involved in *Defenders of Wildlife* ("any person may commence a civil suit . . .") applies to persons with economic interests, not just environmental interests. The *Bennett* plaintiffs were irrigation districts and ranchers using water from a reservoir the Department of the Interior ruled must be kept at a high level to protect two fishes on the endangered list. The Court found these plaintiffs had standing and need not show specific injury under the Act's citizen-suit statute.

Is this decision consistent with *Defenders*? Was the Court more sympathetic with the economic needs of commercial water users than the interests of the zoologists in the prior case? Or are these plaintiffs' interests genuinely more concrete?

In *Steel Co. v. Citizens for a Better Environment*, 523 U.S. 83, 118 S.Ct. 1003, 140 L.Ed.2d 210 (1998), the Court swung back toward a narrower view of standing. This suit by a citizen group contended an industrial facility had failed for eight years to file documents regarding releases of hazardous air pollutants in violation of the Emergency Planning and Citizen Right-to-Know Act, 42 USCA §§ 11001-11050. However, the defendant filled the required information before the plaintiffs' action commenced, once it received the mandatory notice of impending suit. The Court (Scalia, J.) held they lacked standing. No injunction was available to challenge wholly past violations. No declaratory judgment lay since the violations were acknowledged. And the civil penalties sought under the Act were likewise insufficient to redress any injury to the plaintiffs since the money was payable to the Government, not the plaintiffs.

Was this decision correct? Should it apply where the defendant's violations were not halted until after the suit commenced?

FRIENDS OF THE EARTH v. LAIDLAW ENVIRONMENTAL SERVICES, United States Supreme Court, 2000. 528 U.S. 167, 120 S.Ct. 693, 145 L.Ed.2d 610.

Ginsburg, J.: In the Clean Water Act citizen suit now before us, the District Court determined that injunctive relief was inappropriate because the defendant, after the institution of the litigation, achieved substantial compliance with the terms of its discharge permit. The court did, however, assess a civil penalty of $405,800. The "total deterrent effect" of the penalty would be adequate to forestall future violations, the court reasoned, taking into account that the defendant "will be required to reimburse plaintiffs for a significant amount of legal fees and has, itself, incurred significant legal expenses."

The Court of Appeals vacated the District Court's order. The case became moot, the appellate court declared, once the defendant fully complied with the terms of its permit and the plaintiff failed to appeal the denial of equitable relief. "[C]ivil penalties payable to the government," the Court of Appeals stated, "would not redress any injury Plaintiffs have suffered." * * *

We reverse the judgment of the Court of Appeals. The appellate court erred in concluding that a citizen suitor's claim for civil penalties must be dismissed as moot when the defendant, albeit after commencement of the litigation, has come into compliance. In directing dismissal of the suit on grounds of mootness, the Court of Appeals incorrectly conflated our case law on initial standing to bring suit, see, *e.g., Steel Co. v. Citizens for a Better Environment*, with our case law on post-commencement mootness, *see, e.g., City of Mesquite v. Aladdin's Castle, Inc.*, 455 U.S. 283, 102 S.Ct. 1070, 71 L.Ed.2d 152 (1982). A defendant's voluntary cessation of allegedly unlawful conduct ordinarily does not suffice to moot a case. The Court of Appeals also misperceived the remedial potential of civil penalties. Such penalties may serve, as an alternative to an injunction, to deter future violations and thereby redress the injuries that prompted a citizen suitor to commence litigation. * * *

Under § 505(a) of the [Clean Water] Act, a suit to enforce any limitation in [a] permit may be brought by any "citizen," defined as "a person or persons having an interest which is or may be adversely affected." 33 U.S.C. §§ 1365(a), (g). Sixty days before initiating a citizen suit, however, the would-be plaintiff must give notice of the alleged violation to the EPA, the State in which the alleged violation occurred, and the alleged violator. § 1365(b)(1)(A). "[T]he purpose of notice to the alleged violator is to give it an opportunity to bring itself into complete compliance with the Act and thus . . . render unnecessary a citizen suit." *Gwaltney of Smithfield, Ltd. v. Chesapeake Bay Foundation, Inc.*, 484 U.S. 49, 60, 108 S.Ct. 376, 98 L.Ed.2d 306 (1987). Accordingly, we have held that citizens lack statutory standing under § 505(a) to sue for violations that have ceased by the time the complaint is filed. *Id.* * * *

The Act authorizes district courts in citizen-suit proceedings to enter injunctions and to assess civil penalties, which are payable to the United States Treasury.

* * *

Once it received its permit, Laidlaw began to discharge various pollutants into the waterway; repeatedly, Laidlaw's discharges exceeded the limits set by the permit. * * *

On June 12, 1992, FOE filed this citizen suit against Laidlaw under § 505(a) of the Act, alleging noncompliance with the * * * permit and seeking declaratory and injunctive relief and an award of civil penalties. * * *

The record indicates that after FOE initiated the suit, but before the District Court rendered judgment, Laidlaw violated the mercury discharge limitation in its permit 13 times. The District Court also found that Laidlaw had committed 13 monitoring and 10 reporting violations during this period. The last recorded mercury discharge violation occurred in January 1995, long after the complaint was filed but about two years before judgment was rendered.

* * *

[T]he District Court found that Laidlaw had gained a total economic benefit of $1,092,581 as a result of its extended period of noncompliance with the mercury discharge limit in its permit. [It awarded] a civil penalty of $405,800 [but] declined to grant FOE's request for injunctive relief, stating that an injunction was inappropriate because "Laidlaw has been in substantial compliance with all parameters in its NPDES permit since at least August 1992." * * *

The Court of Appeals assumed without deciding that FOE initially had standing to bring the action, but went on to hold that the case had become moot * * * because "the only remedy currently available to [FOE] -- civil penalties payable to the government -- would not redress any injury [FOE has] suffered." *Id.*, at 306-307. The court therefore vacated the District Court's order and remanded with instructions to dismiss the action.

* * *

Laidlaw contends first that FOE lacked standing from the outset even to seek injunctive relief, because the plaintiff organizations failed to show that any of their members had sustained or faced the threat of any "injury in fact" from Laidlaw's activities. In support of this contention Laidlaw points to the District Court's finding, made in the course of setting the penalty amount, that there had been "no demonstrated proof of harm to the environment" from Laidlaw's mercury discharge violations. * * *

The relevant showing for purposes of Article III standing, however, is not injury to the environment but injury to the plaintiff. [And] the District Court found the FOE had demonstrated sufficient injury to establish standing. For example, FOE member Kenneth Lee Curtis averred in affidavits that he lived a half-mile from Laidlaw's facility; that he occasionally drove over the North Tyger River, and that it looked and smelled polluted; and that he would like to fish, camp, swim, and picnic in and near the river between 3 and 15 miles downstream from the facility, as he did when he was a teenager, but would not do so because he was concerned that the water was polluted by Laidlaw's discharges. * * *

Other members presented evidence to similar effect. * * *

These sworn statements, as the District Court determined, adequately documented injury in fact. We have held that environmental plaintiffs adequately allege injury in fact when they aver that they use the affected area and are persons "for whom the aesthetic and recreational values of the area will be lessened" by the challenged activity. *Sierra Club v. Morton.*

* * *

Laidlaw argues that even if FOE had standing to seek injunctive relief, it lacked standing to seek civil penalties. Here the asserted defect is not injury but redressability. Civil penalties offer no redress to private plaintiffs, Laidlaw argues, because they are paid to the government, and therefore a citizen plaintiff can never have standing to seek them. * * *

We have recognized on numerous occasions that "all civil penalties have some deterrent effect." *Hudson* v. *United States*, 522 U.S. 93, 102, 118 S.Ct. 488, 139 L.Ed.2d 450 (1997). More specifically, Congress has found that civil penalties in Clean Water Act cases do more than promote immediate compliance by limiting the defendant's economic incentive to delay its attainment of permit limits; they also deter future violations. This congressional determination warrants judicial attention and respect. * * *

It can scarcely be doubted that, for a plaintiff who is injured or faces the threat of future injury due to illegal conduct ongoing at the time of suit, a sanction that effectively abates that conduct and prevents its recurrence provides a form of redress. Civil penalties can fit that description. To the extent that they encourage defendants to discontinue current violations and deter them from committing future ones, they afford redress to citizen plaintiffs who are injured or threatened with injury as a consequence of ongoing unlawful conduct. * * *

Laidlaw contends that the reasoning of our decision in *Steel Co.* directs the conclusion that citizen plaintiffs have no standing to seek civil penalties under the Act. We disagree. *Steel Co.* established that citizen suitors lack standing to seek civil penalties for violations that have abated by the time of suit. We specifically noted in that case that there was no allegation in the complaint of any continuing or imminent violation, and that no basis for such an allegation appeared to exist.

* * *

Satisfied that FOE had standing under Article III to bring this action, we turn to the question of mootness.

The only conceivable basis for a finding of mootness in this case is Laidlaw's voluntary conduct -- either its achievement by August 1992 of substantial compliance with its * * * permit or its more recent shutdown of the * * * facility. It is well settled that "a defendant's voluntary cessation of a challenged practice does not deprive a federal court of its power to determine the legality of the practice." *City of Mesquite*, 455 U.S., at 289, 102 S.Ct. 1070. "[I]f it did, the courts would be compelled to leave '[t]he defendant . . . free to return to his old ways.'" * * * The "heavy burden of persua[ding]" the court that the challenged conduct cannot reasonably be expected to start up again lies with the party asserting mootness.

The Court of Appeals justified its mootness disposition by reference to *Steel Co.*, which held that citizen plaintiffs lack standing to seek civil penalties for wholly past violations. In relying on *Steel Co.*, the Court of Appeals confused mootness with standing.

* * *

As just noted, a defendant claiming that its voluntary compliance moots a case bears the formidable burden of showing that it is absolutely clear the allegedly wrongful behavior could not reasonably be expected to recur. By contrast, in a lawsuit brought to force compliance, it is the plaintiff's burden to establish standing by demonstrating that, if unchecked by the litigation, the defendant's allegedly wrongful behavior will likely occur or continue, and that the "threatened injury [is] certainly impending." * * *

The plain lesson of these cases is that there are circumstances in which the prospect that a defendant will engage in (or resume) harmful conduct may be too speculative to support standing, but not too speculative to overcome mootness.

* * *

Standing doctrine functions to ensure, among other things, that the scarce resources of the federal courts are devoted to those disputes in which the parties have a concrete stake. In contrast, by the time mootness is an issue, the case has been brought and litigated, often (as here) for years. To abandon the case at an advanced stage may prove more wasteful than frugal. * * *

The District Court denied injunctive relief, but expressly based its award of civil penalties on the need for deterrence. * * * In accordance with this aim, a district court in a Clean Water Act citizen suit properly may conclude that an injunction would be an excessively intrusive remedy, because it could entail continuing superintendence of the permit holder's activities by a federal court -- a process burdensome to court and permit holder alike [-- but nonetheless award a civil penalty.]

Scalia, J., with whom Thomas, J., joins, dissenting:

* * * The Court's treatment of the redressability requirement [is] cavalier. [P]etitioners allege ongoing injury consisting of diminished enjoyment of the affected waterways and decreased property values. They allege that these injuries are caused by Laidlaw's continuing permit violations. But the remedy petitioners seek is neither recompense for their injuries nor an injunction against future violations. Instead, the remedy is a statutorily specified "penalty" for past violations, payable entirely to the United States Treasury. Only last Term, we held that such penalties do not redress any injury a citizen plaintiff has suffered from past violations. *Steel Co.* The Court nonetheless finds the redressability requirement satisfied here, distinguishing *Steel Co.* on the ground that in this case the petitioners allege ongoing violations; payment of the penalties, it says, will

remedy petitioners' injury by deterring future violations by Laidlaw. It holds that a penalty payable to the public "remedies" a threatened private harm, and suffices to sustain a private suit.

That holding has no precedent in our jurisprudence, and takes this Court beyond the "cases and controversies" that Article III of the Constitution has entrusted to its resolution. Even if it were appropriate, moreover, to allow Article III's remediation requirement to be satisfied by the indirect private consequences of a public penalty, those consequences are entirely too speculative in the present case.

* * *

The deterrence on which the plaintiffs must rely for standing in the present case is the marginal increase in Laidlaw's fear of future penalties that will be achieved by adding federal penalties for Laidlaw's past conduct.

I cannot say for certain that this marginal increase is zero; but I can say for certain that it is entirely speculative whether it will make the difference between these plaintiffs' suffering injury in the future and these plaintiffs' going unharmed. In fact, the assertion that it will "likely" do so is entirely farfetched.

* * *

[I]f this case is, as the Court suggests, within the central core of "deterrence" standing, it is impossible to imagine what the "outer limits" could possible be. The Court's expressed reluctance to define those "outer limits" serves only to disguise the fact that it has promulgated a revolutionary new doctrine of standing that will permit the entire body of public civil penalties to be handed over to enforcement by private interests.

Does *Laidlaw* amount to an overruling, in effect, of *Steel Co.*? Or is there a valid distinction between cessation of unlawful conduct before and after suit is filed?

Should standing hinge on whether the plaintiff alleges injury to the environment, as opposed to the plaintiff's own injury (such as inability to fish or swim in polluted waters)? *Laidlaw* holds that personal injury is decisive. Must the plaintiff then show, in order to have standing, that the chemical content of the water (or air) has been altered? *Laidlaw* holds that is not required for standing -- though it may well be needed to prevail at trial.

The Eleventh Amendment, which bars most suits against states in the federal courts, has been held to prohibit a citizen suit to enjoin, and obtain a civil penalty for, pollution from a state-owned source like a prison. See *Burnette v. Carothers*, 192 F.2d 52 (2d Cir. 1999). Correctly decided? The courts have held the Eleventh Amendment does not bar suits for injunctions against state officials, see *Ex Parte Young*, 209 U.S. 123, 28 S.Ct. 441, 52 L.Ed. 714 (1908). Why should it bar such a suit against a state agency?

# 2. NUISANCE

## A. DAMAGES AND INJUNCTION

### Introductory Note

Nuisance is the common law remedy which was in large measure the matrix of environmental law. It furnishes a cause of action to redress acts degrading air, water and land--dust, odors, noise, dumping of chemicals. The list is limitless because nuisance, as a common law action, is constantly being adapted as technology brings forth new forms of injury. And the existence of the host of statutes and government agencies dedicated to environmental protection has in no way made nuisance anachronistic, as the following cases show.

COPART INDUSTRIES, INC. V. CONSOLIDATED EDISON CO., New York Court of Appeals, 1977. 41 N.Y.2d 564, 362 N.E.2d 968, 394 N.Y.S.2d 169.

Cooke, J. "There is perhaps no more impenetrable jungle in the entire law than that which surrounds the word 'nuisance'. It has meant all things to all men" (Prosser, Torts [4th ed], p. 571). From a point someplace within this oft-noted thicket envisioned by Professor Prosser, this appeal emerges.

Plaintiff leased a portion of the former Brooklyn Navy Yard for a period of five years commencing September 1, 1970. On the demised premises during the ensuing eight or nine months it conducted a storage and new car preparation business, the latter entailing over 50 steps ranging from services such as checking brakes to vehicle cleaning, catering to automobile dealers in the metropolitan area of New York City. Adjacent to the navy yard was defendant's Hudson Avenue plant, engaged in the production of steam and electricity since about 1926. This generating system had five smokestacks and during the time in question its burners were fired with oil having sulphur content of 1% or less. Prior to 1968, coal had been the fuel employed and the main boiler was equipped with an electrostatic precipitator to remove or control the discharged fly ash. Upon conversion to oil, the precipitator had been deactivated.

Based on allegations that noxious emissions from defendant's nearby stacks caused damage to the exterior of autos stored for its customers such as to require many to be repainted, that reports were received in early 1971 from patrons of paint discoloration and pitting, and that dealers served by plaintiff terminated their business by early May, plaintiff contends that because of said emissions it was caused to cease doing business on May 28, 1971. This action was instituted seeking $1,300,000 for loss of investment and loss of profit, * * * asserting "a deliberate and willful violation of the rights of plaintiff, constituting a nuisance."* * * The case came on for jury trial in 1974. [T]he trial court charged nuisance based on negligence and nuisance grounded on an intentional invasion of plaintiff's rights.

Negligence was defined and it was pointed out that, although contributory negligence may be a defense where the basis of the nuisance is merely negligent conduct, it would not be where the wrongdoing is founded on the intentional, deliberate, misconduct of defendant. Contending that "nuisance is entirely separate and apart from negligence" and that "defendant's intent or negligence is not * * * an essential element of the cause of action of nuisance", plaintiff excepted to the portions of the charge relating to said subjects.

The jury found in defendant's favor and judgment was entered dismissing the complaint. The Appellate Division, by a divided court, affirmed.* * * On appeal to this court, plaintiff maintains that the trial court erred in charging (1) that plaintiff was required to prove an intent for the defendant to cause damages, and (2) that plaintiff had a burden of proof as to defendant's negligence and plaintiff's freedom from contributory negligence.

Much of the uncertainty and confusion surrounding the use of the term nuisance, which in itself means no more than harm, injury, inconvenience, or annoyance (see Webster's Third New International Dictionary, p. 571; American Heritage Dictionary, p. 900), arises from a series of historical accidents covering the invasion of different kinds of interests and referring to various kinds of conduct on the part of defendants (Prosser, Torts [4th ed], pp. 571-572). The word surfaced as early as the twelfth century in the assize of nuisance, which provided redress where the injury was not a disseisin but rather an indirect damage to the land or an interference with its use of enjoyment. Three centuries later the remedy was replaced by the common-law action on the case for nuisance, invoked only for damages upon the invasion of interests in the use and enjoyment of land, as well as of easements and profits. If abatement by judicial process was desired, resort to equity was required. Along with the civil remedy protecting rights in land, there developed a separate principle that an infringement of the right of the crown, or of the general public, was a crime and, in time, this class of offenses was so enlarged as to include any "act not warranted by law, or omission to discharge a legal duty, which inconveniences the public in the exercise of rights common to all Her Majesty's subjects" (Stephen, General View of Criminal Laws of England [1890], p. 105). At first, interference with the rights of the public was confined to the criminal realm but in time an individual who suffered special damages from a public nuisance was accorded a right of action. (See Restatement, Torts, notes preceding § 822, pp. 217-218; Prosser, Torts [4th ed], pp. 572-573.)

A private nuisance threatens one person or a relative few, an essential feature being an interference with the use or enjoyment of land. It is actionable by the individual person or persons whose rights have been disturbed (Restatement, Torts, notes preceding § 822, p. 217). A public, or as sometimes termed a common, nuisance is an offense against the State, and is subject to abatement or prosecution on application of the proper governmental agency (Restatement, Torts, notes preceding § 822, p. 217; see Penal Law, § 240.45). It consists of conduct or omissions which offend, interfere with or cause damage to the public in the exercise of rights common to all (*New York Trap Rock Corp. v. Town of Clarkstown*, 299

N.Y. 77, 80), in a manner such as to offend public morals, interfere with use by the public of a public place or endanger or injure the property, health, safety or comfort of a considerable number of persons (Restatement, Torts, notes preceding § 822, p. 217).

As observed by Professor Prosser, public and private nuisances "have almost nothing in common, except that each causes inconvenience to someone, and it would have been fortunate if they had been called from the beginning by different names" (Prosser, Torts [4th ed], p. 573).* * *

Despite early private nuisance cases, which apparently assumed that the defendant was strictly liable, today it is recognized that one is subject to liability for a private nuisance if his conduct is a legal cause of the invasion of the interest in the private use and enjoyment of land and such invasion is (1) intentional and unreasonable, (2) negligent or reckless, or (3) actionable under the rules governing liability for abnormally dangerous conditions or activities (Restatement, Torts 2d [Tent. Draft No. 16], § 822; Prosser, Torts [4th ed], p. 574).

In urging that the charge in respect to negligence constituted error, plaintiff's brief opens its discussion with the assertion that "[t]he complaint contained no allegations of negligence and its theory was that of nuisance." This statement is significant in that not only does it miss the fundamental difference between types of conduct which may result in nuisance and the invasion of interests in land, which is the nuisance, but it also overlooks the firmly established principle that negligence is merely one type of conduct which may give rise to a nuisance. A nuisance, either public or private, based on negligence and whether characterized as either negligence or nuisance, is but a single wrong, and "whenever a nuisance has its origin in negligence," negligence must be proven and a plaintiff "may not avert the consequences of his [or her] own contributory negligence by affixing to the negligence of the wrongdoer the label of a nuisance."* * *

Besides liability for nuisance arising out of negligence and apart from consideration of nuisance resulting from abnormally dangerous or ultrahazardous conduct or conditions, the latter of which obviously is not applicable here, one may be liable for a private nuisance where the wrongful invasion of the use and enjoyment of another's land is intentional and unreasonable. It is distinguished from trespass which involves the invasion of a person's interest in the exclusive possession of land (Restatement, Torts, notes preceding § 822, pp. 224-225; Prosser, Torts [4th ed], pp. 594-596). The elements of such a private nuisance, as charged in effect by the Trial Justice, are: (1) an interference substantial in nature, (2) intentional in origin, (3) unreasonable in character, (4) with a person's property right to use and enjoy land, (5) caused by another's conduct in acting or failure to act (Restatement, Torts, § 822).

Thus, plaintiff's exception that "defendant's intent * * * is not * * * an essential element of the cause of action of nuisance" and its criticism of the charge, which was to the effect that as to the private nuisance plaintiff was required to prove that defendant's conduct was intentional, are not well taken. "An invasion of another's interest in the use and enjoyment of land is intentional when the actor

(a) acts for the purpose of causing it; or (b) knows that it is resulting or is substantially certain to result from his conduct" (Restatement, Torts, § 825).* * *

Negligence and nuisance were explained to the jury at considerable length and its attention was explicitly directed to the two categories of nuisance, that based on negligence and that dependent upon intentional conduct. The causes accrued, if at all, prior to the applicable date of [New York's comparative negligence rule], and the trial court properly charged that contributory negligence may be a defense where the nuisance is based on negligent conduct. As to nuisance involving a willful or intentional invasion of plaintiff's rights, the jury was instructed that contributory negligence was not a defense and, in this respect, plaintiff was not prejudiced and has no right to complain (see Prosser, Torts [4th ed], § 91).* * *

*Boomer* v. *Atlantic Cement Co.* [infra,] relied on by plaintiff, does not dictate a contrary result. There, Supreme Court found that defendant maintained a nuisance, same was affirmed by the Appellate Division, and the Court of Appeals concerned itself with the relief to be granted. Although Trial Term did specifically mention the type of nuisance it found it is obvious that it was not a nuisance in which the substance of the wrong was negligence since it was held that "the evidence in this case establishes that Atlantic took every available and possible precaution to protect the plaintiffs from dust." Rather, it would appear that the nuisance found was based on an intentional and unreasonable invasion, as it was stated that "[t]he discharge of large quantities of dust upon each of the properties and excessive vibration from blasting deprived each party of the reasonable use of his property and thereby prevented his enjoyment of life and liberty therein." Contrary to plaintiff's assertion, *Boomer* does not negate the necessity of proving negligence in some nuisance actions involving harmful emissions, since negligence is one of the types of conduct on which a nuisance may depend.

Although there are some Judges in the majority who are of the opinion that the charge did not furnish a model of discussion on some subjects, all of that group agree that reversal on the basis of the charge would not be warranted.

The order of the Appellate Division should be affirmed, with costs.

Fuchsberg, J. (dissenting). I believe, as did Justices Markewich and Kupferman, who dissented at the Appellate Division, that the charge in this case, by repeatedly presenting an admixture of nuisance and negligence in a manner and to an extent that could have misled the jury, should bring a reversal. All the more is that so because of the Trial Judge's insistent refrain that the injury to the plaintiff's property was required to be intentionally inflicted. Accordingly, I must dissent.

In doing so, I should note that, while in the main I am in agreement with the majority of our court in its discussion of the substantive law of nuisance, I believe the readiness with which it uses the term "negligence" in the context of this action for nuisance is counterproductive to the eradication of the confusion which has so long plagued that subject. Words such as "intent," "negligence" and "absolute liability" refer not to the result of the conduct of a defendant who intrudes unreasonably on the use and enjoyment of another's property, but rather to the method of bringing it about. Too often, as here, it serves to divert from focusing on the basic legal issue.

Nuisance traditionally requires that, after a balancing of the risk-utility considerations, the gravity of harm to a plaintiff be found to outweigh the social usefulness of a defendant's activity (Prosser, Torts [4th ed], p. 581). For no matter whether an act is intentional or unintentional, there should be no liability unless the social balance of the activity leads to the conclusion that it is unreasonable[.]

Interestingly, sections 826 and 829A of the Restatement of Torts 2d (Tent. Draft Nos. 17, 18) have now given recognition to developments in the law of torts by moving past the traditional rule to favor recovery for nuisance even when a defendant's conduct is not unreasonable. To be exact, section 826 (Tent. Draft No. 18, pp. 3-4) reads: "An intentional invasion of another's interest in the use and enjoyment of land is unreasonable under the rule stated in section 822, if (a) the gravity of the harm outweighs the utility of the actor's conduct, or (b) the harm caused by the conduct is substantial and the financial burden of compensating for this and other harms does not render infeasible the continuation of the conduct." Indeed, a fair reading of *Boomer* v. *Atlantic Cement Co.* [*infra*] would indicate that the position articulated by the Restatement's Tentative Draft is consistent with the decision of our court in that case.* * *

On the basis of these principles, it follows that on reversal the plaintiff in this case should be permitted to sustain its action for damages on proof that the harm is substantial and that the financial burden of compensating for the harm does not render "infeasible" the continuation of the defendant's business activity.

## Notes

In contrast to *Copart*, many states do not require negligence or intent for a nuisance. *See, e.g., Markey* v. *Danville Warehouse and Lumber, Inc.*, 119 Cal. App. 2d 1, 259 P.2d 19 (1953), and other cases gathered in 82 A.L.R.3d 1004, 1012.

Must the intent that *Copart* holds one of the three bases of nuisance (along with negligence and strict liability for an abnormally dangerous activity) be specific intent? If not, and if the non-negligent nuisance described in *Boomer* v. *Atlantic Cement* was intentional, why is Con Edison's wafting of dust onto Copart's cars not equally so?

What damages are recoverable? For a permanent nuisance, the reduction in value of the plaintiff's land, plus any special damages (medical expenses, lost profits, etc.). For a temporary nuisance, which ends because it's enjoined, or the defendant halts the nuisance – causing activity, the reduction in value for that period, plus special damages. Punitive damages may also be obtained for intentional or grossly negligent nuisances.

Should nuisances be actionable against a former landowner who sold? See *State v. Ole Olsen, Ltd.*, 35 N.Y.2d 979, 324 N.E.2d 886, 365 N.Y.S.2d 528 (1975) (yes). Should farm activities (odors, noise) be actionable? *See Lichtman v. Nadler*, 74 A.D.2d 66, 426 N.Y.S.2d 628 (4th Dept. 1980) (not if restricted to rural areas).

Should "coming to the nuisance," as Copart did, be a defense? Or just an element in balancing the equities for an injunction? Most courts take the latter view.

BOOMER v. ATLANTIC CEMENT CO., New York Court of Appeals, 1970. 26 N.Y.2d 219, 257 N.E.2d 870, 309 N.Y.S.2d 312.

Bergan, J. Defendant operates a large cement plant near Albany. There are actions for injunction and damages by neighboring land owners alleging injury to property from dirt, smoke and vibration emanating from the plant. A nuisance has been found after trial, temporary damages have been allowed; but an injunction has been denied.

The public concern with air pollution arising from many sources in industry and in transportation is currently accorded ever wider recognition accompanied by a growing sense of responsibility in State and Federal Governments to control it. Cement plants are obvious sources of air pollution in the neighborhoods where the operate.

But there is now before the court private litigation in which individual property owners have sought specific relief from a single plant operation. The threshold question raised by the division of view on this appeal is whether the court should resolve the litigation between the parties now before it as equitably as seems possible; or whether, seeking promotion of the general public welfare, it should channel private litigation into broad public objectives.

A court performs its essential function when it decides the rights of parties before it. Its decision of private controversies may sometimes greatly affect public issues. Large questions of law are often resolved by the manner in which private litigation is decided. But this is normally an incident to the court's main function to settle controversy. It is a rare exercise of judicial power to use a decision in private litigation as a purposeful mechanism to achieve direct public objectives greatly beyond the rights and interests before the court.

Effective control of air pollution is a problem presently far from solution even with the full public and financial powers of government. In large measure adequate technical procedures are yet to be developed and some that appear possible may be economically impracticable.

It seems apparent that the amelioration of air pollution will depend on technical research in great depth; on a carefully balanced consideration of the economic impact of close regulation; and of the actual effect on public health. It is likely to require massive public expenditure and to demand more than any local community can accomplish and to depend on regional and interstate controls.

A court should not try to do this on its own as a by-product of private litigation and it seems manifest that the judicial establishment is neither equipped in the limited nature of any judgment it can pronounce nor prepared to lay down and implement an effective policy for the elimination of air pollution. This is an area beyond the circumference of one private lawsuit. It is a direct responsibility for government and should not thus be undertaken as an incident to solving a dispute between property owners and a single cement plant--one of many--in the Hudson River Valley.

The cement making operations of defendant have been found by the court at Special Term to have damaged the nearby properties of plaintiffs in these two actions. That court, as it has been noted, accordingly found defendant maintained a nuisance and this has been affirmed at the Appellate Division. The total damage to plaintiffs' properties is, however, relatively small in comparison with the value of defendant's operation and with the consequences of the injunction which plaintiffs seek.

The ground for the denial of injunction, notwithstanding the findings both that there is a nuisance and that plaintiffs have been damaged substantially, is the large disparity in economic consequences of the nuisance and of the injunction. This theory cannot, however, be sustained without overruling a doctrine which has been consistently reaffirmed in several leading cases in this court and which has never been disavowed here, namely that where a nuisance has been found and where there has been any substantial damage shown by the party complaining an injunction will be granted.

The rule in New York has been that such a nuisance will be enjoined although marked disparity be shown in economic consequence between the effect of the injunction and the effect of the nuisance.

The problem of disparity in economic consequence was sharply in focus in *Whalen* v. *Union Bag & Paper Co.* (208 N.Y. 1 [1913]). A pulp mill entailing an investment of more than a million dollars polluted a stream in which plaintiff, who owned a farm, was "a lower riparian owner." The economic loss to plaintiff from this pollution was small. This court, reversing the Appellate Division, reinstated the injunction granted by the Special Term against the argument of the mill owner that in view of "the slight advantage to plaintiff and the great loss that will be inflicted on defendant" an injunction should not be granted (p.2). "Such a balancing of injuries cannot be justified by the circumstances of this case," [the court] noted (p.4). [It] continued: "Although the damage to the plaintiff may be slight as compared with the defendant's expense of abating the condition, that is not a good reason for refusing an injunction" (p.5).* * * The rule laid down in that case, then, is that whenever the damage resulting from a nuisance is found not "unsubstantial," viz., $100 a year, injunction would follow. This states a rule that had been followed in this court with marked consistency.* * *

Thus if, within *Whalen* v. *Union Bag & Paper Co. (supra)* which authoritatively states the rule in New York, the damage to plaintiffs in these present cases from defendant's cement plant is "not unsubstantial," an injunction should follow.

Although the court at Special Term and the Appellate Division held that injunction should be denied, it was found that plaintiffs had been damaged in various specific amounts up to the time of the trial and damages to the respective plaintiffs were awarded for those amounts. The effect of this was, injunction having been denied, plaintiffs could maintain successive actions at law for damages thereafter as further damage was incurred.

The court at Special Term also found the amount of permanent damage attributable to each plaintiff, for the guidance of the parties in the event both sides stipulated to the payment and acceptance of such permanent damage as a settlement of all the controversies among the parties. The total of permanent damages to all plaintiffs thus found was $185,000. This basis of adjustment has not resulted in any stipulation by the parties.

This result at Special Term and at the Appellate Division is a departure from a rule that has become settled; but to follow the rule literally in these cases would be to close down the plant at once. This court is fully agreed to avoid that immediately drastic remedy; the difference in view is how best to avoid it.*

One alternative is to grant the injunction but postpone its effect to a specified future date to give opportunity for technical advances to permit defendant to eliminate the nuisance; another is to grant the injunction conditioned on the payment of permanent damages to plaintiffs which would compensate them for the total economic loss to their property present and future caused by defendant's operations. For reasons which will be developed the court chooses the latter alternative.

If the injunction were to be granted unless within a short period--e.g., 18 months--the nuisance be abated by improved methods, there would be no assurance that any significant technical improvement would occur.

The parties could settle this private litigation at any time if defendant paid enough money and the imminent threat of closing the plant would build up the pressure on defendant. If there were no improved techniques found, there would inevitably be applications to the court at Special Term for extensions of time to perform on showing of good faith efforts to find such techniques.

Moreover, techniques to eliminate dust and other annoying by-products of cement making are unlikely to be developed by any research the defendant can undertake within any short period, but will depend on the total resources of the cement industry nationwide and throughout the world. The problem is universal wherever cement is made.

For obvious reasons the rate of the research is beyond control of defendant. If at the end of 18 months the whole industry has not found a technical solution a court would be hard put to close down this one cement plant if due regard be given to equitable principles.

On the other hand, to grant the injunction unless defendant pays plaintiffs such permanent damages as may be fixed by the court seems to do justice between the contending parties. All of the attributions of economic loss to the properties on which plaintiffs' complaints are based will been redressed.

The nuisance complained of by these plaintiffs may have other public or private consequences, but these particular parties are the only ones who have sought remedies and the judgment proposed will fully redress them. The limitation of relief

---

*Respondent's investment in the plant is in excess of $45,000,000. There are over 300 people employed there.

granted is a limitation only within the four corners of these actions and does not foreclose public health or other public agencies from seeking proper relief in a proper court.

It seems reasonable to think that the risk of being required to pay permanent damages to injured property owners by cement plant owners would itself be a reasonable effective spur to research for improved techniques to minimize nuisance.

The power of the court to condition on equitable grounds the continuance of an injunction on the payment of permanent damages seems undoubted.* * *

The damage base here suggested is consistent with the general rule in those nuisance cases where damages are allowed. "Where a nuisance is of such a permanent and unabatable character that single recovery can be had, including the whole damage past and future resulting therefrom, there can be but one recovery" (66 C.J.S. Nuisances, § 140, p. 947. It has been said that permanent damages are allowed where the loss recoverable would obviously be small as compared with the cost of removal of the nuisance (*Kentucky-Ohio Gas Co. v. Bowling,* 264 Ky. 470, 477).* * *

There is some parallel to the conditioning of an injunction on the payment of permanent damages in the noted "elevated railway cases" (*Pappenheim v. Metropolitan El. Ry. Co.,* 128 N.Y. 436, and others which followed). Decisions in these cases were based on the finding that the railways created a nuisance as to adjacent property owners, but in lieu of enjoining their operation, the court allowed permanent damages.

Judge Finch, reviewing these cases in *Ferguson v. Village of Hamburg* (272 N.Y. 234, 239-240), said: "The courts decided that the plaintiffs had a valuable right which was being impaired, but did not grant an absolute injunction or require the railway companies to resort to separate condemnation proceedings. Instead they held that a court of equity could ascertain the damages and grant an injunction which was not to be effective unless the defendant failed to pay the amount fixed as damages for the past and permanent injury inflicted."* * *

Thus it seems fair to both sides to grant permanent damages to plaintiffs which will terminate this private litigation. The theory of damage is the "servitude on land" of plaintiffs imposed by defendant's nuisance. (See *United States v. Causby* [Chapter 6], where the term "servitude" addressed to the land was used by Justice Douglas relating to the effect of airplane noise on property near an airport.)

The judgment, by allowance of permanent damages imposing a servitude on land, which is the basis of the actions, would preclude future recovery by plaintiffs or their grantees [.]

The orders should be reversed, without costs, and the cases remitted to Supreme Court, Albany County to grant an injunction which shall be vacated upon payment by defendant of such amounts of permanent damage to the respective plaintiffs as shall for this purpose be determined by the court.

Jasen, J. (dissenting). I agree with the majority that a reversal is required here, but I do not subscribe to the newly enunciated doctrine of assessment of permanent damages, in lieu of an injunction, where substantial property rights have been impaired by the creation of a nuisance.* * *

I see grave dangers in overruling our long-established rule of granting an injunction where a nuisance results in substantial continuing damage. In permitting the injunction to become inoperative upon the payment of permanent damages, the majority is, in effect, licensing a continuing wrong. It is the same as saying to the cement company, you may continue to do harm to your neighbors so long as you pay a fee for it. Furthermore, once such permanent damages are assessed and paid, the incentive to alleviate the wrong would be eliminated, thereby continuing air pollution of an area without abatement.

It is true that some courts have sanctioned the remedy here proposed by the majority in a number of cases, but none of the authorities relied upon by the majority are analogous to the situation before us. In those cases, the courts, in denying an injunction and awarding money damages, grounded their decision on a showing that the use to which the property was intended to be put was primarily for the public benefit. Here, on the other hand, it is clearly established that the cement company is creating a continuing air pollution nuisance primarily for its own private interest with no public benefit.

This kind of inverse condemnation may not be invoked by a private person or corporation for private gain or advantage. Inverse condemnation should only be permitted when the public is primarily served in the taking or impairment of property.* * * The promotion of the interests of the polluting cement company has, in my opinion, no public use or benefit.

Nor is it constitutionally permissible to impose servitude on land, without consent of the owner, by payment of permanent damages where the continuing impairment of the land is for a private use.* * * This is made clear by the State Constitution (art. I, §7, subd.[a]) which provides that "[p]rivate property shall not be taken for *public use* without just compensation" (emphasis added). It is, of course, significant that the section makes no mention of taking for a *private* use.

In sum, then, by constitutional mandate as well as by judicial pronouncement, the permanent impairment of private property for private purposes is not authorized in the absence of clearly demonstrated public benefit and use.

I would enjoin the defendant cement company from continuing the discharge of dust particles upon its neighbors' properties unless, within 18 months, the cement company abated this nuisance.

It is not my intention to cause the removal of the cement plant from the Albany area, but to recognize the urgency of the problem stemming from this stationary source of air pollution, and to allow the company a specified period of time to develop a means to alleviate this nuisance.

I am aware that the trial court found that the most modern dust control devices available have been installed in defendant's plant, but, I submit, this does not mean that *better* and more effective dust control devices could not be developed within the time allowed to abate the pollution.

Moreover, I believe it is incumbent upon the defendant to develop such devices, since the cement company, at the time the plant commenced production (1962), was well aware of the plaintiffs' presence in the area, as well as the probable consequences of its contemplated operation. Yet, it still chose to build and operate the plant at this site.

In a day when there is a growing concern for clean air, highly developed industry should not expect acquiescence by the courts, but should, instead, plan its operations to eliminate contamination of our air and damage to its neighbors.* * *

## Notes

Did the court, in effect, give the company a private right of eminent domain, allowing it to buy up its neighbors' rights to an unpolluted atmosphere? Does this amount to an unconstitutional taking of the neighbors' property, or at least one of the bundle of rights which constitute a property interest, as Judge Jasen's dissent suggests?

Was the air pollution caused by the defendant intentional as the Court of Appeals later used that term in *Copart?*

What is the value of the plaintiffs' right to clean air? On remand, the Appellate Division held the damages to be the difference between the market value of their property before and after the pollution commenced. *Kinley v. Atlantic Cement Co.,* 42 A.D.2d 496, 349 N.Y.S. 2d 199 (3d Dept. 1973). Justice Herlihy, concurring, argued that the plaintiff's damages should be greater than that since the landowner is being deprived of a portion of his fee interest through the servitude being imposed on the land.

Did the New York Court of Appeals in *Copart* clear away much of what it noted Prosser calls the "impenetrable jungle"? It held the decision here was consistent with *Boomer*. But *Boomer* awarded damages and even a conditional injunction for air pollution caused by a non-negligent defendant. If it did so because it found Atlantic Cement discharged dust intentionally, why should not the same result follow here? Is the fact that the defendant in *Copart* is a public utility a factor in the court's decision? Should it be?

Judge Fuchsberg's dissent in *Copart*, relying on the Restatement, concludes that neither negligence nor intent is needed -- just that the conduct be unreasonable. He too finds his position consistent with *Boomer*. Note that the Court of Appeals in *Boomer* did not discuss fault; it assumed the nuisance and concentrated on the remedy. Although the trial court in *Boomer* found "Atlantic took every available and possible precaution," the Court of Appeals emphasized the need for technological advances to end the discharge of dust. Does this amount to a finding of negligence? Or did *Boomer* really find nuisance without fault? Generally, a defendant is not negligent as long as it conforms to the level of technology or skill generally employed in its occupation or profession. But see *Noel v. United Aircraft Corp.*, 219 F. Supp. 556 (D.C. Del. 1963), aff'd 342 F.2d 232 (requiring technical improvements beyond the current state of the art to avoid liability in an aircraft negligence case).

Did the court in *Boomer* really follow the New York rule requiring an injunction where a nuisance causes substantial damage? With friends like the Court of Appeals, does this rule need any enemies?

Is this disposition of a serious nuisance case likely to spur technological improvements by the defendant, as the court suggests? Would an injunction to take effect in a year or two, as Judge Jasen's dissent urges, be more likely to achieve that goal? As Dr. Johnson said of the prospect of hanging, would an imminent injunction be apt to concentrate the defendant's mind wonderfully?

Under Judge Jasen's approach, would it be just to close the plant if, after 18 months of good faith effort, the required technology was still available?

Most other states balance the equities in deciding whether to enjoin nuisances. Is not that what the Court did here despite its professed obeisance to the New York rule? See *Spur Industries, Inc. v. Del E. Webb Development Co.*, 108 Ariz. 178, 494 P.2d 700 (1972) (developer of land near existing cattle feedlot enjoined feedlot but was required to pay costs of moving feedlot to another location).

Should the existence of environmental statutes imposing standards and permit requirements preempt nuisance actions? The courts generally hold these statutes do not bar nuisance actions. See *Leo* v. *General Electric Co.*, 145 A.D. 2d 291, 538 N.Y.S. 2d 844 (2d Dept. 1989); *Miotke* v. *City of Spokane*, 101 Wash. 2d 307, 678 P.2d 803 (1984). Generally, violating a permit is proof of the nuisance; complying with a permit is not a complete defense, just evidence of reasonable conduct.

## B. ESTHETIC NUISANCE

COMMONWEALTH v. NATIONAL GETTYSBURG BATTLEFIELD TOWER, INC., Supreme Court of Pennsylvania, 1973. 454 Pa. 193, 311 A.2d 588.

O'Brien, Justice.

On July 3, 1971, National Gettysburg Battlefield Tower, Inc. (the Tower Corporation) and Thomas R. Ottenstein, two of the appellees, negotiated an agreement with the United States government, acting through the Director of the National Park Service, in which the Tower Corporation conveyed certain land to the government and agreed to abandon construction of an observation tower near the Gettysburg Battlefield, at an area found objectionable to the Park Service, in exchange for the government's cooperation and permission to build the tower in another area near the battlefield. The Tower Corporation also agreed * * * to construct the tower in accordance with certain specifications, with the height of the tower to be limited to 307 feet. The Park Service also conveyed a right of way for limited access to the proposed observation tower site.

What the National Park Service was originally willing to permit,[1] the Commonwealth of Pennsylvania, appellant herein, sought to enjoin. On July 20, 1971, the Commonwealth brought an action in the Court of Common Pleas of Adams County, to enjoin construction of the proposed 307-feet tower, alleging that the proposed construction was "a despoliation of the natural and historical environment."* * *

At the trial, the Commonwealth produced a number of witnesses who generally agreed that the found the tower, in their opinion to be detrimental to the historic, scenic, and esthetic environment of Gettysburg. Appellees, on the other hand, produced experts who found the geometric form of the tower to be esthetically pleasing and its design, while unobtrusive, to be of great educational value because it would provide "the full sweep or overview of a landscape where a significant event in American History took place."

The chancellor concluded that the Commonwealth had failed to show by clear and convincing proof that the natural, scenic, historic or esthetic values of the Gettysburg environment would be injured by the erection of the tower. In order to reach the ultimate issue, the chancellor first found to be without merit the defense interposed by appellees that Article 1, § 27 of the Pennsylvania Constitution, upon which the Commonwealth relied for the authority of the Attorney General to bring this suit--was not self-executing and, therefore, legislative authority was required before the suit could be brought.

On appeal to the Commonwealth Court, all members of the Court agreed that the Commonwealth had failed to carry its burden of proof on the issue of whether the tower would injure the Gettysburg environment. [A]s recognized by Judge Rogers, speaking for the majority of the Commonwealth Court:

> There are no regulations of Cumberland Township, Adams County, the municipality in which the site is located, governing the construction of towers; indeed, there is not one zoning ordinance in all of Adams County.* * *

Similarly, there is no statute of the Pennsylvania Legislature, which would authorize the Governor and the Attorney General to initiate actions like the law suit in the instant case. Rather, authority for the Commonwealth's suit is allegedly based entirely upon Article 1, § 27 of the State Constitution, ratified by the voters of Pennsylvania on May 18, 1971, which reads:

> The people have a right to clean air, pure water, and to the preservation of the natural, scenic, historic and esthetic values of the environment. Pennsylvania's public natural resources are the

---

[1] In May, 1973, after an appeal had been filed in this case, the Park Service's Advisory Council on Historic Preservation finally came out with a report recommending that the United States Government assist the Commonwealth in opposing the construction of the tower. Apparently the report had previously been lost within the bureau.

> common property of all the people, including generations yet to come. As trustee of these resources, the Commonwealth shall conserve and maintain them for the benefit of all the people.

It is the Commonwealth's position that this amendment is self-executing; that the people have been given a right "to the preservation of the natural, scenic, historic and esthetic values of the environment," and "that no further legislation is necessary to vest these rights in the people."

The general principles of law involved in determining whether a particular provision of a constitution is self-executing were discussed at length in O'Neill v. White, 343 Pa. 96, 22 A.2d 25 (1941). In that case, we explained at pages 99-100:

> A Constitution is primarily a declaration of principles of the fundamental law. Its provisions are usually only commands to the purposes of the framers of the Constitution, or mere restrictions upon the power of the legislature to pass laws, yet it is entirely within the power of those who establish and adopt the Constitution to make any of its provisions self-executing," 6 R.C.L. section 52, p.57.* * *
>
> In Davis v. Burke, 179 U.S. 399, 403, 21 S.Ct. 210, 212, 45 L.Ed. 249, the United States Supreme Court said: "Where a constitutional provision is complete in itself it needs no further legislation to put it in force. When it lays down certain general principles, as to enact laws upon a certain subject, or for the incorporation of cities of certain population, or for uniform laws upon the subject of taxation, it may need more specific legislation to make it operative. In other words, it is self-executing only so far as it is susceptible of execution.

[T]he first sentence of § 27 * * * can be read as limiting the right of government to interfere with the people's right to "clean air, pure water, and to the preservation of the natural, scenic, historic and esthetic values of the environment." As such, the first part of § 27, if read alone, could be read to be self-executing.

But the remaining provisions of Section 27, rather than limiting the powers of government, expand these powers. These provisions declare that the Commonwealth is the "trustee" of Pennsylvania's "public natural resources" and they give the Commonwealth the power to act to "conserve and maintain them for the benefit of all the people." Insofar as the Commonwealth always had a recognized police power to regulate the use of land, and thus could establish standards for clean air and clean water, consistent with the requirements of public health, § 27 is merely a general reaffirmation of past law. It must be recognized, however, that up until now, esthetic or historical considerations, by themselves, have not been considered sufficient to constitute a basis for the Commonwealth's exercise of its police power.* * *

Now, for the first time, at least insofar as the state constitution is concerned, the Commonwealth has been given power to act in areas of purely esthetic or historic concern.* * *

It should be noted that § 27 does not give the powers of a trustee of public natural resources to the *Governor* or to the *Attorney General* but to the *Commonwealth*.* * *

Under a constitution providing for a balance of powers, such as Pennsylvania's State Constitution, when power is given simply to the Commonwealth, it is power to be shared by the government's three co-equal branches. The governor cannot decide, alone, how or when he shall exercise the powers of a trustee. It is not for him alone to determine when the "natural, scenic, historic, and esthetic values of the environment" are sufficiently threatened as to justify the bringing of an action. After all, "clean air," "pure water" and "the natural, scenic, historic and esthetic values of the environment," have not been defined. The first two, "clean air" and "pure water," require technical definitions, since they depend, to some extent, on the technological state of the science of purification. The other values, "the natural, scenic, historic and esthetic values" of the environment are values which have heretofore not been the concern of government. To hold that the Governor needs no legislative authority to exercise the as yet undefined powers of a trustee to protect such undefined values would mean that individuals could be singled out for interference by the awesome power of the state with no advance warning that their conduct would lead to such consequences.

If we were to sustain the Commonwealth's position that the amendment was self-executing, a property owner would not know and would have no way, short of expensive litigation, of finding out what he could do with his property. The fact that the owner contemplated a use similar to others that had not been enjoined would be no guarantee that the Commonwealth would not seek to enjoin his use.[4a] Since no executive department has been given authority to determine when to move to protect the environment, there would be no way of obtaining, with respect to a particular use contemplated, an indication of what action the Commonwealth might take before the owner expended what could be significant sums of money for the purchase or the development of the property.

We do not believe that the framers of the environmental protection amendment could have intended such as unjust result, one which raises such serious questions under both the equal protection clause and due process clause of the United States Constitution. In our opinion, to insure that these clauses are not violated, the Legislature should set standards and procedures for proposed executive action.

---

[4a]Appellees contend, in fact, that the relief sought by the Commonwealth would unconstitutionally deny them the equal protection of the laws because the Commonwealth has arbitrarily singled out the proposed tower at a time when the Gettysburg area is becoming "pockmarked" with numerous business establishments and junk yards which, appellees contend, pose even more of a threat to the "historic and esthetic" values of the environment than does the proposed tower.

The Commonwealth also argues that the Pennsylvania environmental protection amendment is self-executing by comparing it with similar constitutional amendments enacted in Massachusetts, Illinois, New York, and Virginia, all of which are obviously not self-executing. The Commonwealth seeks to put great store in the fact that Pennsylvania's amendment, alone, does not specifically provide for legislative implementation. However, we find it more significant that all of these other states, which expanded the powers of their governments over the natural environment in the same way as Article 1, § 27 expanded the powers of the Commonwealth, recognized that legislative implementation was necessary before such new power could be exercised.

To summarize, we believe that the provisions of § 27 of Article 1 of the Constitution merely state the general principle of law that the Commonwealth is trustee of Pennsylvania's public natural resources with power to protect the "natural, scenic, historic, and esthetic values" of its environment. If the amendment was self-executing, action taken under it would pose serious problems of constitutionality, under both the equal protection clause and the due process clause of the Fourteenth Amendment. Accordingly, before the environmental protection amendment can be made effective, supplemental legislation will be required to define the values which the amendment seeks to protect and to establish procedures by which the use of private property can be fairly regulated to protect those values.

By reason of our disposition of this appeal, it is unnecessary to decide the other issues raised by the Commonwealth.

Order of the Commonwealth Court, affirming the Decree of the Court of Common Pleas of Adams County, is affirmed.

Pomeroy, J., joined in this opinion.

Nix, J., concurs in the result.

Roberts, Justice (concurring).

I agree that the order of the Commonwealth Court should be affirmed; however, my reasons for affirmance are entirely different from those expressed in the opinion by Mr. Justice O'Brien (joined by Mr. Justice Pomeroy).

I believe that the Commonwealth, even prior to the recent adoption of Article 1, Section 27, possessed the inherent sovereign power to protect and preserve for its citizens the natural and historic resources now enumerated in Section 27. The express language of the Constitutional amendment merely recites the "inherent and independent rights" of mankind relative to the environment which are "recognized and unalterably established" by Article 1, Section 1 of the Pennsylvania Constitution.* * *

Since natural and historic resources are the common property of the citizens of a state, * * * the Commonwealth can--and always could--proceed as parens patriae acting on behalf of the citizens and in the interests of the community, or as trustee of the state's public resources.

However, in my view, the Commonwealth, on this record, has failed to establish its entitlement to the equitable relief it seeks, either on common-law or constitutional (prior or subsequent to Section 27) theories. The chancellor determined that "[t]he Commonwealth has failed to show by clear and convincing proof that the natural, historic, scenic, and esthetic values of the Gettysburg area will be irreparably harmed by the erection of the proposed tower at the proposed site."

I believe that the chancellor correctly denied equitable relief. The Commonwealth Court concluded that the chancellor's findings should not be disturbed and that the Commonwealth was not entitled to relief.

I am unable, on this record, to find any error in either the chancellor's determination or that of the Commonwealth Court. Moreover, I entertain serious reservations as to the propriety of granting the requested relief in this case in the absence of appropriate and articulated substantive and procedural standards.* * *

Manderino, J., joins in this opinion.

Jones, Chief Justice (dissenting).

This Court has been given the opportunity to affirm the mandate of the public empowering the commonwealth to prevent environmental abuses; instead, the Court has chosen to * * * declari[e] it not to be self-executing. I am compelled to dissent.

Article 1, Section 27, of the Commonwealth's Constitution was passed by the General Assembly and ratified by the voters on May 18, 1971.

Its provisions are clear and uncomplicated:

> The people have a right to clear air, pure water, and to the preservation of the natural, scenic, historic and esthetic values of the environment. Pennsylvania's public natural resources are the common property of all the people, including generations yet to come. As trustee of these resources, the Commonwealth shall conserve and maintain them for the benefit of all the people.

As part of the declaration of rights embraced by Article 1, the amendment confers certain enumerated rights upon the people of the Commonwealth and imposes upon the executive branch a fiduciary obligation to protect and enforce those rights.

If the amendment was intended only to espouse a policy undisposed to enforcement without supplementing legislation, it would surely have taken a different form. But the amendment is not addressed to the General Assembly.* * *

It does not require the legislative creation of remedial measures. Instead, the amendment creates a public trust. The "natural, scenic, historic and esthetic values of the environment" are the trust *res;* the Commonwealth, through its executive branch, is the trustee; the *people of this Commonwealth* are the trust beneficiaries. The amendment thus installs the common law public trust doctrine *as a constitutional right to environmental protection* susceptible to enforcement by an action in equity.

The majority relies on constitutional amendments of Massachusetts, Illinois, New York and Virginia to support its holding that Section 27 is not self-executing. The Court finds it "significant that all of these other states, which expanded the powers of their governments over the natural environment in the same way as Article 1, Section 27 expanded the powers of the Commonwealth, recognized that legislative implementation was necessary before such new power could be exercised." I find no significance in the fact that the constitutional provisions of these several jurisdictions are not self-executing for it is evident to me that each of the cited amendments is materially distinguishable from Article 1, Section 27. Each of these amendments purports to establish a policy of environmental protection, but either omits the mode of enforcement or explicitly delegates the responsibility for implementation to the legislative branch. The Pennsylvania amendment defines enumerated rights within the scope of existing remedies. It imposes a fiduciary duty upon the Commonwealth to protect the people's "right to clean air, pure water, and to the preservation of the natural, scenic, historic and esthetic values of the environment." That the language of the amendment is subject to judicial interpretation does not mean that the enactment must remain *an ineffectual constitutional platitude* until such time as the legislature acts.

Because I believe Article 1, Section 27 is self executing, I believe that our inquiry should have focused upon the ultimate issue of fact: does the proposed tower violate the rights of the people of the Commonwealth as secured by this amendment?

The chancellor's determination that the erection of the tower would not be injurious to the environmental values protected by Article 1, Section 27 was not a "finding of fact," but a conclusion of ultimate fact based upon inferences drawn from the evidence presented at trial. The Commonwealth Court refused to review the chancellor's findings absent a showing of abuse of discretion.* * *

The application of the "abuse of discretion" standard in this context is error. This Court has held on numerous occasions that, although a chancellor's findings of fact have the force and effect of a jury's verdict, the chancellor's conclusions of ultimate fact are reviewable. As long as we give full weight to the chancellor's findings of fact, we are free to draw our own inferences and conclusions from the facts as found.

The facts indicate that the proposed tower is a metal structure rising 310 feet above the ground. It is shaped like an hourglass: about 100 feet in diameter at the bottom, 30 feet in the middle and 70 feet at the top. The top level will include an observation deck, elevator housings, facilities for warning approaching aircraft and an illuminated American flag. The proposed site of the tower is an area around which the third day of the battle of Gettysburg was fought. It is located immediately south of the Gettysburg National Cemetery.

The Commonwealth presented compelling evidence that the proposed observation tower at Gettysburg would desecrate the natural scenic, esthetic and historic values of the Gettysburg environment.

The director of the National Park Service, George Hartzog, testified[:]

> To put a tower 320 feet into this pastoral scene of human scale, a historical event, is just simply to destroy any relationship between the human dimension of this battlefield and this technological achievement of a tower.* * *
>
> I think a monstrous intrusion such as this tower is, into the historical, pastoral scene of that battlefield park and Eisenhower National Site and the National Cemetery and the place where Lincoln spoke, is just destructive of the integrity of its historical value.* * *

Robert Garvey, the Executive Secretary of the President's Advisory Council on Historic Preservation, also testified for the Commonwealth. Mr. Garvey authenticated the Commonwealth's exhibit documenting the Advisory Council's comments to the Secretary of the Interior respecting the Gettysburg tower. The exhibit reads in pertinent part as follows:

> [T]he Undertaking will have an adverse effect upon Gettysburg National Military Park and Gettysburg National Cemetery, both National Register properties.
>
> The Council * * * recommends that the Department of the Interior * * * do everything it can to assist the Commonwealth of Pennsylvania in its legal action to stop the construction of a tower at Gettysburg.* * *

Louis Kahn, distinguished architect and Professor of Architecture at the University of Pennsylvania[,] testified that * * * because the tower will be constructed so out of scale with the battlefield, it will dominate the landscape causing everything to "cringe" beneath it.

Philadelphia architect Vincent Kling testified that the tower is inappropriate to the environment of Gettysburg because it will not blend into the natural surroundings of the area.

Pulitzer prize-winning Civil War historian Bruce Catton testified that the historical integrity of the area was delicate, and that the proposed tower would shatter the visitor's vicarious historical involvement in Gettysburg best experienced by a ground level observation of the area.

In juxtaposition to the eminent expert witnesses offered by the Commonwealth, the appellees offered the testimony of three witness: (1) Harry Biesecker, an Adams County Commissioner, (2) Joel Rosenblatt, a civil engineer who designed the tower and (3) Dr. Mario Menesini, an educational consultant.

Mr. Biesecker testified that the proposed tower would be a significant commercial asset to Adams County, and that a petition approving the construction of the tower had garnered 2200 signatures, about five percent of the county's population. Mr. Rosenblatt testified that the tower was designed to educate its patrons and to stand as unobtrusively as possible. Dr. Menisini offered the opinion that the educational benefits of the tower with respect to the Battle of Gettysburg would be more advantageous than presently existing means of instruction on the subject.

The facts presented, even as construed in a light most favorable to the appellees, permit me only one conclusion: the proposed structure will do violence to the "natural, scenic, historic and esthetic values" of Gettysburg. This Court's decision today imposes unhappy consequences on the people of this Commonwealth. In one swift stroke the Court has disemboweled a constitutional provision which seems, by unequivocal language, to establish environmental control by public trust and, in so doing consequently sanctions the desecration of a unique national monument. I would enjoin the construction of this tower by the authority of Article 1, Section 27 of the Pennsylvania Constitution.* * *

Eagen, J., joins in this dissent.

Notes

Did a majority of the Court hold the constitutional provision was not self-executing? Note the concurring and dissenting opinions.

Could the Commonwealth have prevailed on common-law nuisance principles? See *Parkersburg Builders Material Co. v. Barrack,* 118 W.Va. 608, 191 S.E. 368 (1937) (enjoining an eyesore as an esthetic nuisance); *contra*: *United States v. County Board of Arlington Co.,* 487 F.Supp. 137 (D.C.Va. 1979) (denying an injunction against building construction across the Potomac from the Lincoln Memorial):

> Height alone is not enough--unsightliness or offense to the esthetic senses is not sufficient to constitute a public nuisance.* * * To sustain such an interference with the use of private land without compensation as an exercise of the police power has been farther than the courts have been willing to go. When, however, compensation is provided, such restrictions may be looked upon as easements, created by statute for the benefit of the land on which the park or public building lies, and which have been taken by the public by eminent domain.

The court went on to rule that in any event the plaintiff had failed to prove a visual intrusion.

The tower was completed, but was torn down in 2000 following a suit by the National Park Service. The owner was compensated.

## C. FEDERAL NUISANCE

ILLINOIS v. CITY OF MILWAUKEE, Supreme Court of the United States, 1972. 406 U.S. 91, 92 S.Ct. 1385, 31 L.Ed.2d 712.

Mr. Justice Douglas delivered the opinion of the Court.

This is a motion by Illinois to file a bill of complaint under our original jurisdiction against four cities of Wisconsin, the Sewerage Commission of the City of Milwaukee, and the Metropolitan Sewerage Commission of the County of Milwaukee. The cause of action alleged is pollution by defendants of Lake Michigan, a body of interstate water. According to plaintiff, some 200 million gallons of raw or inadequately treated sewage and other waste materials are discharged daily into the lake in the Milwaukee area alone. Plaintiff alleges that it and its subdivisions prohibit and prevent such discharges, but that the defendants do not take such actions. Plaintiff asks that we abate this public nuisance.

Article III, § 2, cl.2, of the Constitution provides: "In all Cases....in which a State shall be Party, the Supreme Court shall have original Jurisdiction." Congress has provided in 28 USC § 1251 that "(a) the Supreme Court shall have original and exclusive jurisdiction of: (1) All controversies between two or more States."* * * We incline to a sparing use of our original jurisdiction so that our increasing duties with the appellate docket will not suffer. Washington v. General Motors Corp., 406 U.S. 109, 31 L.Ed.2d 727, 92 S.Ct. 1396.

Illinois presses its request for leave to file saying that the agencies named as defendants are instrumentalities of Wisconsin and therefore that this is a suit against Wisconsin which could not be brought in any other forum. [However, we] conclude that the term "States" be used in 28 USC §1251(a)(1) should not be read to include their political subdivisions. That, of course, does not mean that political subdivisions of a State may not be sued under the head of our original jurisdiction, for 28 USC §1251 provides that "(b) the Supreme Court shall have original but not exclusive jurisdiction of: (3) all actions or proceedings by a State against the citizens of another State...."

If the named public entities of Wisconsin may, however, be sued by Illinois in a federal district court, our original jurisdiction is not mandatory.* * *

Title 28 USC § 1331(a) provides that "[t]he district courts shall have original jurisdiction of all civil actions wherein the matter in controversy exceeds the sum or value of $10,000, exclusive of interest and costs, and arises under the Constitution laws, or treaties of the United States."[a] * * *

The question is whether pollution of interstate or navigable waters creates actions arising under the "laws" of the United States within the meaning of §1331(a). We hold that it does; and we also hold that §1331(a) includes suits brought by a State.

---

[a]The $10,000 requirement was removed in 1980 by an amendment to §1331.

Mr. Justice Brennan, speaking for the four members of this Court in Romero v. International Terminal Operating Co. 358 U.S. 354, 393, 3 L.Ed. 2d 368, 394, 79 S.Ct. 468 (dissenting and concurring), who reached the issue, concluded that "laws," within the meaning of §1331(a), embraced claims founded on federal common law.* * *

Judge Harvey M. Johnson in Texas v. Pankey, 441 F.2d 236, 240, stated the controlling principle:

> As the field of federal common law has been given necessary expansion into matters of federal concern and relationship (where no applicable federal statute exists, as there does not here), the ecological rights of a State in the improper impairment of them from sources outside the State's own territory, now would and should, we think, be held to be a matter having basis and standard in federal common law and so directly constituting a question arising under the laws of the United States.

Chief Judge Lumbard, speaking for the panel in Ivy Broadcasting Co. v. American Tel. & Tel. Co. 391 F.2d 486, 492, expressed the same view as follows:

> We believe that a cause of action similarly 'arises under' federal law if the dispositive issues stated in the complaint require the application of Federal common law. . . . The word 'laws' in §1331 should be construed to include laws created by federal judicial decisions as well as by congressional legislation.* * *

Congress has enacted numerous laws touching interstate waters. [The Court discussed the Clean Water Act, the Rivers and Harbors Act, and related legislation, described in Chapter 7, *infra*.]

The remedy sought by Illinois is not within the precise scope of remedies prescribed by Congress. Yet the remedies which Congress provides are not necessarily the only federal remedies available. "It is not uncommon for federal courts to fashion federal law where federal rights are concerned." Textile Workers v. Lincoln Mills, 353 U.S. 448, 457, 1 L.Ed.2d 972, 981, 77 S.Ct. 912. When we deal with air and water in their ambient or interstate aspects, there is a federal common law, as Texas v. Pankey, 441 F.2d 236, recently held.

The application of federal common law to abate a public nuisance in interstate or navigable waters is not inconsistent with [the Clean Water Act]. Congress provided in § 10(b) of that Act that, save as a court may decree otherwise in an enforcement action, "[s]tate and interstate action to abate pollution of interstate or navigable waters shall be encouraged and shall not....be displaced by Federal enforcement action."

The leading air case is Georgia v. Tennessee Copper Co., 206 U.S. 230, 51 L.Ed. 1038, 27 S.Ct. 618, where Georgia filed an original suit in this Court against a

Tennessee company whose noxious gases were causing a wholesale destruction of forests, orchards, and crops in Georgia. The Court said: "The caution with which demands of this sort, on the part of a State, for relief from injuries analogous to torts, must be examined, is dwelt upon in Missouri v. Illinois, 200 U.S. 496, 520, 521 [50 L.Ed. 572, 578, 579, 26 S.Ct. 268]. But is plain that some such demands must be recognized, if the grounds alleged are proved. When the States by their union made the forcible abatement of outside nuisances impossible to each, they did not thereby agree to submit to whatever might be done. They did not renounce the possibility of making reasonable demands on the ground of their still remaining *quasi*-sovereign interests; and the alternative to force is a suit in this court.

"It is a fair and reasonable demand on the part of a sovereign that the air over its territory should not be polluted on a great scale by sulphurous acid gas, that the forests on its mountains, be they better or worse, and whatever domestic destruction they have suffered, should not be further destroyed or threatened by the act of persons beyond its control, that the crops and orchards on its hills should not be endangered from the same source."* * *

Our decisions concerning interstate waters contain the same theme. Rights in interstate streams, like questions of boundaries, "have been recognized as presenting federal questions." Hinderlider v. La Plata Co., 304 U.S. 92, 110, 82 L.Ed. 1202, 1212, 58 S.Ct. 803. The question of apportionment of interstate waters is a question of "federal common law" upon which state statutes or decisions are not conclusive. Ibid.

In speaking of the problem of apportioning the waters of an interstate stream, the Court said in Kansas v. Colorado, 206 US 46, 98, 51 L.Ed. 956, 974, 27 S.Ct. 655, that "through these successive disputes and decisions this court is practically building up what may not improperly be called interstate common law."* * * When it comes to water pollution this Court has spoken in terms of "a public nuisance." * * * It may happen that new federal laws and new federal regulations may in time pre-empt the field of federal common law of nuisance, but until that comes to pass, federal courts will be empowered to appraise the equities of the suits alleging creation of a public nuisance by water pollution. While federal law governs,[9] consideration of state standards may be relevant.* * * Thus, a State with high water-quality standards may well ask that its strict standards be honored and that it not be compelled to lower itself to the more degrading standards of a

[9]"Federal common law and not the varying common law of the individual States is, we think, entitled and necessary to be recognized as a basis for dealing in uniform standard with the environmental rights of a State against improper impairment by sources outside its domain. The more would this seem to be imperative in the present era of growing concern on the part of a State about its ecological conditions and impairments of them. In the outside sources of such impairment, more conflicting disputes, increasing assertions and proliferating contentions would seem to be inevitable. Until the field has been made the subject of comprehensive legislation or authorized administrative standards, only a federal common law basis can provide an adequate means for dealing with such claims as alleged federal rights. And the logic and practicality of regarding such claims as being entitled to be asserted within the federal-question jurisdiction of §1331(a) would seem to be self-evident." Texas v. Pankey, 441 F2d 236, 241-242.

neighbor. There are no fixed rules that govern; these will be equity suits in which the informed judgment of the chancellor will largely govern. We deny, without prejudice, the motion for leave to file. While this original suit normally might be the appropriate vehicle for resolving this controversy, we exercise our discretion to remit the parties to an appropriate district court whose powers are adequate to resolve the issues.

Notes

On remand, Illinois won an injunction banning the discharge of raw sewage by Milwaukee. The Court of Appeals affirmed but eliminated, for failure of proof, the part of the injunction banning discharge of sewerage in excess of limits stricter than those of the EPA. The Supreme Court, in *City of Milwaukee v. Illinois*, 451 U.S. 304, 101 S.Ct. 1784, 68 L.Ed.2d 114 (1981), in an opinion by Justice Rehnquist, reversed that order and dismissed the complaint, holding that the enactment of the Clean Water Act in 1972, six months after the Supreme Court's first decision in *City of Milwaukee,*

> occupied the field through the establishment of a comprehensive regulatory program supervised by an expert administrative agency. The 1972 amendments to the Federal Water Pollution Control Act were not merely another law "touching interstate waters," of the sort surveyed in *Illinois v. City of Milwaukee*, and found inadequate to supplant federal common law. Rather, the amendments were viewed by Congress as a "total restructuring" and "complete rewriting" of the existing water pollution legislation considered in that case [citing the legislative history]. Congress' intent in enacting the amendments was clearly to establish an all-encompassing program of water pollution regulation. *Every* point source discharge is prohibited unless covered by a permit, which directly subjects the discharger to the administrative apparatus established by Congress to achieve its goals.
>
> [T]he action of Congress in supplanting the federal common law is perhaps clearest when the question of effluent limitations for discharges from the two treatment plants is considered. The duly issued permits under which the city commission discharges treated sewage from the Jones Island and South Shore treatment plants incorporate, as required by the Act, see § 402(b)(1), 33 USC § 1342 (b)(1), the specific effluent limitations established by EPA regulations pursuant to § 302s of the Act, 33 USC § 1311.* * * This being so there is no basis for a federal court to impose more stringent limitations than those imposed under the regulatory regime by

reference to federal common law, as the District Court did in this case.* * * Subsection 505(e) provides:

> "Nothing *in this section* shall restrict any right which any person (or class of persons) may have under any statute or common law to seek enforcement of any effluent standard or limitation or to seek any other relief (including relief against the Administrator or a State agency)" (emphasis supplied).

[Illinois] argues that this evinces an intent to preserve the federal common law of nuisance. We, however, are inclined to view the quoted provision as meaning what it says: that nothing *in § 505*, the citizen-suit provision, should be read as limiting any other remedies which might exist.

Subsection 505(e) is virtually identical to subsections in the citizen-suit provisions of several environmental statutes. The subsection is common language accompanying citizen-suit provisions and we think that it means only that the provision of such suit does not revoke other remedies. It most assuredly cannot be read to mean that the Act as a whole does not supplant formerly available federal common-law actions but only that the particular section authorizing citizen suits does not do so. No one, however, maintains that the citizen-suit provision preempts federal common law.

We are thus not persuaded that §505(e) aids respondents in this case, even indulging the unlikely assumption that the reference to "common law" in §505(e) includes the limited *federal* common law as opposed to the more routine state common law.

Dissenting, Justice Blackmun, joined by Justices Marshall and Stevens, characterized the decision as a ruling that the nine-year Lake Michigan litigation "has been just a meaningless charade":

Long before the 1972 decision in *Illinois* v. *Milwaukee*, federal common law enunciated by this court assured each State the right to be free from unreasonable interference with its natural environment and resources when the interference stems from another State or its citizens. *Georgia* v. *Tennessee Copper Co.,* 206 U.S. 230, 237-239 (1907), *Missouri* v. *Illinois*, 200 U.S. 496, 520, 526 (1906).* * * Thus, quite contrary to the statements and intimations of the Court today, * * * *Illinois* v. *Milwaukee* did not create the federal common law of nuisance. [And] Congress cannot be presumed to have been unaware of the relevant common--law history, any more than it can be deemed to have been oblivious to the decision in *Illinois* v. *Milwaukee*, announced six months prior to the passage of the [Act].

In my view, the language and structure of the Clean Water Act leave no doubt that Congress intended to preserve the federal common law of nuisance. Section 505(e) of the Act reads:

"Nothing in this section shall restrict any right which *any person* (or class of persons) may have under *any statute or common law* to seek enforcement of any effluent standard or limitation *or to seek any other relief* (including relief against the Administrator or a State agency)." 33 U.S.C. § 1365(e) (emphasis added).

The Act specifically defines "person" to include States. [A]s succinctly stated by the Court of Appeals in this case: "There is nothing in the phrase 'any statute or common law' that suggests that this provision is limited to state common law." [Moreover,] under the statutory scheme, any permit issued by the EPA or a qualifying state agency does not insulate a discharger from liability under other federal or state law.* * * By eliminating the federal common law of nuisance in this area, the Court in effect is encouraging recourse to state law wherever the federal statutory scheme is perceived to offer inadequate protection against pollution from outside the State.

[This] undermines the Court's prior conclusion that it is federal rather than state law that should govern the regulation of interstate water pollution. *Illinois* v. *Milwaukee*, 406 U.S., at 102. Instead of promoting a more uniform federal approach to the problem of alleviating interstate pollution, I fear that today's decision will lead States to turn to their own courts for statutory or common law assistance in filing the interstices of the federal statute. Rather than encourage such a prospect, I would adhere to the principles clearly enunciated in *Illinois* v. *Milwaukee*, and affirm the judgment of the Court of Appeals.

## Notes

On remand in the *City of Milwaukee* litigation, the Seventh Circuit Court of Appeals ruled Illinois' state nuisance claims were also preempted by the Clean Water Act since they dealt with activity beyond the state's borders. The court read Clean Water Act § 510, 33 U.S.C.A. § 1370 ("nothing in this chapter [the Act] shall . . . be construed as impairing . . . any right or jurisdiction of the States with respect to the waters (including boundary waters) of such States"), as preserving state common law remedies only within that state's boundaries. Hence Illinois could not enforce its law, even within its own waters, with regard to sewage from Milwaukee.

Is this reading consistent with the purposes of the Clean Water Act "to restore and maintain the chemical, physical, and biological integrity of the Nation's waters" (Clean Water Act § 101, 33 U.S.C.A. § 1251)? With the long-standing presumptions against preemption, and against abolition of common-law remedies? May a state (or its citizens) seek to enjoin, or recover damages from, an out-of-state source injuring the plaintiff state's waters if it employs the law of the source state rather than its own? See *International Paper Co.* v. *Ouellette*, 479 U.S. 481, 107 S.Ct. 805, 93 L.Ed.2d 883 (1987), holding such an action valid as long as the law of the source state is used.

## D. TRESPASS AND STRICT LIABILITY

The tort of trespass has also been employed in recent decades against acts involving air pollution, water pollution and other environmentally tortious conduct. The courts usually insist that there be a deposit of matter or some physical damage. Thus noise is not actionable as a trespass. When trespass is used in connection with conduct similar to nuisance, the courts tend to treat it as requiring similar proof of unreasonable conduct.

In *Scribner v. Summers*, 84 F.3d 554 (2d Cir. 1996), the defendants' steel-treating factory discharged sludge containing hazardous waste into drains that fed a ditch entering the plaintiff's land. The court found this to be both a nuisance and a trespass:

> [T]respass is the intentional invasion of another's property. To be liable, the trespasser "need not intend or expect the damaging consequences of his intrusion[;]" rather, he need only "intend the act which amounts to or produces the unlawful invasion." The intrusion itself "must at least be the immediate or inevitable consequence of what [the trespasser] willfully does, or which he does so negligently as to amount to willfulness." [citing cases]

The court likewise found an intentional private nuisance under *Copart* since the defendants "knew that contamination was 'substantially certain to result' from [their] conduct, see *Copart*[.]"

Wasn't Copart's conduct equally likely to cause contamination? Can you reconcile these decisions?

The tort of strict liability for abnormally dangerous activities, stemming from *Rylands* v. *Fletcher*, L.R. 3 H.L. 330 (1868), the English decision well-known to torts students, is also employed in the environmental area. Whether an activity is abnormally dangerous turns on whether it commonly occurs in the area. Thus oil drilling is not abnormally dangerous in Texas, though it might be in Rhode Island, for example.

Sometimes strict liability is imposed by legislation. The Price-Anderson Act, discussed in Chapter 11, imposes it for nuclear accidents.

In Chapter 9 we will examine toxic tort litigation in greater detail.

## 3. LAND USE CONTROLS

### A. ZONING

Introductory Note

Nuisance and the law of riparian rights (Part D of this Chapter) provided, and still provide, means for a land owner, or the state through public nuisance, to redress injurious land uses--odors, fumes, interference with water supply or fishing. But by their very nature these actions are tailored to solve individual grievances. There was no attempt to impose order on the patchwork of land uses which resulted from the 19th century *laissez-faire* attitude that landowners' rights were limited only by the law of nuisance and riparian rights until, early in this century, municipalities began to zone their land to systematically govern its use.

Zoning, which we take for granted, was highly controversial when first enacted. It was regarded as an interference with landowners' rights and soon challenged as an unconstitutional taking of property without due process of law. Observe how the U.S. Supreme Court used the nuisance analogy in examining zoning laws for the first time in the *Euclid* case.

VILLAGE OF EUCLID v. AMBLER REALTY CO.,
Supreme Court of the United States, 1926. 272 U.S. 365, 47 S. Ct. 114, 71 L.Ed. 303.

Mr. Justice Sutherland delivered the opinion of the court:

The village of Euclid is an Ohio municipal corporation. It adjoins and practically is a suburb of the city of Cleveland. Its estimated population is between 5,000 and 10,000, and its area from 12 to 14 square miles, the greater part of which is farm lands or unimproved acreage.* * *

Appellee is the owner of a tract of land containing 68 acres.* * * Adjoining this tract, both on the east and on the west, there have been laid out restricted residential plats upon which residences have been erected.

On November 13, 1922, an ordinance was adopted by the village council, establishing a comprehensive zoning plan for regulating and restricting the location of trades, industries, apartment houses, two-family houses, single family houses, etc., the lot area to be built upon, the size and height of buildings, etc.

The entire area of the village is divided by the ordinance into six classes of use districts, denominated U-1 to U-6, inclusive; three classes of height districts, denominated H-1 to H-3, inclusive; and four classes of area districts, denominated A-1 to A-4, inclusive.

[The Court here detailed the land use allowed in each of the six use districts--from U-1 allowing only single family homes, parks, etc. to U-6 which allows sewerage plants, junk yards and the like. The plaintiff-appellee's tract of land was zoned under three different classes, most of which exclude all industry and a large part of which excludes apartment buildings.]

The ordinance is assailed on the grounds that it is in derogation of § 1 of the 14th Amendment to the Federal Constitution in that it deprives appellee of liberty and property without due process of law and denies it the equal protection of the laws, and that it offends against certain provisions of the Constitution of the state of Ohio. The prayer of the bill is for an injunction restraining the enforcement of the ordinance and all attempts to impose or maintain as to appellee's property any of the restrictions, limitations or conditions. The court below held the ordinance to be unconstitutional and void, and enjoined its enforcement.

Before proceeding to a consideration of the case, it is necessary to determine the scope of the inquiry. The bill alleges that the tract of land in question is vacant and has been held for years for the purpose of selling and developing it for industrial uses, for which it is especially adapted, being immediately in the path of progressive industrial development; that for such uses it has a market value of about $10,000 per acre, but if the use be limited to residential purposes the market value is not in excess of $2,500 per acre; that the first 200 feet of the parcel back from Euclid Avenue, if unrestricted in respect of use, has a value of $150 per front foot, but if limited to residential uses, and ordinary mercantile business be excluded therefrom, its value is not in excess of $50 per front foot.

It is specifically averred that the ordinance attempts to restrict and control the lawful uses of appellee's land so as to confiscate and destroy a great part of its value: that it is being enforced in accordance with its terms: that prospective buyers of land for industrial, commercial and residential uses in the metropolitan district of Cleveland are deterred from buying any part of this land because of the existence of the ordinance and the necessity thereby entailed of conducting burdensome and expensive litigation in order to vindicate the right to use the land for lawful and legitimate purposes; that the ordinance constitutes a cloud upon the land, reduces and destroys its value, and has the effect of diverting the normal industrial, commercial and residential development thereof to other and less favorable locations.

The record goes no farther than to show, as the lower court found, that the normal, and reasonably to be expected, use and development of that part of appellee's land adjoining Euclid Avenue is for general trade and commercial purposes, particularly retail stores and like establishments, and that the normal, and reasonably to be expected, use and development of the residue of the land is for industrial and trade purposes. Whatever injury is inflicted by the mere existence and threatened enforcement of the ordinance is due to restriction in respect of these and similar uses: to which perhaps should be added--if not included in the foregoing--restrictions in respect of apartment houses.* * *

Building zone laws are of modern origin. They began in this country about twenty-five years ago. Until recent years, urban life was comparatively simple; but with the great increase and concentration of population, problems have developed, and constantly are developing, which require, and will continue to require additional restrictions in respect of the use and occupation of private lands in urban communities. Regulations, the wisdom, necessity and validity of which, as applied to existing conditions, are so apparent that they are now uniformly sustained, a century ago, or even half a century ago, probably would have been rejected as arbitrary and oppressive. Such regulations are sustained, under the complex conditions of our day, for reasons analogous to whose which justify traffic regulations, which, before the advent of automobiles and rapid transit street railways, would have been condemned as fatally arbitrary and unreasonable. And in this there is no inconsistency, for while the meaning of constitutional guarantees never varies, the scope of their application must expand or contract to meet the new and different conditions which are constantly coming within the field of their operation.* * *

The ordinance now under review and all similar laws and regulations must find their justification in some aspect of the police power, asserted for the public welfare. The line which in this field separates the legitimate from the illegitimate assumption of power is not capable of precise definition. It varies with circumstances and conditions. A regulatory zoning ordinance, which would be clearly valid as applied to the great cities, might be clearly invalid as applied to rural communities. In solving doubts, the maxim "*sic utere tuo ut alienum non lædas*," which lies at the foundation of so much of the common law of nuisances, ordinarily will furnish a fairly helpful clew. And the law of nuisances, likewise, may be consulted, not for the purpose of controlling, but for the helpful aid of its analogies in the process of ascertaining the scope of the power. Thus the question whether the power exists to forbid the erection of a building of a particular kind or for a particular use, like the question whether a particular thing is a nuisance, is to be determined, not by an abstract consideration of the building or of the thing considered apart, but by considering it in connection with the circumstances and the locality. A nuisance may be merely a right thing in the wrong place--like a pig in the parlor instead of the barnyard. If the validity of the legislative classification for zoning purposes be fairly debatable, the legislative judgment must be allowed to control.

There is no serious difference of opinion in respect of the validity of laws and regulations fixing the height of buildings within reasonable limits, the character of materials and methods of construction, and the adjoining area which must be left open, in order to minimize the danger of fire or collapse, the evils of overcrowding, and the like, and excluding from residential sections offensive trades, industries and structures likely to create nuisances.

Here, however, the exclusion is in general terms of all industrial establishments, and it may thereby happen that not only offensive or dangerous industries will be excluded, but those which are neither offensive nor dangerous will share the same fate. But this is no more than happens in respect of many practice-forbidding laws which this court has upheld, although drawn in general terms so as to include individual cases that may turn out to be innocuous in themselves. The inclusion of a reasonable margin to insure effective enforcement will not put upon a law, otherwise valid, the stamp of invalidity.

It is said that the village of Euclid is a mere suburb of the city of Cleveland; that the industrial development of that city has now reached and in some degree extended into the village and, in the obvious course of things, will soon absorb the entire area for industrial enterprises: that the effect of the ordinance is to divert this natural development elsewhere with the consequent loss of increased values to the owners of the lands within the village borders. But the village, though physically a suburb of Cleveland, is politically a separate municipality, with powers of its own and authority to govern itself as it sees fit within the limits of the organic law of its creation and the state and Federal Constitutions. Its governing authorities, presumably representing a majority of its inhabitants and voicing their will, have determined, not that industrial development shall cease at its boundaries, but that the course of such development shall proceed within definitely fixed lines. If it be a proper exercise of the police power to relegate industrial establishments to localities separated from residential sections, it is not easy to find a sufficient reason for denying the power because the effect of its exercise is to divert an industrial flow from the course which it would follow, to the injury of the residential public if left alone, to another course where such injury will be obviated. It is not meant by this, however, to exclude the possibility of cases where the general public interest would so far outweigh the interest of the municipality that the municipality would not be allowed to stand in the way.

We find no difficulty in sustaining restrictions of the kind thus far reviewed. The serious question in the case arises over the provisions of the ordinance excluding from residential districts, apartment houses, business houses, retail stores and shops, and other like establishments. This question involves the validity of what is really the crux of the more recent zoning legislation, namely, the creation and maintenance of residential districts, from which business and trade of every sort, including hotels and apartment houses, are excluded. Upon that question this court has not thus far spoken. The decisions of the state courts are numerous and conflicting; but those which broadly sustain the power greatly outnumber those which deny it altogether or narrowly limit it; and it is very apparent that there is a constantly increasing tendency in the direction of the broader view. [Many state courts] agree that the exclusion of buildings devoted to business, trade, etc., from residential districts, bears a rational relation to the health and safety of the community. Some of the grounds for this conclusion are--promotion of the health and security from injury of children and others by separating dwelling houses from territory devoted to trade and industry; suppression and prevention of disorder; facilitating the extinguishment of fires, and the enforcement of street traffic regulations and other general welfare ordinances; aiding the health and safety of the community by excluding from residential areas the confusion and danger of fire, contagion and disorder which in greater or less degree attach to the location of stores, shops and factories. Another ground is that the construction and repair of streets may be rendered easier and less expensive by confining the greater part of the heavy traffic to the streets where business is carried on.* * * [Comprehensive reports by experts] concur in the view that the segregation of residential, business and industrial buildings will make it easier to provide fire apparatus suitable for the character and intensity of the development in each section; that it will increase the safety and security of home life; greatly tend to prevent street accidents, especially to children, by reducing the traffic and resulting confusion in residential sections; decrease noise and other conditions which produce or intensify nervous disorders; preserve a more favorable environment in which to rear children, etc. With particular reference to apartment houses, it is pointed out that the development of detached house sections is greatly retarded by the coming of apartment houses, which has sometimes resulted in destroying the entire section for private house purposes: that in such sections very often the apartment house is a mere parasite, constructed in order to take advantage of the open spaces and attractive surroundings created by the residential character of the district. Moreover, the coming of one apartment house is followed by others, interfering by their height and bulk with the free circulation of air and monopolizing the rays of the sun which otherwise would fall upon the smaller homes, and bringing, as their necessary accompaniments, the disturbing noises incident to increased traffic and business, and the occupation by means of moving and parked automobiles, of larger portions of the streets, thus detracting from their safety and depriving children of the privilege of quiet and open spaces for play, enjoyed by those in more favored localities,--until, finally, the residential character of the neighborhood and its desirability as a place of detached residences are utterly destroyed. Under these circumstances, apartment houses, which in a different environment would be not only entirely unobjectionable but highly desirable, come very near to being nuisances.

If these reasons, thus summarized, do not demonstrate the wisdom or sound policy in all respects of those restrictions which we have indicated as pertinent to the inquiry, at least, the reasons are sufficiently cogent to preclude us from saying, as it must be said before the ordinance can be declared unconstitutional, that such provisions are clearly arbitrary and unreasonable, having no substantial relation to the public health, safety, morals, or general welfare.

Decree reversed.

Justice Van Devanter, Justice McReynolds, and Justice Butler dissent.

## Notes

Would a court have likely enjoined an apartment house as a nuisance in the village of Euclid?

In *Euclid* the Supreme Court recognized the possibility of cases arising where "the general public interest would so far outweigh the interest of the municipality that the "municipality would not be allowed to stand in the way." With respect to apartment houses, have we reached the point where the public need for housing outweighs a municipality's interest in prohibiting them? See *Southern*

*Burlington Co. NAACP v. Township of Mt. Laurel* and *Berenson v. Town of New Castle, infra.*

Were the risks of injuries to children, fire, traffic congestion and the rest the genuine concerns of the village in enacting the ordinance? Was the Court pouring some new wine (the zoning ordinance) into some very old bottles (the rights of the state under its police power to control fires, crime and traffic)?

To what extent is the village's motive in enacting a zoning ordinance a factor to be considered by the reviewing court? See *Berman v. Parker*, 348 U.S. 26, 75 S. Ct. 98, 99 L.Ed. 27 (1954). In upholding the condemnation of appellant's property for urban renewal purposes, to be replaced by newly-built private structures, the Court stated: "It is within the power of the legislature to determine that the community should be beautiful as well as healthy, spacious as well as clean, well-balanced as well as carefully patrolled.* * * If those who govern the District of Columbia decide that the Nation's Capital should be beautiful as well as sanitary, there is nothing in the Fifth Amendment that stands in the way." 348 U.S. at 33. See also *Village of Belle Terre v. Boraas,* discussed *infra* in the *Petaluma* case.

## Eminent Domain

*Berman v. Parker* upheld the condemnation of property by eminent domain, a power to acquire land even over the owner's objection that all levels of government have historically enjoyed. Once land is actually acquired by government, it may of course be totally protected from development if government so wishes. But this is by definition a costly way of protecting land, and one that removes it from the tax rolls entirely.

The Constitution imposes two important limits on the power of eminent domain, both stemming from abuses by the Crown. The Fifth Amendment requires eminent domain acquisitions to be for a public use, and requires government to pay the owner "just compensation." These mandates apply to state and local government through the Due Process Clause of the Fourteenth Amendment.

What is "public use"? *Berman v. Parker* held urban renewal constituted public use, even though the particular property acquired was not a blighted building but a viable, functioning department store. The Court nonetheless sustained the taking since the larger area slated for urban renewal, which included Berman's store, was blighted.

A tougher case was *Poletown Neighborhood Council v. City of Detroit*, 410 Mich. 616, 304 N.W.2d 455 (1981), where the city condemned numerous residences to provide a site for an automobile assembly plant. The company had threatened to leave Detroit. The city successfully argued the employment the plant would produce was a public use for the property. A divided court upheld the condemnation. Was the decision correct? Is preserving a wetland or a forest "public use"? What about acquiring a privately-owned farm and leasing it so it may continue operating?

*Poletown* was overruled in *County of Wayne* v. *Hathcock*, 471 Mich. 445, 684 N.W.2d 765 (2004), where condemnation for a private business and technology park was held not to be for a public use.

Later in this chapter (Subsection B) we will discuss the purchase by local governments of the right to develop property, an increasingly popular way of protecting environmental values while keeping the land in private ownership.

Note that the Euclid zoning ordinance did not in fact deprive the plaintiff of all reasonable use of its land, but only the most profitable use. How then could the plaintiff argue it was confiscatory and a taking of its property without the process of law? Should the municipality be required to pay the owner of rezoned property the difference in fair market value between its most profitable permitted use and most profitable use?

If zoning is done under the state's police power, why is it done by municipalities, not the state itself?

From early in the development of zoning, some suburban areas have sought to use minimum lot sizes to keep out low and moderate income residents. Minimums can be set aside as exclusionary zoning, violative of the Constitution's equal protection clause, if they are found to lack a rational basis in valid land-use control. Of late the protection of water supply and related environmental concerns have emerged as justifications for large-lot zoning.

Although some courts have set aside 3-acre and 4-acre zoning, see *National Land & Investment Co. v. Kohn,* 419 Pa. 504, 215 A.2d 597 (1965), New York's Court of Appeals upheld 5-acre zoning in *Robert E. Kurzius, Inc. v. Incorporated Village of Upper Brookville,* 51 N.Y.2d 338, 414 N.E.2d 680, 434 N.Y.S. 2d 180 (1980):

> The zoning power, when properly used, is an effective means to promote the public welfare. Large-lot zoning has also been used to achieve this end, and minimum acre lot restrictions have been upheld on several occasions for varying reasons including, most recently, the preservation of open-space land and the protection of a municipality's residents from the ill-effects of urbanization. We realize, of course, that large-lot zoning may also be used as a means to exclude persons of low or moderate income; and as we have stated before, we will not countenance community efforts at exclusion under any guise *(Matter of Golden v. Planning Bd. of Town of Ramapo [infra]).*
>
> The tests for determining when large-lot zoning has been used in an impermissible manner are suggested by our decision in *Berenson v. Town of New Castle [infra]*. In that case we dealt with the validity of an ordinance excluding multi-family housing as a permitted use. There we expressed our concern for balanced and integrated communities, as well as our concern that regional needs

be met. These concerns gave rise to a two-part test. First, the local board is required to provide a properly balanced and well-ordered plan for the community. Secondly, in enacting the zoning ordinance, consideration must be given to regional needs and requirements. This portion of the test was fashioned to meet the demands of both the Constitution and New York's statutory scheme, because under either basis the regulation must promote the regional welfare. It requires a "balancing of the local desire to maintain the *status quo* with the community and the greater public interest that regional needs be met" (*Berenson v. Town of New Castle [infra]*). In this regard we there noted that "[s]o long as the regional and local needs for such housing were supplied by either the local community or by other accessible areas in the community at large, it cannot be said, as a matter of law, that such an ordinance had no substantial relation to the public health, safety, morals or general welfare."

Generally then, a zoning ordinance enacted for a statutorily permitted purpose will be invalidated only if it is demonstrated that it actually was enacted for an improper purpose or if it was enacted without giving proper regard to local and regional housing needs and has an exclusionary effect. Once an exclusionary effect coupled with a failure to balance the local desires with housing needs has been proved, then the burden of otherwise justifying the ordinance shifts to the defendant. Such is not, however, the case before us.

In the instant case, plaintiffs attempted to show that the enactment of the village ordinance was motivated by an improper purpose by pointing to a portion of the testimony of the architect retained by the village board. In his testimony he stated that he had consulted with people within the village including, of course, large landowners. This testimony does not and cannot sustain the plaintiff's burden of proving an exclusionary purpose, nor does it demonstrate any such purpose, particularly when coupled with the other evidence presented in this case. The record shows clearly that the purpose of the ordinance was to preserve the open-space areas of the village, which may be a legitimate goal of multi-acre zoning. Additionally, plaintiffs have not demonstrated that the ordinance in question was not enacted in accordance with a comprehensive master plan, or that pressing regional needs were ignored in formulating the ordinance.[15] There was no proof that persons of low or moderate incomes were foreclosed from housing in the general

[15]Although regional needs may presently be met, this does not foreclose a zoning ordinance from all future inquiry. As population patterns shift and the demand for housing in a given region necessarily increases, a re-examination of an existing zoning scheme may be warranted.

region because of an unavailability of properly zoned land. In fact, there was no showing of need in the village for lots of less than five acres. Thus, plaintiffs failed to prove that the two-pronged *Berenson* test had not been met. Absent a showing by plaintiff of an exclusionary purpose behind a zoning ordinance, or that the zoning authority had failed to meet the criteria set forth in *Berenson*, the presumption of constitutionality which accompanies the legislative act must prevail unless the ordinance is without a doubt facially invalid. Based upon the record before us, we cannot say that the ordinance in question was an unreasonable and improper exercise of the police power, or beyond the power delegated by Section 7-704 of the Village Law.

Although some courts have assertedly found multi-acre zoning to be per se exclusionary and thus invalid, we do not so hold because of what we perceive to be legitimate purposes of such zoning. In regard to a related question, the Supreme Court has noted that "[a] quiet place where yards are wide, people few, and motor vehicles restricted are legitimate guidelines in a land-use project addressed to family needs" (*Village of Belle Terre v. Boraas* [discussed in *Petaluma*, *infra*]). Although environmental factors may justify large-lot zoning, we do not hold that this type of zoning is permissible without qualification, because minimum lot requirements may involve exclusionary practices.

We recognize that area zoning of this nature might in some circumstances not here present tend to prevent some individuals from making use of zoned land, just as any zoning ordinance tends to prevent certain other desired uses. Therefore, in order to withstand a claim of the potential for an exclusionary effect, these ordinances must be motivated by a proper purpose. The contrary has not here been demonstrated.

## B. LIMITED DEVELOPMENT ORDINANCES

### CONSTRUCTION INDUSTRY ASS'N v. CITY OF PETALUMA,
U.S. Court of Appeals, Ninth Circuit, 1975. 522 F.2d 897,
cert. den. 424 U.S. 934 (1976).

[Petaluma, a city of 25,000 people in 1970, is forty miles north of San Francisco and has become part of the Bay Area metropolitan housing market for commuters. Between 1960 and 1971 the number of housing units built there skyrocketed, leading the City Council to freeze development to allow it to study the situation. After finding that the pattern of building had been haphazard and had created a deficiency in moderately priced multi-family housing on the City's east side, the Council adopted a comprehensive zoning plan to correct the imbalance. The Plan restricts the growth rate of projects containing five or more dwelling units to five hundred dwelling units (homes or apartments) per year. The Plan was limited on its face to five years (1972-1977).]

Choy, Circuit Judge: * * *

The Plan also positions a 200 foot wide "greenbelt" around the City, to serve as a boundary for urban expansion for at least five years[.] The Plan further directs that allocations of building permits are to be divided as evenly as feasible between the west and east sections of the City and between single-family dwellings and multiple residential units (including rental units), and that sections of the City closest to the center are to be developed first in order to cause "infilling" of vacant area, and that 8 to 12 percent of the housing units approved be for low and moderate income persons.

The purpose of the Plan is much disputed in this case. According to general statements in the Plan itself, the Plan was devised to ensure that "development in the next five years, will take place in a reasonable, orderly, attractive manner, rather than in a completely haphazard and unattractive manner." The controversial 500-unit limitation on residential development units was adopted by the city "[i]n order to protect its small town character and surrounding open space." The other features of the Plan were designed to encourage an east-west balance in development, to provide for variety in densities and building types and wide ranges in prices and rents, to ensure infilling of closed-in vacant areas, and to prevent the sprawl of the City to the east and north. The Construction Industry Association of Sonoma County (the Association) argues and the district court found, however, that the Plan was primarily enacted "to limit Petaluma's demographic and market growth rate in housing and in the immigration of new residents."

In 1970 and 1971, housing permits were allotted at the rate of 1,000 annually, and there was no indication that without some governmental control on growth consumer demand would subside or even remain at the 1,000-unit per year level. Thus, if Petaluma had imposed a flat 500-unit limitation on *all* residential housing, the effect of the Plan would clearly be to retard to a substantial degree the natural growth rate of the City. Petaluma, however, did not apply the 500-unit limitation across the board, but instead exempted all projects of four units or less. Because appellees failed to introduce any evidence whatsoever as to the number of exempt units expected to be built during the five-year period, the effect of the 500 *development-unit* limitation on the natural growth in housing is uncertain. For purposes of this decision, however, we will assume that the 500 development-unit growth rate is in fact below the reasonably anticipated market demand for such units and that absent the Petaluma Plan, the City would grow at a faster rate.

According to undisputed expert testimony at trial, if the Plan (limiting housing starts to approximately 6 percent of existing housing stock each year) were to be adopted by municipalities throughout the region, the impact on the housing market would be substantial. For the decade 1970 to 1980, the shortfall in needed housing in the region would be about 105,000 units (or 25 percent of the units needed). Further, the aggregate effect of a proliferation of the Plan throughout the San Francisco region would be a decline in regional housing stock quality, a loss of the mobility of current and prospective residents and a deterioration in the quality and choice of housing available to income earners with real incomes of $14,000 per year or less. If, however, the Plan were considered by itself and with respect to Petaluma only, there is no evidence to suggest that there would be a deterioration in the quality and choice of housing available there to persons in the lower and middle income brackets. Actually, the plan increases the availability of multi-family units (owner-occupied and rental units) and low-income units which were rarely constructed in the pre-Plan days.* * *

Two landowners (the Landowners) and the Association instituted this suit* * * against the City and its officers and council members, claiming that the Petaluma Plan was unconstitutional.

[The court held the plaintiffs lacked standing to challenge the Plan based on a denial of the right to travel, since they would be improperly asserting the rights of third parties.]

Although we conclude that appellees lack standing to assert the rights of third parties, they nonetheless have standing to maintain claims based on violations of rights personal to them. Accordingly, appellees have standing to challenge the Petaluma Plan on the grounds asserted in their complaint that the Plan is arbitrary and thus violative of their due process rights guaranteed by the Fourteenth Amendment and that the Plan poses an unreasonable burden on interstate commerce.* * *

According to appellees, the Plan is nothing more than an exclusionary zoning device,[10] designed solely to insulate Petaluma from the urban complex in

[10] "Exclusionary zoning" is a phrase popularly used to describe suburban zoning regulations which have the effect, if not also the purpose, of preventing the migration of low and middle-income persons. Since a large percentage of racial minorities fall within the low and middle-income brackets, exclusionary zoning regulations may also effectively wall out racial minorities.

which it finds itself. The Association and the Landowners reject, as falling outside the scope of any legitimate governmental interest, the City's avowed purposes in implementing the Plan--the preservation of Petaluma's small town character and the avoidance of the social and environmental problems caused by an uncontrolled growth rate.

In attacking the validity of the Plan, appellees rely heavily on the district court's finding that the express purpose and the actual effect of the Plan is to exclude substantial numbers of people who would otherwise elect to move to the City. The existence of an exclusionary purpose and effect reflects, however, only *one* side of the zoning regulation. Practically all zoning restrictions have as a purpose and effect the *exclusion* of some activity or type of structure or a certain density of inhabitants. And in reviewing the reasonableness of a zoning ordinance, our inquiry does not terminate with a finding that it is for an exclusionary purpose.[11] We must determine further whether the *exclusion* bears any rational relationship to a *legitimate state interest.* The reasonableness, not the wisdom, of the Petaluma Plan is at issue in this suit.

It is well settled that zoning regulations "must find their justification in some aspect of the political power, asserted for the public welfare." *Village of Euclid v. Ambler Realty Co.* The concept of the public welfare, however is not limited to the regulation of noxious activities or dangerous structures. As the Court stated in *Berman v. Parker*, 348 U.S. 26, 33, 75 S. Ct. 98, 102, 99 L.Ed. 27 (1954):

> The concept of the public welfare is broad and inclusive. The values it represents are spiritual as well as physical, esthetic as well as monetary. It is within the power of the legislature to determine that the community should be beautiful as well as healthy, spacious as well as clean, well-balanced as well as carefully patrolled.

*Accord, Village of Belle Terre v. Boraas,* 416 U.S. 1, 6, 9, 94 S. Ct. 1536, 39 L.Ed.2d 797 (1974).

In determining whether the City's interest in preserving its small town character and in avoiding uncontrolled and rapid growth falls within the broad concept of "public welfare," we are considerably assisted by two recent cases. *Belle*

---

* * * Most court challenges to and comment upon so-called exclusionary zoning focus on such traditional zoning devices as height limitations, minimum square footage and minimum lot size requirements, and the prohibition of multi-family dwellings or mobile homes. The Petaluma Plan is unique in that although it assertedly slows the growth rate it replaces the past pattern of single-family detached homes with an assortment of housing units, varying in price and design.

[11] Our inquiry here is not unlike that involved in a case alleging denial of equal protection of the laws. The mere showing of some discrimination by the state is not sufficient to prove an invasion of one's constitutional rights. Most legislation to some extent discriminates between various classes of persons, business enterprises, or other entities. However, absent a suspect classification or invasion of fundamental rights, equal protection rights are violated only where the classification does not bear a rational relationship to a legitimate state interest. *See Ybarra v. City of Town of Los Altos Hills*, 503 F.2d 250, 254 (9th Cir. 1974).

*Terre, supra* and *Ybarra v. City of Town of Los Altos Hills*, 503 F.2d 250 (9th Cir. 1974), each of which upheld as not unreasonable a zoning regulation much more restrictive than the Petaluma Plan, are dispositive of the due process issue in this case.

In *Belle Terre* the Supreme Court rejected numerous challenges[13] to a village's restricting land use to one-family[14] dwellings excluding lodging houses, boarding houses, fraternity houses or multiple-dwelling houses. By absolutely prohibiting the construction of or conversion of a building to other than single-family dwelling, the village ensured that it would never grow, if at all, much larger than its population of 700 living in 220 residences. Nonetheless, the Court found that the prohibition of boarding houses and other multi-family dwellings was reasonable and within the public welfare because such dwellings present urban problems, such as the occupation of a given space by more people, the increase in traffic and parked cars and the noise that comes with increased crowds. According to the Court, a quiet place where yards are wide, people few, and motor vehicles restricted are legitimate guidelines in a land-use project addressed to family needs. This goal is a permissible one within *Berman v. Parker, supra.* The police power is not confined to elimination of filth, stench, and unhealthy places. It is ample to lay out zones where family values, youth values, and the blessings of quiet seclusion, and clean air make the area a sanctuary for people.

Following the *Belle Terre* decision, this court in *Los Altos Hills* had an opportunity to review a zoning ordinance providing that a housing lot shall contain not less than one acre and that no lot shall be occupied by more than one primary dwelling unit. The ordinance as a practical matter prevented poor people from living in Los Altos Hills and restricted the density, and thus the population, of the town. This court, nonetheless, found that the ordinance was rationally related to a legitimate governmental interest--*the preservation of the town's rural environment*--and, thus, did not violate the equal protection clause of the Fourteenth Amendment.

Both the Belle Terre ordinance and the Los Altos Hills regulation had the purpose and effect of permanently restricting growth; nonetheless, the court in each case upheld the particular law before it on the ground that the regulation served a legitimate governmental interest falling within the concept of the public welfare: the preservation of quiet family neighborhoods (Belle Terre) and the preservation of a rural environment (Los Altos Hills). Even less restrictive or exclusionary than the above zoning ordinances is the Petaluma Plan which, unlike those ordinances, does

---

[13] The plaintiffs in *Belle Terre* claimed *inter alia* that the ordinance interfered with a person's right to travel and right to migrate to and settle within a state.

The Supreme Court held that since the ordinance was not aimed at transients, there was no infringement of anyone's right to travel. Although due to appellees' lack of standing we do not reach today the right to travel issue, we note that the Petaluma Plan is not aimed at transients, nor does it penalize those who have recently exercised their right to travel.

[14] The word "family" as used in the ordinance meant one or more persons related by blood, adoption or marriage, living together as a single housekeeping unit. Two or fewer persons living together, though not related by blood, adoption or marriage, were considered a "family."

not freeze the population at present or near-present levels.[15] Further, unlike the Los Altos Hills ordinance and the various zoning regulations struck down by state courts in recent years, the Petaluma Plan does not have the undesirable effect of walling out any particular income class nor any racial minority group.[16] Although we assume that some persons desirous of living in Petaluma will be excluded under the housing permit limitation and that, thus, the Plan may frustrate some legitimate regional housing needs, the Plan is not arbitrary or unreasonable. We agree with appellees that unlike the situation in the past most municipalities today are neither isolated nor wholly independent from neighboring municipalities and that, consequently, unilateral land use decisions by one local entity affect the needs and resources of an entire region.

It does not necessarily follow, however, that the *due process* rights of builders and landowners are violated merely because a local entity exercises in its own self-interest the police power lawfully delegated to it by the state. *See Belle Terre, supra; Los Altos Hills, supra.* If the present system of delegated zoning power does not effectively serve the state interest in furthering the general welfare of the region or entire state, it is the state legislature's and not the federal courts' role to intervene and adjust the system. As stated *supra*, the federal court is not a super zoning board and should not be called on to mark the point at which legitimate local interests in promoting the welfare of the community are outweighed by legitimate regional interests.

We conclude therefore that under *Belle Terre* and *Los Altos Hills* the concept of the public welfare is sufficiently broad to uphold Petaluma's desire to preserve its small town character, its open spaces and low density of population, and to grow at an orderly and deliberate pace.

The district court found that housing in Petaluma and the surrounding areas is produced substantially through goods and services in interstate commerce and that curtailment of residential growth in Petaluma will cause serious dislocation to commerce. Our ruling today, however, that the Petaluma Plan represents a reasonable and legitimate exercise of the police power obviates the necessity of remanding the case for consideration of appellees' claim that the Plan unreasonably burdens interstate commerce.

It is well settled that a state regulation validly based on the police power does not impermissibly burden interstate commerce where the regulation neither

---

[15] Under the Petaluma Plan, the population is expected to increase at the rate of about 1,500 persons annually. This rate approximates the rate of growth in the 1960's and represents about a 6 percent increase per year over the present population.

[16] Contrary to the picture painted by appellees, the Petaluma Plan is "inclusionary" to the extent that it offers new opportunities, previously unavailable, to minorities and low and moderate-income persons. Under the pre-Plan system, single family, middle-income housing dominated the Petaluma market, and as a result low and moderate income persons were unable to secure housing in the area. The Plan radically changes the previous building pattern and requires that housing permits be evenly divided between single-family and multi-family units and that approximately eight to twelve percent of the units be constructed specifically for low and moderate income persons.

discriminates against interstate commerce nor operates to disrupt its required uniformity. *Huron Cement Co. v. [City of] Detroit,* 362 U.S. 440, 448, 80 S. Ct. 813, 4 L.Ed.2d 852 (1960). As stated by the Supreme Court almost 25 years ago:

> When there is a reasonable basis for legislation to protect the social, as distinguished from the economic, welfare of a community, it is not for this Court because of the Commerce Clause to deny the exercise locally of the sovereign power of the [state].

*Breard v. [City of] Alexandria,* 341 U.S. 622, 640, 71 S. Ct. 920, 931, 95 L.Ed. 1233 (1951). It is wholly beyond a court's limited authority under the Commerce Clause to review state legislation by balancing reasonable social welfare legislation against its incidental burden on commerce.

Consequently, since the local regulation here is rationally related to the social and environmental welfare of the community and does not discriminate against interstate commerce or operate to disrupt its required uniformity, appellees' claim that the Plan unreasonably burdens commerce must fail.

Reversed.

## Notes

If Petaluma had restricted individual one-family residences as well, would the result have been the same? What if the city had not specifically provided for low and moderate income residents?

Same result if Petaluma's plan was permanent, rather than for five years?

Will esthetics alone sustain a zoning ordinance? See *People v. Stover,* 12 N.Y.2d 462, 191 N.E.2d 272, 240 N.Y.S.2d 734 (1963) (upholding ordinances forbidding displaying laundry in front of homes, despite appellant's free speech claim that it was in protest at high taxes). Or the locality's desire to maintain family values and privacy? See *Village of Belle Terre v. Boraas,* 416 U.S. 1, 94 S. Ct. 1536, 39 L.Ed.2d 797 (1974), discussed in the *Petaluma* case. Should the court have considered the effect of the Petaluma plan on the surrounding area? Suppose every municipality in the region followed Petaluma's lead?

To what lengths are the courts willing to go to uphold a zoning ordinance in the face of expanding population from a nearby metropolitan area? See the *Golden* case, next.

RUTH GOLDEN v. PLANNING BOARD OF TOWN OF RAMAPO, New York Court of Appeals, 1972. 30 N.Y.2d 359, 285 N.E.2d 291, 334 N.Y.S.2d 138, app. dism. 409 U.S. 1003.

Scileppi, Judge.

[This case arises] out of the 1969 amendments to the Town of Ramapo's Zoning Ordinance.

* * *[P]etitioners, the owner of record and contract vendee,* * * sought an order reviewing and annulling a decision and determination of the Planning Board of the Town of Ramapo which denied their application for preliminary approval of a residential subdivision plat because of an admitted failure to secure a special permit as required by Section 46-13.1 of the Town zoning ordinance prohibiting subdivision approval except where the residential developer has secured, prior to the application for plat approval, a special permit or a variance pursuant to Section F of the ordinance.* * *

The attack by the subdividing landowner is directed against the ordinance in its entirety, and the thrust of the petition and complaint, respectively, is that the ordinance of itself operates to destroy the value and marketability of the subject premises for residential use and thus constitutes a present invasion of the property rights of the complaining landholders.* * *

Experiencing the pressures of an increase in population and the ancillary problem of providing municipal facilities and services,[1] the Town develop[ed] a master plan. The plan's preparation included a four-volume study of the existing land uses, public facilities, transportation, industry and commerce, housing needs and projected population trends. The proposals appearing in the studies were subsequently adopted pursuant to Section 272-a of the Town Law* * *. The master plan was followed by the adoption of a comprehensive zoning ordinance.

[T]he Town subsequently adopted the subject amendments for the alleged purpose of eliminating premature subdivision and urban sprawl. Residential development is to proceed according to the provision of adequate municipal facilities and services, with the assurance that any concomitant restraint upon property use is to be of a "temporary" nature and that other private uses, including the construction of individual housing, are authorized.

The amendments [adopt] a new class of "Special Permit Uses," designated "Residential Development Use." "Residential Development Use" is defined as "The erection or construction of dwellings or any vacant plots, lots or parcels of land" and, any person who acts so as to come within that definition, "shall be deemed to be engaged in residential development which shall be a separate use

---

[1]The Town's allegations that present facilities are inadequate to service increasing demands goes uncontested. We must assume, therefore, that the proposed improvements, both as to their nature and extent, reflect legitimate community needs and are not veiled efforts at exclusion. In the period 1940-1968 population in the unincorporated areas of the Town increased 285.9%.

classification under this ordinance and subject to the requirement of obtaining a special permit from the Town Board."

The standards for the issuance of special permits are framed in terms of the availability to the proposed subdivision plat of five essential facilities or services: specifically (1) public sanitary sewers or approved substitutes; (2) drainage facilities; (3) improved public parks or recreation facilities, including public schools; (4) State, county or town roads--major, secondary or collector; and, (5) firehouses. No special permit shall issue unless the proposed residential development has accumulated 15 development points, to be computed on a sliding scale of values assigned to the specified improvements under the statute. Subdivision is thus a function of immediate availability to the proposed plat of certain municipal improvements; the avowed purpose of the amendments being to phase residential development to the Town's ability to provide the above facilities or services.

Certain savings and remedial provisions are designed to relieve of potentially unreasonable restrictions. Thus, the board may issue special permits vesting a present right to proceed with residential development in such year as the development meets the required point minimum, but in no event later than the final year of the 18-year capital plan. The approved special use permit is fully assignable[.]* * * Finally, upon application to the Town Board, the development point requirements may be varied should the board determine that such a variance or modification is consistent with the on-going development plan.

The undisputed effect of these integrated efforts in land use planning and development is to provide an over-all program of orderly growth and adequate facilities through a sequential development policy commensurate with progressing availability and capacity of public facilities. While its goals are clear and its purposes indisputably laudatory, serious questions are raised as to the manner in which these ends are to be effected, not the least of which relates to their legal liability under present zoning enabling legislation, particularly Sections 261 and 263 of the Town Law. The owners of the subject premises argue * * * that the primary purpose of the amending ordinance is to control or regulate population growth within the Town and as such is not within the authorized objectives of the zoning enabling legislation. We disagree.

In enacting the challenged amendments, the Town Board has sought to control subdivision in all residential districts, pending the provision (public or private) at some future date of various services and facilities. A reading of the relevant statutory provisions reveals that there is no specific authorization for the "sequential" and "timing" controls adopted here. That, of course, cannot be said to end the matter, for the additional inquiry remains as to whether the challenged amendments find their basis within the perimeters of the devices authorized and purposes sanctioned under current enabling legislation. Our concern is, as it should be, with the effects of the statutory scheme taken as a whole and its role in the propagation of a viable policy of land use and planning.

Town, cities and villages lack the power to enact and enforce zoning or other land use regulations. The exercise of that power, to the extent that it is lawful, must be founded upon a legislative delegation to so proceed, and in the absence of such a grant will be held *ultra vires* and void. That delegation, set forth in Section 261 of the Town Law, [grants towns authority to zone for "legitimate zoning purposes," which are] to secure safety from various calamities, to avoid undue concentration of population and to facilitate "adequate provision of transportation, water, sewerage, schools, parks and other public requirements" (Town Law, § 263). In the end, zoning properly effects, and only in the manner prescribed, those purposes detailed under Section 263 of the Town Law. It may not be invoked to further the general police powers of a municipality.[5]

Even so, considering the activities enumerated by Section 261 of the Town Law, and relating those powers to the authorized purposes detailed in Section 263, the challenged amendments are proper zoning techniques, exercised for legitimate zoning purposes. The power to restrict and regulate conferred under Section 261 includes within its grant, by way of necessary implication, the authority to direct the growth of population for the purposes indicated, within the confines of the township.

Of course, zoning historically has assumed the development of individual plats and has proven characteristically ineffective in treating with the problems attending subdivision and development of larger parcels, involving as it invariably does, the provision of adequate public services and facilities. To this end, subdivision control (Town Law, §§ 276, 277) purports to guide community development in the directions outlined here, while at the same time encouraging the provision of adequate facilities for the housing, distribution, comfort and convenience of local residents. It reflects in essence, a legislative judgment that the development of unimproved areas be accompanied by provision of essential facilities.

It is argued, nevertheless, that the timing controls currently in issue are not legislatively authorized since their effect is to prohibit subdivision absent precedent or concurrent action of the Town, and hence constitutes an unauthorized blanket interdiction against subdivision.

It is, indeed, true that the planning Board is not in an absolute sense statutorily authorized to deny the right to subdivide. That is not, however, what is sought to be accomplished here. The Planning Board has the right to refuse approval of subdivision plats in the absence of those improvements specified in Section 277, and the fact that it is the Town and not the subdividing owner or land developer who is required to make those improvements before the plat will be approved cannot be said to transform the scheme into an absolute prohibition any

[5] This distinction, though often unarticulated, is elemental and we have in the past held the exercise of the zoning power *ultra vires* and void where the end sought to be accomplished was not peculiar to the locality's basic land use scheme, but rather related to some general problem, incidental to the community at large.

more than it would be so where it was the developer who refused to provide the facilities required for plat approval.

Undoubtedly, current zoning enabling legislation is burdened by the largely antiquated notion which deigns that the regulation of land use and development is uniquely a function of local government--that the public interest of the state is exhausted once its political subdivisions have been delegated the authority to zone.

Experience, over the past quarter century, however, with greater technological integration and drastic shifts in population distribution has pointed up serious defects and community autonomy in land use controls has come under increasing attack by legal commentators, and students of urban problems alike, because of its pronounced insularism and its correlative role in producing distortions in metropolitan growth patterns, and perhaps more importantly, in crippling efforts toward regional and state-wide problem solving, be it pollution, decent housing, or public transportation.

Recognition of communal and regional interdependence, in turn, has resulted in proposals for schemes of regional and State-wide planning, in the hope that decisions would then correspond roughly to their level of impact.[8] Yet, as salutary as such proposals may be, the power to zone under current law is vested in local municipalities, and we are constrained to resolve the issues accordingly. What does become more apparent in treating with the problem, however, is that though the issues are framed in terms of the developer's due process rights, those rights cannot, realistically speaking, be viewed separately and apart from the rights of others "in search of a [more] comfortable place to live."

There is, then, something inherently suspect in a scheme which, apart from its professed purposes, effects a restriction upon the free mobility of a people until sometime in the future when projected facilities are available to meet increased demands. Although zoning must include schemes designed to allow municipalities to more effectively contend with the increased demands of evolving and growing communities, under its guise, townships have been wont to try their hand at an array of exclusionary devices in the hope of avoiding the very burden which growth must inevitably bring.

Of course, these problems cannot be solved by Ramapo or any single municipality, but depend upon the accommodation of widely disparate interests for their ultimate resolution. To that end, State-wide or regional control of planning would insure that interests broader than that of the municipality underlie various land use policies. Nevertheless, that should not be the only context in which growth devices such as these, aimed at population assimilation, not exclusion, will be sustained.

Hence, unless we are to ignore the plain meaning of the statutory delegation, this much is clear: phased growth is well within the ambit of existing enabling legislation.* * * The answer which Ramapo has posed can by no means be termed

[8] Invariably, the primary responsibility for formulating and implementing zoning policy remains in the hands of local government, with provision for review at county, State and regional levels[.]

definitive; it is however a first practical step toward controlled growth achieved without forsaking broader social purposes.* * *

The subject ordinance is said to advance legitimate zoning purposes as it assures that each new home built in the township will have at least a minimum of public services in the categories regulated by the ordinance.* * *

What we will not countenance, * * * under any guise, is community efforts at immunization or exclusion. But, far from being exclusionary, the present amendments merely seek, by the implementation of sequential development and timed growth, to provide a balanced, cohesive community dedicated to the efficient utilization of land. [And] timed growth, unlike the minimum lot requirements recently struck down by the Pennsylvania Supreme Court as exclusionary, does not impose permanent restrictions upon land use. In sum, Ramapo asks not that it be left alone, but only that it be allowed to prevent the kind of deterioration that has transformed well-ordered and thriving residential communities into blighted ghettos with attendant hazards to health, security, and social stability--a danger not without substantial basis in fact.

We only require that communities confront the challenge population growth with open doors. Where in grappling with that problem, the community undertakes, by imposing temporary restrictions upon development, to provide required municipal services in a rational manner, courts are rightfully reluctant to strike down such schemes.* * *

Without a doubt restrictions upon the property in the present case are substantial in nature and duration. They are not, however, absolute. The amendments contemplate a definite term, as the development points are designed to operate for a maximum period of 18 years and during that period, the Town is committed to the construction and installation of capital improvements. The net result of the on-going development provision is that individual parcels may be committed to a residential development use prior to the expiration of the maximum period. Similarly, property owners under the terms of the amendments may elect to accelerate the date of development by installing, at their own expense, the necessary public services to bring the parcel within the required number of development points.

In sum, where it is clear that the existing physical and financial resources of the community are inadequate to furnish the essential services and facilities which a substantial increase in population requires, there is a rational basis for "phased growth" and hence, the challenged ordinance is not violative of the Federal and State Constitutions.* * *

Breitel, Judge (dissenting).

The limited powers of district zoning and subdivision regulation delegated to a municipality do not include the power to impose a moratorium on land development. [A] municipality has only those powers, and especially land use powers, delegated or necessarily implied.

But there is more involved in these cases than the arrogation of undelegated powers. Raised are vital constitutional issues, and, most important, policy issues trenching on grave domestic problems of our time, without the benefit of a legislative determination which would reflect the interests of the entire State. The policy issues relate to needed housing, planned land development under government control, and the exclusion in effect or by motive, of walled-in urban populations of the middle class and the poor.* * *

The evils of uncontrolled urban sprawl on the one hand, and the suburban and exurban pressure to exclude urban population on the other hand, have created a massive conflict, with social and economic implications of the gravest character.* * *

Generally, there is the view that the conflict requires solution at a regional or State level, usually with local administration, and not by compounding the conflict with idiosyncratic municipal action. The Ramapo ordinance files in the fact of and would frustrate these well-directed efforts.

Decisive of the present appeals, however, is the absence in the town of legislative authorization to postpone growth, let alone to establish unilaterally phased population levels, through the expedient of barring residential development for scheduled periods of up to 18 years. It has always been the rule that a municipality has only those land use powers delegated or necessarily implied. Existing enabling legislation does not grant the power upon which the Ramapo ordinance rests. And for policy reasons, one should not strain the reading of the enabling acts, even if straining would avail, to distort them, beyond any meaning ever attributed to them, except by the ingenious draftsmen of the Ramapo ordinance.* * *

[T]he Ramapo ordinance * * * lacks statutory authorization, and this despite the fact that its reach is more ambitious than any before essayed even with enabling legislation.

By the unsupportable extrapolation from existing enabling acts, one may not usurp the unique responsibility of the Legislature, even where it has failed to act. What is worse, to do this, as a State Legislature would not, without considering the social and economic ramifications for the locality, region, and State, and without limitations essential to an intelligent delegation, is unsound as well as invalid. Moreover, to allow Ramapo's idiosyncratic solution, which would then be available to any other community like Ramapo, may end indefinitely the possibility of commanding better legislation for land planning, just because such legislation requires some diminution in the local control now exercised under the zoning acts.

Judge Jasen joined in this dissent.

Notes

What if the plan wasn't limited to 20 years? Would the court be as willing to uphold a perpetual moratorium on land development?

Judge Breitel, in his dissent, suggests the Ramapo plan is anti-affordable housing. Do you agree?

The dissent also suggests regional planning as a solution. How feasible is this approach? *See Candlestick Properties, Inc. v. San Francisco Bay Conservation & Dev. Comm'n*, 11 Cal. App.3d 557, 89 Cal. Rptr. 897 (1970). Has the state totally delegated to the municipalities its power to zone? Can it be retrieved where, in the language of the *Euclid* Court, "the general public interest would so far outweigh the interest of the municipality that the municipality would not be allowed to stand in the way"?

SOUTHERN BURLINGTON COUNTY NAACP v. TOWNSHIP OF MOUNT LAUREL, Supreme Court of New Jersey, 1975. 67 N.J. 151, 336 A.2d 713, cert. denied 423 U.S. 808.

Hall, J.

This case attacks the system of land use regulation by defendant Township of Mount Laurel on the ground that low and moderate income families are thereby unlawfully excluded from the municipality. The trial court so found and declared the township zoning ordinance totally invalid.* * *

The implications of the issue presented are indeed broad and far-reaching, extending much beyond these particular plaintiffs and the boundaries of this particular municipality.

There is not the slightest doubt that New Jersey has been, and continues to be, faced with a desperate need for housing, especially of decent living accommodations economically suitable for low and moderate income families. The situation was characterized as a "crisis" and fully explored and documented by Governor Cahill in two special messages to the Legislature--*A Blueprint for Housing in New Jersey* (1970) and *New Horizons in Housing* (1972).

Plaintiffs represent the minority group poor (black and Hispanic) seeking such quarters. But they are not the only category of persons barred from so many municipalities by reason of restrictive land use regulations. We have reference to young and elderly couples, single persons and large, growing families not in the poverty class, but who still cannot afford the only kinds of housing realistically permitted in most places--relatively high-priced single-family detached dwellings on sizable lots and, in some municipalities, expensive apartments. We will, therefore, consider the case from the wider viewpoint that the effect of Mount Laurel's land use regulation has been to prevent various categories of persons from living in the township because of the limited extent of their income and resources. In this connection, we accept the representation of the municipality's counsel at oral argument that the regulatory scheme was not adopted with any desire or intent to exclude prospective residents on the obviously illegal bases of race, origin or believed social incompatibility.

[The township's] candid position is that, conceding its land use regulation was intended to result and has resulted in economic discrimination and exclusion of substantial segments of the area population, its policies and practices are in the best present and future fiscal interest of the municipality and its inhabitants and are legally permissible and justified.

[Mount Laurel is a township * * * on the west central edge of Burlington County. It, like most post-World War II municipalities, experienced a prodigious increase in population in the `50s and `60s--from 2,817 in 1950 to 11,221 in 1970. It is part of the South Jersey-Philadelphia metropolitan area, being strategically located in the highway network.

Under Mount Laurel's zoning ordinance, enacted in 1964, approximately 30% of the land is zoned for light industry, approximately 1% for retail business and the rest for residences. The residential area is divided into four types (R-1 to R-4), all of which exclude everything but single family homes on one lot each. By amendment in 1968 a small cluster-zoned area was designated. Cluster-zoning allows multiple dwellings but preserves overall density by demanding that the land left vacant be used as a common ground or donated to the public as parks.]

A variation from conventional development has recently occurred in some parts of Mount Laurel, as in a number of other similar municipalities, by use of the land use regulation device known as "planned unit development" (PUD), [in which] the type, density and placement of land uses and buildings, instead of being detailed and confined to specified districts by local legislation in advance, is determined by contract,* * * as to each development between the developer and the municipal administrative authority, under broad guidelines laid down by state enabling legislation[.]

While the [township's PUD] ordinance was repealed early in 1971, the township governing body in the interim had approved four PUD projects, which were specifically saved from extinction by the repealer.

These projects * * * are very substantial and involve at least 10,000 sale and rental housing units of various types. While multi-family housing in the form of rental garden, medium rise and high rise apartments and attached townhouses is for the first time provided for, as well as single-family detached dwellings for sale, it is not designed to accommodate and is beyond the financial reach of low and moderate income families, especially those with young children. The aim is quite the contrary; as with the single-family homes in the older conventional subdivisions, only persons of medium and upper income are sought as residents. [The township's] approvals also sharply limit the number of apartments having more than one bedroom. Further, they require that the developer must provide in its leases that no school-age children shall be permitted to occupy any one-bedroom apartment and that no more than two such children shall reside in any two-bedroom unit.* * *

All this affirmative action for the benefit of certain segments of the population is in sharp contrast to the lack of action, and indeed hostility, with respect to affording any opportunity for decent housing for the township's own poor living in substandard accommodations, found largely in the section known a Springville (R-3 zone). The 1969 Master Plan Report recognized it and recommended positive action. The continuous official reaction has been rather a negative policy of waiting for dilapidated premises to be vacated and then forbidding further occupancy. An earlier non-governmental effort to improve conditions had been effectively thwarted. In 1968 a private non-profit association sought to build subsidized, multi-family housing in the Springville section with funds to be granted by a higher level governmental agency. Advance municipal approval of the project was required. The Township Committee responded with a purportedly approving resolution, which found a need for "moderate" income housing in the area, but went on to specify that such housing must be constructed subject to all zoning, planning, building and other applicable ordinances and codes. This meant single-family detached dwellings on 20,000 square foot lots. (Fear was also expressed that such housing would attract low income families from outside the township.) Needless to say, such requirements killed realistic housing for this group of low and moderate income families.[8]

The record thoroughly substantiates the findings of the trial court that over the years Mount Laurel "has acted affirmatively to control development and to attract a selective type of growth" and that "through its zoning ordinances has exhibited economic discrimination in that the poor have been deprived of adequate housing and the opportunity to secure the construction of subsidized housing, and has used federal, state, county and local finances and resources solely for the betterment of middle and upper-income persons."

There cannot be the slightest doubt that the reason for this course of conduct has been to keep down local taxes on *property* (Mount Laurel is not a high tax municipality) and that the policy was carried out without regard for non-fiscal consideration with respect to *people*, either within or without its boundaries. This conclusion is demonstrated not only by what was done and what happened, as we have related, but also by innumerable direct statements of municipal officials at public meetings over the years which are found in the exhibits.* * *

This policy of land use regulation for a fiscal end derives from New Jersey's tax structure, which has imposed on local real estate most of the cost of municipal and county government and of the primary and secondary education of the municipality's children. The latter expense is much the largest, so, basically, the fewer the school children, the lower the tax rate. Sizable industrial and commercial

---

[8] The record is replete with uncontradicted evidence that, factually, low and moderate income housing cannot be built without some form of contribution, concession or incentive by some level of government. Such, under various state and federal methods, may take the form of public construction or some sort of governmental assistance or encouragement to private building. Multi-family rental units, at a high density, or, at most, low cost single-family units on very small lots, are economically necessary and in turn require appropriate local land use regulations.

ratables are eagerly sought and homes and the lots on which they are situated are required to be large enough, through minimum lot sizes and minimum floor areas, to have substantial value in order to produce greater tax revenues to meet school costs. Large families who cannot afford to buy large homes and must live in cheaper rental accommodations are definitely not wanted, so we find drastic bedroom restrictions for, or complete prohibition of, multi-family or other feasible housing for those of lesser income.

This pattern of land use regulation has been adopted for the same purpose in developing municipality after developing municipality.* * *

One incongruous result is the picture of developing municipalities rendering it impossible for lower paid employees of industries they have eagerly sought and welcomed with open arms (and, in Mount Laurel's case, even some of its own lower paid municipal employees) to live in the community where they worked.

The situation has become exactly the opposite [in the cities]. Much industry and retail business, and even the professions, have left the cities. Camden is a typical example.* * * [I]t lost thousands of jobs between 1950 and 1970, including more than half of its manufacturing jobs[.] A large segment of retail business faded away with the erection of large suburban shopping centers. The economically better situated city residents helped fill up the miles of sprawling new housing developments, not fully served by public transit. In a society which came to depend more and more on expensive individual motor vehicle transportation for all purposes, low income employees very frequently could not afford to reach outlying places of suitable employment and they certainly could not afford the permissible housing near such locations. These people have great difficulty in obtaining work and have been forced to remain in housing which is overcrowded, and has become more and more substandard and less and less tax productive. There has been a consequent critical erosion of the city tax base and inability to provide the amount and quality of those governmental services--education, health, police, fire, housing and the like--so necessary to the very existence of safe and decent city life. This category of city dwellers desperately needs much better housing and living conditions than is available to them now, both in a rehabilitated city and in outlying municipalities. They make up, along with the other classes of persons earlier mentioned who also cannot afford the only generally permitted housing in the developing municipalities, the acknowledged great demand for low and moderate income housing.* * * The legal question before us * * * is whether a developing municipality like Mount Laurel may validly, by a system of land use regulation, make it physically and economically impossible to provide low and moderate income housing in the municipality for the various categories of persons who need and want it and thereby, as Mount Laurel has, exclude such people from living within its confines because of the limited extent of their income and resources. Necessarily implicated are the broader questions of the right of such municipalities to limit the kinds of available housing and of any obligation to make possible a variety of choice of types of living accommodations.

We conclude that every such municipality must, by its land use regulations, presumptively make realistically possible an appropriate variety and choice of housing. More specifically, presumptively it cannot foreclose the opportunity of the classes of people mentioned for low and moderate income housing and in its regulations must affirmatively afford that opportunity, at least to the extent of the municipality's fair share of the present and prospective regional need therefor. These obligations must be met unless the particular municipality can sustain the heavy burden of demonstrating peculiar circumstances which dictate that it should not be required so to do.[10]

We reach this conclusion under state law and so do not find it necessary to consider federal constitutional grounds urged by plaintiffs.* * *

[I]t is fundamental and not to be forgotten that the zoning power is a police power of the state and the local authority is acting only as a delegate of that power and is restricted in the same manner as is the state. So, when regulation does have a substantial external impact, the welfare of the state's citizens beyond the borders of the particular municipality cannot be disregarded and must be recognized and served.

This essential was distinctly pointed out in *Euclid*, where Mr. Justice Sutherland specifically referred to "* * * the possibility of cases where the general public interest would so far outweigh the interest of the municipality that the municipality would not be allowed to stand in the way."

There cannot be the slightest doubt that shelter, along with food, are the most basic human needs [, as] is implicit in the legislative findings of an extreme, long-term need in this state for decent low and moderate income housing, set forth in the numerous statutes providing for various agencies and methods at both state and local levels designed to aid in alleviation of the need. [Thus a] presumptive obligation arises for each such municipality affirmatively to plan and provide, by its land use regulations, the reasonable opportunity for an appropriate variety and choice of housing, including, of course, low and moderate cost housing, to meet the needs, desires and resources of all categories of people who may desire to live within its boundaries. Negatively, it may not adopt regulations or policies which thwart or preclude that opportunity.* * *

We have spoken of this obligation of such municipalities as "presumptive." The term has two aspects, procedural and substantive. Procedurally, we think the basic importance of appropriate housing for all dictates that, when it is shown that a developing municipality in its land use regulations has not made realistically possible a variety and choice of housing, including adequate provision to afford the opportunity for low and moderate income housing or has expressly prescribed requirements or restrictions which preclude or substantially hinder it, a facial showing of violation of substantive due process or equal protection under the state constitution has been made out and the burden, and it is a heavy one, shifts to the

[10] While, as the trial court found, Mt. Laurel's actions were deliberate, we are of the view that the identical conclusion follows even when municipal conduct is not shown to be intentional, but the effect is substantially the same as if it were.

municipality to establish a valid basis for its action or non-action. The substantive aspect of "presumptive" relates to the specifics, on the one hand, of what municipal land use regulation provisions, or the absence thereof, will evidence invalidity and shift the burden of proof and, on the other hand, of what bases and considerations will carry the municipality's burden and sustain what it has done or failed to do. Both kinds of specifics may we vary between municipalities, according to peculiar circumstances.

The conclusion is irresistible that Mount Laurel permits only such middle and upper income housing as it believes will have sufficient taxable value to come close to paying its own governmental way.

Akin to large lot, single-family zoning restricting the population is the zoning of very large amounts of land for industrial and related uses. Mount Laurel has set aside almost 30% of its are, over 4,100 acres, for that purpose; the only residential use allowed is for farm dwellings. In almost a decade only about 100 acres have been developed industrially. [A]s intimated earlier, it seems plain that the likelihood of anywhere near the whole of the zoned area being used for the intended purpose in the foreseeable future is remote indeed and that an unreasonable amount of land has thereby been removed from possible residential development, again seemingly for local fiscal reasons.
* * *Mount Laurel's zoning ordinance is presumptively contrary to the general welfare and outside the intended scope of the zoning power in the particulars mentioned. A facial showing of invalidity is thus established, shifting to the municipality the burden of establishing valid superseding reasons for its action and non-action. We now examine the reasons it advances.

The township's principal reasons in support of its zoning plan and ordinance housing provisions * * * is the fiscal one previously adverted to, *i.e.,* that by reason of New Jersey's tax structure which substantially finances municipal governmental and educational costs from taxes on local real property, every municipality may, by the exercise of the zoning power, allow only such uses and to such extent as will be beneficial to the local tax rate. In other words, the position is that any municipality may zone extensively to seek and encourage the "good" tax ratables of industry and commerce and limit the permissible types of housing to those having the fewest school children or to those providing sufficient value to attain or approach paying their own way taxwise.

We have previously held that a developing municipality may properly zone for and seek industrial ratables to create a better economic balance for he community *vis-à-vis* educational and governmental costs engendered by residential development, provided that such was "* * * done reasonably as part of and in furtherance of a legitimate comprehensive plan for the zoning of the entire municipality." Gruber v. Mayor and Township Committee of Raritan Township, 39 N.J. 1, 9-11, 186 A.2d 489, 493 (1962). We adhere to that view today. But we were not there concerned with, and did not pass upon, the validity of municipal exclusion by zoning of types of housing and kinds of people for the same local financial end. We have no hesitancy in now saying, and do so emphatically, that, considering the basic importance of the opportunity for appropriate housing for all classes of our citizenry, no municipality may exclude or limit categories of housing for that reason or purpose. While we fully recognize the increasingly heavy burden of local taxes for municipal governmental and school costs on homeowners, relief from the consequences of this tax system will have to be furnished by other branches of government. It cannot legitimately be accomplished by restricting types of housing through the zoning process in developing municipalities.

The propriety of zoning ordinance limitations on housing for ecological or environmental reasons seems also to be suggested by Mount Laurel in support of the one-half acre minimum lot size in that very considerable portion of the township still available for residential development. It is said that the area is without sewer or water utilities and that the soil is such that this plot size is required for safe individual low sewage disposal and water supply. The short answer is that, this being flat land and readily amenable to such utility installations, the township could require them as improvements by developers or install them under the special assessment or other appropriate statutory procedure. The present environmental situation of the area is, therefore, no sufficient excuse in itself for limiting housing therein to single-family dwellings on large lots.

By way of summary, what we have said comes down to this. As a developing municipality, Mount Laurel must, by its land use regulations, make realistically possible the opportunity for an appropriate variety and choice of housing for all categories of people who may desire to live there, of course including those of low and moderate income. It must permit multi-family housing, without bedroom or similar restriction, as well as small dwellings on very small lots, low cost housing of other types and, in general, high density zoning, without artificial and unjustifiable minimum requirements as to lot size, building size and the like, to meet the full panoply of these needs. Certainly when a municipality zones for industry and commerce for local tax benefit purposes, it without question must zone to permit adequate housing within the means of the employees involved in such uses. (If planned unit developments are authorized, one would assume that each must include a reasonable amount of low and moderate income housing in its residential "mix," unless opportunity for such housing has already been realistically provided for elsewhere in the municipality.) The amount of land removed from residential use by allocation to industrial and commercial purposes must be reasonably related to the present and future potential for such purposes. In other words, such municipalities must zone primarily for the living welfare of people and for the benefit of the local tax rate.[20]

---

[20] This case does not properly present the question of whether a developing municipality may time its growth and, if so, how. See e.g. Golden v. Planning Board of Town of Ramapo, Construction Industry Association of Sonoma County v. City of Petaluma (citation of these cases is not intended to indicate either agreement or disagreement with their conclusions). We now say only that, assuming some type of timed growth is permissible, it cannot be utilized as an exclusionary device or to stop all further development and must include early provision for low and moderate income housing.

We have earlier stated that a developing municipality's obligation to afford the opportunity for decent and adequate low and moderate income housing extends at least to "* * * the municipality's fair share of the present and prospective regional need therefor." Some comment on that conclusion is in order at this point. Frequently it might be sounder to have more of such housing, like some specialized land uses, in one municipality in a region than in another, because of greater availability of suitable land, location of employment, accessibility of public transportation or some other significant reason. But, under present New Jersey legislation, zoning must be on an individual municipal basis, rather than regionally.[22] So long as that situation persists under the present tax structure, or in the absence of some kind of binding agreement among all the municipalities of a region, we feel that every municipality therein must bear its fair share of the regional burden.* * *

The composition of the applicable "region" will necessarily vary from situation to situation and probably no hard and fast rule will serve to furnish the answer in every case.* * * Here we have already defined the region at present as "those portions of Camden, Burlington and Gloucester Counties within a semicircle having a radius of 20 miles or so from the heart of Camden City."

[We declare the zoning ordinances void] to the extent and in the particulars set forth in this opinion.* * *

[Pashman, J., concurring, favored ordering affirmative action on the part of the township.]

Notes

Does the decision turn on the municipality's intent to exclude low- and moderate-income residents? See fn. 10, *supra*. Suppose the township hadn't conceded that it discriminated on the basis of wealth? Same result?

Does Mt. Laurel's zoning amount to affirmative action for the wealthy? Anatole France remarked that the law in its majesty forbids the rich and the poor equally from sleeping under bridges.

The court held "peculiar circumstances" might warrant an ordinance such as Mt. Laurel's. What sort of circumstances would be necessary?

Does *Mt. Laurel* conflict with *Golden* or *Petaluma*? With *Belle Terre*?

The New Jersey Supreme Court retained jurisdiction after directing Mt. Laurel to amend its ordinance. The township failed to revise it in any meaningful

---

[22] This court long ago pointed out "* * * the unreality in dealing with zoning problems on the basis of the territorial limits of a municipality." Duffcon Concrete Products, Inc. v. Borough of Cresskill (1 N.J. at 513, 64 A.2d at 350). It is now clear that the Legislature accepts the fact that at least land use planning, to be of any value, must be done on a much broader basis than each municipality separately.* * * Authorization for regional zoning--the implementation of planning--or at least regulation of land uses having a substantial external impact by some agency beyond the local municipality, would seem to be logical and desirable as the next legislative step.

way, and almost no moderate-income people have succeeded in moving into Mt. Laurel since the decision. A second round of litigation commenced before the Supreme Court in 1980. This time ten towns were parties, as well as developers, civil rights groups and the state's public advocate. In 1983 the Supreme Court ruled, in *Southern Burlington Co. NAACP v. Township of Mt. Laurel*, 92 N.J. 158, 456 A.2d, 390 that the State Constitution requires all municipalities to take affirmative steps to provide housing opportunities for low and moderate-income people. The court urged tax incentives and assistance in applying for federal subsidies, as well as zoning to encourage low and moderate-income homes, holding:

> (1) *Every* municipality's land use regulations should provide a realistic opportunity for decent housing for at least some part of its resident poor who now occupy dilapidated housing. The zoning power is no more abused by keeping out the region's poor than by forcing out the resident poor. In other words, each municipality must provide a realistic opportunity for decent housing for its indigenous poor except where they represent a disproportionately large segment of the population as compared with the rest of the region. This is the case in many of our urban areas.
>
> (2) The existence of a municipal obligation to provide a realistic opportunity for a fair share of the region's present and prospective low and moderate income housing needs will no longer be determined by whether or not a municipality is "developing." The obligation extends, instead, to every municipality, any portion of which is designated by the State, through [a State Development Guide Plan, or SDGP, prepared pursuant to statute by the State's Department of Community Affairs,] as a "growth area." This obligation, imposed as a remedial measure, does not extend to those areas where the SDGP discourages growth--namely, open spaces, rural areas, prime farmland, conservation areas, limited growth areas, parts of the Pinelands and certain Coastal Zone areas. The SDGP represents the conscious determination of the State, through the executive and legislative branches, on how best to plan its future. It appropriately serves as a judicial remedial tool. The obligation to encourage lower income housing, therefore, will hereafter depend on rational long-range land use planning (incorporated into the SDGP) rather than upon the sheer economic forces that have dictated whether a municipality is "developing." Moreover, the fact that a municipality is fully developed does not eliminate this obligation although, obviously, it may affect the extent of the obligation and the timing of its satisfaction. The remedial obligation of municipalities that consist of both "growth areas" and other areas may be reduced,

based on many factors, as compared to a municipality completely within a "growth area."

There shall be a heavy burden on any party seeking to vary the foregoing remedial consequences of the SDGP designation.

(3) *Mount Laurel* litigation will ordinarily include proof of the municipality's fair share of low and moderate income housing in terms of the number of units needed immediately, as well as the number needed for a reasonable period of time in the future.

[T]he doctrine does not arise from some theoretical analysis of our Constitution, but rather from underlying concepts of fundamental fairness in the exercise of governmental power. The basis for the constitutional obligation is simple: the State controls the use of land, *all* of the land. In exercising that control it cannot favor rich over poor. It cannot legislatively set aside dilapidated housing in urban ghettos for the poor and decent housing elsewhere for everyone else. The government that controls this land represents everyone. While the State may not have the ability to eliminate poverty, it cannot use that condition as the basis for imposing further disadvantages. And the same applies to the municipality, to which this control over land has been constitutionally delegated.

The clarity of the constitutional obligation is seen most simply by imagining what this state could be like were this claim never to be recognized and enforced; poor people forever zoned out of substantial areas of the state, not because housing could not be built for them but because they are not wanted; poor people forced to live in urban slums forever not because suburbia, developing rural areas, fully developed residential sections, seashore resorts, and other attractive locations could not accommodate them, but simply became they are not wanted. It is a vision only at variance with the requirements that the zoning power be used for the general welfare but with all concepts of fundamental fairness and decency.* * *

The lessons of history are clear, even if rarely learned. One of those lessons is that unplanned growth has a price: natural resources are destroyed, open spaces are despoiled, agricultural land is rendered forever unproductive, and people settle without regard to the enormous cost of the public facilities needed to support them. Cities decay; established infrastructures deteriorate for lack of funds; and taxpayers shudder under a financial burden of public expenditures resulting in part from uncontrolled migration to anywhere anyone wants to settle, roads leading to places they should never be--a pattern of total neglect of sensible conservation of resources, funds, prior public investment, and just plain common sense. These costs in New Jersey, the most highly urbanized state in the nation, are staggering, and our knowledge of our limited ability to support them has become acute. More than money is involved, for natural and man-made physical resources are irreversibly damaged. Statewide comprehensive planning is no longer simply desirable, it is a necessity recognized by both the federal and state governments.* * *

There may be municipalities where special conditions such as extremely high land costs make it impossible for the fair share obligation to be met even after all excessive restrictions and exactions, *i.e.*, those not essential for safety and health, have been removed and all affirmative measures have been attempted. In such cases, *and only in such cases*, the *Mount Laurel* obligation can be met by supplementing whatever lower income housing can be built with enough "least cost" housing to satisfy the fair share. Least cost housing does not, however, mean the most inexpensive housing that developers will build on their own; it does not mean $50,000-plus single family homes and very expensive apartments. Least cost housing means the least expensive housing that builders can provide after removal by a municipality of *all* excessive restrictions and exactions and after thorough use by a municipality of all affirmative devices that might lower costs. Presumably, such housing, though unaffordable by those in the lower income brackets, will be inexpensive enough to provide shelter for families who could not afford housing in the conventional suburban housing market. At the very minimum, provision of least cost housing will make certain that municipalities in "growth" areas of this state do not "grow" only for the well-to-do.

The Development Guide Plan has run into heavy weather. Despite the court's direction, it listed low-density towns as limited-growth areas, essentially exempt from the court's mandate. Critics have charged the Plan with rewarding these areas, in effect, for fencing out low income people in the first place. Opposing the Plan from the opposite direction, other cities have challenged the court decision as judicial legislation, and the Plan as an attempt at statewide zoning. See *N.Y. Times,* Apr. 17, 1983.

The Plan was upheld in *Hills Development Co. v. Township of Bernards,* 103 N.J. 1, 510 A.2d 621 (1986). The court transferred all pending cases on affordable housing to the state's Council on Affordable Housing. Since the decision in *Mt. Laurel II, supra*, thousands of units of moderate-income housing have been built in New Jersey, mostly for senior citizens. Suburban localities may also buy out their obligations to create affordable housing under the New Jersey legislation by paying to build such housing in cities such as Newark and Camden. Not surprisingly, many have played that card.

The New York courts have been reluctant to embrace the *Mt. Laurel* decisions. In *Suffolk Housing Services v. Town of Brookhaven*, 109 A.D.2d 323, 491 N.Y.S.2d 396 (2d Dept. 1985), aff'd 70 N.Y.2d 122, 511 N.E.2d 67, 517 N.Y.S.2d 924, the Appellate Division rejected *Mt. Laurel* and ruled a large Long Island town had no affirmative duty to build low or moderate-income housing. Affirming, the Court of Appeals left open the applicability of *Mt. Laurel* and simply held the town had in fact built some subsidized housing, so the plaintiffs had not proven any intent to exclude lower income families.

Some states have dealt with this issue by statute. Connecticut and Massachusetts laws provide that if a developer dedicates 20% or more of the tract (30% in Connecticut) to affordable housing (based on the area's median income), the locality may zone out the development only for health or safety reasons--not esthetics or community ambiance. Localities with 10% or more of their housing already affordable (or subsidized) are not so restricted. See Conn. Stat. §§ 8-2g - 8-30; Mass. Gen. Laws Ann. ch. 1218, § 28 and ch. 40A, § 9.

In *Village of Arlington Heights v. Metropolitan Housing Development Corp.,* described in Chapter 1, the plaintiffs claimed the village's refusal to rezone a tract for low-income housing was racially discriminatory under both the Equal Protection Clause and the Fair Housing Act, 42 USCA §§ 3601-3631. The Supreme Court (429 U.S. 252, 97 S.Ct. 555, 50 L.Ed.2d 450 [1977]) held racial discrimination is barred by the Equal Protection Clause only if a racially discriminatory intent or purpose is proven, as evidenced by statements by the village legislators or other such proof, and that plaintiffs had failed to prove such intent or purpose. It remanded the case so the Court of Appeals might consider the Fair Housing Act claim.

On remand, the Seventh Circuit found the village had contravened the Act, under which a racially discriminatory effect suffices. 558 F.2d 1283 (1977).

In New York, *Berenson v. Town of New Castle*, 38 N.Y.2d 102, 341 N.E.2d 236, 378 N.Y.S.2d 672 (1975), overturned an ordinance excluding all multi-family housing in a large suburban town just north of White Plains. It directed the town to consider the housing needs of the region, and remanded the case for the lower courts to assess the reasonableness of the ordinance in that light. On remand, the trial court invalidated the ordinance and directed the town to permit 3,500 apartments by 1987. The Appellate Division, 67 A.D.2d 506, 415 N.Y.S.2d 669 (1979), affirmed the annulling of the ordinance but not the affirmative action requirement. It gave the town six months to devise a new plan to accommodate regional needs. *But see Valley View Village v. Proffett*, 221 F.2d 412 (6th Cir. 1955)(village in sparsely settled area had power to exclude apartments completely).

## Comprehensive Planning

Several states have enacted laws subjecting large-scale development--residential, commercial or industrial--to approval by a state agency, in addition to local land-use controls. This is designed to avoid, or reduce, one locality imposing environmental and economic costs on another while gaining the tax benefits of, say, a shopping mall or industrial park. These statutes also provide for land-use planning at the state level.

Vermont and Maine take this approach. See Vt. Stat. Ann. Title 10, §§ 6001 - 6018; Me. Rev. Stat. Ann. Title 30-A, §§ 4301-4454. Hawaii has state, not local, zoning for all purposes. See Haw. Rev. Stat. Ann. §§ 205-1 to 205-18. Florida follows the Vermont two-tiered technique but exempts localities with state-approved land-use plans. Fla. Stat. §§ 163.3161-163.3215.

May a state deny permission to build a mega-store on the outskirts of a town because its likely impact on existing main street shopping, perhaps resulting in store closings and loss of taxes and services. See In re *Pyramid Co.*, 141 Vt. 294, 449 A.2d 915 (1997) (upholding denial of permit). What do these states have in common that enabled them to take these measures?

Some other states have adopted similar legislation for parts of the state regarded as environmentally critical. New York so protects the Adirondacks and the Long Island Pine Barrens, Maryland and Virginia the area surrounding Chesapeake Bay.

## Purchasing Development Rights and Conservation Easements

Another technique is for a local government to prevent development of property by purchasing the development rights of a farm, forest or wetland. Since land is usually taxed at its "highest and best use," eliminating the ability to build on a parcel will substantially reduce its taxes, thus greatly curbing the owner's incentive to sell to a developer. Some states tax agricultural land in lower amounts by placing it in agricultural districts with lower taxes as long as the land is farmed.

A similar technique is the conservation easement, a device through which an owner may convey the right to develop to a not-for-profit land trust in perpetuity. This both reduces real property taxes and provides income tax deductions (like a gift to a museum or school), as well as keeping the parcel in its natural state.

What incentives are there for local governments to purchase development rights, thereby diminishing their property tax base? What reasons might motivate a landowner to place a parcel under a conservation easement, or to convey its development rights?

A related approach is for states and localities to protect critical areas such as wetlands and shoreline, to which we now turn.

## C. CRITICAL AREAS: LANDMARKS, WETLANDS, COASTLINE, FLOOD PLAINS AND TAKINGS

PENN CENTRAL TRANSPORTATION CO. v. CITY OF NEW YORK, Supreme Court of the United States, 1978. 438 U.S. 104, 98 S. Ct. 2646, 57 L.Ed.2d 631.

Mr. Justice Brennan delivered the opinion of the Court.

The question presented is whether a city may, as part of a comprehensive program to preserve historic landmarks and historic districts, place restrictions on the development of individual historic landmarks--in addition to those imposed by applicable zoning ordinances--without effecting a "taking" requiring the payment of "just compensation." Specifically, we must decide whether the application of New York City's Landmarks Preservation Law to the parcel of land occupied by Grand Central Terminal has "taken" its owners' property in violation of the Fifth and Fourteenth Amendments.

Over the past 50 years, all 50 states and over 500 municipalities have enacted laws to encourage or require the preservation of buildings and areas with historic or esthetic importance. These nationwide legislative efforts have been precipitated by two concerns. The first is recognition that, in recent years, large numbers of historic structures, landmarks, and areas have been destroyed without adequate consideration of either the values represented therein or the possibility of preserving the destroyed properties for use in economically productive ways. The second is a widely shared belief that structures with special historic, cultural, or architectural significance enhance the quality of life for all. Not only do these buildings and their workmanship represent the lessons of the past and embody precious features of our heritage, they serve as examples of quality for today. "[H]istoric conservation is but one aspect of the much larger problem, basically an environmental one, of enhancing--or perhaps developing for the first time--the quality of life for people."

New York City, responding to similar concerns and acting pursuant to a New York State enabling Act, adopted its Landmarks Preservation Law in 1965. The city acted from the conviction that "the standing of [New York City] as a world-wide tourist center and world capital of business, culture and government" would be threatened if legislation were not enacted to protect historic landmarks and neighborhoods from precipitate decisions to destroy or fundamentally alter their character. The city believed that comprehensive measures to safeguard desirable features of the existing urban fabric would benefit its citizens in a variety of ways: *e.g.*, fostering "civic pride in the beauty and noble accomplishments of the past," protecting and enhancing "the city's attractions to tourists and visitors;" "support[ing] and stimul[ating] business and industry;" "strengthen[ing] the economy of the city;" and promoting "the use of historic districts, landmarks, interior landmarks and scenic landmarks for the education, pleasure and welfare of the people of the city."

The New York City law is typical of many urban landmark laws in that its primary method of achieving its goals is not by acquisitions of historic properties, but rather by involving public entities in land-use decisions affecting these properties and providing services, standards, controls, and incentives that will encourage preservation by private owners and users. While the law does place special restrictions on landmark properties as a necessary feature to the attainment of its larger objectives, the major theme of the law is to ensure the owners of any such properties both a "reasonable return" on their investments and maximum latitude to use their parcels for purposes not inconsistent with the preservation goals.

The operation of the law can be briefly summarized. The primary responsibility for administering the law is vested in the Landmarks Preservation Commission (Commission), a broad-based, 11-member agency[8] assisted by a technical staff. The Commission first performs the function, critical to any landmark preservation effort, of identifying properties and areas that have "a special character or special historical or esthetic interest or value as part of the development, heritage or cultural characteristics of the city, state or nation." If the Commission determines, after giving all interested parties an opportunity to be heard, that a building or area satisfies the ordinance's criteria, it will designate a building to be a "landmark," situated on a particular "landmark site," or will designate an area to be a "historic district." After the Commission makes a designation, New York City's Board of Estimate, after considering the relationship of the designated property "to the master plan, the zoning resolution, projected public improvements and any plans for the renewal of the area involved," may modify or disapprove the designation, and the owner may seek judicial review of the final designation decision. Thus far, 31 historic districts and over 400 individual landmarks have been finally designated, and the process is a continuing one.

Final designation as a landmark results in restrictions upon the property owner's options concerning use of the landmark site. First, the law imposes a duty upon the owner to keep the exterior features of the building "in good repair" to assure that the law's objectives not be defeated by the landmark's falling into a state of irremediable disrepair. Second, the Commission must approve in advance any proposal to alter the exterior architectural features of the landmark or to construct any exterior improvement on the landmark site, thus ensuring that decisions concerning construction on the landmark site are made with due consideration of both the public interest in the maintenance of the structure and the landowner's interest in use of the property.

In the event an owner wishes to alter a landmark site, three separate procedures are available through which administrative approval may be obtained. First, the owner may apply to the Commission for a "certificate of no effect on protected architectural features": that is, for an order approving the improvement or alteration on the ground that it will not change or affect any architectural feature of

---

[8] The ordinance creating the Commission requires that it include at least three architects, one historian qualified in the field, one city planner or landscape architect, one realtor, and at least one resident of each of the city's five boroughs.* * *

the landmark and will be in harmony therewith. Denial of the certificate is subject to judicial review.

Second, the owner may apply to the Commission for a certificate of "appropriateness." Such certificates will be granted if the Commission concludes--focusing upon esthetic, historical, and architectural values--that the proposed construction on the landmark site would not unduly hinder the protection, enhancement, perpetuation, and use of the landmark. Again, denial of the certificate is subject to judicial review. Moreover, the owner who is denied either a certificate of no exterior effect or a certificate of appropriateness may submit an alternative or modified plan for approval. The final procedure--seeking a certificate of appropriateness on the ground of "insufficient return," provides special mechanisms, which vary depending on whether or not the landmark enjoys a tax exemption,[13] to ensure that designation does not cause economic hardship.

Although the designation of a landmark and landmark site restricts the owner's control over the parcel, designation also enhances the economic position of the landmark owner in one significant respect. Under New York City's zoning laws, owners of real property who have not developed their property to the full extent permitted by the applicable zoning laws are allowed to transfer development rights to contiguous parcels on the same city block. A 1968 ordinance gave the owners of landmark sites additional opportunities to transfer development rights to

---

[13] If the owner of a non-tax-exempt parcel has been denied certificates of appropriateness for a proposed alteration and shows that he is not earning a reasonable return on the property in its present state, the Commission and other city agencies must assume the burden of developing a plan that will enable the landmark owner to earn a reasonable return on the landmark site. The plan may include, but need not be limited to, partial or complete tax exemption, remission of taxes, and authorizations for alterations, construction, or reconstruction appropriate for and not inconsistent with the purposes of the law. The owner is free to accept or reject a plan devised by the Commission and approved by the other city agencies. If he accepts the plan, he proceeds to operate the property pursuant to the plan. If he rejects the plan, the Commission may recommend that the city proceed by eminent domain to acquire a protective interest in the landmark, but if the city does not do so within a specified time period, the Commission must issue a notice allowing the property owner to proceed with the alteration or improvement as originally proposed in his application for a certificate of appropriateness.

Tax-exempt structures are treated somewhat differently. They become eligible for special treatment only if four pre-conditions are satisfied: (1) the owner previously entered into an agreement to sell the parcel that was contingent upon the issuance of a certificate of approval; (2) the property, as it exists at the time of the request, is not capable of earning a reasonable return; (3) the structure is no longer suitable to its past or present purposes; and (4) the prospective buyer intends to alter the landmark structure. In the event the owner demonstrates that the property in its present state is not earning a reasonable return, the Commission must either find another buyer for it or allow the sale and construction to proceed.

But this is not the only remedy available for owners of tax-exempt landmarks. As the case at bar illustrates, if an owner files suit and establishes that he is incapable of earning a "reasonable return" on the site in its present state, he can be afforded judicial relief. Similarly, where a landmark owner who enjoys a tax exemption has demonstrated that the landmark structure, as restricted, is totally inadequate for the owner's "legitimate needs," the law has been held invalid as applied to that parcel. See *Lutheran Church v. City of New York*, 35 N.Y.2d 121, 359 N.Y.S.2d 7, 316 N.E.2d 305 (1974).

other parcels. Subject to a restriction that the floor area of the transferee lot may not be increased by more than 20% above its authorized level, the ordinance permitted transfers from a landmark parcel to property across the street or across a street intersection. In 1969, the law governing the conditions under which transfers from landmark parcels could occur was liberalized. The class of recipient lots was expanded to include lots "across a street and opposite to another lot or lots which, except for the intervention of streets or street intersections, f[or]m a series extending to the lot occupied by the landmark building[, provided that] all lots [are] in the same ownership." In addition, the 1969 amendment permits, in highly commercialized areas like midtown Manhattan, the transfer of all unused development rights to a single parcel.

This case involves the application of New York City's Landmarks Preservation Law to Grand Central Terminal. The Terminal, which is owned by the Penn Central Transportation Co. and its affiliates, is one of New York City's most famous buildings. Opened in 1913, it is regarded not only as providing an ingenious engineering solution to the problems presented by urban railroad stations, but also as a magnificent example of the French beaux-arts style.

The Terminal is located in midtown Manhattan. Its south facade faces 42nd Street and that street's intersection with Park Avenue. The Terminal is one of a number of properties owned by appellant Penn Central in this area of midtown Manhattan.* * * At least eight of these are eligible to be recipients of development rights afforded the Terminal by virtue of landmark designation.

[F]ollowing a public hearing, the Commission designated the Terminal a "landmark" and designated the "city tax block" it occupies a "landmark site."[16] The Board of Estimate confirmed this action * * *. Although appellant Penn Central had opposed the designation before the Commission, it did not seek judicial review of the final designation decision.

[Thereafter] appellant Penn Central, to increase its income, entered into a renewable 50-year lease and sublease agreement with appellant UGP Properties, Inc. UGP was to construct a [55-]story office building above the Terminal. UGP promised to pay Penn Central $1 million annually during construction and at least $3 million annually thereafter.* * *

Appellants UGP and Penn Central then applied to the Commission for permission to construct an office building atop the Terminal. After four days of hearings at which over 80 witnesses testified, the Commission denied this application[,] stating that it found the majestic approach from the south to be still unique in the city and that a 55-story tower atop the Terminal would be * * * detrimental to its south facade * * *. The Commission stated:

---

[16] The Commission's report stated: "Grand Central Station, one of the great buildings of America, evokes a spirit that is unique in this City. It combines distinguished architecture with a brilliant engineering solution, wedded to one of the most fabulous railroad terminals of our time. Monumental in scale, this great building functions as well today as it did when built. In style, it represents the best of the French Beaux Arts."

> [We have] no fixed rule against making additions to designated buildings--it all depends on how they are done. . . But to balance a 55-story office tower above a flamboyant Beaux-Arts facade seems nothing more than an esthetic joke. Quite simply, the tower would overwhelm the Terminal by its sheer mass. The 'addition' would be four times as high as the existing structure and would reduce the Landmark itself to the status of a curiosity.
>
> Landmarks cannot be divorced from their settings--particularly when the setting is a dramatic and integral part of the original concept. The Terminal, in its setting, is a great example of urban design. Such examples are not so plentiful in New York City that we can afford to lose any of the few we have. And we must preserve them in a meaningful way--with alterations and additions of such character, scale, materials and mass as will protect, enhance and perpetuate the original design rather than overwhelm it.

Appellants did not seek judicial review of the denial of either certificate. Because the Terminal site enjoyed a tax exemption, remained suitable for its present and future uses, and was not the subject of a contract of sale, there were no further administrative remedies available to appellants[. Nor did they] avail themselves of the opportunity to develop and submit other plans for the Commission's consideration and approval. Instead, appellants filed suit * * * claiming, *inter alia*, that the application of the Landmarks Preservation Law had "taken" their property without just compensation in violation of the Fifth and Fourteenth Amendments and arbitrarily deprived them of their property without due process of law in violation of the Fourteenth Amendment. Appellants sought a declaratory judgment, injunctive relief barring the city from using the Landmarks Law to impede the construction of any structure that might otherwise lawfully be constructed on the Terminal site, and damages for the "temporary taking" that occurred between August 2, 1967, the designation date, and the date when the restrictions arising from the Landmarks Law would be lifted. The trial court granted the injunctive and declaratory relief, but severed the question of damages for a "temporary taking."

[The] Appellate Division reversed. [It] held that the restrictions on the development of the Terminal site were necessary to promote the legitimate public purpose of protecting landmarks and therefore that appellants could sustain their constitutional claims only by proof that the regulation deprived them of all reasonable beneficial use of the property. The Appellate Division held that the evidence appellants introduced at trial--"Statements of Revenues and Costs, "purporting to show a net operating loss for the years 1969 and 1971, which were prepared for the instant litigation--had not satisfied their burden. First, the court rejected the claim that these statements showed that the Terminal was operating at a loss, for in the court's view, appellants had improperly attributed some railroad operating expenses and taxes to their real estate operations and compounded that error by failing to impute any rental value to the vast space in the Terminal devoted to railroad purposes. Further, the Appellate Division concluded that appellants had failed to establish either that they were unable to increase the Terminal's commercial income by transforming vacant or under-utilized space to revenue-producing use, or that the unused development rights over the Terminal could not have been profitably transferred to one or more nearby sites. The Appellate Division concluded that all appellants had succeeded in showing was that they had been deprived of the property's most profitable use, and that this showing did not establish that appellants had been unconstitutionally deprived of their work.

The New York Court of Appeals affirmed.* * *

The issues presented by appellants are (1) whether the restrictions imposed by New York City's law upon appellants' exploitation of the Terminal for a public use within the meaning of the Fifth amendment, which of course is made applicable to the States through the Fourteenth Amendment, and (2), if so, whether the transferable development rights afforded appellants constitute "just compensation" within the meaning of the Fifth Amendment. We need only address the question whether a "taking" has occurred.

* * *The question of what constitutes a "taking" for purposes of the Fifth Amendment has proved to be a problem of considerable difficulty. While this Court has recognized that the "Fifth Amendment's guarantee [is] designed to bar Government from forcing some people alone to bear public burdens which, in all fairness and justice, should be borne by the public as a whole," *Armstrong v. United States*, 364 U.S. 40, 49, 80 S. Ct. 1563, 1569, 4 L.Ed.2d 1554 (1960), this Court, quite simply, has been unable to develop any "set formula" for determining when "justice and fairness" require that economic injuries caused by public action be compensated by the government, rather than remain disproportionately concentrated on a few persons. See *Goldblatt v. [Town of] Hempstead*, 369 U.S. 590, 594, 82 S. Ct. 987, 990, 8 L.Ed.2d 130 (1962). Indeed, we have frequently observed that whether a particular restriction will be rendered invalid by the government's failure to pay for any losses approximately caused by it depends largely "upon the particular circumstances [in that] case." *United States v. Central Eureka Mining Co.*, 357 U.S. 155, 168, 78 S. Ct. 1097, 1104, 2 L.Ed.2d 1228 (1958)[.]

In engaging in these essentially ad hoc, factual inquiries, the Court's decisions have identified several factors that have particular significance. The economic impact of the regulation on the claimant and, particularly, the extent to which the regulation has interfered with district investment-backed expectation are, of course, relevant considerations. See *Goldblatt v. [Town of] Hempstead, supra*. So, too, is the character of the governmental action. A "taking" may more readily be found when the interferences with property can be characterized as a physical invasion by government, see, *e.g., United States v. Causby,*[a] than when interference arises from some public program adjusting the benefits and burdens of economic life to promote the common good.

---

[a] *Causby*, discussed in Chapter 6, found noise from military aircraft flying over the plaintiff's farm at low altitudes amounted to a *de facto* taking of the property.

"Government hardly could go on if to some extent values incident to property could not be diminished without paying for every such change in the general law," *Pennsylvania Coal Co. v. Mahon,* 260 U.S. 393, 143 S. Ct. 158, 159, 67 L.Ed. 322 (1922), and this Court has accordingly recognized, in a wide variety of contexts, that government may execute laws or programs that adversely affect recognized economic values.

Zoning laws generally do not affect existing uses of real property [see *Euclid*], but "taking" challenges have also been held to be without merit in a wide variety of situations when the challenged governmental actions prohibited a beneficial use to which individual parcels had previously been devoted and thus caused substantial individual harm.* * * *Hadacheck v. Sebastian,* 239 U.S. 394, 36 S. Ct. 143, 60 L.Ed. 348 (1915), upheld a law prohibiting the claimant from continuing his otherwise lawful business of operating a brickyard in a particular physical community on the ground that the legislature had reasonably concluded that the presence of the brickyard was inconsistent with neighboring uses.

*Goldblatt v. [Town of] Hempstead, supra*, is a recent example. There a 1958 city safety ordinance banned any excavations below the water table and effectively prohibited the claimant from continuing a sand and gravel mining business that had been operated on the particular parcel since 1927. The Court upheld the ordinance against a "taking" challenge, although the ordinance prohibited the present and presumably most beneficial use of the property and had, like the regulations, * * * severely affected a particular owner. The Court assumed that the ordinance did not prevent the owner's reasonable use of the property since the owner made no showing of an adverse effect on the value of the land. Because the restriction served a substantial public purpose, the Court thus held no taking had occurred.

*Pennsylvania Coal Co. v. Mahon,* [*supra*], is the leading case for the proposition that a state statute that substantially furthers important public policies may so frustrate distinct investment-backed expectation as to amount to a "taking." There the claimant had sold the surface right to particular parcels of property, but expressly reserved the right to remove the coal thereunder. A Pennsylvania statute, enacted after the transactions, forbade any mining of coal that caused the subsidence of any house, unless the house was the property of the owner of the underlying coal and was more than 150 feet from the improved property of another. Because the statute made it commercially impracticable to mine the coal, and thus had nearly the same effect as the complete destruction of rights claimant had reserved from the owners of the surface land, the Court held that the statute was invalid as effecting a "taking" without just compensation.* * *

In contending that the New York City law has "taken" their property in violation of the Fifth and Fourteenth Amendments, appellants* * * urge that any substantial restriction imposed pursuant to a landmark law must be accompanied by just compensation if it is to be constitutional. Before considering these, we emphasize what is not in dispute. Because this Court has recognized, in a number of settings, that States and cities may enact land-use restrictions or controls to enhance the quality of life by preserving the character and desirable esthetic features of a city, appellants do not contest that New York City's objective of preserving structures and areas with special historic, architectural, or cultural significance is an entirely permissible governmental goal. They also do not dispute that the restrictions imposed on its parcel are appropriate means of securing the purposes of the New York City law. Finally, appellants do not challenge any of the specific factual premises of the decision below. The accept for present purposes both that the parcel of land occupied by Grand Central Terminal must, in its present state, be regarded as capable of earning a reasonable return, and that transferable development rights afforded appellants by virtue of the Terminal's determination as a landmark are valuable, even if not as valuable as the rights to construct above the Terminal. In appellants' view none of these factors derogate from their claim that New York City's law has effected a "taking."

They first observe that the airspace above the Terminal is a valuable property interest, citing *United States v. Causby, supra.* They urge that the Landmarks Law has deprived them of any gainful use of their "air rights" above the Terminal and that, irrespective of the value of the remainder of their parcel, the city has "taken" their right to this superadjacent airspace, thus entitling them to "just compensation" measured by the fair market value of these air rights.

[T]he submission that appellants may establish a "taking" simply by showing that they have been denied the ability to exploit a property interest that they heretofore had believed was available for development is quite simply untenable. Were this the rule, this Court would have erred not only in upholding laws restricting the development of air rights, but also in approving those prohibiting both the subjacent and lateral development of particular parcels. "Taking" jurisprudence does not divide a single parcel into discrete segments and attempt to determine whether rights in a particular segment have been entirely abrogated. In deciding whether a particular governmental action has effected a taking, this Court focuses rather both on the character of the action and on the nature and extent of the interference with rights in the parcel as a whole--here, the city tax block designated as the "landmark site."

Secondly, appellants, focusing on the character and impact of the New York City law, argue that it effects a "taking" because its operation has significantly diminished the value of the Terminal site. Appellants concede that the decisions sustaining other land-use regulations, which like the New York City law, are reasonably related to the promotion of the general welfare, uniformly reject the proposition that a diminution in property value, standing alone, can establish a "taking, " see *Euclid v. Ambler Realty Co.,* (75% diminution in value caused by zoning law); *Hadacheck v. Sebastian,* (87½% diminution in value)[.] Appellants, moreover, also do not dispute that a showing a diminution in property value would not establish a taking if the restriction had been imposed as a result of historic-district legislation, see generally *Maher v. New Orleans* 516 F.2d 1051 (CA5 1975), but appellants argue that New York City's regulation of individual landmarks is fundamentally different from zoning or from historic-district legislation because the controls imposed by New York City's law apply only to individuals who own selected properties.

Stated baldly, appellants' position appears to be that the only means of ensuring that selected owners are not singled out to endure financial hardship for no reason is to hold that any restrictions imposed on individual landmarks pursuant to the New York City scheme is a "taking" requiring the payment of "just compensation." Agreement with this argument would, of course, invalidate not just New York City's law, but all comparable landmark legislation in the Nation. We find no merit in it.

It is true, as appellants emphasize, that both historic-district legislation and zoning laws regulate all properties within given physical communities whereas landmark laws apply only to selected parcels. But, contrary to appellants' suggestions, landmark laws are not like discriminatory, or "reverse spot," zoning: that is, a land-use decision which arbitrarily singles out a particular parcel for different, less favorable treatment than the neighboring ones. In contrast to discriminatory zoning, which is the antithesis of land-use control as part of some comprehensive plan, the New York City law embodies a comprehensive plan to preserve structures of historic or esthetic interest wherever they might be found in the city, and as noted, over 400 landmarks and 31 historic districts have been designated pursuant to this plan.

Equally without merit is the related argument that the decision to designate a structure as a landmark "is inevitably arbitrary or at least subjective, because it is basically a matter of taste," thus unavoidably singling out individual landowners for disparate and unfair treatment. The argument has a particularly hollow ring in this case. For appellants not only did not seek judicial review of either the designation or of the denials of the certificate of appropriateness and of no exterior effect, but do not even now suggest that the Commission's decisions concerning the Terminal were in any sense arbitrary or unprincipled. But, in any event, a landmark owner has a right to judicial review of any Commission decision, and, quite simply, there is no basis whatsoever for a conclusion that courts will have any greater difficulty identifying arbitrary or discriminatory action in the context of landmark regulation than in the context of classic zoning or indeed in any other context.

Next, appellants observe that New York City's law differs from zoning laws and historic-district ordinances in that the Landmarks Law does not impose identical or similar restrictions on all structures located in particular physical communities. It follows, they argue, that New York City's law is inherently incapable of producing the fair and equitable distribution of benefits and burdens of governmental action which is characteristic of zoning laws and historic-district legislation and which they maintain is a constitutional requirement if "just compensation" is not to be afforded. It is, of course, true that the Landmarks Law has a more severe impact on some landowners than on others, but that in itself does not mean that the law effects a "taking." Legislation designed to promote the general welfare commonly burdens some more than others. The owners of the brickyard in *Hadacheck,* * * * and of the gravel and sand mine in *Goldblatt v. [Town of] Hempstead*, were uniquely burdened by the legislation sustained in those cases. Similarly, zoning laws often affect some property owners more severely than others but have not been held to be invalid on the account. For example, the property owner in *Euclid* who wished to use its property for industrial purposes was affected for more severely by the ordinance than its neighbors who wished to use their land for residences.

In any event, appellants' repeated suggestions that they are solely burdened and unbenefited is factually inaccurate. This contention overlooks the fact that the New York City law applies to vast numbers of structures in the city in addition to the Terminal--all the structures contained in the 31 historic districts and over 400 individual landmarks, many of which are close to the Terminal. Unless we are to reject the judgment of the New York City Council that the preservation of landmarks benefits all New York citizens and all structure, both economically and by improving the quality of life in the city as a whole--which we are unwilling to do--we cannot conclude that the owners of the Terminal have in no sense been benefited by the Landmarks Law. Doubtless appellants believe they are more burdened than benefited by the law, but that must have been true, too, of the property owners in *Hadacheck, Euclid, and Goldblatt.* * * *

Rejection of appellants' broad arguments is not however, the end of our inquiry, for all we thus far have established is that the New York City law is not rendered invalid by its failure to provide "just compensation" whenever a landmark owner is restricted in the exploitation of property interests, such as air rights, to a greater extent than provided for under applicable zoning laws. We now must consider whether the interference with appellants' property is of such a magnitude that "there must be an exercise of eminent domain and compensation to sustain [it]." *Pennsylvania Coal Co. v. Mahon*. That inquiry may be narrowed to the question of the severity of the impact of the law on appellants' parcel, and its resolution in turn requires a careful assessment of the impact of the regulation on the Terminal site.

Unlike the governmental acts in *Goldblatt,* * * *Causby, Griggs,* and *Hadacheck*, the New York City law does not interfere in any way with the present uses of the Terminal. Its designation as a landmark not only permits but contemplates that appellants may continue to use the property precisely as it has been used for the past 65 years: as a railroad terminal containing office space and concessions. So the law does not interfere with what must be regarded as Penn Central's primary expectation concerning the use of the parcel. More importantly, on this record, we must regard the New York City law as permitting Penn Central not only to profit from the Terminal but also to obtain a "reasonable return" on its investments.

Appellants, moreover, exaggerate the effect of the law on their ability to make use of the air rights above the Terminal in two respects. First, it simply cannot be maintained, on this record, that appellants have been prohibited from occupying *any* portion of the airspace above the Terminal. While the Commission's actions in denying applications to construct an office building in excess of 50 stories above the Terminal may indicate that it will refuse to issue a certificate of appropriateness for any comparably sized structure, nothing the Commission has said or done suggests an intention to prohibit *any* construction above the Terminal. The Commission's report emphasized that whether any construction would be allowed depended upon whether the proposed addition "would harmonize in scale, material and character with [the Terminal]." Since appellants have not sought approval for the construction of a smaller structure, we do not know that appellants will be denied any use of any portion of the airspace above the Terminal.

Second, to the extent appellants have been denied the right to build above the Terminal, it is not literally accurate to say that they have been denied *all* use of even those pre-existing air-rights. Their ability to use these rights has not been abrogated; they are made transferable to at least eight parcels in the vicinity of the Terminal, one or two of which have been found suitable for the construction of new office buildings. [T]he New York courts here supportably found that, at least in the case of the Terminal, the rights afforded are valuable. While these rights may well not have constituted "just compensation" if a "taking" had occurred, the rights nevertheless undoubtedly mitigate whatever financial burdens the law has imposed on appellants and, for that reason, are to be taken into account in considering the impact of regulation.

On this record, we conclude that the application of New York City's Landmarks Law has not effected a "taking" of appellants' property. The restrictions imposed are substantially related to the promotion of the general welfare and not only permit reasonable beneficial use of the landmark site but also afford appellants opportunities further to enhance not only the Terminal site proper but also other properties.

Affirmed.

Justice Rehnquist, joined by Chief Justice Burger and Justice Stevens, dissented.

## Notes

Is protecting historic landmarks purely a matter of esthetics? In *Penn Central* the court noted the substantial economic benefits to a city of preserving its architectural heritage. If this is true, isn't it an argument for making the city pay for its benefits?

Are an owner's air rights a separable part of his property interest? In *Causby v. United States*, referred to in *Penn Central* and discussed in Chapter 6, the Supreme Court found aircraft noise constituted a taking, or "inverse condemnation," of the plaintiff's farm. Air rights, and underground mineral rights, may be, and often are, sold separately while the owner retains the property itself. How then could the Supreme Court get around the Penn Central's claim that its air rights were a separable part of its property, for which it was entitled to just compensation?

The Supreme Court did not need to reach the issue whether the city's transferred development rights (TDRs) alone would constitute just compensation, since it found there was no taking. For a closer look at TDRs, let us peruse the *Fred F. French* case, which follows.

FRED F. FRENCH INVESTING CO. v. CITY OF NEW YORK, New York Court of Appeals, 1976. 39 N.Y.2d 587, 385 N.Y.S.2d 5, 350 N.E.2d 381. App. dism. 429 U.S. 990.

Chief Judge Breitel.

Plaintiff Fred F. French Investing Co., purchase money mortgagee of Tudor City, a Manhattan residential complex, brought this action to declare unconstitutional a 1972 amendment to the New York City Zoning Resolution and seeks compensation as for "inverse" taking by eminent domain. The amendment purported to create a "Special Park District," and rezoned two private parks in the Tudor City complex exclusively as parks open to the public. It further provided for the granting to the defendant property owners of transferable development (air) rights usable elsewhere. It created the transferable rights by severing the above-surface development rights from the surface development rights, a device of recent invention.

[The trial court] declared the amendment unconstitutional and restored the former zoning classification, R-10, permitting residential and office building development. The Appellate Division unanimously affirmed.

The issue is whether the rezoning of buildable private parks exclusively as parks open to the public, thereby prohibiting all reasonable income productive or other private use of the property, constitutes a deprivation of property rights without due process of law in violation of constitutional limitations.

There should be an affirmance. While the police power of the state to regulate the use of private property by zoning is broad indeed, it is not unlimited. The State may not, under the guise of regulation by zoning, deprive the owner of the reasonable income productive or other private use of his property and thus destroy all but a bare residue of its economic value. Such an exercise of the police power would be void as violative of the due process clauses of the State and Federal Constitutions. In the instant case, the city has, despite the severance of above-surface development rights, by rezoning private parks exclusively as parks open to the public, deprived the owners of the reasonable income productive or other private use of their property. The attempted severance of the development rights with uncertain and contingent market value did not adequately preserve those rights. Hence, the 1972 zoning amendment is violative of constitutional limitations.

Tudor City is a four-acre residential complex built on an elevated level above East 42nd Street, across First Avenue from the United Nations in mid-town Manhattan. Planned and developed as a residential community, Tudor City consists of 10 large apartment buildings housing approximately 8,000 people, a hotel, four brownstone buildings, and two 15,000 square foot private parks. [P]laintiff sold the Tudor City complex to defendant Ramsgate Properties for $36,000,000.* * *

Soon after acquiring the Tudor City property, the new owner announced plans to erect a building, said to be a 50-story tower, over East 42nd Street between First and Second Avenues. This plan would have required New York City Planning Commission approval of a shifting of development rights from the parks to the proposed adjoining site and a corresponding zoning change. Alternatively, the owner proposed to erect on each of the Tudor City park sites a building of maximum size permitted by the existing zoning regulations.

There was immediately an adverse public reaction to the owner's proposals, especially from Tudor City residents. After public hearings, the City Planning Commission recommended [and] the Board of Estimate approved, an amendment to the zoning resolution establishing [a] Special Park District [for] the two Tudor City parks[.]

Under the zoning amendment, "only passive recreational uses are permitted" in the Special Park District and improvements are limited to "structures incidental to passive recreational use." When the Special Park District would be mapped, the parks are required to be open daily to the public between 6:00 A.M. and 10:00 P.M.

The zoning amendment permits the transfer of development rights from a privately owned lot zoned as a Special Park District, denominated a "granting lot," to other areas in midtown Manhattan, bounded by 60th Street, Third Avenue, 38th Street and Eighth Avenue, denominated "receiving lots."

* * *Before development rights may be transferred, however, the Chairman of the City Planning Commission must certify the suitability of a plan for the continuing maintenance, at the owner's expense, of the granting lot as a park open to the public.

It is notable that the private parks become open to the public upon mapping of the Special Park District, and the opening does not depend upon the relocation and effective utilization of the transferable development rights. Indeed the mapping occurred on December 7, 1972, and the development rights have never been marketed or used.

Plaintiff contends that the rezoning of the parks constitutes a compensable "taking" within the meaning of constitutional limitations.* * *

In this case, the zoning amendment is unreasonable and, therefore, unconstitutional because, without due process of law, it deprives the owner of all his property rights, except the bare title and a dubious future reversion of full use. The amendment renders the park property unsuitable for any reasonable income productive or other private use for which it is adapted and thus destroys its economic value and deprives plaintiff of its security for its mortgages.

[D]evelopment rights are an essential component of the value of the underlying property because they constitute some of the economic uses to which the property may be put. As such, they are a potentially valuable and even transferable commodity and may not be disregarded in determining whether the ordinance has destroyed the economic value of the underlying property.

Of course, the development rights of the parks were not nullified by the city's action. In an attempt to preserve the rights they were severed from the real property and made transferable to another section of mid-Manhattan in the city, but not to any particular parcel or place. There was thus created floating development rights, utterly unusable until they could be attached to some accommodating real property, available by happenstance of prior ownership, or by grant, purchase, or devise, and subject to the contingent approvals of administrative agencies. In such case, the development rights, disembodied abstractions of man's ingenuity, float in a limbo until restored to reality by reattachment to tangible real property.* * * The acceptance of this contingency-ridden arrangement, however, was mandatory under the amendment.

The problem with this arrangement * * * is that it fails to assure preservation of the very real economic value of the development rights as they existed when still attached to the underlying property. By compelling the owner to enter an unpredictable real estate market to find a suitable receiving lot for the rights, or a purchaser who would then share the same interest in using additional development rights, the amendment renders uncertain and thus severely impairs the value of the development rights before they severed. Hence, when viewed in relation to both the value of the private parks after the amendment, and the value of the development rights detached from the private parks, the amendment destroyed the economic value of the property. It thus constituted a deprivation of property without due process of law.

None of this discussion of the effort to accomplish the highly beneficial purposes of creating additional park land in the teeming city bears any relation to other schemes, variously described as a "development bank" or the "Chicago Plan" (see Costonis, The Chicago Plan: Incentive Zoning and the Preservation of Urban Landmarks, 85 Harv.L.Rev. 574; Costonis, Development Rights Transfer: An Exploratory Essay, 83 Yale L.J. 75, 86-87). For under such schemes or variations of them, the owner of the granting parcel may be allowed just compensation for his development rights, instantly and in money, and the acquired development rights are then placed in a "bank" from which enterprisers may, for a price, purchase development rights to use on land owned by them. Insofar as the owner of the granting parcel is concerned, his development rights are taken by the State, straightforwardly, and he is paid just compensation for them in eminent domain. The appropriating governmental entity recoups its disbursements when, as, and if, it obtains a purchaser for those rights. In contrast, the 1972 zoning amendment short-circuits the double-tracked compensation scheme but to do this leaves the granting parcel's owner's development rights in limbo until the day of salvation, if ever it comes.* * *

The limits are that unfair or disproportionate burdens may not, constitutionally, be placed on single properties or their owners.* * *

## Notes

1. The privately owned park in *Fred F. French* was ultimately saved. The rent stabilization authorities ruled in 1984 that the park was a "communal back yard" for Tudor City's residents and therefore an amenity that the owners could not take away without compensating the tenants by reducing their rent. Thereafter the buildings were converted to cooperatives and the park, protected by a conservation easement, was conveyed to a corporation wholly owned by the residents of Tudor City.

2. In both *Fred F. French* and *Penn Central* the court was dealing with privately owned, profit making (or seeking) enterprises. What if the owner were a charitable organization? Since charitable organizations are tax exempt this eliminates tax abatement as a possible method of compensation should a "taking" be found. Does this leave no alternative to a regulating authority other than payment outright to the owner? See *Lutheran Church in America v. City of New York,* 35 N.Y.2d 121, 359 N.Y.S.2d 7, 316 N.E.2d 305 (1974), involving the former J.P. Morgan town house on Madison Avenue in Manhattan. Here the church's needs could not be met by the present structure and modifications proved to be inadequate relief. While the Court of Appeals recognized there is no constitutional guarantee to the most profitable use of one's property, the church in this case could make no reasonable use of the present structure. The court held the City could not constitutionally bar the church from demolishing it. A more recent case came to a contrary decision and saved a valuable building from possible demolition where the record showed reasonable uses of the building were feasible. In *Society for Ethical Culture v. Spatt,* 51 N.Y.2d 449, 434 N.Y.S.2d 932, 415 N.E.2d 922 (1980), the Society challenged the designation of its Meeting House as a landmark by New York City's Landmark Preservation Commission, as an unconstitutional taking. Here the court found that the use of the building for charitable and religious purposes was not impaired by the designation. The standard to be used in determining whether a charitable organization is deprived of a reasonable return on its property is whether the designation as a landmark physically or financially prevents or seriously interferes with the owner's charitable purpose. The court admitted the Meeting House was inadequate for the Society's present needs but recognized the ability of the owner to modify the building to make it adequate.

3. *Fred F. French* says, "the ultimate evil of * * * frustration of property rights, under the guise of an exercise of the police power is that it forces the owner to assume the cost of providing a benefit to the public without recoupment." Why was the landmark designation in *Penn Central* not also invalid? Are there different policy reasons there? Was the extent of the diminution in value different? Why are development rights inadequate in *Fred F. French* but valuable compensation in *Penn Central*?

Landmarking Religious Buildings

A landmarked religious institution may argue that preventing construction of an addition, or demolition of a church no longer used, may interfere with its free exercise of religion. See *Rector of St. Bartholomew's Church v. City of New York*, 914 F.2d 348 (2d Cir. 1990), cert. denied 499 U.S. 905 (1991) (no denial of free exercise since church can continue to use existing building). The church sought to build an office building atop its vestry. Its argument that the vast additional income it would earn was "central to its religious mission" was dismissed since landmark law was neutral and only incidentally affected religious concerns.

This issue was considerably complicated by the Supreme Court decision in *Employment Division v. Smith*, 494 U.S. 872, 110 S. Ct. 1595, 108 L. Ed. 2d 876 (1990), holding one asserting a denial of free exercise of religion must prove the government lacked a rational basis for its action (unless the law in question was actually *intended* to limit free exercise). Congress attempted to alter this rule by statute, which the Court ruled unconstitutional in *City of Boerne v. Flores*, 521 U.S. 507, 117 S. Ct. 2157, 138 L. Ed. 2d 624 (1997). Some state courts have held landmark statutes, as applied to churches, interfere with the free exercise clauses of state constitutions. See, *e.g.*, *Society of Jesus of New England v. Boston Landmarks Comm'n*, 409 Mass. 38, 564 N.E.2d 571 (1990) (landmarking interior of church unconstitutionally interferes with worship).

Compensation for Takings

The courts in *Euclid* and *Penn Central* rejected claims that a land-use control amounted to an unconstitutional *de facto* taking of the owner's property. But what if a court finds a regulation so onerous as to effect a taking? The court clearly has the power to set the regulation aside, as it did in *Fred F. French*. Does the state or locality then have to compensate the owner for the deprivation of his or her property during the period the land-use control was in place? The Supreme Court answered that question in the following case.

FIRST ENGLISH EVANGELICAL LUTHERAN CHURCH v. COUNTY OF LOS ANGELES, Supreme Court of the United States, 1987. 482 U.S. 304, 107 S. Ct. 2378, 96 L.Ed.2d 250.

Chief Justice Rehnquist delivered the opinion of the Court.

In this case the California Court of Appeal held that a landowner who claims that his property has been "taken" by a land-use regulation may not recover damages for the time before it is finally determined that the regulation constitutes a "taking" of his property. We disagree, and conclude that in these circumstances the Fifth and Fourteenth Amendments to the United States Constitution would require compensation for that period.

In 1957, appellant First English Evangelical Lutheran Church purchased a 21-acre parcel of land in a canyon along the banks of the Middle Fork of Mill Creek in the Angeles National Forest. The Middle Fork is the natural drainage channel for a watershed area owned by the National Forest Service. Twelve of the acres owned by the church are flat land, and contained a dining hall, two bunkhouses, a caretaker's lodge, an outdoor chapel, and a footbridge across the creek. The church operated on the site a campground, known as "Lutherglen," as a retreat center and a recreational area for handicapped children.

In July 1977, a forest fire denuded the hills upstream from Lutherglen, destroying approximately 3,860 acres of the watershed area and creating a serious flood hazard. Such flooding occurred on February 9 and 10, 1978, when a storm dropped 11 inches of rain in the watershed. The runoff from the storm overflowed the banks of the Mill Creek, flooding Lutherglen and destroying its buildings.

In response to the flooding of the canyon, appellee County of Los Angeles adopted Interim Ordinance No. 11,855 in January 1979. The ordinance provided that "[a] person shall not construct, reconstruct, place or enlarge any building or structure, any portion of which is, or will be, located within the outer boundary lines of the interim flood protection area located in Mill Creek Canyon . . ."* * * The interim flood protection area described by the ordinance included the flat areas on either side of Mill Creek on which Lutherglen had stood.

The church filed a complaint in the Superior Court of California [asserting the ordinance] denies [appellant] all use of Lutherglen.* * * Appellant sought damages * * * for loss of use of Lutherglen. The defendants moved to strike the portions of the complaint alleging that the county's ordinance denied all use of Lutherglen, on the view that the California Supreme Court's decision in *Agins v. [City of] Tiburon,* 24 Cal.3d 266, 157 Cal. Rptr. 372, 598 P.2d 25 (1979), aff'd on other grounds, 447 U.S. 255, 100 S. Ct. 2138, 65 L.Ed.2d 106 (1980), rendered the allegation "entirely immaterially and irrelevant [with] no bearing upon any conceivable cause of action herein."* * *

In *Agins v. [City of] Tiburon, supra,* the Supreme Court of California decided that a landowner may not maintain an inverse condemnation suit in the courts of that State based upon "regulatory" taking.
* * *In the court's view, maintenance of such a suit would allow a landowner to force the legislature to exercise its power of eminent domain. Under this decision, then, compensation is not required until the challenged regulation or ordinance has been held excessive in an action for declaratory relief or a writ of mandamus and the government has nevertheless decided to continue the regulation in effect. Based on this decision, the trial court in the present case granted the motion to strike the allegation that the church had been denied all use of Lutherglen. [The Court of Appeal] affirmed the trial court's decision to strike the allegations concerning appellee's ordinance. The Supreme Court of California denied review.

This appeal followed * * *. Appellant asks us to hold the Supreme Court of California erred in *Agins v. [City of] Tiburon* in determining that the Fifth Amendment, as made applicable to the States through the Fourteenth Amendment, does not require compensation as a remedy for "temporary" regulatory takings--those regulatory takings which are ultimately invalidated by the courts.* * * For reasons explained below, [we] hold that on these facts the California courts have decided the compensation question inconsistently with the requirements of the Fifth Amendment.* * *

Consideration of the compensation question must begin with direct reference to the language of the Fifth Amendment, which provides in relevant part that "private property [shall not] be taken for public use, without just compensation." As its language indicates, and as the Court has frequently noted, this provision does not prohibit the taking of private property, but instead places a condition on the exercise of that power. [T]he Amendment makes clear that it is designed not to limit the governmental interference with property rights per se, but rather to secure compensation in the event of otherwise proper interference amounting to a taking. Thus, government action that works a taking of property rights necessarily implicates the "constitutional obligation to pay just compensation." *Armstrong v. United States,* 364 U.S. 40, 49, 80 S.Ct. 1563, 1569, 4 L.Ed.2d 1554 (1960).

We have recognized that a landowner is entitled to bring an action in inverse condemnation as a result of "'the self-executing character of the constitutional provision with respect to compensation. . . '" [I]t has been established at least since *Jacobs v. United States,* 290 U.S. 13, 54, S.Ct. 26, 78 L.Ed. 142 (1933), that claims for just compensation are grounded in the Constitution itself.* * *

It has also been established doctrine at least since Justice Holmes' opinion for the court in *Pennsylvania Coal Co. v. Mahon* that "[t]he general rule at least is, that while property may be regulated to a certain extent, if regulation goes too far it will be recognized as a taking." While the typical taking occurs when the government acts to condemn property in the exercise of its power of eminent domain, the entire doctrine of inverse condemnation is predicated on the proposition that a taking may occur without such formal proceedings.* * *

While the Supreme Court of California may not have actually disavowed this general rule in *Agins*, we believe that it has truncated the rule by disallowing damages that occurred prior to the ultimate invalidation of the challenged regulation. The Supreme Court of California justified its conclusion at length in the *Agins* opinion, concluding that:

> In combination, the need for preserving a degree of freedom in the land-use planning function and the inhibiting financial force which inheres in the inverse condemnation remedy, persuade us that on balance mandamus or declaratory relief rather than inverse condemnation is the appropriate relief under the circumstances.

We, of course, are not unmindful of these considerations, but they must be evaluated in the light of he command of the Just Compensation Clause of the Fifth Amendment. The Court has recognized in more than one case that the government may elect to abandon its intrusion or discontinue regulations. *See e.g.,* * * * *United States v. Dow,* 357 U.S. 17, 26, 78 S.Ct. 1039, 1046, 2 L.Ed.2d 1109 (1958).

Similarly, a governmental body may acquiesce in a judicial declaration that one of its ordinances has effected an unconstitutional taking of property; the landowner has no right under the Just Compensation Clause to insist that a "temporary" taking be deemed a permanent taking. But we have not resolved whether abandonment by the government requires payment of compensation for the period of time during which regulations deny a landowner all use of his land.

In considering this question, we find substantial guidance in cases where the government has only temporarily exercised its right to use private property. In *United States v. Dow, supra,* though rejecting a claim that the Government may not abandon condemnation proceedings, the Court observed that abandonment "results in an alteration in the property interest taken--from [one of] full ownership to one of temporary use and occupation. . . In such cases compensation would be measured by the principles normally governing the taking of a right to use property temporarily."* * * Each of the cases cited by the *Dow* Court involved appropriation of private property by the United States for use during World War II. Though the takings were in fact "temporary,"* * * there was no question that compensation would be required for the Government's interference with the use of the property; the Court was concerned in each case with determining the proper measure of the monetary relief to which the property holders were entitled.* * *

These cases reflect the fact that "temporary" takings which, as here, deny a landowner all use of his property, are not different in kind from permanent takings, for which the Constitution clearly requires compensation.* * *

In the present case the interim ordinance was adopted by the county of Los Angeles in January 1979, and became effective immediately. Appellant filed suit within a month after the effective date of the ordinance and yet when the Supreme Court of California denied a hearing in the case on October 17, 1985, the merits of appellant's claim had yet to be determined. The United States has been required to pay compensation for leasehold interests of shorter duration than this. The value of a leasehold interest in property for a period of years may be substantial, and the burden on the property owner in extinguishing such an interest for a period of years may be great indeed.* * * Where this burden results from governmental action that amounted to a taking, the Just Compensation Clause of the Fifth Amendment requires that the government pay the landowner for the value of the use of the land during this period. Cf. *United States v. Causby* ("It is the owner's loss, not the taker's gain, which is the measure of the value of the property taken").[a] Invalidation of the ordinance or its successor ordinance after this period of time, though converting the taking into a "temporary" one, is not a sufficient remedy to meet the demands of the Just Compensation Clause.* * *

Once a court determines that a taking has occurred, the government retains the whole range of options already available--amendment of the regulation, withdrawal of the invalidated regulation, or exercise of eminent domain. Thus we do not, as the Solicitor General suggests, "permit a court, at the behest of a private

---

[a] We will visit the *Causby* case again in Chapter 6 (noise).

person, to require the . . . Government to exercise the power of eminent domain. . . " We merely hold that where the government's activities have already worked a taking of all use of property, no subsequent action by the government can relieve it of the duty to provide compensation for the period during which the taking was effective.

We also point out that the allegation of the complaint which we treat as true for purposes of our decision was that the ordinance in question denied appellant all use of its property. We limit our holding to the facts presented, and of course do not deal with the quite different questions that would arise in the case of normal delays in obtaining building permits, changes in zoning ordinances, variances, and the like which are not before us. We realize that even our present holding will undoubtedly lessen to some extent the freedom of flexibility of land-use planners and governing bodies of municipal corporations when enacting land-use regulations. But such consequences necessarily flow from any decision upholding a claim of constitutional right; many of the provisions of the Constitution are designed to limit the flexibility and freedom of governmental authorities and the Just Compensation Clause of the Fifth Amendment is one of them. As Justice Holmes aptly noted more than 50 years ago, "a strong public desire to improve the public condition is not enough to warrant achieving the desire by a shorter cut than the constitutional way of paying for the change." *Pennsylvania Coal Co. v. Mahon.*

Here we must assume that the Los Angeles County ordinances have denied appellant all use of its property for a considerable period of years, and we hold that invalidation of the ordinance without payment of fair value for the use of the property during this period of time would be a constitutionally insufficient remedy. The judgment of the California Court of Appeals is therefore reversed, and the case is remanded for further proceedings not inconsistent with this opinion.

Justices Stevens, Blackmun and O'Connor dissented.

## Notes

Note that *First English* involved an eight-year span between enactment of the ordinance and the Court's ruling. The Court expressly reserved, or left open, whether compensation is required "in the case of normal delays in obtaining building permits, changes in zoning ordinances, variances and the like which are not before us." Are the considerations different there?

On remand, the California court found the flood control ordinance not to be a taking since it did not deny all reasonable use of the property, which could still be used for agriculture, recreation, or parking. In addition, the court ruled, the ordinance was no more than a temporary moratorium enacted for the public's safety, and therefore valid. 210 Cal. App.3d 1353, 258 Cal. Rptr. 893 (1989), cert. den. 110 Sup. Ct. 866.

## Flood Plain Protection

The issue in *First English*, limiting development in areas subject to periodic flooding, or flood-plain areas, has led to legislation at all three levels of government: federal, state and local. *First English* illustrates a local restriction. Some states regulate flood-plain construction or encourage, and fund, localities that do so. Towering over this topic is the federal flood insurance program, enacted in 1968, 42 U.S.C.A. §§ 4001-4129. This legislation subsidizes flood insurance, which would otherwise be too costly to underwrite. But to qualify, the locality where the property is must have land-use and flood-control measures approved by the Federal Emergency Management Agency (FEMA).

This legislation typically does not bar rebuilding in flood-prone areas. What steps, short of outright acquisition of the land, can government take to prevent this? Should government take those steps? What happens when a municipality is not vigorously enforcing its flood-plain ordinance? What can FEMA require in such cases? Is it doing so?

What if a land-use regulation deprives the owner of all reasonable use, but the state argues nonetheless that the regulation is required for public health and safety? We will address this in *Lucas v. South Carolina Coastal Council*, in Subsection F.

In addition to landmarks and flood plains, other environmentally critical areas protected by legislation include wetlands and coastal areas, to which we now turn.

## Wetlands Protection

GAZZA v. NEW YORK STATE DEPARTMENT OF ENVIRONMENTAL CONSERVATION, New York Court of Appeals, 1997. 89 N.Y. 2d 603, 679 N.E..2d 1035, 657 N.Y.S. 2d 555. Cert. denied, 118 S. Ct. 58.

Smith, Judge.

The primary issue in this case is whether the denial of a building variance pursuant to environmental regulation effects an unconstitutional taking (U.S. Const. Fifth Amend.; N.Y. Const., art. I, § 7) for which the landowner must be justly compensated. Petitioner argues that the denial of a variance due to legislation enacted to preserve wetlands is a taking despite the fact that the legislation was fully enacted and in force when he purchased the property. We disagree and affirm the dismissal of the petition.

Petitioner purchased property located in a residentially zoned district in the Village of Quogue, Town of Southampton, Suffolk County, for $100,00. Approximately 65% of the 43,500-square-foot parcel had previously been inventoried as tidal wetlands by the New York State Department of

Environmental Conservation (DEC). As [the trial court] found, the purchase price reflected the fact that a variance would be required to build a residence on the property due to its incorporating tidal wetlands. Petitioner estimates that, assuming a variance were granted and a residence could be constructed on the property, the parcel would be worth $396,000.

Petitioner applied to the DEC for two setback variances * * * to enable him to construct a single-family home on the parcel. The first variance request was from the minimum 75-foot setback required between the tidal wetlands boundary and the dwelling. The second variance request was from the 100-foot setback required between the wetlands boundary and the planned septic system.

The matter was heard by an Administrative Law Judge (ALJ) who recommended that the application be denied. Nevertheless, the ALJ suggested the construction of a dock, catwalk, and/or a small parking lot as possible uses for the property. The Hearing Report of the ALJ was adopted as the decision in the matter by the DEC Commissioner, [who found] [t]he proposed project * * * would eliminate or diminish several tidal wetland benefits, in particular, values related to flood control, wildlife habitat, marine food production and silt/organic material absorption[,] that the proposed construction of a sanitary system threatened both marine life and humans, that other contaminants threatened the area and that flooding problems would be increased.

* * * In 1973, the Legislature concluded that "tidal wetlands constitute one of the most vital and productive areas of our natural world, and that their protection and preservation are essential." The Legislature also noted its concern that much of the State's tidal wetlands had already been irreparably destroyed or despoiled and the remaining wetlands were in imminent danger of the same fate. Pursuant to these findings, the Legislature enacted the Tidal Wetlands Act and struck a balance between ecological and economic considerations by preserving and protecting tidal wetlands while permitting reasonable economic use and development.

To implement this policy, the Legislature directed the Commissioner of Environmental Conservation to inventory all tidal wetlands in the State of New York ([Environmental Conservation Law] 25-0201). The Commissioner was also empowered to regulate the use of inventoried wetlands as well as the areas immediately adjacent there to (ECL 25-0202, 25-0301, 25-0302).

The Legislature also enacted strict guidelines for the application and granting of permits to landowners desiring to conduct regulated activities in and around inventoried wetlands (ECL 25-0402, 25-0403).

* * *

Judicial review is a two-step process. * * * "If the court finds that the permit denial is supported by substantial evidence, then a second determination is made in the same proceeding to determine whether the restriction constitutes an unconstitutional taking requiring compensation."

Turning to the first step in the process, the DEC's denial of the setback variances in this case is supported by substantial evidence.

* * * It must next be "determined whether the wetlands act, coupled with the denial of the * * * permit, has placed such an onerous burden on the property that a taking must be deemed to have occurred" (*Spears v. Berle*, 48 N.Y.2d 254 at 261, 422 N.Y.S.2d 636, 397 N.E.2d 1304).

[P]etitioner's claim that the denial of his variance was a "taking" must fail because he never owned an absolute right to build on his land without a variance. * * * Since the enactment of the wetland regulations, the only permissible uses for the subject property were dependent upon those regulations which were a legitimate exercise of police power. Petitioner cannot base a taking claim upon an interest he never owned. The relevant property interests owned by the petitioner are defined by those State laws enacted and in effect at the time he took title and they are not dependent on the timing of State action pursuant to such laws.

[T]here is support in the record for the conclusion that the economic value of the property had not been extinguished since it could still be used for recreational purposes and that petitioner's reasonable expectations were reflected by his consideration of the inherent limitations on the property when he made the purchase offer for thousands less than its worth without the restrictions. Thus, his "reasonable" expectations were not affected when the property remained restricted. Petitioner argues that the finding of value does not take into account the fact that the non-residential uses proposed by DEC that add value to his land may not be undertaken without a variance from the Village.

In such circumstances, we have stated that petitioner has the burden of showing that it is unreasonable to expect relief from a zoning restriction (*de St. Aubin v. Flacke*, 68 N.Y.2d 66 at 76, 78-79, 505 N.Y.S.2d 859, 496 N.E.2d 879). Although petitioner did not have to complete the application process to meet his burden on the issue, his conclusory assertion that the zoning variance would not be granted is insufficient when the record contains "ample and convincing" evidence to the contrary. The Village Law provides that a variance may be granted if an applicant cannot realize a reasonable return without it (Village Law § 7-712-b[2][b]). The value of the subject property was, at most, diminished as restricted by the regulations.

Here, no per se taking occurred. Moreover, even if petitioner's "bundle of rights" included the "stick" he claims was taken, any burden resulting from the denial of the setback variances would not rise to the level of a taking.

[Affirmed.]

State wetland laws typically require a state environmental agency to balance the need to conserve wetlands for fish and shellfish breeding grounds, flood and storm control, recreation, and migratory bird habitat, against reasonable social and economic development. What factors should these agencies take into account in so doing? Is this akin to court's balancing the equities in deciding whether to enjoin a nuisance (See chapter 2)?

Freshwater wetlands are also important sources of potable water. Is this an added reason to restrict development there?

The Army Corps of Engineers' permit authority under the Clean Water Act over placing fill material in waterways, defined to include wetlands, furnishes another level of protection for these areas, discussed in Chapter 7(B). Why did Congress not simply enact land-use controls over development in wetlands, as the states did?

## D. RIPARIAN RIGHTS

HARRIS v. BROOKS, Supreme Court of Arkansas,
1955. 225 Ark. 436, 283 S.W.2d 129.

Ward, J.

[Plaintiff-appellant,] lessee of riparian landowners, conducts a commercial boating and fishing enterprise. In this business he rents cabins, sells fishing bait and equipment, and rents boats to members of the general public who desire to use the lake for fishing and other recreational purposes. He and his lessors [sued] to enjoin appellees from pumping water from the lake to irrigate a rice crop, alleging that, as of that date, appellees had reduced the water level of the lake to such an extent as to make the lake unsuitable "for fishing, recreation, or other lawful purposes." After a lengthy hearing, the chancellor denied injunctive relief, and this appeal is prosecuted to reverse the chancellor's decision.

[Defendants-appellees] are lessees of Ector Johnson who owns a large tract of land adjacent to the lake, including three-fourths of the lake bed.

For a number of years appellees have intermittently raised rice on Johnson's land and have each year, including 1954, irrigated the rice with water pumped from the lake. [Plaintiff] began operating his business about the first of April, 1954, and fishing and boat rentals were satisfactory from that time until about July 1st or 4th when, he says, the fish quit biting and his income from that source and boat rentals was reduced to practically nothing.

* * *Generally speaking two separate and distinct theories or doctrines regarding the right to use water are recognized.

*[Appropriation Doctrine]*. Generally speaking, under this doctrine, some governmental agency, acting under constitutional or legislative authority, apportions water to contesting claimants. It has never been adopted in this state, but has been in about 17 western states. This doctrine is inconsistent with the common law relative to water rights in force in this and many other states. One principal distinction between this doctrine and the riparian doctrine is that under the former the use is not limited to riparian landowners.[1]

---

[1] Wells A. Hutchins, U.S. Department of Agriculture * * * said: The effect of the repudiation of a common law system and its complete replacement by an appropriative system is to deny the right of an owner of land bordering a stream . . . to divert and make use of the water solely by reason of

*Riparian Doctrine.* This doctrine, long in force in this and many other states, is based on the old common law which gave to the owners of land bordering on streams the right to use the water therefrom for certain purposes, and this right was considered an incident to the ownership of land. Originally it apparently accorded the landowners the right to have the water maintained at its normal level, subject to use for strictly domestic purposes. Later it became evident that this strict limitation placed on the use of water was unreasonable and unutilitarian. Consequently it was not long before the demand for a greater use of water caused a relaxation of the strict limitations placed on its use and this doctrine came to be divided into (a) the natural flow theory and (b) the reasonable use theory.

(a) *Natural Flow Theory.* Generally speaking again, under the natural flow theory, a riparian owner can take water for domestic purposes only such as water for the family, live stock, and gardening, and he is entitled to have the water in the stream or lake upon which he borders kept at the normal level. There are some expressions in the opinions of this court indicating that we have recognized this theory, at least to a certain extent.

(b) *Reasonable Use Theory.* This theory appears to be based on the necessity and desirability of deriving greater benefits from the use of our abundant supply of water. It recognizes that there is no sound reason for maintaining our lakes and streams at a normal level when the water can be beneficially used without causing unreasonable damage to other riparian owners. The progress of civilization, particularly in regard to manufacturing, irrigation, and recreation, has forced the realization that a strict adherence to the uninterrupted flow doctrine placed an unwarranted limitation on the use of water and consequently the courts developed what we now call the reasonable use theory.* * *

In 56 Am. Jur., page 728, it is stated[:"]In general, the special rights of a riparian owner are such as are necessary for the use and enjoyment of his abutting property and the business lawfully conducted thereon, qualified only by the correlative rights of other riparian owners, and by certain rights of the public, and they are to be so exercised as not to injure others in the enjoyment of their rights." It has been stated that each riparian owner has an equal right to make a reasonable use of waters subject to the equal rights of other owners to make the reasonable use, *United States v. Willow River Power Co.,* 324 U.S. 499, 65 S.Ct. 761, 89 L.Ed. 1101. The purpose of the law is to secure to each riparian owner equality in the use of water as near as may be by requiring each to exercise his right reasonably and with due regard to the rights of others similarly situated.* * *

We do not understand that the two theories will necessarily clash in every case, but where there is an inconsistency [it] is our conclusion that the reasonable use theory should control.

---

his ownership of the land; to declare all such waters to be the property of the state, and; to make all water . . . open to appropriation for beneficial use . . . ."

It is recognized that in some instances vested rights may have accrued to riparian landowners and we could not of course constitutionally negate those rights.[3]* * *

The result of our examination of the decision of this court and other authorities relative to the use by riparian proprietors of water in nonnavigable lakes and streams justifies the enunciation of the following general rules and principles:

The right to use water for strictly domestic purposes,,such as for household use,,is superior to many other uses of water,,such as for fishing recreation and irrigation.

Other than the use mentioned above, all other lawful uses of water are equal. Some of the lawful uses of water recognized by this state are: fishing, swimming, recreation, and irrigation.* * *

When one lawful use of water interferes with or detracts from another lawful use, then a question arises as to whether, under all the facts and circumstances of that particular case, the interfering use shall be declared unreasonable and as such enjoined, or whether a reasonable and equitable adjustment should be made, having due regard to the reasonable rights of each.

*Application To This Case.*

(a) Had appellees on July 10, 1954, by the continued use of water from Horseshoe Lake, destroyed appellants' right to fish and conduct the boating enterprise? If so, the injunction should be granted.

(b) If it is found however, that appellant's rights had only been impaired at the stated time then it must be judged, under all the facts are circumstances as before mentioned, whether such impairment is unreasonable. If it is so found then the injunction should issue. If it is found that appellants' rights have not been unreasonably impaired having due regard to all the facts and circumstances and the injury which may be caused appellees as weighed against the benefits accruing to appellants, then the injunction should be denied.

We do not minimize the difficulties attendant upon an application of the reasonable use rule[,] and particularly those present in this instance. It is obvious that there are no definite guide posts provided and that necessarily much must be left to judgment and discretion. [However, s]ubstantial intentional harm to another cannot be justified as reasonable unless the legal merit or utility of the activity which produces it outweighs the legal seriousness or gravity of the harm." [After] careful consideration, an application of the rules above announced to the complicated fact situation set forth in this record leads us to conclude that the chancellor should have issued an order enjoining appellees from pumping water out of Horseshoe Lake when the water level reaches 189.67 feet above sea level for as long as the material facts and circumstances are substantially the same as they appear in this record.* * *

---

[3] In the case of Meriwether Sand & Gravel Co. v. State ex rel. Attorney General, 181 Ark. at page 226, 26 S.W.2d at page 61,this court said: "Riparian rights inhere in the owner of the soil, and are part and parcel of the land itself, and are vested and valuable rights which no more may be destroyed or impaired than any other part of a freehold."

Reversed with direction to the trial court to enter a decree in conformity with this opinion.

Notes

Note that in *Harris v. Brooks* the defendants were enjoined even though their use antedated the plaintiff's. As in nuisance, where "coming to the nuisance" is not a defense but rather one of the elements courts consider in determining whether to issue an injunction, in riparian rights who arrived first is not dispositive. In contrast, under the prior appropriation doctrine used by most of the Rocky Mountain states, and described in *Harris v. Brooks*, in effect time is of the essence. A downstream user may enjoin later diversion by an upstream owner, *State ex rel. Crowley v. Dist. Ct.*, 108 Mont. 89, 88 P.2d 23 (1939), and an upstream owner may continue to divert water needed by a later downstream owner. In the legal shorthand employed by Western courts, "first in time, first in right."

Although a prior appropriator is entitled to divert a watercourse completely, its rights are not unlimited. The use must be "beneficial," *Schodde v. Twin Falls Land & Water Co.*, 224 U.S. 107, 32 S.Ct. 470, 56 L.Ed 686 (1912), and non-polluting, *Arizona Copper Co. v. Gillespie,* 230 U.S. 46, 56-57, 33 S.Ct. 1004, 57 L.Ed. 1384 (1913), and the means used to divert the water must not cause undue waste. *Barrows v. Fox*, 98 Cal. 63, 32 Pac. 811 (1893). Further, the amount of water than can be appropriated is limited to the original use of the water or that allowed by permit. *See* Clark, 1 *Waters & Water Rights* § 51.7 (1967).

Do riparian rights protect quality as well as quantity? In *Harris v. Brooks,* the reasonableness of the quantity of water diverted was at issue. The doctrine of riparian rights has also been used where the quantity diverted is reasonable but the use impairs the quality of water for other users. *See United States v. Willow River Power Co.*, 324 U.S. 499, 505-06, 65 S.Ct. 761, 89 L.Ed. 1101 (1945). Absolute purity is not required, however, and a riparian owner's right to clean water can be limited by reasonable commercial or domestic uses by others that do not substantially impair water quality. *United States v. 531.15 Acres of Land,* 366 F.2d 915, 918-19 (4th Cir. 1966) (discharging untreated waste from textile plant is an unreasonable interference with downstream owner's recreational use).

The Restatement uses a different approach to protect water quality between riparian users. See *Restatement (Second) of Torts* § 847 (1979). Because pollution is not classified as a "use" in the Restatement, its reasonableness is not a defense. As a result, a riparian owner can use nuisance, negligence, trespass and abnormally dangerous activities as theories for recovery against a polluting neighbor. Under the Restatement's view the pollution of water is not the exercise of a riparian right. Does the need to prove unreasonable conduct in most negligence and similar tort actions bring the issue of reasonableness back in anyway?

In *Ancarrow v. City of Richmond*, 600 F.2d 443 (4th Cir. 1979), cert. den. 444 U.S. 992 (1980), the city's pollution of the James River from its sewage treatment plant made the river front "unattractive to the public for recreational purposes, frustrating the Ancarrow's attempts to enhance their property's value as a marina." After the city condemned their property in order to expand the treatment plant, they sued, "seeking damages for the unrealized value of their marina improvements, alleging that the City of Richmond had `taken' their property *prior* to the condemnation by continuing to pollute the river."

The court ordered the complaint dismissed, holding "a citizen's riparian right to use public waters of a particular purity is always subject to the superior right of the public to pollute those waters for sewage disposal."

Nor, it held, may the plaintiffs

> contend that they have some right of beneficial location: in essence, that the city cannot constitutionally use the James River in a way which diminishes the value of land along that river. More particularly, plaintiffs claim that the city has, by its pollution of the river, "taken" the inherent commercial value which attaches to their property by virtue of its location near public waters. This contention fails because no such property right exists.
>
> Although the Fourteenth Amendment protects a property owner from government's direct interference with the use of his property when that interference substantially eliminates the value of his title to it, it does not protect the owner from fluctuations in the value of his property resulting from governmental decisions to put neighboring public property to a lawful, albeit unattractive, use. *Reichelderfer v. Quinn*, 287 U.S. 315 (1932). And, even assuming that plaintiffs have suffered substantial loss in the value of their marina improvements due to the city's continuing lawful pollution, no action under the Fourteenth Amendment will lie unless some distinct property right, personal to plaintiffs, has been taken. Here, plaintiffs have suffered a consequential injury which, "though greater in degree than that of the rest of the public, is the same in kind." *Id.* at 320.
>
> The unattractive use to which the city has put the James River may have a very detrimental effect on the value of property along the river's shore.
>
> But the existence of value alone does not generate interest protected by the Constitution against diminution by the government, however unreasonable its action may be. The beneficial use and hence the value of abutting property is decreased when a public street or canal is closed or obstructed by public authority, or a street grade is raised, or the location of a county seat or of a railroad is changed. But in such cases no private right is infringed. *Id. at 319.* We think this language dispositive of plaintiffs' claim that some

> right of beneficial location was taken in the constitutional sense by the city's decision to continue its lawful pollution of public waters. If the city, by exercising its statutory authority to pollute, were held accountable to riparian owners for indirect, consequential diminution of property value, the admonition of Justice Stone would be apt: "the powers of government would be exhausted by their exercise." *Id.*

But other courts have found a compensable taking where a sewer authority has caused a nuisance and destroyed the value of property by polluting a lake. See *Stoddard v. Western Carolina Regional Sewer Auth.*, 784 F.2d 1200 (4th Cir. 1986).

## E. THE PUBLIC TRUST DOCTRINE AND COASTAL RESOURCES

### ILLINOIS CENTRAL RAILROAD CO. v. ILLINOIS,

Supreme Court of the United States, 1892. 146 U.S. 387, 13 S.Ct. 110, 36 L.Ed. 1019.

[This was an action by the State of Illinois to establish and confirm its title to lands in Chicago under the Lake Michigan shoreline. The State had conveyed a 200-foot strip of land in 1851 by an act of its legislature to the railroad for trackage and depots. In 1869 the legislature further granted to the railroad the underwater lands to a point 400 feet to the east, to build wharves and piers. The railroad accepted the conveyance the following year. In 1873 the legislature repealed the 1869 act. The railroad contended its title had already vested.]

Mr. Justice Field delivered the opinion of the Court.

It is the settled law of this country that the ownership of and dominion and sovereignty over lands covered by tide waters, within the limits of the several states, belong to the respective states within which they are found with the consequent right to use or dispose of any portion thereof, when that can be done without substantial impairment of the interest of the public in the waters, and subject always to the paramount right of Congress to control their navigation so far as may be necessary for the regulation of commerce with foreign nations and among the states.* * *

The same doctrine is in this country held to be applicable to lands covered by fresh water in the Great Lakes over which is conducted an extended commerce with different states and foreign nations. These lakes [in effect] are inland seas, and there is no reason or principle for the assertion of dominion and sovereignty over and ownership by the State of lands covered by tide waters that is not equally applicable to its ownership of and dominion and sovereignty over lands covered by the fresh waters of these lakes.* * *

The State prays a decree establishing and confirming its title to the bed of Lake Michigan and exclusive right to develop and improve the harbor of Chicago by the construction of docks, wharves, piers, and other improvements, against the claim of the railroad company that it has an absolute title to such submerged lands by the Act of 1869, and the right, subject only to the paramount authority of the United States in the regulation of commerce, to fill all the bed of the lake within the limits above stated, for the purpose of its business; and the right, by the construction and maintenance of wharves, docks, and piers, to improve the shore of the lake for the promotion generally of commerce and navigation. And the State, insisting that the company has, without right, erected and proposes to continue to erect wharves and piers upon its domain, asks that such alleged unlawful structures may be ordered to be removed, and the company be enjoined from erecting further structures of any kind. [It contends t]he construction of a pier or the extension of any land into navigable waters for a railroad or other purposes, by one not the owner of lands on the shore, does not give the builder of such pier or extension, whether an individual or corporation, any riparian rights. [However, the] act, if valid and operative to the extent claimed, placed under the control of the railroad company nearly the whole of the submerged lands of the harbor, subject only to the limitations that it should not authorize obstructions to the harbor or impair the public right of navigation, or exclude the legislature from regulating the rates of wharfage or dockage to be charged. With these limitations the act put it in the power of the company to* * * improve [the harbor] as it might choose[.]

The question, therefore, to be considered is whether the Legislature was competent to thus deprive the State of its ownership of the submerged lands in the harbor of Chicago, and of the consequent control of its waters; or, in other words, whether the railroad corporation can hold the lands and control the waters by the grant, against any future exercise of power over them by the State.

That the State holds the title to the lands under the navigable waters of Lake Michigan,* * * we have already shown, and that title necessarily carries with it control over the waters above them whenever the lands are subjected to use. But it is a title held in trust for the people of the State that they may enjoy the navigation of the waters, carry on commerce over them, and have liberty of fishing therein freed from the obstruction or interference of private parties. [It] is grants of parcels of lands under navigable waters, that may afford foundation for wharves, piers, docks, and other structures in aid of commerce, and grants of parcels which, being occupied, do not substantially impair the public interest in the lands and water remaining, that are chiefly considered and sustained in the adjudged cases as a valid exercise of legislative power consistently with the trust to the public upon which such lands are held by the State. But that is a very different doctrine from the one which would sanction the abdication of the general control of the State over lands under the navigable waters of an entire harbor or bay, or of a sea or lake. Such abdication is not consistent with the exercise of that trust which requires the government of the State to preserve such waters for the use of the public. The trust devolving upon the State for the public, and which can only be discharged by the management and control of property in which the public has an interest, cannot be relinquished by a transfer of the property. The control of the State for the purpose of the trust can never be lost.* * *

A grant of all the lands under the navigable waters of a State has never been adjudged to be within the legislative power; and any attempted grant of the kind would be held, if not absolutely void on its face, as subject to revocation. The State can no more abdicate its trust over property in which the whole people are interested, than it can abdicate its police powers in the administration of government and the preservation of the peace.* * *

The harbor of Chicago is of immense value to the people of the State of Illinois in the facilities it affords to its vast and constantly increasing commerce; and the idea that its Legislature can deprive the State of control over its bed and waters and place the same in the hands of a private corporation created for a different purpose, one limited to transportation of passengers and freight between distant points and the city, is a proposition that cannot be defended.* * *

We hold, therefore, that any attempted cession of the ownership and control of the State in and over the submerged lands in Lake Michigan, by the act of April 16, 1869, was inoperative to affect, modify, or in any respect to control the sovereignty and dominion of the State over the lands, or its ownership thereof, and that any such attempted operation of the act was annulled by the repealing act of April 15, 1873, which to that extent was valid and effective. There can be no irrepealable contract in a conveyance of property by a grantor in disregard of a public trust, under which he was bound to hold and manage it.* * *

Justices Shiras, Gray and Brown dissented, arguing the conveyance was valid and thus protected by the Constitutional bar on states impairing the obligation of contracts (Art. I § 10).

## Notes

The public trust doctrine is not limited to conveyances of underwater lands. See *Gould v. Graylock Reservation Comm'n,* 350 Mass. 410, 215 N.E.2d 114 (1966) (parkland). Does it bar *any* state conveyance of trust property? See *Appleby v. City of New York,* 271 U.S. 364, 46 S.Ct. 569, 70 L.Ed. 992 (1926), sustaining a conveyance for pier development as consistent with the public trust doctrine.

Does the Contract Clause (Art. 1, § 10) of the Constitution bar a state from repealing a prior grant of land covered by the public trust doctrine? Or is such a grant deemed unlawful when made and therefore void, or at least voidable? See *Hudson Water Co. v. McCarter,* 209 U.S. 349, 28 S.Ct. 529, 52 L.Ed. 828 (1908), so holding. Was this implicit in *Illinois Central*?

Does a state constitutional provision guaranteeing a right to clean air, pure water and the preservation of natural and scenic resources (see Penna. Const. Art. I § 27; N.Y. Const. Art. XIV, § 4) codify the public trust doctrine? See *Commonwealth v. National Gettysburg Tower,* ch. 2, *supra,* for a discussion of these provisions.

Not only the state as "trustee," but individual citizens as well, may sue to challenge acts in derogation of the public trust doctrine, *Dietz v. King,* 3 Cal. 3d 29,

84 Cal. Rptr. 162, 465 P.2d 50 (1970) (citizens may enjoin beach owner from excluding public). The normal standing requirements are finessed by the plaintiff's status as a beneficiary of the trust.

The public trust doctrine has since been held to apply to all lands that were tidal, that is, subject to the tides, when that state was admitted to the Union, even though now no longer tidal. *Phillips Petroleum Co. v. Mississippi*, 484 U.S. 469, 108 S. Ct. 791, 98 L.Ed.2d 877 (1988).

Does the public trust doctrine require town-owned beaches to be open to all residents of the state? See *Borough of Neptune City v. Borough of Avon-by-the-Sea*, 61 N.J. 296, 294 A.2d 47 (1972) (yes); *Bell v. Town of Wells*, 557 A.2d 168 (Me.1989) (no). Which view makes more sense?

*The Public Trust in Tidal Areas:*
*A Sometime Submerged Traditional Doctrine*
79 Yale Law Journal 762 (1970)*

Roman jurisprudence, developed in a society with heavy commerce, with important urban concentrations, and with a legal heritage from the sea-dependent Greeks, held that by the most basic "natural law" the "air, running water, the sea, and consequently the seashore" were "common to all."

This imperial law is the original foundation from which the common law developed[.]

It has been used in modern cases in which the court has sought to whittle down private claims perceived to be contrary to the public interest. Where subsequent law is found to differ, proponents of the public trust can hold the original Roman law up as a useful model of doctrinal purity to which we should return.

As is well known, with the decline of the Roman Empire, Europe retrogressed in terms of commerce, navigation, and effective governmental administration. Public ownership of waterways and tidal areas frequently gave way to ownership by local powers and feudatories. Many continental princes, for example, came to claim that the right to fish was their personal property and required that all their fishermen be licensed for a fee. In the British Isles, the [English King's jurisdictional and] sovereign claims to tidal areas became confused with a personal private property claim, a confusion handily furthered to this day by successors in interest to the King, notably the American states. The King claimed a private interest in tidal and riverbed soil, and consequently the private right to whatever could be found on or under the soil,,be it sand, stones, minerals, seaweed and shells (for fertilizer), or deserted wrecks or flotsam that washed up onto the shore. He also claimed the right to "several fishery" (an exclusive private right to fish) in these areas.* * * Between what the King claimed for himself and what the lords received by grant or took by prescription, the old common ownership in the public provided for in Roman law was seriously if unevenly eroded.* * * As

* Reprinted by permission of The Yale Journal Company and Fred B. Rothman & Company from *79 Yale Law Journal* 762-789.

England and English commerce continued to grow, statutes and case judgments continued to expand the public's rights in and control over the nation's water resources. Later theorists have attempted to bring this stream of developments together under a "public trust" theory of tidal and navigable waters.

[P]ublic trust theory held that the public had certain important rights in the foreshore, which rights superseded any conflicting private rights, including those claimed by the King. The King was trustee for these public rights, but he could not appropriate them to his own use.

For centuries after Magna Charta there were few reported cases because tidal area resources were still generally abundant. As a result, public trust theory developed only very gradually. With the advent of the commercial and industrial revolutions in the early modern period, [p]ublic trust proponents pushed to expand the scope of the citizens' existing easement rights and to "rediscover" new categories. For a variety of practical and historical reasons [the] dominant approach under the theory was to reserve a series of particular rights to the public, and thus to limit the prerogatives of private ownership.

This "easement" approach is theoretically inconsistent with the traditional Roman concept of common ownership by all the citizenry. It presumes private ownership, which the Roman model denies. This theoretical difference, however, has prevented neither coexistence nor confusion of identity. The Courts have never forsaken the theory of ancestral Roman law, and the Roman approach recently has been gaining ground in practice. In case by case adjudication of controversies between putative owners and other citizens, the broader principles of the Roman model can only lend support to a claimed easement under the public trust theory* * *

By gradually expanding the definition of existing easements and by possibly adding others, it is quite possible that the law could cause private ownership to fade away so completely that the result would ultimately be equivalent to expropriation.

Should the salami tactic of returning tidal areas to common ownership by gradually expanding the scope of public easements on private ownership prove successful, the many significant elements of the original Roman approach that remain imbedded in the common law will have been partly responsible. If the new dominant easement approach proves incapable of such expansion or of providing adequate protection, the currently recessive Roman theory (or its close relative, state ownership for the benefit of the public) does provide a "principled" alternative to private ownership.* * *

*The Grounds for and the Extent of Private Interests*

In today's developed society, the most common method of acquiring a property interest is from a prior owner. Such a vendor may be either a person or a government acting as a private owner. Unfortunately many governments have confused their roles as private owner and sovereign trustee of public interests and have attempted to give or sell portions of their trusteeship powers along with alienable interests. Although some such distributions have since been sanctified by judicial myth-making and/or by prescription, they are theoretically invalid. Where courts and commentators have refused to let time justify such excessive distributions,[49] this refusal is based both on considerations of public policy and, at least for the easement of free navigation, on the exercise of a right uninterrupted since the period of Roman common ownership.[50] * * *

Gradually, the common law has come to recognize the weaknesses of this justification for private alienation and consequently to emphasize prescription increasingly. The common law allowed private prescription (and recognized ancient grants reinforced by use), albeit initially only of incorporeal rights (*e.g.*, a right of way as versus title), by creating the elaborate fictions of usage from time immemorial (*i.e.,* from at least the reign of Richard I), or of a "lost grant" of equal antiquity. The requirements of great antiquity, logically impossible for the United States, have gradually been dropped even from the fictions. Now twenty years prescription in general and sixty years against the state is all that is generally required for private alienation.* * *

The rule of thumb applicable to prescription under the more modern common law has been that the citizen could gain by "user" whatever there was in the tidal area that was not reserved for the people by easement under the public trust theory. Acts of ownership that have been held to provide the basis for prescriptive title include building embankments and filling in parts of the shore, building wharves, piers, access ramps, etc. Thus, those claiming to own tidal areas, unless they previously had long allowed the grant lands (or part of them) to lie idle, have a solid claim.* * *

*A Catalogue of Public Trust Theory Easements*

*Navigation.* The oldest and most completely developed of the rights, the right to navigation, is clearly an easement. In Lord Hale's words, waterways "are in nature of common highwayes, in which all the Kinges people have a liberty of passage. . . ." The easement includes secondary easements, such as the right to anchor[.] Of all the public trust rights, navigation is the only one that has remained unchallenged and rigorously enforced from Roman times to the present.

In dealing with impediments to navigation, no countervailing benefits will be considered.* * *

---

[49] "[N]o length of time will legitimate a public nuisance, so that the acquiescence of twenty years on the part of the public in an interruption of their rights, occasioned by the illegal act of an individual, will not divest these rights, nor prevent the community from proceeding to abate or remedy the nuisance under which they may chance to suffer." Woolrych, A Treatise on the Law of Waters (Phila. Ed. 1853) at 206.

[50] "When a nuisance concerns immediately al[l] men, as the obstruction of a port, the makeinge of a weare in a publique river; this can neither bee licensed or dispenced with, though the Kinge and the owner of the soil of the river should consent thereunto, bycaus it is immediatly a common nuisance, and all are directly or immediatly concerned in it." Hale, First Treatise, 340.

*Ports.* The right of the public in ports is closely connected and similar to its right to free navigation, except that it is policed even more vigorously and that it gives particular [emphasis] to unhindered access to shore facilities for loading and unloading. Lord Hale lists several nuisances particular to ports, including silting or clogging a harbor with rubbish, wrecks, anchors, etc.; allowing the decay of landing facilities such as wharves; the building of weirs or other impediments to navigation and moorage in a harbor; and the building out of a port into areas where ships previously could moor.

*Passage.* Citizens generally have the right of passage over the shore when passage is connected with protected rights, notably the rights of navigation and fishing. Otherwise the property rights of private owners take precedence.

*Fishery.* The right to fish is a public right subject to private invasion, primarily by prescription although initially in early England also in large degree by grant. In case of conflict with the right of navigation, the latter is paramount.* * *

*Bathing (Recreation).* In the case of *Blundell v. Catterall,*[97] the previously open question whether there was a common law right to swim was decided in the negative, and access across a privately owned shore for this purpose was forbidden. One reason given by the court was that swimming could conflict with navigation and fishery, and that it should have the lowest priority. Moreover, Lord C. J. Abbott noted that "public convenience is, in all cases, to be viewed with a due regard to private property. . . ." This exclusion from common law protection of an ancient and universal customary right is a prime example of the needless exclusion of an activity. Although swimming was not felt to be important enough to warrant the same degree of protection that was provided navigation and fishery, local custom often effectively reserved this right for particular sets of people, as long as it did not conflict with priority public interests such as navigation.

The increased need for recreational facilities along the shore has generated considerable [impetus to] reverse *Blundell.* Oregon has seized the customary usage opening and widened it.[102] * * *

*Conservation and Esthetics.* The public interest in conservation is another area in which one can expect growth of the public trust theory.* * *

Almost all the elements of a public trust right of conservation in tidal areas have long existed, because it has long been recognized that adequate conservation is a necessary prerequisite to the employment of protected activities.* * *

Conservation is necessary not only as an adjunct of the right to free navigation, but also to the maintenance of fisheries, any right of bathing and recreation that may exist, [as well as] commerce (tourism)* * *.

---

[97] 106 Eng. Rep. 1191, 5 B. & Ald. 268 (1821).

[102] The Legislative Assembly recognizes that over the years the public has made frequent and uninterrupted use of lands abutting, adjacent, and contiguous to the public highways and state recreation areas and recognizes, further, that where such use has been sufficient to create easements in the public through dedication, prescription, grant or otherwise, that it is in the public interest to protect and preserve such public easements as a permanent part of Oregon's recreational resources. Ore. Rev. Stat. § 390.610(2).

*Public Trust Remedies*

Violations of the public's rights in the foreshore are nuisances that can be challenged by the state and/or affected citizens and are subject to damages, injunction, and/or (especially) abatement.* * * Whether a particular use of the foreshore is a nuisance is a question of fact for jury decision.

## Conclusion

The common law of the foreshore seems to be entering a major period of reformulation. The change in the last half century in the underlying economic ratio of demand to the supply of such resources have been, if anything, more [dramatic] than those that presaged the feudal switch away from Roman common ownership. The present chaotic state of foreshore doctrines reflects not only a long history of adjustments to the demand/supply ratio, but also the law's modern scramble to avoid injustice in particular cases. [N]ew public easements are being created and/or rediscovered,,and the more easements there are, the less any one of them can be absolute or the courts allowed an easy dependence on mechanistic formulae.

We are witnessing a sharp acceleration of a process begun around the time of Magna Charta, the reclamation of the public's interest in the foreshore. Perhaps the day when common law citizens will have as many rights in the foreshore as Roman citizens once did is near at hand.

## Notes

The doctrine also may undercut *de facto* taking claims. For example, in *Just v. Marinette County*, 56 Wis.2d 7, 201 N.W.2d 761 (1972), the court upheld the denial of a permit to build in wetlands, even though the denial assertedly deprived the owner of all reasonable value of his property, on the ground that the restriction prevented construction which would be tantamount to a public nuisance. The court reasoned that the injury to fishing, shellfishing and flood control which would result from filling in the wetland would be a nuisance which a court could enjoin. Since the state need not compensate the owner of a nuisance when it abates it by court order, it need not compensate the owner of a wetland after denying him a permit.

Do you agree with the court? *See Lucas v. South Carolina Coastal Council, infra.*

## F. RECENT TAKING DECISIONS

In California, the public trust doctrine's concept of public access to the coast has been embodied in that state's constitution. But, as the Supreme Court has held, that does not eliminate taking claims, at least where the state's insistence on public access may amount to a physical invasion of the owner's property. The *Nollan* case illustrates this.

NOLLAN v. CALIFORNIA COASTAL COMMISSION, Supreme Court of the United States, 1987. 483 U.S. 825, 107 S. Ct. 3141, 97 L.Ed.2d 677.

Justice Scalia delivered the opinion of the Court.

James and Marilyn Nollan appeal from a decision of the California Court of Appeal ruling that the California Coastal Commission could condition its grant of permission to rebuild their house on their transfer to the public of an easement across their beachfront property.* * * The California Court rejected their claim that imposition of that condition violates the Takings Clause of the Fifth Amendment, as incorporated against the States by the Fourteenth Amendment.* * *

The Nollans own a beachfront lot in Ventura County, California. A quarter-mile north of their property is Faria County Park, an oceanside public park with a public beach and recreation area. Another public beach area, known locally as "the Cove," lies 1,800 feet south of their lot. A concrete seawall approximately eight feet high separates the beach portion of the Nollans' property from the rest of the lot. The historic mean high tide line determines the lot's oceanside boundary.

The Nollans originally leased their property with an option to buy. [U]nder California Public Resources Code §§ 30106, 30212, and 30600, they were required to obtain a coastal development permit from the California Coastal Commission. [T]he Commission * * * recommended that the permit be granted subject to the condition that they allow the public an easement to pass across a portion of their property bounded by the mean high tide line on one side, and their seawall on the other side. This would make it easier for the public to get to Faria County Park and the Cove. The Nollans protested imposition of the condition, but the Commission overruled their objections and granted the permit subject to their recordation of a deed restriction granting the easement.* * *

It found that the new house would increase blockage of the view of the ocean, thus contributing to the development of "a `wall' of residential structures" that would prevent the public "psychologically. . . from realizing a stretch of coastline exists nearby that they have every right to visit."* * * These effects of construction of the house, along with other area development, would cumulatively "burden the public's ability to traverse to and along the shorefront."* * * Therefore, the Commission could properly require the Nollans to offset that burden by providing additional lateral access to the public beaches in the form of an easement across their property.* * *

Had California simply required the Nollans to make an easement across their beachfront available to the public on a permanent basis in order to increase public access to the beach, rather than conditioning their permit to rebuild their house on their agreeing to do so, we have no doubt there would have been a taking. One of the principal uses of the eminent domain power is to assure that the government be able to require conveyance of just such interests, so long as it pays for them. As to property reserved by its owner for private use, "the right to exclude [others is] 'one of the most essential sticks in the bundle of rights that are commonly characterized as property.'" *Loretto v. TelePrompTer Manhattan CATV Corp.*, 458 U.S. 419,

433, 102 S. Ct. 3164, 3175, 73 L.Ed.2d 868 (1982), quoting *Kaiser Aetna v. United States* [Chapter 7, *infra*]. In *Loretto* we observed that where governmental action results in "[a] permanent physical occupation" of the property, by the government itself or by others, * * * our cases uniformly have found a taking to the extent of the occupation[," and] [w]e think a "permanent physical occupation" has occurred, for purposes of that rule, where individuals are given a permanent and continuous right to pass to and fro, so that the real property may continuously be traversed, even though no particular individual is permitted to station himself permanently upon the premises.* * *

Given, then, that requiring uncompensated conveyance of the easement outright would violate the Fourteenth Amendment, the question becomes whether requiring it to be conveyed as a condition for issuing a land use permit alters the outcome. We have long recognized that land use regulation does not effect a taking if it "substantially advance[s] legitimate state interests" and does not "den[y] an owner economically viable use of his land," *Agins v. [City of] Tiburon*, 447 U.S. 255, 260, 100 S. Ct. 2138, 2141, 65 L.Ed.2d 106 (1980). See also *Penn Central.** * * The Commission argues that among these permissible purposes are protecting the public's ability to see the beach, assisting the public in overcoming the "psychological barrier" to using the beach created by a developed shorefront, and preventing congestion on the public beaches. We assume, without deciding, that this is so--in which case the Commission unquestionably would be able to deny the Nollans their permit outright if their new house (alone, or by reason of cumulative impact produced in conjunction with other construction) would substantially impede these purposes, unless the denial would interfere so drastically with the Nollans' use of their property as to constitute a taking. See *Penn Central.* [I]f the Commission attached to the permit some condition that would have protected the public's ability to see the beach notwithstanding construction of the new house--for example, a height limitation, a width restriction, or a ban on fences--so long as the Commission could have exercised its police power (as we have assumed it could) to forbid construction of the house altogether, imposition of the condition would also be constitutional. Moreover (and here we come closer to the facts of the present case), the condition would be constitutional even if it consisted of the requirement that the Nollans provide a viewing spot on their property for passersby with whose sighting of the ocean their new house would interfere. Although such a requirement, constituting a permanent grant of continuous access to the property, would have to be considered a taking if it were not attached to a development permit, the Commission's assumed power to forbid construction of the house in order to protect the public's view of the beach must surely include the power to condition construction upon some concession by the owner, even a concession of property rights, that serves the same end. If a prohibition designed to accomplish that purpose would be a legitimate exercise of the police power rather than a taking, it would be strange to conclude that providing the owner an alternative to that prohibition which accomplishes the same purposes is not.

The evident constitutional propriety disappears, however, if the condition substituted for the prohibition utterly fails to further the end advanced as the justification for the prohibition. When that essential nexus is eliminated, the situation becomes the same as if California law forbade shouting fire in a crowded theater, but granted dispensations to those willing to contribute $100 to the state treasury. While a ban on shouting fire can be a core exercise of the State's police power to protect the public safety, and can thus meet even our stringent standards for regulation of speech, adding the unrelated condition alters the purpose to one which, while it may be legitimate, is inadequate to sustain the ban. Therefore, even though, in a sense, requiring a $100 tax contribution in order to shout fire is a lesser restriction on speech than an outright ban, it would not pass constitutional muster. Similarly here, the lack of nexus between the condition and the original purpose of the building restriction converts that purpose to something other than what it was. The purpose then becomes, quite simply, the obtaining of a easement to serve some valid governmental purpose, but without payment of compensation. Whatever may be the outer limits of "legitimate state interests" in the takings and land use context, this is not one of them.* * * It is quite impossible to understand how a requirement that people already on the public beaches be able to walk across the Nollans' property reduces any obstacles to viewing the beach created by the new house. It is also impossible to understand how it lowers any "psychological barrier" to using the public beaches, or how it helps to remedy any additional congestion on them caused by construction of the Nollans' new house. We therefore find that the Commission's imposition of the permit condition cannot be treated as an exercise of its land use power for any of these purposes.

[T]he Commission [believes] that the public interest will be served by a continuous strip of publicly accessible beach along the coast. The Commission may well be right that it is a good idea, but that does not establish that the Nollans (and other coastal residents) alone can be compelled to contribute to its realization. Rather, California is free to advance its "comprehensive program," if it wishes, by using its power of eminent domain for this "public purpose," see *U.S. Const. Amdt. V*; but if it wants an easement across the Nollans' property, it must pay for it.

Justices Blackmun, Brennan, Marshall and Stevens dissented.

## Notes

What of the uncommon land-use regulation that actually deprives the owner of all reasonable investment-based expectations?

LUCAS v. SOUTH CAROLINA COASTAL COUNCIL, Supreme Court of the United States, 1992. 505 U.S. 1003, 112 S.Ct. 2886, 120 L.Ed.2d 798.

[The owner bought beachfront lots, then zoned for one-family residences. The state then enacted the Beachfront Management Act, which prohibited construction of any permanent habitable structure. The South Carolina Supreme

Court ruled the Act did not effect a taking since it was designed to prevent "serious public harm" to the state's beaches and to its citizens and visitors.]

Scalia, J.

[T]here are good reasons for our frequently expressed belief that when the owner of real property has been called upon to sacrifice all economically beneficial uses in the name of the common good, that is, to leave his property economically idle, he has suffered a taking* * *.

The trial court found Lucas's two beachfront lots to have been rendered valueless by respondent's enforcement of the coastal-zone construction ban. Under Lucas's theory of the case, which rested upon our "no economically viable use" statements, that finding entitled him to compensation. Lucas believed it unnecessary to take issue with either the purposes behind the Beachfront Management Act, or the means chosen by the South Carolina Legislature to effectuate those purposes. The South Carolina Supreme Court, however, thought otherwise. In its view, the Beachfront Management Act was no ordinary enactment, but involved an exercise of South Carolina's "police powers" to mitigate the harm to the public interest that petitioner's use of this land might occasion. By neglecting to dispute the findings enumerated in the Act or otherwise to challenge the legislature's purposes, petitioner "concede[d] that the beach/dune area of South Carolina's shores is an extremely valuable public resource; that the * * * new construction, inter alia, contributes to the erosion and destruction of this public resource; and that discouraging new construction in close proximity to the beach/dune area is necessary to prevent a great public harm." In the court's view, these concessions brought petitioner's challenge within a long line of this Court's cases sustaining against Due Process and Takings Clause challenges the State's use of its "police powers" to enjoin a property owner from activities akin to public nuisances. See *Mugler v. Kansas*, 123 U.S. 623 (1887) (law prohibiting manufacture of alcoholic beverages); *Hadacheck v. Sebastian,* 239 U.S. 394 (1915) (law barring operation of brick mill in residential area); *Miller v. Schoene*, 276 U.S. 272 (1928) (order to destroy diseased cedar trees to prevent infection of nearby orchards); *Goldblatt v. [Town of] Hempstead,* 369 U.S. 590 (1962) (law effectively preventing continued operation of quarry in residential area).

It is correct that many of our prior opinions have suggested that "harmful or noxious uses" of property may be proscribed by government regulation without the requirement of compensation. For a number of reasons, however, we think the South Carolina Supreme Court was too quick to conclude that principle decides the present case. The "harmful or noxious uses" principle was the Court's early attempt to describe in theoretical terms why government may, consistent with the Takings Clause, affect property values by regulation without incurring an obligation to compensate -- a reality we nowadays acknowledge explicitly with respect to the full scope of the State's police power. See, *e.g.*, *Penn Central* (where State "reasonably conclude[s] that 'the health, safety, morals, or general welfare' would be promoted by prohibiting particular contemplated uses of land," compensation need not accompany prohibition); *Nollan* ("Our cases have not elaborated on the standards for determining what constitutes a 'legitimate state interest[,]' [but] [t]hey have made clear . . . that a broad range of governmental purposes and regulations satisfy these requirements"). We made this very point in *Penn Central* where, in the course of sustaining New York City's landmarks preservation program against a takings challenge, we rejected the petitioner's suggestion that *Mugler* and the cases following it were premised on, and thus limited by, some objective conception of "noxiousness":

> "[T]he uses in issue in *Hadacheck, Miller*, and *Goldblatt* were perfectly lawful in themselves. They involved no 'blameworthiness, . . . moral wrongdoing or conscious act of dangerous risk-taking which induce[d society] to shift the cost to a pa[rt]icular individual.' Sax, Takings and the Police Power, 74 Yale L.J. 36, 50 (1964). These cases are better understood as resting not on any supposed 'noxious' quality of the prohibited uses but rather on the ground that the restrictions were reasonably related to the implementation of a policy -- not unlike historic preservation -- expected to produce a widespread public benefit and applicable to all similarly situated property."
>
> "Harmful or noxious use" analysis was, in other words, simply the progenitor of our more contemporary statements that "land-use regulation does not effect a taking if it 'substantially advance[s] legitimate state interests'. . . " *Nollan*[.]

The transition from our early focus on control of "noxious" uses to our contemporary understanding of the broad realm within which government may regulate without compensation was an easy one, since the distinction between "harm-preventing" and "benefit-conferring" regulation is often in the eye of the beholder. It is quite possible, for example, to describe in either fashion the ecological, economic, and esthetic concerns that inspired the South Carolina legislature in the present case. One could say that imposing a servitude on Lucas's land is necessary in order to prevent his use of it from "harming" South Carolina's ecological resources; or, instead, in order to achieve the "benefits" of an ecological preserve.* * *

When it is understood that "prevention of harmful use" was merely our early formulation of the police power justification necessary to sustain (without compensation) *any* regulatory diminution in value; and that the distinction between regulation that "prevents harmful use" and that which "confers benefits" is difficult, if not impossible, to discern on an objective, value-free basis; it becomes self-evident that noxious-use logic cannot serve as a touchstone to distinguish regulatory takings -- which require compensation -- from regulatory deprivations that do not require compensation. *A fortiori* the legislature's recitation of a noxious-use justification cannot be the basis for departing from our categorical rule that total regulatory takings must be compensated. If it were, departure would virtually always be allowed. The South Carolina Supreme Court's approach would essentially nullify *Mahon's* affirmation of limits to the noncompensable exercise of the police power. Our cases provide no support for this: None of them that employed the logic of "harmful use" prevention to sustain a regulation involved an allegation that the regulation wholly eliminated the value of the claimant's land.

Where the State seeks to sustain regulation that deprives land of all economically beneficial use, we think it may resist compensation only if the logically antecedent inquiry into the nature of the owner's estate shows that the proscribed use interests were not part of his title to begin with. This accords, we think, with our "takings" jurisprudence, which has traditionally been guided by the understandings of our citizens regarding the content of, and the State's power over, the "bundle of rights" that they acquire when they obtain title to property. It seems to us that the property owner necessarily expects the uses of his property to be restricted, from time to time, by various measures newly enacted by the State in legitimate exercise of its police powers; "[a]s long recognized, some values are enjoyed under an implied limitation and must yield to the police power." *Pennsylvania Coal Co. v. Mahon*. And in the case of personal property, by reason of the State's traditionally high degree of control over commercial dealings, he ought to be aware of the possibility that new regulation might even render his property economically worthless (at least if the property's only economically productive use is sale or manufacture for sale), see *Andrus v. Allard* [Chapter 4, *infra*] (prohibition on sale of eagle feathers). In the case of land, however, we think the notion [of] the Council that title is somehow held subject to the "implied limitation" that the State may subsequently eliminate all economically valuable use is inconsistent with the historical compact recorded in the Takings Clause that has become part of our constitutional culture.

Where "permanent physical occupation" of land is concerned, we have refused to allow the government to decree it anew (without compensation), no matter how weighty the asserted "public interests" involved, *Loretto v. TelePrompTer Manhattan CATV Corp.*, 458 U.S., at 426 -- though we assuredly *would* permit the government to assert a permanent easement that was a pre-existing limitation upon the landowner's title. [See] *Kaiser Aetna v. United States* [Chapter 7, *infra*] (imposition of navigational servitude on marina created and rendered navigable at private expense held to constitute a taking). We believe similar treatment must be accorded confiscatory regulations, *i.e.,* regulations that prohibit all economically beneficial use of land: Any limitation so severe cannot be newly legislated or decreed (without compensation), but must inhere in the title itself, in the restrictions that background principles of the State's law of property and nuisance already place upon land ownership. A law or decree with such an effect must, in other words, do no more than duplicate the result that could have been achieved in the courts -- by adjacent landowners (or other uniquely affected persons) under the State's law of private nuisance, or by the State under its complementary power to abate nuisances that affect the public generally, or otherwise.

On this analysis, the owner of a lake bed, for example, would not be entitled to compensation when he is denied the requisite permit to engage in a landfilling operation that would have the effect of flooding others' land. Nor the corporate owner of a nuclear generating plant, when it is directed to remove all improvements from its land upon discovery that the plant sits astride an earthquake fault. Such regulatory action may well have the effect of eliminating the land's only economically productive use, but it does not proscribe a productive use that was previously permissible under relevant property and nuisance principles. The use of these properties for what are now expressly prohibited purposes was *always* unlawful, and (subject to other constitutional limitations) it was open to the State at any point to make the implication of those background principles of nuisance and property law explicit. When, however, a regulation that declares "off-limits" all economically productive or beneficial uses of land goes beyond what the relevant background principles would dictate, compensation must be paid to sustain it.

The "total taking" inquiry we require today will ordinarily entail (as the application of state nuisance law ordinarily entails) analysis of, among other things, the degree of harm to public lands and resources, or adjacent private property, posed by the claimant's proposed activities, the social value of the claimant's activities and their suitability to the locality in question, and the relative ease with which the alleged harm can be avoided through measures taken by the claimant and the government (or adjacent private landowners) alike. The fact that a particular use has long been engaged in by similarly situated owners ordinarily imports a lack of any common-law prohibition (though changed circumstances or new knowledge may make what was previously permissible no longer so). So also does the fact that other landowners, similarly situated, are permitted to continue the use denied to the claimant.

It seems unlikely that common-law principles would have prevented * * * any habitable or productive improvements on petitioner's land; they rarely support prohibition of the "essential use" of land. The question, however, is one of state law to be dealt with on remand. We emphasize that to win its case South Carolina must do more than proffer the legislature's declaration that the uses Lucas desires are inconsistent with the public interest, or the conclusory assertion that they violate a common-law maxim such as [use your own property so as not to injure that of another]. As we have said, a State, by ipse dixit, may not transform private property into public property without compensation. . . " *Webb's Fabulous Pharmacies, Inc., v. Beckwith*, 449 U.S. 155, 164 (1980). Instead, as it would be required to do if it sought to restrain Lucas in a common-law action for public nuisance, South Carolina must identify background principles of nuisance and property law that prohibit the uses he now intends in the circumstances in which the property is presently found. Only on this showing can the State fairly claim that, in proscribing all such beneficial uses, the Beachfront Management Act is taking nothing.* * *

Justice Kennedy, concurring, saw the state's powers somewhat more broadly. Justices Blackmun and Stevens dissented, and Justice Souter contended the Court should dismiss the writ of certiorari since the record failed to clearly show Lucas had been deprived of all reasonable use.

On remand, the South Carolina Supreme Court rejected the invitation to find the state's common law would have justified the regulation. It held the Act had taken Lucas's property, 424 S.E.2d 484 (S.C. 1992), and remanded to assess damages.

What kinds of statutory land-use controls, other than Justice Scalia's two examples, would support a denial of all reasonable use based on common-law principles? In addition to nuisance, how helpful are riparian rights and the public trust doctrine here?

Recall *Just v. Marinette County*, discussed after the public trust doctrine material.

DOLAN v. CITY OF TIGARD, Supreme Court of the United States, 1994. 512 U.S. 374, 114 S.Ct. 2309, 129 L.Ed.2d 304.

Chief Justice Rehnquist delivered the opinion of the Court.

Petitioner challenges the decision of the Oregon Supreme Court which held that the city of Tigard could condition the approval of her building permit on the dedication of a portion of her property for flood control and traffic improvements. We granted certiorari to resolve a question left open by our decision in *Nollan*, of what is the required degree of connection between the exactions imposed by the city and the projected impacts of the proposed development.

Petitioner Florence Dolan owns a plumbing and electric supply store located on Main Street in the Central Business District of the city.* * * Fanno Creek flows through the southwestern corner of the lot and along its western boundary. The year-round flow of the creek renders the area within the creek's 100-year floodplain virtually unusable for commercial development. The city's comprehensive plan includes the Fanno Creek floodplain as part of the city's greenway system.

Petitioner applied to the city for a permit to redevelop the site. Her proposed plans called for nearly doubling the size of the store to 17,600 square feet, and paving a 39-space parking lot.* * * The proposed expansion and intensified use are consistent with the city's zoning scheme in the Central Business District.

The City Planning Commission granted petitioner's permit application subject to conditions imposed by the city's [Community Development Code. It] required that petitioner dedicate the portion of her property lying within the 100-year floodplain for improvement of a storm drainage system along Fanno Creek and that she dedicate an additional 15-foot strip of land adjacent to the floodplain as a pedestrian/bicycle pathway. The dedication required by that condition encompasses approximately 7,000 square feet, or roughly 10% of the property. [S]he requested variances [but] [t]he Commission denied the request.

The Commission noted that the site plan has provided for bicycle parking in a rack in front of the proposed building and "[i]t is reasonable to expect that some of the users of the bicycle parking provided for by the site plan will use the pathway adjacent to Fanno Creek if it is constructed." In addition, the Commission found that creation of a convenient, safe pedestrian/bicycle pathway system as an alternative means of transportation "could offset some of the traffic demand on [nearby] streets and lessen the increase in traffic congestion."

The Commission went on to note that the required floodplain dedication would be reasonably related to petitioner's request to intensify the use of the site given the increase in the impervious surface. The Commission stated that the "anticipated increased storm water flow from the subject property to an already strained creek and drainage basin can only add to the public need to manage the stream channel and floodplain for drainage purposes." Based on this anticipated increased storm water flow, the Commission concluded that "the requirement of dedication of the floodplain area on the site is related to the applicant's plan to intensify development on the site." The Tigard City Council approved the Commission's final order, [as did the Land Use Board of Appeals [LUBA], which] concluded that "there is a 'reasonable relationship' between the proposed development and the requirement to dedicate land along Fanno Creek for a greenway." With respect to the pedestrian/bicycle pathway, LUBA noted the Commission's finding that a significantly larger retail sales building and parking lot would attract larger numbers of customers and employees and their vehicles. It again found a "reasonable relationship" between alleviating the impacts of increased traffic from the development and facilitating the provision of a pedestrian/bicycle pathway as an alternative means of transportation.

[The Oregon courts affirmed.]

[The] authority of state and local governments to engage in land use planning has been sustained against constitutional challenge as long ago as our decision in *Euclid v. Ambler Realty Co.* "Government hardly could go on if to some extent values incident to property could not be diminished without paying for every such change in the general law." *Pennsylvania Coal Co. v. Mahon*, 260 U.S. 393, 413, 43 S.Ct. 158, 159, 67 L.Ed. 322 (1922). A land use regulation does not effect a taking if it "substantially advance[s] legitimate state interests" and does not "den[y] an owner economically viable use of his land." *Agins v. [City of] Tiburon*, 447 U.S. 255, 260, 100 S.Ct. 2138, 2141, 65 L.Ed.2d 106 (1980).

The sort of land use regulations discussed in the cases just cited, however, differ in two relevant particulars from the present case. First, they involved essentially legislative determinations classifying entire areas of the city, whereas here the city made an adjudicative decision to condition petitioner's application for a building permit on an individual parcel. Second, the conditions imposed were not simply a limitation on the use petitioner might make of her own parcel, but a requirement that she deed portions of the property to the city. In *Nollan* we held that governmental authority to exact such a condition was circumscribed by the Fifth and Fourteenth Amendments. Under the well-settled doctrine of "unconstitutional conditions," the government may not require a person to give up a constitutional right--here the right to receive just compensation when property is taken for a public use--in exchange for a discretionary benefit conferred by the government where the property sought has little or no relationship to the benefit.

Petitioner contends that the city has forced her to choose between the building permit and her right under the Fifth Amendment to just compensation for the public easements. Petitioner does not quarrel with the city's authority to exact some forms of dedication as a condition for the grant of a building permit, but challenges the showing made by the city to justify these exactions. She argues that the city has identified "no special benefits" conferred on her, and has not identified any "special quantifiable burdens" created by her new store that would justify the particular dedications required from her which are not required from the public at large.

In evaluating petitioner's claim, we must first determine whether the "essential nexus" exists between the "legitimate state interest" and the permit condition exacted by the city. *Nollan*. If we find that a nexus exists, we must then decide the required degree of connection between the exactions and the projected impact of the proposed development. We were not required to reach this question in *Nollan*, because we concluded that the connection did not meet even the loosest standard. Here, however, we must decide this question.

[In *Nollan*,] [t]he absence of a nexus left the Coastal Commission in the position of simply trying to obtain an easement through gimmickry, which converted a valid regulation of land use into "an out-and-out plan of extortion."

No such gimmicks are associated with the permit conditions imposed by the city in this case. Undoubtedly, the prevention of flooding along Fanno Creek and the reduction of traffic congestion in the Central Business District qualify as the type of legitimate public purposes we have upheld. It seems equally obvious that a nexus exists between preventing flooding along Fanno Creek and limiting development within the creek's 100-year floodplain. Petitioner proposes to double the size of her retail store and to pave her now-gravel parking lot, thereby expanding the impervious surface on the property and increasing the amounts of stormwater run-off into Fanno Creek.

The same may be said for the city's attempt to reduce traffic congestion by providing for alternative means of transportation. In theory, a pedestrian/bicycle pathway provides a useful alternative means of transportation for workers and shoppers: "Pedestrians and bicyclists occupying dedicated spaces for walking and/or bicycling . . . remove potential vehicles from streets, resulting in an overall improvement in total transportation system flow."

[But we must still] determine whether the degree of the exactions demanded by the city's permit conditions bear the required relationship to the projected impact of petitioner's proposed development. *Nollan*, quoting *Penn Central* (" '[A] use restriction may constitute a taking if not reasonably necessary to the effectuation of a substantial government purpose' "). Here the Oregon Supreme Court deferred to what it termed the "city's unchallenged factual findings" supporting the dedication conditions and found them to be reasonably related to the impact of the expansion of petitioner's business.

The city required that petitioner dedicate "to the city as Greenway all portions of the site that fall within the existing 100-year floodplain [of Fanno Creek] . . . and all property 15 feet above [the floodplain] boundary." * * * The city relies on the Commission's rather tentative findings that increased stormwater flow from petitioner's property "can only add to the public need to manage the [floodplain] for drainage purposes" to support its conclusion that the "requirement of dedication of the floodplain area on the site is related to the applicant's plan to intensify development on the site."

The city made the following specific findings relevant to the pedestrian/bicycle pathway:

> "In addition, the proposed expanded use of this site is anticipated to generate additional vehicular traffic thereby increasing congestion on nearby collector and arterial streets. Creation of a convenient, safe pedestrian/bicycle pathway system as an alternative means of transportation could offset some of the traffic demand on these nearby streets and lessen the increase in traffic congestion."

The question for us is whether these findings are constitutionally sufficient to justify the conditions imposed by the city on petitioner's building permit. Since state courts have been dealing with this question a good deal longer than we have, we turn to representative decisions made by them.

In some States, very generalized statements as to the necessary connection between the required dedication and the proposed development seem to suffice. See, *e.g., Billings Properties, Inc. v. Yellowstone County*, 144 Mont. 25, 394 P.2d 182 (1964); *Jenad, Inc. v. [Village of] Scarsdale*, 18 N.Y.2d 78, 271 N.Y.S.2d 955, 218 N.E.2d 673 (1966). We think this standard is too lax to adequately protect petitioner's right to just compensation if her property is taken for a public purpose.

Other state courts require a very exacting correspondence, described as the "specifi[c] and uniquely attributable" test. The Supreme Court of Illinois first developed this test in *Pioneer Trust & Savings Bank v. [Village of] Mount Prospect*, 22 Ill.2d 375, 380, 176 N.E.2d 799, 802 (1961). Under this standard, if the local government cannot demonstrate that its exaction is directly proportional to the specifically created need, the exaction becomes "a veiled exercise of the power of eminent domain and a confiscation of private property behind the defense of police regulations." We do not think the Federal Constitution requires such exacting scrutiny, given the nature of the interests involved.

A number of state courts have taken an intermediate position, requiring the municipality to show a "reasonable relationship" between the required dedication and the impact of the proposed development. Typical is the Supreme Court of Nebraska's opinion in *Simpson v. [City of] North Platte*, 206 Neb. 240, 245, 292 N.W.2d 297, 301 (1980), where that court stated:

> "The distinction, therefore, which must be made between an appropriate exercise of the police power and an improper exercise of eminent domain is whether the requirement has some reasonable relationship or nexus to the use to which the property is being made or is merely being used as an excuse for taking property simply because at that particular moment the landowner is asking the city for some license or permit."

Thus, the court held that a city may not require a property owner to dedicate private property for some future public use as a condition of obtaining a building permit when such future use is not "occasioned by the construction sought to be permitted."

Some form of the reasonable relationship test has been adopted in many other jurisdictions.* * *

We think the "reasonable relationship" test adopted by a majority of the state courts is closer to the federal constitutional norm than either of those previously discussed. But we do not adopt it as such, partly because the term "reasonable relationship" seems confusingly similar to the term "rational basis" which describes the minimal level of scrutiny under the Equal Protection Clause of the Fourteenth Amendment. We think a term such as "rough proportionality" best encapsulates what we hold to be the requirement of the Fifth Amendment. No precise mathematical calculation is required, but the city must make some sort of individualized determination that the required dedication is related both in nature and extent to the impact of the proposed development.* * *

It is axiomatic that increasing the amount of impervious surface will increase the quantity and rate of storm-water flood from petitioner's property. Therefore, keeping the floodplain open and free from development would likely confine the pressures on Fanno Creek created by petitioner's development. In fact, because petitioner's property lies within the Central Business District, the Community Development Code already required that petitioner leave 15% of it as open space and the undeveloped floodplain would have nearly satisfied that requirement. But the city demanded more--it not only wanted petitioner not to build in the floodplain, but it also wanted petitioner's property along Fanno Creek for its Greenway system. The city has never said why a public greenway, as opposed to a private one, was required in the interest of flood control.

The difference to petitioner, of course, is the loss of her ability to exclude others. As we have noted, this right to exclude others is "one of the most essential sticks in the bundle of rights that are commonly characterized as property." *Kaiser Aetna.*[a] It is difficult to see why recreational visitors trampling along petitioner's floodplain easement are sufficiently related to the city's legitimate interest in reducing flooding problems along Fanno Creek, and the city has not attempted to make any individualized determination to support this part of its request.

---

[a] This case appears in Chapter 7, Subsection B.

[T]he city wants to impose a permanent recreational easement upon petitioner's property that borders Fanno Creek. Petitioner would lose all rights to regulate the time in which the public entered onto the Greenway, regardless of any interference it might pose with her retail store. Her right to exclude would not be regulated, it would be eviscerated.* * * We conclude that the findings upon which the city relies do not show the required reasonable relationship between the floodplain easement and the petitioner's proposed new building.

With respect to the pedestrian/bicycle pathway, we have no doubt that the city was correct in finding that the larger retail sales facility proposed by petitioner will increase traffic on the streets of the Central Business District. The city estimates that the proposed development would generate roughly 435 additional trips per day. Dedications for streets, sidewalks, and other public ways are generally reasonable exactions to avoid excessive congestion form a proposed property use. But on the record before us, the city has not met its burden of demonstrating that the additional number of vehicle and bicycle trips generated by the petitioner's development reasonably relate to the city's requirement for a dedication of the pedestrian/bicycle pathway easement. The city simply found that the creation of the pathway "could offset some of the traffic demand . . . and lessen the increase in traffic congestion."

As Justice Peterson of the Supreme Court of Oregon explained in his dissenting opinion, however, "[t]he findings of fact that the bicycle pathway system '*could* offset some of the traffic demand' is a far cry from a finding that bicycle pathway system *will*, or is *likely to*, offset some of the traffic demand" (emphasis in original). No precise mathematical calculation is required, but the city must make some effort to quantify its findings in support of the dedication for the pedestrian/bicycle pathway beyond the conclusory statement that it could offset some of the traffic demand generated.

Cities have long engaged in the commendable task of land use planning, made necessary by increasing urbanization particularly in metropolitan areas such as Portland. The city's goals of reducing flooding hazards and traffic congestion, and providing for public greenways, are laudable, but there are outer limits to how this may be done. "A strong public desire to improve the public condition [will not] warrant achieving the desire by a shorter cut than the constitutional way of paying for the change." *Pennsylvania Coal.*

The judgment of the Supreme Court of Oregon is reversed[.]

Justice Stevens, with whom Justice Blackmun and Justice Ginsburg join, dissenting.* * *

Not one of the state cases cited by the Court announces anything akin to a "rough proportionality" requirement. For the most part, moreover, those cases that invalidated municipal ordinances did so on state law or unspecified grounds roughly equivalent to *Nollan's* "essential nexus" requirement. See, *e.g., Simpson v. [City of] North Platte*, 206 Neb. 240, 245-248, 292 N.W.2d 297, 301-302 (1980) (ordinance lacking "reasonable relationship" or "rational nexus" to property's use violated

Nebraska constitution)[.] Although 4 of the 12 opinions mention the Federal Constitution--two of those only in passing--it is quite obvious that neither the courts nor the litigants imagined they might be participating in the development of a new rule of federal law. Thus, although these state cases do lend support to the Court's reaffirmance of *Nollan's* reasonable nexus requirement, the role the Court accords them in the announcement of its newly minted second phase of the constitutional inquiry is remarkably inventive.

In addition, the Court ignores the state courts' willingness to consider what the property owner gains from the exchange in question. The Supreme Court of Wisconsin, for example, found it significant that the village's approval of a proposed subdivision plat "enables the subdivider to profit financially by selling the subdivision lots as home-building sites and thus realizing a greater price than could have been obtained if he had sold his property as unplatted lands." *Jordan v. Village of Menomonee Falls*, 28 Wis.2d 608, 619-620, 137 N.W.2d 442, 448 (1965). The required dedication as a condition of that approval was permissible "[i]n return for this benefit." In this case, moreover, Dolan's acceptance of the permit, with its attached conditions, would provide her with benefits that may well go beyond any advantage she gets from expanding her business. As the United States pointed out at oral argument, the improvement that the city's drainage plan contemplates would widen the channel and reinforce the slopes to increase the carrying capacity during serious floods, "confer[ring] considerable benefits on the property owners immediately adjacent to the creek." * * *

The Court's narrow focus on one stand in the property owner's bundle of rights is particularly misguided in a case involving the development of commercial property. * * *

The city of Tigard has demonstrated that its plan is rational and impartial and that the conditions at issue are "conducive to fulfillment of authorized planning objectives." Dolan, on the other hand, has offered no evidence that her burden of compliance has any impact at all on the value or profitability of her planned development. Following the teaching of the cases on which it purports to rely, the Court should not isolate the burden associated with the loss of the power to exclude from an evaluation of the benefit to be derived from the permit to enlarge the store and the parking lot.

The Court's assurances that its "rough proportionality" test leaves ample room for cities to pursue the "commendable task of land use planning," even twice avowing that "[n]o precise mathematical calculation is required," are wanting given the result that test compels here. Under the Court's approach, a city must not only "quantify its findings," and make "individualized determination[s]" with respect to the nature *and* the extent of the relationship between the conditions and the impact, but also demonstrate "proportionality." The correct inquiry should instead concentrate on whether the required nexus is present and venture beyond considerations of a condition's nature or germaneness only if the developer establishes that a concededly germane condition is so grossly disproportionate to the proposed development's adverse effects that it manifests motives other than land use regulation on the part of the city.

* * *In her objections to the floodplain condition, Dolan made no effort to demonstrate that the dedication of that portion of her property would be any more onerous than a simple prohibition against any development on that portion of her property. Given the commercial character of both the existing and the proposed use of the property as a retail store, it seems likely that potential customers "trampling along petitioner's floodplain" are more valuable than a useless parcel of vacant land. Moreover, the duty to pay taxes and the responsibility for potential tort liability may well make ownership of the fee interest in useless land a liability rather than an asset.

The Court's rejection of the bike path condition amounts to nothing more than a play on words. Everyone agrees that the bike path "could" offset some of the increase traffic flow that the larger store will generate, but the findings do not unequivocally state that it *will* do so, or tell us just how many cyclists will replace motorists. Predictions on such matters are inherently nothing more than estimates. Certainly the assumption that there will be an offsetting benefit here is entirely reasonable and should suffice whether it amounts to 100 percent, 35 percent, or only 5 percent of the increase in automobile traffic that would otherwise occur. If the Court proposes to have the federal judiciary micro-manage state decisions of this kind, it is indeed extending its welcome mat to a significant new class of litigants. Although there is no reason to believe that state courts have failed to rise to the task, property owners have surely found a new friend today.

The Court has made a serious error by abandoning the traditional presumption of constitutionality and imposing a novel burden of proof on a city implementing an admittedly valid comprehensive land use plan. Even more consequential than its incorrect disposition of this case, however, is the Court's resurrection of a species of substantive due process analysis that it firmly rejected decades ago. * * *See *Lochner v. New York*, 198 U.S. 45, 25 S.Ct. 539, 49 L.Ed. 937 (1905).

Justice Souter also dissented.

Does *Dolan* affect cases like *Golden v. Town of Ramapo* (subsection A of this chapter)? Or, perhaps like *Nollan*, does it in fact turn on the virtual physical invasion of the owner's property demanded by the government? The Court looked at that question in the following case.

CITY OF MONTEREY v. DEL MONTE DUNES. Supreme Court of the United States, 1999. 526 U.S. 687, 119 S. Ct. 1624, 143 L.Ed.2d 882.

Justice KENNEDY delivered the opinion of the Court[.]

This case began with attempts by the respondent, Del Monte Dunes, and its predecessor in interest to develop a parcel of land within the jurisdiction of the petitioner, the city of Monterey. The city, in a series of repeated rejections, denied proposals to develop the property, each time imposing stricter demands on the developers. Del Monte Dunes brought suit in the United States District Court [asserting] the city effected a regulatory taking * * * without paying compensation[.] The jury found for Del Monte Dunes, and the Court of Appeals affirmed.

[One] question presented in the city's petition for certiorari [is] whether the Court of Appeals erred in assuming that the rough-proportionality standard of *Dolan v. City of Tigard* applied to this case. * * *

In the course of holding a reasonable jury could have found the city's denial of the final proposal not substantially related to legitimate public interests, the Court of Appeals stated: "[e]ven if the City had a legitimate interest in denying Del Monte's development application, its action must be 'roughly propotional' to furthering that interest . . . . That is, the City's denial must be related 'both in nature and extent to the impact of the proposed development.'"

Although in a .general sense concerns for proportionality animate the Takings Clause, see *Armstrong v. United States*, 364 U.S. 40, 49, 80 S.Ct. 1563, 4 L.Ed.2d 1554 (1960) ("The Fifth Amendment's guarantee . . . was designed to bar the Government from forcing some people alone to bear public burdens which, in all fairness and justice, should be borne by the public as a whole"), we have not extended the rough-proportionality test of *Dolan* beyond the special context of exactions -- land-use decisions conditioning approval of development on the dedication of property to public use. The rule applied in *Dolan* considers whether dedications demanded as conditions of development are proportional to the development's anticipated impacts. It was not designed to address, and is not readily applicable to, the much different questions arising where, as here, the landowner's challenge is based not on excessive exactions but on denial of development. We believe, accordingly, that the rough-proportionality test of *Dolan* is inapposite to a case such as this one.

The instructions given to the jury, however, did not mention proportionality, let alone require it to find for Del Monte Dunes unless the city's actions were roughly proportional to its asserted interests. The Court of Appeals' discussion of rough proportionality, we conclude, was unnecessary to its decision to sustain the jury's verdict. Although the court stated that "[s]ignificant evidence supports Del Monte's claim that the City's actions were disproportional to both the nature and extent of the impact of the proposed development," it did so only after holding that

> "Del Monte provided evidence sufficient to rebut each of these reasons [for denying the final proposal]. Taken together, Del Monte argued that the City's reasons for denying their application were invalid and that it unfairly intended to forestall any reasonable development of the Dunes. In light of the evidence proffered by Del Monte, the City has incorrectly argued that no rational juror could conclude that the City's denial of Del Monte's application lacked a sufficient nexus with its stated objectives."

Given this holding, it was unnecessary for the Court of Appeals to discuss rough proportionality. That it did so is irrelevant to our disposition of the case.

[Affirmed.][a]

PALAZZOLO v. RHODE ISLAND. Supreme Court of the United States, 2001. 533 U.S. 606, 121 S. Ct. 2448, 150 L. Ed. 2d 592.

Justice Kennedy delivered the opinion of the Court.

Petitioner Anthony Palazzolo owns a waterfront parcel of land in the town of Westerly, Rhode Island. Almost all of the property is designated as coastal wetlands under Rhode Island law. After petitioner's development proposals were rejected by respondent Rhode Island Coastal Resources Management council (Council), he sued in state court, asserting the Council's application of its wetlands regulations took the property without compensation in violation of the Takings Clause of the Fifth Amendment [.] Petitioner sought review in this Court, contending the Supreme Court of Rhode Island erred in rejecting his takings claim. We granted certiorari. * * *

When the Council promulgated its wetlands regulations, the disputed parcel was owned not by petitioner but by the corporation of which he was sole shareholder. When title was transferred to petitioner by operation of law [after the corporation was dissolved], the wetlands regulations were in force. The state court held the postregulation acquisition of title was fatal to the claim for deprivation of all economic use, and to the *Penn Central* claim. While the first holding was couched in terms of background principles of state property law, see *Lucas,* and the second in terms of petitioner's reasonable investment-backed expectations, see *Penn Central,* the two holdings together amount to a single, sweeping, rule: A purchaser or a successive title holder like petitioner is deemed to have notice of an earlier enacted restriction and is barred from claiming that it effects a taking. The theory underlying the argument that postenactment purchasers cannot challenge a regulation under the Takings Clause seems to run on these lines: Property rights are created by the State. So, the argument goes, by prospective legislation the State can shape and define property rights and reasonable investment-backed expectations, and subsequent owners cannot claim any injury from lost value. After all, they purchased or took title with notice of the limitation.

The State may not put so potent a Hobbesian stick into the Lockean bundle.*** Were we to accept the State's rule, the postenactment transfer of title would absolve the State of its obligation to defend any action restricting land use,

---

[a] Opinions concurring and dissenting in part as to other issues are omitted.

no matter how extreme or unreasonable. A State would be allowed, in effect, to put an expiration date on the Takings Clause. This ought not to be the rule. Future generations, too, have a right to challenge unreasonable limitations on the use and value of land.

Nor does the justification of notice take into account the effect on owners at the time of enactment, who are prejudiced as well. Should an owner attempt to challenge a new regulation, but not survive the process of ripening his or her claim (which, as this case demonstrates, will often take years), under the proposed rule the right to compensation may not be asserted by an heir or successor, and so may not be asserted at all. The State's rule would work a critical alteration to the nature of property, as the newly regulated landowner is stripped of the ability to transfer the interest which was possessed prior to the regulation. The State may not by this means secure a windfall for itself.*** A blanket rule that purchasers with notice have no compensation right when a claim becomes ripe is too blunt an instrument to accord with the duty to compensate for what is taken.* * *

As the case is ripe, and as the date of transfer of title does not bar petitioner's takings claim, we have before us the alternative ground relied upon by the Rhode Island Supreme Court in ruling upon the merits of the takings claims. It held that all economically beneficial use was not deprived because the uplands portion of the property can still be improved. On this point, we agree with the court's decision. Petitioner accepts the Council's contention and the state trial court's finding that his parcel retains $200,000 in development value under the State's wetlands regulations.*** A regulation permitting a landowner to build a substantial residence on an 18-acre parcel does not leave the property "economically idle." *Lucas*. [The state court] must address, however, the merits of petitioner's claim under *Penn Central*. That claim is not barred by the mere fact that title was acquired after the effective date of the state-imposed restriction.***

For the reasons we have discussed, the State Supreme Court erred in finding petitioner's claims were unripe and in ruling that acquisition of title after the effective date of the regulations barred the takings claims. The court did not err in finding that petitioner failed to establish a deprivation of all economic value, for it is undisputed that the parcel retains significant worth for construction of a residence. The claims under the *Penn Central* analysis were not examined, and for this purpose the case should be remanded.* * *
Justice O'Connor, concurring.* * *

Today's holding does not mean that the timing of the regulation's enactment relative to the acquisition of title is immaterial to the *Penn Central* analysis. Indeed, it would be just as much a error to expunge this consideration from the takings inquiry as it would be to accord it exclusive significance. Our polestar instead remains the principles set forth in *Penn Central* itself and our other cases that govern partial regulatory takings. Under these cases, interference with investment-backed expectations is one of a number of factors that a court must examine. Further, the regulatory regime in place at the time the claimant acquires the property at issue helps to shape the reasonableness of those expectations.* * *

We have "identified several factors that have particular significance" in these "essentially ad hoc, factual inquiries." *Penn Central.* Two such factors are "[t]he economic impact of the regulation on the claimant and, particularly, the extent to which the regulation has interfered with distinct investment-backed expectations."* * * If investment-backed expectations are given exclusive significance in the *Penn Central* analysis and existing regulations dictate the reasonableness of those expectations in every instance, then the State wields far too much power to redefine property rights upon passage of title. On the other hand, if existing regulations do nothing to inform the analysis, then some property owners may reap windfalls and an important indicium of fairness is lost. As I understand it, our decision today does not remove the regulatory backdrop against which an owner takes title to property from the purview of the *Penn Central* inquiry. It simply restores balance to that inquiry. Courts properly consider the effect of existing regulations under the rubric of investment-backed expectations in determining whether a compensable taking has occurred. As before, the salience of these facts cannot be reduced to any "set formula."* * *

Justice Scalia, concurring.* * * In my view, the fact that a restriction existed at the time the purchaser took title (other than a restriction forming part of the "background principles of the State's law of property and nuisance," *Lucas*) should have no bearing upon the determination of whether the restriction is so substantial as to constitute a taking. The "investment-backed expectations" that the law will take into account do not include the assumed validity of a restriction that in fact deprives property of so much of its value as to be unconstitutional. Which is to say that a *Penn Central* taking, no less than a total taking, is not absolved by the transfer of title.* * *

Justice Stevens, concurring in part and dissenting in part. * * *

It by no means follows * * * that, as the Court assumes, a succeeding owner may obtain compensation for a taking of property from her predecessor in interest. A taking is a discrete event, a governmental acquisition of private property for which the State is required to provide just compensation. Like other transfers of property, it occurs at a particular time, that time being the moment when the relevant property interest is alienated from its owner.* * *

To the extent that the adoption of the regulations constitute[s] the challenged taking, petitioner is simply the wrong party to be bringing this action.

If the regulations imposed a compensable injury on anyone, it was on the owner of the property at the moment the regulations were adopted. Given the trial court's finding that petitioner did not own the property at that time, in my judgment it is pellucidly clear that he has no standing to claim that the promulgation of the regulations constituted a taking of any part of the property that he subsequently acquired.* * * [T]he title Palazzolo took by operation of law in 1978 was limited by the regulations then in place to the extent that such regulations represented a valid exercise of the police power. [T]he judgment of the Rhode Island Supreme Court should be affirmed in its entirety. * * *
Justice Ginsburg, with whom Justice Souter and Justice Breyer join, dissenting. * * *

As the Rhode Island Supreme Court saw the case, Palazzolo's claim was not ripe for several reasons, among them, that Palazzolo had not sought permission for "development only of the upland portion of the parcel." The Rhode Island court emphasized the "undisputed evidence in the record that it would be possible to build at least one single-family home on the existing upland area, with no need for additional fill." * * * Palazzolo has conceded the very point on which the State properly relied to resist the simple *Lucas* claim presented below: that Palazzolo can obtain approval for one house of substantial economic value.* * * In sum, as I see this case, we still do not know "the nature and extent of permitted development" under the regulation in question. I would therefore affirm the Rhode Island Supreme Court's judgment.
Justice Breyer, dissenting.

I agree with Justice Ginsburg that Palazzolo's takings claim is not ripe for adjudication, and I join her opinion in full. Ordinarily I would go no further. But because the Court holds the takings claim to be ripe and goes on to address some important issues of substantive takings law, I add that, given this Court's precedents, I would agree with Justice O'Connor that the simple fact that a piece of property has changed hands (for example, by inheritance) does not always and automatically bar a takings claim. [M]uch depends upon whether, or how, the timing and circumstances of a change of ownership affect whatever reasonable investment-backed expectations might otherwise exist. Ordinarily, such expectations will diminish in force and significance—rapidly and dramatically—as property continues to change hands over time. I believe that such factors can adequately be taken into account within the *Penn Central* framework. ***

TAHOE - SIERRA PRESERVATION COUNCIL v. TAHOE REGIONAL PLANNING AGENCY. Supreme Court of the United States, 2002. 535 U.S. 302, 122 S. Ct. 1465, 152 L. Ed. 2d 517.

Justice Stevens delivered the opinion of the Court.

The question presented is whether a moratorium on development imposed during the process of devising a comprehensive land-use plan constitutes a *per se* taking of property requiring compensation under the Takings Clause of the United States Constitution. This case actually involves two moratoria ordered by respondent Tahoe Regional Planning Agency (TRPA) to maintain the status quo while studying the impact of development of Lake Tahoe and designing a strategy for environmentally sound growth. * * * As a result of these two directives, virtually all development on a substantial portion of the property subject to TRPA's jurisdiction was prohibited for a period of 32 months. * * *

The relevant facts are undisputed. * * * All agree that Lake Tahoe is "uniquely beautiful," that President Clinton was right to call it a "'national treasure that must be protected and preserved,'" and that Mark Twain aptly described the clarity of its waters as"' not *merely* transparent, but dazzlingly, brilliantly so.'" Lake Tahoe's exceptional clarity is attributed to the absence of algae that obscures the waters of most other lakes. Historically, the lack of nitrogen and phosphorous, which nourish the growth of algae, has ensured the transparency of its waters. Unfortunately, the lake's pristine state has deteriorated rapidly over the past 40 years; increased land development in the Lake Tahoe Basin has threatened the "'noble sheet of blue water'" beloved by Twain and countless others. As the District Court found, "[d]ramatic decreases in clarity first began to be noted in the late 1950's/early 1960's, shortly after development at the lake began in earnest." The lake's unsurpassed beauty, it seems, is the wellspring of its undoing.

The upsurge of development in the area has caused "increased nutrient loading of the lake largely because of the increase in impervious coverage of land in the Basin resulting from that development." "Impervious coverage--such as asphalt, concrete, buildings, and even packed dirt--prevents precipitation form being absorbed by the soil.["] Those areas in the Basin that have steeper slopes produce more runoff; therefore, they are usually considered "high hazard" lands. [C]onservation efforts have focused on controlling growth in these high hazard areas.

* * *Emphasizing the temporary nature of the regulations, the testimony that the "average holding time of a lot in the Tahoe area between lot purchase and home construction is twenty-five years," and the failure of petitioners to offer specific evidence of harm, the District Court concluded that "consideration of the *Penn Central* factors clearly leads to the conclusion that there was no taking." In the absence of evidence regarding any of the individual plaintiffs, the court evaluated the "average" purchasers' intent and found that such purchasers "did not have reasonable, investment-backed expectations that they would be able to build single-family homes on their land within the * * * period involved in this lawsuit."

The District Court had more difficulty with the "total taking" issue. Although it was satisfied that petitioners' property did retain some value during the moratoria, it found that they had been temporarily deprived of "all economically viable use of their land." The court concluded that those actions therefore constituted "categorical" takings under our decision in *Lucas*. * * *Accordingly, it ordered TRPA to pay damages to most petitioners for the 32-month period[.] Petitioners did not * * * challenge the District Court's findings or conclusions concerning its application of *Penn Central.* With respect to the two moratoria, the Ninth Circuit noted that petitioners had expressly disavowed an argument "that the regulations constitute a taking under the ad hoc balancing approach described in *Penn Central*" and that they did not "dispute that the restrictions imposed on their properties are appropriate means of securing the purpose set forth in the Compact." Accordingly, the only question before the court was "whether the rule set forth in *Lucas* applies--that is, whether a categorical taking occurred because [the moratoria] denied the plaintiffs 'all economically beneficial or productive use of land.'" * * *Contrary to the District Court, the Court of Appeals held that because the regulations had only a temporary impact on petitioners' fee interest in the properties, no categorical taking had occurred.

* * * As we noted in *Lucas*, it was Justice Holmes' opinion in *Pennsylvania Coal Co. v. Mahon* that gave birth to our regulatory takings jurisprudence. In subsequent opinions we have repeatedly and consistently endorsed Holmes' observation that "if regulation goes too far it will be recognized as a taking." * * * In the decades following [*Pennsylvania Coal*] we have "generally eschewed" any set formula for determining how far is too far, choosing instead to engage in "essentially ad hoc, factual inquiries." *Lucas* (quoting *Penn Central*). Indeed, we still resist the temptation to adopt *per se* rules in our cases involving partial regulatory takings, preferring to examine "a number of factors" rather than a simple "mathematically precise" formula. * * * In ***First English***, the Court unambiguously and repeatedly characterized the issue to be decided as a "compensation question" or a "remedial question." [W]e identified two reasons why a regulation temporarily denying an owner all use of her property might not constitute a taking. First, we recognized that "the county might avoid the conclusion that a compensable taking had occurred by establishing that the denial of all use was insulated as a part of the State's authority to enact safety regulations." Second, we limited our holding "to the facts presented" and recognized "the quite different questions that would arise in the case of normal delays in obtaining building permits, changes in zoning ordinances, variances, and the like which [were] not before us."

Similarly, our decision in *Lucas* is not dispositive of the question presented. * * * Certainly, our holding [in *Lucas*] that the permanent "obliteration of the value" of a fee simple estate constitutes a categorical taking does not answer the question whether a regulation prohibiting any economic use of land for a 32-month period has the same legal effect. Petitioners seek to bring this case under the rule announced in *Lucas* by arguing that we can effectively sever a 32-month segment from the remainder of each landowner's fee simple estate, and then ask whether that segment has been taken in its entirety by the moratoria. Of course, defining the property interest taken in terms of the very regulation being challenged is circular. With property so divided, every delay would become a total ban; the moratorium and the normal permit process alike would constitute categorical takings. Petitioners' * * * argument is unavailing because it ignores *Penn Central's* admonition that in regulatory takings cases we must focus on "the parcel as whole." * * *

Neither *Lucas*, nor *First English,* nor any of our other regulatory takings cases compels us to accept petitioners' categorical submission. In fact, these cases make clear that the categorical rule in *Lucas* was carved out for the "extraordinary case" in which a regulation permanently deprives property of all value; the default rule remains that, in the regulatory taking context, we require a more fact specific inquiry. Nevertheless, we will consider whether the interest in protecting individual property owners from bearing public burdens "which, in all fairness and justice, should be borne by the public as a whole," justifies creating a new rule for these circumstances.

[T]he ultimate constitutional question is whether the concepts of "fairness and justice" that underlie the Takings Clause will be better served by one of these categorical rules or by a *Penn Central* inquiry into all of the relevant circumstances in particular cases. From that perspective, the extreme categorical rule that any deprivation of all economic use, no matter how brief, constitutes a compensable taking surely cannot be sustained. Petitioners' broad submission would apply to numerous "normal delays in obtaining building permits, changes in zoning ordinances, variances, and the like," as well as to orders temporarily prohibiting access to crime scenes, businesses that violate health codes, fire-damaged buildings, or other areas that we cannot now foresee. Such a rule would undoubtedly require changes in numerous practices that have long been considered permissible exercises of the police power. As Justice Holmes warned in *Mahon,* "[g]overnment hardly could go on if to some extent values incident to property could not be diminished without paying for every such change in the general law." A rule that required compensation for every delay in the use of property would render routine government processes prohibitively expensive or encourage hasty decisionmaking.

* * *A narrower rule that excluded the normal delays associated with processing permits, or that covered only delays of more than a year, would certainly have a less severe impact on prevailing practices, but it would still

impose serious financial constraints on the planning process. Unlike the "extraordinary circumstance" in which the government deprives a property owner of all economic use, *Lucas,* moratoria * * * are used widely among land-use planners to preserve the status quo while formulating a more permanent development strategy. In fact, the consensus in the planning community appears to be that moratoria, or "interim development controls" as they are often called, are an essential tool of successful development. Yet even the weak version of petitioners' categorical rule would treat these interim measures as takings regardless of the good faith of the planners, the reasonable expectations of the landowners, or the actual impact of the moratorium on property values.

* * * The interest in facilitating informed decisionmaking by regulatory agencies counsels against adopting a *per se* rule that would impose such severe costs on their deliberations. Otherwise, * * * compensating property owners during a moratorium may force officials to rush through the planning process or to abandon the practice altogether. To the extent that communities are forced to abandon using moratoria, landowners will have incentives to develop their property quickly before a comprehensive plan can be enacted, thereby fostering inefficient and ill-conceived growth.

* * * It may well be true that any moratorium that lasts for more than one year should be viewed with special skepticism. But given the fact that the District Court found that the 32 months required by TRPA to formulate the 1984 Regional Plan was not unreasonable, we could not possibly conclude that every delay of over one year is constitutionally unacceptable. * * * We conclude, therefore, that the interest in "fairness and justice" will be best served by relying on the familiar *Penn Central* approach when deciding cases like this, rather than by attempting to craft a new categorical rule.

Accordingly, the judgment of the Court of Appeals is affirmed.

Chief Justice Rehnquist, with whom Justice Scalia and Justice Thomas join, dissenting. For over half a decade petitioners were prohibited from building homes, or any other structures, on their land. Because the Takings Clause requires the government to pay compensation when it deprives owners of all economically viable use of their land, see *Lucas*, and because a ban on all development lasting almost six years does not resemble any traditional land-use planning device, I dissent. [T]he Court ignores much of the impact of respondent's conduct on petitioners. Instead, it relies on the flawed determination of the Court of Appeals that the relevant time period lasted only from August 1981 until April 1984. During that period, Ordinance 81-5 and Regulation 83-21 prohibited development pending the adoption of a new regional land-use plan. The adoption of the 1984 Regional Plan did not, however, change anything from petitioners' standpoint.

After the adoption of the 1984 Plan, petitioners still could make no use of their land.

The Court of Appeals disregarded this post-April 1984 deprivation on the ground that respondent did not "cause" it * * * because the Plan actually allowed permits to issue for the construction of single-family residences. Those permits were never issued because the District Court immediately issued a temporary restraining order, and later a permanent injunction that lasted until 1987, prohibiting the approval of any building projects under the 1984 Plan. Thus, the Court of Appeals concluded that the "1984 Plan itself could not have constituted a taking," because it was the injunction, not the Plan, that prohibited development during this period. The Court of Appeals is correct that the 1984 Plan did not cause petitioners' injury. But that is the right answer to the wrong question. The causation question is not limited to whether the 1984 Plan caused petitioners' injury; the question is whether respondent caused petitioners' injury. * * *

The injunction in this case issued because the 1984 Plan did not comply with the 1980 Tahoe Regional Planning Compact and regulations issued pursuant to the Compact. And, of course, respondent is responsible for the Compact and its regulations. * * * It follows that respondent was the "moving force" behind petitioners' inability to develop their land from April 1984 through the enactment of the 1987 plan. Without the environmental thresholds established by the Compact and Resolution 82-11, the 1984 Plan would have gone into effect and petitioners would have been able to build single-family residences. And it was certainly foreseeable that development projects exceeding the environmental thresholds would be prohibited; indeed, that was the very purpose of enacting the thresholds. Because respondent caused petitioners' inability to use their land from 1981 through 1987, that is the appropriate period of time from which to consider their takings claim. * * *

The Court does not dispute that petitioners were forced to leave their land economically idle during this period. But the Court refuses to apply *Lucas* on the ground that the deprivation was "temporary." Neither the Takings Clause nor our case law supports such a distinction. For one thing, a distinction between "temporary" and "permanent" prohibitions is tenuous. The "temporary" prohibition in this case that the Court finds is not a taking lasted almost six years. The "permanent" prohibition that the Court held to be a taking in *Lucas* lasted less than two years.

[E]ven if a practical distinction between temporary and permanent deprivations were plausible, to treat the two differently in terms of takings law would be at odds with the justification for the *Lucas* rule. The *Lucas* rule is derived from the fact that a "total deprivation of beneficial use is, from the landowner's point of view, the equivalent of a physical appropriation." The regulation in *Lucas* was the "practical equivalence" of a long-term physical appropriation, *i.e.*, a condemnation, so the Fifth Amendment required compensation. * * *From petitioners' standpoint, what happened in this case is no different than if the government had taken a 6-year lease of their property.

* * * *Lucas* is implicated when the government deprives a landowner of "all economically beneficial or productive use of land." The District Court found, and the Court agrees, that the moratorium "temporarily" deprived petitioners of "all economically viable use of their land." Because the rationale for the *Lucas* rule applies just as strongly in this case, the "temporary" denial of all viable use of land for six years is a taking. * * *

We noted in *First English* that our discussion of temporary takings did not apply "in the case of normal delays in obtaining building permits, changes in zoning ordinances, variances, and the like." * * *But a moratorium prohibiting all economic use for a period of six years is not one of the longstanding, implied limitations of state property law. * * *As for moratoria that prohibit all development, these do not have the lineage of permit and zoning requirements and thus it is less certain that property is acquired under the "implied limitation" of a moratorium prohibiting all development.

But this case does not require us to decide as a categorical matter whether moratoria prohibiting all economic use are an implied limitation of state property law, because the duration of this "moratorium" far exceeds that of ordinary moratoria. * * *Because the prohibition on development of nearly six years in this case cannot be said to resemble any "implied limitation" of state property law, it is a taking that requires compensation. * * *

## G. THE COASTAL ZONE MANAGEMENT ACT.

In the Coastal Zone Management Act, 16 U.S.C.A. §§ 1451-1464, Congress encouraged the states, through grants of federal funds and authority to veto federal projects, to control development of their coastal areas. See Weinberg, *Coastal Area Legislation*, 6 Seton Hall Legis. Journal 317 (1983):[a]

---

[a]Reprinted by permission of the publisher.

Congress found that there was a "national interest in the effective management, beneficial use, protection and development of the coastal zone." The coastal zone encompasses coastal waters and adjacent shorelands and wetlands, including the shores of the Great Lakes. Under its terms, the federal government will pay up to eighty percent of a state's costs of developing a management program approved by the Secretary of Commerce. In addition, the Coastal Zone Management Act's most dramatic provision requires federal agencies conducting, funding, or permitting activities directly affecting a state's coastal zone to conform with the state's coastal zone management plan to the maximum extent practicable.[b] Generally, the Coastal Zone Management Act encourages state control over land use in coastal areas.

California responded to the congressional invitation to states to manage their coastal and offshore resources by enacting a coastal management program; it was approved by the Secretary of Commerce in 1977. In addition, the State created the Coastal Commission with jurisdiction throughout its shorelands and offshore areas to control land use by issuing permits for development. California's management program was upheld by the federal courts against the claim that it unduly restricted offshore drilling for oil and gas. In *California v. Watt* [520 F.Supp. 1359 (S.D.Cal. 1981)], the State was able to enjoin the Secretary of the Interior from preparing an offshore oil lease sale in federal waters nine miles off the California coast.

The controversy in *California v. Watt* arose when the Secretary of the Interior announced the lease sale of twenty-nine tracts in the Santa Maria Basin, off Santa Barbara, California. The State argued that the drilling and the risk of spills would endanger water quality, fishing and shellfishing, recreation and the existence of the southern sea otter and the gray whale.

> The District Court had "no difficulty in finding. . . a direct effect [on] the coastal zone." The court enjoined the Secretary of the Interior, James Watt, from proceeding with pre-leasing activities as not conforming to the State's management plan to the maximum extent practicable. This action was taken even though leases are expressly exempted from the conformity provisions of the Act. Shortly after this decision, the Secretary withdrew other proposed lease sales in four other basins off the California coast because of the * * * ruling.

The Court of Appeals affirmed, 683 F.2d 1253. The Supreme Court, however, reversed in a 5-4 decision, *Secretary of Interior v. California*, 464 U.S. 312, 104 S. Ct. 656, 78 L.Ed.2d 496 (1984), holding the lease sale did not "directly

---

[b] *Cf.* Clean Water Act § 401, discussed in Chapter 7, allowing a state to bar a federally licensed project which it finds will contravene state water quality standards.

affect the coastal zone," as required by the Act. The majority conceded that subsequent exploration and drilling pursuant to the lease sale would do so, and thus could be barred by the state.

A 1990 amendment to the Act expressly requires oil and gas leases to be consistent with approved state coastal plans. 16 U.S.C.A. § 1456(c)(3)(B).

## H. STRIP MINING

Another environmentally critical activity regulated by Congress is that of strip mining, a now-prevalent form of mining that, unless closely controlled, levels forests, causes erosion and silting of streams, and destroys farm land. The Surface Mining Control and Reclamation Act of 1977, 30 U.S.C.A. §§ 1201-1328, requires strip mining operators to restore land to its approximate original contours, and has particularly stringent provisions mandating the operator to demonstrate its capacity to restore prime farmland to its original agricultural yield.

This statute was upheld against the predictable claims of lack of federal power, Tenth Amendment interference with state sovereignty and *de facto* taking in *Hodel v. Virginia Surface Mining and Reclamation Assn.*, 452 U.S. 264, 101 S. Ct. 2352, 69 L.Ed.2d 1 (1981), and *Hodel v. Indiana*, 452 U.S. 314, 101 S. Ct. 2376, 69 L.Ed. 2d 40 (1981). The Court held Congress had ample power under the Commerce Clause and did not interfere with any constitutionally protected right of the states. It ruled a taking claim premature in a challenge to the statute on its face, noting that a landowner is free to claim a taking in a suit based on a specific showing that the Act bars him or her from earning a reasonable return.

An important decision involving strip mining and the Clean Water Act is discussed in Chapter 7, Subsection B.

## I. BILLBOARDS AND ESTHETIC CONTROLS

We saw in Chapter 2 the reluctance of the courts to render essentially esthetic decisions, such as the propriety of the Gettysburg tower. Courts are far more comfortable in the role of reviewing determinations made by a local board of architectural review. See *Iodice v. Architectural Access Bd.*, 424 Mass. 370, 676 N.E.2d 1130 (1997). In addition, the *Scenic Hudson* decision (Chapter 1[A]) was largely about the proposed power plant's visual impacts.

Localities may regulate billboards along streets and highways, where both esthetics and safety (distraction to drivers) converge. Is such regulation requiring the removal of a billboard a taking of the owner's property? See *Modjeska Sign Studios, Inc. v. Berle*, 43 N.Y.2d 468, 373 N.E.2d 255, 402 N.Y.S.2d 359 (1977) (not if done for safety). Is it a violation of First Amendment rights of free expression?

*Metromedia, Inc. v. City of San Diego*, 453 U.S. 490, 101 S.Ct. 2882, 69 L.Ed.2d 800 (1981), upheld the power of a locality to prohibit commercial billboards, rejecting a free speech challenge. But the regulation failed because it allowed on-site commercial billboards ("Eat at Joe's" atop Joe's Restaurant) while banning on-site billboards with political, religious or other messages entitled to greater protection than commercial speech.

The taking issue as to highway billboards has been clouded by a federal statute. The Highway Beautification Act of 1965, 23 U.S.C.A. § 131, reduced federal highway funds to states that failed to remove billboards within 660 feet of federally-funded highways. It was initially quite effective. However, a 1978 amendment mandates "compensation" to the owner of any billboard, whether or not near a federally-aided road, if a state or local government requires its removal. See § 131(g).

This naturally deterred state and local billboard regulation. Did it exceed what the Fourteenth Amendment would require on de facto taking principles? Can Congress so legislate?

The New York courts take the view that "compensation" under this statute is furnished if the billboard's cost is amortized at the time it is removed. See *Suffolk Outdoor Advertising Co. v. Town of Southampton,* 60 N.Y.2d 70, 455 N.E.2d 1265, 468 N.Y.S.2d 450 (1983).

Auto junkyards are subject to a similar Highway Beautification Act provision, 23 U.S.C.A. § 136, reducing federal highway funds to states that fail to require junkyards to be screened from highways. Here, too, owners must be compensated if the state or locality requires the junkyard to be removed or relocated.

# 4. PROTECTION OF FISH AND WILDLIFE

## Introductory Note

Along with nuisance and riparian rights, regulation of the taking of fish and game is one of the oldest and most fundamental areas of conservation law. Statutes limiting the harvest of fish and wildlife, establishing seasons and requiring licenses were enacted in the last century. The courts have recognized this subject as one of the basic areas for exercise of the states' police power. Indeed, until recently fish and wildlife were deemed the property of the state under a common law rule recognized by the Supreme Court in *Geer v. Connecticut*, 161 U.S. 519, 16 S.Ct 600, 40 L.Ed. 793 (1896), and followed until *Hughes v. Oklahoma, infra.*

Significant Federal intervention in the area commenced with treaties protecting migratory birds, such as the Supreme Court dealt with in *Missouri v. Holland.*

## A. POWER TO REGULATE WILDLIFE

MISSOURI v. HOLLAND, Supreme Court of the United States, 1920. 252 U.S. 416, 40 S.Ct. 382, 64 L.Ed. 641.

Mr. Justice Holmes delivered the opinion of the court.

This is a bill in equity brought by the State of Missouri to prevent a game warden of the United States from attempting to enforce the Migratory Bird Treaty Act of July 3, 1918, c. 128, 40 Stat. 755, and the regulations made by the Secretary of Agriculture in pursuance of the same. The ground of the bill is that the statute is an unconstitutional interference with the rights reserved to the States by the Tenth Amendment and that the acts of the defendant done and threatened under that authority invade the sovereign right of the State and contravene its will manifested in statues. The State also alleges a pecuniary interest, as owner of the wild birds within its borders and otherwise, admitted by the Government to be sufficient, but it is enough that the bill is a reasonable and proper means to assert the alleged quasi sovereign rights of a State. A motion to dismiss was sustained by the District Court on the ground that the act of Congress is constitutional.

On December 8, 1916, a treaty between the United States and Great Britain was proclaimed by the President. It recited that many species of birds in their annual migrations traversed certain parts of the United States and of Canada, that they were of great value as a source of food and in destroying insects injurious to vegetation, but were in danger of extermination through lack of adequate protection. It therefore provided for specified close seasons and protection in other forms, and agreed that the two powers would take or propose to their law-making bodies the necessary measurers for carrying the treaty out.

[The resulting Act of Congress] prohibited the killing, capturing or selling any of the migratory birds included in the terms of the treaty except as permitted by regulations compatible with those terms, to be made by the Secretary of Agriculture. Regulations were proclaimed on July 31, and October 25, 1918.

[The issue before us is] whether the treaty and statute are void as an interference with the rights reserved to the States.

To answer this question it is not enough to refer to the Tenth Amendment, reserving the powers not delegated to the United States, because by Article II, § 2, the power to make treaties is delegated expressly, and by Article VI treaties made under the authority of the United States along with the Constitution and laws of the United States made in pursuance thereof, are declared the supreme law of the land. If the treaty is valid there can be no dispute about the validity of the statute under Article I, § 8, as a necessary and proper means to execute the powers of the Government. The language of the Constitution as to the supremacy of treaties being general, the question before us is narrowed to an inquiry into the ground upon which the present supposed exception is placed.

It is said that a treaty cannot be valid if it infringes the Constitution, that there are limits, therefore, to the treaty-making power, and that one such limit is that what an act of Congress could not do unaided, in derogation of the powers reserved to the States, a treaty cannot do. An earlier act of Congress that attempted by itself and not in pursuance of a treaty to regulate the killing of migratory birds within the States had been held bad in the District Court. *United States v. Shauver*, 214 Fed. Rep. 154. *United States v. McCullagh*, 221 Fed. Rep. 288. Those decisions were supported by arguments that migratory birds were owned by the States in their sovereign capacity for the benefit of their people, and that under cases like *Geer v. Connecticut*, this control was one that Congress had no power to displace. The same argument is supposed to apply now with equal force.

Whether the two cases cited were decided rightly or not they cannot be accepted as a test of the treaty power. Acts of Congress are the supreme law of the land only when made in pursuance of the Constitution, while treaties are declared to be so when made under the authority of the United States. [T]here may be matters of the sharpest exigency for the national well being that an act of Congress could not deal with but that a treaty followed by such an act could, and it is not lightly to be assumed that, in matters requiring national action. "a power which must belong to and somewhere reside in every civilized government" is not to be found. *Andrews v. Andrews,* 188 U.S. 14, 33. What was said in that case with regard to the powers of the States applies with equal force to the powers of the nation in cases where the States individually are incompetent to act. We are not yet discussing the particular case before us but only are considering the validity of the test proposed. With regard to that we may add that when we are dealing with words that also are a constituent act, like the Constitution of the United States, we must realize that they have called into life a being the development of which could not have been foreseen completely by the most gifted of its begetters. It was enough for them to realize or to hope that they had created an organism; it has taken a century and has cost their successors much sweat and blood to prove that they created a nation. The case before us must be considered in the light of our whole experience and not merely in that of what was said a hundred years ago. The treaty in question does not contravene any prohibitory words to be found in the Constitution. The only question is whether it is forbidden by some invisible radiation from the general terms of the Tenth Amendment. We must consider what this country has become in deciding what that Amendment has reserved.

The State * * * founds its claim of exclusive authority upon an assertion of title to migratory birds, an assertion that is embodied in statute. No doubt it is true that as between a Sate and its inhabitants the State may regulate the killing and sale of such birds, but it does not follow that its authority is exclusive of paramount powers. To put the claim of the State upon title is to lean upon a slender reed. Wild birds are not in the possession of anyone; and possession is the beginning of ownership. The whole foundation of the State's rights is the presence within their jurisdiction of birds that yesterday had not arrived, tomorrow may be in another State and in a week a thousand miles away. If we are to be accurate we cannot put the case of the State upon higher ground than that the treaty deals with creatures that for the moment are within the state borders, that it must be carried out by officers of the United States within the same territory, and that but for the treaty the State would be free to regulate this subject itself.

As most of the laws of the United States are carried out within the States and as many of them deal with matters which in the silence of such laws the State might regulate, such general grounds are not enough to support Missouri's claim. Valid treaties of course "are as binding within the territorial limits of the States as they are elsewhere throughout the dominion of the United States." *Baldwin v. Franks*, 120 U.S. 678, 683. No doubt the great body of private relations usually fall within the control of the State, but a treaty may override its power.* * *

Here a national interest of very nearly the first magnitude is involved. It can be protected only by national action in concert with that of another power. The subject-matter is only transitorily within the State and has no permanent habitat therein. But for the treaty and the statute there soon might be no birds for any powers to deal with. We see nothing in the Constitution that compels the Government to sit by while a food supply is cut off and the protectors of our forests and our crops are destroyed. It is not sufficient to rely upon the States. The reliance is vain and were it otherwise, the question is whether the United States is forbidden to act. We are of opinion that the treaty and statute must be upheld.

Notes

Note that the state based its claim of exclusive power to regulate the taking of migratory birds on its title to wildlife as established in *Geer* v. *Connecticut*, discussed *supra*. As early as 1920 Justice Holmes in *Missouri v. Holland* described this title as "a slender reed" on which to support a claim of exclusive authority. The reed snapped in *Hughes v. Oklahoma*.

HUGHES v. OKLAHOMA, Supreme Court of the United States, 1979. 441 U.S. 332, 99 S.Ct. 1727, 60 L.Ed.2d 250.

Mr. Justice Brennan delivered the opinion of the Court.

The question presented for decision is whether Okla. Stat., Title 29, § 4-115(b) violates the Commerce Clause, Art I, § 8, cl.3, of the United States Constitution, insofar as it provides that "No person may transport or ship minnows for sale outside the state which were seined or procured within the waters of this state.* * *

Appellant William Hughes holds a Texas license to operate a commercial minnow business near Wichita Falls, Tex. An Oklahoma Game Ranger arrested him on a charge of violating § 4-115(b) by transporting from Oklahoma to Wichita Falls a load of natural minnows purchased from a minnow dealer licensed to do business in Oklahoma. Hughes' defense that § 4-115(b) was unconstitutional because it was repugnant to the Commerce Clause was rejected, and he was convicted and fined. The Oklahoma Court of Criminal Appeals affirmed, stating:

> The United States Supreme Court has held on numerous occasions that the wild animals and fish within a state's border are, so far as capable of ownership, owned by the state in its sovereign capacity for the common benefit of all its people. Because of such ownership, and in the exercise of its police power, the state may regulate and control the taking, subsequent use and property rights that may be acquired therein. [T]he law serve[s] to protect against the depletion of minnows in Oklahoma's natural streams through commercial exportation. No person is allowed to export natural minnows for sale outside of Oklahoma. Such a prohibition is not repugnant to the commerce clause* * *

We reverse. *Geer* v. *Connecticut*, on which the Court of Criminal Appeals relied, is overruled. In that circumstance, § 4-115(B) cannot survive appellant's Commerce Clause attack.

*Geer* sustained against a Commerce Clause challenge a statute forbidding the transportation beyond the State of game birds that had been lawfully killed within the State. The decision rested on the holding that no interstate commerce was involved. This conclusion followed in turn from the view that the State had the power, as representative for its citizens, who "owned" in common all wild animals within the State, to control not only the *taking* of game but the *ownership* of game that had been lawfully reduced to possession. By virtue of this power, Connecticut could qualify the ownership of wild game taken within the State by, for example, prohibiting its removal from the State: "The common ownership imports the right to keep the property, if the sovereign so chooses, always within its jurisdiction for every purpose." Accordingly, the State's power to qualify ownership raised serious doubts whether the sale or exchange of wild game constituted "commerce" at all; in any event the Court held that the qualification imposed by the challenged statute removed any transactions involving wild game killed in Connecticut from *interstate* commerce.* * *

Mr. Justice Field and the first Mr. Justice Harlan dissented, rejecting as artificial and formalistic the Court's analysis of "ownership" and "commerce" in wild game. They would have affirmed the State's power to provide for the protection of wild game, but only "so far as such protection . . . does not contravene the power of Congress in the regulation of interstate commerce." Their view was that "[w]hen an animal . . . is lawfully killed for the purposes of food or other uses of man, it becomes an article of commerce, and its use cannot be limited to the citizens of one state to the exclusion of citizens of another state."

The view of the Geer dissenters increasingly prevailed in subsequent cases. Indeed, not only has the Geer analysis been rejected when natural resources other than wild game were involved, but even state regulations of wild game have been held subject to the strictures of the Commerce Clause under the pretext of distinctions from Geer.* * *

Today's principle is that stated in *Pike v. Bruce Church, Inc.*, 397 U.S. 137, 142, 90 S.Ct. 844, 25 L.Ed.2d 174 (1970):

Where the statute regulates evenhandedly to effectuate a legitimate local public interest, and its effects on interstate commerce are only incidental, it will be upheld unless the burden imposed on such commerce is clearly excessive in relation to the putative local benefits. . . If a legitimate local purpose is found, then the question becomes one of degree. And the extent of the burden that will be tolerated will of course depend on the nature of the local interest involved, and on whether it could be promoted as well with a lesser impact on interstate activities.

This formulation was employed only last Term to strike down New Jersey's attempt to "conserve" the natural resource of landfill areas within the State for the disposal of waste generated within the State. *[City of] Philadelphia v. New Jersey.*[a]

The Geer analysis has also been eroded to the point of virtual extinction in cases involving regulation of wild animals. The first challenge to Geer's theory of

---

[a]Discussed in Chapter 9.

a State's power over wild animals came in *Missouri* v. *Holland* [, where] Justice Holmes upheld the Act as a proper exercise of the treatymaking power. He commented in passing on the artificiality of the *Geer* rationale: "To put the claim of the State upon title is to lean upon a slender reed."* * *

[See also] *Douglas v. Seacoast Products, Inc.*, 431 U.S. 265, 97 S.Ct. 1740, 52 L.Ed.2d 304 (1977), rejecting the argument that Virginia's "ownership" of fish swimming in its territorial waters empowered the State to forbid fishing by federally licensed ships owned by nonresidents while permitting residents to fish, Seacoast Products explicitly embraced the analysis of the Geer dissenters:

A State does not stand in the same position as the owner of a private game preserve and it is pure fantasy to talk of "owning" wild fish, birds, or animals. Neither the States nor the Federal Government, any more than a hopeful fisherman or hunter, has title to these creatures until they are reduced to possession by skillful capture. . . . *Geer v. Connecticut* (Field, J., dissenting). The "ownership" language of cases such as those cited by appellant must be understood as no more than a 19th-century legal fiction expressing "the importance to its people that a State have power to preserve and regulate the exploitation of an important resource." . . . Under modern analysis, the question is simply whether the State has exercised its police power in conformity with the federal laws and the Constitution.

The case before us is the first in modern times to present facts essentially on all fours with *Geer*. We now conclude that challenges under the Commerce Clause to state regulations of wild animals should be considered according to the same general rule applied to state regulations of other natural resources, and therefore expressly overrule Geer. We thus bring our analytical framework into conformity with practical realities. Overruling Geer also eliminates the anomaly, created by the decisions distinguishing Geer, that statutes imposing the most extreme burdens on interstate commerce (essentially total embargoes) were the most immune from challenge. At the same time, the general rule we adopt in this case makes ample allowance for preserving, in ways not inconsistent with the Commerce Clause, the legitimate state concerns for conservation and protection of wild animals underlying the 19th century legal fiction of state ownership.

Section 4-115(B) on its face discriminates against interstate commerce. It forbids the transportation of natural minnows out of the State for purposes of sale and thus "overtly blocks the flow of interstate commerce at [the] State's border." *[City of] Philadelphia v. New Jersey, supra*. Oklahoma argues that § 4-115(b) serves a legitimate local purpose in that it is "readily apparent as a conservation measure."

The State's interest in maintaining the ecological balance in state waters by avoiding the removal of inordinate numbers of minnows may well quality as a legitimate local purpose. We consider the States' interests in conservation and protection of wild animals as legitimate local purposes similar to the States' interests in protecting the health and safety of their citizens.* * * But the scope of legitimate state interests in "conservation" is narrower under this analysis than it was under Geer. A State may no longer "keep the property, if the sovereign so chooses, always within its jurisdiction for every purpose." *Geer v. Connecticut.* The fiction of state ownership may no longer be used to force those outside the State to bear the full costs of "conserving" the wild animals within its borders when equally effective nondiscriminatory conservation measures are available.* * *

Far from choosing the least discriminatory alternative, Oklahoma has chosen to "conserve" its minnows in the way that most overtly discriminates against interstate commerce. The State places no limits on the numbers of minnows that can be taken by licensed minnow dealers; nor does it limit in any way how these minnows may be disposed of within the State. Yet it forbids the transportation of any commercially significant number of natural minnows out of the State of sale. Section 4-115(B) is certainly not a "last ditch" attempt at conservation after nondiscriminatory alternatives have proven unfeasible. It is rather a choice of the most discriminatory means even though nondiscriminatory alternatives would seem likely to fulfill the State's purported legitimate local purpose more effectively.* * *

The overruling of Geer does not leave the States powerless to protect and conserve wild animal life within their borders. Today's decision makes clear, however, that States may promote this legitimate purpose only in ways consistent with the basic principle that "our economic unit is the Nation," *H.P. Hood & Sons, Inc. v. Du Mond*, 336 U.S. at 537, 69 S.Ct. 657, 93 L.Ed. 865, and that when a wild animal "becomes an article of commerce . . . its use cannot be limited to the citizens of one State to the exclusion of citizens of another State." *Geer v. Connecticut* (Field, J., dissenting).

We therefore hold that § 4-115(b) is repugnant to the Commerce Clause.

Reversed.

## Notes

Suppose the Oklahoma legislature hadn't fished in such troubled waters, and had written a statute which did not discriminate against interstate commerce? How much power do the states retain over fish and wildlife within their borders?

For an example of a statute that p assed the *Hughes* test, see *Maine v. Taylor*, 477 U.S. 131, 106 S. Ct. 2440, 91 L.Ed.2d 110 (1986), sustaining a provision barring the importation of baitfish. The court found concern over a parasite, not easily detected, that Maine baitfish could catch, justified the ban.

*Baldwin* v. *Fish and Game Commission*, 436 U.S. 371, 98 S.Ct. 1852, 56 L.Ed.2d 354 (1978), upheld a Montana law imposing a $225 fee on non-resident elk hunters. Residents paid between $9 and $30 to hunt elk. The vast disparity in fees was upheld as not contravening the Privileges and Immunities Clause since "[t]he elk supply, which has been entrusted to the care of the State by the people of Montana, is finite and must be carefully tended in order to be preserved." The Court also rejected a challenge based on the Equal Protection Clause, finding a rational basis for the disparity since non-residents, who do not pay significant taxes to the state, may be required to help support conservation and forestry programs.

All states charge non-residents more for hunting and fishing licenses. *Baldwin* upheld a far greater disparity than most as against Privileges and Immunities and Equal Protection Clause claims.

In *Douglas v. Seacoast Products, Inc.*, 431 U.S. 265, 97 S.Ct. 1740, 52 L.Ed.2d 304 (1977), also discussed in *Hughes*, the Court held that under the Supremacy Clause Virginia was preempted by federal law from limiting the right of non-residents to fish in Virginia's waters. The Court did not reach the Commerce Clause issue. It held the plaintiffs' federal licenses "to be employed in carrying on the * * * mackerel fishery" preempted the State from restricting non-residents' fishing rights.

The Interior Department's offshore oil drilling program, discussed in Chapter 7, raises serious issues of protection of fishing and shell-fishing grounds. See in particular *Commonwealth v. Andrus*. The Marine Protection, Research and Sanctuaries Act allows the Secretary of Commerce to select as marine sanctuaries areas he decides are "necessary for the purpose of preserving or restoring" for, among other things, conservation of fisheries. The same purpose, more specifically preventing over-fishing and depletion of stocks, motivated Congress to enact the Magnuson-Stevens Fishery Conservation and Management Act, known as the Magnuson Act, creating a 200-mile economic unit off the coast of the United States, within which federal fishery protection laws must be obeyed. See 46 U.S.C.A. § 1811 (1977).

The over-fishing issue has international dimensions. It led Newfoundland to impose a moratorium on cod fishing in the 1990s in hopes that depleted stocks would restore themselves. Much of the over-fishing in Canada's Grand Banks and elsewhere has been done by factory trawlers from other countries. This has resulted in the Straddling Stocks Treaty of 1995, restricting over-fishing of stocks that straddle national 200-mile economic zones. The treaty authorizes the boarding and inspection of ships of member states and bans on ships found in violation of catch limits. Non-member states' ships can be barred from areas subject to over-fishing. See Mack, *International Fisheries Management: How the U.N. Conference on Straddling and Highly Migratory Fish Stocks Changes the Law of Fishing on the High Seas*, 26 Cal. W. Intl. L.J. 313 (1996).

## B. PROTECTION OF ENDANGERED SPECIES

A.E. NETTLETON CO. v. DIAMOND, New York Court of Appeals, 1971. 27 N.Y.2d 182, 264 N.E.2d 118, 315 N.Y.S.2d 625. App. dism. *sub nom. Reptile Products Assn. v. Diamond,* 401 U.S. 969.

Scileppi, J.

Appellants, consisting of several officials of the State of New York (hereinafter referred to as the State) have taken a direct appeal to our court from a judgment of the Supreme Court, Onondaga County, which declared section 358-a of the Agriculture and Markets Law[a] to be contrary to the Fourteenth Amendment of the Constitution of the United States and article I (§ 6) of the New York State Constitution and enjoined enforcement of the aforesaid statute.

This appeal presents a problem of critical importance. Throughout history, man has relied upon the lower forms of life for food, clothing and shelter. Indeed, long before the advent of what historians have come to term the Commercial Revolution, the skins and pelts of animals had played an essential role in the development of man and his trade. In recent years, however, the scientific community has warned that since the year 1600, 130 animal species and 228 subspecies have become extinct and numerous other species will soon be lost the world forever unless something is done to curtail man's commercial exploitation of the wildlife of the world.

It was in response to the great need to preserve wildlife that the Legislature, sharing the concern expressed by the people of our State, Nation and planet, recently enacted * * * section 358-a of the Agriculture and Markets Law (hereinafter referred to as the Mason Law) which provides that after September 1, 1970: "1. No part of the skin or body, whether raw or manufactured, of the following species of wild animals or the animal itself may be sold or offered for sale by any individual, firm, corporation, association or partnership within the state of New York after the effective date of this section: Leopard, Snow Leopard, Clouded Leopard, Tiger, Cheetah, Alligators, Caiman or Crocodile of the Order Crocodylia, Vicuna, Red Wolf, or Polar Bear, nor after a period of twelve months from the effective date of this section, of the following species: Mountain Lion, sometimes called Cougar, Jaguar, Ocelot, or Margay." The Mason Law further provides for the issuance of warrants for the search and seizure and forfeiture of all goods held in violation of its provisions and for the issuance of licenses permitting the import of the forbidden species for "zoological, educational, and scientific purposes."

As a result of this legislation, the A.E. Nettleton Company, which has for over 90 years engaged in the manufacture, sale and distribution of men's footwear made from alligator, crocodile and caiman skins, initiated the instant action for a judgment declaring * * * the Mason Law to be unconstitutional and for an injunction enjoining [its] enforcement. [T]he sole question before us is the constitutional validity of the Mason Law. This requires a two-step analysis: (1) Does the State of New York have the power to legislate in this area and, if the answer is in the affirmative, (2) was that power validly exercised.

The Industry has made a two-fold attack on the power of the State of promulgate legislation in the area of wildlife preservation arguing that the Mason

[a]Now N.Y. Environmental Conservation Law § 11-0536.

Law violates both the Supremacy Clause (art. VI, § 2) and the Commerce Clause (art. I, § 8, cl. 3) of the Federal Constitution.* * *

Taking the Supremacy issue first, it is argued by the Industry that the recent Federal Endangered Species Conservation Act of 1969 is an elaborate, comprehensive and pervasive scheme of Federal regulations which necessitates the conclusion that State power has been curtailed and that the field of wildlife preservation has been preempted by Congress. This argument was rejected by the court below and we are in agreement with that court's resolution of this issue.

It is true that the Federal Act is a piece of comprehensive legislation which provides for the systematic prohibition of the importation into our country of certain species designated as endangered by the Secretary of the Interior, and requires the Secretary of State to promote the protection of threatened species in their countries or origin and regulates the importation of other species of animals by restricting points of entry and requiring documentation of origin.

The Industry's pre-emption argument is, however, not persuasive. In *Florida Avocado Growers v. Paul* (373 U.S. 132) the Supreme Court sustained the constitutionality of a California statute which prohibited the marketing within that State of a certain avocado which was marketable under Federal standards, and rejected the argument that the Federal legislation pre-empted State action, holding that pre-emption could only occur if there was "such actual conflict between the two schemes of regulation that both cannot stand in the same area [or] evidence of a congressional design to pre-empt the field." Turning to the first test (State power to legislate), there is no real conflict between the Federal statute and the Mason Law. While it is true that our State statute includes species which are not on the Federal list * * * there has been no showing that compliance with both the Federal and State law is an impossibility. Nor has it been demonstrated that the Mason Law could not be enforced without impairing the effectiveness of the Federal Act. The Industry has not shown that wildlife conservation is a matter exclusively within the sphere of Federal competence. On the contrary, it is almost axiomatic that wildlife conservation has been a matter traditionally left to the States (see *Barrett v. State of New York,* 220 N.Y. 423, 427). Thus, it would seem that the preemption question narrows down to whether Congress by the 1969 Act has evidenced its design to exclude State action. We think it has not. Federal displacement of the "historic police powers of the States" should not be decreed "unless that was the clear and manifest purpose of Congress" (*Rice v. Santa Fe Elevator Corp.,* 331 U.S. 218, 230). "In other words, we are not to conclude that Congress legislated the ouster [of the Mason Law by the Federal Act] in the absence of an unambiguous congressional mandate to that effect" (*Florida Avocado Growers v. Paul, supra,* at pp. 146-147). We find no such mandate. On the contrary, the Federal statute specifically provides for the enforcement of State laws such as the Mason Law. Section 7 of the Federal Act makes any person who: "(a)* * * (2) delivers, carries, transports, or ships, by any means whatever, or causes to be delivered, carried, transported, or shipped for commercial or noncommercial purposes or sells or causes to be sold in interstate or foreign commerce *any wildlife taken, transported, or sold in any manner in violation of any law or regulation of any State or foreign country*" (emphasis added) subject to the enforcement provisions of the Act.* * *

The Industry's argument that these sections refer only to State regulations of indigenous species lacks merit. We find no such requirement in the statute. At most the statute is ambiguous in this regard and thus falls short of the unequivocal intent which is necessary before we can decree pre-emption. Moreover, Congress has specifically given the State the power to enact legislation involving non-indigenous species. This statute (U.S. Code, title 16, § 667e) reads as follows: "§ 667e. Dead bodies of game animals or game or song birds, subject to laws of State. All dead bodies, or parts thereof, of any foreign game animals, or game or song birds the importation of which is prohibited, or the dead bodies, or parts thereof, of any wild game animals or game or song birds transported into any State or Territory, or remaining therein for use, consumption, sale, or storage therein, *shall upon arrival in such State or Territory be subject to the operation and effect of the laws of such State or Territory enacted in the exercise of its police powers, to the same extent and in the same manner as though such animals or birds had been produced in such State or Territory.*" (Emphasis added.)

The above-quoted statute is also dispositive of the Industry's contention that the Legislature lacked the power to enact the Mason Law under the Commerce Clause. In *People v. Bootman* (180 N.Y. 1) we construed section 667e and said: "The action of Congress has taken away all questions of interstate commerce, so that the state can act with entire freedom and can prevent the shipment of game into or out of its own territory; and if game is imported, it can regulate or prohibit the sale thereof." In any event, the Mason Act merely prohibits the sale or offer for sale, within New York State, of skins or products made from the forbidden species and it is our view that the Industry's Commerce Clause argument is untenable.

Inasmuch as the State clearly had the power to enact the Mason Law, the next question is whether that legislation represents a constitutional exercise of that power. The issue is again double-edged: (1) Is the Mason Law a valid exercise of the police power and, (2) does it deprive the Industry of property without due process of law.

At the outset it must be emphasized that "[t]he police power of the State is the least limitable of all the powers of government" (*Matter of Engelsher v. Jacobs*, 5 N.Y.2d 370, 373, cert. den. 360 U.S. 902) and we have sustained its application to the conservation of fish and wildlife (*Barrett v. State of New York, supra*) and other areas of beauty and esthetics. In *Barrett* (*supra*, at p. 428) we said: "The police power is not to be limited to guarding merely the physical or material interests of the citizen. His moral, intellectual and spiritual needs may also be considered. The eagle is preserved not for its use for its beauty."

Since wildlife conservation is within the police power, our inquiry is limited to the question whether the means employed are reasonable.* * *

A strong presumption of validity attaches to legislative enactments and a party who is attacking the constitutionality of a statute bears the heavy burden of establishing unconstitutionality beyond a reasonable doubt.

We find that in the instant case, the Industry has not met its burden. ["I]n order for an exercise of the police power to be valid, there must be 'some fair, just and reasonable connection' between it and the promotion of the health, comfort, safety and welfare of society." Viewed in this light, the Mason Law would be an unreasonable exercise of the police power only if we are able to say that it is *unreasonable* for the State of New York to declare that the interdiction of all sales or offers for sale of skins of certain animals or products made therefrom is necessary for the continued existence of those animals. Such a conclusion is not warranted in the instant case. The wildlife of the world is a vital asset to the people of this State. As the Legislature stated in the Harris Act:[b] "The legislature of the state of New York hereby finds that the protection of endangered species of wildlife is a matter of general state concern. The recently enacted Federal Endangered Species Conservation Act of 1969 provides for the protection of species of wildlife threatened with worldwide extinction and for restricting and regulating the interstate transportation of wildlife taken in violation of state, national or foreign laws. The states, however, must assume the responsibility of restricting the transportation, possession and sale of these species within their respective jurisdictions to assure the continued survival of many of the nation's endangered species of fish and wildlife. The legislature hereby finds that by eliminating the market for these species in New York State, the potential for their continued existence will be strengthened." The protection of the animals listed in the Mason Act is necessary not only for their natural beauty and for the purpose of biological study, but for the key role that they play in the maintenance of the life cycle. Thus, the protection of these animals is essential for the welfare of our society, and we do not agree with the Industry that the Mason Law goes too far.

The Industry, conceding that some degree of protection is necessary for the preservation of wildlife since it may ultimately affect the continued existence of their own business, argues that the Mason Law is a superfluous curtailment of their rights because adequate protection is afforded by both the Federal statute and the Harris Law and for the additional reason that some of the animals named in the Mason Act are not listed as endangered by the Secretary of the Interior. The wisdom of a particular statute is beyond the scope of judicial review (*Ferguson v. Skrupa*, 372 U.S. 726, 730; *Wasmuth v. Allen,* 14 N.Y.2d 391) and we should not substitute our judgment for that employed by the Legislature in enacting the statute in question. Implicit in the Industry's argument is the assumption that animals not on the Federal list are not threatened with extinction and do not require protection. The minutes of a hearing held prior to the enactment of the Mason Law reveal that the Legislature specifically considered whether the tiger, vicuna, red wolf, polar bear, mountain lion, jaguar, ocelot, margay, leopard,

---

[b]The Harris Act, now New York Environmental Conservation Law § 11-0535, also challenged in this case, makes possession of animals on the Secretary of Interior's endangered list unlawful.

cheetah, and crocodile are subjects of commercial exploitation and are threatened. Thus, it appears that the Legislature rejected the Industry's assumption and found otherwise. Accordingly, we do not have the power to disturb these findings.

The mere fact that an animal is not on the Federal list does not mean it is not endangered, since there is no agreement among experts in this field. For example, the Secretary of the Interior lists only four varieties of leopard and one Asian cheetah on the Federal list while the president of the East African Wildlife Society says that "all spotted cats in Africa [are] endangered, owing to the over commercialization of their skins." As we have seen, the Mason Law will, however, protect all of these animals and other threatened animals * * * which, though not within the Secretary of the Interior's technical definition of endangered species, are the subject of indiscriminate killing.

While it is true that the banning of "Alligators, Caiman or Crocodile of the Order Crocodylia" may include some reptiles which are in adequate supply, it is clear that the Legislature did so because it is practically impossible to determine, without expert detection at great expense, whether a given skin is from a threatened species or one that is not threatened. Thus, by preventing the sale or offer for sale within the State of skins or products made from the skins of animals listed in the Mason Law, one market for these goods is removed and the killing of these animals is rendered less lucrative. In so doing the Mason Law contributes to the effective enforcement of the Harris Law and the Federal Law. Moreover, it is also evident that poachers are not concerned with the niceties of animal classification and the prospective purchasers of animal skin products have no way of knowing which skins are from endangered species and which are not. If the Industry wishes to take issue with this view, it is our opinion that the proper procedure is for them to seek amendment of the statute. Furthermore, the Mason Law should provide an impetus to the Industry to develop methods of sustained yield breeding which would guarantee the existence of their business in the years to come.

[T]he evil in the instant case which the Legislature sought to prevent is as broad as the statute itself. All the listed animals need protection either because they are endangered or, in the case of the crocodiles, because processed skins of endangered animals for all practical purposes are indistinguishable from those in abundant supply.

As to the Industry's contention that the Mason Law is confiscatory, in that it bars all sales or offers for sale after September 1, 1970 thus rendering valueless the inventory on hand and imported into the State while it was legal to do so, we do not think that such a result was the intent of the Legislature. Such a prohibition could in no way effectuate the purpose of the Mason Law since it could not afford protection to the animals already destroyed. It is, therefore, our view that the Mason Law does not apply to skins, hides, or products therefrom which arrived in the United States of America on or before August 31, 1970.

Reversed.

Judges Fuld and Burke dissented.

Notes

The federal Endangered Species Act, 16 U.S.C.A. §§ 1531-1544, enacted in 1973 to supersede the Lacey Act discussed in *Nettleton*, preempts inconsistent state laws which "prohibit what is authorized pursuant to a [federal] exemption or permit." 16 U.S.C.A. §1535(f). Since alligators can now be taken and sold pursuant to federal permit, state efforts to bar the sale of such items must yield to the amended federal law--but only where the seller has a valid federal permit. *Fouke Co. v. Brown*, 463 F. Supp. 1142 (E. D. Cal 1979). However, if the federal permit is conditioned on the holder's also obeying state laws, then it does not shield him from state enforcement. *H.J. Justin & Sons, Inc. v. Brown*, 519 F. Supp. 1383, 1390 (E.D. Cal. 1981).

How far may state endangered species laws extend beyond a state's borders in "eliminating the market for these species" in that state? Suppose a New York corporation's salespeople write orders in Chicago for articles made of the hide of an animal proscribed by the Mason Law. Is that a sale or offer for sale "within the State of New York"? See *People v. Corum Watch Company*, 39 A.D.2d 513, 330 N.Y.S. 2d 186 (1st Dept. 1972), holding such sales illegal where the home office in New York must approve the order.

In *Nettleton* the court held the statute inapplicable to goods in New York the date it took effect, since "such a prohibition could in no way effectuate the purpose of the Mason Law,* * *." This holding avoided the plaintiffs' claim that such a construction would be an unconstitutional deprivation of property without due process of law. Several years later the Supreme Court dealt with that problem in the context of the federal law protecting eagles, and upheld the power of Congress to so legislate.

ANDRUS v. ALLARD, Supreme Court of the United States, 1979. 444 U.S. 51, 100 S.Ct. 318, 62 L.Ed.2d 210.

Brennan, J.

[Pursuant to the Eagle Protection Act, 16 U.S.C.A. § 668, the Secretary of the Interior promulgated regulations prohibiting commercial transactions in products made of bird parts including parts from birds legally killed prior to the passage of the Act. Appellees traded in Native American artifacts and sought compensation for their pre-existing inventory of eagle feathers.] In this case, it is crucial that appellees retain the rights to possess and transport their property, and to donate or devise the protected birds . . . [W]here an owner possesses a full 'bundle' of property rights, the destruction of one 'strand' of the bundle is not a taking.* * * It is, to be sure, undeniable that the regulations here prevent the most profitable use of appellees' property. Again, however, that is not dispositive. [I]t is not clear that appellees will be unable to derive economic benefit from the artifacts; for example, they might exhibit the artifacts for an admissions charge. At any rate, loss of future profits--unaccompanied by any physical property restriction--provides a slender reed upon which to rest a takings claim.* * * Regulations that bar trade in goods have been upheld against claims of unconstitutional taking. For example, the court has sustained regulations prohibiting the sale of alcoholic beverages despite the fact that individuals were left with previously acquired stocks.* * * We hold that the simple prohibition of the sale of lawfully acquired property in this case does not effect a taking in violation of the Fifth Amendment.

## Notes

Should a ban on foods processed with a preservative discovered to be carcinogenic result in a compensable taking with regard to pre-existing supplies? What about pre-existing stockpiles of a banned pesticide? Would it be valid to argue that society at large should bear these costs rather than manufacturers, processors, retailers or other holders in the chain of commercial distribution who were trading in goods society believed were beneficial, or at least harmless? In what way(s) are eagle feathers distinguishable from these other cases?

TENNESSEE VALLEY AUTHORITY v. HILL, Supreme Court of the United States, 1978. 437 U.S. 153, 98 S.Ct. 2279, 57 L.Ed.2d 117.

[The Tellico Dam was authorized by Congress in 1967 and funds were appropriated that year and every year thereafter. The snail darter, a 3-inch, previously unknown, species of perch, was discovered in 1973 in the waters of the Little Tennessee River in an area that the dam would inundate. The Secretary of the Interior declared the snail darter an endangered species under the Endangered Species Act of 1973, 16 U.S.C.A. §§ 1531 -1544, and the area its critical habitat. The act (§ 1536) requires all federal agencies to take "action necessary to insure that actions authorized, funded, or carried out by them do not jeopardize the continued existence of such endangered species * * * or result in the destruction or modification of [their critical] habitat * * *."]

Chief Justice Burger delivered the opinion of the Court.

The questions presented in this case are (a) whether the Endangered Species Act of 1973 requires a court to enjoin the operation of a virtually completed federal dam -- which had been authorized prior to 1973 -- when, pursuant to authority vested in him by Congress, the Secretary of the Interior has determined that operation of the dam would eradicate an endangered species; and (b) whether continued congressional appropriations for the dam after 1973 constituted an implied repeal of the Endangered Species Act, at least as to the particular dam.* * *

In explaining the expected impact of this provision on federal agencies, the House Committee's Report states:

> This subsection requires the Secretary and the heads of all other Federal departments and agencies to use their authorities in order to carry out programs for the protection of endangered species, and it further *requires* that those agencies take *the necessary action* that will *not jeopardize* the continuing existence of endangered species or result in the destruction of critical habitat of those species.* * *

The House manager of the bill, Representative Dingell, provided an interpretation of what the Conference bill would require, making it clear that the mandatory provisions of § 7 were not casually or inadvertently included: * * *

> [As] to the continental population of grizzly bears which may or may not be endangered, but which is surely threatened . . . Once this bill is enacted, the appropriate Secretary, whether of Interior, Agriculture or whatever, *will have to take action* to see that this situation is not permitted to worsen, and that these bears are not driven to extinction. The purposes of the bill included the conservation of the species and of the eco-systems upon which they depend, and *every agency of government is committed* to see that those purposes are carried out . . . [T]he agencies of Government can no longer plead that they can do nothing about it. *They can, and they must. The law is clear.* (Emphasis added.)

It is against this legislative background that we must measure TVA's claim that the Act was not intended to stop operation of a project which, like Tellico Dam, was near completion when an endangered species was discovered in its path. While there is no discussion in the legislative history of precisely this problem, the totality of congressional action makes it abundantly clear that the result we reach today is wholly in accord with both the words of the statute and the intent of Congress. The plain intent of Congress in enacting this statute was to halt and reverse the trend toward species extinction whatever the cost. This is reflected not only in the stated policies of the Act, but in literally every section of the statute. All persons, including federal agencies, are specifically instructed not to "take" endangered species, meaning that no one is "to harass, harm,[1] pursue, hunt, shoot, wound, kill, trap, capture, or collect" such life forms.* * *

---

[1] We do not understand how TVA intends to operate Tellico Dam without "harming" the snail darter. The Secretary of the Interior has defined the term "harm" to mean "an act or omission which actually injures or kills wildlife, including acts which annoy it to such an extent as to significantly disrupt essential behavioral patterns, which include, but are not limited to, *breeding, feeding or sheltering; significant environmental modification or degradation which has such effects is included within the meaning of 'harm.'*" 50 C.F.R. § 17.3.

Agencies in particular are directed by §§ 2(c) and 3(2) of the Act to "use * * * *all methods* and procedures which are necessary" to preserve endangered species (emphasis added). In addition, the legislative history undergirding § 7 reveals an explicit congressional decision to require agencies to afford first priority to the declared national policy of saving endangered species. The pointed omission of the type of qualifying language previously included in endangered species legislation reveals a conscious decision by Congress to give endangered species priority over the "primary missions" of federal agencies.* * *

One might dispute the applicability of these examples to the Tellico Dam by saying that in this case the burden on the public through the loss of millions of unrecoverable dollars would greatly outweigh the loss of the snail darter. But neither the Endangered Species Act nor Art. III of the Constitution provides federal courts with authority to make such fine utilitarian calculations. On the contrary, the plain language of the Act, buttressed by its legislative history, shows clearly that Congress viewed the value of endangered species as "incalculable." Quite obviously, it would be difficult for a court to balance the loss of a sum certain -- even $100 million--against a congressionally declared "incalculable" value, even assuming we had the power to engage in such a weighing process, which we emphatically do not.* * *

Notwithstanding Congress' expression of intent in 1973, we are urged to find that the continuing appropriations for Tellico Dam constitute an implied repeal of the 1973 Act at least insofar at it applies to the Tellico Project.* * *

There is nothing in the appropriations measures, as passed, which states that the Tellico Project was to be completed irrespective of the requirements of the Endangered Species Act. These appropriations, in fact, represented relatively minor components of the lump-sum amounts for the *entire* TVA budget. To find a repeal of the endangered Species Act under these circumstances would surely do violence to the "cardinal rule . . . that repeals by implication are not favored." *Morton v. Mancari*, 417 U.S. 535, 549, 94 S.Ct. 2474, 41 L.Ed.2d 290 (1974).* * *

The doctrine disfavoring repeals by implication "applies with full vigor when . . the subsequent legislation is an *appropriations* measure." *Committee for Nuclear Responsibility v. Seaborg*, 149 U.S. App. D.C. 380, 382, 463 F.2d 783, 785 (1971) (emphasis added). This is perhaps an understatement since it would be more accurate to say that the policy applies with even *greater* force when the claimed repeal rests solely on an Appropriations measures, legislators are entitled to operate under the assumption that the funds will be devoted to purposes which are lawful and not for any purposes forbidden. Without such an assurance, every appropriations measure would be pregnant with prospects of altering substantive legislation, repealing by implication any prior statute which might prohibit the expenditure. Not only would this lead to the absurd result of requiring Members to review exhaustively the background of every authorization before voting on an appropriation, but it would flout the very rules the Congress carefully adopted to avoid this need.* * *

Having determined that there is an irreconcilable conflict between operation of the Tellico Dam and the explicit provisions of § 7 of the Endangered Species Act, we must now consider what remedy, if any, is appropriate.* * *

Here we are urged to view the Endangered Species Act "reasonably," and hence shape a remedy "that accords with some modicum of common sense and the public weal" [quoting Justice Powell's dissenting opinion.] But is that our function? We have no expert knowledge on the subject of endangered species, much less do we have a mandate from the people to strike a balance of equities on the side of the Tellico Dam. Congress has spoken in the plainest of words, making it abundantly clear that the balance has been struck in favor of affording endangered species the highest of priorities, thereby adopting a policy which it described at "institutionalized caution."

Our individual appraisal of the wisdom or unwisdom of a particular course consciously selected by the Congress is to be put aside in the process of interpreting a statute. Once the meaning of an enactment is discerned and its constitutionality determined, the judicial process comes to an end.

***

We agree with the Court of Appeals that in our constitutional system the commitment to the separation of powers is too fundamental for us to pre-empt congressional action by judicially decreeing what accords with "common sense and the public weal." Our Constitution vests such responsibilities in the political branches.

Affirmed.

Justices Powell, Blackmun and Rehnquist dissented.

Notes

Shortly after this case was decided, the proponents of the dam in Congress succeeded in amending the Endangered Species Act to establish an intergovernmental seven-agency board with the power to exempt public projects it found to be of national or regional significance and in the public interest where no reasonable or prudent alternative exists to destroying an endangered species' habitat. The board unanimously refused to exempt Tellico Dam. It based its decision on the ground that the dam's costs outweighed its benefits. -- the dam was to flood out valuable farmland, and was not needed to generate electricity.

Congress thereupon, at the urging of Senator Howard H. Baker, Jr. and Representative John J. Duncan of Tennessee, amended an appropriations bill to specifically authorize funds to complete the dam and exempted it from any statutes, including the Endangered Species Act, which would otherwise bar its completion. This time Congress in effect said: "Keep off the grass. This means you." The dam was completed. And ironically, additional snail darters were later found in nearby streams, causing the fish to be taken off the endangered species list.

Note that the opinion explicitly rejects the argument that the yearly appropriations measures passed by Congress impliedly authorized the dam despite the Endangered Species Act. For a case holding appropriations by Congress for a dam effectively repealed a federal law which would have otherwise protected Rainbow Bridge National Monument in Utah, from flooding, see *Friends of the Earth v. Armstrong*, 485 F.2d 1 (10th Cir. 1973), cert. den. 414 U.S. 1171.

Note that the majority said the Court has "no expert knowledge on the subject of endangered species." However, in his dissent, Justice Powell observed, "Although the snail darter is a distinct species, it is hardly an extraordinary one. Even ichthyologists have trouble distinguishing it from several related species. Moreover, new species of darter are discovered in Tennessee at the rate of about one a year; 8 to 10 have been discovered in the last 5 years. All told, there are some 130 species of darters, 85 to 90 of which are found in Tennessee, 40 to 45 in the Tennessee River System, and 11 in the Little Tennessee itself." Should this matter? Do you think the same kind of arguments and media ballyhoo would have attended the destruction of the principal habitat of a species with a larger public profile -- say the whale, or condor?

The Supreme Court studiously avoided balancing the equities in *TVA v. Hill*. In fact, do not courts balance the equities every day in deciding whether, as here, to issue injunctions? See, for example, *Boomer v. Atlantic Cement Co.* in Chapter 2. Why was the snail darter different? Was the Supreme Court here piously tossing a hot potato back to Congress?

The Endangered Species Act also makes it a federal crime to "take" an endangered species, that is, to kill it. Does this provision apply to acts that destroy the habitat of such a species? The Supreme Court said yes in *Babbitt v. Sweet Home Chapter of Communities for a Great Oregon*, 515 U.S. 687, 115 S.Ct. 2407, 132 L.Ed.2d 597 (1995). The Court noted that the Act defines "take" as "harass, harm, pursue, hunt," and the like -- a definition broad enough to encompass degrading a species' habitat.

Does the Act's requirement that federal agencies consult with the Department of the Interior before actions destructive of the critical habitat of an endangered species apply to United States – funded activities outside the country? That was the issue the Supreme Court finessed in *Lujan v. Defenders of Wildlife* (Chapter 1 [B]) when it ruled the plaintiffs lacked standing. That left in effect a Department regulation limiting these provisions to acts within the United States.

## The CITES Treaty

Since 1975 an international treaty, the Convention on International Trade in Endangered Species (CITES), has had a profound effect on traffic in hides, skins, bone, and products made from them. Most countries are signatories. Each must issue import and export permits for listed species through a scientific authority that certifies the particular shipment is not detrimental to the survival of the species, and a management authority that certifies the animal was lawfully taken. In the United States, the Department of the Interior is both the scientific and management authority. See 16 U.S.C.A. § 1537a.

CITES has virtually ended international traffic in ivory, except for ivory from three southern African nations -- Zimbabwe, Botswana and Namibia -- that assert the only ivory they export is from elephants whose herds are lawfully culled in national parks. In 1997 the signatory nations to CITES agreed to allow a sale of accumulated tusks from those three countries. The three contended that allowing limited culling, with the profits to be shared by local residents, will discourage poaching and encourage the local population to help protect elephants. The converse argument, advanced by Kenya and Tanzania as well as many developed nations, is that any legal traffic in ivory will spur poaching in other habitat countries. The dispute continues.

CITES has been less successful to date in curbing traffic in rhinoceros horns, and the killing of those severely endangered animals unfortunately continues.

## The GATT and NAFTA Agreements

The General Agreement on Tariffs and Trade (GATT) and the North American Free Trade Agreement (NAFTA) have been used as arguments against import bans of endangered species as well as restrictions on fishing designed to protect dolphin and sea turtles. Opponents of these restrictions contend they amount to protectionist limits on free trade. GATT as originally interpreted allowed nations to safeguard the environment within their borders only.

The international tribunal administering GATT ruled in 1994 that a United States law, the Marine Mammal Protection Act, requiring an embargo on tuna caught without mechanisms in the vessel's nets to enable dolphin to escape, in fact violated GATT.

In 1998 that tribunal, the World Trade Organization, ruled a United States ban on shrimp imports from countries not requiring turtle excluder devices (TEDs) was a measure to conserve natural resources, which GATT article XX (g) authorizes. However, it found the ban discriminatory and invalidated it since it was effectively applied only against India, Malaysia, Pakistan and Thailand. All those nations require TEDs, although their provisions are not identical to the United States law.

CITES takes precedence over GATT as an international agreement adopted later. (GATT was adopted in 1947.) NAFTA contains an express provision barring any signatory from violating CITES.

Federal courts in this country have upheld import bans on foreign fish netted without turtle-excluding devices, *Earth Island Institute v. Christopher*, 922 F.Supp. 616 (Ct. of Intl. Trade 1996), and fish caught with drift-nets that capture huge numbers of turtles, dolphin and other sea life, *Humane Society of U.S. v. Brown*, 920 F.Supp. 178 (Ct. of Intl. Trade 1996).

Whales and Dolphins

A treaty older than CITES, entered into by the major former-whaling nations in 1946, protects these mammals through the International Whaling Commission. Commercial whaling has essentially been banned since 1986. Indigenous peoples, like Indians and Inuit, are permitted to continue their traditional whaling as long as this does not jeopardize the survival of any species of whale. Should this exception exist?

The chief problem under the treaty has been continued violations by Japan in the guise of taking whales for "scientific purposes," allowed by the treaty. In fact the number of whales killed by Japanese ships far exceeds any legitimate scientific exception, and whale meat has shown up in Japanese shops.

A statute known as the Pelly Amendment to the Magnuson Act regulating fishing, 22 USCA § 1978, appears to require the United States to ban fish imports from any country whose actions "diminish the effectiveness" of the treaty. When the Secretary of Commerce refused to take this step, a conservation group brought suit. However, in *Japan Whaling Association* v. *American Cetacean Society*, 478 U.S. 221, 106 S. Ct. 2860, 92 L.Ed.2d 166 (1986), the Supreme Court, by a 5-4 decision, ruled the Secretary has discretion to determine whether the violations diminish the treaty's effectiveness, and went on to hold the Secretary acted reasonably in agreeing to allow limited Japanese whaling for another few years. But the whaling has continued with the failure to impose sanctions.

What further steps might be taken to prevent this?

Notes

Since shrinking habitat has largely replaced poaching as the primary threat to endangered species, some have suggested domesticating species such as herbivores and turtles in order to guarentee their habitat. Is this a good solution? What about concerns over diseases, such as brucellosis that bison may carry, that could infect livestock? Is the limited gene pool of domesticated species another concern?

Developing countries' zeal for protecting endangered species like elephants has been somewhat curtailed by increasing human population and these large animals' propensities for devouring crops.

## 5. AIR QUALITY

### Introductory Note

Although the law relating to air quality seems to have been born fully clothed, like Athena, with the Clean Air Act, in fact it stems from common law nuisance cases which antedate the Act by decades. Many of the leading nuisance decisions relate to air pollution and its effect on land use, property values and health. See Chapter 2, *supra*.

### A. NUISANCE

Reexamine the *Copart* and *Boomer* decisions in Chapter 2, Part A. Note the court's invitation in *Boomer* to have government deal with air quality problems administratively through regulations and permits, rather than placing the gorilla on the judicial back.

### B. STATE AND LOCAL LAWS

ORIENTAL BLVD. CO. v. HELLER, New York Court of Appeals, 1970. 27 N.Y. 2d 212, 265 N.E.2d 72, 316 N.Y.S.2d 226. Appeal dismissed, 401 U.S. 986.

Breitel, J.

Plaintiffs question the power of the City of New York to regulate by a particular local ordinance the use of fuel burners and refuse incinerators to control the emission of aerial pollutants. The original plaintiffs and several hundred intervenors, all apartment house owners, sought a declaratory judgment to annual and enjoin enforcement of the ordinance on the ground of its unconstitutionality.* * *

The principal contentions are: the State has pre-empted the regulation of air pollution; the local ordinance is impossible of compliance within the time schedule provided; the upgrading of equipment is disproportionately costly; the daily accumulative penalties are confiscatory and would discourage justifiable resistance to the ordinance; and the provisions for summary sealing of incinerators and fuel burners are violative of constitutional limitations. Plaintiffs particularly urge that the effect of the ordinance in reducing air pollution would be either nonexistent or so minimal as not to justify the extraordinary expense imposed on property owners.* * *

The amended ordinance * * * requires the commissioner of air pollution control to issue operating certificates for fuel burners and incinerators [in apartment houses, which must comply] with the new standards [for air quality in the ordinance.] Installation of apparatus in the fuel burners, entailing substantial outlays, was required within two years[.] Varying with the number of apartments dependent upon an incinerator, owners are required to install additional apparatus within staggered periods up to two years[.] After compliance dates have passed, the commissioner is empowered to seal any equipment for which permits have not been obtained[, and,] after notice and hearing, to seal any other equipment which is emitting harmful substances[.] A fine from $25 to $200 a day and imprisonment up to 60 days may be imposed for each day of improper operation of an incinerator[.]

The ponderous argument made that pollution caused by incinerators and oil burning equipment is of trivial effect in the overall solution of a massive problem is fallacious. Accepting the contention that there is only a 2% daily contribution [it] still aggregates over 186 tons per day. Moreover, government is and must be entitled to attack massive problems piecemeal, and to select those most susceptible areas which permit of the least destructive effect on the economy (see *United States v. Carolene Prods. Co.*, 304 U.S. 144, 151).* * * So long as there is reasonable basis in available information, and rationality in chosen courses of conduct to alleviate an accepted evil, there is no constitutional infirmity [citations omitted]. * * *

Also unsound is plaintiffs' argument of State pre-emption. The Environmental Conservation Law was recently enacted, effective July 1, 1970. Section 10 provides that "It shall further be the policy of the state to improve and coordinate the environmental plans, functions, powers and programs of the state, in cooperation with the federal government, regions and local governments."

Paragraph 21 of section 14 empowers the newly created department to: "Encourage activities consistent with the purposes of this chapter by advising and assisting local governments, institutions, industries and individuals." These provisions explicitly recognize that local units of government are intended to function in the air pollution area.* * *

## Notes

It is almost axiomatic in environmental law that truly effective action by government at any level will be challenged by aggrieved parties as beyond the jurisdiction of that level of government. State action will be attacked as preempted by federal law (see *A. E. Nettleton Co. v. Diamond,* Chapter 4, *supra*), local as preempted by the state (as in *Oriental Boulevard*). Federal action will be challenged, predictably, on the ground that it has invaded the states' jurisdiction as protected by the Tenth Amendment. See *Brown v. Environmental Protection Agency*, 521 F.2d 827 (9th Cir. 1975), vacated as moot, 431 U.S. 99, 97 S.Ct. 1635, 52 L.Ed.2d 166.

State and municipal air pollution statutes were traditionally held valid exercises of the police power and not preempted by federal laws. The landmark decision in this area, *Huron Portland Cement Co. v. City of Detroit*, 362 U.S. 440, 80 S.Ct. 813, 4 L.Ed. 2d 852 (1960), held a Detroit municipal-anti-smoke ordinance valid as applied to a vessel in interstate commerce and not preempted by federal laws regulating boilers on such vessels. The federal statute in *Huron* dealt with safety and did not purport to control air pollution. See also *Phillips Petroleum Co. v. Illinois Environmental Protection Agency*, 72 Ill. App.3d 217, 390 N.E.2d 620 (1979), upholding state jurisdiction to impose a civil penalty for a discharge of ammonia resulting from a railroad accident, as against the claim that federal railroad safety laws preempted the state.

Enactment of the Clean Air Act in 1970, the major federal air quality statute, might have opened new vistas for litigants seeking to argue that it preempted state and local laws, but for Congress' carefully specifying when the Act was to preempt, as the next case illustrates.

EXXON CORPORATION v. CITY OF NEW YORK, United States Court of Appeals, Second Circuit, 1977. 548 F.2d 1088.

[In 1971 the City of New York enacted regulations which provided for a staggered reduction in the lead content of gasoline sold in the City. By 1973 gasoline was to contain no more than .5 grams of lead per gallon and by 1974 no more than .075 grams per gallon.

Meanwhile, the Administrator of the United States Environmental Protection Agency issued regulations governing the lead content of gasoline in February 1973. 42 USCA § 1857f-6c(a) (now § 7545) authorizes the Administrator to issue regulations controlling or prohibiting the use of a fuel or fuel additive if he finds that its use endangers the public health or welfare or significantly impairs the performance of any emission control device.

Exxon commenced this action claiming that 42 USCA § 1857f-6c (present § 7545) preempted the City regulation.]

Mulligan, Circuit Judge:

* * * We note at the outset that this is not a case where we are asked to infer preemption because the Congress has legislated in the same area as the City of New York, but rather this is the unusual case where explicit preemption language appears in the Act. We recognize that the exercise of federal supremacy is not lightly to be presumed and that there must be a clear manifestation of a congressional purpose to supersede the exercise of power by the state.* * *

Nonetheless there are three basic provisions in the statute from which a pattern of preemption arises which is fatal to the City's ordinances and requires reversal here, the granting of summary judgment for the appellants and the nullification of both of the City regulations in issue.

1) The prime section involved, and the only provision considered below, is section § 1857f-6c(4)(A) [now § 7545(c)(4)(A)].

That section explicitly precludes a state or any political subdivision thereof from prescribing or attempting to prescribe any controls or prohibition respecting the use of fuels or fuel additives in motor vehicles, if the Administrator has prescribed an applicable control or prohibition unless the state prohibition or control is identical to that prescribed by the Administrator. There is no question but that the Administrator has promulgated standards prescribing controls and prohibitions with respect to the lead content of gasoline used in motor vehicles, 40 C.F.R. § 80.20 *et seq*. Neither is there any question that N.Y.C. Admin. Code § 1403.2-13.11 which prescribes a lead content for gasoline used in the City of New York is not identical to the federal regulations. Indeed, the local ordinance is more demanding as to both lead content and the time limitations within which such reduction must be achieved. In face of the clear preemption language of section 1857f-6c(4)(A) it is difficult to perceive how the non-identical City regulation can survive.* * *

The City argues that the preemption language of a statute must be narrowly construed where the exercise of the local police power serves the purpose of the federal act. We do not cavil at the principle but find that the City ordinances here do not serve the purpose of federal act but in fact disrupt it. The problems faced by the Administrator in determining the quality of national ambient air are made evident from a reading of the text accompanying the promulgation of the amended regulations of 40 C.F.R. § 80.20 revising the lead content phasedown schedule and providing for its enforcement by controls now effective. [T]he E.P.A. concluded that due to the gasoline industry's inability to produce sufficient high octane gasoline enforcement of the then promulgated lead phase-down schedule could result in a gasoline shortage of about 6.6% of demand in 1977 and 9% in 1978. The Administrator stated that "the intent of these regulations is to achieve the desired reduction of lead in gasoline as expeditiously as practicable for protection of public health without causing a gasoline shortage." 41 Fed.Reg. 42676.[a]

These considerations account for the amendments to the phase-down schedule which took into consideration both the technological problems of the industry which must add equipment and plant capacity on an expedited basis and the concern for preserving energy in a period of national shortage. What consideration the City of New York may have given these factors in 1971 does not appear in the record before us. In sum, logic as well as the express language of section 1857f-6c(4)(A) mandate that the City regulation be identical to that of the Administrator. Fragmented, piecemeal local legislation could only bring chaos particularly in view of the national character of the industry supplying motor vehicle fuel and the technical problems associated with the production of unleaded gasoline.

2) Our inquiry into this question does not cease here. We find that the federal scheme does not impose a complete strait jacket on the states or their subdivisions. Section 1857f-6c(4) which in subdivision (A) precludes local regulation unless identical to federal regulation, provides a relevant exception in subdivision (C). That section allows a state to prescribe a control or prohibition

---

[a]These regulations were sustained in *Ethyl Corporation v. EPA*, discussed in Chapter 1.

respecting the use of a fuel or fuel additive in a motor vehicle if such restriction is included as a provision in an applicable implementation plan for such state as provided under section 1857c-5 [now § 7410]. The state restrictions so allowed could be more severe than the federal regulations. The Administrator may approve a state plan with a provision governing automotive fuels "if he finds that the State control or prohibition is necessary to achieve the national primary or secondary ambient air quality standard which the plan implements." 42 U.S.C. § 1857f-6c(4)(C). Thus the Act provides a mechanism which would allow New York to set up standards concerning fuels that varied from the federal norms.* * * We conclude therefore that with respect to standards for moving sources such as the gasoline utilized in motor vehicles, the Congress has explicitly provided that state or local regulation is preempted unless such control or prohibition is identical with the federally promulgated standards. Variation is permitted only if it is accomplished through the mechanism of a state implementation plan, a procedure not followed here. The right of a state or subdivision to proceed on its own without approval of the Administrator is limited to the regulation of fuel in stationary sources and therefore not pertinent to the issue before us.

[Since the court held the City's regulations were preempted, it did not need to reach the Commerce Clause challenge also raised by the plaintiffs.]

Notes

California was expressly exempted from the Clean Air Act's preemptive requirements as to fuels and pollution-control devices in automobiles since it had legislated in these areas prior to the advent of the Clean Air Act, 42 U.S.C.A. §§ 7543(b), 7545(c)(4), discussed in Part E.

The Clean Air Act's Structure

Except for its provisions regarding fuels and pollution-control devices in autos and a few others relating to aircraft, the Clean Air Act does not preempt the states but rather envisions tandem federal-state enforcement.

Why did Congress choose this approach? Why have federal legislation at all in this area? What are some reasons why Congress believed it could not be left with the states? The level of enforcement varied greatly from state to state, with some competing to attract industry by offering minimal environmental regulation. In addition, air does not respect state borders, so federal controls are needed to prevent on state's sources damaging air quality in other states.

Given these concerns, why did Congress leave clean air regulation largely in state hands? As the following cases indicate, the Act requires states to submit implementation plans showing how they will meet these standards. These State Implementation Plans, or SIPs, require the EPA's approval.

This basic format was followed in the Clean Water Act and other major federal environmental legislation.

## C. THE CLEAN AIR ACT: CRITERIA AND STANDARDS

KENNECOTT COPPER CORP. v. ENVIRONMENTAL PROTECTION AGENCY, United States Court of Appeals, District of Columbia Circuit, 1972. 462 F.2d 846.

Leventhal, Circuit Judge:

In this appeal, Kennecott Copper Corporation attacks the "national secondary ambient air quality standards" for sulfur oxides, promulgated by the Environmental Protection Agency on April 30, 1971. It raises as objections that the standards (1) were not "based on" the underlying "air quality criteria" issued by the Government, as required by Section 109 of the Clean Air Act (Act), as amended in 1970; (2) were not accompanied by a "concise general statement of their basis and purpose" as required by § 4(c) of the Administrative Procedure Act, and in any event (3) were not adequately supported by a statement of their basis necessary to insure adequate judicial review.

The Act provides for the establishment of national primary and secondary ambient air quality standards, to prescribe maximum concentrations of pollutants that will be permitted in the air of our country. Primary standards are those "requisite to protect the public health," while secondary standards are those "requisite to protect the public welfare," which is defined as including, but not limited to, "effects on soils, water, crops, vegetation, manmade materials, animals, wildlife, weather, visibility, and climate, damage to and deterioration of property, and hazards to transportation, as well as effects on economic values and on personal comfort and well-being."

This appeal involves the non-health-related "secondary" standards for sulfur oxides, which are more stringent than the "primary" standards, though greater time flexibility is provided for attaining secondary standards. In particular, this appeal has come to focus on the requirement in the secondary air quality standard limiting the annual arithmetic mean amount of sulfur oxides (sulfur dioxide) to: "60 micrograms per cubic meter-annual arithmetic mean."

Sections 108 and 109 of the Act[1] are the key sections for present purposes. The statute requires air quality criteria, if not issued prior to the 1970 amendments, to be issued by the Administrator within 12 months after the listing of an air pollutant. The Administrator is required to publish and revise a list which includes each pollutant present in the ambient air from numerous or diverse mobile or stationary sources, which in the judgment of the Administrator "has an adverse effect on public health or welfare."

Section 108 makes clear that the term "air quality criteria" is not used in the law with the conventional meaning of "criterion," as referring to a standard.

---

[1] Now 42 U.S.C.A. §§ 7408 and 7409.

What the term refers to is a document which "shall accurately reflect the latest scientific knowledge useful in indicating the kind and extent of all identifiable effects on public health or welfare which may be expected from the presence of such pollutant in the ambient air, in varying quantities."

Section 109 of the Act provides for expeditious issuance of air quality standards "based on" the criteria. They were required within 30 days after the 1970 enactment of [the Act] for each air pollutant for which air quality criteria had been issued prior to such enactment. As for criteria issued subsequent to the 1970 law, the Administrator is required, simultaneously, to publish proposed national air quality standards. In either event the air quality standards prescribe a level of air quality "the attainment and maintenance of which in the judgment of the Administrator, based on such criteria" is requisite to protect the public interest--in the case of primary standards, "requisite to protect the public health," in the case of secondary standards, "requisite to protect the public welfare from any known or anticipated adverse effects associated with the presence of such air pollutant in the ambient air."

* * *In the case before us the air quality criteria were published in January 1969, prior to the 1970 law, by the Department of Health, Education and Welfare. No contention is made that they were not adequate to serve the function contemplated of criteria under the 1970 law, of reflecting pertinent scientific knowledge concerning effects that may be expected from the presence of the pollutant. The complaint is that there is no adequate indication of the basis of the 1971 standard of 60 micrograms per cubic meter. It is particularly stressed that the summarizing "Resume" paragraph, reproduced in the footnote,[2] of the 1969 Criteria refer to no effects at a level below 85 micrograms per cubic meter. While the statement of the purpose and nature of the regulation set forth the basis for the primary standards, simultaneously adopted, in some detail, as to secondary standards the Administrator said only:

---

[2] RESUME

> In addition to health considerations, the economic and esthetic benefits to be obtained from low ambient concentrations of sulfur oxides as related to visibility soiling, corrosion, and other effects should be considered by organizations responsible for promulgating ambient air quality standards. Under the conditions prevailing in areas where the studies were conducted, adverse health effects were noted when 24-hour average levels of sulfur dioxide exceeded 300 *ug*/m$^3$ (0.11 ppm) for 3 to 4 days. Adverse health effects were also noted when the annual mean level of sulfur dioxide exceeded 115 *ug*/m$^3$ (0.12 ppm) and adverse effects on vegetation were observed at an annual mean of 85 *ug*/m$^3$ (0.03 ppm). It is reasonable and prudent to conclude that when promulgating ambient air quality standards, consideration should be given to requirements for margins of safety which take into account long-term effects on health, vegetation, and materials occurring below the above levels.

National secondary ambient air quality standards are those which, in the judgment of the Administrator, based on the air quality criteria, are requisite to protect the public welfare from any known or anticipated adverse effects associated with the presence of air pollutants in the ambient air.

In support of the EPA's annual standard of 60 micrograms per cubic meter, the Government * * * refer[s] to lower figures in the material in the body of the Criteria, saying that the Resume is not conclusive. In the alternative [it] argue[s] that the 85 figure in the Resume supports a 60 standard, on the basis of the Administrator's judgment as to anticipated effects and a margin necessary to avoid the adverse effects noted at the 85 level.

We do not undertake to rule on these particular matters. This court has been assigned special responsibility for determining challenges to EPA's air quality standards. This judicial review rests on the premise that agency and court "together constitute a partnership in furtherance of the public interest, and are collaborative instrumentalities of justice. The court is in a real sense part of the total administrative process." *Greater Boston Television Corp. v. FCC*, 143 U.S. App.D.C. 383, 444 F.2d 841, 851-852, cert. denied, 403 U.S. 923 (1971). Inherent in the responsibility entrusted to this court is a requirement that we be given sufficient indication of the basis on which the Administrator reached the 60 figure so that we may consider whether it embodies an abuse of discretion or error of law.[3]

The provision for statutory judicial review contemplates some disclosure of the basis of the agency's action. *Citizens to Preserve Overton Park v. Volpe; Securities and Exchange Commission v. Chenery Corp.*, 318 U.S. 80, 94, 63 S.Ct. 454, 87 L.Ed. 626 (1943). We are not to be taken as specifying that the agency must provide the same articulation as is required for orders or regulations issued after evidentiary hearings. We are keenly aware of the need to avoid procedural strait jackets that would seriously hinder this new agency in the discharge of the novel, sensitive and formidable, tasks entrusted to it by Congress. This concern is emphasized by the fact that in the 1970 Amendments Congress was significantly concerned with expedition and avoidance of previous cumbersome and time-consuming procedures in effect under prior law.

The provision by Congress of only informal rule-making, as a preliminary to the issuance of standards, and the contemplation of expedition, yield as reasonable corollaries some latitude in the requirement for delineation of

---

[3]As to any agency approach based on "margin of error," the appellant concedes some latitude for a figure below the 85 level which was identified as in the criteria as producing harm to vegetation. But appellant contends that a figure as low as 60 is inconsistent with the law's failure to include, as to secondary standards, the phrase "margin of safety" set forth in § 109(b) for primary standards. We intimate no view on this contention. We point it out to identify the kind of legal issue that cannot meaningfully be disposed of without some awareness of the basis of the Administrator's action.

approach. While the provision in § 4 of the [Administrative Procedure Act] for a "concise general statement" of the basis and purpose of regulations is not to be interpreted over-literally, the regulation before us contains sufficient exposition of the purpose and basis of the regulation as a whole to satisfy this legislative minimum. Particularly as applied to environmental regulations, produced under the tension of need for reasonable expedition and need for resolution of a host of nagging problems, we are loath to stretch the requirement of a "general statement" into a mandate for reference to all the specific issues raised in comments.

There are contexts, however, contexts of fact, statutory framework and nature of action, in which the minimum requirements of the Administrative Procedure Act may not be sufficient. In the interest of justice, and in aid of the judicial function, centralized in this court, of expeditious disposition of challenges to standards, the record is remanded for the Administrator to supply an implementing statement that will enlighten the court as to the basis on which he reached the 60 standard from the material in the Criteria.* * *

## Notes

The secondary standard for sulfur oxides was withdrawn and the court's invitation to issue a new and documented standard remains unanswered.

Later standards promulgated by the EPA, however, have been accompanied by a "Kennecott statement" of the basis for the standard. See Rodgers, *Environmental Law,* 2d Ed. (West Publishing Co. 1994), at 161.

Note that the court found the standard satisfied the Administrative Procedure Act but not the requirements of the Clean Air Act itself.

Why did the court find it improper for the EPA to provide the reasonable margin for safety recommended by the Department of Health, Education and Welfare when it adopted the criteria for sulfur oxides (see n. 2)? Is this carrying the hard look doctrine (Chapter 1, *supra*) beyond the point of public usefulness? In the nuclear field, maximum safe exposure levels to radiation adopted by the Nuclear Regulatory Commission and its predecessor, the Atomic Energy Commission, have been repeatedly reduced in the light of new evidence of hazards. Is a safety margin of 60 micrograms of sulfur dioxide per cubic meter where the criteria state 85 is the maximum safe exposure really beyond the scope of reasonable discretion usually accorded administrative agencies?

Clemenceau once said "government regulation is the substitution of error for chance in human events."

More recently, the Supreme Court upheld the EPA's standards for particulate matter (soot and fly ash, often discharged from truck exhaust pipes) and ozone, rejecting a claim that Congress had unconstitutionally delegated legislative power to the Agency. *Whitman* v. *American Trucking Associations*, 531 U.S. 457, 121 S. Ct. 903, 149 L. Ed.2d 1 (2001). On remand, the Court of Appeals likewise upheld the standards on the merits as not arbitrary, 283 F.3d 355 (D.C. Cir. 2002).

## D. THE CLEAN AIR ACT: IMPLEMENTATION PLANS

UNION ELECTRIC CO. v. ENVIRONMENTAL PROTECTION AGENCY, United States Supreme Court, 1976. 427 U.S. 246, 96 S.Ct. 2518, 49 L.Ed.2d 474.

[Petitioner is an electric utility company serving the St. Louis metropolitan area and portions of Missouri, Illinois, and Iowa. Two years after the Administrator of the Environmental Protection Agency (hereinafter EPA) approved Missouri's implementation plan the company petitioned for review of that approval, arguing economic and technical unfeasibility.]

Justice Marshall delivered the opinion of the court.

The Administrator's position is that he has no power whatsoever to reject a state implementation plan on the ground that it is economically or technologically infeasible, and we have previously accorded great deference to the Administrator's construction of the Clean Air Act. After surveying the relevant provisions of the [Act and its] legislative history, we agree that Congress intended claims of economic and technological unfeasibility to be wholly foreign to the Administrator's consideration of a state implementation plan. [T]he Act [was] a drastic remedy to what was perceived as a serious and otherwise uncheckable problem of air pollution. [It] place[s] the primary responsibility for formulating pollution control strategies on the States, but nonetheless subject[s] the States to strict minimum compliance requirements. These requirements are of a "technology-forcing character," * * * and are expressly designed to force regulated sources to develop pollution control devices that might at the time appear to be economically or technologically infeasible.

This approach is apparent on the face of § 110(a)(2). The provision sets out eight criteria that an implementation plan must satisfy, and provides that if these criteria are met and if the plan was adopted after reasonable notice and hearing, the Administrator "shall approve" the proposed state plan. The mandatory "shall" makes it quite clear that the Administrator is not to be concerned with factors other than those specified, * * * and none of the eight factors appears to permit consideration of technological or economic infeasibility. Nonetheless, it a basis is to be found for allowing the Administrator to consider such claims, it must be among the eight criteria, and so it is here that the argument is focused.

It is suggested that consideration of claims of technological and economic infeasibility is required by the first criterion--that the primary air quality standards be met "as expeditiously as practicable but . . . in no case later than three years . . ." and that the secondary air quality standards be met within a "reasonable time." § 110(a)(2)(A). The argument is that what is "practicable" or "reasonable" cannot be determined without assessing whether what is proposed is possible. This argument does not survive analysis.

Section 110(a)(2)(A)'s three-year deadline for achieving primary air quality standards is central to the Amendments' regulatory scheme and, as both the language and the legislative history of the requirement make clear, it leaves no room for claims of technological or economic infeasibility.

[In the words] of the Senate committee:

In the Committee discussions considerable concern was expressed regarding the use of the concept of technical feasibility as the basis of ambient air standards. The Committee determined that 1) the health of people is more important than the question of whether the early achievement of ambient air quality standards protective of health is technically feasible; and 2) the growth of pollution load in many areas, even with application of available technology, would still be deleterious to public health.

Therefore, the Committee determined that existing sources of pollutants either should meet the standard of the law or be closed down . . .

The Conference Committee made clear that the States could not procrastinate until the deadline approached. Rather, the primary standards had to be met in less than three years if possible; they had to be met "as expeditiously as practicable." § 110(a)(2)(A).* * *

It is argued that when such a state plan calls for proceeding more rapidly than economics and the available technology appear to allow, the plan must be rejected as not "practicable." Whether this is a correct reading of § 110(a)(2)(A) depends on how that section's "as expeditiously as practicable" phrase is characterized. The Administrator's position is that § 110(a)(2)(A) sets only a minimum standard that the States may exceed in their discretion, so that he has no power to reject an infeasible state plan that surpasses the minimum federal requirements--a plan that reflects a state decision to engage in technology forcing on its own and to proceed more expeditiously than is practicable. On the other hand, petitioner argue[s] that § 110(a)(2)(A) sets a mandatory standard that the States must meet precisely, and conclude[s] that the Administrator may reject a plan for being too strict as well as for being too lax.* * * They claim that the States are precluded from submitting implementation plans more stringent than federal law demands by § 110(a)(2)'s second criterion--that the plan is not "necessary" for attainment of the national standards and so must be rejected by the Administrator.

[However,] the most natural reading of the "as may be necessary" phrase in context is simply that the Administrator must assure that the minimal, or "necessary," requirements are met, not that he detect and reject any state plan more demanding than federal law requires.* * *

Beyond that, if a State makes the legislative determination that it desires a particular air quality by a certain date and that it is willing to force technology to attain it--or lose a certain industry if attainment is not possible--such a determination is fully consistent with the structure and purpose of the

Amendments, and § 110(a)(2)(B) provides no basis for the EPA Administrator to object to the determination on the ground of infeasibility.

In sum, we have concluded that claims of economic or technological infeasibility may not be considered by the Administrator in evaluating a state requirement that primary ambient air quality standards be met in the mandatory three years. And, since we further conclude that the States may submit implementation plans more stringent than federal law requires and that the Administrator must approve such plans if they meet the minimum requirements of § 110(a)(2), it follows that the language of § 110(a)(2)(B) provides no basis for the Administrator ever to reject a state implementation plan on the ground that it is economically or technologically infeasible. Accordingly, a court of appeals reviewing an approved plan under § 307(b)(1) cannot set it aside on those grounds, no matter when they are raised.

Our conclusion is bolstered by recognition that the Amendments do allow claims of technological and economic infeasibility to be raised * * * before the state agency formulating the implementation plan. So long as the national standards are met, the State may select whatever mix of control devices it desires, and industries with particular economic or technological problems may seek special treatment in the plan itself.

* * *Moreover, if the industry is not exempted from, or accommodated by, the original plan, it may obtain a variance, [and]
take its claims of economic or technological infeasibility to the state courts.

[In addition,] technological and economic factors may be considered in at least one other circumstance. When a source is found to be in violation of the state implementation plan, the Administrator may, after a conference with the operator, issue a compliance order rather than seek civil or criminal enforcement. Such an order must specify a "reasonable" time for compliance with the relevant standard, taking into account the seriousness of the violation and "any good faith efforts to comply with applicable requirements." § 113(a)(4) * * *.

In short, the Amendments offer ample opportunity for consideration of claims of technological and economic infeasibility. Always, however, care is taken that consideration of such claims will not interfere substantially with the primary goal of prompt attainment of the national standards. Allowing such claims to be raised by appealing the Administrator's approval of an implementation plan, as petitioner suggests, would frustrate congressional intent. It would permit a proposed plan to be struck down as infeasible before it is given a chance to work, * * *. And it would permit the Administrator or a federal court to reject a State's legislative choices in regulating air pollution, even though Congress plainly left with the States, so long as the national standards were met, the power to determine which sources would be burdened by regulation and to what extent.* * *

SIERRA CLUB v. RUCKELSHAUS, 344 F. Supp. 253. United States District Court of Columbia, 1972. Affirmed --F.2d--; affirmed without opinion *sub nom. Fri v. Sierra Club*, 412 U.S. 541, 93 S.Ct. 2770, 37 L.Ed.2d 140.

John H. Pratt, District Judge.

The Administrator, [of the EPA], in recent testimony before Congress, indicated that he had declined to require state implementation plans to provide against significant deterioration of the existing clear air areas--i.e., areas with levels of pollution lower than the secondary standard--because he believed that he lacked the power to act otherwise.* * *

Previously, the Administrator had promulgated a regulation permitting states to submit plans which would allow clean air areas to be degraded, so long as the plans were merely "adequate to prevent such ambient pollution levels from exceeding such secondary standard." 40 C.F.R. § 51.12(b)(1972).

Plaintiffs claim that the Administrator's interpretation of the extent of his authority is clearly erroneous.* * *

In Section 101(b) of the Clean Air Act, Congress states four basic purposes of the Act, the first of which is "to protect and enhance the quality of the Nation's air resources so as to promote the public health and welfare and the productive capacity of its population." 42 U.S.C. § 1857(b)(1) [now § 7401(b)(1)]. On its face, this language would appear to declare Congress' intent to improve the quality of the nation's air and to prevent deterioration of that air quality, no matter how presently pure that quality in some sections of the country happens to be.

[B]oth Secretary Finch and Under Secretary Veneman of HEW testified before Congress that neither the 1967 Act nor the proposed Act would permit the quality of air to be degraded.* * *

More important, of course, is the language of the Senate Report accompanying the bill which became the Clean Air Act of 1970. The Senate Report, in pertinent part, states:

> In areas where current air pollution levels are already equal to or better than the air quality goals, the Secretary shall not approve any implementation plan which does not provide, to the maximum extent practicable, for the continued maintenance of such ambient air quality. S.Rep.No. 1196, 91st Cong., 2d Sess., at 2 (1970).

On the other hand, the present Administrator, in remarks made in January and February of 1972 before certain House and Senate Subcommittees, has taken the position that the 1970 Act allows degradation of clean air areas. Several Congressional leaders voiced their strong disagreement with the Administrator's interpretation. [Citing statements of the House and Senate subcommittee chairman and vice-chairman to that effect.]

The Administrator's interpretation of the 1970 Act, as disclosed in his current regulations, appears to be self-contradictory. On the one hand, 40 C.F.R. § 50.2(c)(1970) provides:

> The promulgation of national primary and secondary air quality standards shall not be considered in any manner to allow significant deterioration of existing air quality in any portion of any State.

Yet, in 40 C.F.R. § 51.12(b), he states:

> In any region where measured or estimated ambient levels of a pollutant are below the levels specified by an applicable secondary standard, the State implementation plan shall set forth a control strategy which shall be adequate to prevent such ambient pollution levels from exceeding such secondary standard.

The former regulation appears to reflect a policy of nondegradation of clean air but the latter mirrors the Administrator's doubts as to his authority to impose such a policy upon the states in their implementation plans. In our view, these regulations are irreconcilable and they demonstrate the weakness of the Administrator's position in this case.

Having considered the stated purpose of the Clean Air Act of 1970, the legislative history of the Act and its predecessor, and the past and present administrative interpretation of the Acts, it is our judgment that the Clean Air Act of 1970 is based in important part on a policy of non-degradation of existing clean air and that 40 C.F.R. § 51.12(b), in permitting the states to submit plans which allow pollution levels of clean air to rise to the secondary standard level of pollution, is contrary to the legislative policy of the Act and is, therefore, invalid.* * *

Notes

The court correctly diagnosed the EPA's schizophrenia and enjoined it. The Court of Appeals and ultimately the Supreme Court, by a 4-4 vote, affirmed. (Citations before the District Court's opinion, *supra.*)

Thereafter the EPA amended its regulations to provide for dividing each state into air quality zones. The state environmental agency has the power to rezone to reflect development of areas within the state. In Class I areas any deterioration is deemed "significant." In Class II areas the deterioration in air quality which accompanies moderate development is deemed insignificant, and in Class III areas deterioration is deemed insignificant unless it exceeds the national standards for particulates and sulfur dioxide. See 42 U.S.C.A. § 7471.

Does the "no significant deterioration" policy of the Act effectively thrust the federal government into the land-use control area, a subject historically regarded by the courts as one within the states' jurisdiction under the police power?

Where does "no significant deterioration" tend to direct development? Is it more equitable, or socially and environmentally beneficial, to foster major industrial and commercial construction in areas already suffering from impaired air quality? Will such a policy actually broaden the disparity in air quality between, say, the Adirondacks and the New York City area, or the Sierras and Los Angeles, so that the environmentally rich get richer and the poor poorer?

Often Class I areas, with superior air quality, are remote and economically poor, and offer little employment to their residents. Is the government, by consciously directing development away from these regions, bestowing an unwanted gift? Or helping protect these regions from inappropriate development whose long-term harm may far outweigh its short-term economic benefits?

## Performance Standards

Once the EPA establishes the National Ambient Air Quality Standards described in *Kennecott*, and states adopt the state implementation plans (SIPs) described in *Union Electric* for each listed pollutant, how are emission limits set for individual sources? The Act contemplates specific performance standards for stationary sources (factories, incinerators, power plants and the like) and requires "new sources" -- those built or significantly altered since the Act took effect in 1970 -- to have permits. The Act's 1990 amendments require permits for all stationary sources, new and existing.

How are these limits on emission of pollutants determined? The Act sets levels for categories of stationary sources. In attainment areas -- those areas that have attained the primary NAAQS for a specific pollutant -- new sources are to meet a best available control technology (BACT) standard. 42 U.S.C.A. § 7479. In non-attainment areas, new sources must meet the lowest available emission rate (LAER), a more stringent standard. *Id.* § 7501(3). The standard for existing (pre-1970) sources is the most lenient: reasonably available control technology (RACT). *Id.* § 7502(c)(1).

The 1990 amendments impose a permit requirement (§§ 7661-7661f) for new sources. The permits are issued by the state environmental agency. Does the EPA have power to overturn a state permit it finds to have been issued in violation of the Act's standards? The Supreme Court upheld the EPA's authority to do just that in *Alaska Dept. of Envtl. Conserv.* v. *EPA*, 540 U.S. 461, 124 S. Ct. 983, 157 L. Ed. 2d 967 (2004). The EPA had found the state's permit for a zinc mine did not meet the BACT standard since it allowed the discharge of excessive nitrogen oxide.

## The Bubble Policy

The EPA has developed an emission offset policy, universally known as the bubble policy, under which a stationary source may use gains in air quality to offset increases in air pollution. The key is the agency's plant-wide definition of a "source" in its regulations. By defining a source to encompass an entire facility, the EPA can justify balancing off reductions from some buildings against increased air emissions from others. The rules apply in both attainment and non-attainment areas.

After a checkered history in the courts under earlier, less explicit, rules, these rules were sustained as consistent with the Act in *Chevron U.S.A., Inc. v. Natural Resources Defense Council, Inc.*, 467 U.S. 837, 104 S. Ct. 2778, 81 L.Ed.2d 694 (1984). But are they consistent with the Act's general purpose "to protect and enhance the quality of the Nation's air resources so as to promote the public health and welfare" (42 U.S.C.A. § 7401[b][1]?

## Acid Rain

The vexing problem of acid rain first became evident in the 1970s with lakes in areas such as the Adirondacks, New England and Eastern Canada becoming so acid as to kill fish. Caused by sulfur dioxide and nitrogen oxide emissions, acid rain is now known to be damaging to forests, soil and even buildings and statues. It is an issue of international dimensions, involving not only deposits from United States sources landing in Canada, and vice versa, but also emissions crossing borders within Europe, typically traveling from west to east with the prevailing winds. In the United States acid rain is mainly generated at Midwestern power plants burning high-sulfur coal and deposited hundreds of miles further east. Since the Midwestern states' SIPs (State Implementation Plans) permit those sources to burn high-sulfur coal, what legal recourse do Eastern states or their residents have?

The EPA, which had the power to disapprove the Midwestern SIPs, failed to do so throughout the 1970s and 1980s despite the urging of New York, in league with several other Northeastern states and environmental groups. These states then sued under Clean Air Act provisions which authorize the EPA to find a state's SIP in violation of the Act if it prevents another state from attaining the Act's primary standards. The courts rejected this claim, contending the plaintiff state must prove specific individual sources in the offending states prevented it from obtaining the standards. See *Air Pollution Control District of Jefferson County* v. *EPA*, 739 F.2d 1071 (6th Cir. 1984). Other legal techniques also proved unavailing.

The 1990 Clean Air Act amendments finally furnished a mechanism to curtail acid rain. The Act now imposes stringent limits on sulfur dioxide and required the EPA to set standards for nitrogen oxides. See §§ 404-407, 42 U.S.C.A. §§ 7651c-7651f. The nitrogen oxide standards were upheld in

*Appalachian Power Co.* v. EPA, 135 F.3d 791 (D.C. Cir. 1998). But the Northeastern states have brought suit to curtail emissions from Midwestern power plants that allegedly violate the new standards. The acid test, one might say, is to see how effective these remedies will be.

### Hazardous Air Pollutants

Section 112 of the Act, 42 U.S.C.A. § 7412, authorizes the EPA to regulate hazardous air pollutants directly. The 1970 Act defined such pollutants as those that cause or contribute to air pollution reasonably anticipated to result in greater mortality or serious illness. Section 112(a)(1), 42 U.S.C.A. § 7412(a)(1). The statute required the EPA to name such pollutants and adopt emission standards for them that "provide[ ] an ample margin of safety to protect the public health. . . ." This created a dilemma. Standards literally meeting the statute's mandate would mean zero emissions for some pollutants and would prevent oil refineries, copper smelters (which emit arsenic), and coal-burning power plants from operating. The EPA's response was to name few hazardous air pollutants -- only four in the first seven years of the Act's history -- and enact even fewer standards. When it belatedly adopted a standard for vinyl chloride, the Agency essentially required the industry to meet a "best available technology" standard, taking into account cost and feasibility along with health. This standard was annulled by the courts, which held the EPA could consider feasibility but had to first decide on a health-related "ample margin of safety." *Natural Resources Defense Council, Inc.* v. *EPA*, 824 F.2d 1146 (D.C. Cir., *en banc*, 1987).

The 1990 Act cut this Gordian Knot. Revised § 112 now lists 189 hazardous air pollutants and allows the EPA to add others. In addition, the Act now requires the Agency to set a standard based on their maximum achievable control technology (MACT), weighing both health and feasibility.

## E. THE CLEAN AIR ACT: MOBILE SOURCES

Motor vehicles are a chief culprit in air pollution, and the Act attempts to curtail emissions from vehicles, or mobile sources, in four ways: emission standards, engine testing and certification, warranty provisions for catalytic converters, and requirements for fuels. In addition, states with major metropolitan areas that are non-attainment areas, that is, that have not attained the primary ambient air quality standards for vehicle-related pollutants, are required to submit transportation control plans (TCPs) as part of their SIPs.

The Act provides specific emission standards for hydrocarbons, carbon monoxide and nitrogen oxides created by automobiles and light-duty trucks. Section 202, 42 U.S.C.A. § 7521. The 1990 amendments require long-overdue emission standards for diesel-powered vehicles, including heavy trucks. In addition, the Act empowers the EPA to test engines at the assembly plant, or loading dock, § 206, 42 U.S.C.A. § 7525, and requires catalytic converters, protected by a 50,000 mile or 5-year warranty. Section 207, 42 U.S.C.A. § 7541. The 1990 law increases the warranty period to 100,000 miles or 10 years for new requirements.

But catalytic converter and warranty requirements are only effective if vehicle owners know whether their emission controls are operating properly. This, of course, means the inspection of exhaust systems -- a strategy not provided for in the Clean Air Act. Whey wasn't it? Congress left inspection, along with reductions in parking and driving, to the states in the transportation control plans mandated by § 110 of the Act, 42 U.S.C.A. § 7410.

FRIENDS OF THE EARTH v. CAREY, United States Court of Appeals, Second Circuit, 1976, 535 F.2d 165.

Mansfield, Circuit Judge:

[The State of New York] submitted to the EPA a plan called the Transportation Control Plan for the Metropolitan New York City Area ("the Plan"), containing 32 mandatory "strategies" or schedules of specific actions to be taken by certain dates to abate air pollution. The strategies were designed to meet the 1975 primary air quality deadline, to maintain air quality beyond that date, to create contingency steps or procedures should the primary strategies fail, and to plan for attainment of the secondary ambient air quality standards. The Plan was approved by the EPA on June 22, 1973, with certain revisions. [W]ith the acceptance by the EPA and judicial ratification by this court, [on review in 1974] the Plan became binding upon and enforceable against state and local officials, subject only to the narrow revision and postponement provisions allowed by the Act.

Nevertheless, enforcement of the Plan's strategies suffered because of inaction on the part of those legally obligated to put it into effect. * * * The Act expressly provides only two methods for securing enforcement; a suit initiated by the EPA, § 113, 42 U.S.C. [§ 7413,] or a citizen suit pursuant to § 304, 42 U.S.C. [§ 7604,] which authorizes citizens, as private attorneys general, to enforce state implementation plans provided (a) the citizen gives 60 days' notice of a violation to the EPA, the state and the alleged violator, and (b) the EPA or state has failed within the 60-day period to secure compliance or to bring an action for enforcement. Section 304(a)(1) provides that upon meeting these requirements

[a]ny person may commence a civil action on his own behalf

"(1) against any person (including (i) the United States, and (ii) any other governmental instrumentality or agency to the extent permitted by the Eleventh Amendment to the Constitution) who is alleged to be in violation of (a) an emission standard or limitation under this chapter or (B) an order issued by the Administrator or a State with respect to such a standard or limitation. . . .

[P]laintiffs served their citizen suit notice of violation, and, after the required 60-day notice period had expired without compliance by the State and without the initiation of enforcement proceedings by the EPA, plaintiffs on October 11, 1974, commenced their action in the Southern District of New York and applied for preliminary relief. The City sought to avoid injunctive relief on the ground that the Plan was in the process of being formally revised. The State's Assistant Attorney General, on the other hand, * * * acknowledged that the Plan "is a legally enforceable plan, is a legally adequate plan and that the state is committed. . . to fulfilling its responsibilities thereunder." However, he then informed the court that the "State apparently has no intention of implementing certain strategies," while admitting that "[i]f there is a valid legal ground for such a refusal, we have not been able to find it, your honor." In addition, he disputed the legal contention of both the city officials and the State Department of Environmental Conservation "that the proposed revision precluded enforcement of the plan," by noting that the revision was "speculative at best" and that the Governor-elect had opposed any such revision. Events a mere four days later proved the speaker correct concerning the uncertain nature of the "pending" revision.

The district court, Kevin T. Duffy, Judge, recognized that the State and City in effect conceded that they were in noncompliance with the Plan. However, * * * Judge Duffy denied relief, stating that in light of the proposed revision he would await clarification of the EPA's position and that the court lacked the expertise to supervise enforcement, which would involve "highly technical" problems.

Four days later the EPA ruled that the State had failed to complete its application for a revision and on January 8, 1975, issued notices of violation with respect to 12 of the 32 strategies contained in the Plan, § 113(a)(1),* * *. The EPA, however, refused to initiate judicial enforcement proceedings as authorized by § 113 of the Act and instead attempted to negotiate consensual administrative orders. By July, 1975, three months after the March 31 deadline for satisfaction of the primary ambient standards had expired, the City and State remained in explicit violation of four of the most important strategies,[4] and had consented to eight other strategies.[5] Administrative action apparently had not even been commenced to enforce the remaining twenty. As of that date, although the Plan was designed to reduce carbon monoxide pollution by 78%, carbon monoxide levels in the City (95% of which are attributable to motor vehicles) had actually increased since pre-Plan days by some 25% and were now five times the level set by federal health standards. Thus these violations were significantly harmful to public health.

[4]These strategies are: reductions in business district parking, selective ban on taxicab cruising, tolls on the East and Harlem River bridges, and night-time freight movement.* * *

[5]Emission inspections of cars, trucks, and taxicabs, mechanic training, enforcing existing traffic regulations, traffic management, increased express bus services, and retrofit of trucks. Even here, however, the plaintiffs allege that city and State officials have failed to comply with the administrative order. The EPA recently has filed separate suit to enforce the taxicab-inspection strategy.

In late July the Transit Authority announced a pending transit fare increase from 35 cents to 50 cents. Believing that such an increase would undermine implementation of the Plan, plaintiffs returned to the district court * * * and, through an order to show cause, sought a preliminary injunction restraining the fare increase and ordering Plan enforcement. [P]laintiffs moved for partial summary judgment enforcing four strategies that indisputably were being violated and that were cited as violations by the EPA. See note 7 *supra*. In addition, plaintiffs again requested the enforcement of the entire Plan.

[T]he district court again denied plaintiffs' request for relief on several grounds. In refusing to enjoin the fare increase Judge Duffy noted that the original complaint and statutory notice required by § 304(b)(1) had failed to name the Transit Authority ("TA"), the agency to which responsibility for the fare increase had been delegated. Therefore, although notice was given to its sister agency, the Metropolitan Transportation Authority, and to the state authorities officially responsible for compliance with the Plan, and although TA officials had notice in fact, the district court dismissed the complaint as to the TA for violating "[s]tandards of fairness and due process." In addition, the court found that there was a "substantial question" as to whether the court had subject matter jurisdiction over the fare increase since the terms of the Plan did not prohibit such an increase.

The district court also refused enforcement of the Plan. Even though the defendants had not denied plaintiffs' allegations that they were in outright violation of at least four important strategies and were in various stages of noncompliance with the remaining twenty-eight, the district court, apparently proceeding on the basis of unsupported assumptions derived from "a plethora of paper emanating from the parties," concluded that "there exist many true issues of fact. . . ."[6] The court also apparently relied upon the fact that several orders were "presently under negotiation" between the EPA and the State. However, the court neither defined these "issues of fact" nor explained the reasons for its unwillingness to enforce those strategies as to which the defendants were clearly in default other than to state that enforcement would necessitate excessive supervision by the district court "where there is already a federal agency charged with the enforcement of the Plan." Accordingly, he ordered that the action be dismissed unless plaintiffs joined the EPA as a party within 10 days. * * *

In enacting § 304 of the 1970 Amendments, Congress made clear that citizen groups are not to be treated as nuisances or troublemakers but rather as welcomed participants in the vindication of environmental interests. Fearing that

---

[6]Judge Duffy, referring to the eight strategies with respect to which formal administrative consent orders had been negotiated between the State and the EPA, see note 8 supra, noted that plaintiffs alleged that even these orders had not been complied with and proceeded to surmise that "[i]t must be assumed that defendants would disagree with this allegation." From this he apparently concluded that, since "it must be assumed" that at least these eight of the 32 strategies remain in dispute, relief is properly denied as to all of the Plan's provisions.

administrative enforcement might falter or stall, "the citizen suits provision reflected a deliberate choice by Congress to widen citizen access to the courts, as a supplemental and effective assurance that the Act would be implemented and enforced." *Natural Resources Defense Council, Inc., v. Train,* 166 U.S. App. D.C. 312, 510 F.2d 692, 700 (1975). The Senate Committee responsible for fashioning the citizen suit provision emphasized the positive role reserved for interested citizens:

Government initiative in seeking enforcement under the Clean Air Act has been restrained. Authorizing citizens to bring suits for violations of standards should motivate governmental agencies charged with the responsibility to bring enforcement and abatement proceedings.* * *

And the Congress apparently was sufficiently pleased with the operation of the citizen suit section of the Clean Air Act to essentially duplicate the provision in the subsequently enacted Water Pollution Control Act of 1972, § 505, 33 U.S.C. § 1365 [now the Clean Water Act].

Thus the Act seeks to encourage citizen participation rather than to treat it as curiosity or a theoretical remedy. Possible jurisdictional barriers to citizens actions, such as amount in controversy and standing requirements, are expressly discarded by the Act. As additional encouragement the Act expressly authorizes courts to award costs of litigation to any party when "appropriate," § 304(d); * * * Once a citizen suit to enforce an EPA-approved state implementation plan has been properly commenced, the district court is obligated, upon a showing that the state has violated the plan, to issue appropriate orders for its enforcement. The court may not, over the plaintiff's objection, escape this obligation on the ground that the EPA is attempting to negotiate consent orders or has not been joined as a party in the citizen suit. Indeed, since it is EPA's failure to obtain compliance and to seek enforcement that brings the citizen suit into play, it would defeat the very purpose of that enforcement mechanism to require that the EPA be dragged reluctantly into the enforcement proceedings. The statute simply obligates the citizen plaintiff to provide the EPA with notice of the Plan's violation and of the upcoming private enforcement suit, § 304(b)(1)(A). The agency can then decide for itself whether or not to participate in the proceedings. "[T]he Administrator has the right to intervene in the suit, but he is not required to be a participant in such litigation and his absence does not render the action infirm." *Metropolitan Washington Coalition for Clean Air v. District of Columbia*, 167 U.S. App. D.C. 243, 511 F.2d 809, 814-15 (1975).

Of course the EPA's participation in a citizen enforcement suit is welcomed by the court, since the EPA, as the agency vested by Congress with important overall responsibilities related to the matter under consideration, possesses expertise which should enable it to make a major contribution. But both the underlying rationale and legislative history surrounding the citizen suit provision demonstrate that Congress intended the district court to enforce the mandated air quality plan irrespective of the failings of agency participation. As noted earlier, the very purpose of the citizens' liberal right of action is to stir slumbering agencies and to circumvent bureaucratic inaction that interferes with the scheduled satisfaction of the federal air quality goals.

Nor may the district court deny citizen enforcement of an approval state implementation plan on the ground that the task of supervising enforcement would be unduly burdensome or require the court to grapple with "highly technical" problems. Whatever may be the wisdom of having added this chore to the others imposed by new legislation upon the federal judiciary, Congress' intention that the courts must accept the duty is clear and unmistakable. Realizing that the responsibility for enforcement would thus fall upon the courts, Congress nevertheless viewed a plan's strategies as containing sufficiently clear and specific guidelines to enable a federal judge to direct compliance, armed as he is with the power to obtain such expert advice and assistance as may be necessary to guide him. [I]n adopting § 304, Congress specifically considered but rejected arguments advocating the deletion or weakening of the citizen suit section of the Act on the ground that enforcement difficulties would overburden the courts.

With these principles in mind we turn to the issues which are the immediate subject of this appeal: whether the district court erred in (1) refusing to enjoin the transit fare increase, and (2)refusing to enforce those strategies of the Plan which admittedly are being violated and to take steps toward enforcement of the other provisions of the Plan. With respect to the first of these two matters the fare increase we hold that the district court did not abuse its discretion in denying preliminary relief. As for the enforcement of the Plan's strategies, we direct the district court immediately to issue such orders as are necessary to enforce those strategies admittedly being violated and to conduct an expeditious hearing to determine the remaining violations and to enforce the other strategies as required by the Plan.

The district court's primary basis for refusing to enjoin the transit fare increase was its finding that the notice given by the plaintiffs to the TA, the governmental agency to which responsibility for the transit fare schedules is delegated by the state, was inadequate. We disagree and find that the notice [to the Governor and the MTA] was clearly sufficient. [The District Court's] technical, crabbed reading of the statute's notice requirement [was] clearly erroneous[. Its] excessively restrictive construction of the citizen suit notice requirement is completely at odds with the announced purpose of the statute, which looks to substance rather than to form in an effort to facilitate citizen involvement.* * *

Looking both to the letter of the statute and to the purposes underlying the citizen suit provision, plaintiffs adequately performed their responsibility of providing informative notice. Under the Act the parties required to be notified were the "Administrator," § 304(b)(1)(A)(i), the "State in which the violation occurs," § 304(b)(1)(A)(ii), and the "alleged violator," § 304(b)(1)(A)(iii). It is undisputed that the Administrator and the State were both notified The only remaining question is whether the requirement of notice to the "alleged violator" obligates the citizen to give formal notice directly to all of the involved agencies of the State in addition to notice to the primary State officials. Since the agencies merely act as delegates of the State, we hold that it does not.

As evident here, a state air pollution plan is likely to involve participation on the part of literally dozens of state and local agencies. To require that precise formalistic notice be provided to each is to erect wholly unrealistic barriers to citizen access to the courts as insured by Congress. The citizen would be relegated to a guessing-game reminiscent of strict common-law pleading long ago discarded. [I]t is undisputed that actual notice was provided both to [the TA] and to the MTA. Regardless of the hat being worn by the joint officials of the MTA and TA, this notification in fact advised them of the proposed citizen suit and afforded them the requisite opportunity and time to investigate and to act on the alleged violation. Accordingly, we reinstate the TA as a defendant in action.

As a further ground for refusing to enjoin the transit fare increase the district court stated that "[t]here is also [a] substantial question in my mind as to whether this Court has subject matter jurisdiction over the fare increase," since jurisdiction was grounded upon the Clean Air Act, § 304(a)(1), and the Plan promulgated thereunder "does not contain any language prohibiting a fare increase." We agree that jurisdiction is not available in this enforcement proceeding to test the validity of the fare increase.

The citizen suit provision of the Act speaks in specific terms, conferring jurisdiction on the court to entertain any citizen suit claiming a violation of "an emission standard or limitation under this chapter" or of "an order issued by the Administrator or a State with respect to such a standard or limitation. . . ." § 304(a)(1). The stabilization of transit fares is not an expressed strategy of the Plan[.] As a result, the fare increase is not an overt violation of the above provisions of § 304 and we lack subject matter jurisdiction to review the propriety of the TA's action.* * *

The primary relief sought by the citizen plaintiffs is enforcement of the Plan, which was approved by the EPA pursuant to § 110(a)(2) of the Clean Air Act,* * * and upheld by this court some 20 months ago[.]

In denying relief under the citizen suit provision the court [below] referred to the existence of ongoing negotiations between the EPA and the State and City Authorities designed to reach consent decrees carrying out the Plan's mandated strategies. We join the district court in recognizing the utility of such deliberations and the desirability of attaining compliance through consensual means. But it is equally clear that the statute empowers neither the EPA nor the State to delay the approved Plan's strategies through negotiations, be they formal or otherwise. Negotiations are no substitute for enforcement and for timely compliance with the Plan's mandated strategies. Consequently, the district court erred in permitting the continuation of EPA State discussions to bar suit by citizen groups seeking judicial enforcement of the Plan's expressed provisions. The Act authorizes only two procedural routes for modifying the Plan: a §110(a)(3) revision or a § 110(f) postponement. In all other instances, the State is relegated to a lone option: compliance.

We are aware that enforcement of the air quality plan might well cause inconvenience and expense to both governmental and private parties, particularly when a congested metropolitan community provides the focal point of the controversy. But Congress decreed that whatever time and money otherwise might be saved should not be gained at the expense of the lungs and health of the community's citizens[.]

The record before us is one that cries out for prompt and effective relief if the congressional clean air mandate is to have any meaning and effect in New York City. [I]t is beyond serious dispute that the defendants are now almost a year in default in carrying out the principal strategies of the mandated Plan, which are central to achieving the primary ambient air quality standards prescribed by Congress, with the result that the public of New York City is exposed to carbon monoxide pollution that has in the meantime climbed to over five times the federal health standards. The court cannot consistently with its duty be a party to the delaying process that has led to this situation.* * *

## Notes

Several of the strategies in the New York TCP proved politically controversial, notably tolls on the East River and Harlem River bridges. The state and the city, which had incorporated that strategy in the plan, under subsequent administrations vigorously opposed it. The Act was amended in 1977 to resolve the impasse. Under amended § 110 (42 U.S.C.A. § 7410(c)(5)), known as the Moynihan-Holtzman amendment after its sponsors, a governor may remove bridge tolls within a city from a plan provided he or she revises the plan to expand or improve public transportation and to implement transportation control measures to obtain an equal gain in air quality.

Transit fare increases in cities like New York, where most residents and commuters use public transportation, clearly have enormous air quality implications. The courts have recognized the major impact of fare increases. See *ACORN* v. *Southeastern Penna. Public Transp. Admin.*, 462 F. Supp. 879 (E.D.Pa. 1978).

Most states, unlike New York, failed to produce adequate TCPs, or transportation control plans. After an initial series of skirmishes over the EPA's authority to write a plan where the state has failed, see *Brown* v. *EPA*, 521 F.2d 827 (9th Cir. 1975),vacated as moot, 431 U.S. 99, 97 S.Ct. 1635, 52 L.Ed.2d 166 (federal government lacks power to direct the states to legislate), Congress found a way to achieve the result. The 1977 Clean Air Act amendments furnished the EPA the authority to withhold federal funds for highways or for air quality enforcement, as well as permits for new sources, to states not submitting TCPs approved by the Agency. See 42 U.S.C.A. § 7506(a).

This effective brandishing of the carrot in place of the legally questionable stick made all the difference. States began to adopt inspection and maintenance ("I & M") programs for in-use vehicles, requiring their exhaust systems and catalytic converters to be inspected as part of vehicle owners' annual safety inspections. New York has had such a program for the Metropolitan area since 1981.

In the late 1980s states with worsening traffic and air pollution have recognized the need to take further steps. Yearly increases in vehicle-miles traveled in and around major cities have more than canceled out the improvements in air quality that resulted from emission reductions. California, expressly exempt from the Act's federal preemption of motor vehicle equipment since the state required catalytic converters as early as 1966, adopted a series of stringent and dramatic traffic and vehicular controls in 1989. These measures, applicable to the Los Angeles area, would have limited the number of automobiles one family might own and imposed higher parking fees for cars occupied by one person. By 1998, 40% of cars, 70% of trucks and all buses would have to run on a non-polluting fuel, and by 2007 no gasoline-powered vehicles could be operated in the Los Angeles area.

However, California later retreated from these draconian measures. Under 2001 rules it now requires 4% of new cars sold to be zero emission vehicles and 6% to use alternative fuels to gasoline or diesel oil. In addition, its South Coast Air Quality Management District, a regional agency with jurisdiction over air quality in the Los Angeles area, enacted rules requiring owners of fleets of vehicles, including trucks and buses as well as cars, to purchase solely alternative-fuel or low emission vehicles. These were promptly challenged as preempted by Clean Air Act § 209, which exempts states, but not political subdivisions, from the EPA standards. 42 U.S.C.A. § 7543. The Supreme Court largely agreed that the rules were preempted, though it remanded for the lower courts to decide whether the agency might regulate state-owned, leased, or used vehicles, which the Act does not clearly preempt. *Engine Manufacturers Ass'n* v. *South Coast Air Quality Management Dist.*, __ U.S. __, 124 S. Ct. 1756, 158 L. Ed. 2d 529 (2004).

In addition, California has stricter requirements for catalytic converters, and New York has followed suit with similar requirements under a provision of the Act allowing states to adopt controls like those of California. Section 177, 42 U.S.C.A. § 7507.

The 1990 Act requires any federally-funded highway or mass transit program to conform to the state's SIP, a potentially powerful weapon for air quality improvement -- the "conformity provision." Congress continues to add mechanisms to reduce vehicular air pollution and most states continue to balk.

The Supreme Court ruled that allowing trucks registered in Mexico to use United States roads did not trigger this conformity provision. The Court held it was the lifting of a ban on those trucks by the President, acting pursuant to the North American Free Trade Agreement (NAFTA), and not any action by a federal agency subject to the conformity provision, that authorized the trucks to enter. The Federal Motor Carrier Safety Administration, part of the Department of Transportation, an agency subject to the conformity provision, must adopt safety rules before the trucks may use United States highways. And Mexican-registered vehicles are not covered by Clean Air Act requirements. Nonetheless, the Court found it was the President's action, not the agency's, that would case the environmental effects. *Department of Transportation* v. *Public Citizen*, __ U.S. __, 124 S. Ct. 2204, 159 L. Ed. 2d 60 (2004).

Fuel Standards

The Act expressly allows the EPA to regulate fuels used in motor vehicles; and as we saw in *Exxon* (subsection A), this is a federally-preempted area. It was through this provision, 42 U.S.C.A. § 7545, that lead was phased out as a gasoline additive. Recall the *Ethyl Corp.* case in Chapter 1. The removal of lead is the single unalloyed success story in air pollution for vehicles. The other vehicle-related pollutants continue to increase with increased vehicle-miles traveled, even though each individual vehicle emits far fewer pollutants. The 1990 amendments to the Act (§ 211[k], 42 USCA § 7545[k]) require "reformulated" gasoline, desgined to reduce ozone-producing pollutants that cause smog. But one additive aimed at achieving this, MTBE (methyl tertiary butyl ether), turned out to be a serious water pollutant, and New York and California have banned its use.

Since California has commenced a gradual phase-out of gasoline-powered vehicles from the Los Angeles area, as discussed in the previous note, the race is now on to develop a zero-emission vehicle, or ZEV, and New York and several other northeastern states have adopted California's mandate for a ZEV, along with the stricter emission controls discussed earlier.

Compressed natural gas, already in large-scale use in New Zealand and Brazil, is one likely choice. Electric vehicles are also being considered, and hybrid gasoline–electric powered vehicles, in which the gasoline engine recharges the electric battery, are now available, eliminating the need for recharging every 100 miles or so. Which would be better? What are the advantages and drawbacks of each? Still in the wings, but apt to enter soon, is the prospect of a totally pollution-free hydrogen-powered vehicle. This would enormously reduce energy concerns, which we will look at in Chapter 8.

Aircraft Emissions

The third mobile source area federally preempted under the Act, along with new motor vehicles and fuels for mobile sources, is that of emissions from aircraft. This dovetails with the larger federal preemption of the entire field of aviation through the Federal Aviation Act, discussed in the next chapter.

The EPA adopts regulations limiting air emissions from aircraft, but only after consultation with the Federal Aviation Agency (FAA), to ensure that the rules are consistent with safety. Enforcement is done by the FAA. The citizen suit remedy, described later in this chapter, is not available here since the rules are not enforced by the EPA.

## F. THE CLEAN AIR ACT: ENFORCEMENT

UNITED STATES v. TIVIAN LABORATORIES, INC., United States Court of Appeals, First Circuit, 1978. 589 F.2d 49, cert. denied 442 U.S. 942.

Levin H. Campbell, Circuit Judge.

Appellant Tivian Laboratories, Inc. challenges the constitutionality of the provisions of the [Clean Water Act,] 33 U.S.C. § 1318(a)(1)(A)(v), and the [Clean Air Act,] 42 U.S.C. § 7414(a)(i)(1)(E))[,] which authorize the Environmental Protection Agency (EPA) to "require the owner or operator of any [emission or point] source. . . to provide [the agency with] such information as [it] may reasonably require" to carry out its responsibilities under the Acts. These provisions, Tivian contends, violate the fourth amendment's prohibition of unreasonable searches and seizures, the thirteenth amendment's bar against involuntary servitude, and the fifth amendment's guarantee of due process.

Tivian is a small corporation engaged in the production of plating solutions, resins, waxes, and chemical specialties for metal casting and finishing. In October 1975 the EPA sent it a letter, requesting detailed information concerning the company's acquisition, use, and disposal of polychlorinated biphenyls (PCBs) and comparable chemical substances. The letter stated that the agency was "attempting to determine the sources and amounts of these chemical substances entering the environment" as part of an investigation into "the nature and extent of the possible adverse effects resulting from [their] presence. . . ." Section 1318 of the [Clean Water] Act and [§ 7414] of the [Clean Air] Act were cited as the agency's authority for requesting the information.

Tivian persistently refused to comply with EPA's request. In May 1976 the United States, on behalf of the EPA and pursuant to its authority under the Acts, commenced suit in federal district court to obtain judicial enforcement of its request, [and] to have civil fines imposed on Tivian for its refusal to supply the data voluntarily.

[T]he government moved for summary judgment. Tivian responded by challenging the constitutionality of the Acts. At the hearing on the motion, the district court ruled against Tivian on each of its constitutional claims, granted the motion for summary judgment, and ordered Tivian to supply the data sought forthwith.* * * The procedure followed by the EPA to obtain information from Tivian was in accordance with the authority conferred upon it under the two Acts. Each Act requires the EPA, in cooperation with other state and federal agencies, to identify and reduce or eliminate the discharge of pollutants into the environment. To achieve these objectives the agency is authorized to request the owner or operator of a company using chemicals which may be hazardous to the environment to supply the agency with whatever information it "may reasonably require" to carry out its statutory responsibilities. Upon a company's refusal to comply with the request, the EPA may go to court to have the request enforced. It may also seek penalties for violations of the Acts.

Tivian complains that EPA warned it in a letter requesting data that should it fail to provide the data sought, it would be subjected to substantial fines. This attempt by the EPA, allegedly acting to compel Tivian to produce records without first obtaining a court order or warrant is claimed to have violated appellant's fourth amendment rights.

We find Tivian's contention of a fourth amendment violation to be without merit. In making the contention, Tivian misstates the facts. EPA's letter to Tivian did not refer to the penalty provisions of the Acts or even address the issue of noncompliance. Thus, even assuming the matter were of legal consequence, there is no record support for Tivian's assertion that it was threatened with fines prior to the commencement of this suit. Threats or no, the agency's request for information is not enforceable under the Acts, nor may fines be imposed, until a court order is obtained. Consequently, any contention that the Acts permit the EPA, without first obtaining judicial leave, to force Tivian to produce records is simply untrue. The agency may ask for the data without a court order, but must turn to the court to have its request enforced.

The procedure for data gathering authorized by the Acts is similar to another procedure, the issuance of subpoenas duces tecum, which agencies are commonly authorized to use to procure corporate records. Subpoenas duces tecum used by agencies to obtain evidence relevant not only to pending charges, but also to investigations into whether charges should issue, have withstood fourth amendment challenges. *See, e.g., Oklahoma Press Publishing Co. v. Walling,* 327 U.S. 186, 201, 208-09, 66 S. Ct. 494, 90 L.Ed. 614 (1946). A subpoena may be issued without first obtaining a court's permission, and may be judicially enforced without a showing that probable, or even reasonable, cause exists to believe that a violation of law has occurred.* * *

In general, what the fourth amendment requires as a condition to enforcement of any agency subpoena is a showing by the agency (1) that its investigation is authorized by Congress and is for a purpose Congress can order and (2) that the documents sought are relevant to the investigation and adequately described. *Oklahoma Press Publishing Co. v. Walling*[.]

Tivian has not established that EPA's request fails to meet the grounds in (1), nor does it contend that the requested documents are inadequately described or irrelevant to the agency's investigation. Nothing on the face of the request transgresses these bounds. Hence, we find no fourth amendment violation.

Tivian's thirteenth amendment challenge is based on the argument that the practical effect of the demand for records is to compel Tivian to incur an otherwise unnecessary expense, overtime wages, so that its employees can find and transmit the requested data while keeping up with their normal duties. Being compelled to incur this expense allegedly constitutes involuntary servitude within the thirteenth amendment. Even assuming, however, that a corporation has rights under the thirteenth amendment and that the amendment is not otherwise inapplicable, we find no violation. The thirteenth amendment "has no application to a call for service made by one's government according to law to meet a public need. . . ." *Heflin v. Sanford*, 142 F.2d 798, 799 (5th Cir. 1944).* * *

Tivian's final challenge to the constitutionality of the * * * Acts, that the taking of its records was without the procedural due process required by the fifth amendment, is also without merit. The Acts provide for procedural due process. When Tivian refused to comply voluntarily, the EPA had to institute suit to obtain enforcement of its request. Before compliance was ordered, Tivian received ample opportunity in the district court to contest the request.

[W]e thus find no merit whatever in Tivian's constitutional attacks upon the statutes and the agency's actions[.]

AIR POLLUTION VARIANCE BOARD OF COLORADO v. WESTERN ALFALFA CORP., Supreme Court of the United States, 1974. 416 U.S. 861, 94 S. Ct. 2114, 40 L.Ed.2d 607.

Justice Douglas delivered the opinion of the Court.

An inspector of a division of the Colorado Department of Health entered the outdoor premises of respondent without its knowledge or consent. It was daylight and the inspector entered the yard to make a Ringelmann test[7] of plumes of smoke being emitted from respondent's chimneys. Since that time Colorado has adopted a requirement for a search warrant for violations of air quality standards. At the time of the instance inspection the state law required no warrant and none was sought. Indeed, the inspector entered no part of respondent's plant to make the inspection.* * *

[T]he sole question presented [is] whether Colorado has violated federal constitutional procedures in making the inspection in the manner described.* * *

Colorado's Air Pollution Variance Board * * * held a hearing and found that respondent's emissions were in violation of the state Act.* * *

The Colorado Court of Appeals [held] under *Camara* v. *Municipal Court,* 387 U.S. 523, 87 S. Ct. 1727, 18 L.Ed.2d 930, and *See* v. *City of Seattle,* 387 U.S. 541, 87 S.Ct. 1737, 18 L.Ed.2d 943, the act of conducting the tests on the premises of respondent without either a warrant or the consent of anyone from respondent constituted an unreasonable search within the meaning of the Fourth Amendment. We adhere to *Camara* and *See* but we think they are not applicable here. The field inspector did not enter the plant or offices. He was not inspecting stacks, boilers, scrubbers, flues, grates, or furnaces; nor was his inspection related to respondent's files or papers. He had sighted what anyone in the city who was

---

[7]This test is prescribed by Colo. Rev. Stat. Ann. § 66-29-5 (Supp 1967). It requires a trained inspector to stand in a position where he has an unobstructed view of the smoke plume, observe the smoke, and rate it according to the opacity scale of the Ringelmann chart. The person using the chart matches the color and density of the smoke plume with the numbered example on the chart. The Ringelmann test is generally sanctioned for use in measuring air pollution. * * *

near the plant could see in the sky plumes of smoke. The Court in *Hester* v. *United States*, 265 U.S. 57, 59, 44 S.Ct. 445, 68 L.Ed. 898, speaking through Mr. Justice Holmes, refused to extend the Fourth Amendment to sights seen in "the open fields." The field inspector was on respondent's property but we are not advised that he was on premises from which the public was excluded. The invasion of privacy, * * * if it can be said to exist, is abstract and theoretical.* * *

Notes

On remand the company, like the British Empire in the adage, lost every battle except the last. The Colorado courts held due process required that the state notify Western at the time that its smoke was being inspected, 534 P.2d 796, 35 Colo. App. 207 (1975), affirmed, 553 P.2d 811, 191 Colo. 455:

> [T]he Board ruled that the only probative evidence [against the company] was evidence relating to the alleged violation of June 4, 1969. Since Western had no representative present at the time the test was administered, and since the smoke was constantly dissipating, Western was effectively precluded from entering any affirmative evidence to rebut the evidence against it. Thus, it was forced to rely exclusively on cross-examination of the investigator.* * * However, no effective cross-examination of the investigator was possible to offset the prejudice to Western caused by the Division's failure to notify Western of the inspection until months after it took place. [Since] the defense had no reference upon which to base its questions nor independent knowledge as to what occurred, its opportunity to cross-examine was merely a hollow gesture.

Is this ruling good law?

When, if ever, does the Fourth Amendment's restriction on searches and seizures authorize inspection *inside* a source? As the cases marshaled in *Western Alfalfa* indicate, in general a warrant is needed for a government search of the interior of business premises. Some courts, however, have found a lesser expectation of privacy in a closely regulated business. See *Donovan v. Dewey*, 452 U.S. 598, 101 S.Ct. 937, 67 L.Ed.2d 108 (1981) (coal mine); *New York v. Burger*, 482 U.S. 691, 107 S.Ct. 2636, 96 L.Ed.2d 601 (1987) (auto dismantler).

The states are free to adopt stricter rules under state constitutional provisions, and some have. See, *e.g.*, *People v. Scott*, 79 N.Y.2d 474, 593 N.E.2d 1328, 583 N.Y.S.2d 920 (1992) (warrantless search of open fields violates state constitution).

Clean Air Act permits require the source to consent to inspection. What about an aerial search? Infra-red photography can reveal a great deal about a source's operations. One was sustained in *Dow Chemical Co. v. United States*, 476 U.S. 227, 106 S.Ct. 1819, 90 L.Ed.2d 226 (1986) (aerial search of interior regions of plant between buildings). Within buildings? See *Florida v. Riley*, 488 U.S.445, 109 S.Ct. 693, 102 L.Ed.2d 835 (1989) (sustaining helicopter search of greenhouse for marijuana).

ADAMO WRECKING CO. v. UNITED STATES, Supreme Court of the United States, 1978. 434 U.S. 275, 98 S.Ct. 566, 54 L.Ed.2d 538.

Justice Rehnquist delivered the opinion of the Court.

The Clean Air Act authorizes the Administrator of the Environmental Protection Agency to promulgate "emission standards" for hazardous air pollutants "at the level which in his judgment provides an ample margin of safety to protect the public health." § 112(b)(1)(B) [42 U.S.C.A. § 7412.] The emission of an air pollutant in violation of an applicable emission standard is prohibited by § 112(c)(1)(B) * * *. The knowing violation of the latter section, in turn, subjects the violator to fine and imprisonment under the provisions of § 113(c)(1)(C) * * *. The final piece in this statutory puzzle is § 307(b) [42 U.S.C.A. § 7607,] which provides in pertinent part:

(1) A petition for review of action of the Administrator in promulgating . . . any emission standard under section 112 . . . may be filed only in the United States Court of Appeals for the District of Columbia . . . Any such petition shall be filed within 30 days from the date of such promulgation or approval, or after such date if such petition is based solely on grounds arising after such 30th day.

(2) Action of the Administrator with respect to which review could have been obtained under paragraph (1) shall not be subject to judicial review in civil or criminal proceedings for enforcement.

It is within this legislative matrix that the present criminal prosecution arose.

Petitioner was indicted in the United States District Court for the Eastern District of Michigan for violation of § 112(c)(1)(B). The indictment alleged that petitioner, while engaged in the demolition of a building in Detroit, failed to comply with 40 C.F.R. § 61.22(d)(2)(i) (1975). That regulation, described in its caption as a "National Emission Standard for Asbestos," specifies procedures to be followed in connection with building demolitions, but does not by its terms limit emissions of asbestos which occur during the course of a demolition. The District Court granted petitioner's motion to dismiss the indictment on the ground that no violation of § 112(c)(1)(B), necessary to establish criminal liability under § 113(c)(1)(C), had been alleged, because the cited regulation was not an "emission standard" within the meaning of § 112(c). The United States Court of Appeals for the Sixth Circuit reversed, holding that Congress had in § 307(b) precluded petitioner from questioning in a criminal proceeding whether a regulation ostensibly promulgated under § 112(b)(1)(B) was in fact an emission standard. We granted certiorari, and we now reverse.

We do not intend to make light of a difficult question of statutory interpretation when we say that the basic question in this case may be phrased: "When is an emission standard not an emission standard?" Petitioner contends, and the District Court agreed, that while the preclusion and exclusivity provisions of § 307(b) of the Act prevented his obtaining "judicial review" of an emission standard in this criminal proceeding, he was nonetheless entitled to claim that the administrative regulation cited in the indictment was actually not an emission standard at all. The Court of Appeals took the contrary view. It held that a regulation designated by the Administrator as an "emission standard," however different in content it might be from what Congress had contemplated when it authorized the promulgation of emission standards, was sufficient to support a criminal charge based upon
' 112(c), unless it had been set aside in an appropriate proceeding commenced in the United States Court of Appeals for the District of Columbia Circuit pursuant to § 307(b).

The Court of Appeals in its opinion relied heavily on *Yakus* v. *United States*, 321 U.S. 414, 64 S. Ct. 660, 88 L.Ed. 834 (1944), in which this Court held that Congress in the context of criminal proceedings could require that the validity of regulatory action be challenged in a particular court at a particular time, or not at all. That case, however, does not decide this one. Because § 307(b) expressly applies only to "emission standards," we must still require as to the validity of the Government's underlying assumption that the Administrator's mere designation of a regulation as an "emission standard" is sufficient to foreclose any further inquiry in a criminal prosecution under § 113(c)(1)(C) of the Act. For the reasons hereafter stated, we hold that one such as [petitioner] who is charged with a criminal violation under the Act may defend on the ground that the "emission standard" which he is charged with having violated was not an "emission standard" within the contemplation of Congress when it employed that term, even though the "emission standard" in question has not been previously reviewed under the provisions of § 307(b) of the Act.

[Under the statute, n]ot only is the Administrator's promulgation of the standard not subject to judicial review in the criminal proceeding, but no prior notice of violation from the Administrator is required as a condition for criminal liability.[8] Since Congress chose to attach these stringent sanctions to the violation of an emission standard, in contrast to the violation of various other kinds of orders that might be issued by the Administrator, it is crucial to determine whether the Administrator's mere designation of a regulation as an "emission standard" is conclusive as to its character.

---

[8]The severity of the scheme is accentuated by the fact that persons subject to the Act, including innumerable small businesses, may protect themselves against arbitrary administrative action only by daily perusal of proposed emission standards in the Federal Register and by immediate initiation of litigation in the District of Columbia to protect their interests.

The stringency of the penalty imposed by Congress lends substance to petitioner's contention that Congress envisioned a particular type of regulation when it spoke of an "emission standard." The fact that Congress dealt more leniently, either in terms of liability, of notice, or of available defenses, with other infractions of the Administrator's orders suggests that it attached a peculiar importance to compliance with "emission standards." Unlike the situation in *Yakus*, Congress in the Clean Air Act singled out violators of this generic form of regulation, imposed criminal penalties upon them which would not be imposed upon violators of other orders of the Administrator, and precluded them from asserting defenses which might be asserted by violators of other orders of the Administrator. All of this leads us to conclude that Congress intended, within broad limits, that "emission standards" be regulations of a certain type, and that it did not empower the Administrator, after the manner of Humpty Dumpty in Through the Looking-Glass, to make a regulation an "emission standard" by his mere designation.* * *

In sum, a survey of the totality of the statutory scheme does not compel agreement with the Government's contention that Congress intended that the Administrator's designation of a regulation as an emission standard should be conclusive in a criminal prosecution. At the very least, it may be said that the issue is subject to some doubt. Under these circumstances, we adhere to the familiar rule that, "where there is ambiguity in a criminal statute, doubts are resolved in favor of the defendant."

We conclude, therefore, that a federal court in which a criminal prosecution under § 113(c)(1)(C) of the Clean Air Act is brought may determine whether or not the regulation which the defendant is alleged to have violated is an "emission standard" within the meaning of the Act. We are aware of the possible dangers that flow from this interpretation; district courts will be importuned, under the guise of making a determination as to whether a regulation is an "emission standard," to engage in judicial review in a manner that is precluded by § 307(b)(2) of the Act. This they may not do. The narrow inquiry to be addressed by the court in a criminal prosecution is not whether the Administrator has complied with appropriate procedures in promulgating the regulation in question, or whether the particular regulation is arbitrary, capricious, or supported by the administrative record. Nor is the court to pursue any of the other familiar inquiries which arise in the course of an administrative review proceeding. The question is only whether the regulation which the defendant is alleged to have violated is on its face an "emission standard" within the broad limits of the congressional meaning of that term.

[The Court examined the language of the Act and defined an "emission standard" as a quantitative level of particles allowed to be discharged into the air. It then looked at the regulation which the petitioner had violated. Since that regulation only specified work procedures at a demolition site and did not limit the quantity of asbestos allowed to be discharged into the air, the court said it was a work practice standard and not an "emission standard."]

For all of the foregoing reasons, we conclude that the work-practice standard involved here was not an emission standard. The District Court's order dismissing the indictment was therefore proper, and the judgment of the Court of Appeals is reversed.

Justices Stewart, Brennan, Blackmun, and Stevens dissented.

Notes

Does the regulation look like an "emission standard" to you? Is the Court's definition of "emission standard" too restrictive? Can you formulate a more appropriate one? Should the Administrator or the courts decide what constitutes an "emission standard?"

Following this decision the EPA adopted a work practice standard barring the conduct involved in *Adamo.*

The general rule is that where Congress prescribes a particular method of judicial review of an administrative regulation, the regulation may not later be challenged by the defendant in enforcement proceedings. See *Friends of the Earth* v. *Carey*, *supra* Part E:

> Since the City [of New York] could have advanced its present contentions by way of a petition for review of the Administrator's approval of the Plan in 1973 and chose instead voluntarily to commit itself to enforcement of the Plan, we hold that the city has waived its right to assert these contentions and is precluded by § 307(b)(2) of the Act from raising them in an enforcement proceeding instituted under § 304.

The Citizen Suit Provision

In *Friends of the Earth* v. *Carey*, Part E, we saw how the Court of Appeals' broad and hospitable construction of the citizen-suit provision of §304 "to stir slumbering agencies" has furnished a powerful weapon in air quality cases. Note that the section allows fees for attorneys and expert witnesses for a successful plaintiff. Even the construction of a stationary source may be reviewed through a citizen suit if controls on that source are part of an implementation plan. *Citizens Association of Georgetown* v. *Washington*, 383 F. Supp. 136 (D.D.C. 1974), reversed on other grounds, 535 F.2d 1318.

When is a citizen suit under §304 against a polluter barred by ongoing governmental action? The statute itself precludes a citizen suit if court action by the state or federal government is in progress. What about administrative enforcement at the level of the agency, not the courts? *Baughman* v. *Bradford Coal Co.*, 592 F.2d 215 (3d Cir. 1979), cert. denied 441 U.S. 961, holds an administrative agency proceeding is a bar if the agency has substantially the enforcement powers of a court. But *Gardeski* v. *Colonial Sand and Stone Co.*,

501 F. Supp. 1159 (S.D.N.Y. 1980), holds that even ongoing administrative enforcement efforts of a state's environmental protection agency may not always bar a citizen suit on the same matter. The court may examine the steps the agency has taken and assess its diligence. If the court finds that the matter has not been "diligently prosecuted" by the agency it may retain jurisdiction and act on the matter concurrently.

In addition to the injunctive relief available under § 304, the 1990 amendments to the Act also authorize a civil penalty, payable to the United States, not to the citizen plaintiff, who presumably has loftier motives.

## Environmental Audits

Companies now routinely audit their own operations to determine whether they are complying with the Clean Air Act and other environmental regulations, thus becoming aware of violations before government inspection takes place. Should the information gleaned from a self-audit be available to the EPA and the states' enforcement agencies?

Several states have legislated to make this material privileged, in order to encourage voluntary remediation. Is this a good idea? The EPA has ruled that corporate audit material is not privileged, but it will not seek punitive penalties or prosecute criminally on the basis of this information, except in the case of sources with a record of repeated offenses.

# 6. NOISE CONTROLS

## Introductory Note

Noise is generally defined as excessive, or unwanted, sound. Its adverse impact on health--physical and mental--has been well documented. It can no longer be regarded as merely esthetically unpleasing, and in fact exposure to aircraft or similar noise lowers property values and gives rise to actions in inverse condemnation, a species of *de facto* taking. A federal statute, the Noise Control Act, provides a modicum of regulation in this area.

## A. SURFACE NOISE

### The Noise Control Act

The federal Noise Control Act (42 U.S.C.A. §§ 4901-4918), enacted in 1972, empowers the EPA to prescribe maximum ambient noise levels, as well as maximum noise limits for major sources as manufactured, like the air pollution standards for motor vehicles in the Clean Air Act. Standards have been set for trucks, air compressors, motorcycles, compactors and motor homes. The Act goes on to prescribe warranty, labeling and anti-tampering requirements. But the analogy with the Clean Air Act ends there, and control of noise from the subsequent operation of these sources is left to the states. Only noise from trucks and railroad engines in operation is directly controlled by the Act. As to these, the states are preempted from imposing different requirements (though they are free to set identical limits, which they may then enforce).

Despite the existence of a host of state and local laws regulating noise, enforcement under them tends to be sporadic and penalties trivial. Here, at least as much as in other areas of environmental law, nuisance remains an effective remedy.

STATE OF NEW YORK v. WATERLOO STOCK CAR RACEWAY, INC., Supreme Court of New York, Seneca County, 1978. 96 Misc. 2d 350, 409 N.Y.S.2d 40.

John J. Conway, J.

This is an action brought by the State of New York, for itself and as *parens patriae* on behalf of the citizens of New York, seeking to enjoin permanently the use of certain property in the Village of Waterloo for stock car [racing at] the Seneca County Fairgrounds [by the] Waterloo Stock Car Raceway, Inc., [weekly from April to October].

The hours of operation are such that the cars begin to warm up before the scheduled 7:00 P.M. starting time and the last race does not end until approximately midnight.* * *

At trial the plaintiff produced 16 lay witnesses, residents of the Village of Waterloo, who, in general, testified to the disturbance created in the neighborhood by the stock car racing. In addition, the plaintiff produced two expert witnesses. The first, William Burnett, Director of Engineering Research and Development for the New York State Department of Transportation, testified as to the inadequacy of the guiderail surrounding the race track. Dr. Fred G. Haag, Principal Accoustical Engineer for the Department of Environmental Conservation, followed, and testified as to the noise levels created on race night by the operation of the raceway. The court found the technical evidence presented by Dr. Haag, as well as his opinion as to the injurious effect the loud noise can have on the populous of the community, to be highly persuasive.

The evidence introduced by Dr. Haag [showed that] on the average, during the approximately three and one-half hours of racing while he tested, noise levels were from two to eight times as loud as normal [and] exceed[ed] the EPA maximum acceptable day-night sound level by a wide margin. In fact, the intensity was so great that normal conversation at the seven locations was found to be impossible at a distance greater than four feet, and at four of those locations, beyond two feet.* * *

The 16 lay witnesses who testified at trial were neighbors in the vicinity of the racetrack.* * * The[ir] nearly universal description of the noise is that of a constant roar. As a consequence of this audio intrusion upon their lives, the witnesses testified to a serious alteration of their lifestyles in a futile attempt to adapt. Some keep their windows closed regardless of the heat, others make it a point to absent themselves from their homesteads on race nights, and most of them have been forced to cease using their out-of-doors property for entertainment of guests and for recreation on these nights. Conversation, whether in the homes or outside, has become exceedingly difficult due to the loud noise. A common complaint was that sleep both for the adults and their children has been inhibited. As a consequence of this lack of rest plus the constant roar, nervous tension and wracked nerves have resulted.

The noise is not the only suffering for the residents of the area. They also testified to clouds of dust being produced by the races which accumulated on their property. Apparently the range of the falling dust is as great as that of the noise. For those upon whom it comes to rest it necessitates washing of items of personal property after the day of the race.

Also of concern to the residents is that there is a definite danger [of] safety in the vicinity of the raceway from launched projectiles. Undisputed testimony was had at trial that at one time a racing tire flew across the street and hit a witness's garage, that on their occasions steel guiderails have fallen apart upon impact from the autos and have even been projected as far as the public street, and that on May 30, 1977 at one of the races a car was forced off the track and landed on three parked cars, not far from a resident's property.* * * The intrusions and hazards accompanying the operation of the raceway * * * add up to the severe alteration of an otherwise tranquil neighborhood.* * *

The complaints generated and the facts established in this case by the operation of the race track are not of a private nature; rather they expose an assault on the community as a whole. The common right involved is that of the neighborhood to its normal peace and quiet, which is one of its essential characteristics. Practically all the witnesses at trial agreed that this is a tranquil community. Were it not for the existence of the racetrack operations it would continue as such. As it is, everyone in the vicinity of the track has found their eardrums to be hammered away at during the nights the races take place, to expect an aftermath of dust accumulated on their property, and to live in fear for their continued safety * * * because of the danger from flying guiderails, racing tires, wood and errant cars.* * *

Defendants have countered that the operation of the racetrack is being lawfully conducted and is not in violation of zoning ordinances, being a prior existing use in a residentially zoned area, and therefore is not subject to attack as a nuisance. As recently as in the case of *Little Joseph Realty v.Town of Babylon* (41 N.Y.2d 738) the Court of Appeals stated that the use may be in full compliance with zoning ordinances but that it may still be enjoined as a nuisance. Every business has a duty to conduct its operations in a reasonable manner such that it does not materially interfere with the general well-being, health or property rights of neighbors or of people generally.* * * [W]hile there is nothing unlawful about the operation of a stock car raceway under proper circumstances, its use at its present location * * *, under all the circumstances, constitutes a public nuisance and should be discontinued. "A nuisance may be merely a right thing in the wrong place." (*Euclid v. Ambler Co.* [Chapter 3]).* * *

[The court enjoined stock car racing at the defendants' premises, except for a three-day period each year during the county fair.]

## Note: Nuisance and State Noise Control Statutes

A brief look at the legislative attempts to regulate noise will suffice to show why nuisance remains a valuable weapon in curbing excessive sound. Municipal laws tend to provide minor criminal penalties for "excessive" or "unreasonable" noise, with no provisions for regulating through permits, or injunctive measures. In what seemed an exception, the City of New York enacted an impressively detailed noise code in 1972 (New York City Administrative Code § 1403.3). It provides for noise-sensitive areas within the city and emission standards for construction equipment, jackhammers and other noise makers. But enforcement has been spotty and penalties have often been mild. The code removes noise from the criminal courts and turns enforcement over to an administrative agency, the Environmental Control Board.

Among the few states which regulate noise in more than rudimentary fashion, Illinois furnishes a comprehensive system of controls in its Environmental Protection Act (Illinois Rev. Stat. ch. 111 1/2, § 1023), prescribing emission limits for sources based on the use of the adjacent land--lower for residences, higher for industrial zones.

Is a statute proscribing "unreasonable noise" unconstitutionally vague? See *People v. New York Trap Rock Corp.*, 57 N.Y.2d 371, 442 N.E.2d 1222, 456 N.Y.S.2d 711 (1982) (no; "reasonable person" test firmly embedded in common law). But a law against "unnecessary" noise has been held unduly subjective, *Jim Crockett Promotion v. City of Charlotte,* 706 F.2d 846 (4th Cir. 1983).

### Highway Noise

The Federal-Aid Highway Act requires the Department of Transportation to set ambient noise standards for land adjacent to federally-aided highways, such as the Interstate System. These may be met through shielding, elevating or depressing the road, or purchasing land to create buffer zones around it.

### Workplace Noise

Noise, like other environmental and safety concerns in the workplace, is governed by OSHA, the Occupational Safety and Health Act, 29 U.S.C.A. §§ 651-678. This act, administered by the Occupational Safety and Health Administration, an arm of the Department of Labor, empowers that agency (also universally known as OSHA) to adopt rules regarding safety in workplaces. OSHA has adopted rules requiring hearing conservation measures for workers exposed to 85 decibels or more, and mandatory use of hearing protectors for workers experiencing hearing loss or who are exposed to high noise levels.

Should hearing protectors (worn over the ears) be the prime means of reducing excessive noise in the workplace, as opposed to installing quieter machinery and equipment? Are there safety concerns stemming from reliance on hearing protectors?

## B. AIRCRAFT NOISE

GRIGGS v. ALLEGHENY COUNTY, Supreme Court of the United States, 1962. 369 U.S. 84, 82 S.Ct. 531, 7 L.Ed. 2d 585.

Justice Douglas delivered the opinion of the Court.

[The plaintiff, a homeowner aggrieved by low-flying aircraft from the county-owned Greater Pittsburgh Airport, claimed the respondent county] has taken an air easement over petitioner's property for which it must pay just compensation as required by the Fourteenth Amendment.* * * The Greater Pittsburgh Airport [is] in conformity with the rules and regulations of the Civil Aeronautics Administration[a] within the scope of the National Airport Plan provided for in [the Airports and

---

[a]Now the Federal Aviation Administration [FAA].

Airways Development Act], 49 U.S.C. §§ 1101 [-1120]. By this Act the federal Administrator is authorized and directed to prepare and continually revise a "national plan for the development of public airports," § 1102(a), and to make grants to "sponsors" for airports development.* * * The United States agrees to share from 50% to 75% of the "allowable project costs," depending, so far as material here, on the class and location of the airport. § 1109.

Allowable costs payable by the Federal Government include "costs of acquiring land or interest therein or easements through or other interests in air space . . ." * * *

Respondent executed three agreements with the Administrator of Civil Aeronautics in which it agreed, among other things, to abide by and adhere to the rules and Regulations of C.A.A. and to "maintain a master plan of the airport," including "approach areas." It was provide that the "airport approach standards to be followed in this connection shall be those established by the Administrator;" and it was also agreed that respondent "will acquire such easements or other interests in lands and air space as may be necessary to perform the covenants of this paragraph." The "master plan" laid out and submitted by respondent included the required "approach areas;" and that "master plan" was approved. One "approach area" was to the northeast runway. As designed and approved, [there is] a clearance of 11.36 feet between the bottom of the glide angle and petitioner's chimney.* * *

The airlines that use the airport are lessees of respondent; and the leases give them, among other things, the right "to land" and "take off." No flights were in violation of the regulations of C.A.A.; nor were any flights lower than necessary for a safe landing or take-off. The planes taking off from the northeast runway observed regular flight patterns ranging from 30 feet to 300 feet over petitioner's residence; and on let-down they were within 53 feet to 153 feet.

On take-off the noise of the planes is comparable "to the noise of a riveting machine or steam hammer." On the let-down the planes make a noise comparable "to that of a noisy factory." * * *

We start with United States v.Causby, 328 U.S. 256, 90 L. Ed. 1206, which held that the United States by low flights of its military planes over a chicken farm made the property unusable for that purpose and that therefore there had been a "taking," in the constitutional sense, of an air easement for which compensation must be made.* * * The use of land presupposes the use of some of the airspace above it. Otherwise no home could be built, no tree planted, no fence constructed, no chimney erected. An invasion of the "super-adjacent airspace" will often "affect the use of the surface of the land itself."

It is argued that though there was a "taking," someone other than respondent was the taker--the airlines or the C.A.A. acting as an authorized representative of the United States. We think, however, that respondent, which was the promoter, owner, and lessor of the airport, was in these circumstances the one who took the air easement in the constitutional sense. Respondent decided, subject to the approval of the C.A.A., where the airport would be built, what runways it would need, their direction and length, and what land and navigation easements would be needed.

The Federal Government takes nothing; it is the local authority which decides to build an airport [or not], and where it is to be located. We see no difference between its responsibility for the air easements necessary for operation of the airport and its responsibility for the land on which the runways were built. Nor did the Congress when it designed the legislation for a National Airport Plan.* * * Congress provided for the payment to the owners of airports, whose plans were approved by the Administrator, a share of "the allowable project costs," including the "costs of acquiring land or interests therein or easements through or other interests therein or easements through or other interests in air space." ' 1112(a)(2).* * * That the instant "taking" was "for public use" is not debatable. For respondent agreed with the C.A.A. that it would operate the airport "for the use and benefit of the public" that it would operate "on fair and reasonable terms and without unjust discrimination." * * * Respondent in designing it had to acquire some private property. Our conclusion is that by constitutional standards it did not acquire enough.

Reversed.

Justice Black, with whom Justice Frankfurter concurs, dissenting.

I think that the United States, not the Greater Pittsburgh Airport, has "taken" the airspace over Griggs' property necessary for flight. While the County did design the plan for the airport including the arrangement of its takeoff and approach areas, in order to comply with federal requirements it did so under the supervision of and subject to the approval of the Civil Aeronautics Administrator of the United States.

Congress has over the years adopted a comprehensive plan for national and international air commerce, regulating in minute detail virtually every aspect of air transit--from construction and planning of ground facilities to safety and methods of flight operations.[13] As part of this overall scheme of development, Congress in 1938 declared that the Unites States has "complete and exclusive national sovereignty in the air space above the United States" and that every citizen has "a public right of freedom of transit in air commerce through the navigable air space of the United States." * * *

These airspaces are so much under the control of the Federal Government that every takeoff from and every landing at airports such as the Greater Pittsburgh Airport is made under the direct signal and supervisory control of some federal agent.* * * Congress has * * * appropriated the airspace necessary to approach the Pittsburgh airport as well as all the other airports in the country.* * * Merely because local communities might eventually be reimbursed for the acquisition of necessary easements does not mean that local communities must acquire easements that the United States has already acquired.* * * Congress has already declared airspace *free* to all--a fact not denied by the Court--pretty clearly it need not again be

---

[13] The Federal Aviation Agency Administrator is directed to prepare and maintain a "national plan for the development of public airports in the United States" taking "into account the needs of both air commerce and private flying, the probable technological developments in the science of aeronautics, [and] the probable growth and requirements of civil aeronautics." 49 U.S.C. § 1102.

acquired by an airport.* * * Having taken the airspace over Griggs' private property for a public use, it is the United States which owes just compensation.* * *

The construction of the Greater Pittsburgh Airport was financed in large part by funds supplied by the United States as part of its plan to induce localities like Allegheny County to assist in setting up a national and international air-transportation system. The Court's imposition of liability on Allegheny County, however, goes a long way toward defeating that plan because of the greatly increased financial burdens (how great one can only guess) which will hereafter fall on all the cities and counties which till now have given or may hereafter give support to the national program. I do not believe that Congress ever intended any such frustration of its own purpose.

Nor do I believe that Congress intended the wholly inequitable and unjust saddling of the entire financial burden of this part of the national program on the people of local communities like Allegheny County. The planes that take off and land at the Greater Pittsburgh Airport wind their rapid way through space not for the peculiar benefit of the citizens of Allegheny County but as part of a great, reliable transportation system of immense advantage of the whole nation.

## Notes

Is the inverse condemnation, or *de facto* taking, basis for *Griggs* a distortion of the "taking" doctrine? Normally, a taking of one's property under the Fifth Amendment occurs only when the owner has been deprived of all reasonable use of that property. See the *Penn Central* case, Chapter 3. But in aircraft noise cases a compensable taking by the airport proprietor occurs even though the plaintiff still has use of his or her property, albeit reduced in value. Is this because of the physical invasion of the owner's airspace?

Is the inverse condemnation remedy in reality more akin to nuisance than to an unconstitutional taking? Are cases like *Griggs* troublesome in keeping the law of *de facto* takings clear?

CITY OF BURBANK v. LOCKHEED AIR TERMINAL, INC., Supreme Court of the United States, 1973. 411 U.S. 624, 93 S.Ct. 1854, 36 L.Ed.2d 547.

Justice Douglas delivered the opinion of the Court.* * *

This suit * * * asked for an injunction against the enforcement of an ordinance adopted by the City Council of Burbank, California, which made it unlawful for a so-called pure jet aircraft to take off from the Hollywood-Burbank Airport between 11 p.m. of one day and 7 a.m. the next day, and making it unlawful for the operator of that airport to allow any such aircraft to take off from that airport during such periods.* * *

The Federal Aviation Act of 1958, [now] 49 [App.] USC §§ 1301 [-1557], as amended by the Noise Control Act of 1972, [is] central to the question of pre-emption.

Section 1508 provides in part, "The United States of America is declared to possess and exercise complete and exclusive national sovereignty in the airspace of the United States . . . " By § 1348(a), (c) the Administrator of the Federal Aviation Administration (FAA) has been given broad authority to regulate the use of the navigable airspace, "in order to insure the safety of aircraft and the efficient utilization of such airspace . . ." and "for the protection of persons and property on the ground . . ." * * *

The Solicitor General, though arguing against pre-emption, concedes that as respects "airspace management" there is pre-emption. That, however, is a fatal concession, for as the District Court found: "The imposition of curfew ordinances on a nationwide basis would result in a bunching of flights in those hours immediately preceding the curfew. This bunching of flights during these hours would have the twofold effect of increasing an already serious congestion problem and actually increasing, rather than relieving, the noise problem by increasing flights in the period of greatest annoyance to surrounding communities. Such a result is totally inconsistent with the objectives of the federal statutory and regulatory scheme." It also found "[t]he imposition of curfew ordinances on a nationwide basis would cause a serious loss of efficiency in the use of the navigable airspace."

Curfews such as Burbank has imposed would, according to the testimony at the trial and the District Court's finding, increase congestion, cause a loss of efficiency, and aggravate the noise problem.

[The] FAA has consistently opposed curfews, unless managed by it, in the interests of its management of the "navigable airspace." * * *

The Noise Control Act of 1972, * * * by amending § 611 of the Federal Aviation Act, also involves the Environmental Protection Agency (EPA) in the comprehensive scheme of federal control of the aircraft noise problem. Under the amended § 611(b)(1), FAA, after consulting with EPA, shall provide "for the control and abatement of aircraft noise and sonic boom, including the application of such standards and regulations in the issuance, amendment, modification, suspension, or revocation of any certificate authorized by this title." Section 611(b)(20), as amended, provides that future certificates for aircraft operations shall not issue unless the new aircraft noise requirements are met.* * *

The Noise Control Act reaffirms and reinforces the conclusion that FAA, in conjunction with EPA, has full control over aircraft noise, preempting state and local control.* * *

There is, to be sure, no express provision of pre-emption in the 1972 Act. That, however, is not decisive.* * * It is the pervasive nature of the scheme of federal regulation of aircraft noise that leads us to conclude that there is pre-emption. As Mr. Justice Jackson stated, concurring in Northwest Airlines, Inc. v. Minnesota, 322 U.S. 292, 303, 64 S.Ct. 950, 88 L.Ed. 1283:

Federal control is intensive and exclusive. Planes do not wander about in the sky like vagrant clouds. They move only by federal permission, subject to federal inspection, in the hands of federally certified personnel and under an intricate system of federal command. The moment a ship taxis onto a runway it is caught up in an elaborate and detailed system of controls.

Both the Senate and House Committees included in their Reports clear statements that the bills would not change the existing pre-emption rule.* * * The Senate Report stated: "States and local governments are pre-empted from establishing or enforcing noise emission standards for aircraft unless such standards are identical to standards prescribed under this bill. This does not address responsibilities or powers of airport operators, and no provision of the bill is intended to alter in any way the relationship between the authority of the Federal government and that of State and local governments * * *." * * *

The Secretary [of Transportation in] a written opinion [in response to a Congressional inquiry,] dated June 22, 1968, stated:

> The courts have held that the Federal Government presently preempts the field of noise regulation insofar as it involves controlling the flight of aircraft . . . [This bill] would merely expand the Federal Government's role in a field already preempted. It would not change this preemption. State and local governments will remain unable to use their police powers to control aircraft noise by regulating the flight of aircraft.

According to the Senate Report, it was "not the intent of the committee in recommending this legislation to effect any change in the existing apportionment of powers between the Federal and State and local governments," and the Report concurred in the views set forth by the Secretary in his letter.[14] [Further,] Congressman Staggers, Chairman of the House Committee on Interstate and Foreign Commerce, in urging the House to accept the [act,] said:

---

[14] The letter from the Secretary of Transportation also expressed the view that "the proposed legislation will not affect the rights of a State or local public agency, *as the proprietor of an airport*, from issuing regulations or establishing requirements as to the permissible level of noise which can be created by aircraft using the airport. Airport owners *acting as proprietors* can presently deny the use of their airports to aircraft on the basis of noise considerations so long as such exclusion is nondiscriminatory." (Emphasis added.) This portion as well was quoted with approval in the Senate Report. *Ibid.*

Appellants and the Solicitor General submit that this indicates that a municipality with jurisdiction over an airport has the power to impose a curfew on the airport, notwithstanding federal responsibility in the area. But, we are concerned here not with an ordinance imposed by the City of Burbank as "proprietor" of the airport, but with the exercise of police power. While the Hollywood-Burbank Airport may be the only major airport which is privately owned, many airports are owned by one municipality yet physically located in another. For example, the principal airport serving Cincinnati is located in Kentucky. Thus, authority that a municipality may have as landlord is not necessarily congruent with its police power. We do not consider here what limits, if any, apply to a municipality as a proprietor.

> * * *We have evidence that across America some cities and States are trying to * * * pass noise regulations. Certainly we do not want that to happen. It would harass industry and progress in America. That is the reason why I want to get this bill passed during this session.* * *

Control of noise is of course deep seated in the police power of the States. Yet the pervasive control vested in EPA and in FAA under the 1972 Act seems to use to leave no room for local curfews or other local controls. What the ultimate remedy may be for aircraft noise which plagues many communities and tens of thousands of people is not known.* * *

The Administration has imposed a variety of regulations relating to takeoff and landing procedures and runway preferences. The Federal Aviation Act requires a delicate balance between safety and efficiency, 49 U.S.C. § 1348a, * * * and the protection of persons on the ground... Any regulations adopted by the Administrator to control noise pollution must be consistent with the "highest degree of safety." 49 U.S.C. § 1431(d)(3).* * * The interdependence of these factors requires a uniform and exclusive system of federal regulation if the congressional objectives underlying the Federal Aviation Act are to be fulfilled.

If we were to uphold the Burbank ordinance and a significant number of municipalities followed suit, it is obvious that fractionalized control of the timing of take-offs and landings would severely limit the flexibility of the FAA in controlling air traffic flow. The difficulties of scheduling flights to avoid congestion and the concomitant decrease in safety would be compounded. In 1960 the FAA rejected a proposed restriction on jet operations at the Los Angeles airport between 10 p.m. and 7 a.m. because such restrictions could "create critically serious problems to all air transportation patterns." * * * [The FAA added:]

> The network of airports throughout the United States and the constant availability of these airports are essential to the maintenance of a sound air transportation system. The continuing growth of public acceptance of aviation as a major force in passenger transportation and the increasingly significant role of commercial aviation in the nation's economy are accomplishments which cannot be inhibited if the best interest of the public is to be served. It was concluded therefore that the extent of relief from the noise problem which this provision might have achieved would not have compensated the degree of restriction it would have imposed on domestic and foreign Air Commerce.

This decision, announced in 1960, remains peculiarly within the competence of the FAA, supplemented now by the input of the EPA. We are not at liberty to diffuse the powers given by Congress to FAA and EPA by letting the State or municipalities in on the planning. If that change is to be made Congress alone must do it.

Justice Rehnquist, with whom Justice Stewart, Justice White, and Justice Marshall join, dissenting.* * *

Appellees do not contend that the noise produced by jet engines could not reasonably be deemed to affect adversely the health and welfare of persons constantly exposed to it; control of noise, sufficiently loud to be classified as a public nuisance at common law, would be a type of regulation well within the traditional scope of the police power possessed by States and local governing bodies. Because noise regulation has traditionally been an area of local, not national, concern, in determining whether congressional legislation has, by implication, foreclosed remedial local enactments "we start with the assumption that the historic police powers of the States were not to be superseded by the Federal Act unless that was the clear and manifest purpose of Congress." Rice v.Santa Fe Elevator Corp., 331 U.S. 218, 230, 67 S. Ct. 1146, 91 L.Ed. 1447 (1947).* * *

The 1958 Act was intended * * * to regulate federally all aspects of air safety, * * * and, once aircraft were in "flight," air-space management.* * * While the Act might be broad enough *to permit* the Administrator to promulgate takeoff and landing rules to avoid excessive noise at certain hours of the day, see 49 U.S.C. § 1348(c), Congress was not concerned with the problem of noise created by aircraft and did not intend to pre-empt its regulation.* * *

The 1968 noise abatement amendment to the 1958 Act, 49 U.S.C. § 1431[,] was the first congressional legislation dealing with the problem of aircraft noise. On its face, the present § 611 neither pre-empts the general field of regulation of aircraft noise nor deals specifically with the more limited question of curfews.* * * [It] established exclusive federal control of the technological methods for reducing the output of noise by jet aircraft, but that is a far cry from saying that it prohibited any local regulations of the times at which the local airport might be available for the use of jet aircraft.

The Court of Appeals found critical to its decision the distinction between the local government as an airport proprietor and the local government as a regulatory agency, which was reflected in the views of the Secretary of Transportation outlined in the Senate Report on the 1968 Amendment. Under its reasoning, a local government unit that owned and operated an airport would not be pre-empted by § 611 from totally, or, as here, partially, excluding noisy aircraft from using its facilities, but a municipality having territorial jurisdiction over the airport would be pre-empted from enacting an ordinance having a similar effect. If the statute actually enacted drew this distinction, I would of course respect it. But since we are dealing with "legislative history,' rather than the words actually written by Congress into law, I do not believe it is of the controlling significance attributed to it by the court below.

The pre-emption question to which the Secretary's letter was addressed related to "the field of noise regulation insofar as it involves controlling the *flight* of aircraft" (emphasis added), and thus included types of regulation quite different from that enacted by the city of Burbank that would be clearly precluded. But more important is the highly practical consideration that the Hollywood-Burbank Airport is probably the only nonfederal airport in the country used by federally certified air carriers that is not owned and operated by a state or local government. There is no indication that this fact was brought to the attention of the Senate Committee, or that the Secretary of Transportation was aware of it in framing his letter. It simply strains credulity to believe that the Secretary, the Senate Committee, or Congress intended that all airports except the Hollywood-Burbank Airport could enact curfews.

A local governing body that owns and operates an airport is certainly not, by the Court's opinion, prohibited from permanently closing down its facilities. A local governing body could likewise use its traditional police power to prevent the establishment of a new airport or the expansion of an existing one within its territorial jurisdiction by declining to grant the necessary zoning for such a facility. Even though the local government's decision in each case were motivated entirely because of the noise associated with airports, I do not read the Court's opinion as indicating that such action would be prohibited by the Supremacy Clause merely because the Federal Government has undertaken the responsibility for some aspects of aircraft noise control. Yet if this may be done, the Court's opinion surely does not satisfactorily explain why a local governing body may not enact a far less "intrusive" ordinance such as that of the city of Burbank.

The history of congressional action in this field demonstrates, I believe, an affirmative congressional intent to allow local regulation. But even if it did not go that far, that history surely does not reflect "the clear and manifest purpose of Congress" to prohibit the exercise of "the historic police powers of the States" which our decisions require before a conclusion of implied pre-emption is reached.* * *

## Notes

Clearly, the last line of footnote 14, "We do not consider here what limits, if any, apply to a municipality as a proprietor," substantially limits the applicability of this case. More than likely judicial activists such as Justices Douglas and Rehnquist would have preferred to have settled the question with respect to all airports, albeit in diametrically opposed ways, but neither could find a consensus for his views.

Do you agree with Justice Rehnquist in his dissent when he argued that Burbank was probably the only airport this ruling would affect, and that "it simply strains credulity to believe that the Secretary, the Senate Committee, or Congress intended that all airports except the Hollywood-Burbank Airport could enact curfews?" As the following cases make clear, the majority opinion and its well-traveled footnote would not prevent the proprietor of the Airport from enacting a non-discriminatory curfew. (The Hollywood-Burbank Airport is in fact no longer privately owned.) Similarly, the holding in *Burbank* would, for example, prevent New York City from enacting similar regulations pursuant to its police power which would affect Kennedy International Airport, owned and operated by the Port Authority of New York and New Jersey.

Note that the plaintiff in *Burbank* also claimed the city's ordinance was an unconstitutional burden on interstate commerce. The court did not have to reach that question since it found the local law to be preempted. Does such a law, or an airport proprietor's regulation, unduly burden commerce?

AIR TRANSPORT ASSOCIATION OF AMERICA v. CROTTI, United States District Court, Northern District of California, 1975. 389 F. Supp. 58.

East, Senior District Judge:

The [plaintiff] Airlines contend that Sections 21669 to 21669.4, inclusive, of the California Public Utilities Code, and the implementing regulations, * * * referred to as California Noise Standards, * * * are invalid and unenforceable by virtue of Article VI, Clause 2, (Supremacy Clause) and Article I, Section 8, Clause 3, (Commerce Clause) of the Constitution of the United States, as implemented by controlling federal legislation and regulations, and seek a declaratory judgment to that effect and injunctive relief thereon.* * *

The federal statutes intending to regulate the intensity of noise generated by aircraft in flight and incident thereto are the Noise Control Act of 1972 and the regulations now and to be promulgated thereunder. Of particular note is Section 2(a)(3) of the Noise Control Act, 42 U.S.C. § 4901(1)(3), which reads:

> The Congress finds . . . "(3) that, while primary responsibility for control of noise rests with State and local governments, Federal action is essential to deal with major noise sources in commerce control of which require national uniformity of treatment." * * *

Sections 21669 and 21669.5, inclusive, of the California Public Utilities Code, *inter alia* required the California Department of Aeronautics to adopt noise regulations governing the operations of airports and of aircraft at all airports in California operating mandatorily under a permit issued by the Department of Aeronautics * * *. California Public Utilities Code § 21669.4 provides that the violation by any aircraft of the noise regulations so adopted is deemed a misdemeanor and the operator or such aircraft is punishable by a fine of $1,000 for each infraction. Pursuant to the same § 21669.4, the county in which the airport is situated is given responsibility to enforce the noise regulations adopted by the Department. The airport's non-compliance subjects their permit to suspension or cancellation.* * * The objective of the regulations in §§ 5000-5080.5 [is to achieve] a gradual reduction of noise to be suffered at airports operating under California permits to a level at which no residential community is exposed to more than 65 dB as of December 31, 1985 (California Administrative Code § 5012); that level is designated as the Community Noise Equivalent Level (CNEL). By that date, absent the granting of a variance (California Administrative Code §§ 5062, 5075), no incompatible land use is to exist with the 65 dB Noise Impact Boundary (residential usage is not a compatible one within the Noise Impact Boundary). Airports with a noise problem are responsible for establishing the Noise Impact Boundary by monitoring and measuring aircraft nose emissions.

Some of the means available in order to meet California's airport noise standards are set out in Section 5011 of the Administrative Code[:]

The methods whereby the impact of airport noise shall be controlled and reduced include but are not limited to the following:

> (a) Encouraging use of the airport by aircraft classes with lower noise level characteristics and discouraging use by higher noise level aircraft classes;
>
> (b) Encouraging approach and departure flight paths and procedures to minimize the noise in residential areas;
>
> (c) Planning runway utilization schedules to take into account adjacent residential areas, noise characteristics of aircraft and noise sensitive time periods;
>
> (d) Reduction of the flight frequency, particularly in the most noise sensitive time periods and by the noisier aircraft;
>
> (e) Employing shielding for advantage, using natural terrain, buildings, . . . and
>
> (f) Development of a compatible land use within the noise impact boundary.

Preference shall be given to actions which reduce the impact of airport noise on existing communities. Land use conversion involving existing residential communities shall normally be considered the least desirable action for achieving compliance with these regulations.

Hence, the Code recommends certain procedures which can be employed in order to attain the established noise reduction standards, but no particular procedure is mandatory. Airport authorities are left to choose among the suggested means at their own discretion, tailoring their own programs to their peculiar needs and inclinations. Furthermore, airport authorities are left free to devise and employ other noise control measures beyond those suggested in the Code.

In addition to the continuing CNEL standards prescribed for airports, the California regulations also require the establishment of maximum Single Event Noise Exposure Levels (SENEL) * * * to the noise generated by an aircraft directly engaged in flight.

We envision the regulations promulgated as a commendable progressive state-sponsored effort towards the future safety and protection of its citizenry from the ever increasing aircraft produced noise nuisances. We deem it most worthy of advisory consideration to the EPA, which is engaged in promulgating its advice to FAA pursuant to the Noise Control Act of 1972. However, portions thereof hover in direct confrontation with the avowed exclusive domain of federal power under the Noise Control Act of 1972 in the control of noise emitted by aircraft during flight operations and generally air space management. City of Burbank v. Lockheed Air Terminal.* * *

The Airlines' position narrows to the simple contention that any control and regulation of the levels of noise generated by aircraft in direct flight is preempted by the federal government; accordingly, each of the CNEL standards and related monitoring requirements and SENEL prohibitions are per se void and unenforceable under the holdings of *Burbank.* * * *

The [defendant] Airports counter and thrust at that position the exemption of a *proprietor of an airport* from the pre-emption by the federal government, which such exemption flows from * * * footnote 14 to *Burbank* [, *supra*].

At the outset, we pay homage and respect to the "presumption of constitutionality with which [the SENEL and CNEL provisions] come to us [."] It is now firmly established that the airport proprietor is responsible for the consequences which attend his operation of a public airport; his right to control the use of the airport is a necessary concomitant, whether it be directed by state police power or his own initiative.* * * That correlating right of proprietorship control is recognized and exempted from judicially declared federal pre-emption by footnote 14. Manifestly, such proprietary control necessarily includes the basic right to determine the type of air service a given airport proprietor wants its facilities to provide, as well as the type of aircraft to utilize those facilities. The intent of Congress not to interfere with such basic airport control is made clear in the legislative history of § 611 of the Federal Aviation Act of 1958 [:]

> The Federal Government is in no position to require an airport to accept service by larger aircraft and, for that purpose to obtain longer runways. Likewise, the Federal Government is in no position to require an airport to accept service by noisier aircraft, and for that purpose to obtain additional noise easements. The issue is the service desired by the airport owner and the steps it is willing to take to obtain the service. In dealing with this issue, the Federal Government should not substitute its judgment for that of the States or elements of local government who, for the most part, own and operate our Nation's airports. The proposed legislation is not designed to do this and will not prevent airport proprietors from excluding any aircraft on the basis of noise considerations.

The preamble to 14 C.F.R., Part 36 [the FAA noise regulations,] emphasizes that local air proprietors have the responsibility for determining the permissible noise levels for aircraft using their airport:

> Compliance with Part 36 is not to be construed as a Federal determination that the aircraft is "acceptable," from a noise standpoint, in particular airport environments. Responsibility for

> determining the permissible noise levels for aircraft using an airport remains with the proprietor of that airport. The noise limits specified in Part 36 are the technologically practicable and economically reasonable limits of aircraft noise reduction technology at the time of type certification and are not intended to substitute federally determined noise levels for those more restrictive limits determined to be necessary by individual airport proprietors in response to the locally determined desire for quiet and the locally determined need for the benefit of air commerce;

and Section 36.5 of 14 C.F.R. provides:

> . . . [t]he noise levels in this part have been determined to be as low as is economically reasonable, technologically practicable, and appropriate to the type or aircraft to which they apply. No determination is made, under this part, that these noise levels are or should be acceptable or unacceptable for operation at, into, or out of, any airport.

The monitoring provisions in the California airport noise abatement scheme are innocuous to aircraft traffic * * * and in no wise intrude upon or affect flight operations and air space management in commerce.

The State dictated employment of shielding and ground level facility configurations, as well as development of compatible land uses under the provisions of CNEL, is so patently within local police power control and beyond the intent of Congress in the federal legislation that further discussion would be wasteful.

We do not here consider what limits, if any, apply to any of the CNEL provisions and requirements. While we are satisfied from the record that threatening action has been taken, and § 5011(d) [reduction of flight frequency] appears suspect, none of the Airports have as yet taken definite affirmative action in the field of controlling aircraft traffic under CNEL. So further delineation of any airport proprietor's authority or limitations thereof in the enforcement of CNEL must await another day.

We conclude that the CNEL provisions and regulations are not per se invalid as delving into and regulating a field of aircraft operation engaged in direct flight, which is pre-empted unto the federal government.* * *

Whether or not the CNEL requirements and regulations are *in fact* unrealistic, arbitrary and unreasonable, and an abuse of police powers constituting an unlawful burden or infringement upon any United States constitutional right or privilege held by a proprietor of an airport, or an unreasonable burden upon interstate and foreign commerce as utilized by aircraft, is not before us upon undisputed facts and must await a future day of judgment.

The SENEL provisions and regulations are not so favored. We are satisfied and conclude that the SENEL provisions and regulations of noise levels which occur when an aircraft is in direct flight, and for the levying of criminal fines for violation, are a per se unlawful exercise of police power into the exclusive federal domain of control over aircraft flights and operation, and air space management and utilization in interstate and foreign commerce. The thrust of the Single Event Noise Exposure Levels is clear and direct and collides head-on with the federal regulatory scheme for aircraft flights delineated by and central to the Burbank decision.

[They are] void and unenforceable as in contravention of the Constitution and laws of the United States.* * *

NATIONAL AVIATION v. CITY OF HAYWARD, CALIFORNIA, United States District Court, Northern District of California, 1976. 418 F. Supp. 417.

Peckham, Chief Judge.

This is an action by four related commercial airplane operators who seek to have Hayward City Ordinance 75-023 declared unconstitutional. That ordinance, enacted on October 14, 1975, pursuant to defendant Hayward's capacity as proprietor of the Hayward Air Terminal, prohibits all aircraft which exceed a noise level of 75 dBA from landing or taking off from the Hayward Air Terminal between the hours of 11:00 p.m. and 7:00 a.m.* * *

Plaintiffs * * * contend that the Noise Control Act of 1972, * * * and the regulations promulgated thereunder preempt the area of noise regulation and render the Hayward ordinance unconstitutional. The leading case on this question is *Burbank v. Lockheed Air Terminal*, [holding] that the "pervasive nature of the scheme of federal regulation of aircraft noise" constituted preemption. [However,] the *Burbank* court's finding of preemption was made only with regard to a nonproprietor municipality's attempt to regulate aircraft noise pursuant to its police power. Indeed, in footnote 14 of the majority opinion, Mr. Justice Douglas expressly acknowledges that the court "do[es] not consider here what limits, if any, apply to a municipality as a proprietor." As a result, this court must now attempt to do so. We begin with an examination of the ordinance in question.* * *

Section 2 of the Hayward City Ordinance 75-023 recites that the City of Hayward as the owner, operator, and proprietor of an airport located within its corporate limits, possesses the authority to adopt reasonable rules regulating the use of such airport. Nevertheless, the ordinance appears to greatly resemble a measure that a municipality would pass pursuant to its police power. It was enacted as an amendment to the Municipal Code, by the Hayward City Council, and subjects violators to criminal penalties of six months in jail and/or a $500.00 fine. The ordinance further states that it was passed in order to preserve "the public peace, health, and safety in order to provide relief from noise pollution to occupants of residential property surrounding the Hayward Air Terminal."

Thus, it seems clear that if this ordinance was passed by a state or other local government not the proprietor of the airport, it would run afoul of *Burbank* and would constitute an impermissible exercise of police power in an area preempted by Congress. The question presented here is whether the City of Hayward's status as proprietor of the Hayward Air Terminal leaves the city free to exercise its police powers without constraint by federal preemption.

*Air Transport Association v. Crotti* [held that]:

> It is now firmly established that the airport proprietor is responsible for the consequences which attend his operation of a public airport; his right to control the use of the airport is a necessary concomitant, whether it be directed by state police power or his own initiative . . . *That correlating right of proprietorship control is recognized and exempted from judicially declared federal pre-emption by footnote 14.* * * *

Indeed the only regulation promulgated to date by the FAA pursuant to its authority to "prescribe and amend such regulations as [it] may find necessary to provide for the control and abatement of aircraft noise and sonic boom" (49 U.S.C. § 1431(b)(1)) is Part 36 of the Federal Aviation Regulations. But even the FAA in its original preface to Part 36 disclaimed that it was intending to preempt noise control regulation and emphasized that local airport owners have the responsibility for determining the permissible noise levels for aircraft using their airport.* * *

Thus, the import of *Burbank* and the legislative history discussed therein, as well as the nature of the subsequent noise regulations implemented by the FAA, is, as the *Crotti* court stated, that the right of airport proprietorship control is recognized and exempted from preemption. Such an interpretation does, however, overlook the explicit statement of the *Burbank* majority that the court was not considering "what limits, if any, apply to a municipality as a proprietor." * * *

Moreover, the *Crotti* court's interpretation of Burbank would produce a result, which plaintiffs strenuously contend would be anomalous; namely, that a municipality that owns an airport would be free to exercise police powers in the field of airport noise regulation which powers, if identically exercised by a different municipality or state, would unlawfully intrude into an area said to have been preempted by Congress.

Therefore, we cannot merely rely on the *Crotti* court's interpretation of this problem. Rather, we must examine further to see whether Congress or the Supreme Court ever intended such a result.

[As the court held in *Burbank:*]

> If we were to uphold the Burbank ordinance and a significant number of municipalities followed suit, it is obvious that fractionalized control of the timing of take-offs and landings would severely limit the flexibility of FAA in controlling air traffic flow. The difficulties of scheduling flights to avoid congestion and the concomitant decrease in safety would be compounded.* * *

[To] allow municipal airport proprietors to restrict the use of their facilities by imposing jet curfews or other noise regulations would certainly undermine the rationale underlying Justice Douglas' finding of preemption. This is particularly so in light of the fact that most of the airports in this country are owned by the municipalities in which they are located.

However, the majority was well aware of this fact, as well as of the clear Congressional intention that airport proprietors continue to be permitted to deny the use of their airports to aircraft on the basis of noise considerations so long as such exclusion was nondiscriminatory. The rationale underlying this special treatment for airport proprietors can be traced to another Justice Douglas opinion--*Griggs v. Allegheny County*.* * *

*Griggs* held that an airport operator is financially responsible to nearby property owners for property damage resulting from aircraft noise from overflying commercial flights.* * *

Thus, this court finds itself caught on the horns of a particularly sharp dilemma: If on one hand, we follow the dicta in footnote 14 of the *Burbank* opinion, which is intended to comport with the court's holding in *Griggs*, we will severely undercut the rationale of *Burbank's* finding of preemption. If on the other hand, we disregard the proprietor exception as dicta in order to fully effectuate the *Burbank* rationale, we impose upon airport proprietors the responsibility under *Griggs* for obtaining the requisite noise easements, yet deny them the authority to control the level of noise produced at their airports. This is, of course, exactly what the Senate Commerce Committee indicated that the 1972 amendment to section 611 of the Federal Aviation Act was *not* intended to do.* * *

In the opinion of this court, it is ultimately this clear expression of legislative intent which must control our decision, for, to echo the analysis of Justice Douglas, when "Congress legislate[s] in a field which the States have traditionally occupied . . . [the] powers of the States [are] not to be superseded by the Federal Act unless that [is] the clear and manifest purpose of Congress . . ." Accordingly, while the Congressional purpose was undoubtedly clear enough to the *Burbank* majority to rule that a municipality's police power regulations regarding aircraft noise at an airport, which it was not the proprietor of, invaded an area exclusively reserved for federal control, this court cannot, in light of the clear Congressional statement that the amendments to the Federal Aviation Act were not designed to and would not "prevent airport proprietors from excluding any aircraft on the basis of noise considerations," make the same finding with respect to regulations adopted by municipal airport proprietors. If Justice Douglas' comments regarding the need for an "uniform and exclusive system of federal regulation" prove correct, Congress and the FAA can take appropriate steps to provide such a regulatory system. However, at the present time, Congress and the FAA do not appear to have preempted the area, and therefore, the City of Hayward, as proprietor of Hayward Air Terminal, cannot be enjoined form enforcing ordinance 75-023 on preemption grounds. Nor do we think that this ordinance can be enjoined under the "Commerce Clause."

[A]ny effect on interstate commerce produced by the ordinance seems to be incidental at best and clearly not excessive when weighed against the legitimate and concededly laudable goal of controlling the noise levels at the Hayward Air Terminal during late evening and morning hours.

Perhaps recognizing this, the real thrust of plaintiffs' * * * argument is directed at the potential for conflicting legislation which itself is alleged to constitute an impermissible burden on interstate commerce. [But] the record here contains "nothing to suggest the existence of any such competing or conflicting local regulation." * * *

The possibility that other municipalities will sometime in the future enact similar ordinances, which will together then create an impermissible burden on interstate commerce is mere speculation.* * *

## Notes

The court here dismissed the plaintiffs' argument that other local governments might impose similar restrictions by saying that none had in fact done so. But what if a significant number of localities were to pass such an ordinance? Air travel, especially long flights through several time zones, might be impossible, or at least unacceptably complicated, by a multiplicity of such ordinances. Would a proliferation of Hayward-type ordinances lead to a Supreme Court decision redressing the line of lower court decisions interpreting *Burbank?* Or are the airport proprietor's rights now firmly entrenched?

Does giving the proprietor, rather than the state or municipality, these powers reduce public influence over noise limits? Airports are often owned by public-benefit corporations, such as the Port Authority of New York and New Jersey, one step removed from the political process. What about airports, such as Cincinnati's, located in a different county or state from the city they serve?

GREATER WESTCHESTER HOME OWNERS ASSOCIATION v. CITY OF LOS ANGELES, Supreme Court of California, 1979. 26 Cal.3d 86, 603 P.2d 1329, 160 Cal. Rptr. 733. Cert. denied, 446 U.S. 933 (1980).

Richardson, Justice.

Is a municipality which owns and operates an airport liable on a nuisance theory for personal injuries sustained by nearby residents and caused by noise from aircraft using the facility? We will conclude that it is. The resolution of this issue requires a careful weighing of two conflicting interests and policies. On the one hand, by ancient law, the owners and occupants of land are entitled to the peaceful use, possession, and enjoyment of their property. On the other, the general public has a strong interest in the transportation and related services furnished by commercial aviation. These two interests, the private and the public, are solidly founded in the common law and deeply rooted in established constitutional doctrine.

When locked in confrontation, which interest prevails and under what circumstances?

[P]laintiffs, multiple homeowners and their families living in the Westchester area adjacent to Los Angeles International Airport (LAX), sought damages from the defendant, City of Los Angeles (City), which owns and operates LAX. The condition of nuisance giving rise to their claim of emotional and mental distress was the noise generated by the arrival and departure of jet aircraft at LAX, the nation's third largest commercial aviation facility.

In 1968 plaintiffs, as owners and occupants of homes situated near LAX's two north runways, sued the City in inverse condemnation for property damage and, on a nuisance theory, for personal injuries allegedly caused by noise, smoke, and vibrations emanating from aircraft using LAX.* * * Trial of the direct condemnation and nuisance actions was bifurcated, and substantial direct and inverse condemnation judgments in favor of plaintiffs were entered and fully satisfied.

The nuisance phase of the case, tried before the court, resulted in findings of fact to the effect that the noise created by jet aircraft using the two north runways of LAX "interfered with person-to-person conversation in the home, . . . [with] normal telephonic communication, with the ability to enjoy the use of the out-of-doors' portion of their property and . . . to hear and enjoy television programs; that such noise caused frequent arousal from sleep and, in some cases, interfered with the ability . . . of school age members of the families to study in their homes." On the basis of the foregoing findings the trial court concluded that plaintiffs had established the existence of an actionable nuisance giving rise to damages for "annoyance, inconvenience, discomfort, mental distress, and emotional distress," and that a nuisance recovery was independent of plaintiffs' claim for diminution of their property values.

In the nuisance proceeding 41 plaintiffs were awarded damages in the aggregate sum of $86,000 for personal injuries sustained during the period 1967-1975. [The] City has consistently argued that plaintiffs' nuisance claim must fail for two reasons. First, the noise in question originates from flying aircraft over which the United States government exercises exclusive dominion and therefore any attempted noise control by an airport operator is federally preempted. Second, the operation of aircraft being expressly sanctioned by statutory law, any aircraft noise emissions cannot constitute a nuisance because of Civil Code section 3482, which provides: "Nothing which is done or maintained under the express authority of a statute can be deemed a nuisance." We review, and will reject, each of these contentions.* * *

Certain fundamental principles expressed by the United States Supreme Court guide our analysis of the preemption issue. When respective federal and state sovereignties are juxtaposed, "the proper approach is to reconcile the operation of both statutory schemes with one another rather than holding one completely ousted." (*Merrill Lynch, Pierce, Fenner & Smith v. Ware* (1973), 414 U.S. 117, 127, 94 S.Ct. 383, 389-90, 38 L.Ed.2d 348.) The courts thereby attempt "the necessary accommodation between local needs and the overriding requirement of freedom for the national commerce . . ." * * *

The United States Supreme Court has described, generally, the scope of the preemption doctrine. It has said that federal regulation of an area of commerce may preempt state actions upon the same subject matter if (1) there is an apparent congressional intent to blanket the field, (2) the federal and state schemes directly conflict, or (3) any state intervention would burden or frustrate the full purposes and objectives of Congress.

The preemptive intent of Congress may be explicit or implicit, but where the effect of preemption is to impede the exercise of historic state powers the high court has held that the intent must be "clear and manifest." * * * Furthermore, preemption exists only to the extent necessary to serve congressional objectives.* * *

Consistent with the foregoing general principles and with specific application to aviation, we have previously acknowledged that commercial flights which are conducted in strict compliance with federal regulations may not be enjoined as nuisances, both because of the continuing public interest in air transportation, and because of the likelihood of direct conflict with federal law. (*Loma Portal Civic Club v. American Airlines, Inc.*, 61 Cal.2d 582, 591, 39 Cal. Rptr. 708, 714, 394 P.2d 548, 554.) In so holding, however, we expressly cautioned that our decision did not determine the "rights of landowners who suffer from airplane annoyances to seek damages from the owners or operators of aircraft *or to seek compensation from the owner or operator of an airport.*" Preemption, we observed, did not operate *per se* to preclude the enforcement of private state remedies for aircraft noise damage, and only a "compelling federal interest" would support a finding that Congress intended to nullify state-created rights.

Is there a "compelling federal interest" which precludes state imposition of nuisance liability upon the proprietor of an airport? [*Burbank* held that the Federal Aviation] Act, as amended by 1968 and 1972 federal noise control laws had completely preempted local regulation of "aircraft in flight" for the purpose of aviation noise abatement. [It] concluded that the widespread imposition of local curfews would frustrate flight scheduling and navigational patterns nationwide, thus hindering commerce, aviation safety, and the general FAA management of the national air traffic network. [But] the *Burbank* court expressly refrained from imposing similar limitations on the rights and obligations of a *proprietorship-landlord* to control aircraft noise levels.* * *

As the *Burbank* court suggests, considering the inverse condemnation burden imposed upon airport owners of *Griggs*, Congress apparently intended to preserve the principle of substantial proprietary control over airport planning, design, and use.* * * Nonetheless, the related congressional enactments contemplate very considerable federal involvement in the planning and operation of airports. The FAA has apparently invoked both contractual and regulatory authority on several occasions to oppose unilateral proprietor use restrictions.* * * Furthermore, the *Burbank* opinion strongly suggests that any local noise or use restrictions, by whomever imposed, which substantially upset current air schedules or prevented the use of commercial aircraft which were currently operational would burden to an unacceptable degree both federal aviation policy and interstate commerce.

On the other hand, the citizen's rights to the full use, possession, and enjoyment of his property are given a protected status under the law. [A] property owner has an inverse condemnation remedy, constitutionally founded, against the proprietor of an airport for *property* damage or loss caused by noise generated at the facility. We discern no reason either in law or policy why the * * * remedy of nuisance * * * should not under similar circumstances equally protect the *person* of the owner or the occupant.

We find significance in the depth and continuous nature of City's involvement in the creation and maintenance of the nuisance in question. City concedes that it, and not the federal government, decided to build and then to expand the airport in the immediate vicinity of a residential area. It is undeniable that City chose the particular location and direction of the airport runways. It approved their usage by jet aircraft. It entered into service agreements with commercial air carriers all with full and prior knowledge of the potential noise impact.* * * Admittedly, some of the foregoing actions by City followed federal advice, approval, and perhaps even encouragement. Nonetheless, City chose, and was not forced by anyone, to develop LAX in its particular location. City voluntarily elected to expand the facility, with foreknowledge of the preexisting nature and usage of the surrounding area.* * *

Nor has City lacked the means to meet the obligations herein imposed. Since at least 1965, public entities have had statutory power to condemn "aircraft noise easements," and to secure, in appropriate quantities, land which might otherwise be the subject of noise damage actions.

[P]laintiff's acoustician testified at trial that early as 1967 he had suggested to LAX officials the economic feasibility of constructing ground barriers to defeat and diminish LAX noise. The soundproofing of adjacent structures and restrictions on noise generated by static engine tests were additional proposed alternatives. Accordingly, City cannot fairly argue that federal law has rendered City powerless to prevent or reduce the damages of which plaintiffs complain. [Moreover,] the Act specifically provides that its terms shall not abridge "remedies now existing at common law or by statute, . . ." (§ 1506). This would seem to preserve the validity of preexisting nuisance causes of action.* * *

Finally, we are not persuaded that preemption is mandated because recognition of a state nuisance remedy would impermissibly hinder commerce or conflict with federal policy. We cannot assume that the imposition of liability on a proprietor for personal injury would burden commerce to an appreciably greater degree than that represented by the well accepted, indeed constitutionally compelled, exposure of the proprietor to property damage claims. While it is true that the probable number of claimants will increase and the nature of the claims enlarge, we discern no basis for any reasoned distinction between claims for property damage and personal injury arising from the same activity and cause.* * *

We therefore hold that the claims for personal injuries founded upon nuisance have not been federally preempted.* * *

City contends that LAX cannot be liable for nuisance because the noise generating activity complained of is specifically sanctioned by statutes, federal and state. Particularly, City relies upon Civil Code section 3482 [, *supra*]. We have consistently applied a narrow construction to section 3482 and to the principle therein embodied. Thus, a number of years ago we observed, "'A statutory sanction cannot be pleaded in justification of acts which by the general rules of law constitute a nuisance, unless the acts complained of are authorized by the express terms of the statute under which the justification is made, or by the plainest and most necessary implication from the powers expressly conferred, so that it can be fairly stated that the legislature contemplated the doing of the very act which occasions the injury.'" [S]tatutes which broadly authorize or regulate airports and aircraft flights do not create a legislative sanction for their maintenance as a nuisance.

The argument is made that because aviation and noise are necessarily inseparable, governmental approval and encouragement of aviation activity necessarily implies legislative approval of aviation noise which results in interference with neighboring land uses. We disagree. Both federal and state authorities have attempted vigorously to abate aircraft and airport noise.* * * In addition, as previously noted, the California Legislature has granted airports express and expanded condemnation and compensation authority to reduce and minimize the effects of noise on the private use and enjoyment of neighboring land.* * * Reasonably construed, the foregoing legislation preserves both the authority and responsibility of an airport proprietor to acquire adequate noise easement and to institute reasonable noise abatement procedures which do not conflict with federal law.

[W]e hold that no * * * immunity derives from section 3482 or any other related federal or state statute.* * *

Notes

The court drew an analogy between nuisance and inverse condemnation, finding no reason either in law or policy why nuisance should not under similar circumstances protect the "person" of an affected landowner just as inverse condemnation protects his property. Is this analogy sound in view of the fact that in an inverse condemnation action preemption can never be an issue because federal regulation can never preempt constitutionally protected rights? Chief Justice Bird, in a concurring opinion, rejected the analogy. She felt the court reached the proper result but should have based its finding exclusively on the wealth of legislative history [outlined in *Burbank, Crotti, Hayward* and this case] which emphasizes the clear intention of both the legislative and executive branches that local airport operators retain the responsibility for controlling airport noise through reasonable nondiscriminatory regulation.

It is interesting to note, in view of Justice Richardson's analogy and Chief Justice Bird's questioning of it, how a perhaps somewhat attenuated argument born of need has become so deeply ingrained in our common law. *Burbank*, as we have seen, was written to comport with *Griggs*, which, over Justice Black's vigorous dissent, identified the airport operator as the proper defendant in the inverse condemnation actions created by *U.S. v. Causby*, the first aircraft noise case to reach the Supreme Court. At the time Mrs. Causby was planning to sue the military for the noise that damaged her chicken farm, the issue to be circumvented was sovereign immunity. There was no Federal Tort Claims Act and actions against the federal government were brought under the Tucker Act, which required the plaintiff to assert a constitutional question. This marriage of inverse condemnation and aircraft noise actions has had many offspring. In the absence of the *Causby* precedent do you think this line of cases could have developed under nuisance theory?

BRITISH AIRWAYS BOARD v. THE PORT AUTHORITY OF NEW YORK & NEW JERSEY, United States Court of Appeals, Second Circuit, 1977. 558 F.2d 75.

Irving R. Kaufman, Chief Judge:

Our task is to review the judgment of the district court dissolving the Port Authority's temporary ban on SST [supersonic transport] flights at John F. Kennedy International Airport.* * *

The Port Authority of New York and New Jersey, operator of New York's Kennedy International Airport, was one of the first to recognize the environmental challenge of civil jet aviation. In 1951, the Authority adopted a regulation, still in force, prohibiting any jet from landing or taking off without permission at any facility operated by the Authority. The purpose of this regulation was to make it clear to the developers of the first commercial jets that elimination of excessive noise was as important an element of design as safety or speed. [A] consulting firm was retained and charged with evolving a measure of noise that would reflect subjective reactions to the irritating high-pitched whine of jet airplanes. Careful study revealed that an ordinary person heard 112 PNdB (perceived noise in decibels) emitted by a jet as substantially equivalent to the sound produced by the standard DC-6B propeller aircraft. This single-event noise level, as registered at selected sites, was adopted as the permissible maximum.* * * Thereafter, until the Port Authority's resolution of March 11, 1976, which banned the supersonic transport "Concorde" from Kennedy Airport and spawned this litigation, the 112 PNdB standard was uniformly applied to all aircraft seeking landing permission at Kennedy.* * *

Britain and France decided in 1962 to embark upon a dramatic joint venture: the development of a supersonic jet airliner, the Concorde. [They] were well aware of the importance of minimizing noise [, and] spent more than $100 million just to moderate the noise of the Concorde.

[Its] success, our allies maintain, must remain an idle dream unless the supersonic airliner is permitted to land in New York, the principal gateway between Europe and the United States. The operators of the Concorde urge that their plane can meet the 112 PNdB standard that Port Authority applies to other aircraft and desire merely to prove, by actual experience, that the airliner will not cause an intolerable deterioration in the noise environment around Kennedy Airport.* * * Approval of the airlines' applications could hardly have been entrusted to the routine processes of the FAA: the potential promise of supersonic jet aviation, the special importance of the Concorde to two of America's closest allies, and the serious environmental questions raised by the aircraft, all required a decision by the cabinet officer responsible for transportation, on the basis of a carefully prepared environmental impact statement. Secretary William T. Coleman's decision is the very paragon of a clear and considered administrative action.

He directed * * * each carrier to conduct up to two Concorde flights daily into John F. Kennedy International Airport and one per day into Dulles International Airport [for] 16 months from the commencement of commercial service [, revocable] immediately in the event of an emergency or at any time on four months notice. [I]n addition, the plane was required to observe a 10 p.m. to 7 a.m. curfew and to abide by noise abatement procedures, including a sharp left turn upon takeoff, as prescribed by the FAA.* * * The Concorde differs from other jets because the sound produced by its engines is of a relatively low pitch. The plane's deep rumble causes minor structural rattling and an increased likelihood of penetration of the sound into buildings. Coleman concluded, however, on the basis of a comprehensive survey of the evidence, that "these vibrations do not present any danger of structural damage and little possibility of annoyance." The principal difference between the Concorde and subsonic aircraft, we are told, is that the SST's sound carries farther. Secretary Coleman found, however, that the addition of eight Concorde flights a day at Kennedy, under the restriction imposed by his order, would have but a marginal impact on the noise environment near the airport. Secretary Coleman, his successor Brock Adams, and President Carter have all repeatedly avowed that the Coleman order did not preempt the Port Authority's right to exclude the Concorde pursuant to a reasonable, non-discriminatory noise regulation. The United States has reaffirmed this position in its *amicus* brief to this Court.* * *

The Port Authority did not apply its 112 PNdB rule to the Concorde. Rather, it raised what it considered significant questions regarding the adequacy of its existing noise rule to regulate special characteristics of the SST's low frequency sound. Thus, the Port Authority considered the adverse environmental effects of the Concorde's low-pitched noise worthy of more study. And, the Port Authority expressed concern that the total area exposed to the rumble of Concorde flights would be considerably greater than the equivalent area for subsonic aircraft.

The Port Authority agreed with Secretary Coleman that the subjective reaction of people exposed to Concorde noise needed further inquiry under actual operating conditions but declared that further evidence was needed before the large number of people living near John F. Kennedy Airport were exposed to Concorde noise. Accordingly, on March 11, 1976, the Concorde was banned from Kennedy pending a six-month study of operating experience at Dulles in the United States, and Charles DeGaulle and Heathrow Airports in Europe. The Concorde began commercial flights to Washington in May, 1976, over 13 months ago. The Authority has not concluded its inquiry and, accordingly, has not considered what noise regulation would be appropriate for the special characteristics of the Concorde--assuming that the existing and well established 112 PNdB rule were found inadequate.

Air France and British Airways urge that the Authority's action violates U.S. treaty commitments, interferes with the foreign affairs power of the federal government, and is preempted by Secretary Coleman's authorization of Concorde landings at JFK and provision of detailed regulations for noise control at the airport.* * * We believe the ground for [the district court's] grant of summary judgment, that Secretary Coleman's order preempted the conflicting exercise of power by the Port Authority, is simply untenable and erroneous. Accordingly, we will reverse.

[T]he United States position confirms our independent assessment of the public record. In view of the repeated disavowal by federal officials of any attempt to preempt the Port Authority's right to subject the Concorde to reasonable noise regulations, we are compelled to hold the Secretary's order did not preclude the exercise of power by the Authority.* * * Since the reasonableness of the Port Authority's delay has been raised for the first time by the United States as *amicus* on appeal, we cannot appropriately decide the issue. Basic tenets of fairness require that a federal appellate court should not consider an issue involving questions of fact not resolved below.

We do believe, however, that the government has raised an important and viable point. Implicit in the federal scheme of noise regulation, which accords to local airport proprietors the critical responsibility for controlling permissible noise levels in the vicinity of their airports, is the assumption that this responsibility will be exercised in a fair, reasonable and nondiscriminatory manner. Although 13 months have already elapsed since the commencement of commercial Concorde operations at Dulles, we cannot on the state of this record find that this delay is unreasonable. The Port Authority desires an evidentiary hearing to submit facts justifying this delay.

[Since] there remains the question of whether the 13 months delay by the Port Authority in promulgating reasonable noise regulations applicable to supersonic aircraft is so excessive as to constitute unfair discrimination and an undue burden on commerce, [we] direct that the district court on remand proceed to conduct an evidentiary hearing on the reasonableness of the Port Authority's thirteen month ban on Concorde landings at JFK.

In the event that the evidence does not support a finding of unreasonable delay, we nevertheless believe it is in the interest of all concerned that this interminable strife be brought to an end. Accordingly, we urge the Port Authority to conclude its study and fix reasonable noise standards with dispatch.

Notes

Judge Kaufman's urging went unheeded. Instead, as he held in *British Airways Board v. Port Authority of New York and New Jersey*, 564 F.2d 1002 (1977), on appeal from the district court proceedings directed by the Court of Appeals in his first opinion,

> Five days before the mandated hearing, on July 7, 1977, the Port Authority's Commissioners voted to indefinitely extend the "temporary" ban imposed sixteen months earlier.* * * On August 17, the district judge again struck down the Port Authority's ban of SST flights after concluding that for over a year the agency had been "reploughing old ground and doing re-reviews of scientific and theoretical data previously available." [Prior to] review of the district judge's order * * * President Carter decided to permit existing Concordes to fly into thirteen American cities, including New York[.]* * *
>
> To this day the Port Authority has demonstrated total resistance in responding to the airlines' desire to secure a fair test of their aircraft in New York. Moreover, it is plain from its public statements that the Authority has no intention to resolve this critical issue in the foreseeable future. We cannot countenance such abdication. Accordingly, we will affirm the order of the district court, enjoining further prohibition of Concorde operations at Kennedy Airport until the Port Authority promulgates a reasonable nonarbitrary and nondiscriminatory noise regulation that all aircraft are afforded an equal opportunity to meet.* * *

Why was the federal government unwilling to preempt the airport proprietors in aircraft noise regulation?

Why did the government as *amicus* seek to reverse the district court's holding that Secretary of Transportation Coleman's decision to accord the Concorde limited permission to land in this country "preempted any contrary exercise of local authority" when it was clearly the federal government's desire that the Concorde be granted such permission? Was it because the government did not wish to be saddled with the liability for damages which the law now places on the proprietor?

If Justice Black had had his way in *Griggs*, *supra*, might the Port Authority conceivably have been a plaintiff in this kind of an action? Against whom?

In fact the Concorde did not create the excessive noise its opponents feared. Tests in New York and Washington have shown its takeoff and landing noise has been well within permitted levels. But the public concern over excessive noise required the courts to determine the proprietor's rights--the issue unresolved by *Burbank.*

## The FAA's Controls

The FAA Part 36 regulations referred to in *National Aviation v. City of Hayward* imposed a 107-decibel effective limit on large commercial aircraft. These rules, adopted in 1969, apply to "Stage 2" aircraft built after they took effect. Four years later the FAA enacted fleet noise regulations imposing the same limits on existing "Stage 1" aircraft, but affording the airlines a long period within which to comply -- essentially until 1985. Airlines could comply by either retrofitting aircraft or simply phasing them out and replacing them with quieter planes.

The Airport Noise and Capacity Act of 1990, 49 App. U.S.C.A. §§ 2151-2158, obligates the Secretary of Transportation to develop a national aviation noise policy. This is to include Department of Transportation (DOT) review of airport noise regulations adopted after Oct. 1, 1990. Rules of airports for "Stage 2" aircraft require public notice and consideration of alternatives. Rules for newer "Stage 3" planes require DOT approval, unless agreed to by all airlines using the airport.

Airports enforcing "Stage 3" rules without DOT approval forfeit the right to receive federal funding or to impose passenger facility charges (arrival or departure fees). Conversely, if DOT disapproves a rule, the United States is liable in any inverse condemnation suit brought by a landowner for aircraft noise. Finally, "Stage 2" aircraft are to be phased out by 1999.

Another significant federal statute, the Airport and Airway Improvement Act, 49 App. U.S.C.A. §§ 2201-2227, requires DOT to certify, as a condition of federal grants for airport expansion adversely affecting the community, that no feasible or prudent alternative exists. In addition, under the Aviation Safety and Noise Abatement Act, 49 App. U.S.C.A. §§ 2101-2125, airports may file noise exposure maps indicating where noise will likely occur. Once a map is filed, no subsequent purchaser may recover for inverse condemnation unless the airport significantly changes its operations.

# 7. WATER QUALITY

## Introductory Note on Water Resources

At common law, water quality was protected by the riparian rights doctrine, giving a downstream property owner a cause of action for damages or an injunction against diversion of water by an upstream user. Shore-lines and wetlands were protected by the public trust doctrine, which itself ebbed and flowed with the passage of time. See Chapter 2, *supra*.

The first meaningful statute protecting water quality was the Rivers and Harbors Act of 1899 (33 U.S.C. §§401-420), enacted pursuant to Congress's power to further interstate commerce, which bars the dumping of refuse and dredging or filling in navigable waters without a permit.

Regulation of emissions into the nation's waters under a permit program began with the Clean Water Act (33 U.S.C. §§1251-1387) in 1972, which, like the Clean Air Act, shares enforcement with those states with federally-approved programs.

## A. REFUSE DISCHARGE: THE RIVERS AND HARBORS ACT

UNITED STATES v. REPUBLIC STEEL CORP., Supreme Court of the United States, 1960. 362 U.S. 482, 80 S. Ct. 884, 4 L.Ed.2d 963.

Justice Douglas delivered the opinion of the Court.

This is a suit by the United States to enjoin respondent companies from depositing industrial solids in the Calumet River (which flows out of Lake Michigan and connects eventually with the Mississippi) without first obtaining a permit from the Chief of Engineers of the Army providing conditions for the removal of the deposits and to order and direct them to restore the depth of the channel to 21 feet by removing portions of existing deposits.

The District Court found that the Calumet was used by vessels requiring a 21-foot draft, and that depth has been maintained by the Corps of Engineers. Respondents, who operate mills on the banks of the river for the production of iron and related products, use large quantities of the water from the river, returning it through numerous sewers. The processes they use create industrial waste containing various solids. A substantial quantity of these solids is recovered in settling basins but, according to the findings, many fine particles are discharged into the river and they flocculate into larger units and are deposited in the river bottom. Soundings show a progressive decrease in the depth of the river in the vicinity of respondents' mills. But respondents have refused, since 1951, the demand of the Corps of Engineers that they dredge that portion of the river. The shoaling conditions being created in the vicinity of these plants were found by the District Court to be created by the waste discharged from the mills of respondents. This shoaling was found to have reduced the depth of the channel to

17 feet in some places and to 12 feet in others. The District Court made findings which credited respondents with 81.5% of the waste deposited in the channel, and it allocated that in various proportions among the three respondents.

* * *Section 10 of the Rivers and Harbors Act of 1899, 33 U.S.C. '403, provides in part:

That the creation of *any obstruction* not affirmatively authorized by Congress, *to the navigable capacity* of any of the waters of the United States is hereby prohibited; . . . ." (Italics added.)

Section 10 then states that "it shall not be lawful to excavate or fill, or in any manner to alter or modify the . . . .capacity of. . . .the channel of any navigable water of the United States, unless the work has been recommended by the Chief of Engineers and authorized by the Secretary of the Army prior to beginning the same."

* * *Section 13 forbids the discharge of "any refuse matter of any kind or description whatever other than that flowing from streets and sewers and passing therefrom in a liquid state, into any navigable water of the United States;" but § 13 grants authority of the Secretary of the Army to permit such deposits under conditions prescribed by him.

Our conclusions are that the industrial deposits placed by respondents in the Calumet have, on the findings of the District Court, created an "obstruction" within the meaning of § 10 of the Act and are discharges not exempt under §13. We also conclude that the District Court was authorized to grant the relief.

The history of federal control over obstructions to the navigable capacity of our rivers and harbors goes back to *Willamette Iron Bridge Co. v. Hatch*, 125 U.S. 1, 8, S. Ct. 811, 31 L.Ed. 629, 632, where the Court held "there is no common law of the United States" which prohibits "obstructions" in our navigable rivers. Congress acted promptly, forbidding by § 10 of the Rivers and Harbors Act of 1890, "the creation of any obstruction, not affirmatively authorized by law, to the navigable capacity" of any waters of the United States. * * *

It is argued that "obstruction" means some kind of structure. The design of § 10 should be enough to refute the argument, since the ban of "any obstruction," unless approved by Congress, appears in the first part of § 10, followed by a semicolon and another provision which bans various kinds of structures unless authorized by the Secretary of the Army.

The reach of § 10 seems plain. Certain types of structures, enumerated in the second clause, may not be erected "in" any navigable river without approval by the Secretary of the Army. Nor may excavations or fills, described in the third clause, that alter or modify "the course location, condition, or capacity of" a navigable river be made unless "the work" has been approved by the Secretary of the Army.* * *

The decision in *Sanitary Dist.* v. *United States* [226 U.S. 405, 45 S. Ct. 143, 69 L.Ed. 352] seems to be decisive. There the Court affirmed a decree enjoining the diversion of water from Lake Michigan through this same river. Mr. Justice Holmes, writing for the Court, did not read § 10 narrowly but in the spirit in which Congress moved to fill the gap created by *Willamette Iron Bridge Co. v. Hatch, supra.* That which affects the water level may, he said, amount to an "obstruction" within the meaning of § 10: ["A] withdrawal of water on the scale directed by the statute of Illinois threatens and will affect the level of the Lakes, and that is a matter which cannot be done without the consent of the United States.["]

The teaching of those cases is that the term "obstruction" as used in § 10 is a broad enough to include diminution's of the navigable capacity of a waterway by means not included in the second or third clauses. In the *Sanitary District* case it was caused by lowering the water level. Here it is caused by clogging the channel with deposits of inorganic solids. Each affected the navigable "capacity" of the river. The concept of "obstruction" which was broad enough to include the former seems to us plainly adequate to include the latter.

As noted, § 13 bans the discharge in any navigable water of "any refuse material of any kind or description whatever other than that flowing from streets and sewers and passing therefrom in a liquid state." The materials carried here are "industrial solids," as the District Court found. The particles creating the present obstruction were in suspension, not in solution. Articles in suspension, such as organic matter in sewage, may undergo chemical change. Others settle out. All matter in suspension is not saved by the exception clause in §13. Refuse flowing from "sewers" in a "liquid state" means to us "sewage." Any doubts are resolved by a consistent administrative construction which refused to give immunity to industrial wastes resulting in the deposit of solids in the very river in question.[5] The fact that discharges from streets and sewers may contain some articles in suspension that settle out and potentially impair navigability is no reason for us to enlarge the group to include these industrial discharges. We follow the line Congress has drawn and cannot accept the invitation to broaden the exception in §13 because other matters "in a liquid state" might logically have been treated as favorably as sewage is treated. We read the 1899 Act charitably in light of the purpose to be served. The philosophy of the statement of Mr. Justice Holmes in *New Jersey* v. *New York*, 283 U.S. 336, 342, 1106, 51 S. Ct. 478, 75 L.Ed. 1104, that "A river is more than an amenity, it is a treasure," forbids a narrow, cramped reading either of § 13 or of § 10.* * *

Section 10 of the present Act defines the interest of the United States which the injunction serves. Protection of the water level of the Great Lakes

---

[5] We have a rather precise history of administrative construction of the 1899 Act as it applies to the deposit of solids in the Calumet River by mills located on it. The Army Engineers, beginning in 1909, warned a steel company of the accumulation of solids from industrial wastes being poured into the Calumet. In 1918, 1920, 1924, 1927, 1928, 1931, and 1937 the District Engineer required these deposits to be removed. * * *

through injunctive relief, *Sanitary Dist. v. United States, supra*, is precedent enough for ordering that the navigable capacity of the Calumet River [be restored.] Congress has legislated and made its purpose clear; it has provided enough federal law in § 10 from which appropriate remedies may be fashioned even though they rest on inferences. Otherwise we impute to Congress a futility inconsistent with the great design of this legislation.* * *

Justices Harlan, Frankfurter, Whittaker and Stewart dissented:

[Section] 13 expressly exempts refuse "flowing from streets and sewers and passing therefrom in a liquid state." The Court says that materials in "a liquid state" must mean materials which do not settle out. But it is difficult to believe that nineteenth century Congress, in carving out an exception for liquid sewage, meant to establish an absolute standard of purity which not only bore no relation to the prevailing practice of sewage disposal at the time, but also is impossible to achieve even under present-day technology. It is conceded that despite respondents' best efforts to separate out industrial solids, a few minute particles remain. These comprise a small fraction of 1% of the total solution and the most damaging of them are too small to be seen under a microscope. One need not be an expert to say that the refuse discharged by an ordinary sewer pipe today, and a fortiori 60 years ago, undoubtedly contains far more solid matter in suspension than respondents' discharges. And the statute affords no basis for differentiating, as the Court suggests, between industrial and domestic refuse.* * *

What has happened is clear. In order to reach what it considers a just result the Court, in the name of "charitably" construing the Act, has felt justified in reading into the statute things that actually are not there. However appealing the attempt to make this old piece of legislation fit modern day conditions may be, such a course is not permissible one for a court of law, whose function it is to take a statute as it finds it. The filling of deficiencies in the statute, so that the burdens of maintaining the integrity of our great navigable rivers and harbors may be fairly allocated between those using them and the Government, it is a matter for Congress, not for this Court.

I would affirm.

UNITED STATES v. STANDARD OIL CO., Supreme Court of the United States, 1966. 384 U.S. 224, 86 S. Ct. 1427, 16 L.Ed.2d 492.

Justice Douglas delivered the opinion of the Court.

The question presented for decision is whether the statutory ban on depositing "any refuse matter of any kind or description" in a navigable water covers the discharge of commercially valuable aviation gasoline.

Section 13 of the Rivers and Harbors Act provides:

> "It shall not be lawful to throw, discharge, or deposit. . . .any refuse matter of any kind or description whatever other than that flowing from streets

and sewers and passing therefrom in a liquid state, into any navigable water of the United States. . . ."

The indictment charged appellee, Standard Oil (Kentucky), with violating § 13 by allowing to be discharged into the St. Johns River "refuse matter" consisting of 100-octane aviation gasoline. Appellee moved to dismiss the indictment, * * * stat[ing] that the gasoline was commercially valuable and that it was discharged into the St. Johns only because a shut-off valve at dock-side had been "accidentally" left open.* * *

The statutory words are "any refuse matter of any kind or description." We said in *United States v. Republic Steel* [that] the history of this provision and of related legislation dealing with our free-flowing rivers "forbids a narrow, cramped reading" of § 13. The District Court recognized that if this were waste oil it would be "refuse matter" within the meaning of § 13 but concluded that it was not within the statute because it was "valuable" oil. That is "a narrow, cramped reading" of § 13 in partial defeat of its purpose.

Oil is oil and whether usable or not by industrial standards it has the same deleterious effect on waterways. In either case, its presence in our rivers and harbors is both a menace to navigation and a pollutant.* * *

Section 13 codified pre-existing statutes [making it unlawful to discharge] into navigable waters "any ballast, stone, slate, gravel, earth, rubbish, wreck, filth, slabs, edgings, sawdust, slag, cinders, ashes, refuse, or other waste of any kind.. . . which shall tend to impede or obstruct navigation." [In these statutes] valuable pre-discharge materials were included.* * *

The 1899 Act now before us was no more than an attempt to consolidate these prior Acts into one. It was indeed stated by the sponsor in the Senate to be "in accord with the statutes now in existence * * *."

It is plain from [the] legislative history [of the 1899 Act] that the "serious injury" to our watercourses * * * sought to be remedied was caused in part by obstacles that impeded navigation and in part by pollution--"the discharge of sawmill waste into streams" and the injury of channels by "deposits of ballast, steam-boat ashes, oysters, and rubbish from passing vessels." The list is obviously not an exhaustive list of pollutants. The words of the Act are broad and inclusive: "any refuse matter of any kind or description whatever." * * *

Justice Harlan, with whom Justice Black and Justice Stewart join, dissenting.

[T]he language of the present statute, which is penal in nature, is in itself explicit and unambiguous.

The purpose of § 13 was essentially to eliminate obstructions to navigation and interference with public works projects. This 1899 enactment, like the two preexisting statutes which it was intended to codify, was a minor section attached to a major appropriation act together with other measures dealing with sunken wrecks, trespassing at public works sites, and obstructions caused by improperly constructed bridges, piers, and other structures. These statutes were rendered necessary primarily because navigable rivers, which the Congress was appropriating funds to improve, were being obstructed by depositing of waste materials by factories and ships. It is of course true, as the Court observes, that "oil is oil," * * * and that the accidental spillage of valuable oil may have substantially the same "deleterious effect on waterways" as the wholesale depositing of waste oil. But the relevant inquiry is not the admittedly important concerns of pollution control, but Congress' purpose in enacting this anti-obstruction Act, and that appears quite plainly to be a desire to halt through the imposition of criminal penalties the depositing of obstructing refuse matter in rivers and harbors.

The Court's construction eschews the everyday meaning of "refuse matter"--waste, rubbish, trash, debris, garbage, see Webster's New International Dictionary, 3rd ed.--and adopts instead an approach that either reads "refuse" out of the Act altogether, or gives to it a tortured meaning. The Court declares, at one point, that "The word refuse includes all foreign substances and pollutants apart from those `flowing from streets and sewers and passing therefrom in a liquid state' into the watercourse." * * * Thus, dropping anything but pure water into a river would appear to be a federal misdemeanor. At the same time, the Court also appears to endorse the * * * view that "refuse matter" refers to any material, however valuable, which becomes unsalvageable when introduced into the water.* * * On this latter approach, the imposition of criminal penalties would in effect depend in each instance on a prospective estimate of salvage costs. Such strained definitions of a phrase that is clear as a matter of ordinary English hardly commend themselves, and at the very least raise serious doubts as to the intended reach of § 13.

Given these doubts as to the proper construction of "refuse matter" in § 13, we must reckon with a traditional canon that a penal statute will be narrowly construed.* * *

In an area in which state or local law has traditionally regulated primary activity, there is good reason to restrict federal penal legislation within the confines of its language. If the Federal Government finds that there is sufficient obstruction or pollution of navigable waters caused by the introduction of commercial oil or other non-refuse material, it is an easy matter to enact appropriate regulatory or penal legislation. Such legislation can be directed at specific types of pollution, and the remedies devised carefully to ensure compliance.* * *

## Notes

*What is refuse?*

Following the lead of the Court in *Republic Steel*, courts typically interpret refuse "charitably in light of the purpose to be served." See *United States v. Kennebec Log Driving Co.*, 530 F.2d 446 (1st Cir. 1976) (log deposits which are normal incident of lawful navigation on river violate § 13).

*The "sewage" exception.*

While prohibiting the deposit of refuse in rather absolute terms without regard to the polluter's willfulness or negligence, Congress excepted refuse "flowing from streets and sewers and passing therefrom in a liquid state." One noted commentator has suggested that Congress intended to exclude only material flowing from municipal sewers and subject to municipal control. Rodgers, Industrial Water Pollution and the Refuse Act: A Second Chance for Water Quality, 119 U. Pa. L. Rev. 761, 777-78, 781-82 (1971). Although this is the dominant view regarding Congressional intent about the exception, *e.g. United States v. Pennsylvania Industrial Chemical Corp.*, 461 F.2d 468 (3d Cir. 1972), modified and remanded, 411 U.S. 655 (1973), it is still not clear whether all material flowing through municipally-controlled sewers is excepted. *Republic Steel* has been interpreted by some as an exclusion of all industrial wastes from the statutory "sewage" exception, *e.g., United States v. Genoa Cooperative Creamery Co.*, 336 F. Supp. 539 (W.D. Wis. 1972). In this view, "sewage" is defined as "organic solid matter. . . .typically, human and animal and domestic wastes, as distinguished from industrial wastes." *But see United States v. Dexter Corp.*, 507 F.2d 1038 (7th Cir. 1974) (excepting from the Act a liquid chemical discharged by an industrial source into Lake Michigan through public sewers with municipal approval). In this view, "sewage" is not limited to "refuse of domestic origin." Which view seems more consistent with *Republic Steel*?

*Private enforcement of § 13.*

Is § 13 enforceable by private plaintiffs? *National Sea Clammers Assn. v. City of New York*, 616 F.2d 1222 (3d Cir. 1980), aff'd (on other grounds) *sub nom. Middlesex Co. Sewage Authority v. National Sea Clammers Association,* 453 U.S. 1, 101 S. Ct. 2515, 69 L.Ed.2d 435, (1981), holds it gives no private right of action. The same is true of the rest of the Rivers and Harbors Act. Only the government may enforce it.

## B. DREDGING AND FILLING: RIVERS AND HARBORS ACT § 10, CLEAN WATER ACT § 404.

CITIZENS COMMITTEE FOR THE HUDSON VALLEY v. VOLPE, United States District Court, Southern District of New York, 1969. 302 F. Supp. 1083, aff'd 425 F.2d 97 (1970).

Thomas F. Murphy, District Judge.

These four actions, consolidated for trial, challenge the construction of the proposed Hudson River Expressway on a variety of grounds.

The Expressway, as proposed by the New York State Department of Transportation, is planned to be a six lane arterial highway which will * * * extend approximately nine miles along the east shore of the Hudson River from the Tappan Zee Bridge at Tarrytown north to Crotonville, New York. Approximately 22,000 feet of the road will rest on 9,500,000 cubic yards of fill which will extend at its widest point 1,300 feet into the river.

[T]he State Department of Transportation, pursuant to [§ 10 of the] Rivers and Harbors Act, applied to the Corps of Engineers for a permit * * * issued by the Corps. [The] plaintiffs' major claim is that since the Expressway project involves *dikes, causeways and bridges* to be built over or in a navigable waterway of the United States, the Corps exceeded its statutory authority in issuing the permit without the prior approval of Congress and/or the federal Department of Transportation, as required by [§ 9] of the same Rivers and Harbors Act. Section [10], under which the Corps issued the permit, provides:

> The creation of any obstruction not affirmatively authorized by Congress, to the navigable capacity of any of the waters of the United States is prohibited * * * and it shall not be lawful to excavate or fill [in a navigable waterway of the United States] unless the work has been recommended by the Chief of Engineers and authorized by the Secretary of the Army prior to beginning the same.

Section [9], claimed by the plaintiffs to be applicable, provides:

> It shall not be lawful to construct or commence the construction of any bridge, dam, dike, or causeway over or in any port, roadstead, haven, harbor, canal, [or] navigable river * * * of the United States until the consent of Congress to the building of such structures shall have been obtained and until plans for the same shall have been submitted to and approved by the Chief of Engineers and by the Secretary of the Army.

The needed approval of the Secretary of Transportation of the United States becomes a factor in the case as a result of the evolution of Section [9]. [T]he Department of Transportation Act transferred certain powers and duties of other federal departments to the Secretary of Transportation. [49 U.S.C.A. §1655(g)] transferred jurisdiction over bridges and causeways in navigable waters of the United States from the Secretary of the Army to the Secretary of Transportation.

Consequently, the construction of a bridge over or in navigable waters now requires approval of the Corps of Engineers acting under the Secretary of the Army and the Secretary of Transportation; the construction of a dike require the consent of Congress and the Corps of Engineers when authorized by the Secretary of the Army; the construction of a causeway requires the consent of Congress and the approval of the Secretary of Transportation.* * *

It is undisputed that the Hudson River is a navigable waterway of the United States, and that in both the permit issued by the Corps, and the New York State plans accompanying the permit there are numerous references to "dikes."

* * *The main type, the rock dike, will run along the entire length of the western side of the fill in order to prevent the fill from returning to the river.

We hold, based on the evidence presented at trial, that "dikes, characterized as such by the defendants, are to be constructed along the western side of the fill and that Congress, when it said "any dike" over or in any navigable river, meant exactly that. Therefore, the Corps of Engineers exceeded its statutory authority in issuing the permit * * *.

* * *In addition to the consent of Congress being required because of the presence of dikes, we hold that approval of the Secretary of Transportation of the United States is required since causeways are also involved in the construction of the project. We * * * accept the defendants' definition of a causeway, i.e., its ordinary meaning connotes a raised road across water or marshy land with the water or marshy land on both sides of the road.

[T]he proof at trial clearly shows a * * * portion of the Expressway to clearly be a causeway within the definition urged by the defendants. [T]he Corps of Engineers exceeded its statutory authority in ignoring the presence of the causeway when it issued the permit without prior approval of the Secretary of Transportation.

[The court enjoined construction of the road.]

## Notes

Since *Citizens' Committee* was decided, the courts have held that § 9, like the rest of the Rivers and Harbors Act, is enforceable only by the Government. See *Sierra Club v. United States Army Corps of Engineers*, 701 F.2d 1001 (2d Cir. 1982).

In *Zabel v. Tabb*, 430 F.2d 199 (5th Cir. 1970), cert, den. 401 U.S. 910, landowners sued to compel the Secretary of the Army to issue a dredge and fill permit under § 10 of the Rivers and Harbors Act to create a trailer park on an arm of Tampa Bay. The United States Fish and Wildlife Service and the county navigation control authority opposed the permit, the former because it "would have a distinctly harmful effect on the fish and wildlife resources of Boca Ciega Bay." Secretary of the Army Tabb denied the permit for that reason. The Court (John R. Brown, Ch. J.) held:

> The question for us is whether under the Act the Secretary may include conservation considerations as conditions to be met to make the proposed project acceptable.

* * *The Fish and Wildlife Coordination Act [16 U.S.C.A. §§ 661-666] clearly requires the dredging and filling agency (under a governmental permit), whether public or private, to consult with the Fish and Wildlife Service, with a view of conservation of wildlife resources.

[P]roof that the Secretary is directed and authorized by the Fish and Wildlife Coordination Act to consider conservation is found in the legislative history. The Senate Report on the Fish and Wildlife Coordination Act states:

> Finally, the nursery and feeding grounds of valuable crustaceans, such as shrimp, as well as the young valuable marine fishes, may be affected by dredging, filling, and diking operations often carried out to improve navigation and provide new industrial or residential land.* * *

The intent of the three branches [of government] has been unequivocally expressed: The Secretary must weigh the effect a dredge and fill project will have on conservation before he issues a permit lifting the congressional ban.* * *

In rejecting a permit on non-navigational grounds, the Secretary of the Army does not abdicate his sole ultimate responsibility and authority. Rather, in weighing the application, the Secretary of the Army is acting under a Congressional mandate to collaborate and consider all of these factors.* * *

Clean Water Act § 404

In 1972 Congress enacted the Clean Water Act, a comprehensive regulatory statute, modeled on the Clean Air Act, to deal with water quality. The provisions of the Act requiring permits to discharge pollutants, dealt with later in this chapter, are enforced by the EPA. But § 404, requiring a permit to dispose of dredge spoil or to place fill in the waters of the United States, is built on Rivers and Harbors Act § 10 and is for that reason administered by the Army Corps of Engineers like the older statute. Note that the jurisdictional reach of § 404 is considerably broader, in keeping with the broader reading of the commerce power of Congress given by the courts since the 1930s.

*Minnehaha Creek Watershed Dist. v. Hoffman,* 597 F.2d 617 (8th Cir. 1979), involved permits under § 10 and § 404 to place riprap and construct dams in a lake in Minnesota, Lake Minnetonka. "The lake's single outlet is [non navigable] Minnehaha Creek, which flows eastward [to] the Mississippi River." Steamboats plied the lake for many years, and its present use is "primarily recreational" by both local residents and travelers from other states."

As to § 10 of the Rivers and Harbors Act, the Court held that waters are "navigable waters of the United States," as held in *The Daniel Ball v. United States*, 77 U.S. 557, 563, 19 L.Ed. 999 (1871): "when they form in their ordinary condition by themselves, or by uniting with other waters, a continuing highway over which commerce is or may be carried on with other States or foreign countries in the customary modes in which such commerce is conducted by water." The Court went on:

> Applying *The Daniel Ball* test to the waters at issue here, we agree with the District Court that Lake Minnetonka, and that portion of Minnehaha Creek above Minnetonka Mills, are not "navigable waters of the United States" as required for federal regulatory jurisdiction under § 10 of the Rivers and Harbors Act of 1899. *The Daniel Ball* test is bipartite: first the body of water must be navigable in fact,[6] and second, it must itself, or together with other waters, form a highway over which commerce may be carried on with other states. All parties agree that both Lake Minnetonka, and that portion of Minnehaha Creek above Minnetonka Mills, are navigable in fact. These waters do not, however, form themselves, or in conjunction with other navigable waters, a continued highway over which interstate commerce can be conducted. Lake Minnetonka is located entirely within the State of Minnesota, with Minnehaha Creek as its sole connecting waterway. Although the portion of Minnehaha Creek above Minnetonka Mills is navigable, the remainder of the creek is not. Lake Minnetonka and the upper, navigable portion of Minnehaha Creek are not, therefore, part of a navigable interstate waterway, and federal regulatory jurisdiction under the Rivers and Harbors Act over these waters does not exist.
>
> The Corps of Engineers contends, however, that federal regulatory jurisdiction under the Rivers and Harbors Act does not require that a body of water be part of an interstate waterway system, as long as it is a segment of a commercial highway, which may consist of water, rail or road connections. The Corps contends that since Lake Minnetonka and the upper portion of Minnehaha Creek have interstate road and rail connections, this is enough to make them "navigable waters of the United States" for the purposes of regulatory jurisdiction under the Act.

[6] "Navigability in fact" has been broadened by later decisions of the Supreme Court to include bodies of water which were navigable in their natural state although they may not presently be so. *Economy Light & Power Co. v. United States*, 256 U.S. 113, 123, 41 S. Ct. 409, 65 L.Ed. 847 (1921), or which, although traditionally considered to be nonnavigable, might be made navigable with reasonable improvements. *United States v. Appalachian Electric Power Co.*, 311 U.S. 377, 404-410, 61 S. Ct. 291, 85 L.Ed. 243 (1940).

We disagree.

[However, as to § 404], all parties agree that Lake Minnetonka and Minnehaha Creek above Minnetonka Mills are "navigable waters" as that term is used in the [Clean Water] Act, and thus, the Corps of Engineers has jurisdiction under the § 404 of the Act to regulate the discharge of dredge or fill material into these waters.* * *

Does Rivers and Harbors Act § 10 create a private right of action to enjoin the obstruction of a navigable waterway? The Supreme Court held it does not in *California v. Sierra Club,* 451 U.S. 287, 101 S. Ct. 1775, 68 L.Ed.2d 101 (1981):

> The language of the statute and its legislative history do not suggest that the Act was intended to create federal rights for the especial benefit of a class of persons but rather was intended to benefit the public at large through a general regulatory scheme to be administered by the then Secretary of War. Nor is there any evidence that Congress anticipated that there would be a private remedy.

*Natural Resources Defense Council, Inc. v. Callaway*, 392 F. Supp. 685 (D.D.C. 1975) ("Definition of Waters" Case) challenged the Army Corps of Engineers regulations implementing § 404, which limited the Corps' jurisdiction to waters meeting the *Daniel Ball* test used for the Rivers and Harbors Act. See the *Minnehaha Creek* case, supra. The court held:

> Congress, by defining the term "navigable waters" in Section 502(7) of the [Clean Water Act] to mean "the waters of the United States, including the territorial seas," asserted federal jurisdiction over the nation's waters to the maximum extent permissible under the Commerce Clause of the Constitution. Accordingly, as used in the Water Act, the term is not limited to the traditional tests of navigability.
>
> [Defendants] Secretary of the Army [and] Army Corps of Engineers are without authority to amend or change the statutory definition of navigable waters and they are hereby declared to have acted unlawfully an in derogation of their responsibilities under Section 404 of the Water Act by the adoption of the definition of navigability described [in their regulations.]

Following this decision the Army amended its regulations (33 CFR § 328.3) to assert jurisdiction over navigable waters, their tributaries, wetlands contiguous to navigable waters, interstate waters and wetlands, and intrastate waters and wetlands whose degradation or destruction could affect interstate commerce.

Wetlands are broadly defined in the Army Corps of Engineers regulations in terms of the vegetation. They must be areas flooded frequently enough to support wetlands plants. This has been construed to include a tract flooded only five times in 80 years. *United States v. Riverside Bayview Homes, Inc.*, 474 U.S. 121, 106 S. Ct. 455, 88 L. Ed.2d 419 (1985). The Army Corps' regulation of dredging and filling in wetlands exists alongside the state land-use controls described in Chapter 2(C).

Are there Constitutionally-imposed limits on Congressional power to regulate wetlands and other non-navigable waters under § 404? Are they met by the need to protect wetlands that are a habitat for ducks, geese and other migratory birds that are viewed, and hunted, by numerous persons who travel from one state to another?

*In Solid Waste Agency of Northern Cook County* v. *Corps of Engineers*, 531 U.S. 159, 121 S. Ct. 675, 148 L. Ed. 2d 576 (2001), the Supreme Court ruled isolated ponds not connected to navigable waters are not part of the "navigable waters" defined in the Act. It thus avoided the constitutional issue as to whether Congress may regulate such areas under its commerce power. Note, however, that the Court did not overrule *Riverside Bayview*, so that even a tenuous connection to navigable waters suffices.

NATURAL RESOURCES DEFENSE COUNCIL, INC. v. CALLAWAY ("Thames Dredging" case), United States Court of Appeals, Second Circuit, 1975. 524 F.2d 79.

Mansfield, Circuit Judge:

The Natural Resources Defense Council, Inc., * * * along with other environmental and citizen groups, brought this action in the District of Connecticut against the Secretary of the Army, the Secretary of the Navy and other related federal officials seeking declatory and injunctive relief against further dumping by the United States Navy of highly polluted dredged spoil at the New London Dumping Site in Long Island Sound. The complaint charges violations of the National Environmental Policy Act of 1969 ("NEPA"), [discussed in chapter 10] and the [Clean Water Act.]

The action arises out of a project undertaken by the United States Navy at New London, Connecticut. In order to accommodate a new class of submarine, the SSN 688 class, at the Navy's Submarine Base in Groton, Connecticut, the Navy has determined that it is necessary to dredge the Thames River from Long Island Sound to the north boundary of Groton, a distance of 7.5 miles. [This] dredging operation requires the removal from the Thames River bottom and disposal of approximately 2.8 million cubic yards of highly polluted material containing volatile solids, industrial wastes and Kjeldahl nitrogen.* * *

Plaintiffs and intervenors do not object to the dredging project itself, choosing to restrict their legal challenge to the Navy's use of the New London Dumping Site as the disposal area. All parties agree that, because the polluted material is likely to cause great harm to the ocean ecosystem if allowed to disperse after being dumped, it is important that if it is dumped in the ocean it be deposited at a "containment site," an area of the ocean floor where currents and other water movement will not cause it to move or disperse. The underlying disagreement between plaintiffs and the government defendants is over the relative merits of the New London Dumping Site as a containment site and the existence of more suitable sites for disposal both in the ocean and on land. Plaintiffs adduced substantial evidence that because of the shallow depth of the site, the fact that the bottom currents there were higher than at some alternative sites, and the prospective impact of storms, the sludge dumped at the New London Dumping Site, although it would remain in place for a while, would eventually break up and disperse to the northwest where it would contaminate and destroy the fish nurseries and marine resources on the coast.

Plaintiffs raised three principal claims before the district court: 1) that the Army Corps of Engineers issued a dumping permit to the Navy in violation of § 404 of [the Clean Water Act], 2) that the Navy and the Corps failed to comply with NEPA in reaching the decision to dump at New London in that a) The Corps, not the Navy, was the proper party required to prepare the necessary Environmental Impact Statement ("EIS"), b) the EIS inadequately discussed other dumping projects and alternative dumping sites, c) the NEPA decision-making procedures were short-circuited, and d) there were errors in the EIS, and 3) that the substantive decision by the Navy to use the New London site was arbitrary and [capricious].

We hold that jurisdiction exists under [the Clean Water Act] and that the discussion in EIS of other dumping projects and alternative dump sites was inadequate under NEPA. Accordingly, we reverse and remand as to those issues. Since there is a substantial risk that additional amounts of highly polluted spoil will be dredged and dumped in non-compliance with the [Act] and NEPA we direct that the Navy be enjoined from such activity until it has satisfied the requirements of these laws. In all other aspects we affirm the district court's opinion.

[Under] § 404 the disposal of dredged material at the New London site requires a permit from the Army Corps of Engineers. Appellants argued below that the permit for this dumping was issued in violation of § 404(b) because it was not, as required by that section, issued in accordance with dumping guidelines developed by the Administrator of the Environmental Protection Agency ("EPA"). [The] only guidelines that have been issued to date by the EPA for use under § 404(b) are the Ocean Dumping Criteria, 40 C.F.R. Part[s] 220 [-233], which are not directly applicable to this dumping project in inland waters. (Long Island Sound has been deemed by the government to be inland waters, both in nautical charts and under a definition found in § 3(b) of the Marine Protection, Research, and Sanctuaries Act of 1972.) Because of this lack of guidelines, the government argues, there cannot have been any failure by the Corps to issue the dumping permit in violation of EPA guidelines. However, we are not here dealing with non-existent guidelines. In its notice of intent to issue the dumping permit to the EPA, the Corps made specific reference to the Ocean Dumping Criteria, stating that § 227.64 thereof, which *prohibits dumping in areas where prevailing currents would carry the dumped material into nursery, fishing or shoreline areas*, would not be violated by disposal at the New London site. Having relied at least in part upon the standards of the Ocean Dumping Criteria to support its selection of the New London site, the Corps cannot now be heard to say that those standards are irrelevant to its issuance of the permit for this dumping project. By its own use of the standards it has made them applicable to this case. The federal courts therefore have the power and the duty to review the application of the Criteria to the extent that they were used by the Corps.

The record also contains evidence that would support findings to the effect that dumping at the New London site violates the Ocean Dumping Criteria as set forth in § 227.64. Plaintiffs introduced considerable proof to the effect that because of the depth and ocean current conditions in the area the highly polluted dredged spoil, despite its initial cohesiveness as a gelatinous mass, would eventually break up and drift northwestward to the Connecticut coast where it would destroy productive fishing and shellfish nurseries and spawning.* * * In response the Navy relies principally upon a study of currents in the area, which plaintiffs label as of little or no value because it was limited to a 25-hour period.* * * The Navy also relies upon a current-monitoring program that it has been required by EPA to undertake. However, plaintiffs point out that since the polluted spoil would not break up and disperse to the northwest for a few years the monitoring program would not avoid the damage, which would already have been done and would be irreversible once the dumping had been completed. Furthermore, say the plaintiffs, the monitoring program will be terminated in two years, which is too soon to determine the long-term polluting effect on coastal fisheries of the dumping at the New London site.

Rather than resolve these * * * issues upon the record as it stands we prefer to remand the case for findings by the district court which will have the benefit not only of observation of the witnesses who have already testified but also of such additional expert testimony and documentary proof as the parties may offer. Furthermore, should the district court conclude that further Navy dumping on the New London site would violate the Ocean Dumping Criteria which have been adopted and applied as guidelines it may then be called upon to determine whether the Corps is able to sustain its burden of showing that selection of the New London site, as distinguished from some other alternative site which satisfies the Criteria, is justified because of the New London site's economic impact on navigation and anchorage.

[The court held the Navy had the right to prepare the EIS. This part of the decision appears in Chapter 10.]

The Final EIS filed by the Navy discussed and evaluated only the environmental impact of this particular Navy project. It did not mention other pending proposals for dumping of approximately an additional 2 million cubic yards of polluted spoil at the New London site or at other nearby areas. The Corps of Engineers proposes, subject to approval and funding by Congress, to dredge the channel of the Thames River to a depth of 41 feet, generating approximately 1,400,000 cubic yards of spoil, with the New London site as a likely dumping spot. The United States Coast Guard, according to a draft EIS recently issued by it, proposes to use the New London site for the dumping of approximately 250,000 cubic yards of spoil. Maintenance of the Thames River channel through 1980 will create approximately an additional 200,000 cubic yards of spoil. The Electric Boat Division of General Dynamics has applied to dredge 300,000 cubic yards from the Thames River near its plant and to dump the spoil at the New London site.

In view of the failure of the Navy's Final EIS to make any mention whatsoever of all of these proposed projects or to analyze the possible cumulative effects of the Navy's dumping of 2.8 million cubic yards of highly polluted spoil with the proposals for dredging of an additional 2.15 million cubic yards, which must be dumped somewhere, appellants renew their contention, rejected below, that the EIS is deficient. We agree that in this respect the EIS failed to furnish information essential to the environmental decision-making process.

The district court concluded that the environmental impact of the Navy's project may be considered in isolation for the reason that the other dumping projects are tentative or speculative in nature and * * * the Navy's dumping of spoil is unrelated to that required by other projects. The court furthermore concluded that the Navy's use of the New London site, unlike some federal projects, will not have a "band wagon effect" leading inevitably to the use of the same site for the dumping output of the other projects[.] Although the district court recognized the threat of incremental harm posed by the other proposals for dumping of polluted spoil in the area, it was persuaded that the development of an impact statement for a larger ecosystem was neither feasible nor reasonable. Accordingly the court drew the line at the Navy's single project, reasoning that "The duty to discuss the impact of all possible pollutants cannot be imposed on each isolated project." We believe that this represents too constricted a view of the informative function of an EIS and of the duty of the responsible agency in preparing it. We agree with the Navy that NEPA does not require it to make a "crystal ball" inquiry, *National Resources Defense Council, Inc. v. Morton,* [also discussed in Chapter 10] and that an EIS is required to furnish only such information as appears to be reasonably necessary under the circumstances for evaluation of the project rather than to be so all-encompassing in scope that the task of preparing it would become either fruitless or well nigh impossible. [But] an agency may not go to the opposite extreme of treating a project as an isolated "single-shot" venture in the face of persuasive evidence that it is but one of several substantially similar operations, each of which will have the same polluting effect in the same area. To ignore the prospective cumulative harm under such circumstances could be to risk ecological disaster.

The Navy's failure to consider these and possibly other proposed dredging projects in the New London area is an example of the isolated decision-making sought to be eliminated by NEPA. The cumulative environmental impact of disposal of all of this dredged spoil at or near the New London site would clearly be greater than the impacts of the projects individually and the risk of serious environmental consequences (such as the movement of the spoil toward shore) may be correspondingly greater. If the total amount and type of spoil to be disposed of in this area in the foreseeable future is studied objectively by the Navy and the Corps, they may well conclude that some other method of disposal, such as a containment island large enough to contain the spoil dredged from all of these and similar projects, should be urged upon Congress as the only effective way of dealing with the problem. The Navy's piecemeal approach to environmental consideration prevented any such comprehensive planning. [I]t is required at least to disclose in its EIS other planned or proposed dredging projects in the area of New London and other plans or proposals to dispose of dredged spoil at or near New London, with a discussion and analysis of the combined environmental impact of its own and these other projects.

Plaintiffs finally attack the procedure followed by the Navy in selecting the New London Disposal Site, contending (1) that it violated NEPA for the reason that the site was chosen without first considering its environmental impact, the Final EIS amounting to nothing more than a post hoc rationalization of a decision already made, and (2) that there was a failure to furnish sufficient information in the Final EIS with respect to reasonable alternative sites to permit a fair consideration and comparison of their respective impacts with that of the New London site.

In the Revised Draft EIS of May 1973 the Navy indicated that it had chosen to dispose of the dredged spoil at Brenton Reef, a site located in Rhode Island Sound off Newport, Rhode Island. Although the site is some 23 miles from the Thames River mouth, it was thought at that time to be the most suitable disposal area because it had previously been used successfully as a site for disposal of some 8.2 million cubic yards of dredged spoil which had been dumped there in 1967 and 1970 with no adverse effect. Based on the relatively great depth at the Brenton Reef site, the low velocity of bottom currents, and the fact that material previously dumped at the site had stayed in place, the probability was high that material deposited there in the future would not disperse. Sites in Long Island Sound were not considered at that time because Navy studies and EPA comments indicated it to be a poor disposal area.

Just before the Revised Draft was circulated the Navy applied to the Army Corps of Engineers for a permit for dumping at Brenton Reef pursuant to § 404. The Corps rejected the application as "premature" and questioned the economics of dumping at Brenton Reef. Over the next three months, May-July, 1973, the Corps decided, apparently independently of the Navy, that the New London site should be used. The basis for the Corps' decision is not altogether clear, but the choice seems to have been based upon economics,[7] sketchy information regarding the extent to which sediment at the New London site was moved by currents, the fact that the latter site had been previously used, and the abandonment by the EPA of its objections to disposal in Long Island Sound. Since the Corps is the permit-granting agency, its views prevailed and the Navy issued an Addendum to the Revised Draft EIS on August 9, 1973, changing the primary disposal site from Brenton Reef to New London. [T]he Final EIS was published in December 1973, designating New London as the disposal site, and the dumping permit for New London was issued by the Corps in April 1974.

Plaintiffs charge that these events have amounted to a short-circuiting of the agency decision-making process mandated by NEPA[.]

Although an EIS may be supplemented, the critical agency decision must, of course, be made after the supplement has been circulated, considered and discussed in the light of the alternatives, not before. Otherwise the process becomes a useless ritual, defeating the purpose of NEPA, and rather making a mockery of it. The district court here found that the supplemental information was made available by the Navy to the Corps and considered by the latter in good faith before the New London site was finally chosen and a permit issued. Plaintiffs vigorously attack this finding as clearly erroneous, pointing to documentary evidence indicating that the Corps had decided as early as June, 1973 that the New London site must be used by the Navy instead of Brenton Reef, which the Navy had previously chosen, i.e., long before the Navy's brief study of the movement of sediment at the New London site was made and the Addendum prepared. We find it unnecessary to resolve this issue, in view of our conclusion that the permit cannot in any event stand because the Corps was not presented with adequate information on alternative dump sites before issuing it.

The district court, applying a "rule of reason[,"] found the consideration of alternatives to be adequate. We disagree with this finding. In our view, even when judged by the "rule of reason" the Addendum failed adequately to explain and evaluate the change of the primary dump site from Brenton Reef to New London and failed to make an adequate analysis of the comparative environmental merits and disadvantages of the New London site and the alternative sites that had figured prominently in the Navy's earlier decision.* * *

By failing to present a complete analysis and comparison of the possible dumping sites, the Final EIS fails to perform its vital task of exposing the reasoning and data of the agency proposing the action to scrutiny by the public and by other branches of the government.* * *
It leaves the reader completely in the dark as to why the New London site was suddenly chosen over Brenton Reef after the latter had been selected as the most suitable site and it gives only sketchy information as to other sites that had been runners-up to Brenton Reef.

---

[7] Use of the Brenton Reef site instead of the New London site was estimated to cost approximately $7,000,000 more.

[In sum] we hold that the district court has jurisdiction to hear plaintiffs' claimed violation of [the Clean Water Act]. The Corps of Engineers' voluntary application of part of the Ocean Dumping Criteria makes that part of the Criteria relied upon by the Corps enforceable against it.

The final EIS does not meet NEPA standards because of its failure to discuss other dumping and dredging projects in the New London area and their cumulative impact, combined with the Navy's project, on the ocean environment. The Addendum evaluating the change in primary dump site from Brenton Reef to New London fails adequately to compare New London with other dump sites and to explain the Navy's choice. Similarly, the Final EIS fails to present a comprehensible and thorough discussion of all the alternative dumping sites suggested by the Navy and the reasons for choosing New London over the others.

The Navy should not be permitted to proceed with further dumping at the New London site until the [§ 404] claim has been resolved and the serious deficiencies in the EIS remedied. Otherwise application of a "rule of reason" would convert an EIS into a mere rubber stamp for post hoc rationalization of decisions already made. If the spirit as well as the letter of NEPA is to have any real meaning in this case, the Navy should prepare and circulate for consideration and comment a supplemental statement that will furnish detailed information with respect to (1) other dredging and dumping projects, existing and proposed, in the New London area and their anticipated cumulative impact, when combined with the Navy's Thames River project, on the ocean's environment, (2) all of the alternative dumping sites proposed in the Revised Draft EIS and Final EIS. The supplemental statement must then make a genuine effort in a truly objective fashion to evaluate and compare the qualities of all of the containment sites and to select one on the basis of clearly stated data and reasoning.* * *

Mulligan, Circuit Judge, dissented.

KAISER AETNA v. UNITED STATES, Supreme Court of the United States, 1979. 444 U.S. 164, 100 S. Ct. 383, 62 L.Ed.2d 332.

[Kaiser Aetna wished to dredge a privately owned pond in Hawaii in order to create a marina with access to the ocean. The pond had previously been a lagoon. The Army Corps notified Kaiser Aetna it required a § 10 permit to dredge the channel and that once completed the channel would make the pond a part of the "navigable waters of the United States," requiring access by the public. The issue in the Supreme Court, as seen by Rehnquist, J., was whether]
petitioners' improvements to Kuapa Pond caused its original character to be so altered that it become subject to an overriding federal navigational servitude[.]

The Government contends that petitioners may not exclude members of the public from the Hawaii Kai Marina because "[t]he public enjoys a federally protected right of navigation over the navigable waters of the United States."

[Although] the Government is clearly correct in maintaining that the now dredged Kuapa Pond falls within the definition of "navigable waters" [this Court] has never held that the navigational servitude creates a blanket exception to the Takings Clause whenever Congress exercises its Commerce Clause authority to promote navigation. Thus, while Kuapa Pond may be subject to regulation by the Corps of Engineers, acting under the authority delegated it by Congress in the Rivers and Harbors Appropriation Act, it does not follow that the pond is also subject to a public right of access.* * * In light of its expansive authority under the Commerce Clause, there is no question but that Congress could assure the public a free right of access to the Hawaii Kai Marina if it so chose. Whether a statute or regulation that went so far amounted to a "taking," however, is an entirely separate question.* * * When the "taking" question has involved the exercise of the public right of navigation over interstate waters that constitute highways for commerce, however, this Court has held in many cases that compensation may not be required as a result of the federal navigational servitude.* * *

The navigational servitude is an expression of the notion that the determination whether a taking has occurred must take into consideration the important public interest in the flow of interstate waters that in their natural condition are in fact capable of supporting public navigation. [Thus] in *United States v. Chandler-Dunbar Co.,* 229 U.S. 53, 33 S. Ct. 667, 57 L.Ed. 1063, this Court stated that "the running water in a great navigable stream is [incapable] of private ownership. [However, here,] the Government's attempt to create a public right of access to the improved pond goes so far beyond ordinary regulation or improvement for navigation as to amount to a taking.

What petitioners now have is a body of water that was private property under Hawaiian law, linked to navigable water by a channel dredged by them with the consent of the Government. While the consent of individual officials representing the United States cannot "estop" the United States, * * * it can lead to the fruition of a number of expectancies embodied in the concept of "property"--expectancies that, if sufficiently important, the Government must condemn and pay for before it takes over the management of the land-owner's property. In this case, we hold that the "right to exclude," so universally held to be a fundamental element of the property right, falls within this category of interests that the Government cannot take without compensation. This is not a case in which the Government is exercising its regulatory power in a manner that will cause an insubstantial devaluation of petitioners' private property; rather, the imposition of the navigational servitude in this context will result in an actual physical invasion of the privately owned marina.

* * *If the Government wishes to make what was formerly Kuapa Pond into a public aquatic park after petitioners have proceeded as far as they have here, it may not, without invoking its eminent domain power and paying just compensation, require them to allow free access to the dredged pond[.]

Justice Blackmun, dissenting, joined by Brennan and Marshall, JJ.:

To sustain its holding today, I believe that the Court must prove [that] the navigational servitude does not extend to waters that are clearly navigable and fully subject to use as a highway for interstate commerce.

The Court holds, in essence, that the extent of the servitude does not depend on whether a waterway is navigable under any of the tests, but on whether the navigable waterway is "natural" or privately [developed.]

In my view, the power we describe by the term "navigational servitude" extends to the limits of interstate commerce by water; accordingly, I would hold that is coextensive with the "navigable waters of the United States."

* * *The National Government is guardian of a public right of access to navigable waters of the United States. The navigational servitude[,] in order to safeguard the Federal Government's paramount control over waters used in interstate commerce, limits the power of the States to create conflicting interests based on local law. That control does not depend on the form of the water body or the manner in which it was created, but on the fact of navigability and the corresponding commercial significance the waterway attains. Wherever that commerce can occur, be it Kuapa Pond or Honolulu Harbor, the navigational servitude must extend.

[W]hen the Government exercises [the navigational] servitude, it is exercising its paramount power in the interest of navigation, rather than taking the private property of anyone.

[The] developers of Kuapa Pond have acted at their own risk and are not entitled to compensation for the public access the Government now asserts. [The] chief value of the Pond in its present state obviously is a value of access to navigable water. Development was undertaken to improve and enhance [this value]. Whatever expectancy petitioners may have had in control over the Pond for use as a fishery was surrendered in exchange for the advantages of access when they cut a channel into the Bay.

[T]he Government's interest in vindicating a public right of access to the Pond is substantial. It is the very interest in maintaining "common highways,. . . .forever free." After today's decision, it is open to any developer to claim that private improvements to a waterway navigable in interstate commerce have transformed "navigable water of the United States" into private property, at least to the extent that he may charge for access to the portion improved. Such appropriation of navigable waters for private use directly injures the freedom of commerce that the navigational servitude is intended to safeguard.

BRAGG v. ROBERTSON, U.S. District Court, Southern District of West Virginia, 1999. 72 F.Supp. 2d. 642, affirmed in part, reversed in part *sub nom.* Bragg v. West Virginia Coal Association, 248 F.3d 275 (4th Cir. 2001), cert. denied, 534 U.S. 1113 (2002).

***

The coalfields of southern West Virginia are mountainous, with steep wooded slopes. Coal in these mountains is found in seams of varying thickness sandwiched between layers of rock and dirt. In mountaintop removal mining, the rock and dirt overburden or "spoil" is removed, layer by layer, and the coal is mined at the exposed surface, as it appears. The ultimate effect is to remove the mountaintop to a depth where deep mining is the practical method of recovery.

The Surface Mining Control and Reclamation Act of 1977 ("SMCRA"), 30 U.S.C. §§ 1201-1328, require[s] coal mining operations "as [sic] a minimum" to "restore the approximate original contour [AOC] of the land." 30 U.S.C. § 1265(b)(3). Where the volume of overburden is large relative to the amount of coal removed, *** not all the earth and rock removed during mining is needed to restore AOC. The unneeded overburden is called "excess spoil."

Valley fills are composed of excess spoil, that is coal mine waste material, which is disposed of by placing it in a valley. The topography of the coalfields and gravity dictate that valleys contain streams, so that valley fills also are generally placed in streams and streambeds.

[The] "buffer zone rule," a SMCRA rule[,] provides:

> No land within one hundred feet of an intermittent or perennial stream shall be disturbed by surface mining operations including roads unless specifically authorized by the Director. The Director will authorize such operations only upon finding that surface mining activities will 1) not adversely affect the normal flow or 2) gradient of the stream, 3) adversely affect fish migration or 4) related environmental values, 5) materially damage the water quantity or 6) quality of the stream and 7) will not cause or contribute to violations of applicable State or Federal water quality standards. ***

The Director [of Environmental Protection] and his agents consistently admit that he made none of the required findings *** for buffer zone variances when authorizing valley fills.

***Surface mine permit applications support the agency testimony that the required findings were not made. A typical application relates:

> The normal flow and gradient of the stream will be adversely affected in the areas of the proposed durable rock [valley] fills and the required sediment control for each. Surface mining activities as proposed in this application make disturbance in these areas necessary.
>
> . . .
>
> Fish migration and related environmental values will be adversely affected in the areas of the proposed durable rock [valley] fills and the required

sediment control for each. Surface mining activities as proposed in this application make disturbance in these areas necessary.

Based on applicant assertions that contend the buffer zone requirements could not be met, buffer zone variances, without required findings, were granted for numerous valley fills.

Further, Defendants have never denied that the stream segments buried under a valley fill no longer exist, Defendants agree the required findings about stream flow, environmental values and water quantity and quality cannot be made.
***

Defendants advance that in August 1999 the DEP, United States Environmental Protection Agency ("EPA"), Office of Surface Mining ("OSM"), and the United States Army Corps of Engineers ("Corps") entered into a Memorandum of Understanding ("MOU"). The August 1999 MOU allows 1) that valley fills may be constructed in intermittent and perennial streams and 2) that the findings for the buffer zone authorization are to be met through compliance with the ostensibly comparable Clean Water Act ("CWA") requirements necessary to carry out dredge and fill activities under CWA § 404. According to Defendants, therefore, *** CWA § 404 permits fill operations and, thus, the Director is not precluded from authorizing valley fills in intermittent and perennial streams under the MOU interpretation. ***

SMCRA's first enumerated purpose is "establish[ing] a nationwide program to protect society and the environment from the adverse effects of surface coal mining operations." 30 U.S.C. § 1202(a). SMCRA contemplates "a continuing partnership between the states and the federal government, with the Secretary [of the Interior] providing oversight, advice, and back-up authority, and the states bearing the major responsibility for implementation of the Act." *In re Permanent Surface Mining Regulation Litigation,* 653 F.2d 514, 516 (D.C. Cir. 1980).

Under an approved state program, such as in West Virginia, the state regulatory authority decides whether mining companies' permit applications meet the State and federal SMCRA requirements. The state agency is the issuer of surface mining permits. *See* 30 U.S.C. § 1260. In West Virginia, the state regulatory agency is the DEP. Mining operations must also obtain permits under CWA including a Section 401 permit certifying any proposed discharge will comply with standards, 33 U.S.C. § 1341; a Section 402 permit allowing discharge of pollutants from a point source into waters of the United States, 33 U.S.C. § 1342; and a Section 404 permit allowing discharge of dredge and fill material into waters of the United States, 33 U.S.C. § 1344.

OSM promulgated the buffer zone rule in 1979 to implement SMCRA Sections 515(b)(10) and (24) (codified at 30 U.S.C. § 1265(b)(18) and (24)), [which] require the operation *at a minimum to*
***

(24) *to the extent possible using the best technology currently available, minimize disturbances and adverse impacts of the operation on fish, wildlife, and related environmental values, and achieve enhancement of such resources where practicable.* (emphasis added).

To carry out this statutory program, the *federal* buffer zone rule provides:

(a) No land within 100 feet of a perennial stream or an intermittent stream shall be disturbed by surface mining activities, unless the regulatory authority specifically authorizes surface mining activities closer to, or through such a stream. The regulatory authority may authorize such activities only upon finding that —

(1) Surface mining activities will not cause or contribute to the violation of applicable State or Federal water quality standards, and will not adversely affect the water quantity and quality or other environmental resources of the stream.

30 C.F.R. § 816.57.

The *state* buffer zone regulation is similar[.]

Defendants read the OSM's stream protections to apply to a stream's entirety, so that one part of a stream, usually the headwaters and upper reaches, may be filled, i.e., covered by a valley fill, as long as stream quantity and quality are not adversely affected downstream. This interpretation, however, leads, to the *reductio ad absurdum* that miles of streams could be filled and deeply covered with rock and dirt, but if some stretch of water downstream of the fill remains undiminished and unsullied, the stream has been protected. The regulations provide otherwise. Under State regulations, an intermittent stream is "a stream or reach of a stream," that is, a portion of a stream. ***

Federal regulations also refer to a perennial stream *or part of a stream* and an intermittent stream *or reach* thereof. *See* 30 C.F.R. § 701.5 Where such streams or their parts exist, they are to be protected by application of the buffer zone rule. [But] defendants propose § 404 of the CWA specifically permits "fills" in the waters of the United States and therefore authorizes valley fills for disposing of excess spoil, as provided in the August 9, 1999 MOU.

[CWA] Section 404 permits, issued by the Corps, authorize dredge and fill operations in waters of the United States. "Dredged material" is "material that is excavated or dredged from waters of the United States." 33 C.F.R. § 323.2(c). It is undisputed the overburden originating from mountaintop mining is not excavated or dredged from the waters of the United States. The Corps defines "fill material," for which Section 404 permits also may be issued, as:

> any material used for the primary purpose of replacing an aquatic area with dry land or of changing the bottom elevation of an [sic] waterbody. *The term does not include any pollutant discharged into the water primarily to*

> *dispose of waste, as that activity is regulated under section 402 of the Clean Water Act.*

33 C.F.R. § 323.3(e) (emphasis added). This "primary purpose" definition explicitly excludes "pollutants" discharged into the water primarily to dispose of waste.

Under Section 404, the Corps regulates the "discharge of fill material," which:

> includes, without limitation, the following activities: Placement of fill that is necessary for the construction of any structure in a water of the United States; the building of any structure or impoundment requiring rock, sand, dirt, or other material for its construction; site-development fills for recreational, industrial, commercial, residential, and other uses; causeways or road fills; dams and dikes; artificial islands, property protection and/or reclamation devices such as riprap, groins, seawalls, breakwaters, and revetments; beach nourishment; levees; fill for structures such as sewage treatment facilities, intake and outfall pipes associated with power plants and subaqueous utility lines; and artificial reefs.

33 C.F.R. § 323.3(f). These uses are all constructive and do not include any sort of waste disposal.

While valley fills in intermittent or perennial streams have the incidental effect of replacing an aquatic area with dry land and changing the bottom elevation of streams, their primary purpose is the disposal of rock and dirt, that is, industrial waste, the overburden or excess spoil which must be removed to mine the coal in mountaintop removal mining.

***

As Judge Copenhaver previously analyzed and stated the law of this district:

> [B]ecause the [Corps'] definition of fill material includes only material placed for the "primary purpose" of "changing the bottom elevation of a waterbody," it would appear that the [Corps] never intended to regulate the disposal of waste or spoil in valley fills. The primary purpose of the fills. . .is to dispose of waste. . ., not to create dry land such as is needed for construction of buildings or land development, as contemplated by the [Corps'] definition above. [*West Virginia Coal Association* v.]

*Reilly*, 728 F. Supp. [1276] at 1285-87.

Our Court of Appeals, affirming *Reilly* in an unpublished opinion, similarly stated, "The discharge of fill material at issue here is expressly for the purpose of disposing of waste or spoil from the mining operations." *West Virginia Coal Assoc. v. Reilly*, 932 F.2d 964 (4th Cir. 1991).

The Court finds and concludes that overburden or excess spoil, being a pollutant and waste material, is not "fill material" subject to Corps' authority under Section 404 of the CWA when it is discharged into waters of the United States for the primary purpose of waste disposal. The Corps' § 404 authority to permit fills in the waters of the United States does not include authority to permit valley fills for coal mining waste disposal. Accordingly the August MOU is inconsistent with the CWA to extent it bases its proposal on the Corps' authority to authorize waste fills in the waters of the United States.

***

Federal and State water quality standards require the waters of the United States shall not be used for waste assimilation nor be degraded. The Director cannot make the required finding that valley fills will not cause or contribute to violations of applicable State or federal water quality standards. In the stream portion filled, those standards, are inevitably violated. Accordingly, the Court *** holds the Director has a nondiscretionary duty under the buffer zone rule to deny variances for valley fills in intermittent and perennial streams because they necessarily adversely affect stream flow, stream gradient, fish migration, related environmental values, water quality and quantity, and violate state and federal water quality standards. * * *

On appeal, the Fourth Circuit ruled the suit against the state was barred by the Eleventh Amendment, 248 F.3d 275 (4th Cir. 2001), cert. denied, 534 U.S. 1113 (2002).

In 2002 the Army Corps of Engineers promulgated a revised rule that redefined "fill material" to authorize the disposal of mining waste found unlawful in *Bragg*. The new rule was itself unsuccessfully challenged as inconsistent with the Clean Water Act. See *Kentuckians for the Commonwealth, Inc.* v. *Rivenburgh*, 317 F. 3d 425 (4th Cir. 2003).

## C. THE CLEAN WATER ACT: WATER QUALITY

### Introductory Note

In the Clean Water Act, Congress enacted a comprehensive scheme to control water quality, modeled on the Clean Air Act but with some important differences. Each source, new or existing, must have a permit. States may assume control of the permit program within their borders with EPA approval.

It is important to note that the Clean Water Act only applies to surface waters. Groundwater, which furnishes the water supply for half the nation, is regulated by the Safe Drinking Water Act (42 U.S.C.A. §§ 300f to 300j-26), requiring permits and establishing EPA and state criteria for potable water.
The EPA is empowered to require that public or private water supply systems be filtered to remove pollutants. New York City's water supply, stemming from upstate reservoirs, was the subject of great controversy in the 1990s over the need for filtration, an enormously expensive remedy. In the end a compromise was reached under which the older, more endangered, Croton Reservoir System will require filtration. The newer and more pristine Catskill and Delaware systems,

providing about 85% of the City's water, will not. The City is to purchase land and upgrade local sewage treatment systems in order to safeguard its water supply, and upstate farms and industrial dischargers are subject to restrictions on their effluent.

Groundwater protection is exemplified by the measures adopted to insure the integrity of Long Island's aquifer, including restrictions on development in Long Island's Pine Barrens (a "recharge area" from which the aquifer replenishes itself), and on landfills and petroleum storage atop the recharge area, as well as bans on septic tank cleaners and other toxic substances that could impair the aquifer.

What about the vast increase in population and water use in areas like Long Island? This too can place its aquifer at risk. If water is removed faster than rain and snow can replace it, salt water from the ocean and Long Island Sound can seep into the edges of the aquifer, a process known as salt water intrusion. This is heightened by the use of sewers (discharging into the ocean and sound) in place of septic systems as population density increases.

Section 401: State Water Quality Certification

Section 401 of the Clean Water Act (33 U.S.C.A. §§ 1251-1387) requires an applicant for a federal permit to conduct any activity "which may result in any discharge into the navigable waters of the United States" to provide the licensing agency "a certification from the State [of] reasonable assurance [that the activity will meet] applicable water quality standards." Con Edison's proposed construction of the Storm King pumped-storage hydroelectric power plant on the Hudson River required a permit from the then Federal Power Commission, now the Federal Energy Regulatory Commission. See the *Scenic Hudson* case, Ch. 1. The utility therefore had to obtain § 401 certification from the State of New York.

In *De Rham v. Diamond*, 32 N.Y.2d 34, 295 N.E.2d 763, 343 N.Y.S.2d 84 (1973), New York's Court of Appeals sustained the § 401 certificate, rebuffing the challengers' claims that the State Department of Environmental Conservation was obliged to consider the power plant's effect on the Hudson River fishery, the scenic beauty of the Hudson Highlands and the danger it posed to the City of New York's aqueduct by blasting near the point where it tunneled beneath the river. The court adopted the lower court's view that the claim of danger to the aqueduct "has no bearing on water quality," adding:

> [T]he petitioners' argument misconceives the proper scope of the limited certificate proceeding pursuant to [§ 401]. That provision * * * requires the State Commissioner merely to consider the water quality standards which may be affected by discharges from a proposed project into navigable waterways. The Aqueduct is, of

> course, a water main, not a stream. But even more important, the Cornwall Project will not discharge into the Aqueduct, and there is not the slightest suggestion that its contents would be polluted by the project.

This view of "water quality" also disposed of the scenic beauty claim. With regard to the asserted effect on fish life the Court held:

> [T]he subject of Hudson River fishery was extensively considered by the Federal Power Commission. At the hearing before that body, fishery biologists, experts in the design and operation of screening devices and others testified. One witness (Dr. Alfred Perlmutter of New York University) declared that the project "will have no measurable effect on the Hudson River fishery" and a staff member of the Commission itself stated that fish losses caused by the project's operation "would not significantly affect the Hudson River fishery resources." And * * * the Hudson River Policy Committee--consisting of top-flight experts of the New York State Conservation Department, the New Jersey Division of Fish and Game, the United States Bureau of Commercial Fisheries and the United States Bureau of Sports Fisheries and Wildlife--following a three-year study (1965-1968) of the effect of the project on aquatic life, reported that "there would not be any significant adverse effects to the striped bass and American shad fisheries of the Hudson River from a pumped storage generating plant in Cornwall."

It is noteworthy that the Federal Power Commission reached the same conclusion after a careful investigation of the entire project. Beyond that, under the terms of the of the Federal Power Commission license, Con Ed is required to conduct further studies relating to the entire subject and, indeed, the license is conditioned upon the utility's installing fish protective facilities and making any modifications that may be ordered by the Commission.

Ironically, the hearings were reinstated later to reconsider the impact of the plant on the fishery. See the discussion after *Scenic Hudson* in Chapter 1.

What if a proposed hydroelectric plant will increase the turbidity, or turbulence, of a stream used for water supply? See *Power Authority of State of New York v. Williams*, 101 A.D.2d 659, 475 N.Y.S.2d 901 (3d Dept. 1984), lv. app. den. 63 N.Y.2d 605, 471 N.E.2d 462, 481 N.Y.S.2d 1023, holding the state properly denied § 401 certification on those facts.

Does § 401 authorize a state to deny certification to a federally-licensed project because it will reduce water *quantity*? See *Public Util. Dist. No. 1 of Jefferson County v. Washington Department of Ecology*, 511 U.S. 700, 114 S.Ct. 1900, 128 L. Ed.2d 716 (1994) (O'Connor, J.):

Petitioners propose to build the Elkhorn Hydroelectric Project on the Dosewallips River. * * * The project would divert water from a 1.2-mile reach of the River (the bypass reach), run the water through turbines to generate electricity and then return the water to the River below the bypass reach. Under the Federal Power Act, the Federal Energy Regulatory Commission has authority to license new hydroelectric facilities. As a result, the petitioners must get a FERC license to build or operate the Elkhorn Project. Because a federal license is required, and because the project may result in discharges into the Dosewallips River, petitioners are also required to obtain State certification of the project pursuant to § 401 of the Clean Water Act, 33 U.S.C. § 1341.

The water flow in the bypass reach, which is currently undiminished by appropriation, ranges seasonally between 149 and 738 cubic feet per second (cfs). The Dosewallips supports two species of salmon, Coho and Chinook, as well as Steelhead trout. As originally proposed, the project was to include a diversion dam which would completely block the River's water into a tunnel alongside the streambed. About 25% of the water would remain in the baypass reach, but would be returned to the original riverbed through sluice gates or a fish ladder. Depending on the season, this would leave a residual minimum flow of between 65 and 155 cfs in the River. [The State Department of Ecology] undertook a study to determine the minimum stream flows necessary to protect the salmon and steelhead fisheries in the bypass reach [and] issued a § 401 water quality certification imposing a variety of conditions on the project, including a minimum stream-flow requirement of between 100 and 200 cfs depending on the season.

The Washington Supreme Court held that the antidegradation provisions of the State's water quality standards require the imposition of minimum stream flows [and] that § 401(d), which allows States to impose conditions based upon several enumerated sections of the Clean Water Act and "any other appropriate requirement of State law," authorized the stream flow condition. * * *

The principal dispute in this case concerns whether the minimum stream flow requirement that the State imposed on the Elkhorn project is a permissible condition of a § 401 certification under the Clean Water Act. To resolve this dispute we must first determine the scope of the State's authority under § 401. We must then determine whether the limitation at issue here, the requirement that petitioners maintain minimum stream flows, falls within the scope of that authority. * * * Section 401(d) provides that any certification shall set forth "any effluent limitations and other limitations . . . necessary to assure that *any applicant*" will comply with various provisions of the Act and appropriate state law requirements. (emphasis added). The language of this subsection contradicts petitioners' claim that the State may only impose water quality limitations specifically tied to a "discharge." The text refers to the compliance of the applicant, not the discharge. Section 401(d) thus allows the State to impose "other limitations" on the project in general to assure compliance with various provisions of the Clean Water Act and with "any other appropriate requirement of State law."

* * * Although § 401(d) authorizes the State to place restrictions on the activity as a whole, the authority is not unbounded. The State can only ensure that the project complies with "any applicable effluent limitations and other limitations, under [33 U.S.C. §§ 1311, 1312]" or certain other provisions of the Act, "and with any other appropriate requirement of State law." 33 U.S.C.
§ 1341(d). The State asserts that the minimum stream flow requirement was imposed to ensure compliance with the state water quality standards adopted pursuant to § 303 of the Clean Water Act, 33 U.S.C. § 1313.

We agree with the State that ensuring compliance with § 303 is a proper function of the § 401 certification. Although § 303 is not one of the statutory provisions listed in § 401(d), the statute allows states to impose limitations to ensure compliance with § 301 of the Act, 33 U.S.C. § 1311. Section 301 in turn incorporates § 303 by reference. As a consequence, state water quality standards adopted pursuant to § 303 are among the "other limitations" with which a State may ensure compliance through the § 401 certification process.

[W]e [next] consider whether the minimum flow condition is such a limitation. Under § 303, state water quality standards must "consist of the designated uses of the navigable waters involved and the water quality criteria for such waters based upon such uses." In imposing the minimum stream flow requirement, the State determined that construction and operation of the project as planned would be inconsistent with one of the designated uses of Class AA water, namely "[s]almonid [and other fish] migration, rearing, spawning, and harvesting." The designated use of the River as a fish habitat directly reflects the Clean Water Act's goal of maintaining the "chemical, physical, and biological integrity of the Nation's waters." 33 U.S.C. § 1251(a). [T]he Act expressly

requires that, in adopting water quality standards, the State must take into consideration the use of waters for "propagation of fish and wildlife." 33 U.S.C.
§ 1313(c)(2)(A).

* * * Petitioners also assert more generally that the Clean Water Act is only concerned with water "quality," and does not allow the regulation of water "quantity." This is an artificial distinction. In many cases, water quantity is closely related to water quality; a sufficient lowering of the water quantity in a body of water could destroy all of its designated uses, be it for drinking water, recreation, navigation or, as here, as a fishery. In any event, there is recognition in the Clean Water Act itself that reduced stream flow, *i.e.*, diminishment of water quantity, can constitute water pollution. First, the Act's definition of pollution as "the man-made or man induced alteration of the chemical, physical, biological, and radiological integrity of water" encompasses the effects of reduced water quantity. 33 U.S.C. § 1362(19). This broad conception of pollution--one which expressly evinces Congress' concern with the physical and biological integrity of water--refutes petitioner's assertion that the Act draws a sharp distinction between the regulation of water "quantity" and water "quality." Moreover, § 304 of the Act expressly recognizes that water "pollution" may result from "changes in the movement, flow, or circulation of any navigable waters . . . including changes caused by the construction of dams." 33 U.S.C. § 1314(f). This concern with the flowage effects of dams and other diversions is also embodied in the EPA regulations, which expressly require existing dams to be operated to attain designated uses. 40 CFR § 131.10(g)(4).

[W]e hold that the State may include minimum stream flow requirements in a certification issued pursuant to § 401 of the Clean Water Act insofar as necessary to enforce a designated use contained in a state water quality standard. * * *

## Point Sources and Permits

The Clean Water Act originally regulated, and still chiefly regulates, "point sources" of water pollution. As explained in *Natural Resources Defense Council* v. *Costle*, a point source is a pipe, ditch or similar definite point from which pollutants are discharged. Each point source must obtain a permit to discharge pollutants. The National Pollutant Discharge Elimination System (NPDES) described in *NRDC* v. *Costle* is administered by the EPA, though states may take over the permit program, subject to EPA supervision, as is discussed in the *General Electric* decision later in this section. About three quarters of the states have done so.

What are some reasons why a state might want, or not want, to administer a permit program under the Act?

NATURAL RESOURCES DEFENSE COUNCIL, INC. v. COSTLE, United States Court of Appeals, District of Columbia Circuit, 1977. 568 F.2d 1369.

[The Natural Resources Defense Council (NRDC) sought a declaratory judgment that regulations of the EPA exempting discharges from some classes of point sources from the permit requirements of Clean Water Act § 402 were illegal. NRDC contended the EPA Administrator exceeded his authority in enacting such regulations in light of clear statutory language that the intent of the Act was to prohibit discharges of pollutants from all point sources unless a permit had been secured pursuant to § 402 or unless the statute specifically exempted the point source. The EPA contended that administrative necessity required that it concern itself with the most egregious discharges rather than with minor pollutants.]

Leventhal, Circuit Judge.

In 1972 Congress passed the Federal Water Pollution Control Act Amendments [hereafter referred to as the "FWPCA" or the "Act"--today known as the Clean Water Act.] It was a dramatic response to accelerating environmental degradation of rivers, lakes and streams in this country. The Act's stated goal is to eliminate the discharge of pollutants into the Nation's waters by 1985. This goal is to be achieved through the enforcement of the strict time-tables and technology-based effluent limitations established by the Act.

The FWPCA sets up a permit program, the National Pollutant Discharge Elimination System (NPDES), as the primary means of enforcing the Act's effluent limitations. At issue in this case is the authority of the Administrator of the Environmental Protection Agency to make exemptions from this permit component of the FWPCA.

Section 402 of the FWPCA, 33 U.S.C. § 1342, provides that under certain circumstances the EPA Administrator "may. . . . issue a permit for the discharge of any pollutant" notwithstanding the general proscription of pollutant discharges found in § 301 of the Act. 33 U.S.C. § 1311. The discharge of a pollutant is defined in the FWPCA as "any addition of any pollutant to navigable waters from any point source" or "any addition of any pollutant to the waters of the contiguous zone or the ocean from any point source other than a vessel or floating craft." 33 U.S.C. § 1362 (12). In 1973 the EPA Administrator issued regulations that exempted certain categories of "point sources" of pollution from the permit requirements of § 402. The Administrator's purported authority to make such exemptions turns on the proper interpretation of § 402.

A "point source" is defined in § 502(14) as "any discernible, confined and discrete conveyance, including but not limited to any pipe, ditch, channel, tunnel, conduit, well, discrete fissure, container, rolling stock, concentrated animal feeding operation, or vessel or other floating craft, from which pollutants are or may be discharged."

The 1973 regulations exempted discharges from a number of classes of point sources from the permit requirements of § 402, including all silvicultural point sources; all confined animal feeding operations below a certain size; all irrigation return flows from areas of less than 3,000 contiguous acres that use the same drainage system; all non-feedlot, non-irrigation agricultural point sources; and separate storm sewers containing only storm runoff uncontaminated by an industrial or commercial activity. The EPA's rationale for these exemptions is that in order to conserve the Agency's enforcement resources for more significant point sources of pollution, it is necessary to exclude these smaller sources of pollutant discharges from the permit program.* * *

The principal purpose of the FWPCA is "to restore and maintain the chemical, physical, and biological integrity of the nation's waters." The Act's ultimate objective, to eliminate the discharge of pollutants into the navigable waters by 1985, is to be achieved by means of two intermediate steps. As of July 1, 1977, all point sources other than publicly owned treatment works were to have achieved effluent limitations that require application of the "best practicable control technology," These same point sources must reduce their effluent discharges by July 1, 1983, to meet limitations determined by application of the "best available technology economically achievable" for each category of point source.

The technique for enforcing these effluent limitations is straightforward. Section 301(a) of the FWPCA provides:

> Except as in compliance with this section and Sections 302, 306, 307, 318, 402 and 404 of this Act, the discharge of any pollutant by any person shall be unlawful.

Appellants concede that if the regulations are valid it must be because they are authorized by § 402; none of the other sections listed in § 301(a) afford grounds for relieving the exempted point sources from the prohibition of § 301.* * *

The NPDES permit program established by § 402 is central to the enforcement of the FWPCA. It translates general effluent limitations into the specific obligations of a discharger.* * *

The appellants argue that § 402 not only gives the Administrator the discretion to grant or refuse a permit, but also gives him the authority to exempt classes of point sources from the permit requirements entirely. They argue that this interpretation is supported by the legislative history of § 402 and the fact that unavailability of this exemption power would place unmanageable administrative burdens on the [EPA.]

Putting aside for the moment the appellants' administrative infeasibility argument, * * * the legislative history makes clear that Congress intended the NPDES permit to be the only means by which a discharger from a point source may escape the total prohibition of § 301(a). This intention is evident in both Committee Reports. In discussing § 301 the House Report stressed:

> Any discharge of a pollutant without a permit issued by the Administrator under Section 318, or by the Administrator or the State under Section 402 or by the Secretary of the Army under Section 404 is unlawful. Any discharge of a pollutant not in compliance with the conditions or limitations of such a permit is also unlawful.* * *

The EPA argues that since § 402 provides that "the Administrator *may*. . . issue a permit for the discharge of any pollutant" (emphasis added), he is given the discretion to exempt point sources from the permit requirements altogether. This argument, as to what Congress meant by the word "may" in § 402, is insufficient to rebut the plain language of the statute and the committee reports. We say this with due awareness of the deference normally due "the construction of a new statute by its implementing agency." The use of the word "may" in § 402 means only that the Administrator has discretion either to issue a permit or to leave the discharger subject to the total proscription of § 301. This is the natural reading, and the one that retains the fundamental logic of the statute.

Under the EPA's interpretation the Administrator would have broad discretion to exempt large classes of point sources from any or all requirements of the FWPCA. This is a result that the legislators did not intend. Rather they stressed that the FWPCA was a tough law that relied on explicit mandates to a degree uncommon in legislation of this type. A statement of Senator Jennings Randolph of West Virginia, Chairman of the Senate Committee responsible for the Act, is illustrative.

I stress very strongly that Congress has become very specific on the steps it wants taken with regard to environmental protection. We have written into law precise standards and definite guidelines on how the environment should be protected. We have done more than just provide broad directives for administrators to follow.* * *

The wording of the statute, legislative history, and precedents are clear: The EPA Administrator does not have authority to exempt categories of point sources from the permit requirements of § 402. Courts may not manufacture for an agency a revisory power inconsistent with the clear intent of the relevant statute.* * *

The appellants have stressed * * * the extraordinary burden on the EPA that will be imposed by the above interpretation of the scope of the NPDES program. The spectre of millions of applications for permits is evoked both as part of appellants' legislative history argument--that Congress could not have intended to impose such burdens on the EPA--and as an invitation to this court to uphold the regulations as deviations from the literal terms of the FWPCA necessary to permit the agency to realize the general objectives of that act.

EPA argues that the regulatory scheme intended under * * * the FWPCA requires, first, that the Administrator establish national effluent limitations and, second, that these limitations be incorporated in the individual permits of dischargers. EPA argues that the establishment of such limitations is simply not possible with the type of point sources involved in the 1973 regulations, which essentially involve the discharge of runoff--i.e., wastewaters generated by rainfall that drain over terrain into navigable waters, picking up pollutants along the way.* * *

EPA contends that certain characteristics of runoff pollution make it difficult to promulgate effluent limitations for most of the point sources exempted by the 1973 regulations:

> The major characteristic of the pollution problem which is generated by runoff. . . . is that the owner of the discharge point. . . has no control over the quantity of the flow or the nature and amounts of the pollutants picked up by the runoff. The amount of flow obviously is unpredictable because it results from the duration and intensity of the rainfall event, the topography, the type of ground cover and the saturation point of the land due to any previous rainfall. Similar factors affect the types of pollutants which will be picked up by that runoff, including the type of farming practices employed, the rate and type of pesticide and fertilizer application, and the conservation practices employed. . . .
>
> An effluent limitation must be a precise number in order for it to be an effective regulatory tool; both the discharger and the regulatory agency need to have an identifiable standard upon which to determine whether the facility is in compliance. That was the principle of the passage of the 1972 Amendments.

Federal Appellants' Memorandum on "Impossibility" at 7-8. Implicit in EPA's contention is the premise that there must be a uniform effluent limitation prior to issuing a permit. That is not our understanding of the law.* * *

[T]he existence of uniform national effluent limitations is not a necessary precondition for incorporating into the NPDES program pollution from agricultural, silvicultural, and storm water runoff point sources. The technological or administrative infeasibility of such limitations may result in adjustments in the permit programs * * * but it does not authorize the Administrator to exclude the relevant point source from the NPDES program.* * *

Finally, EPA argues that the number of permits involved in the absence of an exemption authority will simply overwhelm the Agency. Affidavits filed with the District Court indicate, for example, that the number of silviculture point sources may be over 300,000 and that there are approximately 100,000 separate storm sewer point sources. We are and must be sensitive to EPA's concerns of an intolerable permit load. But the District Court and the various parties have suggested devices to mitigate the burden--to accommodate within a practical regulatory scheme Congress's clear mandate that all point sources have permits. All that is required is that EPA make full use of its interpretational authority. [For example,] NRDC and the District Court have suggested the use of area or general permits. The Act allows such techniques.* * * We find a plain Congressional intent to require permits in any situation of pollution from point sources. We also discern an intent to give EPA flexibility in the structure of the permits, in the form of general or area permits.* * * Imagination conjoined with determination will likely give EPA a capability for practicable administration. If not, the remedy lies with Congress.* * *

## Notes

Accepting the court's suggestion that group permits comply with the Act, the oil industry has successfully challenged the EPA's practice of requiring separate permits for individual mobile offshore oil drilling rigs at each new location. *American Petroleum Institute v. Costle*, 15 Envt. Rptr. Cases 1138 (W.D.La. 1980).

The 1987 amendments to the Act bring storm sewers and non-point sources--the latter not required to obtain permits under the 1972 Act--under the permit program. See 33 U.S.C. §§ 1329 (non-point sources), 1342(p) (storm sewers). Non-point sources are discussed later in this subsection.

IN RE GENERAL ELECTRIC COMPANY, File No. 2833 (N.Y. Dept of Envtl. Conservation, Feb. 9, 1976). 6 Envtl. Law. Rptr. 30007.

Sofaer, Hearing Officer.[a]

This proceeding was commenced by the Department of Environmental Conservation ("Department") to enforce against the General Electric Company ("GE") §§ 17-0501,[8] 17-0511,[9] and 11-0503[10] of the Environmental Conservation

---

[a]Later, a United States District Judge in the Southern District of New York.

[8] ECL 17-0501 *General prohibition against pollution*[.] It shall be unlawful for any person, directly or indirectly, to throw, drain, run or otherwise discharge into such waters organic or inorganic matter that shall cause or contribute to a condition in contravention of the standards adopted by the department pursuant to Section 17-0301.

[9] ECL 17-0511 *Restrictions on discharge of sewage, industrial waste or other wastes*[.] The use of existing or new outlets or point sources which discharge sewage, industrial waste or other wastes into waters of this state is prohibited unless such use is in compliance with all standards,

Law of the State of New York ("ECL") and of water quality and purity standards promulgated pursuant to ECL 17-0301. The complaint alleges that GE is polluting the waters of the Hudson River by directly and indirectly discharging a toxic substance, polychlorinated biphenyls ("PCB's"), into the river from the Company's facilities at Hudson Falls and Fort Edward (ECL 17-0501, 17-0511), and that the discharged PCB's are injurious to fish life of the Hudson River (ECL 11-0503.1). The Department seeks far-reaching relief including: an order that GE cease its discharge of PCB's from all point and non-point sources, that GE restore the health of the Hudson River and other natural resources to the extent its PCB discharges have despoiled them; and that these objectives be attained through a procedure under Department's supervision, including a requirement that GE file a surety bond of $2,000,000 to guarantee its compliance.

GE answers that it discharges do not violate the ECL and raises as an affirmative defense compliance with its permit under the National Pollutant Discharge Elimination System (NPDES), now a State Pollutant Discharge Elimination Permit (SPDES), issued originally by the U.S. Environmental Protection Agency (EPA). GE argues that no basis exists for the imposition of any remedy. At the same time, the Company represents that "it is going forward voluntarily with a program to achieve maximum treatment and containment." At the hearing, its manager of Engineering and Product Development, Dr. Michael Modan, testified that GE was in the process of reducing its discharge of PCB's from a claimed daily average of about two pounds, to a maximum daily amount of one hundred grams by the end of 1976. Tr. 1322. These amounts are in sharp contrast to the combined daily discharge level of 30 pounds from the plants at Fort Edward and Hudson Falls described in GE's SPDES permit.

[T]he record in this case overwhelmingly demonstrates violations of ECL 17-0501 and 17-0511, within the applicable statutory period. PCB's are toxic substances, capable in sufficient quantities of causing skin lesions, destroying cells in vital body organs, adversely affecting reproduction, and inducing cancer and death. GE has discharged PCB's in quantities that have breached applicable standards of water quality. The PCB's have injured fish, and have destroyed the viability of recreational fishing in various parts of the Hudson River by rendering its fish dangerous to consume. Fish analyses in evidence present a grim picture in which PCB contamination reaches over 100 times the temporary tolerance level established by the U.S. Food and Drug Administration ("FDA") in 1971.

These unlawful consequences are the product of both corporate abuse and regulatory failure: corporate abuse in that GE caused the PCB's to be discharged without exercising sufficient precaution and concern; regulatory failure in that GE

---

criteria, limitations, rules and regulations promulgated or applied by the department pursuant to this article.

[10] ECL 11-0503 *Polluting streams prohibited*[.] No dyestuffs, coal tar, * * * acid, oil or other deleterious or poisonous substance shall be thrown or allowed to run into any waters, either private or public, in quantities injurious to fish life, protected wildlife or waterfowl inhabiting those waters or injurious to the propagation of fish, protected wildlife or waterfowl therein.

informed the responsible federal and state agencies of its activities, and they too exercised insufficient caution and concern until this action was instituted by New York's present Commissioner of Environmental Conservation.* * *

GE is responsible for its conduct and must be compelled to abide by the law. It will at a minimum be ordered drastically to limit its discharges, as it claims itself willing and able to do; to consider and use substitute products wherever feasible; to take other steps that may be appropriate to prevent intentional and non-intentional future discharges; and to rectify the effects of its prior violations where lawfully proper, and economically and environmentally practicable. The public must not be made to pay a continuing price for past bureaucratic insufficiency. But neither should the legislature and public be deceived by this focus on GE's activities into assuming that government has otherwise dealt in a meaningful, institutional fashion with PCB's, or with other hazardous substances being discharged into our environment. Effective regulatory surveillance would have prevented much of the harm that GE has inflicted.

GE "has not contested that it has been a source of certain PCB's in the Upper Hudson River in the vicinity of its discharges." But it claims that "the evidence does not permit,. . . .by the legal standards which exclude conjecture as a basis for penalties, a finding that the high levels of PCB's reported in these fish are attributable to Respondent's discharges." In particular, the company asserts there is "no evidence" excluding other PCB sources earlier than September 1975, "no evidence" relating downstream fish concentrations to Respondent's discharges, and "no evidence" as to when the accumulations occurred.

The Department has the burden of proof in this proceeding. The burden involved is that normally applied in civil and administrative proceedings to prove the alleged violations by a preponderance of the evidence. [And] the Department has * * * carried its burden on this issue beyond any reasonable doubt. The evidence that GE is responsible for the high concentration of PCB's in the Upper Hudson's water, sediment, organisms and fish is overwhelming.

Not only has GE been shown to have discharged large quantities of PCB's into the Hudson over long periods of time, the Department has established that other sources contribute negligible amounts of PCB's to the river. During September 1975, * * * the Department tested effluent from 28 municipal and industrial discharges in the Upper Hudson. The Hudson Falls Village Treatment Plant showed a discharge of 2.45 lbs. PCB's per day, which has been shown to be attributable to GE. Four other sources had amounts of 0.005, 0.001, 0.22 and 0.095 lbs. per day. All of the remaining sources indicate no recordable amounts of PCB's.* * *

The strongest evidence of GE's responsibility for existing PCB levels is in the contrasting results obtained, in all the studies in evidence, of PCB concentration upstream as opposed to downstream of GE plants. Thus, in the EPA study during August 1974, a reading of 2800 ppb[b] PCB's in water was taken

---

[b]ppb = part(s) per billion; ppm = part(s) per million.

at the junction of GE's Fort Edward Plant's discharge and the Hudson River. The concentration of a station one-half mile above Bakers Falls, upstream of the GE plants, was less than 1 ppb.* * *

Sediment samples taken above the GE plants also had concentrations of PCB's that were much lower than those below the plants.* * *

Plentiful evidence gathered concerning PCB concentration in fish also shows that GE's plants are the only important sources of PCB contamination in that area.* * * The Department's study during 1975 revealed that, in 29 samples taken from upstream stations (above the Hudson Falls sewage plant), all contained less than 1 ppm PCB's. In contrast, the average concentration for the numerous fish sampled at Fort Edward was 176.83 ppm PCB's for the whole fish, and other, very high concentrations were found at most downstream stations.

By any reasonable standard, then, GE has been shown to be responsible for the PCB contamination of the Upper Hudson.* * * The Department cannot be required to prove that specific PCB molecules, discharged by GE, reached specific fish or parts of the river.* * *

Given the natural flow of rivers, and the nature of the issues, the evidence of GE's responsibility is more than sufficient.

[Under] ECL 17-0301(1) * * * the Department is instructed to group designated waters into classes, after notice and hearing. Then, after proper study and further hearings, the Department is to "adopt and assign (necessary) standards of quality and purity for each such classification. . . ." Acting pursuant to this mandate, the Department classified the waters at and immediately below Fort Edward and Hudson Falls as "Class D." * * * Class D waters must be "suitable for fish survival" * * *.

[A]n overall standard, applicable to waters classified A through D, is that they shall not contain "toxic wastes and deleterious substances. . . in amounts that will be injurious to fish life or which in any manner shall adversely affect the flavor, color or odor therefor, or impair the waters for any best usage" assigned.

Compliance with these standards is mandated by ECL 17-0501, which GE has been charged with violating. That section makes it unlawful to discharge, "directly or indirectly," any matter that shall "cause or contribute" to a condition in contravention of the water quality standards established pursuant to ECL 17-0301. The issues posed by this provision, therefore, are whether PCB's in the quantities discharged by GE have "caused or contributed" to a breach of standards that (1) prohibit the discharge of "toxic wastes" or "deleterious substances" in amounts "injurious to fish life" or (2) "impair the waters for any best usage," in particular fishing.

The federal government long ago moved to regulate water pollution through effluent limitations, rather than merely the setting of stream standards. In 1972, the Federal Water Pollution Control Act (FWPCA) [now the Clean Water Act] was amended to give the states primary responsibility for pollution abatement, but only if they adopted a program based both on stream standards and effluent limitations. New York adopted a State Pollution Discharge Elimination System (SPDES).* * *

The resulting legal structure requires any would-be discharger of pollutants to seek a certification from the state in which the waters are involved are located. [Clean Water Act § 401,] 33 U.S.C. § 1341. After state approval, the applicant must obtain a federal discharge permit for the activities permitted by the state. Discharging without a state permit violates ECL 17-0505; and increasing or altering a permitted discharge violates ECL 17-0507. In addition, ECL 17-0511, the second statute under which GE has been charged, prohibits any industrial discharge from outlets or point sources "unless such use is in compliance with all standards, criteria, limitations, rules and regulations promulgated or applied by the department pursuant to this article." The article involved, 17 ECL, includes provisions that make unlawful violations of both the permit and water classification systems.* * * On August 23, 1973, the Department received GE's application under its new SPDES system. The application indicated that a daily average of 30 pounds of "chlorinated hydrocarbons" were being discharged * * *. Department personnel appear to have been well aware by August 1973 of GE's PCB discharges, having already conducted studies of their effects.* * *

On November 13, 1973, the Department certified that * * * "the classification and standards governing the quality and purity of waters of New York State" are applicable [to GE's permit,] and set forth certain specific and some general limitations to assure compliance.* * *

The certification limited effluent of "toxic wastes" or "deleterious substances" in the following manner: "None alone or in combination with other substances or wastes in sufficient amounts or at such temperatures as to prevent fish survival or impair the waters for agricultural purposes or any other best usage as determined for the specific waters which are assigned to this class." The certification then went on to limit discharges "at all times so as to be in full compliance with all applicable requirements of [the Department's] regulations establishing the classification and standards governing New York waters."

* * *EPA issued an NPDES permit to GE on December 20, 1974, [complying] with the requirement that conditions of state certification must appear in the federal permit.

In paragraph 6, it warns that it issuance does not "authorize. . . .any infringement of Federal, State or local laws or regulations. . . ." And before detailing the applicable limitations in paragraph 9, it recites: "Nothing in this permit shall be deemed to * * * relieve the permittee from any responsibilities, liabilities or penalties to which the permittee is or may be subject. . . .under any other Federal or state law or regulations." The permit authorized "chlorinated hydrocarbon" discharges of 10 and 20 lbs. * * *.

GE claims that it has complied with its state certification and federal permit. Consequently, it asserts, it cannot be found to have violated any statute for its discharges until the permit is duly modified in accordance with the applicable regulations. "If the SPDES permit program is to be meaningful and effective, . . . it cannot, by its very nature as a permit system, allow the imposition of penalties for permitted discharges. It is axiomatic that penalties may not be imposed by a governmental agency for acts permitted by law," GE Brief, p. 21. GE notes that the Department was fully aware of GE's PCB discharges, and thus suggests that it implicitly found them lawful.

GE's argument has more than superficial appeal. The effluent limitation system is intended and well designed to serve as a supplement to the water classification system. Both the state and federal governments are presented, when a discharge application is filed, with an opportunity to regulate so as to insure that water quality objectives are attained. Thus, when GE filed its application the Department should have been made aware that GE proposed to continue discharging PCB's at an average rate of 30 lbs. daily. A relatively simple calculation at that point would have indicated that such a discharge rate was destined to cause the present situation. Had this anticipated result been unacceptable, the Department could then have denied or conditioned its certification.

[However,] [t]he system seems clearly to place on the would-be discharger * * * the burden of insuring that the discharge violates no other federal, state or local prohibitions. It would defeat the legislature's objectives to impose the costs of such failures on the public rather than upon the discharging party.

[In addition, the Clean Water Act] guaranteed that the states would be free to impose additional limitations, including those implicit in a water classification approach. Section 401 of the federal act requires that a state's conditions to its own permit becomes a part of the federal permit[.]

If consumed in sufficient quantities by fish, animals or men, there is no doubt that PCB's can have the effects described in the ECL as "toxic." * * * That they are non-biodegradable, for example, may be useful in capacitors, but it also makes them persistent. They are virtually indissolvable in water, and their effects in the Hudson are felt long after their discharge into the river. PCB's also bioaccumulate.* * * They tend to remain suspended in water, attached to plankton and other organisms, or they fall into the river sediment. In either case, they pass into snails and other aquatic organisms, including fish, and become stored in their bodies, particularly in areas with high lipid content. The significance of bioaccumulation is that the PCB's are accumulated in fish and other high lipid organisms to points far higher than the PCB concentrations to which the organisms are exposed. Experimental results introduced at the hearing showed, for example, that Fathead Minnows accumulate PCB's to a point 200,000 times greater than the concentrations in which they are placed.* * *

Fish also accumulate PCB's through the food chain, by means of bio-magnification. At each level of the food chain, organisms absorb the collected accumulations of PCB's in the lower-level organisms. Fish are relatively high on the chain. Humans are higher. Consequently, PCB levels in fish predicted on the basis of concentration in water alone will tend to understate the actual level of

PCB's because of accumulation from sediment and by bio-magnification from the food chain.

Due to these characteristics, PCB's have been observed to cause toxic effects in fish food, a variety of estuarine organisms, fresh water fish, birds, rats, mink, monkeys and humans.* * *

GE has violated ECL 17-0501 and 17-0511, as charged, by causing or contributing to a condition in contravention of the water quality standards adopted pursuant to ECL 17-0301. Two separate standards have been violated: GE has discharged wastes injurious to fish; and the company's conduct has caused and contributed to the impairment of a protected usage of the waters -- fishing.

[The] nature of this case makes it unnecessary that the Department prove that specific fish were directly affected.* * * ECL 17-0301 sets a water quality standard, and is part of a plan adopted in part to avoid the rigidities of the law aimed at punishing for harm done to identifiable fish.* * * The experimental results in evidence show that fish, among other living things, have suffered toxic effects from PCB exposures equal to or lower than those to which fish taken from the Hudson were subjected.* * *

The theory on which GE argues in effect that its unlawful conduct should go unremedied is that no injunction may be issued to require a level of discharge that has already been achieved. This is simply incorrect. The Department is not required to accept GE's representations--mainly unsupported and equivocal--as a substitute for an order requiring discharges at a lawful level.* * * Nor is the Department precluded by any equitable principle from attempting to require GE to take steps to rectify its prior violations. However negligent the Department may have been in granting GE a permit to discharge those large amounts, the permit and the ECL required GE to conform its effluent to stream classification standards. This proceeding is designed to protect public resources, and cannot be made into a forum for determining the relative fault of GE and the Department.

The ECL and its regulations are also violated by discharges that cause or contribute to an impairment of recreational fishing.

Recreational fishing is impaired when fish, though healthy enough to survive, are dangerous to use as food. GE argued at the hearing that recreational fishing does not require fish that are edible.* * * This may be true as a matter of abstract theory, but in reality recreational fishermen frequently consume the fish they catch, as the testimony shows.* * *

The regulations themselves contemplate fish consumption by prohibiting the discharge of substances that adversely affect the "flavor, color and odor" of fish. 6 NYCRR 701.5.* * *

Hudson River fish have been rendered inedible by GE's PCB discharges. The Department properly relies in proving this fact in part upon the FDA's temporary tolerance limit of 5 ppm for the edible portion of fish.* * *

The Department claims GE has violated ECL 11-0503(1) by discharging a poisonous or deleterious substance into a public water in quantities "injurious" to fish or wildlife, or to the propagation of fish or protected wildlife. The evidence that proves a violation of ECL 17-0501 and 17-0511, the Department contends, likewise proves a violation of ECL 11-0503(1). Further, it offers proof that mink reside in the Hudson River basin, and that they are wildlife that would be injured and whose propagation would be adversely affected if they consumed fish with the quantities of PCB's shown to exist in the river.

ECL 11-0503(1) is however, very different in background and purpose than ECL 17-0501 and 17-0511. The former has nineteenth century roots, and is an isolated provision and aimed specifically at protecting fish and wildlife. The latter are relatively modern parts of an overall system of water classification. [A] relatively narrow purpose for the [former] provision is also strongly suggested by ECL 17-0925(5), which states that "any act" in violation of ECL 11-0503(1) may be punished by a fine of from $500 to $1,000 "for each offense and an additional penalty of ten dollars for each fish killed in violation thereof . . . "The statute seems aimed at specific, identifiable "acts" and "offenses" that injure or kill fish.* * *

GE's conduct is not the sort against which ECL 11-0503 was written.* * * The Department has shown injury, but not in a context to which ECL 11-0503 should be applied.* * * The allegation must be dismissed as inappropriate and unproven.

The Department has proven violations of ECL 17-0501 and 17-0511. It has also shown itself entitled at the very least to an order requiring GE to reduce its PCB discharges to a lawful level. Whether the levels GE represents it has and can attain are lawful is only the first of several issues to be examined when the proceeding reconvenes. Other issues include:

> 1. The extent to which GE should be ordered to rectify the effects of its prior discharges, including whether any practicable and environmentally safe method exists or can be devised to remove PCB's from the river bottom, and the expected duration and extent PCB contamination if not remedial steps are taken;
> 2. The extent to which GE should be required to remove PCB-contaminated earth and equipment from around its plants, and the manner in which this operation should be conducted.* * *

* * *These are complicated matters that will require technical proof. The Department will have to go forward on these issues. GE is hereby ordered, however, to provide the parties and the Hearing Officer, within two weeks of the date of this opinion, with as comprehensive as possible a description of its present abatement plans. The hearing should proceed with a full appreciation for what GE is prepared to accomplish without compulsion.

## Notes

Following this landmark opinion, GE and the Department reached an agreement. A Settlement Advisory Committee was established to determine how best to dispose of the PCBs which lined the bottom of the Hudson. It proposed a three-year dredging program to remove three quarters of the PCBs from the river between Ft. Edward and Troy, where they are most highly concentrated, or about half the total. That stretch of the river remains closed to commercial fishing. Funding for this project has not been obtained, nor has a disposal site for the dredge spoil been selected. The publicity attendant to the case, however, led to the federal ban on PCBs adopted soon thereafter by the EPA under both the hazardous substance provisions of Clean Water Act § 307 (33 U.S.C.A. § 1317) and in the Toxic Substances Control Act (TSCA), 15 U.S.C.A. §§ 2601-2629, discussed in Chapter 9.

Lengthy litigation ensued over a proper disposal site for the PCB-laden spoil to be removed from the river bed. A landfill in the area was chosen but the courts overturned that decision. See *Washington County Cease, Inc., v. Persico*, 64 N.Y.2d 923, 477 N.E.2d 1084, 488 N.Y.S.2d 630 (1985). The PCBs remain in the Hudson, and striped bass caught there may not be consumed. GE has urged the use of bacteria that consume PCBs. Finally, in 2000, the EPA ordered GE to dredge much of the PCB-laden sediment in the upper Hudson, acting under CERCLA, the Superfund hazardous-substance cleanup statute discussed in Chapter 9. A site for disposal, though, has yet to be chosen.

The Clean Water Act requires permits for all significant sources of effluent, as described in the *General Electric* decision. Permits must take into account both effluent limitations based on technology (measuring the actual discharge) and water quality (measuring the purity of the water body). All sources were mandated to achieve the best practicable technology (BPT) by 1977, meaning the best technology readily achievable in 1972 when the Act was enacted. By 1989 sources were to reach the best available technology economically achievable (BATEA). In other words, the Act compels industry to develop mechanisms to curb pollution beyond what existed before. As with the Clean Air Act (see Chapter 5), toxic water pollutants are treated more stringently.

## Publicly Owned Treatment Works

Discharges from publicly owned treatment works (POTWs) -- sewage treatment plants -- are subject to the Clean Water Act's requirements. Recall that sewage was exempt from regulation under the Rivers and Harbors Act. See the *Republic Steel* case in subsection A. Technology developed since then enables municipalities to treat their sewage, and the Clean Water Act mandates "secondary treatment" -- defined as the removal of at least 85% of biological material. Industrial dischargers placing their effluent into POTWs must pretreat it to ensure that it will not cause the POTW to malfunction. The Act also requires that industrial dischargers into POTWs be assessed a fee based on their discharge.

## Non-Point Sources

As noted earlier, the Act originally dealt only with discharges from point sources. It is clear that much severe water pollution stems from non-point sources like agricultural runoff, irrigation return flows and the like that do not enter a waterway through a pipe, ditch or other point source. These were unregulated until the 1987 amendments to the Act. States are now required to devise plans to deal with non-point source pollution and submit them for EPA approval. 33 U.S.C.A. § 1329.

## Enforcement

Clean Water Act enforcement is largely similar to that under the Clean Air Act. See Chapter 5 (F). However, there are some noteworthy decisions and one important statutory difference.

The Supreme Court has held a defendant is entitled to a jury trial in a suit by the United States for civil penalties under the Act. *Tull v. United States*, 481 U.S. 412, 107 S.Ct. 1831, 95 L. Ed.2d 365 (1987). The court analogized the suit to an action to recover a debt, where there was a right to trial by jury at common law. But, it noted, the court, not the jury, sets the penalty.

The court denied an injunction against repeated water pollution by the United States Navy in *Weinberger v. Romero-Barcelo*, 456 U.S. 305, 102 S.Ct. 1798, 72 L. Ed.2d 91 (1982). Traditionally, an injunction is available only when the plaintiff lacks an adequate remedy at law, such as damages. Here, the Court took the view that a civil penalty was an adequate remedy. Was this decision based in part by a reluctance on the Court's part to enjoin defense operations?

The Clean Water Act's citizen-suit provision, 33 U.S.C.A. § 1365, requires the plaintiff to have "an interest which is or may be affected" by the conduct involved. See § 1365(g). Recall the discussion in *City of Milwaukee v. Illinois*, Chapter 2 (C), over this language as a bar to federal common-law nuisance actions. The language has been interpreted to require a plaintiff to be "aggrieved" in the sense of having an injury, or being threatened with one. But it has not been a serious bar to citizen suits under the Act, many of which have been brought.

A citizen suit will lie only against a current water polluter. Past violations will not support such an action unless they were so egregious as to make future violations likely. *Gwaltney of Smithfield, Ltd. v. Chesapeake Bay Foundation, Inc.*, 484 U.S. 49, 108 S. Ct. 376, 98 L. Ed.2d 306 (1987). See also the *Laidlaw* decision, Chapter 1(B), holding cessation of pollution does not render a pending Clean Water Act citizen suit moot.

As noted earlier, the civil penalty recoverable in a citizen suit is payable to the Government, not the individual plaintiffs. However, in Clean Water Act litigation a common form of settlement is for a defendant to agree to perform a supplemental environmental project -- for example, restoring a wetland, or some other beneficial act not otherwise required by law.

## Controlling Ocean Dumping

See *Coastal Area Legislation,* 6 Seton Hall Legis. J. 317, continued (from Chapter 3, Part G).[a]

The offshore waters near our major cities have been a major dumping ground for sewage sludge and industrial waste, the volume of which, ironically, has increased as a result of improved sewage treatment. To combat the problem of dumping and to control water pollution within the territorial limits of the United States, the Congress enacted the Clean Water Act and the Rivers and Harbors Act.

[But these] did not directly address the problems resulting from ocean dumping, because permits continue to be routinely issued by the EPA and the states. Such routine and continuous dumping over a prolonged period may kill all but the most hardy fish and shellfish.

The Marine Protection Act, 33 U.S.C.A. §§ 1401-1444, enacted in 1972, recognized that "[u]nregulated dumping of material into ocean waters endangers human health, welfare, and amenities, and the marine environment, ecological systems, and economic potentialities." The Act established a permit system to regulate ocean dumping and makes provisions for the initiation of "comprehensive and continuing programs of research with respect to the possible long-range effects of pollution, over-fishing, and man-induced changes of ocean ecosystems." The Administrator of the EPA is given the responsibility of issuing permits for ocean dumping, and for promulgating criteria for evaluating permit applications, after consultation with federal, state, and local officials and interested members of the general public.

The Act's jurisdiction depends upon the origins of the material being transported. If the vessel is carrying material from the United States then the Act's jurisdiction begins outside the territorial sea, defined as water within three

---

[a]Reprinted by permission of the publisher.

miles of the coast. If the material is transported from outside the United states the Act's jurisdiction shall include the territorial sea as well as the contiguous zone "extending to a line twelve nautical miles seaward from the base line from which the breadth of the territorial sea is measured."

The [EPA] grants permits under the Act, except for * * * dredged material which is regulated by the Army Corps of Engineers. Both entities use essentially the same criteria, but the EPA may veto the Army's grant of a permit. If the Secretary of the Army, after notice and hearing, finds no economically feasible method or site available, a waiver may be requested from the EPA. The waiver must be granted within thirty days after receipt of the request, unless the EPA finds an "unacceptable adverse impact on municipal water supplies, shell-fish beds, wildlife, fisheries (including spawning and breeding areas), or recreational areas." The EPA therefore has the final say[.]

The Marine Protection Act's 1981 amended deadline for the cessation of ocean dumping has been largely successful, with over two hundred municipal dumpers already using alternative disposal methods. The City of New York, however, continues to resist the deadline, and dumps about 260 dry tons a day into an area of the ocean known as the New York Bight Apex, which is off the central New Jersey coast. New York's sewage sludge dumping is uniquely massive and environmentally hazardous. The city insists that dumping its sludge on land or incinerating it would be more harmful than burial at sea.

[In *City of New York v. EPA*, 543 F. Supp. 1084 (S.D.N.Y., 1981), t]he city sued to compel the EPA to consider its evidence, relying on the general provisions of the Marine Protection Act requiring the EPA to weigh the costs and risks of the dumping against land-based alternatives. Ironically, the city's long-term dumping into the Bight Apex has so degraded the water quality that the court found, "cessation of the dumping would result in no discernible improvement in the bight in the foreseeable future. . ."

Although section 1412(a) of the Marine Protection Act, as amended, states that the EPA "shall end the dumping of sewage sludge into ocean waters . . .as soon as possible after November 4, 1977, but in no case may the [EPA] Administrator issue any permit . . . which authorizes any such dumping after December 31, 1981," the court held this seemingly crystal-clear language not dispositive. The district court pointed out that the Act defines sewage sludge as municipal waste "the ocean dumping of which may *unreasonably* degrade or endanger" health or the marine environment. [Emphasis supplied.] Therefore, it held the 1977 amendment "does not purport to modify in any way the factors that [the Act] . . . required EPA to consider in determining whether dumping would unreasonably degrade the environment; it simply provides that EPA may not, after 1981, permit dumping that fails the test established by the 1972 Act."

The court found New York's dumping did not unreasonably degrade the environment under the Act and that the EPA regulations adopted pursuant to the Act were so strict they effectively deprived the agency of discretion to grant a permit and were therefore contrary to the intent of Congress. It directed the EPA to consider the city's evidence that ocean dumping is a less harmful alternative than land disposal.

The aftermath of the decision was a settlement under which the EPA agreed to adopt the court's view of the statute. The EPA will apply the 1981 deadline only to dumping which will "unreasonably degrade the environment as its particular site, in view of all relevant statutory criteria," and to evaluate the city's application for a continued permit. Under the settlement, the agency also will continue to evaluate an alternate site one hundred and six miles offshore. The site was proposed earlier as an interim dumping location to relieve the * * * present dumping site. This provision caught the EPA * * * between the city's resistance to a far more distant dumping area and fishermen's demands that offshore dumping of sewage sludge be halted completely.

## Notes

In 1988 Congress again amended the Act, this time explicitly prohibiting the ocean dumping of sludge from sewage treatment plants after December 31, 1991. The City of New York, which had earlier agreed to haul its sludge to an interim site chosen by the EPA 106 miles offshore, agreed to cease dumping altogether by the end of 1991. It was the last municipality to halt sludge dumping; others, such as Philadelphia, had done so earlier. Sewage sludge is now disposed of in landfills, incinerated, or used as fertilizer for grass and similar non-edible vegetation.

Ocean dumping of dredge spoil is allowed under the Act, subject to an Army Corps of Engineers permit. This has been controversial where the dredge spoil may contain toxic material.

## D. OIL SPILL ENFORCEMENT AND LIABILITY

### 1. Penalties

UNITED STATES v. TEX-TOW, INC., United States Court of Appeals, Seventh Circuit, 1978. 589 F.2d 1310.

Castle, Senior Circuit Judge.

Tex-Tow, Inc. appeals from the district court's enforcement by way of summary judgment of a $350 civil penalty assessed by the United States Coast Guard against Tex-Tow under section 1321(b)(6) of the Federal Water Pollution Control Act (FWPCA) [now the Clean Water Act] for a discharge of oil into navigable waters in violation of section 1321(b)(3) of the Act [Clean Water Act § 311].

Tex-Tow operated a tank barge which was being loaded with a cargo of gasoline at a dock on the Mississippi River owned and operated by Mobil Oil Company. As the barge was filled with gasoline, it sank deeper into the water, settling on an underwater steel piling that was part of the dock structure. The piling punctured the hull of the barge, resulting in a discharge of 1600 gallons of gasoline into the river. Concededly Tex-Tow was not at fault as there is no reasonable way it could have known of the piling and it received no warning from Mobil.* * *

The FWPCA was enacted "to restore and maintain the chemical, physical, and biological integrity of the Nation's waters." 33 U.S.C. § 1251(a). Toward that end, Congress set the goal of eliminating the discharge of all pollutants into navigable waters by 1985. § 1251(a)(1). Section 1321, dealing with oil and hazardous substance liability, sets a "no discharge" policy of immediate effect and prohibits any discharge in harmful quantities. The section holds owners or operators of discharging facilities liable for clean-up costs, subject to the defenses of act of God, act of war, negligence of the United States Government, or act or omission of a third party. § 1321(f).* * * Finally, section 1321(b)(6), the immediate focus of our concern here, makes owners and operators liable to a civil penalty of up to $5,000,[a] with no provision for any defenses but with the amount of the penalty to be determined by the Coast Guard, which is instructed to take into account ability to pay and "gravity of the violation." * * *

First, Tex-Tow argues that the third party causation defense contained in the provisions dealing with clean-up liability and liquidated damages liability should also be read into the civil penalty provision. We decline to do so.* * *

The statutory language is not ambiguous, and a literal interpretation according no third party or other defenses to the civil penalty furthers the overall statutory scheme of shifting the cost of pollution onto the polluting enterprise. [A]bsolute liability in the case of the civil penalty is not unduly harsh or unreasonable in view of the * * * flexibility afforded by the statutory directive that the Coast Guard, in setting the amount of the penalty, take into account the charged party's ability to pay and the "gravity of the violation," which has been interpreted by the Coast Guard to include degree of culpability.

Tex-Tow, however, asserts that a causation requirement must be implied in the civil penalty provision because no liability may exist in the absence of causation. We agree that causation is required even under a strict liability statute[;] however, Tex-Tow has conceded that the presence of its barge at the pier was a cause in fact of the spill. The only question is whether legal, or proximate, cause also exists. [Tex-Tow] argues that the mere presence of its barge at the dock is not sufficient to constitute legal cause. We believe, however that more than "mere presence" was involved here. Tex-Tow was engaged in the type of enterprise which will inevitably cause pollution and on which Congress has determined to shift the cost of pollution when the additional element of an actual discharge is present. These two elements, actual pollution plus statistically foreseeable pollution attributable to a statutorily defined type of enterprise, together satisfy the requirement of cause in fact and legal cause.* * * An

---

[a]The maximum has since been raised to $125,000.

enterprise such as Tex-Tow engaged in the transport of oil can foresee that spills will result despite all precautions and that some of these will result from the acts or omissions of third parties. Although a third party may be responsible for the immediate act or omission which "caused" the spill, Tex-Tow was engaged in the activity or enterprise which "caused" the spill.* * *

We hold that the "cause" of a spill is the *polluting enterprise* rather than the *conduct* of the charged party or a third party. Accordingly, an owner or operator of a discharging facility is liable to a section 1321(b)(6) civil penalty even where it exercised all due care and a third party's acts or omission was the immediate cause of the spill.* * *

Notes

The Clean Water Act's provisions regarding oil spills extend far beyond the 3-mile limit generally applicable to pollutant discharge. They control oil discharges connected with offshore oil drilling under the Outer Continental Shelf (described in Part D [4] of this chapter), as well as waters managed by the United States under the Magnuson-Stevens Fishery Conservation and Management Act (described in Chapter 4[A]), reaching 200 miles offshore. See § 311(b)(3), 33 U.S.C.A. § 1321(b)(3).

The Act requires the reporting to the Government of oil spills. Since there are criminal penalties for intentional discharges, under § 13 of the Rivers and Harbors Act (discussed in Part A of this Chapter), does this raise self-incrimination concerns?

UNITED STATES v. WARD, Supreme Court of the United States, 1980. 448 U.S. 242, 100 S.Ct. 2636, 65 L.Ed. 2d 742.

Justice Rehnquist:

The United States seeks review of a decision of the United States Court of Appeals for the Tenth Circuit that a proceeding for the assessment of a "civil penalty" under § 311(b)(6) of the [Clean Water Act] is a "criminal case" within the meaning of the Fifth Amendment's guarantee against compulsory self-incrimination. We granted certiorari and now reverse.

At the time this case arose, § 311(b)(3) * * * prohibited the discharge into navigable waters or onto adjoining shorelines of oil or hazardous substances in quantities determined by the President to the "harmful." Section 311(b)(5) of the Act imposed a duty upon "any person in charge of a vessel or of an onshore facility or an offshore facility" to report any discharge of oil or a hazardous substance into navigable waters to the "appropriate agency" of the United States Government. Should that person fail to supply such notification, he or she was liable to a fine of not more than $10,000 or imprisonment of not more than one year. Section 311(b)(5) also provided for a form of "use immunity," specifying that "notification received pursuant to this paragraph or information obtained by the exploitation of such notification shall not be used against any such person in any criminal case, except a prosecution for perjury or for giving a false statement."

Section 311(b)(6) provided for the imposition of a "civil penalty" against "any owner or operator of any vessel, onshore facility, or offshore facility from which oil or a hazardous substance is discharged in violation" of the Act.

* * *On or about March 23, 1975, oil escaped from an oil retention pit at a drilling facility * * * being leased by respondent L.O. Ward who was doing business as L. O. Ward Oil & Gas Operations. On April 2, 1975, respondent Ward notified the regional office of the Environmental Protection Agency (EPA) that a discharge of oil had taken place. Ward later submitted a more complete written report of the discharge, which was in turn forwarded to the Coast Guard, the agency responsible for assessing civil penalties under § 311(b)(6).

After notice and opportunity for hearing, the Coast Guard assessed a civil penalty against respondent in the amount of $500. Respondent * * * contend[ed] that the report requirements of § 311(b)(5) of the Act violated his privilege against compulsory self-incrimination.* * *

The distinction between a civil penalty and a criminal penalty is of some constitutional import. The Self-Incrimination Clause of the Fifth Amendment, for example, is expressly limited to "any criminal case . . ."

[W]hether a particular statutorily-defined penalty is civil or criminal is a matter of statutory construction.

Our inquiry in this regard has traditionally proceeded on two levels. First, we have set out to determine whether Congress, in establishing the penalizing mechanism, indicated either expressly or impliedly a preference for one label or the other.* * *

Second, where Congress has indicated an intention to establish a civil penalty, we have inquired further whether the statutory scheme was so punitive either in purpose or effect as to negate that intention. [And] "only the clearest proof could suffice to establish the unconstitutionality of a statute on such a ground." * * *

As for our first inquiry in the present case, we believe it quite clear that Congress intended to impose a civil penalty upon persons in Ward's position. Initially, and importantly, Congress labeled the sanction authorized in § 311(b)(6) a "civil penalty," a label that takes on added significance given its juxtaposition with the criminal penalties set forth in the immediately preceding subparagraph, § 311(b)(5). Thus, we have no doubt that Congress intended to allow imposition of penalties under § 311(b)(6) without regard to the procedural protections and restrictions available in criminal prosecutions.

We turn then to consider whether Congress, despite its manifest intention to establish a civil, remedial mechanism, nevertheless provided for sanctions so punitive as "transform[s] what was clearly intended as a civil remedy into a criminal penalty." In making this determination, both the District Court and the Court of Appeals found it useful to refer to the seven considerations listed in *Kennedy v. Mendoza-Martinez*, [372 U.S. 144, 83 S.Ct. 544, 9 L. Ed. 2d 644, (1963)].[11] Of these, only one, the fifth, aids respondent. That is a consideration of whether "the behavior to which [the penalty] applies is already a crime[.]" In this regard, respondent contends that § 13 of the Rivers and Harbors Act of 1899 makes criminal the precise conduct penalized in the present case.* * *

While we agree that this consideration seems to point toward a finding that § 311(b)(6) is criminal in nature, that indication is not as strong as it seems at first blush. We have noted on a number of occasions that "Congress may impose both a criminal and a civil sanction in respect to the same act or omission." [And here] the placement of criminal penalties in one statute and the placement of civil penalties in another statute enacted 70 years later tends to dilute the force of the fifth Mendoza-Martinez criterion in this case. In sum, we believe that [no facts exist] sufficient to render unconstitutional the congressional classification of the penalty established in § 311(b)(6) as civil.

[Ward further argues that] the penalty imposed in this case, although clearly not "criminal" enough to trigger the protections of the Sixth Amendment, the Double Jeopardy Clause of the Fifth Amendment, or the other procedural guarantees normally associated with criminal prosecutions, is nevertheless "so far criminal in [its] nature" as to trigger the Self-Incrimination Clause of the Fifth Amendment. [But] respondent is protected by § 311(b)(5), which expressly provides that "notification received pursuant to this paragraph or information obtained by the exploitation of such notification shall not be used against any such person in any criminal case, except for prosecution for perjury or for giving a false statement."

[I]n the light of what we have found to be overwhelming evidence that Congress intended to create a penalty civil in all respects and quite weak evidence of any countervailing punitive purpose or effect it would be quite anomalous to hold that § 311(b)(6) created a criminal penalty for the purposes of the Self-Incrimination Clause but a civil penalty for all other purposes.

## Notes

Does reporting a spill immunize the owner of the ship or onshore facility that employs the person who reports it? The answer is no. Section 311(b)(5) was amended in 1990 to provide that "[n]otification received pursuant to this

[11] The standards set forth were "[w]hether the sanction involves an affirmative disability or restraint, whether it has historically been regarded as a punishment, whether it comes into play only on a finding of scienter, whether its operation will promote the traditional aims of punishment--retribution and deterrence, whether the behavior to which it applies is already a crime, whether an alternative purpose to which it may rationally be connected is assignable for it, and whether it appears excessive in relation to the alternative purpose assigned. . ."

paragraph shall not be used against any such *natural person* in any criminal case[.]" (emphasis supplied)

2. Cleanup Cost and Liability; the Oil Pollution Act

The same § 311 of the Clean Water Act imposes liability on dischargers for oil spill cleanup costs incurred by the Coast Guard. There are financial limits, and the discharger may assert (and must prove) the defenses of act of God, act of war or act of a third party. Is the pilot of a tanker, an independent contractor, not an employee, a third party exempting the shipowner from liability? See *United States* v. *Hollywood Marine, Inc.*, 625 F.2d 524 (5th Cir. 1980), cert. den. 451 U.S. 994: no. Is a tug? See *United States v. Le Beouf Bros. Towing Co.*, 537 F.2d 149 (5th Cir. 1980), cert. den. 430 U.S. 987: no.

Can a state legislate further, imposing strict liability without limits, or its it preempted by § 311? The Supreme Court ruled in *Askew v. American Waterways Operators, Inc.*, 411 U.S. 325, 93 S.Ct. 1590, 36 L.Ed.2d 280 (1973), that § 311 was no bar to a Florida strict-liability statute since the federal statute is limited to cleanup costs owed to the Coast Guard. States, it held, are free to legislate as to cleanup costs incurred by state and local governments and private parties.

However, Florida repealed its statute after this victory. Tankers simply avoided Florida waters because of the unlimited strict liability provided by this statute.

Until 1990 a greater bar to state legislation was the Limited Liability Act of 1851, 45 U.S.C.A. §§ 181-189. This statute, a relic of the clipper-ship era, limits liability following a marine collision to the value of the ship and its cargo after the accident, unless the accident took place with the privity or knowledge of the shipowner (defined to mean the owner's negligence).

The Oil Pollution Act, the 1990 legislation creating the Oil Spill Liability Trust Fund, belatedly ended preemption by the 1851 statute. 33 U.S.C.A. § 2718 expressly provides that the Limitation of Liability Act no longer preempts state laws imposing liability for oil spills. The Act was prompted by the catastrophic *Exxon Valdez* oil spill from a tanker off the Alaska coast.

The Oil Pollution Act also establishes a one billion dollar liability trust fund for oil spill damages and cleanup, financed by a 54-per-barrel tax on both domestic and imported oil. Damages include lost profits. The fund is strictly liable to claimants, and has a right of subrogation against the discharger, who may assert the three defenses available under § 311 -- act of God, act of war, or act of a third party. But a third party is defined here as one who is not an agent, employee or contractor of the discharger (except for a railroad). See 33 U.S.C.A. §§ 1321(s) and 2701-2719.

3. Tanker Regulation

RAY v. ATLANTIC RICHFIELD CO., Supreme Court of the United States, 1978. 435 U.S. 151, 98 S. Ct. 988, 55 L. Ed.2d 179.

Justice White:

Pursuant to the Ports and Waterways Safety Act of 1972 (PWSA), 33 U.S.C. §§ 1221-[1236], navigation in Puget Sound, a body of inland water lying along the northwest coast of the State of Washington, is controlled in major respects by federal law. The PWSA also subjects to federal rule the design and operating characteristics of oil tankers.

This case arose when Wash. Rev. Code §§ 88.16.170[-88.16.200] ([the] Tanker law), was adopted with the aim of regulating in particular respects the design, size, and movement of oil tankers in Puget Sound. Located adjacent to Puget Sound are six oil refineries[;] tankers will * * * be used to transport oil there from the terminus of the Trans-Alaska Pipeline at Valdez, Alaska [, mostly] by means of tankers in excess of 40,000 deadweight tons (DWT), and, prior to the effective date of the Tanker Law, 15 [deliveries] by means of tankers in excess of 125,000 DWT.* * *

On the day the Tanker Law became effective, ARCO brought suit [asserting] that the statute was pre-empted by * * * the PWSA, and that it was thus invalid under the Supremacy Clause. It was also alleged that the law imposed an undue burden on interstate commerce in violation of the Commerce Clause, Art. I, § 8, cl. 3, and that it interfered with the federal regulation of [foreign affairs].

We address first Wash. Rev. Code § 88.16.180, which requires both enrolled and registered oil tankers of at least 50,000 DWT to take on a pilot licensed by the State of Washington while navigating Puget Sound. The District Court held that insofar as the law required a tanker "enrolled in the coastwise trade" to have a local pilot on board, it was in direct conflict with 46 U.S.C. §§ 215, 364. We agree.

Section 364 provides that "every coastwise seagoing steam vessel subject to the navigation laws of the United States, . . . not sailing under register, shall, when under way, be under the control and direction of pilots licensed by the Coast Guard." Section 215 adds that "[n]o State or municipal government shall impose upon pilots of steam vessels any obligation to procure a State or other license in addition to that issued by the United States . . ." It goes on to explain that the statute shall not be construed to "affect any regulation established by the laws of any State, requiring vessels entering or leaving a port in any such State, *other than coastwise steam vessels*, to take a pilot duly licensed or authorized by the laws of such State . . ." (Emphasis added.) The Court has long held that these two statutes read together give the Federal Government exclusive authority to regulate pilots on enrolled [coastwise] vessels and that they preclude a State from imposing its own pilotage requirements upon them. Thus, to the extent that the Tanker Law requires enrolled tankers to take on state-licensed pilots, the District Court correctly concluded, as the State now concedes, that it was in conflict with federal law and was therefore invalid.

[However, states] are free to impose pilotage requirements on registered [foreign-trade] vessels entering and leaving their ports. Not only does § 215 so provide, as was noted above, but so also does § 101(5) of the PWSA, 33 U.S.C. § 1221(5), which authorizes the Secretary of Transportation to "require pilots on self-propelled vessels engaged in the foreign trades * * * where a pilot is not otherwise required by State law to be on board[."] Accordingly, * * * the State was free to require registered tankers in excess of 50,000 DWT to take on a state-licensed pilot upon entering Puget Sound.

We next deal with § 88.16.190(2) of the Tanker Law, which requires enrolled and registered oil tankers of from 40,000 to 125,000 DWT to possess * * * [t]win screws; [d]ouble bottoms, underneath all oil and liquid cargo compartments; and [t]wo radar's in working order and operating[.] [These] design requirements * * * are invalid in the light of the PWSA and its regulatory implementation. [PWSA] Title II begins by declaring that the protection of life, property, ad the marine environment from harm requires the promulgation of "comprehensive minimum standards of design, construction, alteration, repair, maintenance, and operation" for vessels carrying certain cargoes in bulk, primarily oil and fuel tankers. To implement the twin goals of providing for vessel safety and protecting the marine environment, it is provided that the Secretary of [Transportation,] in which the Coast Guard is located[,] "shall establish" such rules and regulations as may be necessary with respect to the design, construction, and operation of the covered vessels[.]

Congress, insofar as design characteristics are concerned, has entrusted to the Secretary the duty of determining which oil tankers are sufficiently safe to be allowed to proceed in the navigable waters of the United States. This indicates to us that Congress intended uniform national standards for design and construction of tankers that would foreclose the imposition of different or more stringent state requirements.

We do not question in the slightest the prior cases holding that enrolled and registered vessels must conform to "reasonable, nondiscriminatory conservation and environmental protection measures . . ." imposed by a State. [See, for example,] *Huron Portland Cement Co. v. City of Detroit*, [discussed in Chapter 5]. [T]he mere fact that a vessel has been inspected and found to comply with the Secretary's vessel safety regulations does not prevent a State or city from enforcing local laws having other purposes, such as a local smoke abatement law. But in none of the relevant cases sustaining the application of state laws to federally licensed or inspected vessels did the federal licensing or inspection procedure implement a substantive rule of federal law addressed to the object also sought to be achieved by the challenged state regulation. *Huron Portland Cement Co. v. [City of] Detroit*, for example, made it plain that there was "no overlap between the scope of the federal ship inspection laws and that of the municipal ordinance . . ." there involved. The purpose of the "federal inspection statutes [was] to insure the seagoing safety of vessels . . . to affor[d] protection from the perils of maritime navigation," while "[b]y contrast, the sole aim of the Detroit ordinance [was] the elimination of air pollution to protect the health and enhance the cleanliness of the local community." * * *

Here, we have the very situation that *Huron Portland Cement Co. v. [City of] Detroit* * * * put aside. Title II aims at insuring vessel safety and protecting the marine environment; and the Secretary must issue all design and construction regulations that he deems necessary for these ends, after considering the specified statutory standards. Refusing to accept the federal judgment, however, the State now seeks to exclude from Puget Sound vessels certified by the Secretary as having acceptable design characteristics, unless they satisfy the different and higher design requirements imposed by state law. The Supremacy Clause dictates that the federal judgment that a vessel is safe to navigate United States waters prevail over the contrary state judgment.

Enforcement of the state requirements would at least frustrate what seems to us to be the evident congressional intention to establish a uniform federal regime controlling the design of oil tankers.

In our view, both enrolled and registered vessels must also comply with the provision of the Tanker Law that requires tug escorts for tankers over 40,000 DWT that do not satisfy the design provisions specified in § 88.16.190(2). [PWSA] Title I authorizes the Secretary to establish and operate "vessel traffic services and systems" for ports subject to congested traffic[.] The Secretary may "control vessel traffic" under various hazardous conditions by specifying the times for vessel movement, by establishing size and speed limitations and vessel operating conditions, and by restricting vessel operation to those vessels having the particular operating characteristics which he considers necessary for safe operation under the circumstances.

A tug escort provision is not a design requirement, such as is promulgated under Title II. It is more akin to an operating rule arising from the peculiarities of local waters that call for special precautionary measures, and, as such, is a safety measure clearly within the reach of the Secretary's authority under §§ 1221(3)(iii) and (iv) to establish "vessel size and speed limitations and vessel operating conditions" and to restrict vessel operation to those with "particular operating characteristics and capabilities . . ." Title I, however, merely authorizes and does not require the Secretary to issue regulations to implement the provisions of the Title[.]

The relevant inquiry under Title I with respect to the State's power to impose a tug-escort rule is thus whether the Secretary has either promulgated his own tug requirement for Puget Sound tanker navigation or has decided that no such requirement should be imposed at all. It does not appear to us that he has yet taken either course. It may be that rules will be forthcoming that will pre-empt the State's present tug-escort rule, but until that occurs, the State's requirement need no give way under the Supremacy Clause.

* * *We cannot arrive at the same conclusion with respect to the remaining provision of the Tanker Law at issue here. Section 88.16.190(1) excludes from Puget Sound under any circumstances any tanker in excess of 125,000 DWT. In our view, this provision is invalid [since] the Secretary has the authority to establish "vessel size and speed limitations," § 1221(3)(iii), and § 1222(b), by permitting the State to impose higher equipment or safety standards "for structures only," impliedly forbids higher state standards for vessels. [A Coast Guard] rule with respect to Rosario Strait * * * prohibits the passage of more than one 70,000 DWT vessel through Rosario Strait in either direction at any given time, and in periods of bad weather, the "size limitation" is reduced to approximately 40,000 DWT. On the record before us, it appears sufficiently clear that federal authorities have indeed dealt with the issue of size and have determined whether and in what circumstances tanker size is to limit navigation in Puget Sound.* * * Because under § 1222(b) the State may not impose higher safety standards than those prescribed by the Secretary under Title I, the size limitation of § 88.16.190(1) may not be enforced. [Further,] the size regulation imposed by the Tanker Law, if not pre-empted under Title I, is similar to or indistinguishable from a design requirement which Title II reserves to the federal regime. This may be true if the size limit represents a state judgment that, as a matter of safety and environmental protection generally, tankers should not exceed 125,000 DWT. In that event, the State should not be permitted to prevail over a contrary design judgment made by federal authorities in pursuit of uniform national and international goals.* * *

We reject appellees' additional constitutional challenges to the State's tug-escort requirement [as violating] the Commerce Clause because it is an indirect attempt to regulate the design and equipment of tankers, an area of regulation that appellees contend necessitates a uniform national rule. [T]he Commerce Clause does not prevent a State from enacting a regulation of this type. Similar in its nature to a local pilotage requirement, a requirement that a vessel take on a tug escort when entering a particular body of water is not the type of regulation that demands a uniform national rule. Accordingly, we hold that § 88.16.190(2) of the Tanker Law is not invalid under the Commerce Clause.* * *

Justice Marshall with whom Justice Brennan and Justice Rehnquist join, concurring in part and dissenting in part.* * *

I * * * cannot agree with the Court's conclusion * * * that the size limitation contained in the Tanker Law is invalid under the Supremacy Clause.

* * *The Coast Guard's unwritten "local navigation rule," which prohibits passage of more than one 70,000 DWT vessel through Rosario Strait at any given time, is the sole evidence cited by the Court to show that size limitations for Puget Sound have been considered by federal authorities. On this record, however, the rule cannot be said to reflect a determination that the size limitations set forth in the Tanker Law are inappropriate or unnecessary. First, there is no indication that in establishing the vessel traffic rule for Rosario Strait the Coast Guard considered

the need for promulgating size limitations for the entire Sound. Second, even assuming that the Rosario Strait rule resulted from consideration of the size issue with respect to the entire area, appellees have not demonstrated that the rule evinces a judgment contrary to the provisions of the Tanker Law. Under the express terms of the PWSA, the existence of local vessel-traffic-control schemes must be weighed in the balance in determining whether, and to what extent, federal size limitations should be imposed. There is no evidence in the record that the Rosario Strait "size limitation" was in existence or even under consideration prior to passage of the Tanker Law. Thus appellees have left unrebutted the inference that the Coast Guard's own limited rule was built upon, and is therefore entirely consistent with, the framework already created by the Tanker Law's restrictions.

[Nor is] the size limitation imposed by the Tanker Law * * * pre-empted under Title II of the PWSA. [T]he Court theorizes that the state rule might be pre-empted if it "represents a state judgment that, as a matter of safety and environmental protection *generally*, tankers should not exceed 125,000 DWT." (emphasis added). It is clear, however, that the Tanker Law was not merely a reaction to the problems arising out of tanker operations in general, but instead was a measure tailored to respond to unique local conditions--in particular, the unusual susceptibility of Puget Sound to damage from large oil spills and the peculiar navigational problems associated with tanker operations in the Sound. Thus, there is no basis for pre-emption under Title II.* * *

Justice Stevens and Powell dissented in part, ruling

> the tug-escort requirement is merely a proviso in § 88.16.190(2)--the section of the Washington Tanker Law that prescribes the design requirements; it is imposed only on tankers that do not comply with those requirements. The federal interest that prohibits state enforcement of these requirements should also prohibit state enforcement of a special penalty for failure to comply with them.

## Notes

Here too, the Oil Pollution Act, locking the barn door after many horses were stolen, mandates double hulls on all new tankers of 5000 tons or more. Existing tankers are required to retrofit on a schedule between 1995 and 2010, depending on their age. 46 U.S.C.A. § 3703a.

Tankers carry water as ballast when not carrying oil, and this water in their tanks often mixes with oil residue from previous shipments. A Coast Guard rule prohibits discharging ballast containing a visible trace of oil. Is a state statute barring the discharge of *all* ballast (whether or not showing a visible sheen) in state waters preempted by the Coast Guard rule? See *Chevron USA, Inc. v. Hammond*, 726 F.2d 483 (9th Cir. 1984), cert. den. 471 U.S. 1140 (not preempted, since unlike the Ports and Waterways Safety Act tanker design provisions in *Ray v. Arco*, there was no Congressional interest to preempt or need for uniformity).

How about state laws and regulations requiring tanker operators to report collisions and near-collisions, record their position every fifteen minutes, and monitor crew performance, and mandating state inspection of tankers' navigation and propulsion systems? In *United States* v. *Locke*, 529 U.S. 89, 120 S.Ct. 1135, 146 L.Ed.2d 69 (2000), the Court found the Ports and Waterways Safety Act preempted state laws by occupying the fields of tanker operation and personnel qualifications.

Tankers carrying liquefied natural gas (LNG), which must be shipped at extremely low temperatures in order to remain in a liquid state, are subject to stringent Coast Guard rules. LNG will easily catch fire if the ship's tank is breached by a collision, or if the cooling system malfunctions and the LNG gasifies. LNG tankers are therefore required to have double hulls and must notify the Coast Guard before entering United States ports.

## The Marine Pollution (MarPol) Treaty

Oil frequently travels between countries by tanker. Indeed, the United States imports about half the oil it voraciously consumes. Since 1973 a treaty known as MarPol, the Marine Pollution Treaty, has existed, and currently the nations shipping most of the world's oil and other cargo are signatories. MarPol requires tankers to be certified and to meet safety standards. For example, all large tankers built since 1993 require double hulls. The treaty also restricts oil discharges. It is administered by the International Maritime Organization. However, enforcement is left largely to the "flag state" where a tanker is registered, and many of these are small nations with few resources for enforcing safety and environmental standards. Countries where a tanker is docked also may enforce certain MarPol provisions, and may inspect and detain vessels in case of major damage, or threat, to safety, or pollution. But flag state enforcement largely preempts activity by port or coastal states, so the treaty has not been overly effective.

A federal statute, the Act to Prevent Pollution from Ships, 33 U.S.C.A. §§ 1901-1915, makes it unlawful to violate MarPol or regulations enacted under MarPol.

## The Exxon Valdez Spill

The severe oil spill caused when the tanker *Exxon Valdez* hit rocks off the Alaska coast in 1989 led not only to the Oil Pollution Act (discussed in Subsection D[2] of this Chapter) but also to major litigation against the company. Exxon pleaded guilty to Clean Water Act and state criminal charges and paid $900 million in civil penalties and fines to the United States and Alaska. In addition it paid $5 billion in punitive damages, as well as compensatory damages, to fishermen and others injured by the spill, which killed prodigious amounts of fish, seals, birds and other wildlife.

4. The Outer Continental Shelf Drilling Program

For decades oil has been extracted from underwater lands. In the 1940s oil from the outer continental shelf (OCS), lands extending from 80 to 120 miles offshore, started to become a major source of domestic petroleum, and the states soon disputed the federal government's claim of ownership and resulting right to collect royalties. This resulted in a political compromise, the Submerged Lands Act of 1953, ancestor of the current Outer Continental Shelf Lands Act, 43 U.S.C.A. §§ 1344-1356. The states won ownership of the first three miles of undersea land from shore, except that Texas and Florida won 10.5 (three marine leagues). Undersea lands further out are owned by the United States and administered by the Department of the Interior. The Supreme Court has rejected the claims of the Atlantic Coast states that they own undersea lands beyond three miles based on colonial grants, holding the 1953 Submerged Lands Act itself submerged whatever rights had been bestowed by the British and Spanish crowns. *United States v. Maine*, 420 U.S. 515, 95 S.Ct. 1155, 43 L.Ed.2d 363 (1975). The states, under a 1985 amendment to the OCS Lands Act, now receive 27% of the federal royalties on near-shore leases of OCS lands.

Since 1978 the Interior Department has had explicit power to suspend or cancel a lease of undersea land for environmental violations.

After the 1973 OPEC energy crisis raised the price of imported oil dramatically, the federal government insistently promoted exploration for OCS oil. Some states and municipalities, along with fishing and environmental groups, just as strongly opposed this expansion of the program. Recall the California coastal zone management litigation discussed in Chapter 3, Part G, and the subsequent amending of the Coastal Zone Management Act to allow a state veto of offshore oil drilling contrary to a US-approved state coastal zone management plan.

COMMONWEALTH v. ANDRUS, United States District Court, Mass., 1978. 11 Envl. Rptr. Cases 1138.

[The Commonwealth of Massachusetts and a group of conservation organizations sued to enjoin the Secretary of the Interior from receiving bids for a sale of leases of offshore lands pursuant to the Outer Continental Shelf Act. The lands involved are part of the Georges Bank fishing grounds.

The Court, Garrity, J., granted the plaintiffs' motion for a preliminary injunction.]

[A]s much as 15 percent of the world's fish protein is derived from George's Bank sources. This is no ordinary fishing ground. It is as important a natural resource as the people of this state and region will ever have to rely upon.

It is the basis for one of the leading industries in this state and in this section.* * * The OCS Lands Act provides in pertinent part: "This subchapter shall be construed in such manner" * * * "that the character as high seas of the waters above the Outer Continental Shelf and the right to navigation and fishing therein shall not be affected."* * *

This duty of the Secretary to be especially concerned and to be the guardian in a sense of fishing in the Outer Continental Shelf waters, is underscored by the enactment of the Fishery Conservation and Management Act [16 U.S.C.A. §§ 1801-1882].

In my opinion, it would be a violation of this duty for the Secretary of the Interior to receive the bids on the George's Bank area previous to final Congressional action on the legislation pending before it, whose enactment is expected in the near future.

One of the provisions has to do with the establishment of a fund that would provide for payment to a person who is damaged by oil spills in situations where the source of the spill or the blame for the damage could not be ascertained.

Another provision has to do with the compensation of fishermen for damage to their fishing gear under similar circumstances.* * *

In not waiting for this legislation to be enacted, the Secretary has done less than he should, in my opinion, to preserve the natural resource on the George's Bank which he is bound to do. The effect of the two proposals having to do with the establishment of compensation funds would in effect compel the lessees of these tracts to pay for damages even when their liability could not be established. The effect of such an absolute liability provision would * * * strengthen and increase measures taken by the lessees to prevent accidental damage and accidental spills of oil and accidental leakage of oil and damage of other sorts.

[Further,] the Secretary of the Interior, we find, would violate not only the duties flowing directly from the statute, but also the National Environmental [Policy] Act, by relying on an inadequate Environmental Impact Statement in the matter of the costs and benefits of the delay which the Court says he is bound under the law to grant.* * *

The fact of the pending legislation is referred to and a mention made to the problem of the retroactivity [but it] is altogether inadequate in the Court's opinion. [T]he ecological aspect of this proposed legislation is not even adverted to. By that I refer to the benefit that this would arguably have on reducing damage.* * *

The likelihood of this type of damage, measures to be taken to reduce it, arguments pro and con, the enactment of this legislation, all are treated in a cursory manner in my opinion.

[The EIS] states, "If this proposed sale were held prior to the establishment of oil spill liability legislation, the legislation could be made applicable to operations on leases issuing from this sale." That simply is an over-simplification of the problem and it is an inadequate over-simplification.* * *

Another deficiency in the EIS is the omission to discussion of the possible use of this area as a marine sanctuary [under the Marine Protection, Research and Sanctuaries Act, 16 USCA §§ 1431-1434 (1972), a] valuable long-range important alternative use which did * * * not even rate so much as a paragraph in the EIS. [The EIS did not deal with] the possibility that this area is more valuable to the country over the indefinite future as a breeding ground for fish and other marine life than it is as a source of oil and gas.* * *

Notes

The Court of Appeals, deciding the case after the oil spill liability and compensation fund and a special fund for fishermen's gear were enacted (43 USCA §§ 1810-1866), amending the Outer Continental Shelf Lands Act, reversed the judgment as moot as to that issue. The Court of Appeals went on to reject the NEPA basis for the injunction, finding the failure to discuss the pending legislation now moot, and remanding to the District Court the claim that the EIS should have considered the declaration of George's Bank as a marine sanctuary for reconsideration in light of the 1978 amendment. 594 F.2d 872 (1979). The Court of Appeals tentatively held, however, that the EIS "should be extended to include a discussion of the marine sanctuary alternative."

Thereafter the Interior Department issued a supplemental EIS discussing, among other things, the possibility of declaring George's Bank a marine sanctuary. The plaintiffs again moved for a preliminary injunction, this time contending a separate EIS should be prepared by the National Oceanic and Atmospheric Administration (NOAA), the agency with jurisdiction to name marine sanctuaries, in order to adequately consider that prospect. The court denied the motion, 481 F. Supp. 685, aff'd 623 F.2d 712 (1979). In December 1980 the suit was settled. Interior agreed to conduct biological studies before development of the tracts and to insist that the oil company lessees use the best available and safest technology. NOAA agreed to again consider naming the area a marine sanctuary. The Government agreed to prepare an EIS before drilling, and the plaintiffs discontinued their action with the understanding that they can renew it should these conditions not be met.

For similar complex litigation regarding leases off New York's shores, see *County of Suffolk v. Secretary of the Interior*, 562 F.2d 1368 (2d Cir. 1977). The court there also reversed an injunction issued by the District Court, which had ruled the EIS inadequate for several reasons, including failure to adequately take into account (1) the possibility that localities might bar pipelines to bring offshore oil to the coast and (2) the advantages of separating exploration from the leasing itself to "give the government detailed data upon which to base resource estimates and evaluate tracts before leasing."

President George H.W. Bush later declared a moratorium on new offshore oil drilling sites, which is still in effect. A current controversy relates to whether oil drilling should be allowed in the National Arctic Wildlife Refuge in northern Alaska, an extremely fragile ecosystem and habitat to whales, bears, caribou and other species that drilling might place at risk.

# 8. ENERGY CONSERVATION

## Environmental Significance

The vital importance of energy use, and particularly the need to conserve energy, in environmental protection is plain. The burning of fossil fuels -- coal, natural gas and especially petroleum products -- contributes heavily to global warming, discussed in Chapter 12. Additionally, using coal and oil results in air pollution, and, as we have seen, the strip mining of coal and the extraction, refining and transport of oil all have profound environmental risks.

The United States, with six percent of the world's population, consumes about 34 percent of its energy. This profligate use of energy, largely oil and oil products, vastly exceeds the amount used in most other countries, including those with standards of living much like our own. The consumption of energy in British thermal units (BTUs) for each dollar of gross national product, for example, is 12,000 BTUs in Britain, 10,000 in Japan . . . and 20,000 in the United States.

Using petroleum as a fuel for transportation accounts for the lion's share of this disparity. In this country, a far greater degree of automobile use exists. The reasons range from land-use to our neglect of public transportation, notably railroads. Rail moves both passengers and freight far more efficiently than road transport. For instance, a gallon of fuel moves a ton of cargo 200 miles by rail as against 58 miles by road. But the United States in recent decades has allowed its once-efficient rail system to deteriorate, and has permitted -- indeed, encouraged -- land-use patterns favoring the private automobile.

Consider the words of historian Bruce Catton:

> [i]t is fairly easy for man to assert his mastery over his early environment, but once he has asserted that mastery he has to go on exercising it no matter where the exercise takes him. The age of applied technology has one terrible aspect -- each new technique has to be exploited to its absolute limit, until man becomes the victim of his own skills. The conquest of nature cannot end in a negotiated peace. Invent a single device like the automobile, to get you from here to there more quickly than you could go without it; before long you are in bondage to it, so that you build your cities and shape your countryside and reorder your entire life in the light of what will be good for the machine instead of what will be good for you.*

* B. CATTON, WAITING FOR THE MORNING TRAIN 5-6 (1972).

In 1975, in the wake of the OPEC oil crisis that sharply curtailed imports, enacted the Energy Policy and Conservation Act, 15 U.S.C.A. §§ 2601-2629. The Act attempted to reduce petroleum consumption by making automobiles and appliances more fuel-efficient.

Another major facet of energy conservation, relating to the generation and use of electricity, will be discussed in Chapter 11.

## The Fuel Economy Standards

The Energy Policy and Conservation Act, 49 USCA § 32902, mandated improvements in the fuel economy of automobiles. It legislated the corporate average fuel economy (CAFE) standards that required both domestic and imported automobiles to operate more efficiently -- from 18 miles per gallon (mpg) in 1978 to 27.5 mpg in 1985. After that year, the Secretary of Transportation may set CAFE levels as low as 26 mpg, and has in fact done just that. The CAFE standards do not govern trucks, buses or the sport-utility vehicles that have become popular in recent years. They preempt state laws on the subject.

Does Congress need to revisit this CAFE? How does the adoption of alternative fuels such as natural gas and hybrid and electric vehicles (see Chapter 5[E]) affect this issue? Would increasing taxes on gasoline (as in Europe and Japan) be helpful? If so, why hasn't this occurred?

## Appliance Standards

The Act also contains efficiency standards (42 USCA §§ 6291-6309) for appliances such as furnaces, air conditioners, refrigerators, ranges and washing machines. Not only must these appliances be manufactured so as to use less energy, but consumers must be notified as to the relative efficiency of various machines prior to purchase.

What other steps to conserve energy would be appropriate? What levels of government should take them? Does this issue relate to international concern over global warming, discussed in Chapter 12?

# 9. SOLID WASTE AND TOXIC SUBSTANCES

## A. SOLID WASTE

### Introductory Note

Solid waste, which was not subject to serious regulation until the mid-1970s, became a subject of critical importance with the dramatic emergence of hazardous waste sites such as the Love Canal in Niagara Falls, N.Y. and Times Beach, Mo. The severe health hazards raised by these improperly chosen and policed disposal areas led to much tort litigation raising fascinating, as yet mainly unresolved, issues of burden of proof, statute of limitations, liability among unknown tortfeasors and class actions, discussed in Part B of this chapter. It also brought about the enactment of the third of the triad of major federal substantive environmental laws, the Resource Conservation and Recovery Act, or RCRA, 42 U.S.C.A. §§ 6901-6992k.

But, even prior to its metamorphosis, the field of solid waste, though prosaic, had its share of litigation as well as attempts by statute to curb the mounting volume of litter by controlling excess packaging and encouraging the recycling of beverage containers and other particularly obtrusive forms of solid waste.

ORTEGA CABRERA v. MUNICIPALITY OF BAYAMON, United States Court of Appeals, First Circuit, 1977. 562 F.2d 91.

Coffin, Chief Judge.

Plaintiffs are the occupants of four tracts of land in * * * Bayamon, Puerto Rico. In January, 1972, the municipality opened a sanitary landfill near plaintiffs' properties, the operation of which interfered in a variety of ways with plaintiffs' peaceful enjoyment of their lands. Plaintiffs instituted this action to obtain injunctive and monetary relief from the municipality[.] [T]he district court entered an injunction that essentially ordered the municipality to engage in construction at the dump site that would minimize the damage to plaintiffs' property. Following a separate hearing on damages, the district court set aside substantial jury verdicts rendered in favor of each of the plaintiffs[.]

Beginning in the late 1960's, the municipality of Bayamon decided that it needed a new city dump. Because open air burning had been prohibited, the new dump was to be operated as a "sanitary landfill," a method of disposing of solid wastes which, if established and operated in accordance with sound engineering practices, will present no dangers whatsoever to the environment or to public health. At such landfills, wastes are deposited in a highly controlled manner. A portion of the site is first excavated. When the solid wastes arrive, they are compacted and spread in thin layers over prepared areas. The wastes will be covered daily, or more frequently if necessary, with at least six inches of top soil, and the cover material is itself compacted daily. When the site is completely filled with waste, additional topsoil is laid down and grass planted. At this point, there will be no traces of the solid wastes, and the land will be suitable for a variety of uses, normally recreational ones.

While "sanitary landfills" have been employed successfully throughout the United States, the Bayamon project was, by any standard, a failure. The primary, although not only, reason was that the planners selected a wholly inappropriate site for the landfill. Solid wastes ordinarily contain many contaminants and infectious materials. Since serious health hazards can result if such pollutants are permitted to enter water supplies, it is critical that sanitary landfills be located in places where there is no danger that water will pass through the solid waste and cause ground or surface water pollution.

The site the municipality selected could scarcely have been worse. Presumably because it wished the new dump to be close to the old one, the city located the landfill in the uppermost part of a ravine in a mountainous section of the municipality which enjoys a heavy average annual rainfall of between 75 and 80 inches. The site is right above the headwaters of a creek which flows into the La Plata River, one of Puerto Rico's largest sources of drinking water, and is both the site of at least one major underground spring and the terminal point of several other creeks.* * *

The landfill opened in January, 1972, and sometime thereafter it reached its full operational capacity of 400 tons of garbage per day. The baleful effects of the dump began immediately. Water entered the solid waste mass from the several creeks that flowed into it, from the internal springs within it, and from the rainfall that seeped through the cover soil. Initially, the solid waste absorbed the water, but it eventually reached a point of total saturation. The addition of further water then resulted in the production of "leachate"--that is, water which had percolated through a solid waste mass carrying with it contaminates in a soluble and suspended state. The leachate, which was yellowish brown, would ooze out the tail of the landfill into the headwaters of the creek, polluting it with contaminants which included unsafe amounts of arsenic, lead, mercury, fecal coliform, and fecal streptococci. Because of the leachate, the creek waters emitted malodorous fumes and turned a brownish color.

The dump was closed by court order in January, 1974, and thereafter, the maintenance of the landfill became sporadic, if there was any at all. The steady flow of water through the landfill caused erosion in the top soil, which was the most pronounced at the perimeters of the site. The result was that much of the solid waste was exposed, contributing to the noisome odors in the area and creating an environment highly conducive to rodents and insects. Because of the erosion, portions of the waste mass would fall into the creek and be carried downstream, exacerbating the already existing problems and adding garbage to the brown polls of leachate.

Plaintiffs all occupy land located within several hundred meters of the landfill[.]

The properties that have been most directly affected by the operation of the dump are those parcels adjacent to the creek that runs to the La Plata river. Prior to the establishment of the landfill, this creek had enriched plaintiffs' lives in a number of ways. Its water had been determined to be safe for drinking, so plaintiffs' families drilled wells next to it and received all their water from these wells. They also permitted their animals to drink from it. Equally significantly, the creek was used for recreation. For some fifty years, the plaintiffs had swum, boated, and fished in it. The opening of the dump, of course, ended all that. The toxic substances in the water preclude its use for any domestic purposes--indeed, the farm animals that drank from it died. The brown, toxic leachate and garbage not only make it impossible to use the creek for recreational purposes, but also have converted the creek into a source of stench and into a health risk.* * * Quite apart from the pollution of the creek, the dump, in its present condition, has made the immediate surrounding area a far less pleasant place to live.* * *

A real estate appraiser testified and fixed the total damage to [plaintiffs'] parcels at approximately $191,000.* * *

The lion's share of the loss of value--$116,828--resulted from the fact that, in the appraiser's view, the presence of the dump in the area made the land unsuitable for what had heretofore been its highest and best use: a residential subdivision. [But] the appraiser's report * * * states that, notwithstanding all the problems arising from the presence of the dump, the land remains suitable for residential and limited agricultural purposes.

Shortly after the dump opened[,] plaintiffs instituted the present action [claiming] the operation of the dump violated their federal constitutional rights both by taking their property without just compensation in violation of the Fifth Amendment and by arbitrarily and discriminatorily interfering with their property rights. They also sought relief on several local law theories.

The district court exercise[d] pendent jurisdiction over the local law claims, and * * * held that the dump was a nuisance under local law, that the mayor had violated Puerto Rico's Public Policy Environmental Act, and that the operation of the dump violated a Commonwealth regulation concerning water purity. Each violation, the district court believed, was a sufficient ground for the issuance of an injunction to prevent the continuation of the harm to the plaintiffs.

Fashioning equitable relief, however, proved to be difficult. The district court thought the broad relief plaintiffs requested--ordering either that the entire landfill be relocated or that the city condemn all plaintiffs' lands--was inappropriate. Although the court confessed not to know what steps could feasibly be taken, it was convinced that construction work could be done at the dump to eliminate the evil and make the landfill "work correctly," and, on January 31, 1974, it ordered defendants to perform the "necessary remedial construction" work and to report to the court within ninety days.* * *

The issues before us concerning the injunctive relief are narrow. Because defendants have not sought appellate review of the January 31, 1974 order, they are bound by it and by future orders implementing it. The sole question before us is * * * whether the district court was obliged to grant plaintiffs' prayer to order defendants either to relocate the landfill or to condemn the * * * land plaintiffs occupy.* * * We have little difficulty deciding that the district court acted well within its discretion in declining to order that the entire landfill be relocated. The reason the district court gave for refusing to enter this relief was that it believed that "removing hundreds of thousands of tons of decayed matter and moving it through the public highways . . . would be a risky, if not altogether impossible maneuver that would endanger the public health of a whole community" and thought it manifestly unsound to remedy the health hazard created by the dump in such a way that a greater health hazard would arise.

But we need not rest our decision on this ground alone.* * * While Puerto Rico's sanitary regulation Number 129 prohibits the pollution of surface waters by municipal governments, nothing therein suggests that the remedy for any such violation should be the dismantling of the municipal operation that caused the pollution and not -- as the district court required -- construction that would eliminate or significantly reduce the pollution.* * *

Plaintiffs' alternative prayer that the district court order defendants to institute eminent domain proceedings in local court and condemn all four parcels [is] based entirely upon the fact that, in the view of their expert, the four tracts had lost some $191,119 in value because of the presence and operation of the dump. This loss of value, which is a consequence of the bad odors, and proximity of the land to a health hazard, represents a diminution in value of approximately 53 percent, 41 percent, 34 percent, and 29 percent for the four parcels. Notably, some $116,000 of the decline results from the unsuitability of the land for a subdivision.

[However,] a long line of Supreme Court cases appears to establish that the facts of substantial economic loss and significant diminution in value alone do not establish compensable takings.[a]* * *

Although plaintiffs have not specifically advanced this argument on appeal, we note that the plaintiffs inhabiting the land next to the creek have a very plausible claim that there has been a partial taking of their property. There is a suggestion in the record that the pollution of the creek with highly toxic substances has not only prevented any continuation of the recreational and other present uses of the land that includes and is immediately adjacent to the creek, but also has converted it into such a danger to health that the plaintiffs must fence off the area to prevent any use whatsoever of that land. If that pollution of the creek has had this effect, it would seem plaintiffs have a strong argument that the government action destroyed the value of this portion of the land to the same extent as if the city had regularly flooded it or deposited sewage upon it.* * *

---

[a] See discussion of this issue in Penn Central Transportation Co. v. City of New York, Chapter 3 [C], supra.

If such a partial taking were found, the measure of just compensation would be the pre-January, 1972, value of the property to the plaintiffs. *See United States v. Causby* [Chapter 6, *supra*].

[We therefore] remand the case for a determination of defendants' responsibilities under the decree, and, if necessary, for consideration of the partial taking claim.

## Notes

Although an improperly operated landfill may not deprive an adjacent owner of all reasonable use of his property so as to constitute a taking, it may well be a nuisance at common law. See *Village of Wilsonville v. SCA Services, Inc.*, 86 Ill.2d 1, 426 N.E.2d 824 (1981).

RCRA mandates that all solid waste areas meet at least proper sanitary landfill conditions--those described in *Ortega Cabrera* as the standards the landfill failed to satisfy. But the Act leaves enforcement largely to the states. How can states reduce the avalanche of solid waste within their borders without running afoul of the kind of constitutional restrictions discussed in *Hughes v. Oklahoma*, Chapter 4, *supra?*

CITY OF PHILADELPHIA v. NEW JERSEY, Supreme Court of the United States, 1978. 437 U.S. 617, 98 S.Ct. 2531, 57 L.Ed.2d 475.

Justice Stewart delivered the opinion of the Court.

A New Jersey law prohibits the importation of most "solid or liquid waste which originated or was collected outside the territorial limits of the State . . . ." In this case we are required to decide whether this statutory prohibition violates the Commerce Clause of the United States Constitution.

[T]he operators of private landfills in New Jersey, and several cities in other States that had agreements with these operators for waste disposal[,] brought suit against New Jersey and its Department of Environmental Protection in state court, attacking the statute[.]

The New Jersey Supreme Court [upheld the Legislation, holding that it] advanced vital health and environmental objectives with no economic discrimination against, and with little burden upon, interstate commerce, and that the law was therefore permissible under the Commerce Clause of the Constitution. The court also found * * * no federal pre-emption of the state law[.] We agree with the New Jersey court that the state law has not been pre-empted by [RCRA].

Before it addressed the merits of the appellants' claim, the New Jersey Supreme Court questioned whether the interstate movement of those wastes banned by [the statute, known as] ch. 363[,] is "commerce" at all within the meaning of the Commerce Clause. Any doubts on that score should be laid to rest at the outset. [There are, it is true,] several old cases of this Court holding that States can prohibit the importation of some objects because they "are not legitimate subjects of trade and commerce." *Bowman v. Chicago & Northwestern R. Co.,* 125 U.S. 465, 489, 8 S.Ct. 689, 31 L. Ed. 700.[a] These articles include items "which, on account of their existing condition, would bring in and spread disease, pestilence, and death, such as rags or other substances infected with the germs of yellow fever or the virus of small-pox, or cattle or meat or other provisions that are diseased or decayed, or otherwise, from their condition and quality, unfit for human use or consumption." The state court found that ch. 363 * * * banned only "those wastes which can[not] be put to effective use," and therefore those wastes were not commerce at all[."]

[In] saying that innately harmful articles "are not legitimate subjects of trade and commerce," the Bowman Court was stating its conclusion, not the starting point of its reasoning. All objects of interstate trade merit Commerce Clause protection; none is excluded by definition at the outset. In Bowman and similar cases, the Court held simply that because the articles' worth in interstate commerce was far outweighed by the dangers inhering in their very movement, States could prohibit their transportation across state lines. Hence, we reject the state court's suggestion that the banning of "valueless" out-of-state wastes by ch. 363 implicates no constitutional protection. Just as Congress has power to regulate the interstate movement of these wastes, States are not free from constitutional scrutiny when they restrict that movement.

The opinions of the Court through the years have reflected an alertness to the evils of "economic isolation" and protectionism, while at the same time recognizing that incidental burdens on interstate commerce may be unavoidable when a State legislates to safeguard the health and safety of its people. Thus, where simple economic protectionism is effected by state legislation, a virtually per se rule of invalidity has been erected. The clearest example of such legislation is a law that overtly blocks the flow of interstate commerce at a State's borders [see *Hughes v. Oklahoma*, Chapter 4 *supra*]. But where other legislative objectives are credibly advanced and there is no patent discrimination against interstate trade, the Court has adopted a much more flexible approach, the general contours of which were outlined in Pike v. Bruce Church, Inc. 397 U.S. 137, 142, 90 S.Ct. 844, 25 L.Ed.2d 174:

> Where the statute regulates even-handedly to effectuate a legitimate local public interest, and its effects on interstate commerce are only incidental, it will be upheld unless the burden imposed on such commerce is clearly excessive in relation to the putative local benefits . . . If a legitimate local purpose is found,

---

[a] This 1888 case struck down an Iowa statute that restricted railroads from shipping beer into the then "dry" Iowa. Subsequent decisions held that items such as lottery tickets "pollute" commerce and therefore could be excluded from it by Congress. See *Champion v. Ames*, 188 U.S. 321, 23 S.Ct. 321, 47 L.Ed. 492 (1903).

> then the question becomes one of degree. And the extent of the burden that will be tolerated will of course depend on the nature of the local interest involved, and on whether it could be promoted as well with a lesser impact on interstate activities.

* * *The crucial inquiry, therefore, must be directed to determining whether ch. 363 is basically a protectionist measure, or whether it can fairly be viewed as a law directed to legitimate local concerns, with effects upon interstate commerce that are only incidental.* * *

The purpose of ch. 363 is set out in the statute itself as follows:

> The Legislature finds and determines that . . . the volume of solid and liquid waste continues to rapidly increase, that the treatment and disposal of these wastes continues to pose an even greater threat to the quality of the environment of New Jersey, that the available and appropriate land fill sites within the State are being diminished, that the environment continues to be threatened by the treatment and disposal of waste which originated or was collected outside the State, and that the public health, safety and welfare require that the treatment and disposal within this State of all wastes generated outside of the State be prohibited.

The New Jersey Supreme Court accepted this statement of the state legislature's purpose. The state court additionally found that New Jersey's existing landfill sites will be exhausted within a few years; that to go on using these sites or to develop new ones will take a heavy environmental toll, both from pollution and from loss of scarce open lands; that new techniques to divert waste from landfills to other methods of disposal and resource recovery processes are under development, but that these changes will require time; and finally, that "the extension of the lifespan of existing landfills, resulting from the exclusion of out-of-state waste, may be of crucial importance in preventing further virgin wetlands or other undeveloped lands from being devoted to landfill purposes." Based on these findings, the court concluded that ch. 363 was designed to protect, not the State's economy, but its environment, and that its substantial benefits outweigh its "slight" burden on interstate commerce.* * *

The appellants strenuously contend that ch. 363, "while outwardly cloaked `in the currently fashionable garb of environmental protection,' . . . is actually no more than a legislative effort to suppress competition and stabilize the cost of solid waste disposal for New Jersey residents . . ." They cite passages of legislative history suggesting that the problem addressed by ch. 363 is primarily financial: Stemming the flow of out-of-state waste into certain landfill sites will extend their lives, thus delaying the day when New Jersey cities must transport their waste to more distant and expensive sites.

The appellees, on the other hand, deny that ch. 363 was motivated by financial concerns or economic protectionism.* * *

This dispute about ultimate legislative purpose need not be resolved, because its resolution would not be relevant to the constitutional issue to be decided in this case. [I]t does not matter whether the ultimate aim of ch. 363 is to reduce the waste disposal costs of New Jersey residents or to save remaining open lands from pollution, for we assume New Jersey has every right to protect its residents' pocketbooks as well as their environment. And it may be assumed as well that New Jersey may pursue those ends by slowing the flow of *all* waste into the State's remaining landfills, even though interstate commerce may incidentally be affected. But whatever New Jersey's ultimate purpose, it may not be accomplished by discriminating against articles of commerce coming from outside the State unless there is some reason, apart from their origin, to treat them differently. Both on its face and in its plain effect, ch. 363 violates this principle of nondiscrimination. The Court has consistently found parochial legislation of this kind to be constitutionally invalid[.]

Also relevant here are the Court's decisions holding that a State may not accord its own inhabitants a preferred right of access over consumers in other States to natural resources located within its borders. These cases stand for the basic principle that a "State is without power to prevent privately owned articles of trade from being shipped and sold in interstate commerce on the ground that they are required to satisfy local demands or because they are needed by the people of the State."

The New Jersey law at issue in this case falls squarely within the area that the Commerce Clause puts off limits to state regulation. On its face, it imposes on out-of-state commercial interests the full burden of conserving the State's remaining landfill space. It is true that in our previous cases the scarce natural resource was itself the article of commerce, whereas here the scarce resource and the article of commerce are distinct. But that difference is without consequence. In both instances, the State has overtly moved to slow or freeze the flow of commerce for protectionist reasons. It does not matter that the State has shut the article of commerce inside the State in one case and outside the State in the other. What is crucial is the attempt by one State to isolate itself from a problem common to many by erecting a barrier against the movement of interstate trade.

The appellees argue that not all laws which facially discriminate against out-of-state commerce are forbidden protectionist regulations. In particular, they point to quarantine laws, which this Court has repeatedly upheld even though they appear to single out interstate commerce for special treatment.

In the appellees' view, ch. 363 is analogous to such health-protective measures, since it reduces the exposure to New Jersey residents to the allegedly harmful effects of landfill sites.

It is true that certain quarantine laws have not been considered forbidden protectionist measures even though they were directed against out-of-state commerce.* * *

But those quarantine laws banned the importation of articles such as diseased livestock that required destruction as soon as possible because their very movement risked contagion and other evils. Those laws thus did not discriminate against interstate commerce as such, but simply prevented traffic in noxious articles, whatever their origin.

The New Jersey statute is not such a quarantine law. There has been no claim here that the very movement of waste into or through New Jersey endangers health, or that waste must be disposed of as soon as and as close to its point of generation as possible. The harms caused by waste are said to arise after its disposal in landfill sites, and at that point, as New Jersey concedes, there is no basis to distinguish out-of-state waste from domestic waste. If one is inherently harmful, so is the other. Yet New Jersey has banned the former while leaving its landfill sites open to the latter. The New Jersey law blocks the importation of waste in an obvious effort to saddle those outside the State with the entire burden of slowing the flow of refuse into New Jersey's remaining landfill sites. That legislative effort is clearly impermissible under the Commerce Clause of the Constitution.

Today, cities in Pennsylvania and New York find it expedient or necessary to send their waste into New Jersey for disposal, and New Jersey claims the right to close its borders to such traffic. Tomorrow, cities in New Jersey may find it expedient or necessary to send their waste into Pennsylvania or New York for disposal, and those States might then claim the right to close their borders. The Commerce Clause will protect New Jersey in the future, just as it protects her neighbors now from efforts by the State to isolate itself in the stream of interstate commerce from a problem shared by all.

The judgment is reversed.

Justice Rehnquist, with whom the Chief Justice [Burger] joins, dissenting.

The Court holds that New Jersey must either prohibit *all* landfill operations, leaving itself to cast about for a presently nonexistent solution to the serious problem of disposing of the waste generated within its own borders, or it must accept waste from every portion of the United States, thereby multiplying the health and safety problems which would result if it dealt only with such wastes generated within the State. Because past precedents establish that the Commerce Clause does not present appellee with such a Hobson's choice, I dissent.

Under [precedents upholding quarantine laws,] New Jersey may require germ-infected rags or diseased meat to be disposed of as best as possible within the State, but at the same time prohibit the *importation of* such items for disposal at the facilities that are set up within New Jersey for disposal of such material generated *within* the State. The physical fact of life that New Jersey must somehow dispose of its own noxious items does not mean that it must serve as a depository for those of every other State. Similarly, New Jersey should be free under our past precedents to prohibit the importation of solid waste because of the health and safety problems that such waste poses to its citizens. The fact that New Jersey continues to, and indeed must continue to, dispose of its own solid waste does not mean that New Jersey may not prohibit the importation of even more solid waste into the State. I simply see no way to distinguish solid waste, on the record of this case, from germ-infected rags, diseased meat, and other noxious items.* * *

According to the Court, the New Jersey law is distinguishable from these other laws, and invalid, because the concern of New Jersey is not with the *movement* of solid waste but of the present inability to safely *dispose* of it once it reaches its destination. But I think it far from clear that the State's law has as limited a focus as the Court imputes to it: solid waste which is a health hazard when it reaches its destination may in all likelihood be an equally great health hazard to transit.

Even if the Court is correct in its characterization of New Jersey's concerns, I do not see why a State may ban the importation of items whose movement risks contagion, but cannot ban the importation of items which, although they may be transported into the State without undue hazard, will then simply pile up in an ever increasing danger to the public's health and safety. The Commerce Clause was not drawn with a view to having the validity of state laws turn on such pointless distinctions.

[T]his Court has repeatedly upheld quarantine laws "even though they appear to single out interstate commerce for special treatment." The fact that New Jersey has left its landfill sites open for domestic waste does not, of course, mean that solid waste is not innately harmful. Nor does it mean that New Jersey prohibits importation of solid waste for reasons other than the health and safety of its population. New Jersey must, out of sheer necessity, treat and dispose of its solid waste in some fashion, just as it must treat New Jersey cattle suffering from hoof-and-mouth disease. It does not follow that New Jersey must, under the Commerce Clause, accept solid waste or diseased cattle from outside its borders and thereby exacerbate its problems.

## Notes

Would *City of Philadelphia* bar a state from prohibiting the importation of nuclear waste? Or would that, unlike the solid waste involved in *City of Philadelphia*, be hazardous to ship, like diseased meat? See Note, Transporting and Disposing of Nuclear Materials, Chapter 11, Part C.

If states may not restrict incoming waste, what steps may they take to deal with the problems described in *City of Philadelphia v. New Jersey?*

What if, instead of totally excluding out-of-state waste, a state charges a separate fee? In *Chemical Waste Management, Inc. v. Hunt,* 504 U.S. 334, 112 S.Ct. 2009, 119 L.Ed.2d 121 (1992), the Supreme Court, relying on *City of Philadelphia*, held an Alabama law imposing a state fee of $72 per ton on out-of-state hazardous waste placed in Alabama landfills discriminated against interstate commerce. The Court held, in line with earlier decisions:

> No State may attempt to isolate itself from a problem common to the several States by raising barriers to the free flow of interstate trade.

The fee for in-state hazardous waste in Alabama was $26.50 per ton. What about a state fee of $2.25 per ton on out-of-state solid (not hazardous) waste, as opposed to an 85¢ per ton fee on in-state waste? *See Oregon Waste Systems v. Oregon Dept. of Envtl. Quality,* 511 U.S. 93, 114 S.Ct. 1345, 128 L.Ed.2d 13 (1994), following *Chemical Waste* and overturning the fee.

Suppose a county excludes waste from outside that county from all landfills within its borders? In *Fort Gratiot Sanitary Landfill, Inc. v. Michigan Department of Natural Resources,* 504 U.S. 353, 112 S.Ct. 2019, 119 L.Ed.2d 139 (1992), decided together with *Chemical Waste,* the Court held that, too constitutes discrimination against interstate commerce. It was no defense that the law also barred in-state waste from other counties.

However, a state or local regulation of a landfill or other facility operated by that level of government -- as distinguished from a police power regulation or fee applicable to both private and public facilities -- may be immune from Commerce Clause challenge since the government has itself entered the marketplace. *See Swin Resources Systems, Inc. v. Lycoming County,* 883 F.2d 245 (3d Cir. 1989), *cert. denied,* 493 U.S. 1077 (1990) (upholding higher fee for out-of-county solid waste at county-run landfill).

What about a local law requiring all waste to be brought to a sole private transfer station, which charges a higher fee than other disposal facilities? Localities may actually seek a flow of solid waste to feed an incinerator. See *C&A Carbone, Inc. v. Town of Clarkstown,* 511 U.S. 383, 114 S.Ct. 1677, 128 L.Ed. 2d 399 (1994) (rejecting law as discrimination against commerce). However, a municipality may contract to have all solid waste generated within its borders hauled to an incinerator. The court in *SSC Corp. v. Town of Smithtown,* 66 F.3d 502 (2d Cir. 1995), cert. den. 116 S.Ct. 911 and 1453, viewed the town as a market participant as in *Swin Resources,* and not as a regulator.

Suppose Congress legislated to allow states to bar waste from beyond their borders. Would that finesse the "dormant Commerce Clause" issue? See *Western & Southern Life Ins. Co. v. State Board of Equalization,* 451 U.S. 648, 101 S.Ct. 2070, 68 L.Ed.2d 514 (1981):

> [It is] well settled that Congress may use its powers under the Commerce Clause to "[confer] upon the States an ability to restrict the flow of interstate commerce that they would not otherwise enjoy."

Would a state law restricting out-of-state waste still raise questions of denial of equal protection of the laws under the Fourteenth Amendment? See *Metropolitan Life Ins. Co. v. Ward,* 470 U.S. 869, 105 S.Ct. 1676, 84 L.Ed.2d 751

(1985) (Alabama's higher tax on premiums written by out-of-state insurers, though not a Commerce Clause violation because Congress explicitly allows states to regulate insurance, was nonetheless invalid as "the very sort of parochial discrimination that the Equal Protection Clause was designed to prevent").

## Recycling and Incineration

The United States generates 4.3 billion tons of solid waste each year -- 180 million tons of household and commercial waste alone. The rest is generated chiefly by industry and government. In the Northeast, landfill capacity is stretched to its limit, causing enormous quantities of waste to be shipped to other parts of the country. How can this prodigious volume of solid waste be reduced?

Many localities have instituted recycling programs for waste paper, cans, glass and plastic. Are these readily enforceable? More difficult to administer in cities where many reside in apartment houses?

Are there markets for recycled paper, plastic and the like? Sometimes the price of recycled items is not high enough to furnish an incentive to use them. In such cases, what can governments do to foster the use of recycled materials?

Incinerating solid waste, an old device that was phased out because of air pollution (see the *Oriental Boulevard* case in Chapter 5), had a renaissance in recent decades as landfill space became crowded. As an added benefit, solid waste incinerators can generate electricity, or steam for industrial uses. However, the air pollution problems remain, and have increased with the greater use of plastics. Further, the ash residue from garbage burning must be disposed of, usually in landfills. If the ash contains metals and residue from plastics, may it be a hazardous waste, requiring far more stringent regulation under RCRA? See *Environmental Defense Fund, Inc. v. City of Chicago*, 511 U.S. 328, 114 S.Ct. 1588, 128 L.Ed.2d 302 (1994) (yes; even though RCRA exempts household waste from its definition of hazardous waste, the ash from incinerating household waste may be within the definition of hazardous waste in RCRA).

MINNESOTA v. CLOVER LEAF CREAMERY CO., Supreme Court of the United States, 1981. 449 U.S. 456, 101 S.Ct. 715, 66 L.Ed.2d 659.

Justice Brennan delivered the opinion of the Court.

In 1977, the Minnesota Legislature enacted a statute banning the retail sale of milk in plastic nonreturnable, nonrefillable containers, but permitting such sale in other nonreturnable, nonrefillable containers, such as paperboard milk cartons [and plastic pouches]. Respondents contend that the statute violates the Equal Protection and Commerce Clauses of the Constitution.* * *

The Act was [designed to] promote resource conservation, ease solid waste disposal problems, and conserve energy.

[T]he State Supreme Court held that "the evidence conclusively demonstrates that the discrimination against plastic nonrefillables is not rationally related to the Act's objectives." We reverse.* * * The parties agree that the purposes of the Act cited by the legislature -- promoting resource conservation, easing solid waste disposal problems, and conserving energy -- are legitimate state purposes. Thus, the controversy in this case centers on the narrow issue whether the legislative classification between plastic and nonplastic nonreturnable milk containers is rationally related to achievement of the statutory purposes. Respondents produced impressive supporting evidence at trial to prove that the probable consequences of the ban on plastic nonreturnable milk containers will be to deplete natural resources, exacerbate solid waste disposal problems, and waste energy, because consumers unable to purchase milk in plastic containers will turn to paperboard milk cartons, allegedly a more environmentally harmful product. [However, w]here there was evidence before the legislature reasonably supporting the classification, litigants may not procure invalidation of the legislation merely by tendering evidence in court that the legislature was mistaken.* * *

The State identifies four reasons why the classification between plastic and nonplastic nonreturnables is rationally related to the articulated statutory purposes. If any one of the four substantiates the State's claim, we must reverse the Minnesota Supreme Court and sustain the Act.

First, the State argues that elimination of the popular plastic milk jug will encourage the use of environmentally superior containers. There is no serious doubt that the plastic containers consume energy resources and require solid waste disposal, nor that refillable bottles and plastic pouches are environmentally superior. [T]he State argues that the ban on plastic nonreturnables will buy time during which environmentally preferable alternatives may be further developed and promoted.* * *

We find the State's approach fully supportable under our precedents. This Court has made clear that a legislature need not "strike at all levels at the same time or in the same way," and that a legislature "may implement [its] program step by step,....adopting regulations that only partially ameliorate a perceived evil and deferring complete elimination of the evil to future regulations." The Equal Protection Clause does not deny the State of Minnesota the authority to ban one type of milk container conceded to cause environmental problems, merely because another type, already established in the market, is permitted to continue in use. Whether *in fact* the Act will promote more environmentally desirable milk packaging is not the question: the Equal Protection Clause is satisfied by our conclusion that the Minnesota Legislature *could rationally have decided* that its ban on plastic nonreturnable milk jugs might foster greater use of environmentally desirable alternatives.

Second, the State argues that its ban on plastic nonreturnable milk containers will reduce the economic dislocation foreseen from the movement toward greater use of environmentally superior containers. The State notes that plastic nonreturnables have only recently been introduced on a wide scale in

Minnesota, and that, at the time the legislature was considering the Act, many Minnesota dairies were preparing to invest large amounts of capital in plastic container production.* * *

Moreover, the State explains, to ban both the plastic and the paperboard nonreturnable milk container at once would cause an enormous disruption in the milk industry because few dairies are now able to package their products in refillable bottles or plastic pouches. Thus, by banning the plastic container while continuing to permit the paperboard container, the State was able to prevent the industry from becoming reliant on the new container, while avoiding severe economic dislocation.* * * The state legislature concluded that nonreturnable, nonrefillable milk containers pose environmental hazards, and decided to ban the most recent entry into the field. The fact that the legislature, in effect, "grandfathered" paperboard containers, at least temporarily, does not make the Act's ban on plastic nonreturnables arbitrary or irrational.

Third, the State argues that the Act will help to conserve energy. It points out that plastic milk jugs are made from plastic resin, an oil and natural gas derivative, whereas paperboard milk cartons are primarily composed of pulpwood, which is a renewable resource.* * *

The Minnesota Supreme Court held, in effect, that the legislature misunderstood the facts [and] concluded that "production of plastic nonrefillables requires less energy than production of paper containers."

[W]e reiterate that "it is up to legislatures, not courts, to decide on the wisdom and utility of legislation."

Fourth, the State argues that the Act will ease the State's solid waste disposal problem. Most solid consumer wastes in Minnesota are disposed of in landfills. A reputable study before the Minnesota Legislature indicated that plastic milk jugs occupy a greater volume in landfills than other nonreturnable milk containers. This was one of the legislature's major concerns.* * *

We therefore conclude that the ban on plastic nonreturnable milk containers bears a rational relation to the State's objectives, and must be sustained under the Equal Protection Clause.* * *

The District Court also held that the Minnesota statute is unconstitutional under the Commerce Clause because it imposes an unreasonable burden on interstate commerce. We cannot agree.* * *

Minnesota's statute does not effect "simple protectionism" [,as in *City of Philadelphia v. New Jersey, supra,*] but "regulates even-handedly" by prohibiting all milk retailers from selling their products in plastic, nonreturnable milk containers, without regard to whether the milk, the containers, or the sellers are from outside the State.

Since the statute does not discriminate between interstate and intrastate commerce, the controlling question is whether the incidental burden imposed on interstate commerce by the Minnesota Act is "clearly excessive in relation to the putative local benefits."

The burden imposed on interstate commerce by the statute is relatively minor. Milk products may continue to move freely across the Minnesota border, and since most dairies package their products in more than one type of containers, the inconvenience of having to conform to different packaging requirements in Minnesota and the surrounding States should be slight.

The judgment of the Minnesota Supreme Court is reversed.

Justice Powell concurred in part, agreeing with the majority with respect to the Equal Protection Clause, and dissented in part contending the case should have been remanded because the Minnesota Supreme Court never considered the Commerce Clause issue. Justice Stevens dissented.

Notes

A prior and more general Minnesota statute banning packaging causing or exacerbating waste disposal problems within the state withstood vagueness and Commerce Clause challenges in *Can Manufacturers' Institute, Inc. v. Minnesota*, 289 N.W.2d 416 (Minn. 1979).

It is hard to imagine what evidence the industry produced that convinced the state court in *Cloverleaf* that paperboard milk cartons could be "more environmentally harmful" than plastic jugs. Even treated or "water-proofed" paperboard is biodegradable. Plastics remain in the environment virtually in perpetuity. The plastic pouches referred to in the case are preferable only because they are reusable, at which point their relative unbreakability (as opposed to glass) and durability (as opposed to paper products) become tangible assets without a significant debit.

Measures to Limit Packaging

One special type of solid waste has generated legislation to deal with the particular difficulties it causes. At the cutting edge, so to speak, of the solid waste problem lie beer and soda bottles and cans, which are discarded in huge numbers along roads and streets, on beaches and vacant lots. The anti-litter laws are ineffectual in reducing this tide. In recent years several states--led by Oregon and now including California, Michigan and New York--and some municipalities, have enacted laws requiring glass, metal and plastic beverage containers to be sold with a deposit refundable on return of the container to a retailer. What benefits accrue from a law like this, other than a reduction in litter? What objections are likely to be voiced? Are such laws a deprivation of due process or equal protection? An undue burden on commerce? See *American Can Co. v. Oregon Liquor Control Comm'n*, 15 Or. App. 618, 517 P.2d 691 (1973) (statute upheld). Should these laws be extended to cover bottled water and juice drinks?

Although an ounce of feathers weighs the same as an ounce of lead, it can cost significantly more to ship a ton of scrap steel than a ton of newly-forged steel.

This marked disparity in government-approved freight rates was, you will recall, the subject of the challenge in *SCRAP v. United States*, discussed in Chapter 1, holding the plaintiff law student group had standing. The merits were reached in *National Association of Recycling Industries, Inc. v. Interstate Commerce Comm'n*, 585 F.2d 522 (D.C. Cir. 1978), cert. denied, 440 U.S. 929. The court held the Commission ignored the mandate of Congress in § 204 of the Regulatory Reform Act, now 49 App. U.S.C.A. § 10710, to end unjust discrimination in freight rates and in particular to end the higher rates for scrap metal.

Germany and some other European countries impose far stricter measures to limit waste, including requiring manufacturers to bear the cost of disposing of packaging. Is this an effective way of curtailing excess packaging? Who should bear these costs, as between the manufacturer, the consumer, and the municipality?

## B. HAZARDOUS WASTE

UNITED STATES v. MIDWEST SOLVENT RECOVERY, INC., United States District Court, Northern District of Indiana, 1980. 484 F. Supp. 138.

McNagny, District Judge.

[The United States alleged defendants' activities presented an imminent and substantial endangerment to health and the environment and moved for a preliminary injunction under § 7003 of RCRA, 42 U.S.C.A. § 6973. Defendant has conducted its business--reclaiming solvents as well as storing and disposing of various solid and hazardous wastes--in open pits on two tracts of Land, Midco No. 1 & No. 2. Each site has experienced a major fire. The Midco No. 1] fire caused the generation of toxic fumes and caused a large number of the 55-gallon drums to rocket up to 250 feet in the air. A number of Gary (Indiana) Fire Department members were injured and/or made ill in the course of fighting the fire.

[The Midco No. 2 Fire] fed for a number of days upon the chemical wastes stored in thousands of drums there.] At the present time the perimeter of Midco No. 1 is not fenced, there is easy access to the site, and the site is not otherwise secured or guarded. There are presently about 14,000 or so 55-gallon drums on the site. Drums are stacked on the ground or on top of each other, two, three or four drums high. The drums are not stored inside any buildings. Thousands of the drums were damaged in the December 21, 1976 fire. Many other drums are rusted out and/or severely corroded. A number are in good condition. Large amounts of poisonous chemical wastes have permeated much of the topsoil at the site, whether because of purposeful dumping, spillage, or fire-induced or corrosion-induced seepage. Soil sampling done at Midco No. 1 by the Indiana State Board of Health revealed that much of the Midco No. 1 topsoil contained inordinately high amounts of chromium, arsenic, cyanide, lead and other poisonous materials.

In many of the drums at the site, one or several of a number of compounds are present [that] are extremely flammable with dangerously low flashpoints.

Presently stacked on Midco No. 2 in disarray are thousands of 55-gallon drums. The majority of these drums are fire-damaged. Other drums are badly corroded. Others are rusted to various degrees. Some drums are in good condition. At one time or another a fence has ringed the front and both sides of the Midco No. 2 property. What fence that remains, however, is in such poor condition that it is not difficult for an individual to walk onto the Midco No. 2 site. The site is not patrolled or otherwise secured.
* * *The chemical wastes that have entered and are entering the soil at Midco No. 1 and at Midco No. 2 and the nature of the soil at the two sites are such that the wastes have seeped and are seeping through the soil and have reached or will reach the water tables lying beneath the two sites. [RCRA] § 7003 provides:

> [U]pon receipt of evidence that the handling, storage, treatment, transportation or disposal of any solid waste or hazardous waste is presenting an imminent and substantial endangerment of health or the environment, the [EPA] Administrator may bring suit on behalf of the United States in the appropriate district court to immediately restrain any person contributing to the alleged disposal to stop such handling, storage, treatment, transportation, or disposal or to take such other action as may be necessary.

[T]he government [argues that if it] makes all of the showings deemed at common law to be prerequisites to preliminary injunctive relief, except the showing that the plaintiff would be irreparably harmed in the absence of such relief, then a preliminary injunction should issue. In effect, the government urges both that in petitions for preliminary injunctive relief jurisdictionally rooted in § 7003, a showing that activities present "an imminent and substantial endangerment to health or the environment" is sufficient and that irreparable harm to the plaintiff in the absence of preliminary injunctive relief need not be demonstrated.

The Court disagrees. [T]he Court is persuaded for a number of reasons that § 7003 of the Act is in purpose only jurisdictional. [T]he section that immediately precedes § 7003 is a private attorney general provision that confers standing for purposes of enforcing the Act upon any "person," as that term is defined in § 1004(15) of the Act, 42 U.S.C. § 6903(15). Section 7002 does not, however, confer standing for this purpose upon the United States. Because the drafters of the Act would have been impelled by logic to organize the Act so as to place provisions relating to standing and jurisdiction in the same portion of the Act, the placement of the provision entitled § 7003 in immediate proximity of the provision entitled § 7002 is * * * evidence that § 7003 was not meant to create substantive tests of liability under the Act. [Further,] because § 7003 is as broadly worded as it is, if it were intended to function as a liability-creating provision, it would appear to make liable even those who contribute to the handling, storage, treatment, transportation or disposal of solid or hazardous wastes in such a way that an imminent and substantial endangerment to health or the environment is created. Any provision that could logically be read so to expand the set of persons liable under the federal solid and hazardous waste regulatory scheme would surely be identified as such in the legislative history. Finally, the Act elsewhere establishes by regulations the standards of conduct that must be followed by those who generate, transport, or own or operate facilities that treat, store, or dispose of hazardous wastes. 42 U.S.C. §§ 6922, 6923. and 6924.

In sum, the Court finds that the tests of when preliminary injunctive relief may issue in cases brought under the Act, are provided not by § 7003, but by Federal Rule of Civil Procedure 65 and by the common law. The tests identified in § 7003 are merely evidentiary tests which, if satisfied, permit the Administrator to petition in some situations for immediate injunctive relief. In the great majority of controversies that the Court can envision that involve the disposal, storage, treatment or handling of solid or hazardous wastes, if an endangerment of the sort described in § 7003 can be made out, the common law prerequisite to the issuance of preliminary injunctive relief will also be existent. But in those actions in which plaintiff shows a § 7003 endangerment but fails to demonstrate that in the absence of preliminary injunctive relief irreparable harm will result, a preliminary injunction cannot issue.* * *

[A] preliminary injunction can issue only upon findings that : 1) the plaintiff has no adequate remedy at law and will be irreparably harmed if the injunction is not imposed, 2) the threatened injury to the plaintiff outweighs the threatened harm the injunction may inflict on the defendant, 3) the plaintiff has at least a reasonable likelihood of success on the merits and 4) the granting of the preliminary injunction will not disserve the public interest.* * *

## Notes

RCRA contains, in addition to the injunction provisions illustrated in *Midwest Solvent*, authority for important EPA regulations controlling the transport and disposal of hazardous waste. These regulations establish a manifest system under which generators, transporters and disposers of hazardous waste (such as landfills) must keep records, and report to the EPA (or the state, if the state has an approved program) each shipment of such wastes. There are also financial responsibility requirements and detailed provisions for hazardous waste treatment, storage and disposal facilities (landfills, incinerators and warehouses). These regulations are codified at 40 CFR Parts 260-272.

Who is a more likely defendant in a suit by government -- the generator, transporter or disposer? Typically, all three are named as defendants. But the generator is likely to have the deepest pockets and is therefore a prime target.

A 1988 amendment to RCRA subjects medical waste to many of the same requirements as hazardous chemical waste. See 42 U.S.C.A. §§ 6992-6992k.

RCRA contains a citizen suit provision similar to those found in the Clean Air Act and Clean Water Act. Under it, plaintiffs may obtain an injunction requiring the clean up of waste endangering the environment, as the government did in *Midwest Solvent*. May they also recover their costs of cleaning up hazardous waste deposited by the defendant in the past, which no longer threatens the environment? The Supreme Court addressed this issue in *Meghrig v. KFC Western, Inc.*

MEGHRIG v. KFC WESTERN, INC. Supreme Court of the United States, 1996. 516 U.S. 479, 116 S.Ct. 1251, 134 L.Ed.2d 121.

O'Connor, J.

We consider whether § 7002 of the Resource Conservation and Recovery Act of 1976 (RCRA), 42 USC § 6972, authorizes a private cause of action to recover the prior cost of cleaning up toxic waste that does not, at the time of suit, continue to pose an endangerment to health or the environment. We conclude that it does not.

Respondent KFC Western, Inc. (KFC), owns and operates a "Kentucky Fried Chicken" restaurant on a parcel of property in Los Angeles. In 1988, KFC discovered during the course of a construction project that the property was contaminated with petroleum. The County of Los Angeles Department of Health Services ordered KFC to attend to the problem, and KFC spent $211,000 removing and disposing of the oil-tainted soil.

Three years later, KFC brought this suit under the citizen suit provision of RCRA,[*] seeking to recover these cleanup costs from petitioners Alan and Margaret Meghrig.

KFC claimed that the contaminated soil was a "solid waste" covered by RCRA, that it had previously posed an "imminent and substantial endangerment to health or the environment," and that the Meghrigs were responsible for "equitable restitution" of KFC's cleanup costs under § 6972(a) because, as prior owners of the property, they had contributed to the waste's "past or present handling, storage, treatment, transportation, or disposal." * * *

RCRA is a comprehensive environmental statute that governs the treatment, storage, and disposal of solid and hazardous waste. Unlike the Comprehensive Environmental Response, Compensation and Liability Act of

---

[*] Section 6972(a) provides, in relevant part:

> "[A]ny person may commence a civil action on his own behalf -- * * * against any person, including . . . . any past or present generator, past or present transporter, or past or present owner or operator of a treatment, storage, or disposal facility, who has contributed or who is contributing to the past or present handling, storage, treatment, transportation, or disposal of any solid or hazardous waste which may present an imminent and substantial endangerment to health or the environment.* * * The district court shall have jurisdiction to restrain any person who has contributed or who is contributing to the past or present handling, storage, treatment, transportation, or disposal of any solid or hazardous waste[,] to order such person to take such other action as may be necessary, or both. * * * "

1980 (CERCLA), 42 USC §§ 9601 *et seq.*, RCRA is not principally designed to effectuate the cleanup of toxic waste sites or to compensate those who have attended to the remediation of environmental hazards. Cf. *General Electric Co. v. Litton Industrial Automation Systems, Inc.*, 920 F.2d 1415, 1422 (CA8 1990) (the "two . . . main purposes of CERCLA" are "prompt cleanup of hazardous waste sites and imposition of all cleanup costs on the responsible party"). RCRA's primary purpose, rather, is to reduce the generation of hazardous waste and to ensure the proper treatment, storage, and disposal of that waste which is nonetheless generated, "so as to minimize the present and future threat to human health and the environment." 42 USC § 6902(b). * * *

Two requirements of § 6972(a) defeat KFC's suit against the Meghrigs. The first concerns the necessary timing of a citizen suit brought under § 6972(a)(1)(B): That section permits a private party to bring suit against certain responsible persons, including former owners, "who ha[ve] contributed or who [are] contributing to the past or present handling, storage, treatment, transportation, or disposal of any solid or hazardous waste which *may present* an *imminent* and substantial endangerment to health or the environment." (Emphasis added.) The second defines the remedies a district court can award in a suit brought under § 6972(a)(1)(B): Section 6972(a) authorizes district courts "*to restrain* any person who has contributed or who is contributing to the past or present handling, storage, treatment, transportation, or disposal of any solid or hazardous waste . . ., *to order such person to take such other action as may be necessary,* or both." (Emphasis added.)

It is apparent from the two remedies described in § 6972(a) that RCRA's citizen suit provision is not directed at providing compensation for past cleanup efforts. Under a plain reading of this remedial scheme, a private citizen suing under § 6972(a)(1)(B) could seek a mandatory injunction, *i.e.,* one that orders a responsible party to "take action" by attending to the cleanup and proper disposal of toxic waste, or a prohibitory injunction, *i.e.*, one that "restrains" a responsible party from further violating RCRA. Neither remedy, however, * * * contemplates the award of past cleanup costs, whether these are denominated "damages" or "equitable restitution."

In this regard, a comparison between the relief available under RCRA's citizen suit provision and that which Congress has provided in the analogous, but not parallel, provisions of CERCLA is telling. CERCLA was passed several years after RCRA went into effect, and it is designed to address many of the same toxic waste problems that inspired the passage of RCRA. Compare 42 USC § 6903(5) (RCRA definition of "hazardous waste") * * * with § 9601(14) (CERCLA provision incorporating certain "hazardous substance[s]," but not [all] the hazardous and solid wastes defined in RCRA, and specifically not petroleum). CERCLA differs markedly from RCRA, however, in the remedies it provides. * * * CERCLA expressly permits the Government to recover "all costs of removal or remedial action," § 9607(a)(4)(A), and it expressly permits the recovery of any "necessary costs of response, incurred by any . . . person consistent with the national contingency plan." § 9607(a)(4)(B). CERCLA also provides that "[a]ny person may seek contribution from any other person who is liable or potentially liable" for these response costs. See § 9613(f)(1). Congress thus demonstrated in CERCLA that it knew how to provide for the recovery of cleanup costs, and that the language used to define the remedies under RCRA does not provide that remedy.

The RCRA's citizen suit provision was not intended to provide a remedy for past cleanup costs is further apparent from the harm at which it is directed. Section 6972(a)(1)(B) permits a private party to bring suit only upon a showing that the solid or hazardous waste at issue "may present an imminent and substantial endangerment to health or the environment." The meaning of this timing restriction is plain: An endangerment can only be "imminent" if it "threaten[s] to occur immediately," Webster's New International Dictionary of English Language 1245 (2d ed. 1934), and the reference to waste which "may present" imminent harm quite clearly excludes waste that no longer presents such a danger. * * *

Other aspects of RCRA's enforcement scheme strongly support this conclusion. Unlike CERCLA, RCRA contains no statute of limitations, compare § 9613(g)(2) (limitations period in suits under CERCLA § 9607), and it does not require a showing that the response costs being sought are reasonable, compare §§ 9607(a)(4)(A) and (B) (costs recovered under CERCLA must be "consistent with the national contingency plan"). If Congress had intended § 6972(a) to function as a cost-recovery mechanism, the absence of these provisions would be striking. * * *

RCRA does not prevent a private party from recovering its cleanup costs under other federal or state laws, see § 6972(f) (preserving remedies under statutory and common law), but the limited remedies described in § 6972(a), along with the stark differences between the language of that section and the cost recovery provisions of CERCLA, amply demonstrate that Congress did not intend for a private citizen to be able to undertake a clean up and then proceed to recover its costs under RCRA. * * *

Notes

Should *Meghrig* also bar recovery under RCRA of *future* cleanup costs? See *Avondale Fed. Savings Bank v. Amoco Oil Co.,* 170 F.3d 692 (7th Cir. 1999) (yes).

Can a state obtain civil penalties or criminal fines against an agency of the United States under RCRA? Section 6961 expressly allows those remedies, overruling *Department of Energy v. Ohio*, 503 U.S. 607, 112 S.Ct. 1627, 118 L.Ed.2d 255 (1992), which had denied them based on the United States' sovereign immunity.

Despite its title, the Resource Conservation and Recovery Act (RCRA) does little to foster conservation, or hazardous waste reduction. The Act does provide that reducing the generation of hazardous waste is the national policy, section 6902 (b). But the liability provisions of CERCLA, the Superfund statute discussed later in this chapter, likely do far more to encourage the reduction of hazardous wastes.

## Environmental Justice

Hazardous waste, as well as nuclear, sites tend to be located disproportionately in low-income and minority communities. This issue, which has become known as the environmental justice, or environmental equity, issue, has come to the fore in the past few years. How can this gross imbalance be remedied? What are its causes? Are the considerations different as to existing and future facilities?

Where, as is often the case, the facility is either operated by a government agency or requires government approval, does siting it in a predominantly racial or ethnic minority community constitute a denial of equal protection of the laws under the Fourteenth Amendment? Proof of such a denial requires a showing of a discriminatory intent. See *Washington v. Davis*, 426 U.S. 229, 96 S.Ct. 2040, 48 L.Ed.2d 597 (1976). Can this likely be shown in selecting the site for a hazardous waste facility? See *Rozar v. Mullis*, 85 F.3d 556 (11th Cir. 1996) (no proof of discriminatory intent in siting of landfill).

An EPA regulation bars recipients of grants from that agency from actions having a discriminatory effect. This obviates the need to prove intent. Is the rule , adopted pursuant to Title VI of the Civil Rights Act of 1964, 42 U.S.C.A. §§ 2000d to 2000d-4a, which bars discrimination in federal and federally-funded agencies, enforceable by parties other than the government? See *Chester Residents Concerned for Quality Living v. Pennsylvania Dept. of Envtl. Prot.,* 132 F.3d 925 (3d Cir. 1997) (yes), vacated as moot, 524 U.S. 915 (1998).

Thereafter, the Supreme Court ruled in *Alexander* v. *Sandoval*, 532 U.S. 275, 121 S. Ct. 1511, 149 L. Ed. 2d 517 (2001), that suits under Title VI require proof of intent to discriminate, not just a discriminatory effect, and that no private right of action exists under federal agency regulations adopted to implement Title VI. These rules combined to derail much environmental justice litigation. In *South Camden Citizens in Action* v. *New Jersey Dept. of Envtl. Prot.*, 274 F.3d 771 (3d Cir. 2001), cert. denied, 536 U.S. 939 (2002), for example, the court reversed a preliminary injunction against building a state-permitted cement plant in a predominantly minority area, relying on *Sandoval*. It also held the plaintiffs could not sue under 42 U.S.C.A. § 1983, the all-purpose civil rights procedural statute, without a claim that a federal statute (or the Constitution) had been violated. On remand, the district court allowed the suit to proceed based on a claim that the state agency had intentionally discriminated based on race in approving the permit. 254 F. Supp. 2d 486 (D.N.J. 2003).

An Executive Order issued by President Clinton bars such discrimination. The order was the basis for the 1997 denial of a permit to construct a nuclear power plant in a predominantly black community in Louisiana. The denial, by the Nuclear Regulatory Commission's Atomic Safety and Licensing Board, was appealed to the Commission itself, See N.Y. Times, May 4, 1997; M. Gerrard and M.J. Bose, The Emerging Arena of "Justice," N.Y. Law Journal, July 25, 1997, p. 3, but the applicant withdrew its permit application, which, the Commission ruled, made the Board's ruling moot. See *Louisiana Energy Services*, 47 N.R.C. 113 (1998).

## C. HAZARDOUS WASTE CLEANUP

### The Comprehensive Environmental Response, Compensation and Liability Act (CERCLA)

As *Meghrig* held, RCRA deals with hazardous waste chiefly on a prospective basis. It failed to create an effective means of cleaning up hazardous waste deposited before the Act took effect in 1976, and even as to subsequent waste it provides a remedy for injunctive relief but not a fund for cleanup cost.

To deal with these issues, Congress in 1980 enacted CERCLA, the Comprehensive Environmental Response, Compensation and Liability Act, 42 U.S.C.A. §§ 9601-9675. This act establishes the well-known Superfund, a fund available for the removal of hazardous substances and remediation of areas where such materials were placed, or areas contaminated by them. The fund is derived chiefly (77%) from a tax on oil and chemical feedstocks (the raw materials from which hazardous substances are made). The remaining 23% stems from the United States Treasury. "Hazardous substance" is defined to exclude oil, gas and products derived from them. 42 U.S.C.A. § 9601(14). (Had *Meghrig* not concerned oil, CERCLA would have furnished a remedy.) However, waste oil and petroleum sludge may be hazardous substances under CERCLA because of the non-petroleum chemicals they may contain. *See Cose v. Getty Oil Co.*, 4 F.3d 700 (9th Cir. 1993).

### Liability

The fund is strictly liable for the cost of removal or remediation ("response costs") by the federal government, a state, or a private party if done under the National Contingency Plan created by the Act and administered by the EPA. The fund is also liable for damage to natural resources -- water supply, parklands and the like -- caused by hazardous substances, but only at the suit of the federal government or a state. Natural resources owned by a municipality or private person or corporation are not covered by CERCLA.

Sources, in turn, are liable to the fund. They may assert the defenses of an act of God, act of war or act of a third party, and have the burden or proving that the damage was solely due to one of those causes. A third party is defined as someone other than an agent, employee or contractor of the defendant, except that a railroad may be a third party. CERCLA § 107 (42 U.S.C.A § 9607). Even in asserting the third-party defense, the defendant must prove it acted with due care considering the nature of the substance.

In addition, parties that incur response costs may sue the responsible party directly, a common scenario. However, private plaintiffs may recover the costs of long-term remediation (as opposed to short-term removal) only where the site is listed in the National Contingency Plan. The defenses available under the Act are quite narrowly construed by the courts. For example, the act of God defense has been held not to apply to heavy rainfall or lightning, as those are foreseeable occurrences. *See United States v. Stringfellow*, 661 F. Supp. 1053 (C.D. Cal. 1987); *Wagner Seed Co. v. United States*, 946 F.2d 918 (D.C. Cir. 1991), cert. denied, 503 U.S. 970.

CERCLA originally preempted similar state funds derived from a tax on industry. Under its 1986 amendments, it no longer does, and states are free to establish their own funds. Many have.

The Act does not deal with liability for personal injury, wrongful death, or property damage (other than to natural resources). A study that took place under CERCLA § 301(e) (42 U.S.C.A § 9651[e]), under the tutelage of Professor Frank Grad of Columbia Law School, recommended further legislation to enact an administrative remedy under which injured persons may recover medical costs and a proportion of lost earnings. At this tribunal there would be a presumption that the exposure to hazardous waste caused the injury and that the source was responsible. The study recommended that tort recovery be allowed if claimants sought additional damages, such as for pain and suffering, unlike the workers' compensation structure where such suits are barred. But successful plaintiffs would have to deduct what they recovered from the administrative tribunal. And unsuccessful ones would have to pay significant costs to the defendant. See Developments in Victim Compensation Legislation: A Look Beyond the Superfund Act of 1980, 10 Colum. J. Envtl. L. 271 (1985).

CERCLA has given birth to a federal common law of joint and several liability for defendants where the harm is indivisible. See *United States v. Chem-Dyne Corp.*, 572 F.Supp. 802 (S.D. Ohio 1983). The federal courts also allow contribution among jointly liable defendants, irrespective of state law, where suit is brought under § 113 of CERCLA, 42 U.S.C.A. § 9613. Where the harm is divisible, courts weigh the amount and toxicity of each defendant's share, its degree of care and involvement, and similar factors, in apportioning liability.

An owner or operator is responsible under CERCLA even though it did not place the hazardous waste on the site, as long as it knew or had reason to know of it. 42 U.S.C.A. § 9601(35). The test is whether the purchaser made all appropriate inquiry, consistent with good customary practice. See *United States v. Serafini*, 706 F.Supp. 346 (M.D.Pa. 1988).

Private plaintiffs may sue under CERCLA to recover response and cleanup costs, though not their attorneys' fees. *Key Tronic Corp. v. United States*, 511 U.S. 809, 114 S. Ct. 1960, 128 L.Ed.2d 797 (1994) (actually a suit for reimbursement, not response costs). What about lost profits? Medical monitoring of a water supply?

Lenders' Liability

Difficult issues surround the role of banks and other lenders. Until 1991 they became the owner or operator following foreclosure, *United States v. Maryland Bank & Trust Co.*, 632 F.Supp. 573 (D. Md. 1986). What about a mortgagee or other secured creditor prior to foreclosure? Is it responsible under CERCLA if it exercised day-to-day control? If it could have, even though it did not? See *United States v. Fleet Factors Corp.*, 901 F.2d 1550 (11th Cir. 1990); cert. denied 111 S.Ct. 752 (yes); *In re Bergsoe Metal Corp.*, 910 F.2d 668 (9th Cir. 1990) (no). In 1991 the EPA adopted regulations holding lenders to be responsible parties under CERCLA only if they actually exercise control, the *Bergsoe* rule, and holding they do not become responsible parties when they foreclose (overruling *Maryland Bank and Trust Co.*). Although the regulation was challenged, Congress amended the Act (present § 9601 [20][E], [F]) in 1996 to codify that result.

State-operated Sites

Can a state be a defendant if it operates a site? The Eleventh Amendment bars suits against states in the federal courts, but the courts permit such suits where Congress has expressly authorized them. Has CERCLA in effect authorized actions against states? The statute allows citizen suits "against any person (including the United States and any other governmental instrumentality or agency, to the extent permitted by the eleventh amendment . . .)." This language, the Supreme Court held in *Pennsylvania v. Union Gas Co.*, 491 U.S. 1, 109 S.Ct. 2273, 105 L.Ed.2d 1 (1989), supported suit against a state-operated facility. But *Union Gas* was soon overruled by *Seminole Tribe v. Florida,* 517 U.S. 44, 116 S. Ct. 1114, 134 L.Ed.2d 252 (1996) (not a CERCLA case), which held Congress lacks power under the Commerce Clause to override the Eleventh Amendment. So suits in federal court against states as operators of hazardous waste sites to recover response costs are not available.

Insurance

Is an owner or operator's liability insurance responsible for hazardous waste response costs? Often the insurance policy was written before the vast extent of liability existed, and the premium was fixed accordingly. Is a release of hazardous waste an "occurrence" under such a policy? Are cleanup costs "property damage"? See *Avondale Industries, Inc.* v. *Travelers Indemnity Co.*, 887 F.2d 1200 (2d Cir. 1989), cert. denied 496 U.S. 906 (yes). This is a state law issue, and the results vary accordingly from state to state.

Since CERCLA many insurers added pollution exclusion clauses, limiting their coverage to "sudden and accidental" discharges. Does this wording take the insurer off the hook? See *FL Aerospace* v. *Aetna Casualty & Surety Co.*, 897 F.2d 214 (6th Cir. 1990), cert. denied 498 U.S. 911 (policy excludes releases over gradual period; not "sudden and accidental"). More recent pollution exclusion clauses exempted all discharges of hazardous substances. But liability insurance is once again available (at a price reflective of the heightened risk) to cover hazardous discharges.

## Bankruptcy

Suppose an owner or operator files for bankruptcy. Does the Bankruptcy Code bar claims under CERCLA or similar state laws? The Code generally protects the bankrupt from civil suits seeking money damages. Is a suit seeking cleanup such an action? The Supreme Court first dealt with this issue in *Ohio v. Kovacs*, 469 U.S. 274, 105 S.Ct. 705, 83 L.Ed.2d 649 (1985). There the state appointed a receiver to clean up the property, a landfill, since the owner had refused to do so. The owner then filed for bankruptcy. The Court held the state's order was really a debt dischargeable in bankruptcy since it amounted to a demand for money. It left open the question of a cleanup order issued by the government itself without the appointment of a receiver. And in *Midlantic National Bank v. New Jersey Dept. of Envtl. Prot.*, 474 U.S. 494, 106 S.Ct. 755, 88 L.Ed.2d 859 (1986), the Court ruled that the Bankruptcy Code's provision allowing a bankrupt to abandon worthless property does not preempt state cleanup orders. Most recently, a court has held cleanup costs incurred prior to petitioning for bankruptcy are dischargeable in bankruptcy, while those incurred after the petition is filed are not, and must be paid in full. But that court went on to hold an injunction requiring cleanup is not a dischargeable debt. *In re Chateaugay Corp.*, 944 F.2d 997 (2d Cir. 1991).

Some states have enacted "Superlien" statutes making hazardous waste cleanup a priority lien in bankruptcy. CERCLA creates a lien as to the federal government's response costs, but does not mention bankruptcy. See § 107(1), 42 U.S.C.A. § 9607(1). Another approach, taken by New Jersey's Industrial Site Recovery Act (ISRA), N.J. Stat. Ann. §§ 13:1 K-6 to 13:1 K-14, is to require state approval of a cleanup plan before property used for the manufacture, transport, storage or disposal of hazardous substances may be conveyed. Funds to remediate, if that proves necessary, must be shown to be available as well.

Under CERCLA, when is an owner responsible for waste placed on the site by a prior owner?

NEW YORK v. LASHINS ARCADE CO., United States Court of Appeals, Second Circuit, 1996. 91 F.3d 353.

[The State of New York sued the owner of a shopping arcade under CERCLA § 107, 42 U.S.C.A. § 9607, to recover its costs of cleaning of perchloroethylene (PCE) and related chemicals used as solvents in dry-cleaning.]

Mahoney, Circuit Judge:

* * * The district court awarded Lashins summary judgment based upon the third-party defense provided by §107(b)(3) of CERCLA, 42 U.S.C. § 9607(b)(3),[3] and dismissed the action "as against the Lashins defendants." * * *

On this appeal, New York contests * * * the dismissal of its claims against Lashins[.] We affirm the judgment of the district court.

This appeal involves the release of hazardous substances at the Arcade, which resulted in groundwater contamination in the area. The Arcade, a 6,800 square foot one-story building housing six retail stores, was built in 1955, and was owned by Holbrook B. Cushman until his death in 1966. The property was then held in trust by Cushman's widow, Beatrice Cushman, and the Bank of New York until 1972. Cushman leased a store in the Arcade to Astrologo from about 1958 to 1963, where Astrologo operated a dry cleaning business. The store was next leased to defendant Rocco Tripodi * * * in 1963, who maintained the dry cleaning business at the Arcade until 1971. During this period, Tripodi dumped powdered wastes from his dry cleaning machines, which contained the volatile organic compound ("VOC") PCE, on the ground outside the Arcade behind his store. In December 1971, Tripodi moved his dry cleaning business out of the Arcade, and no other dry cleaning establishment has operated there since that time. In November 1972, the trust sold the Arcade to Miriam Baygell, who owned the

---

[3] Section 9607(b) provides:

> There shall be no liability under subsection (a) of this section for a person otherwise liable who can establish by a preponderance of the evidence that the release or threat of release of a hazardous substance and the damages resulting therefrom were caused solely by--

(1) an act of God;

(2) an act of war;

(3) an act or omission of a third party other than an employee or agent of the defendant, or than one whose act or omission occurs in connection with a contractual relationship, existing directly or indirectly, with the defendant (except where the sole contractual arrangement arises from a published tariff and acceptance for carriage by a common carrier by rail), if the defendant establishes by a preponderance of the evidence that (a) he exercised due care with respect to the hazardous substance concerned, taking into consideration the characteristics of such hazardous substance, in light of all relevant facts and circumstances, and (b) he took precautions against foreseeable acts or omissions of any such third party and the consequences that could foreseeably result from such acts or omissions; or

(4) any combination of the foregoing paragraphs.

property until her death in 1977, when it was inherited by her husband, Milton Baygell.

In 1978, the Westchester County Department of Health (the "WCDOH") conducted a countywide survey regarding possible groundwater contamination by VOCs. The survey found elevated VOC levels in the [area]. Further sampling of private wells in Bedford Village conducted by the WCDOH in 1979 revealed groundwater contamination in an area southeast of the Arcade. These samples contained high concentrations of PCE and its breakdown compounds, TCE and DCE. The WCDOH issued "boil water" notices to affected homeowners.

In 1982, the New York State Department of Environmental Conservation (the "NYSDEC") authorized state funds for an investigation and remediation of the groundwater problem at the Arcade[, which] revealed fluctuating levels of VOC contamination in the wells adjacent to the Arcade [, particularly] in the area formerly occupied by the dry cleaning establishment.

Following the Phase I investigation, the "Bedford Village Wells" site was lised on the New York State Registry of Inactive Hazardous Waste Disposal Sites (the "Registry"). The Registry is published annually by the NYSDEC pursuant to § 27-1305(1) of the New York Environmental Conservation Law, which requires the NYSDEC annually to "transmit a report to the legislature and the governor identifying every inactive hazardous waste disposal site in the state known to the [NYSDEC]." * * * In the 1983 Registry, the Bedford Village Wells site was designated as a Class "2a" site, based in part upon information that disposition of dry cleaning solvents had probably occurred at the Arcade. Class "2a" sites are those that are suspected to be hazardous waste disposal sites, but which require further investigation to confirm the presence of hazardous wastes. * * * By letter dated October 12, 1983 and addressed to Miriam Baygell (who by that time was deceased), the NYSDEC advised that it intended to conduct a Phase I investigation of the Bedford Village Wells, and also stated that Mrs. Baygell had the right to conduct such an investigation herself. Milton Baygell did not respond to this letter, which he may never have received. In any event, Wehran [the State's consultant] conducted the Phase II fieldwork for the NYSDEC commencing in 1984, and reported its final conclusions in June 1985. During this period, the WCDOH requested in a letter to Milton Baygell dated March 6, 1984 that he install a granular activated carbon ("GAC") filter in the well supplying the Arcade with water to remedy the VOC problem; Baygell installed the GAC filter in May 1985.

The final Phase II Report concluded that VOC contamination persisted at the Arcade site.* * * As a result of these findings, the Bedford Village Wells Site was reclassified from Class "2a" to Class "2" in the 1986 Registry. A Class "2" site is defined as a "[s]ignificant threat to the public health or environment--action required." N.Y. Envtl.Conserv.Law § 27-1305(4)(b)(2). Milton Baygell was informed about the reclassification in a certified letter for which he signed a receipt on June 20, 1986.

In 1986, the United States Environmental Protection Agency (the "EPA") joined with the WCDOH to investigate the Arcade. Their joint surveys confirmed that VOCs persisted in three private wells at the Bedford Village Wells site, and low VOC concentrations also appeared east and southeast of the Arcade in water supplies that had previously been uncontaminated. In view of this problem, the NYSDEC requested and obtained approval from the EPA for a Remedial Investigation/Feasibility Study ("RI/FS") of the entire Bedford Village Wells site. The NYSDEC retained Dvirka and Bartilucci Consulting Engineers ("Dvirka and Bartilucci") to perform the RI/FS in December 1986, and the firm began its field work the following summer.

Meanwhile, in January 1987, Milton Baygell entered into negotiations with Lashins for the sale of the Arcade[.] In the course of these negotiations, Baygell's attorney * * * wrote Lashins' attorney * * * on March 20, 1987 to inform him that "there are chemicals in the ground being treated by ultra violet and activated carbon machines situated in the rear of the building to clean the water. Chemicals have to be replaced approximately every 8-9 months." Prior to executing the contract of sale, Lashins contacted the Arcade's water service contractor, Environmental Recovery Co., who advised Lashins that the well on the premises had a water filter, but assured Lashins that the filter was "routine" and had been installed in response to an area-wide groundwater contamination problem, and that the suspected source of the contamination was a nearby Exxon gas station.

In addition, Lashins states that it contacted the Town of Bedford prior to purchasing the Shoping Arcade to determine whether there were any violations or other present or past problems with the property, and was assured that there were none. Lashins further asserts that it interviewed the Arcade's tenants, all of whom spoke enthusiastically about the property. New York contends, however that Lashins made no inquiry concerning the groundwater contamination (other than the discussion with Environmental Recovery Co.) prior to purchasing the Arcade. In any event, Lashins executed a contract of sale with Baygell on April 6, 1987, and the transaction closed on June 26, 1987.

Lashins claims that at the time of the closing, it was unaware that the NYSDEC was conducting an administrative proceeding involving the Arcade, or that it had contracted with a firm to conduct the RI/FS concerning the Bedford Village Wells site. Baygell did not transmit any NYSDEC notices to Lashins, no public notice was issued, and the Arcade tenants, the Town of Bedford, and the local bank were allegedly unaware of the situation.

Lashins was first informed that the NYSDEC was conducting a formal investigation of the Arcade by letter dated August 13, 1987. That letter advised Lashins of the impending RI/FS requested by the NYSDEC, and stated that NYSDEC representatives intended to enter the Arcade property "for the purpose of drilling, installing and operating groundwater monitoring wells and taking samples of soil, septage, surface water, and groundwater."

New York also informed Milton Baygell of the RI/FS by letter dated September 18, 1987[.]

After purchasing the Arcade, Lashins maintained the existing GAC filter and took water samples which were analyzed by a laboratory for VOC contamination on a semiannual basis. It also instructed all tenants to avoid discharging any hazardous substances into the waste and septic systems, subsequently incorporated this requirement into the tenant leases, and conducted peeriodic inspections of the tenants' premises to assure compliance with this obligation.

The RI/FS was completed in February 1990. It concluded, inter alia, that the contamination in the affected wells,

> "although unconfirmed, most probably originated from a former dry cleaning establishment located in the Shopping Arcade [and these sources] may be continuing to release organic chemicals to the surrounding environment." * * *

The district court concluded that all elements for strict liability as to Lashins under § 9607(a) were satisfied in this case, but that Lashins was entitled to summary judgment on its affirmative defense under § 9607(b)(3), *supra* note 3. [It] noted that "Lashins had no direct or indirect contractual relationship with either of the third party dry cleaners who released the VOCs, or with the owners of the Shopping Arcade at the time the dry cleaners operated and when the pollution occurred," and that Lashins had done "everything that could reasonably have been done to avoid or correct the pollution." * * *

Since Lashins is a current owner of the Shopping Arcade, it is a potentially responsible defendant under § 9607(a)(1), notwithstanding the fact that it did not own the Arcade at the time of disposal of the hazardous substances. * * *

Section 9607(b)(3) provides an affirmative defense for a party who can establish that the offending "release . . . of a hazardous substance and the damages resulting therefrom were caused solely by . . . an act or omission of a third party," provided that: (1) the third party is not "one whose act or omission occurs in connection with a contractual relationship, existing directly or indirectly, with the defendant," (2) the defendant "took precautions against foreseeable acts or omissions of any such third party and the consequences that could foreseeably result from such acts or omissions," and (3) the defendant "exercised due care with respect to the hazardous substance concerned, taking into consideration the characteristics of such hazardous substance, in light of all relevant facts and circumstances."

The offending release here was clearly caused by third parties (Tripodi, Bedford Village Cleaners, Inc., Astrologo, and (New York contends) Milton Baygell). Although paragraphs (1)-(3) of § 9607(b) speak exclusively in the singular, referring to events and damages "caused solely by -- (1) an act of God; (2) an act of war; [or] (3) and act or omission of a third party," § 9607(b), paragraph (4) of § 9607(b) refers to "any combination of the foregoing paragraphs," *id.*, see *supra* note 3. We read paragraph (4) as allowing consideration of multiple causes within, as well as among, the several preceding paragraphs. Thus, in our view, damage that resulted from an earthquake and a subsequent flood would fall within paragraph (1) of § 9607(b), and damages caused by a number of acts by a single third party (as typically occurs when pollution is caused by a course of conduct), or a number of acts by several third parties (as in this case), would fall within paragraph (3).

* * * In this case, the only one of the allegedly offending third parties with whom Lashins had a contractual relationship was Milton Baygell. Further, Baygell's allegedly offending conduct did not "occur in connection with a contractual relationship . . . with [Lashins]" within the meaning of § 9607(b)(3), and therefore Lashins may not be disqualified from the protection afforded by § 9607(b)(3) because of its contractual relationship with Baygell. [See] *Westwood Pharmaceuticals, Inc. v. National Fuel Gas Distribution Corp.*, 964 F.2d 85 (2d Cir. 1992): "[A] landowner is precluded from raising the third-party defense only if the contract between the landowner and the third party somehow is connected with the handling of hazardous substances." The straightforward sale of the Arcade by Baygell to Lashins clearly did not "relate to hazardous substances" or vest Lashins with authority "to exert some element of control over [Baygell's] activities" within the contemplation of our ruling in *Westwood.*

The second requirement for the successful assertion of a third-party defense demands that the defendant shall have taken adequate precautions against actions by the third party that would lead to a release of hazardous waste. Given that the last release in the instant case happened more than fifteen years before Lashins' purchase of the Arcade, there was obviously nothing Lashins could have done to prevent actions leading to a release.

Thus, the resolution of this appeal turns upon the validity of the district court's ruling that Lashins was entitled to summary judgment on the question whether Lashins "exercised due care with respect to the hazardous substance concerned . . . in the light of all relevant facts and circumstances" within the meaning of § 9607(b)(3). This requirement is not defined in the statute. CERCLA's legislative history, however, provides some guidance: "[T]he defendant must demonstrate that he took all precautions with respect to the particular waste that a similarly situated reasonable and prudent person would have taken in light of all relevant facts and circumstances." H.R.Rep. No. 1016, 96th Cong., 2d Sess., pt. 1, at 34 (1980), reprinted in 1980 U.S.C.C.A.N. 6119, 6137. Further, "due care 'would include those steps necessary to protect the public from a health or environmental threat.'" *United States v. A & N Cleaners & Launderers, Inc.*, 854 F. Supp. 229, 238 (S.D.N.Y. 1994)[.]

Against this background, New York contends that Lashins inadequately investigated the contamination problem before buying the Arcade despite being notified about it, and after its purchase "did nothing to contain, control or clean up the pollution except to continue to maintain a filter on its own property." New

York points to cases such as *A & N Cleaners* and *Kerr-McGee Chemical Corp.* where § 9607(a) liability was imposed because the defendant did not take active measures to address a hazardous waste problem, and adds that *Kerr-McGee Chemical Corp.* [*v. Lefton Iron & Metal Co.*, 14 F.3d 321 (7th Cir. 1994)] established that the "due care" standard does not permit a landowner to remain passive simply because public environmental authorities are addressing a hazardous waste situation.

We are not persuaded by New York's arguments, or by the authorities that New York cites to us. The pertinent language of § 9607(b)(3) focuses the "due care" inquiry upon "all relevant facts and circumstances" of the case at hand. In this case, the RI/FS by Dvirka and Bartilucci had been commissioned six months before Lashins purchased the Arcade, and before Lashins had even learned that the Arcade was for sale. It would have been pointless to require Lashins to commission a parallel investigation once it acquired the Arcade and became more fully aware of the environmental problem. * * *

Nor do we discern any policy reasons for imposing such a rule. We agree with *HRW Systems, Inc. v. Washington Gas Light Co.*, 823 F.Supp. 318 (D. Md. 1993), that the "due care" mandate of § 9607(b)(3) does not "impose a duty on a purchaser of land to investigate prior to purchase, in order to determine whether there is pollution on the land caused by someone with whom the purchaser is not in contractual privity." *Id.* at 349. No claim is made that Lashins' purchase of the Arcade deprived New York of any remedy available to it against any predecessor owners or operators under § 9607(a); consent decrees were in fact entered against Tripodi and Astrologo[.] It is surely the policy of CERCLA to impose liability upon parties responsible for pollution, rather than the general taxpaying public, but this policy does not mandate precluding a "due care" defense by imposing a rule that is tantamount to absolute liability for ownership of a site containing hazardous waste.

Finally, the cases cited by New York do not require the negation of Lashins' "due care" defense. None involved a defendant who played no role in the events that led to the hazardous waste problem and came on the scene after public authorities were well along in a program of investigation and remediation. *Kerr-McGee Chemical Corp.* involved in a landowner who was aware of the environmental problem and made no attempt to address it after preliminary investigative efforts by federal and state authorities provided notice of the contamination. In *A & N Cleaners*, the defendant landowners' sublessee (who subsequently became a lessee) was operating the offending dry cleaning establishment throughout the entire period of the defendant's ownership. * * *

In sum, we perceive no basis for reversal of the district court's award of summary judgment to Lashins on the basis that Lashins satisfied its obligation to "exercise[] due care" with respect to the Arcade within the meaning of § 9607(b)(3). In so ruling, we proclaim no broad rule of exemption from the liability imposed by § 9607(a). Rather, mindful of the mandate of § 9607(b)(3) that the "due care" inquiry focus upon "all relevant facts and circumstances" of the case presented for decision, we conclude that Lashins' "due care" obligation did not require it to go beyond the measures that it took to address the contamination problem at the Arcade, and to supplant, duplicate, or underwrite the RI/FS previously commissioned by the EPA and NYSDEC to address pollution that ensued from activities which occurred more than fifteen years before Lashins purchased the Arcade.

The judgment of the district court is affirmed.

## Notes

After *Lashins*, what must the government or private plaintiffs show under CERCLA to impose liability on a purchaser of contaminated property? Did the court unduly broaden the third-party defense? Who will bear the costs of cleanup in these situations?

## The Brownfields Issue

When CERCLA mandates cleanup of a contaminated site as in *Lashins*, how clean is clean? This is what has become known as the "brownfields" controversy. If sites in industrial areas must be cleaned as if they were used as residences or farms, not only do the costs escalate, but the resulting disincentives to decontaminate these sites will often cause them to remain toxic. New industrial development will occur outside cities, using (and perhaps contaminating) agricultural land, woodlands and similar areas. In addition, these new sites will usually be accessible only by road, and thus likely to heighten air pollution. They will also be not readily accessible to urban workers.

Conversely, if urban industrial sites are held to a lower ("brownfields" instead of "greenfields") standard, is this fair to urban residents, who often live near these sites and may remain exposed to hazardous materials that would otherwise have been cleaned up?

Some states have enacted, or are considering, legislation to require only a "brownfields" cleanup. See Ill. Rev. Stat. ch. 415, para. 5/22b (1995); New York Envtl. Conserv. Law §§ 27-1401 to 27-1431 (2004). Should they?

## Community Right-to-Know Laws

How do residents of areas near factories and warehouses know whether hazardous chemicals are stored near them? The 1986 amendments to CERCLA included Community Right-to-Know provisions to deal with this issue, 42 U.S.C.A. §§ 11001-11050, the Emergency Planning and Community Right-to-Know Act. Each state is to establish an emergency response commission. Facilities must report their storage or release (routine or accidental) of toxic chemicals listed by the EPA. The vehicles for this notification are material safety data sheets and toxic chemical release forms. Facilities are also required to prepare emergency response plans for state approval, and are subject to inspection.

## D. PESTICIDES AND OTHER TOXIC SUBSTANCES

### 1. Pesticides

DOW CHEMICAL COMPANY v. BLUM, United States District Court, Eastern District of Michigan, 1979. 469 F.Supp. 892.

James Harvey, District Judge.

[P]laintiffs brought this action seeking judicial review of a decision by the Environmental Protection Agency to order an emergency ban of two herbicides manufactured primarily by the plaintiff Dow Chemical Company (Dow). The herbicides are commonly known as 2,4,5,T and Silvex. In ordering the ban, EPA was acting, for the first time, pursuant to its emergency powers under Section 6(c)(3) of the Federal Insecticide, Fungicide and Rodenticide Act (FIFRA), 7 U.S.C. §136d(c)(3). Such action is subject to immediate review in the district courts solely to determine whether the order of suspension was arbitrary, capricious, or otherwise not in accordance with the law.

* * *Having reviewed the testimony and exhibits, the relevant portions of the administrative record cited to the Court by the parties, as well as the law on the matter, the Court believes that the request for a stay of the EPA emergency suspension orders of February 28, 1979 should be denied.

On February 28, 1979, EPA issued two emergency suspension orders which had the effect of immediately suspending the distribution, sale, and use of: (1) 2,4,5-T for forestry, rights-of-way, and pasture uses; and (2) Silvex for the foregoing uses, as well as home and garden, aquatic week control/ditch bank, and commercial/ornamental turf uses. The emergency suspension orders were based on a judgment by EPA that pregnant women at the time of exposure to the banned uses of 2,4,5-T and Silvex faced an immediate unreasonable risk of spontaneous abortions. [T]his judgment was based on* * *: (1) laboratory tests which indicated that the contaminant TCDD, which is present in small amounts in both 2,4,5-T and Silvex, produced feto-toxic and teratogenic effects in animals at extremely low dose levels; and (2) an epidemiological study, labeled "Alsea II," which claimed to have found a statistically significant correlation between the spraying of 2,4,5-T and the occurrence of spontaneous human abortions in women residing in the Alsea basin region on the western coast of Oregon.* * * At present, 2,4,5-T and Silvex cannot be manufactured without producing as a by-product the contaminant TCDD. The studies relied upon by EPA reflect that TCDD is a highly feto-toxic and embryo-lethal substance for which a no-effect level has not, at present, been determined.* * *

EPA also considered the prospective benefits from the continued use of 2,4,5-T and Silvex during the three and one-half month period that the emergency suspension order would be in effect. Due to the relatively short period that the emergency suspension orders would be in effect, as well as the availability of alternative herbicides, EPA concluded that the benefits of continued us of 2,4,5-T and Silvex during the suspension process would be nominal.

After considering the risks to human health and the environment posed by 2,4,5-T and Silvex, the prospective benefits of continued use of 2,4,5-T and Silvex during the suspension process, as well as the imminency of the March spraying period for 2,4,5-T, EPA concluded that emergency action was necessary.* * *

The ultimate issue to be decided by the Court in this matter is a simple one: whether the EPA decision that an emergency existed with respect to the uses in question of 2,4,5-T and Silvex, which did not permit a hearing prior to suspension was arbitrary, capricious, or an abuse of discretion or otherwise not made in accordance with the procedures established by law. This ultimate issue leads to a secondary legal issue: what is the meaning of the term "emergency."* * * FIFRA generally requires that all pesticides be registered with the Administrator after a determination that the pesticide meets registration requirements, set forth in Section 3(c)(5) of FIFRA, 7 U.S.C. §136a(c)(5), which requires a determination that the pesticide to be registered will not cause "unreasonable adverse effects on the environment." Section 6 of FIFRA, 7 U.S.C. §136d requires the Administrator to exercise a continuous review of pesticides that have been registered.

If it appears to the Administrator that a pesticide no longer meets registration requirements and appears to cause unreasonable adverse effects on the environment, the Administrator may * * * (1) cancel a registration; (2) suspend a registration pending cancellation ("ordinary suspension"); and (3) suspend a registration pending suspension ("emergency suspension").

This case involves the third type[.]

The ordinary suspension provision (Section 6(e)(1) of FIFRA provides that the Administrator may, by order, suspend the registration of a pesticide if he "determines that action is necessary to prevent an imminent hazard during the time required for cancellation. . ." The term "imminent hazard" is defined to mean "a situation which exists when the continued use of a pesticide during the time required for cancellation proceeding would be *likely* to result in unreasonable adverse effects on the environment. . . ." (emphasis added). The term "unreasonable adverse effects on the environment" is defined to mean "unreasonable risk to man or the environment taking into account the economic, social and environmental costs and benefits." FIFRA §2 (bb) (7 U.S.C. §136(bb)).

* * *The emergency suspension provision, Section 6(c)(3) of FIFRA, provides that the Administrator may, by order, suspend the registration of a pesticide immediately upon issuance of an emergency suspension order--prior to hearing and prior to notifying the registrant--whenever he determines that an emergency exists which does not permit the Administrator to hold a hearing prior

to suspension. An emergency suspension order remains in effect until the cancellation decision unless an expedited hearing is requested. If an expedited hearing is requested on the issue of imminent hazard, the emergency order continues in effect until the issuance of a final suspension order.

In this connection, the plaintiffs have requested a suspension hearing[.] Following the suspension hearing, the Administrator may affirm, modify or vacate the emergency suspension order, and his decision is then reviewable in the Courts of Appeal.* * *

FIFRA was enacted for three basis reasons: (a) To impose restrictions on the use of pesticides; prior law imposed labeling requirements, but did not restrict the actual use, of pesticides; (b) Extend Federal pesticide regulation to *intrastate*, by contrast to, interstate commerce; and (c) Strengthen and streamline pesticide regulation.

* * *The term "emergency" is not defined in the Act, legislative history, regulations, or the cases. EPA has interpreted the term to mean a threat of harm to humans and the environment so immediate that the continuation of pesticide use is likely to result in unreasonable adverse effects during a suspension hearing. EPA Decision and Emergency Order (2,4,5-T) at 7 (February 28, 1979).

Because there is no precedent for the Court to follow in this action, it is appropriate to define the term "emergency" by reference to the principles and rationale for the granting by a court of a temporary restraining order. The purpose of a temporary restraining order is to prevent immediate and irreparable harm to the complaining party during the period necessary to conduct a hearing on a preliminary injunction.

[T]he standard of review in this instance is whether there is a substantial likelihood that serious harm will be experienced during the year or two required in any realistic projection of the administrative process.* * * This * * * suggests the necessity to examine five factors:

(1) The seriousness of the threatened harm;
(2) The immediacy of the threatened harm;
(3) The probability that the threatened harm would result;
(4) Benefits to the public of the continued use of the pesticide in question during the suspension process; and
(5) The nature and extent of the information before the Administrator at the time he made his decision.

Compare *Ethyl Corp. v. EPA* [, Chapter 1.] Further, in accordance with the legislative history outline above, these factors should be applied in the spirit of avoiding delay and recognition of broad powers on the part of EPA in regulating pesticides.* * *

The ultimate standard of review, however, is a narrow one -- the Court is not empowered to substitute its judgment for that of the agency: *Ethyl Corp. v. EPA, supra.** * *

[T]he Court is unable to say that EPA made a clear error of judgment with regard to the probability that the uses in question of 2,4,5-T and Silvex are associated with spontaneous human abortions. There is evidence in the record that the animal studies and the Alsea II Study, although certainly inconclusive, are nevertheless suggestive of the conclusions reached by EPA in this regard.

[T]here is evidence in the record to show that pregnant women in the Study Area are potentially exposed to 2,4,5-T and TCDD through drinking water and food supplies, as well as a risk of dermal exposure. The Court believes that this evidence, together with evidence that a no-effect level of TCDD has not been established, are sufficient reasons to hold that EPA made no clear error of judgment in relying on the Alsea II conclusions.* * *

EPA also relied on the Alsea II Report in deciding to issue an emergency ban of Silvex. This was based on the assumption that, because of the chemical similarity between 2,4,5-T and Silvex and the fact TCDD is present in both substances, one could reasonably expect the spraying of Silvex to have an association with spontaneous human abortions similar to the association found in the Alsea II Study between spontaneous human abortions and 2,4,5-T.

[T]he Court is unable to say that EPA made a clear error of judgment regarding its possible risks.* * *

## FIFRA, the Federal Insecticide, Fungicide and Rodenticide Act

FIFRA, 7 U.S.C.A. §§ 136-136y, was enacted in 1947. The cancellation and suspension provisions discussed in *Dow*, above, are contained in amendments passed in 1972. The older provisions of the statute provide a regulatory scheme for the registration and proper labeling of all pesticides, built, as the court noted in *Dow*, on earlier federal statutes chiefly aimed at protecting users from defective pesticides, as opposed to protecting all of us from dangerous ones.

To register a pesticide under the Act the manufacturer must certify that it will:

(1) do what it is supposed to do,
(2) meet all labeling requirements, and
(3) not be unreasonably harmful to the environment on balance with its economic benefit.

Registration is for 5-year renewable periods and is for either general or restricted use. Restricted use pesticides may be limited to sales to certified pesticide applicators, and must be clearly so labeled. Certification for registration may be delegated to the states and variances in the form of emergency use permits and experimental use permits are available at the Administrator's discretion in certain instances. Pesticides manufactured for export are exempt, but imported pesticides must meet the Act's requirements.

Labeling is broadly construed to include advertisements and promotional material accompanying the product. All labels must include a statement of treatment in the event of accidental ingestion, giving rise to the syllogism that substances for which no treatment exists cannot be properly labeled, and consequently cannot be properly registered. All highly toxic substances must have a skull and crossbones on the label. Under the statute EPA may impose civil penalties for mislabeling and cancel, suspend, or halt on an emergency basis, the registration of a pesticide as described in *Dow*.

Should conformity with the Act's labeling requirements bar a tort suit for failure to warn as federally preempted? See *Cox v. Velsicol Chemical Corp.*, 704 F.Supp. 85(?) (E.D. Pa. 1989) (no); *Papas v. Upjohn Corp.*, 985 F.2d 516 (11th Cir. 1993) (yes).

Is it realistic to expect or require, the agency to set a tolerance for human ingestion of a pesticide -- even a zero tolerance -- where the overwhelming scientific evidence shows the substance is dangerous to health but it is presently impossible to totally remove it from food?

The problems highlighted here are not limited to DDT. States have stocked lakes with fish even after finding unacceptable amounts of PCBs and similar hazardous substances in those lakes. What are some of the economic motives for such acts? How much proof is necessary before a ban should issue? See *Matter of General Electric*, Chapter 7, Part C.

Is a substance, like a person, innocent until proven guilty? Or does the need for prudence in protecting the public health outweigh any justification for a presumption of innocence for pesticides or toxic chemicals? Is the criminal-prosecution analogy a good one?

UNITED STATES v. GOODMAN, United States Court of Appeals, Seventh Circuit, 1973. 486 F.2d 847.

Sprecher, Circuit Judge.

Upon the complaints of the United States, the district court * * * permanently enjoined five distributors of fish known as raw chubs from distributing in interstate commerce such fish in which the total amount of DDT and its derivative exceeds the interim limit of 5 parts per million. This limit was established by the [United States Food and Drug Administration (FDA) in 1969] for all fish[.] [T]he Food, Drug and Cosmetic Act (21 U.S.C. §331(a) (FDCA)) prohibits the "introduction or delivery for introduction into interstate commerce of any food . . . that is adulterated . . ." Section 402 of FDCA provides in part that:

> A food shall be deemed to be adulterated * * * if it is a raw agricultural commodity and it bears or contains a pesticide chemical which is unsafe within the meaning of section 346a(a) of this title . . .

A pesticide chemical is deemed "unsafe" by FDCA as follows:

> (a) Any poisonous or deleterious pesticide chemical which is not generally recognized, among experts qualified by scientific training and experience to evaluate the safety of pesticide chemicals, as safe for use, added to a raw agricultural commodity, shall be deemed unsafe for the purposes of the application of clause (2) of section 342(a) of this title unless--
>
> (1) a tolerance . . . has been prescribed [by regulations promulgated] by the Administrator of the Environmental Protection Agency under this section and the quantity of such pesticide chemical in or on the raw agricultural commodity is within the limits of the tolerance so prescribed; or
>
> (2) . . . the pesticide chemical has been exempted from the requirement of a tolerance [by regulations promulgated] by the Administrator under this section.

The parties stipulated that there is neither a regulation nor an exemption covering the situation at issue.

The issue [is,] did the raw chubs distributed by the five defendants contain a poisonous or deleterious pesticide chemical which is not generally recognized, among experts qualified by scientific training and experience to evaluate the safety of pesticide chemicals, as safe for use?* * *

The pesticide DDT[1] became "one of the most widely used chemicals to control various insect populations and to protect agricultural crops from destruction by insects" but "[r]ecent scientific studies have . . . raised serious questions about the effect on the environment and on human health of the continued use of DDT." *Environmental Defense Fund, Inc. v. United States Department of HEW*, 428 F.2d 1083, 1085 (D.C. Cir. 1970).

On April 22, 1969, the FDA issued in the form of a public press release a "guideline" establishing 5 parts per million as the maximum amount of DDT permissible in fish shipped in interstate commerce.* * *

As a result of overwhelming evidence in the form of virtually undisputed expert testimony the district court found that "DDT is not generally recognized, among experts qualified by scientific training and experience to evaluate the safety of pesticide chemicals, to be safe at levels in excess of five ppm in fish for human consumption."

The court concluded that raw chubs containing DDT in excess of 5 parts per million are an adulterated food under 21 U.S.C. §342(a)(2)(B), that the

[1] DDT is an abbreviation for dichloro-diphenyl-trichloroethane.

The pesticide controversy is chronicled in Carson, Silent Spring (1962); Graham, Since Silent Spring (1970).

introduction or delivery for introduction into interstate commerce of such chubs is in violation of §331(a), and such introduction or delivery is subject to restraint pursuant to §332(a).* * *

The only issue upon appeal is whether Section 346a of FDCA makes it mandatory for EPA to promulgate regulations establishing tolerance.

The defendants contended that the use of the word "shall" establishes the mandatory requirement of regulations either (1) to set a tolerance at some level, (2) to exempt a particular pesticide from the necessity of any tolerance, or (3) as further provided in Section 346a(b) to "establish the tolerance * * * at zero level if the scientific data before the Administrator does not justify the establishment of a greater tolerance."* * *

EPA has recently banned almost all agricultural uses of DDT, effective December 31, 1972. This decision represented the culmination of almost three years of intensive administrative inquiry which resulted in the conclusion that the long-range risk of DDT at the present total volume of use is unacceptable and that DDT presents a carcinogenic risk.* * * The language of Section 346a(b) provides for promulgation of regulations establishing tolerances "to the extent necessary to protect the public health." EPA has determined that a regulation for DDT in raw fish is not necessary at this time. In fact, they have refrained from promulgating such a regulation because DDT levels in the environment are in a state of flux, a state partially induced by their other control activities concerning DDT.

In the absence of a tolerance or exemption, the Secretary of HEW[a] is charged with the enforcement of the ban of interstate shipment of adulterated agricultural commodities. 21 U.S.C. § 331(a).

[T]he Commissioner of Food and Drugs, as the delegate of the Secretary of HEW, had the authority under FDCA to abide by the interim guidelines, * * * in so doing his acts were not arbitrary, capricious, an abuse of discretion or otherwise not in accordance with law or without observance of procedure required by law, and, * * * the district court's findings are not clearly erroneous.* * *

Affirmed.

## Notes

The Ninth Circuit later directed the EPA to implement a zero tolerance level for pesticide residues in jams and other processed foods. *Les v. Reilly*, 968 F.2d 985 (9th Cir. 1992), *cert. denied* 113 S.Ct. 1361 (1993). This was based on a provision of the Federal Food, Drugs and Cosmetics Act known as the Delaney Clause, 21 U.S.C.A. § 409, that forbade the use of additives or other substances in processed foods that were found to be carcinogenic to animals. This meant that the EPA could not set a tolerance for such pesticide residues. However, in 1996 Congress repealed the Delaney Clause, allowing tolerance levels to be set and overruling *Les v. Reilly*. See 21 U.S.C.A. § 346a(b)(2)(A).

---

[a] Health, Education and Welfare, the predecessor agency to the United States Department of Health and Human Services.

Enforcement of FIFRA includes provisions prohibiting the sale or distribution of unregistered, adulterated or misbranded pesticides or the use of pesticides inconsistent with their labeling. The Government may indemnify persons damaged economically by the suspension or cancellation of a pesticide's registration, such as farmers who cannot legally market produce on which such a pesticide has been applied. Does this provision encourage enforcement (by eliminating that economic disincentive to banning a pesticide), or deter it (by costing the Government money)?

## State Regulation of Pesticides

The states may, and many do, regulate pesticides in the areas not preempted by FIFRA. Labeling is so preempted, but states may require warnings on lawns notifying the public that pesticides have been applied. *New York Pesticide Coalition Inc. v. New York Dept. of Envtl. Conserv.*, 704 F.Supp. 26 (N.D.N.Y.), aff'd 874 F.2d 115 (2d Cir. 1989). Local laws regulating pesticide use (as opposed to labeling) are not preempted by FIFRA, the Supreme Court held in *Wisconsin Public Intervenor v. Mortier*, 501 U.S. 597, 111 S.Ct. 2476, 115 L.Ed.2d 532 (1991). And states may likewise ban the registration or sale of pesticides even though the EPA allows them. The states also license the applicators of restricted-use pesticides.

## Dioxin and the Agent Orange Litigation

The injuries sustained by military personnel in Vietnam as a result of exposure to the defoliant Agent Orange became the subject of a complex action in the United States District Court in New York's Eastern District, one of the most significant environmental tort actions that are a result of some of the more injudicious uses to which modern advances in chemical engineering have been put.

The plaintiffs instituted the suit as a class action on behalf of all veterans exposed to Agent Orange, members of their families exposed through them, and their estates in cases where the exposure was claimed to have been fatal. The district court held the complaint stated a valid claim for relief under federal common law since the veterans had been exposed to the defoliant while in government employ and the defendants, manufacturers of the chemical, were government contractors. *In re Agent Orange Product Liability Litigation*, 506 F.Supp. 737 (E.D.N.Y. 1979). That order was reversed, 635 F.2d 987 (1981), holding no federal claim for relief exists. The action continued as a suit based on diversity jurisdiction under 28 U.S.C.A. § 1332, which authorizes federal courts to hear cases arising under state law where the plaintiffs reside in different states from the defendants.

Although the defendants impleaded the United States under the Federal Tort Claims Act (28 U.S.C.A. §§ 1346(b), 2674), the district court dismissed the third-party complaints, holding them barred by the *Feres* Doctrine, announced in *Feres v. United States*, 340 U.S. 135, 71 S.Ct. 153, 95 L.Ed. 152 (1950). That rule prevents Armed Forces personnel from suing the United States for damages sustained "incident to their service," and the court held it extends to impleader against the government, immunizing the United States from liability here. 506 F.Supp. 762 (1980). The court went on to hold the action to be a valid class action.

The defendants asserted they produced Agent Orange at the government's command, and that all of the alleged injuries, if caused by Agent Orange at all, were due to the supervening acts of the government over which the defendants had no control and should not be held accountable.

If the action continued as a diversity suit, would that mean 50 different statutes of limitation and rules as to negligence, burden of proof and assumption of risk would apply?

Is it a valid defense for the manufacturers to assert they made Agent Orange under government contract, pursuant to government specifications, for use in a government venture? Would that be a valid defense for a bus manufacturer? Does the fact that the chemical was made for war make it different?

The *Agent Orange* litigation was settled in 1984 with the defendants' agreement to establish a $180 million trust fund -- the largest product liability payment ever. But divided among over 46,000 claimants, it resulted in an average death benefit of $1800 and an average payment for total disability of $5700. Forty-five million dollars were devoted to a foundation to furnish assistance for birth defects and diseases attributed to exposure to Agent Orange.

This disposition left major legal issues unresolved. May veterans obtain government disability payments for Agent Orange exposure-related ailments? Such payments require proof the disability is service-connected. What about the government's liability to the defendants on an indemnity theory? The Supreme Court rejected such liability in *Hercules Inc. v. United States*, 516 U.S. 417, 116 S.Ct. 981, 134 L.Ed.2d 47 (1996), holding the government never agreed to reimburse the manufacturers of Agent Orange for tort liability to third parties.

2. Other Toxic Substances

## The Toxic Substances Control Act

The Toxic Substances Control Act (TSCA), 15 U.S.C.A. §§ 2601-2692, is designed to monitor potentially harmful chemicals at the development stage, before they are unleashed, just as the Food, Drug and Cosmetic Act does for those substances. The statute requires that 90-day notice of intent to use a new chemical, or to use an old chemical in a new way, be filed with the EPA. EPA must then conduct tests and then ban or restrict the new chemical or new use if it finds (1) a significant risk of cancer, mutation or birth defects, (2) the possibility of an unreasonable risk to health and data are insufficient, or (3) that a substantial number of people would be exposed and data are insufficient.

The EPA has power to restrict the use of a new chemical pending testing, but if the manufacturer objects the Agency must obtain a court injunction. Why might a manufacturer *not* object to an EPA restriction pending further testing?

After testing, the EPA may restrict a chemical's sale or use if it finds an unreasonable risk to public health or the environment. It has done so with regard to PCBs (recall the *General Electric* case in Chapter 7). Or the Agency may require labeling to inform the public of risks.

TSCA preempts state action except that states may restrict a substance under the same terms as the EPA has, or ban a substance totally. And state controls on the *disposal* of chemicals are not preempted. The Act exempts substances covered by the Food, Drug and Cosmetic Act, pesticides and other substances regulated pursuant to other federal legislation.

## Cost Benefit Analysis and Risk Assessment

Unquestionably, many toxic and hazardous substances serve, at the very least, extremely useful purposes, protecting our food supply from insects, and meeting our fuel and energy needs, for example.

Whether administrative agencies should employ cost-benefit analysis in deciding whether to ban or restrict the use of a dangerous substance has been the subject of considerable controversy in recent years. How much risk to health is ever justifiable?

In *Industrial Union Department, AFL-CIO v. American Petroleum Institute*, 448 U.S. 607, 100 S.Ct. 2844, 65 L.Ed.2d 1010 (1980), the Supreme Court dealt with this highly charged issue.

The Secretary of Labor, acting pursuant to his authority under the Occupational Safety and Health Act ("OSHA") (29 U.S.C.A. §§ 651-678) to set workplace standards "which most adequately assure . . . that no employee will suffer material impairment of health or functional capacity," lowered the permissible level of airborne exposure to benzene from 10 ppm to 1 ppm on the basis of a causal connection between exposure to benzene and disease.

Justice Stevens, joined by Chief Justice Burger and Justices Stewart and Powell, held that the Secretary had failed to make the threshold finding of a significant risk to health which can be lessened by changing work practices, since lowering exposure to all carcinogens to a minimum feasible level would "impose enormous costs that might produce little, if any, discernible benefit." The agency, he added, improperly adopted an "absolute, no-risk policy" which the Act did not permit.

Justice Rehnquist concurred on the ground that the Act, which authorized the Secretary to set a standard "which most adequately assures, to the extent feasible, * * * that no employee will suffer material impairment of health * * *," was invalid as an unconstitutional delegation of legislative power to the executive branch. Four justices dissented on the grounds that the Secretary's standard was supported by "substantial evidence in the record considered as a whole."

Shortly thereafter, in *American Textile Manufacturers' Inst. v. Donovan*, 452 U.S. 490, 101 S.Ct. 2478, 69 L.Ed.2d 185 (1981), the Court, in a case under the same statute challenging an OSHA standard relating to cotton dust, ingestion of which causes brown lung, held OSHA did not mandate a cost-benefit analysis. In that case the agency met the threshold finding of risk which it had failed to satisfy in the benzene case. Three justices dissented.

The Clean Air Act has been held not to require the Administrator to use cost-benefit analysis in setting standards. *Lead Industries Ass'n v. EPA*, 647 F.2d 1130 (D.C. Cir. 1980). Repeated proposals to write cost-benefit requirements into the statute have been rebuffed by the EPA and Congress. FIFRA and TSCA, in contrast, provide for some degree of cost-benefit analysis. For example, FIFRA requires the EPA to determine whether a pesticide has unreasonable adverse effects "taking into account the economic...costs."

Ironically, cost-benefit analysis, a tool earlier used by conservationists to resist costly Army Corps of Engineers and Bureau of Reclamation dams, stream channelizations and irrigation projects, has been employed in recent years by the opponents of environmental standards.

Should environmental controls consider cost? To what extent? What about risk assessment, as distinguished from weighing costs against benefits? Risk assessment consists of scientifically measuring the degree of risk imposed by exposure to a particular substance. What factors should be taken into account in assessing risk? Should fear of illness be considered? Should exposure over, say, a 40-year period be somehow discounted in assessing risk? See *Corrosion Proof Fittings v. EPA*, 947 F.2d 1201 (5th Cir. 1991) (setting aside TSCA decision for failure to so discount).

Environmental Torts

While a full study of the cases involving environmental tort actions is beyond the scope of this course, it would be remiss not to briefly examine some of the major issues in this rapidly mushrooming area of litigation. We have already looked at the torts of nuisance and riparian rights (Chapters 2 and 3) as well as the Agent Orange litigation relating to a pesticide. It is useful at this point, having also examined the major regulatory statutes dealing with hazardous substances, to consider the types of legal issues that recur in environmental tort actions.

Standard of proof. Is causing the plaintiff to be exposed to a hazardous substance an abnormally dangerous activity incurring strict liability? A few states, including California, have statutes imposing strict liability for exposure to hazardous waste. If neither statute nor common law impose such liability, the plaintiff must prove the defendant was negligent or acted intentionally. Compare *Jersey City Redevelopment Auth. v. PPG Industries*, 655 F.Supp. 1257 (D.N.J. 1987), aff'd 866 F.2d 1411 (strict liability) with *Indiana Harbor Belt R.R.* v. *American Cyanamid Co.*, 916 F.2d 1174 (7th Cir. 1990) (no strict liability; due care could have prevented injury).

Duty of Care. A continuing concern in tort cases is the extent of the defendant's duty of care. Recall the issues in the landmark *Palsgraf v. Long Island Rail Road,* 248 N.Y. 339, 162 N.E. 99 (1928), as to the railroad's duty to a passenger on a station platform. This question recurs in environmental tort litigation.

For example, may commercial fishermen recover for the contamination of a river by a chemical spill? Sport fishermen? Marinas, bait and tackle shops? Seafood merchants? See *Pruitt v. Allied Chemical Co.*, 523 F.Supp. 975 (E.D. Va. 1981) (all may, except seafood merchants); *Leo v. General Electric Co.*, 145 A.D.2d 291, 538 N.Y.S.2d 844 (2d Dept. 1989) (commercial fisherman may; no others were involved). Are lost profits, or emotional distress, recoverable absent physical injury? This varies from state to state.

Proof. Often it is unclear how many defendants contributed to, say, the contamination of water supply caused by hazardous waste leaching from a landfill. Some courts use a market-share theory of liability derived from the DES litigation. Each defendant who might have caused the injury is liable up to its share of the market, but not jointly and severally. See *Hymowitz v. Eli Lilly & Co.*, 73 N.Y.2d 487, 539 N.E.2d 1069, 541 N.Y.S.2d 941 (1989), cert. denied 110 S.Ct. 350; *Sindell v. Abbott Laboratories,* 26 Cal.3d 588, 607 P.2d 924, 163 Cal. Rptr. 132 (1980), cert. denied 449 U.S. 912. Other courts impose joint and several liability; as we have seen, this is done under CERCLA. Which is fairer?

Common law concerns about causation are also being severely tested by toxic tort actions. Historically, the plaintiff had to prove the defendant caused the injury by a preponderance of the evidence. Suppose, however, the medical or other scientific proof is that the defendant is 20% likely to have caused the injury -- say, an increased risk of cancer? Perhaps the defendant should be required to pay that proportion of the damage, particularly where there are numerous plaintiffs.

If the plaintiffs' wells are exposed to hazardous substances through the defendant's negligence, may they recover, absent proof they became ill, for medical monitoring? Emotional distress? Reduced quality of life? See *Ayers v. Township of Jackson,* 106 N.J. 557, 525 A.2d 287 (1987) (medical monitoring allowed; emotional distress damages held to be barred by statute restricting such damages against municipalities); *Sterling v. Velsicol Chemical Corp.*, 647 F.Supp. 303 (W.D. Tenn. 1986) (emotional distress damages allowed). In a suit against a railroad under the Federal Employers' Liability Act, the Supreme Court ruled in *Metro North R.R. v. Buckley,* 521 U.S. 424, 117 S.Ct. 2113, 138 L.Ed.2d 560 (1997), that no cause of action exists for emotional distress based on the fear of illness resulting from exposure to asbestos, in the absence of proven injuries.

Suits against Government. Suit against the United States in tort is governed by the Federal Tort Claims Act, 28 U.S.C.A. §§ 2671-2680. That statute waives the government's sovereign immunity for its torts, but bars jury trials and punitive damages. The Act also exempts "discretionary" acts. Some courts have ruled that government decisions as to how to remediate a landfill, or whether to warn neighbors of nuclear testing, fall within the discretionary exception. Other courts have held the exception inapplicable to federal employees following a specific agency policy. See *Dickerson, Inc. v. United States*, 857 F.2d 1577 (11th Cir. 1989), based on *Berkovitz v. United States*, 486 U.S. 531, 108 S.Ct. 1954, 100 L.Ed.2d 531 (1988) (polio vaccination policy). Similar rules generally limit suits against states.

Does the discretionary acts exception make sense when applied to EPA or Nuclear Regulatory Commission decisions about waste cleanup?

Jurisdiction. The Bhopal, India catastrophe, resulting in thousands of deaths and over 500,000 claimants, stemmed from a discharge of methyl isocyanate, a hazardous air pollutant, at a plant operated by the Indian subsidiary of Union Carbide. The litigation led to the paradox of the Indian plaintiffs, including the government of India, suing in the United States courts, and the American-owned defendant seeking to transfer the actions to India. Why this seeming role reversal?

The court cut the baby in half. It held it clearly had jurisdiction over the defendant, but dismissed the cases based on the forum non conveniens doctrine since virtually all the witnesses were in India, provided the defendant agreed to submit to the jurisdiction of the Indian courts. However, it ordered Union Carbide to also consent to abide by American discovery rules, far broader than those of India. The Court of Appeals affirmed as to all but the discovery requirement. As to that, it held the requirement was one-sided since the plaintiffs were not bound to broader American discovery as well. It ruled the Indian courts were free to permit mutual discovery under the Federal Rules; otherwise both sides were limited to discovery under the narrower Indian procedures. *In re Union Carbide Corp. Gas Plant Disaster*, 809 F.2d 195 (2d Cir. 1987), cert. denied 484 U.S. 871.

The litigation was settled in the Supreme Court of India. The plaintiffs received $470 million--about $800 for each. N.Y. Times, February 15, 1989. Specific amounts were then set by claims commissioners.

Can Bhopal plaintiffs relitigate their claims in the United States? The court held they may not in *Bi v. Union Carbide Chemicals and Plastics, Inc.*, 984 F.2d 582 (2d Cir. 1993), cert. denied 510 U.S. 862, holding the act-of-state doctrine bars a United States court from rehearing the decision of a court in a country with an equitable legal system, such as India's.

A federal court has more recently allowed suit in New York over the alleged oil pollution of forests and rivers in Ecuador by a United States defendant. The court held the forum non conveniens doctrine inappropriate unless the defendant consented to suit in Ecuador. *Jota v. Texaco Inc.*, 157 F.3d 153 (2d Cir. 1998). Correctly decided?

Bankruptcy. Here, as under CERCLA, the effect of the Bankruptcy Code on litigation can lead to complex problems. Tort litigation plunged Johns Manville, a major asbestos manufacturer, into reorganization under Chapter XI of the Bankruptcy Code. Where assets are thus limited, the interests of present and future claimants clash. Should part of a bankrupt corporation's remaining funds be set aside for future claimants, whose symptoms have not yet appeared because of the long latency period of asbestosis and similar diseases? Is this fair to the present claimants, whose recoveries are already sharply circumscribed? To the company's other creditors? Is the solution a CERCLA-type fund? If so, who should finance it--the industry or the public?

Class Actions. Traditionally the courts have frowned on class actions in tort suits, even those involving air crashes and other major disasters. Many courts allow joint discovery and even joint trials. See *Snyder v. Hooker Chemicals & Plastics Corp.*, 104 Misc.2d 735, 429 N.Y.S.2d 153 (Sup. Ct. Niagara Co. 1980). Of late, some courts have permitted class actions for environmental torts, as in the *Agent Orange* and *Jackson Township* cases already noted. Should they? The United States Supreme Court has rejected class actions in two major suits seeking damages against manufacturers of asbestos. In *Amchem Products Inc. v. Windsor*, 521 U.S. 591, 117 S. Ct. 2231, 138 L.Ed.2d 689 (1997), it held there were insufficient common questions of law of fact to warrant a class suit on behalf of over 100,000 future claimants. And in *Ortiz v. Fibreboard Corp.*, 527 U.S. 815, 119 S. Ct. 2295, 144 L.Ed.2d 715 (1999), the Court noted the conflict between present and future claimants (some represented by the same attorneys) and held a "limited fund" class action inappropriate where there was serious question as to whether the fund at issue, an insurance policy, was in fact limited.

Insurance. As under CERCLA, many liability insurance policies have been ruled inapplicable to discharges that are not "sudden and accidental." See *Technicon Electronics Corp. v. American Home Assurance Co.*, 74 N.Y.2d 66, 542 N.E.2d 1048, 544 N.Y.S.2d 531 (1989); *United States Fidelity & Guar. Co. v. Star Fire Coals Inc.*, 856 F.2d 31 (6th Cir. 1988). Is contamination of water supply by leachate flowing from landfill "sudden and accidental"? See *Just v.*

*Land Reclamation Ltd.*, 155 Wis.2d 737, 456 N.W.2d 570 (1990) (yes). Are cleanup costs "damages" within the meaning of a liability policy? See *Avondale Industries, Inc. v. Travelers Indemnity Co.*, 887 F.2d 1200 (2d Cir. 1989), cert. denied 496 U.S. 906 (yes).

Even where insurance exists, some questions remain. Suppose an insured has a policy written by insurer A at the time of exposure of hazardous waste to the plaintiffs, but another policy by insurer B by the time the plaintiffs' injuries manifest themselves. Which company is liable? Are both? See *Keene Corp. v. Insurance Co. of North America*, 667 F.2d 1034 (D.C. Cir. 1981), cert. denied 455 U.S. 1007 (both); *Eagle-Picher Industries v. Liberty Mut. Ins. Co.*, 682 F.2d 12 (1st Cir. 1982), cert. denied 460 U.S. 1028 (manifestation period); *Insurance Co. of North America v. 48 Insulations, Inc.*, 633 F.2d 1212 (6th Cir. 1980), aff'd on reh. 657 F.2d 814, cert. denied 454 U.S. 1109 (exposure period).

Is it fairer to impose liability on the company that was the insurer when the exposure occurred? The later insurer was, or could have been, more aware of the risks, and may have charged a higher premium accordingly, or sought to exclude those risks. But that company did not insure when the exposure took place.

An insurer's duty to defend an insured (*i.e.*, to pay for the insured's defense) is broader than its duty to pay, so that insurers often must furnish lawyers for their insureds even though the insurer may seek to argue that the policy does not cover the acts involved. In such cases, is the insured well represented by a lawyer chosen by the insurer? Should the insured retain its own counsel (at the insurer's expense)?

Workplace Risks. Normally, you will doubtless recall from Torts, an employee may not sue his or her employer for workplace injuries, but is limited to a workers' compensation claim. In compensation the employee need not prove fault, or be concerned about his or her own culpable conduct, but may only recover for medical costs, lost wages, and specific scheduled amounts for loss of a limb or the like. On the other hand, the employee is free to sue the manufacturer of an article causing an injury, as long as the defendant is not the plaintiff's employer.

When the injury is environmental, these rules apply. Some courts, however, have ruled that a manufacturer may defend on the ground that the employer failed to warn its employees of a hazardous substance--a sort of "sophisticated user" defense. See *Goodbar v. Whitehead Bros.*, 591 F.Supp. 552 (W.D.Va. 1984), aff'd *sub nom. Beale v. Hardy*, 769 F.2d 213.

Remember, too, that employees may sue employers for their intentional torts. Intent need not be a specific intent to cause harm, just the usual tort-law intent to cause the reasonable consequences of one's acts. We will look at these issues again in the *Silkwood* case in Chapter 11.

Statute of Limitations. Most states now have statutes of limitations running from discovery (or when a reasonable person would have discovered his or her injury), not from exposure as was once the case. Statutes running from exposure impose Herculean obstacles on plaintiffs in environmental torts, where diseases often have long latency periods.

Does the date of discovery (triggering the statute of limitations) mean the date the illness is discovered, or the date its cause is discovered? In *In re New York County DES Litigation*, 238 A.D.2d 209, 656 N.Y.S.2d 858 (1997), the court held plaintiffs time-barred when they sued only after discovering the cause, ruling the statute runs from the time the injury is discovered.

Discovery and Settlement. Should plaintiffs be able to share with others information obtained through discovery -- depositions, interrogatories and the like? Defendants, fearing a proliferation of suits, often seek a protective order from the court preventing this, as well as adverse publicity, by barring the plaintiff from publicizing the information gained. Is this a valid means of avoiding a biased jury? Or are other techniques available to accomplish that goal? What are they?

Sometimes defendants seek to condition settlements on the plaintiff not disclosing the amount obtained, or any information gained through discovery. Should this be permitted? Are the considerations the same as they are with discovery before the litigation is concluded?

Expert Testimony. For decades courts allowed scientific evidence only when the underlying theory was "generally accepted." *See Frye v. United States,* 293 F. 1013 (D.C. Cir. 1923). More recently the Supreme Court in the landmark *Daubert v. Merrell Dow Pharmaceuticals*, 509 U.S. 579, 113 S. Ct. 2786, 125 L.Ed.2d 469 (1993), held such evidence admissible as long as the trial judge finds it was derived through the scientific method, was subject to testing, and that a reasonable juror could accept it. But not all states have accepted *Daubert*, see, *e.g., People v. Wesley,* 83 N.Y.2d 417, 633 N.E.2d 451, 611 N.Y.S.2d 97 (1994), and much environmental tort litigation occurs in state courts.

Punitive Damages. Punitive damages are often sought in environmental torts. Should they bear a reasonable relationship to the compensatory damages recovered? Should they be limited by state legislatures? Are they consistent with due process, or do juries lack adequate guidelines for setting them? See *Pacific Mut. Life Ins. Co. v. Haslip*, 499 U.S. 1, 111 S.Ct. 1032, 113 L.Ed.2d 1 (1991), holding the trial court's instructions to the jury sufficient to meet due process concerns.

But in *Honda Motor Co. Ltd. v. Oberg,* 512 U.S. 415, 114 S.Ct. 2331, 129 L.Ed.2d 336 (1994), the Court held Oregon's courts failed to adequately review punitive damages set by juries. And in *BMW of North America v. Gore,* 517 U.S. 559, 116 S.Ct. 1589, 134 L.Ed.2d 809 (1996), the Court overturned punitive damages of $2 million based on compensatory damages of $4,000 as so excessive as to deny the defendant due process of law. And in *State Farm Mutual Ins. Co.* v. *Campbell*, 538 U.S. 408, 123 S.Ct. 1513, 155 L.Ed.2d 585 (2003), the Court ruled punitives should almost never exceed nine times the compensatory damages, and that the defendant's wealth should not be an element in setting punitives.

## 10. THE NATIONAL ENVIRONMENTAL POLICY ACT

### Introductory Note

No single statute in the environmental field has had the impact of NEPA, the National Environmental Policy Act (42 U.S.C.A. §§ 4321-4370d). Enacted in 1969, the Act soon dramatically heightened the weapons available to litigants challenging federal projects on environmental grounds. Equally important, it requires all federal agencies to consider the environmental consequences of their actions beforehand. It has also become the model for similar state statutes in about half the states (examined in subsection E of this chapter), as well as statutes in many other countries.

After a statement affirming Congressional policy to restore and maintain environmental quality (§ 2 of the Act; 42 U.S.C.A. § 4321), NEPA specifies (§ 101(b); 42 U.S.C.A. § 4331[b]) that;

> (b) In order to carry out the policy set forth in this chapter, it is the continuing responsibility of the Federal Government to use all practical means, consistent with other essential considerations of national policy, to improve and coordinate Federal plans, functions, programs, and resources to the end that the Nation may --
>
> (1) fulfill the responsibilities of each generation as trustee of the environment for succeeding generations;
> (2) assure for all Americans safe, healthful, productive, and esthetically and culturally pleasing surroundings;
> (3) attain the widest range of beneficial uses of the environment without degradation, risk to health or safety, or other undesirable and unintended consequences;
> (4) preserve important historic, cultural and natural aspects of our national heritage, and maintain, wherever possible, an environment which supports diversity and variety of individual choice;
> (5) achieve a balance between population and resource use which will permit high standards of living and a wide sharing of life's amenities, and
> (6) enhance the quality of renewable resources and approach the maximum attainable recycling of depletable resources.

The keystone of NEPA is its § 102 (42 U.S.C.A. § 4332), which requires all federal government agencies to:

(A) utilize a systematic, interdisciplinary approach which will insure the integrated use of the natural and social sciences and the environmental design arts in planning and in decisionmaking which may have an impact on man's environment;

(B) identify and develop methods and procedures, in consultation with the Council on Environmental Quality * * *, which will insure that presently unqualified environmental amenities and values may be given appropriate consideration in decisionmaking along with economic and technical considerations;

(C) include in every recommendation or report on proposals for legislation and other major Federal actions significantly affecting the quality of the human environment, a detailed statement by the responsible official on--

(i) the environmental impact of the proposed action;

(ii) any adverse environmental effects which cannot be avoided should the proposal be implemented,

(iii) alternatives to the proposed action,

(iv) the relationship between local short-term uses of man environment and the maintenance and enhancement of long-term productivity, and

(v) any irreversible and irretrievable commitments of resources which would be involved in the proposed action should it be implemented.

Prior to making any detailed statement, the responsible Federal official shall consult with and obtain the comments of any Federal agency which has jurisdiction by law or special expertise with respect to any environmental impact involved. Copies of such statement and the comments and views of the appropriate Federal, State, and local agencies, which are authorized to develop and enforce environmental standards, shall be made available to the President, the Council on Environmental Quality and to the public as provided by section 552 of Title 5, and shall accompany the proposal through the existing agency review processes; * * *

(E) study, develop, and describe appropriate alternatives to recommended courses of action in any proposal which involves unresolved conflicts concerning alternative uses of available resources; * * *

## The Background to NEPA's Enactment

By the late 1960s, the environment had become a major legislative issue.[1] Of the 695 bills signed into law during the 91st Congress (1969-70), 121 were listed by the Congressional Research Service as "environment oriented." Meanwhile, several congressional committees issued a number of reports on environmental policy.

In 1969 Senator Jackson reintroduced a bill addressing national environmental protection. The only Senate hearing on this bill occurred on April 16. It was at this point that the concept of an Environmental Impact Statement (EIS) was integrated into the bill. The need for an action-forcing provision to obtain compliance from the federal agencies had been recognized by commentators on environmental protection legislation. During the hearing, in response to a question by Senator Jackson, Lynton K. Caldwell[2] testified that a declaration of environmental policy must be operational to be effective – written so that its principles could not be ignored. Caldwell declared that "a statement of policy by the Congress should at least consider measures to require federal agencies, in submitting proposals, to contain within those proposals an evaluation of their effect upon the state of the environment. William Van Ness and Daniel A. Dreyfus, both of whom were staff members of the Committee on Interior and Insular Affairs, drafted detailed language for the impact statement requirement.

### The Intention of the Framers

The legislative history of NEPA provides a clear indication of the framers' intent when they drafted the Act. From a macro perspective, the framers intended NEPA to be the most important piece of environmental legislation in the history of the United States. According to the Senate sponsor of the law, Senator Jackson, NEPA "is the most important and far-reaching environmental and conservation measure ever enacted by the Congress." Dr. Lynton K. Caldwell, a consultant to the Senate Committee on Interior and Insular Affairs and one of the architects of NEPA, asserts that "the purpose of NEPA, as the Act declares, was to adopt a national policy for the environment within the context of the planetary biosphere. The intent of the legislation is general, but hardly vague . . . ."

NEPA provisions were designed to accomplish four goals. First, the Act includes a statement of national environmental policy. According to Senator Jackson:

> A statement of environmental policy is more than a statement of what we believe as a people and as a nation. It establishes priorities and gives

---

[1] Paul S. Weiland, Amending the National Environmental Policy Act: Federal Environmental Protection in the 21st Century, 12 J. LAND USE AND ENVIRONMENTAL LAW 275 (1997). Reprinted with the permission of the Publisher, Florida State University.

[2] Professor of Political Science, Indiana University, widely regarded as the author of NEPA.

> expression to our national goals and aspirations. It provides a statutory foundation to which administrators may refer to it [sic] for guidance in making decisions which find environmental values in conflict with other values.

The Act's statement of policy is designed to provide federal decision makers with a statutory referent when they are confronted with a situation in which they must balance competing economic, environmental, political, and social concerns.

Second, the Act includes an action-forcing provision designed to ensure that the policies and goals of the Act are carried out by the federal government. This action-forcing provision, the Environmental Impact statement (EIS) was designed to improve decision-making by forcing the federal agencies to consider the environmental implications of their activities. Section 102(2)(C) of NEPA applies to "proposals for legislation and other major federal actions significantly affecting the quality of the human environment."

According to Caldwell, who is credited with the creation of the EIS concept, section 102(2)(C) is designed to promote better planning and decisionmaking. The authors of NEPA decided to include an action-forcing provision in order to ensure that the statement of national environmental policy could be implemented and would not be ignored.

Third, the Act establishes a Council on Environmental Quality (CEQ). The CEQ, according to Senator Jackson, was established to provide: (1) a locus at the highest level for the concerns of environmental management; (2) objective advice to the President and a comprehensive, integrated overview of Federal actions as they related to the environment; and (3) a system for monitoring the state of the environment.

The CEQ was purposely placed in the Executive Office of the President (EOP) and not the White House to lessen the President's control over the Council. The design of the CEQ is based on the design of the Council of Economic Advisers (CEA). In order to understand the logic behind the creation of the CEA and the CEQ, the historical context in which the CEA was proposed must be examined. The Brownlow Report to the President, which preceded the creation of the CEA, provides significant insights into important changes in the Executive Branch that were considered and made under President Franklin D. Roosevelt.[3] The drafters of the Brownlow Report envisioned an executive characterized by a distinction between politics and administration.[4] The purpose of creating a White House staff

---

[3] The Brownlow Report is named for its author, Louis Brownlow, who headed the President's Committee on Administrative Management. *See* PRESIDENT'S COMM. ON ADMIN. MGMT., REPORT OF THE ADMINISTRATIVE MANAGEMENT IN THE FEDERAL GOVERNMENT (1937) [HEREINAFTER BROWNLOW REPORT].

[4] See id. The Brownlow Report states:

Our Presidency unites at least three important functions. From one point of view the President is a political leader. . . .From another point of view he is head of the Nation in the ceremonial sense of the term. . . .From still another point of view the President is the Chief Executive and the administrator within the Federal system and service.

separate from the Executive Office of the President was to institutionalize the politics/administration distinction.

Fourth, the Act requires that the President submit to Congress an annual environmental quality report. This report provides Congress and the people with an assessment of the state of the environment.

Note

Although the environmental impact statement (EIS) requirement of § 102(2)(c) of NEPA has generated the greatest controversy, that provision is limited to "major federal actions significantly affecting the quality of the human environment." The other major sections of NEPA, notably § 102(2)(E) requiring agencies to consider alternatives, are not so limited. But, as the statute makes clear, it applies only to federal action--whether actually performed by a federal agency, or funded or licensed by such an agency.

## A. ENVIRONMENTAL IMPACT STATEMENTS

CALVERT CLIFFS' COORDINATING COMMITTEE v. U.S. ATOMIC ENERGY COMMISSION, United States Court of Appeals, D.C. Circuit, 1971. 449 F.2d 1109, cert. denied., 404 U.S. 942.

J. Skelly Wright, Circuit Judge:

[In this case] we must for the first time interpret the broadest and perhaps most important of the [recently enacted environmental] statutes: the National Environmental Policy Act of 1969 (NEPA). We must assess claims that one of the agencies charged with its administration has failed to live up to the congressional mandate. Our duty, in short, is to see that important legislative purposes, heralded in the halls of Congress, are not lost or misdirected in the vast hallways of the federal bureaucracy.

NEPA, like so much other reform legislation of the last 40 years, is cast in terms of a general mandate and broad delegation of authority to new and old administrative agencies. It takes the major step of requiring all federal agencies to consider values of environmental preservation in their spheres of activity, and it prescribes certain procedural measures to ensure that those values are in fact fully respected. Petitioners argue that rules recently adopted by the Atomic Energy Commission to govern consideration of environmental matters fail to satisfy the rigor demanded by NEPA. * * * We conclude that the Commission's procedural rules do not comply with the congressional policy. Hence we remand these cases for further rule making. * * *

NEPA, first of all, makes environmental protection a part of the mandate of every federal agency and department. The Atomic Energy Commission, for example, had continually asserted, prior to NEPA, that it had no statutory authority to concern itself with the adverse environmental effects of its actions. Now, however, [i]t is not only permitted, but compelled, to take environmental values into account. Perhaps the greatest importance of NEPA is to require the Atomic Energy Commission and other agencies to *consider* environmental issues just as they consider other matters within their mandates. This compulsion is most plainly stated in Section 102. There, "Congress authorizes and directs that, to the fullest extent possible: (1) the policies, regulations, and public laws of the United States shall be interpreted and administered in accordance with the policies set forth in this Act * * * ." Congress also "authorizes and directs" that "(2) all agencies of the Federal Government shall" follow certain rigorous procedures in considering environmental values. * * *

In order to include all possible environmental factors in the decisional equation , agencies must "identify and develop methods and procedures * * * which will insure that presently unquantified environmental amenities and values may be given appropriate consideration in decisionmaking along with economic and technical considerations." "Environmental amenities" will often be in conflict with "economic and technical considerations." To "consider" the former "along with" the latter must involve a balancing process. In some instances environmental costs may outweigh economic and technical benefits and in other instances they may not. But NEPA mandates a rather finely tuned and "systematic" balancing analysis in each instance. * * *

To ensure that the balancing analysis is carried out and given full effect, Section 102(2)(C) requires that responsible officials of all agencies prepare a "detailed statement" covering the impact of particular actions on the environment, the environmental costs which might be avoided, and alternative measures which might alter the cost-benefit equation[,] to aid in the agencies' own decision making process and to advise other interested agencies and the public of the environmental consequences of planned federal action.

* * * Section 102 duties are not inherently flexible. They must be complied with to the fullest extent, unless there is a clear conflict of *statutory* authority. Considerations of administrative difficulty, delay or economic cost will not suffice to strip the section of its fundamental importance.

[In this case w]e must review the Commission's recently promulgated rules which govern consideration of environmental values in all [its] individual decisions. The rules were devised strictly in order to comply with the NEPA procedural requirements--but petitioners argue that [four specific parts of the rules] fall far short of the congressional mandate[:]

(1) [E]nvironmental factors * * * need not be considered by the hearing board conducting an independent review of staff recommendations, unless affirmatively raised by outside parties or staff members. (2) Another part of the procedural rules prohibits any such party from raising non-radiological environmental issues at any hearing if the notice for that hearing appeared in the Federal Register before March 4, 1971. (3) Moreover, the hearing board is prohibited from conducting an independent evaluation and balancing of certain environmental factors if other responsible agencies have already certified that their

own environmental standards are satisfied by the proposed federal action. (4) Finally, the Commission's rules provide that when a construction permit for a facility has been issued before NEPA compliance was required and when an operating license has yet to be issued, the agency will not formally consider environmental factors or require modifications in the proposed facility until the time of the issuance of the operating license.

> [The rules state:]
>
> When no party to a proceeding * * * raises any [environmental] issue * * * such issues will not be considered by the atomic safety and licensing board. Under such circumstances, although the Applicant's Environmental Report, comments thereon, and the Detailed Statement will accompany the application through the Commission's review processes, they will not be received in evidence, and the Commission's responsibilities under the National Environmental Policy Act of 1969 will be carried out in toto outside the hearing process.

The question here is whether the Commission is correct in thinking that its NEPA responsibilities may "be carried out in toto outside the hearing process"--whether it is enough that environmental data and evaluations merely "accompany" an application through the review process, but receive no consideration whatever from the hearing board.

We believe that the Commission's crabbed interpretation of NEPA makes a mockery of the Act. What possible purpose could there be in the Section 102(2)(C) requirement (that the "detailed statement" accompany proposals through agency review processes) if "accompany" means no more than physical proximity--mandating no more than the physical act of passing certain folders and papers, unopened, to reviewing officials along with other folders and papers? What possible purpose could there be in requiring the "detailed statement" to be before hearing boards, if the boards are free to ignore entirely the contents of the statement? NEPA was meant to do more than regulate the flow of papers in the federal bureaucracy. The word "accompany" in Section 102(2)(C) must not be read so narrowly as to make the Act ludicrous. It must, rather, be read to indicate a congressional intent that environmental factors, as compiled in the "detailed statement," be *considered* through agency review processes.

Beyond Section 102(2)(C), NEPA requires that agencies consider the environmental impact of their actions "to the fullest extent possible." The Act is addressed to agencies as a whole, not only to their professional staffs. Compliance to the "*fullest*" possible extent would seem to demand that environmental issues be considered at every important stage in the decision making process concerning a particular action--at every stage where an overall balancing of environmental and nonenvironmental factors is appropriate and where alterations might be made in the proposed action to minimize environmental costs.

* * * The rationale of the Commission's limitation of environmental issues to hearings in which parties affirmatively raise those issues may have been one of economy. It may have been supposed that, whenever there are serious environmental costs overlooked or uncorrected by the staff, some party will intervene to bring those costs to the hearing board's attention. [But it is] unrealistic to assume that there will always be an intervenor with the information, energy and money required to challenge a staff recommendation which ignores environmental costs. NEPA establishes environmental protection as an integral part of the Atomic Energy Commission's basic mandate. The primary responsibility for fulfilling that mandate lies with the Commission. Its responsibility is not simply to sit back, like an umpire, and resolve adversary contentions at the hearing stage. Rather, it must itself take the initiative of considering environmental values at every distinctive and comprehensive stage of the process beyond the staff's evaluation and recommendation.

Congress passed the final version of NEPA in late 1969, and the Act went into full effect on January 1, 1970. Yet the Atomic Energy Commission's rules prohibit any consideration of environmental issues by its hearing boards at proceedings officially noticed before March 4, 1971. This is 14 months after the effective date of NEPA. And the hearings affected may go on for as much as a year longer until final action is taken. The result is that major federal actions having a significant environmental impact may be taken by the Commission, without full NEPA compliance, more than two years after the Act's effective date. In view of the importance of environmental consideration during the agency review process, * * * such a time lag is shocking.

[T]he Commission indicates that it will refer totally to water quality standards devised and administered by state agencies and approved by the federal government under [the Water Quality Improvement Act, predecessor to the Clean Water Act.] [Its] rules provide for similar abdication of NEPA authority to the standards of other agencies; * * * . The most the Commission will do is include a condition in all construction permits and operating licenses requiring compliance with the water quality or other standards set by such agencies. The upshot is that the NEPA procedures, viewed by the Commission as superfluous, will wither away in disuse, applied only to those environmental issues wholly unregulated by any other federal, state or regional body.

We believe the Commission's rule is in fundamental conflict with the basic purpose of the Act. NEPA mandates a case-by-case balancing judgment on the part of federal agencies. In each individual case, the particular economic and technical benefits of planned action must be assessed and then weighed against the environmental costs; alternatives must be considered which would affect the balance of values. * * *

Certification by another agency that its own environmental standards are satisfied involves an entirely different kind of judgment. Such agencies, without overall responsibility for the particular federal action in question, attend only to one aspect of the problem: the magnitude of certain environmental costs. They simply determine whether those costs exceed an allowable amount. * * *

The * * * Commission, abdicating entirely to other agencies' certifications, neglects the mandated balancing analysis. Concerned members of the public are thereby precluded from raising a wide range of environmental issues in order to affect particular Commission decisions. And the special purpose of NEPA is subverted.

[Finally, for nuclear plants] for which construction permits were granted without consideration of environmental issues, but for which operating licenses have yet to be issued[,] [w]hatever environmental damage the reports and statements may reveal, the Commission will allow construction to proceed on the original plans. It will not even consider requiring alterations in those plans (beyond compliance with external standards which would be binding in any event), though the "detailed statements" must contain an analysis of possible alternatives and may suggest relatively inexpensive but highly beneficial changes. [The] Commission has, as a blanket policy, refused to consider the possibility of temporarily halting construction in particular cases pending a full study of a facility's environmental impact. * * *

By refusing to consider requirement of alterations until construction is completed, the Commission may effectively foreclose the environmental protection desired by Congress. * * *

[T]he Commission must revise its rules governing consideration of environmental issues. We do not impose a harsh burden on the Commission. For we require only an exercise of substantive discretion which will protect the environment "to the fullest extent possible." No less is required if the grand congressional purposes underlying NEPA are to become a reality.

## Notes

The environmental impact statement, or EIS, described in *Calvert Cliffs*, has become the key requirement of NEPA and a lever for much litigation seeking to enjoin federal projects for want of an EIS, or because of its inadequacy.

In *Vermont Yankee Nuclear Power Corp.* v. *NRDC*, discussed in Part C and in Chapter 11, Part C, the Supreme Court upheld as reasonable an Atomic Energy Commission (now Nuclear Regulatory Commission) rule requiring intervenors at licensing proceedings raising energy conservation alternatives to a nuclear power plant to meet a "threshold test" of materiality:

> [W]hile it is true that NEPA places upon an agency the obligation to consider every significant aspect of the environmental impact of a proposed action, it is still incumbent upon intervenors who wish to participate to structure their participation so that it is meaningful, so that it alerts the agency to the intervenors' position and contentions. This is especially true when the intervenors are

requesting the agency to embark upon an exploration of uncharted territory, as was the question of energy conservation in the late '60s and early '70s.

> [C]omments must be significant enough to step over a threshold requirement of materiality before any lack of agency response or consideration becomes of concern. The comment cannot merely state that a particular mistake was made; it must show why the mistake was of possible significance in the results. . . . [citation omitted]

Indeed, administrative proceedings should not be a game or a forum to engage in unjustified obstructionism by making cryptic and obscure reference to matters that "ought to be" considered and then, after failing to do more to bring the matter to the agency's attention, seeking to have that agency determination vacated on the ground that the agency failed to consider matters "forcefully presented."

Does this represent a step back from the strong holding of *Calvert Cliffs?*

At what point should an intervenor be deemed to have risen above the cryptic and obscure?

Where is an EIS required? As we have seen, the touchstone under the Act is that the project be "major federal action significantly affecting the quality of the human environment." *Hanly* v. *Kleindienst* illustrates the courts' difficulties with this definition.

HANLY v. KLEINDIENST, United States Court of Appeals, Second Circuit, 1972. 471 F.2d 823, cert. denied 412 U.S. 908 (1973).

Mansfield, Circuit Judge:

This case, which presents serious questions as to the interpretation of the National Environmental Policy Act ("NEPA"), the language of which has been characterized as "opaque" and "woefully ambiguous," is here on appeal for the second time. Following the district court's denial for the second time of a preliminary injunction against construction of a jail and other facilities known as the Metropolitan Correction Center ("MCC") we are called upon to decide whether a redetermination by the General Services Administration ("GSA") that the MCC is not a facility "significantly affecting the quality of the human environment," * * * satisfies the requirements of NEPA and thus renders it unnecessary for GSA to [prepare] a formal, detailed environmental impact statement.

* * * Appellants are members of groups residing or having their businesses in an area of lower Manhattan called "The Manhattan Civic Center" which comprises not

only various courthouses, government buildings and businesses, but also residential housing, including cooperative apartments in two buildings close to the MCC and various similar apartments and tenements in nearby Chinatown. GSA * * * is engaged in the construction of an Annex to the United States Courthouse, Foley Square, Manhattan, located on a site to the east of the Courthouse and immediately to the south of Chinatown and the aforementioned two cooperative apartments. The Annex will consist of two buildings, each approximately 12 stories high, * * * an office building for the staffs of the United States Attorney and the United States Marshal, presently located in the severely overcrowded main Courthouse building, and the other * * * the MCC.

* * * The MCC will serve * * * as the detention center for approximately 449 persons awaiting trial or convicted to short term federal offenses. It will replace the present drastically overcrowded and inadequate facility on West Street, Manhattan, and will be large enough to provide space not only for incarceration but for diagnostic services, and medical, recreational and administrative facilities. Up to 48 of the detainees, mostly those scheduled for release within 30 to 90 days, may participate in a community treatment program whereby they will be permitted to spend part of each day in the city engaged in specific work or study activity, returning to the MCC after completion of each day's business. A new program will provide service for out-patient non-residents. The MCC will be serviced by approximately 130 employees, only 90 of whom will be present on the premises at any one time.

In February 1972, appellants sought injunctive relief against construction of the MCC on the ground that GSA had failed to comply with the mandates of § 102 of NEPA, which requires the preparation of a detailed environmental impact statement with respect to major federal actions "significantly affecting the quality of the human environment."

[T]he application was denied by the district court on the ground that GSA had concluded that the Annex would not have such an effect and that its findings were not "arbitrary" within the meaning of § 10 of the Administrative Procedure Act ("APA"). The Government concedes that construction of the Annex is a "major" federal action within the meaning of § 102 of NEPA.

Upon appeal [*Hanly I*][a] this Court affirmed the district court's order as to the office building but reversed and remanded as to the detention center, the MCC, on the ground that the GSA's threshold determination, which had been set forth in a short memorandum entitled "Environmental Statement" * * * was too meager to satisfy NEPA's requirements. That statement confined itself to a brief evaluation of the availability of utilities, the adequacy of mass transportation, the removal of trash, the absence of a relocation problem and the intention to comply with existing zoning regulations. In remanding the case this Court, although finding the GSA statement sufficient to support its threshold determination with respect to the proposed office building, concluded that the detention center "stands on a different

[a]*Hanly v. Mitchell*, 460 F.2d 640, cert. denied *sub nom. Hanly v. Kleindienst*, 409 U.S. 990 (1972).

footing," and that the agency was required to give attention to other factors that might affect human environment in the area, including the possibility of riots and disturbances in the jail which might expose neighbors to additional noise, the dangers of crime to which neighbors might be exposed as the consequence of housing an out-patient treatment center in the building, possible traffic and parking problems that might be increased by trucks delivering food and supplies and by vans taking prisoners to and from the Eastern District and New Jersey District Courts, and the need for parking space for prison personnel and accommodations for visitors, including lawyers or members of the family.

We further noted that in making the threshold determination authorized by § 102(2)(C) of NEPA the agency must "affirmatively develop a reviewable environmental record" in lieu of limiting itself to perfunctory conclusions with respect to the MCC.

[A] new threshold determination in the form of a 25-page "Assessment of the Environmental Impact" ("Assessment" herein) was made by the GSA[.] This document * * * analyzes the size, exact location, and proposed use of the MCC; its design features, construction and esthetic relationship to its surrounding; the extent to which its occupants and activities conducted in it will be visible by the community; the estimated effects of its operation upon traffic, public transit and parking facilities; its approximate population, including detainees and employees; its effect on the level of noise, smoke, dirt, obnoxious odors, sewage and solid waste removal; and its energy demands. It also sets forth possible alternatives, concluding that there is none that is satisfactory. Upon the basis of this Assessment * * * concluded * * * that the MCC was not an action significantly affecting the quality of the human environment.

[A]ppellants renewed their application * * * for a preliminary injunction, arguing that the Assessment * * * amounted to nothing more than a rewrite of the earlier statement that had been found inadequate, and that some of its findings were incorrect or insufficient. * * * Judge Tenney, in a careful opinion, denied appellants' motions, from which the present appeal was taken. * * *

We are confronted with a question [as to] the standard of review that must be applied by us in reviewing GSA's action. The action involves both a question of law--the meaning of the word "significantly" in the statutory phrase "significantly affecting the quality of the human environment"--and a question of fact--whether the MCC will have a "significantly" adverse environmental impact. Strictly speaking, our function as a reviewing court is to determine *de novo* "all relevant questions of law," Administrative Procedure Act § 10e, and, with respect to GSA's factual determinations, to determin[e] [only] whether its findings are "arbitrary, capricious, an abuse of discretion, or otherwise not in accordance with law" or "without observance of procedure required by law," APA § 10(e).

[W]e believe that the appropriate criterion in the present case is the "arbitrary, capricious" standard established by the Administrative Procedure Act, since the meaning of the term "significantly" as used in § 102(2)(C) of NEPA can be isolated as a question of law.

* * * Upon attempting, according to the foregoing standard, to interpret the amorphous term "significantly," as it is used in § 102(2)(C), we [note that the] [g]uidelines issued by the [Council of Environmental Quality (CEQ)] suggest that a formal impact statement should be prepared with respect to "proposed actions, the environmental impact of which is likely to be highly controversial."

However, the term "controversial" apparently refers to cases where a substantial dispute exists as to the size, nature or effect of the major federal action rather than to the existence of opposition to a use, the effect of which is relatively undisputed.[1a] * * *

In the absence of any Congressional or administrative interpretation of the term, we are persuaded that in deciding whether a major federal action will "significantly" affect the quality of the human environment the agency in charge, although vested with broad discretion, should normally be required to review the proposed action in the light of at least two relevant facts: (1) the extent to which the action will cause adverse environmental effects in excess of those created by existing uses in the area affected by it, and (2) the absolute quantitative adverse environmental effects of the action itself, including the cumulative harm that results from its contribution to existing adverse conditions or uses in the affected area. Where conduct conforms to existing uses, its adverse consequences will usually be less significant than when it represents a radical change. * * * For instance, one more highway in an area honeycombed with roads usually has less of an adverse impact than if it were constructed through roadless public park.

[But] it must be recognized that even a slight increase in adverse conditions that form an existing environmental milieu may sometimes threaten harm that is significant. One more factory polluting air and water in an area zoned for industrial use may represent the straw that breaks the back of the environmental camel. Hence the absolute, as well as comparative, effects of a major federal action must be considered.

[Here,] [t]he office building would not differ substantially from the makeup of the surrounding area. Nor would it in absolute terms give rise to sizeable adverse environmental effects. Most of the employees occupying the building would merely be transferred from the existing Courthouse where the newly created space will be used primarily for courtrooms and desperately needed office space for court personnel. On the other hand, the proposed jail * * * might have adverse effects differing both qualitatively and quantatively from those associated with existing uses in the area. Moreover there was insufficient evidence that the absolute

---

[1a]To require an impact statement whenever a threshold determination dispensing with one is likely to face a court challenge, as the dissent suggests, would surrender the determination to opponents of a major federal action, no matter how insignificant its environmental effect when viewed objectively. Experience in local zoning disputes demonstrates that it is the rare case where some neighbors do not oppose a project, no matter how beneficial, and that their opposition is usually accompanied by threats of litigation.

environmental effect with respect to the jail had been analyzed and considered by the GSA. * * *

The GSA's finding that the MCC would harmonize architecturally with existing buildings in the area, * * * is supported by details of the proposed building, architectural renditions, and photographs of the area.

[T]here will be no fortress walls or unsightly steel-barred windows[.] In short, the building will not look like a correctional center.

The Assessment further describes efforts that will be made to minimize any contact between detainees and members of the community. In addition to the recessed, darkened windows, all prisoners will enter the building through an entrance * * * located on the side opposite from and out of view of neighborhood residential apartments. Although there will be a roof-top recreational area for detainees, a 20-foot wall will minimize their visibility from the apartments.

The Assessment further notes that any increase in traffic from MCC will be extremely slight. One van will take and return detainees on one daily round trip during weekdays to the Eastern District Courthouse and to the Newark District Courthouse. * * *

The GSA Assessment projected on the basis of past experience that approximately 130 visitors will arrive per day with no more than 20 on the premises at any one time. This would not impose any excessive burden on mass transportation facilities[.] There will be only four truck deliveries of supplies per day to the premises.

The windows of the MCC are designed to minimize any noise from within the premises, in addition to which detainees will be under constant supervision when outside on the roof-top for recreational purposes. During the past five years there have been only two small inside disturbances at the present detention facility at West Street, Manhattan, and three outside disturbances, the latter confined to non-violent picketing, marching and the like, incidents which have been common occurrence in the Foley Square area during the same period.

The Assessment makes clear that the MCC will not produce any unusual or excessive amounts of smoke, dirt, obnoxious odors, solid waste, or other forms of pollution. The utilities required to heat and air-condition the building are readily available and the MCC is designed to incorporate energy-saving features, so that no excessive power demands are posed.

* * * Appellants offer little or no evidence to contradict the detailed facts found by the GSA. For the most part their opposition is based upon a psychological distaste for having a jail located so close to residential apartments, which is understandable enough. It is doubtful whether psychological and sociological effects upon neighbors constitute the type of factors that may be considered in making such a determination since they do not lend themselves to measurement. However we need not decide that issue because these apartments were constructed within two or three blocks of another existing jail, The Manhattan House of Detention for Men, which is much larger than the proposed MCC and houses approximately 1,200 prisoners. Furthermore the area in which the MCC is located

has at all times been zoned by the City of New York as a commercial district designed to provide for a wide range of uses, *specifically including "Prisons."* * * *

Despite the GSA's scrupulous efforts the appellants do present one or two factual issues that merit further consideration and findings by the GSA. One bears on the possibility that the MCC will substantially increase the risk of crime in the immediate area, a relevant factor as to which the Assessment fails to make an outright finding despite the direction to do so in *Hanly I.* Appellants urge that the Community Treatment Program and the program for observation and study of non-resident out-patients will endanger the health and safety of the immediate area by exposing neighbors and passersby to drug addicts visiting the MCC for drug maintenance and to drug pushers and hangers-on who would inevitably frequent the vicinity of a drug maintenance center. If the MCC were to be used as a drug treatment center, the potential increase in crime might tip the scales in favor a mandatory detailed impact statement. The Government has assured us by post-argument letter addressed to the Court that:

> Neither the anticipated nonresident presentence study program nor any program to be conducted within the Metropolitan Correction Center will include drug maintenance.

While we do not question the Government's good faith, a finding in the matter by GSA is essential, since the Assessment is ambiguous as to the scope of the non-resident out-patient observation program and makes no finding on the subject of whether the MCC will increase the risk of crime in the community.[2] In addition one of the appellants, Sien Wei Liu, has furnished to the district court an affidavit taking issue with certain facts found by the GSA, including the visibility of the jail's rear entrance from nearby apartment buildings, the distance of the MCC from the closest apartment, the possible use of nearby overcrowded community medical facilities by prisoners, and the claim that certain city officials are opposed to the location of the MCC.

[W]e find that § 102(2)(E) was complied with insofar as the GSA specifically considered the alternatives to continuing operation at the present facility at West Street and evaluated the selected site as compared with other specified possibilities. Although the assessment of the alternative sites was not as intensive as we might hope, its failure to analyze them in further detail does not warrant reversal.

A more serious question is raised by the GSA's failure to comply with § 102(2)(B), which requires the agency to "identify and develop methods and procedures . . . which will insure that presently unquantified environmental amenities and values may be given appropriate consideration in decisionmaking along with economic and technical considerations." Since an agency, in making a

---

[2] If the Government should later change the use of the premises to include a drug treatment center, or any other change that might significantly affect the quality of the human environment, then a detailed § 102(C) impact statement would be required at that time. See [CEQ] Guidelines § 11.

threshold determination as to the "significance" of an action, is called upon to review in a general fashion the same factors that would be studied in depth for preparation of a detailed environmental impact statement, § 102(2)(B) requires that some rudimentary procedures be designed to assure a fair and informed preliminary decision. Otherwise the agency, lacking essential information, might frustrate the purpose of NEPA by a threshold determination that an impact statement is unnecessary. Furthermore, an adequate record serves to preclude later changes in use without consideration of their environmental significance as required by NEPA.

Where a proposed major federal action may affect the sensibilities of a neighborhood, the prudent course would be for the agency in charge, before making a threshold decision, to give notice to the community of the contemplated action and to accept all pertinent information proffered by concerned citizens with respect to it. Furthermore, in line with the procedure usually followed in zoning disputes, particularly where emotions are likely to be aroused by fears, or rumors of misinformation, a public hearing serves the dual purpose of enabling the agency to obtain all relevant data and to satisfy the community that its views are being considered. However, neither NEPA nor any other federal statute mandates the specific type of procedure to be followed by federal agencies. There is no statutory requirement that a public hearing be held[.]

* * * We now * * * hold that before a preliminary or threshold determination of significance is made the responsible agency must give notice to the public of the proposed major federal action and an opportunity to submit relevant facts which might bear upon the agency's threshold decision. We do not suggest that a full-fledged formal hearing must be provided before each such determination is made, although it should be apparent that in may cases such a hearing would be advisable for reasons already indicated. The necessity for a hearing will depend greatly upon the circumstances surrounding the particular proposed action and upon the likelihood that a hearing will be more effective than other methods in developing relevant information and an understanding of the proposed action. The precise procedural steps to be adopted are better left to the agency[.]

In view of the Assessment's failure to make findings with respect to the possible existence of a drug maintenance program at the MCC, the increased risk of crime that might result from the operation of the MCC, and the fact that appellants have challenged certain findings of fact, we remand the case for the purpose of requiring the GSA to make a further investigation of these issues, with directions to accept from appellants and other concerned citizens such further evidence as they may proffer within a reasonable period, to make supplemental findings with respect to these issues, and to redetermine whether the MCC "significantly affects the quality of the human environment." If, as a result of such further investigation, the GSA concludes that a detailed environment impact statement is required, a preliminary injunction will be granted restraining further construction of the MCC until the agency has complied with the procedures required by § 102(2)(C) of NEPA. In the event that the GSA reaffirms its initial determination, the district court will determine, should a further request be made, whether preliminary injunctive relief is warranted. * * *

Friendly, Chief Judge (dissenting):

One of the purposes of the impact statement is to insure that the relevant environmental data are before the agency and considered by it prior to the decision to commit Federal resources to the project; the statute must not be construed so as to allow the agency to make its decision in a doubtful case without the relevant data or a detailed study of it. * * * What Congress was trying to say was "You don't need to make an impact statement, with the consequent expense and delay, when there is no sensible reason for making one." I thus agree with [the] view that "a statement is required whenever the action *arguably* will have an adverse environmental impact," * * * with the qualification, doubtless intended, that the matter must be *fairly* arguable. * * *

The CEQ Guidelines lend additional support to the conclusion that the threshold determination of significance must be set at a low level. They provide and they state[:]

> Proposed actions, the environmental impact of which is likely to be highly controversial, should be covered in all cases. * * *

* * * I would think it clear that this includes action which the agency should know is likely to arouse intense opposition, even if the actual environmental impact is readily apparent.

[T]he CEQ may well have had in mind that when action having some environmental impact "is likely to be highly controversial," an agency assessment that the action does not constitute major Federal action significantly affecting the environment is almost certain to evoke challenge in the courts. The CEQ could well have believed that rather than to incur the delay incident to such a suit, and the further delay if a court sustains the challenge--both vividly illustrated in this case where nearly two years have elapsed since the initial assessment that an impact statement was not required and a further remand is being directed--the agency would do better to prepare an impact statement in the first instance. In addition to possibly providing new information making reconsideration or modification of the project appropriate, such a policy has the added benefits of allowing opponents to blow off steam and giving them the sense that their objections have been considered--an important purpose of NEPA.

[But even a]ccepting the majority's standard of review, I would think that, even with the fuller assessment here before us, the GSA could not reasonably conclude that the MCC does not entail potentially significant environmental effects. I see no ground for the majority's doubt "whether psychological and sociological effects upon neighbors constitute the type of factors that may be considered in making such a determination [of significant environmental effect] since they do not lend themselves to measurement." [NEPA] directs that "presently unquantified environmental amenities and values.... be given appropriate consideration in decisionmaking along with economic and technical considerations." I cannot believe my brothers would entertain the same doubt concerning the relevance of psychological and sociological factors if a building like the MCC were to be constructed at Park Avenue and East 72nd Street, assuming that zoning allowed it.

The energies my brothers would require GSA to devote to still a third assessment designed to show that an impact statement is not needed would better be devoted to making one.

I would reverse and direct the issuance of an injunction until a reasonable period after the making of an impact statement.

## Notes

Following this decision the GSA prepared a supplemental environmental assessment and again concluded the possibility of drug sales and increased crime would not create significant impact so as to trigger the EIS requirement. This time the courts agreed. 484 F.2d 448 (2d Cir. 1973), cert. den. 416 U.S. 936.

The CEQ regulations referred to in *Hanly* v. *Kleindienst* are of vital importance in interpreting NEPA. The regulations speak of the "context" and "intensity" of the project. 40 CFR § 1508.27. Do these terms embody the two criteria in the decision of "adverse environmental effects in excess of those created by existing uses" and "the absolute quantitative environmental effects of the action"?

Does the work "major" in "major federal action" add anything to "significantly affecting the quality of the human environment"? Could there be minor government action having a significant environmental impact? If not, is the word "major" redundant? See *Minnesota Pub. Int. Research Group* v. *Butz*, 498 F.2d 1314 (8th Cir. 1974), cert. den. 430 U.S. 922, holding, effect, that federal action "significantly affecting" the environment is "major." This view is now mandated by the CEQ regulations. 40 CFR § 1508.18: "Major reinforces but does not have a meaning independent of significantly."

Should the controversial nature of the federal action by a touchstone for significant environmental impact? Or does that give the ball to the project's opponents, as the majority in *Hanly* v. *Kleindienst* suggests?

A related question, also touched on in *Hanly* v. *Kleindienst*, is whether psychological impacts (the fear engendered by a project) are environmental impacts under NEPA. The Supreme Court ruled in *Metropolitan Edison Co. v. People Against Nuclear Energy,* 460 U.S. 766, 103 S.Ct. 1556, 75 L.Ed.2d 534 (1983) (involving the reopening of the Three Mile Island nuclear power plant after its closing following an accident), that an EIS need not consider psychological concerns.

Should the test for reviewing an agency's decision not to prepare an EIS be whether it was arbitrary or capricious? Or is the issue one of law, which a court should review *de novo*?

Can "no action" be federal action triggering an EIS? In *National Helium Corp.* v. *Morton,* 455 F.2d 650 (10th Cir. 1971), the Department of the Interior decided to no longer stockpile helium.. The company which had supplied it contended an EIS was required. It argued the environmental impact was the depletion of helium resources available to the government if its purchases ended. Helium is a by-product of natural gas; if not extracted, it disappears into the air. The court held:

> The Secretary in the instant case proposes to take an action which has environmental consequences, namely rapid depletion of the helium resources of the country. Whether the Secretary's proposed action has significant long-range consequences, or whether the environmental effects are insignificant in relationship to the countervailing government interests, are decisions which are left to the Secretary. The important thing is that he must consider the problem.

Is socio-economic impact, such as the loss of employment and relocation of personnel if an Air Force base is closed, environmental impact within NEPA? See *Jackson County* v. *Jones,* 571 F.2d 1004 (8th Cir. 1978) (yes; the Court found that the physical environment of two cities would be affected); *City of Rochester* v. *United States Postal Service,* 541 F.2d 967 (2d Cir. 1976) (yes, as to relocation of the city's main post office); but see *Image of Greater San Antonio* v. *Brown*, 570 F.2d 517 (5th Cir. 1978) (socio-economic impact requires an EIS only where the primary impact is traditionally environmental, such as air or water quality).

What about a Navy decision to store nuclear weapons at a post near historic sites and the habitat of an endangered species? See *Weinberger* v. *Catholic Action of Hawaii*, 454 U.S. 139, 102 S.Ct. 197, 70 L.Ed.2d 298 (1981), holding that since information regarding nuclear weapons is confidential any statement would have to be a "hypothetical EIS," which NEPA does not require. The Court agreed an internal EIS would be needed for storage of nuclear weapons, but held:

> It does not follow, however, that the Navy is required to prepare an EIS in this case. The Navy is not required to prepare an EIS regarding the hazards of storing nuclear weapons at West Loch simply because the facility is "nuclear capable." As we held in *Kleppe* v. *Sierra Club*, [*infra*,] an EIS need not be prepared simply because a project is *contemplated*, but only when the project is *proposed*. To say that the West Loch facility is "nuclear capable" is to say little more than that the Navy has contemplated the possibility that nuclear weapons of whatever variety, may at some time be stored here. It is the proposal to *store* nuclear weapons at West Loch that triggers the Navy's obligation to prepare an EIS. Due to national security reasons, however, the Navy can neither admit nor

> deny that it proposes to store nuclear weapons at West Loch. In this case, therefore, it has not been and cannot be established that the Navy has proposed the only action that would require the preparation of an EIS dealing with the environmental consequences of nuclear weapons storage at West Loch.
>
> Ultimately, whether or not the Navy has complied with NEPA "to the fullest extent possible" is beyond judicial scrutiny in this case. In other circumstances, we have held that "public policy forbids the maintenance of any suit in a court of justice, the trial of which would inevitably lead to the disclosure of matters which the law itself regards as confidential, and respecting which it will not allow the confidence to be violated." We confront a similar situation in the instant case.

How can NEPA be enforced to insure that defense agencies prepare at least an internal EIS before making a decision with significant environmental impacts, such as to store nuclear weapons? Should the Act be amended to deal with this problem? Is it sufficient for the court to admit that whether the Navy has satisfied NEPA is "beyond judicial scrutiny in this case"?

Although § 102(c) mandates an EIS for proposals for legislation, as well as major federal actions, which significantly affect the environment, the Supreme Court has held federal agencies' budget requests do not require an EIS. *Andrus* v. *Sierra Club*, 442 U.S. 347, 99 S. Ct. 2335, 60 L.Ed.2d 943 (1979). The court relied heavily, as it did in *Hanly* v. *Kleindienst*, on the CEQ's regulations regarding the preparation of impact statements, which exempted budget requests. Although not then binding on federal agencies, the CEQ regulations were found by the court to be highly persuasive.

The CEQ, referred to here, is the Council on Environmental Quality, a small but important agency whose responsibility under NEPA is to develop and recommend national policies and review government agency programs with an eye to furthering the goals of the Act. For a vivid instance of CEQ influence in rejecting an EIS, see *National Resources Defense Council, Inc.* v. *Nuclear Regulatory Commission,* 539 F.2d 824 (2d Cir. 1976), vac. to consider mootness 434 U.S. 1030:

> [T]he President's Council on Environmental Quality ("CEQ"), by letter, informed the Commission that in its opinion [the draft EIS] was inadequate, particularly since it failed to address adequately the special dangers of sabotage and theft posed by large-scale transportation of plutonium materials. The CEQ recommended that these special problems be addressed before any final decision on wide-scale use. Further, the CEQ directed the Commission to avoid taking any licensing steps in the interim period which could result in the foreclosure of alternative safeguards or which could result in

unnecessary "grandfathering" of existing facilities' safeguards systems.

As we have seen, the CEQ has adopted regulations implementing NEPA which bind federal agencies (40 CFR §§ 1500-1517) and its authority to recommend national policies and review programs, together with its prestige, gave it sufficient clout in this instance to affect a major ongoing program of the Nuclear Regulatory Commission.

Does NEPA apply to United States government actions beyond the borders of the country? See *Environmental Defense Fund, Inc. v. National Science Foundation*, 986 F.2d 528 (D.C.Cir. 1993) (yes, at least as to Antarctica, an area without sovereignty). Would it apply to United States funded projects in other sovereign countries?

Are treaties such as GATT and NAFTA, discussed in Chapter 4, federal actions significantly affecting the environment under NEPA? See *Public Citizen v. Office of U.S. Trade Rep.*, 804 F. Supp. 385 (D.D.C. 1992) (GATT amendments: environmental injury too remote and speculative); *Public Citizen v. United States Trade Rep.,* 5 F.3d 549 (D.C.Cir. 1993), cert. denied 510 U.S. 1041 (NAFTA: held plaintiff lacked standing, but also suggested in dicta that President probably not a federal agency and therefore not subject to NEPA).

A devastating event of low probability may not qualify as significantly affecting the environment under the Act. *City of New York v. Department of Transportation*, 715 F.2d 732 (2d Cir. 1983), cert. denied 465 U.S. 1055 (low likelihood of traffic accident severe enough to cause nuclear materials to spill).

KLEPPE v. SIERRA CLUB, Supreme Court of the United States, 1976. 427 U.S. 390, 96 S.Ct. 2718, 49 L.Ed.2d 576.

Justice Powell:

[S]ince 1973 the [Interior] Department has engaged in a complete review of its coal-leasing program for the entire Nation. On February 17 of that year the Secretary announced the review and announced also that during study a "short-term leasing policy" would prevail, under which new leasing would be restricted to narrowly defined circumstances and even then allowed only when an environmental impact statement had been prepared if required under NEPA. The purpose of the program review was to study the environmental impact of the Department's entire range of coal-related activities and to develop a planning system to guide the national leasing program. The impact statement, known as the "coal Programmatic EIS," * * * proposed a new leasing program based on a complex planning system and assessed the prospective environmental impact of the new program as well as the alternatives to it. * * *

The major issue [is] whether NEPA requires petitioners to prepare an environmental impact statement on the entire Northern Great Plains region. [We hold it does not.] [Section] 102(2)(C) requires an impact statement [for "] major Federal actions significantly affecting the quality of the human environment." [T]he controlling phrase in this section of the Act, for this case, is "major Federal actions." Respondents can prevail only if there has been a report or recommendation on a proposal for major federal action with respect to the Northern Great Plains region. Our statement of the relevant facts shows there has been none; instead, all proposals are for actions of either local or national scope. * * *

The local actions are the decisions by the various petitioners to issue a lease, approve a mining plan, issue a right-of-way permit, or take other action to allow private activity at some point within the region[.] [Clearly,] an impact statement must be included in the report or recommendation on a proposal for such action if the private activity to be permitted is one "significantly affecting the quality of the human environment" within the meaning of § 102(2)(C). * * *

The [Department does] not dispute this requirement in this case, and indeed ha[s] prepared impact statements on several proposed actions of this type in the Northern Great Plains. Similarly, [it] agreed that § 102(2)(C) required the Coal Programmatic EIS that was prepared in tandem with the new national coal-leasing program and included as part of the final report on the proposal for adoption of that program. [Its] admission is well made, for the new leasing program is a coherent plan of national scope, and its adoption surely has significant environmental consequences.

But there is no evidence in the record of an action or a proposal for an action of regional scope. The District Court, in fact, expressly found that there was no existing or proposed plan or program on the part of the Federal Government for the regional development of the area of any plan or program to develop or encourage [coal] development of the Northern Great Plains. That court found no evidence that the individual coal development projects undertaken or proposed by private industry and public utilities in that part of the country are integrated into a plan or otherwise interrelated. * * *

Quite apart from the fact that the statutory language requires an impact statement only in the event of a proposed action, respondents' desire for a regional environmental impact statement cannot be met for practical reasons. In the absence of a proposal for a regional plan of development, there is nothing that could by the subject of the analysis envisioned by the statute for an impact statement. * * *

The Court of Appeals, in reversing the District Court, did not find that there was a regional plan or program for development of the Northern Great Plains region. It accepted all of the District Court's findings of fact, but concluded nevertheless that the petitioners "contemplated" a regional plan or program[.] We think the court was mistaken in concluding, on the record before it, that the petitioners were "contemplating" a regional development plan or program. It considered the several studies undertaken by the [Department] to represent attempts to control development on a regional scale. This conclusion was based on a finding by the District Court that those studies, as well as the new national coal-leasing policy, were "attempts to control development by individual companies in a manner consistent with the policies and procedures of [NEPA."] But in context, that finding meant only that the named studies were efforts to gain background environmental information for subsequent application in the decisionmaking with respect to individual coal-related projects.

Even had the record justified a finding that a regional program was contemplated by the [Department], the legal conclusion drawn by the Court of Appeals cannot be squared with the Act. The court recognized that the mere "contemplation" of certain action is not sufficient to require an impact statement. But it believed the statute nevertheless empowers a court to require the preparation of an impact statement to begin at some point prior to the formal recommendation or report on a proposal. The Court of Appeals accordingly revised its own four-part "balancing" test for determining when, during the contemplation of a plan or other type of federal action, an agency must begin a statement. The factors to be considered were identified as the likelihood and imminence of the program's coming to fruition, the extent to which information is available on the effects of implementing the expected program and on alternatives thereto, the extent to which irretrievable commitments are being made and options precluded "as refinement of the proposal progresses," and the severity of the environmental effects should the action be implemented. * * * The court's reasoning and action find no support in the language or legislative history of NEPA. The statute clearly states when an impact statement is required, and mentions nothing about a balancing of factors. Rather, as we noted last Term, under the first sentence of § 102(2)(C) the moment at which an agency must have a final statement ready "is the time at which it makes a recommendation or report on a *proposal* for federal action." *Aberdeen & Rockfish R. Co.* v. *SCRAP* (SCRAP II).[a] A court has no authority to depart from the statutory language and, by a balancing of court-devised factors, determine a point during the termination process of a potential proposal at which an impact statement *should be prepared.* Such an assertion of judicial authority would leave the agencies uncertain as to their procedural duties under NEPA, would invite judicial involvement in the day-to-day decisionmaking process of the agencies, and would invite litigation. As the contemplation of a project and the accompanying study thereof do not necessarily result in a proposal for major federal action, it may be assumed that the balancing process devised by the Court of Appeals also would result in the preparation of a good many unnecessary impact statements.

[Alternatively, r]espondents insist that, even without a comprehensive federal plan for the development of the Northern Great Plains, a "regional" impact statement nevertheless is required on all coal-related projects in the region because they are intimately related.

[We agree] with respondents' basic premise that § 102(2)(C) may require a comprehensive impact statement in certain situations where several proposed actions are pending at the same time. * * * A comprehensive impact statement may be necessary in some cases [; for example,] when several proposals for coal-related

[a] Discussed later in the section.

actions that will have cumulative or synergistic environmental impact upon a region are pending concurrently before an agency, their environmental consequences must be considered together. Only through comprehensive consideration of pending proposals can the agency evaluate different courses of action. [But that] does not require acceptance of their conclusion that all proposed coal-related actions in the Northern Great Plains region are so "related" as to require their analysis in a single comprehensive impact statement.

Respondents concede * * * that to prevail they must show that petitioners have acted arbitrarily in refusing to prepare one comprehensive statement on this entire region, and we agree.

* * *Absent a showing of arbitrary action, we must assume that the agencies have exercised this discretion appropriately. Respondents have made no showing to the contrary.

Respondents' basic argument is that one comprehensive statement on the Northern Great Plains is required because all coal-related activity in that region is "programmatically," "geographically," and "environmentally" related [, *i.e.*, that proper] study in this area [should be] on a regional basis. Respondents point primarily to the [Northern Great Plains Resources Program study, or] NGPRP, which claim * * * focused on the region described in the complaint. [But] its irrelevance to the delineation of an appropriate area for analysis in a comprehensive impact statement has been well stated by the Secretary:

> Resource studies [like the NGPRP] are one of many analytical tools employed by the Department to inform itself as to general resource availability, resource need and general environmental considerations so that it can intelligently determine the scope of environmental analysis and review specific actions it may take. Simply put, resource studies are a prelude to informed agency planning, and provide the data base on which the Department may decide to take specific actions for which impact statements are prepared. The scope of environmental impact statements seldom coincide[s] with that of a given resource study, since the statements evolve from specific proposals for federal action while the studies simply provide an educational backdrop.

As for the alleged "environmental" relationship, respondents contend that the coal-related projects "will produce a wide variety of cumulative environmental impacts" throughout the Northern Great Plains region. They described them as follows: diminished availability of water, air and water pollution, increases in population and industrial densities, and perhaps even climatic changes. Cumulative environmental impacts are, indeed, what require a comprehensive impact statement. But determination of the extent and effect of these factors, and particularly identification of the geographic area within which they may occur, is a task assigned to the special competency of the appropriate agencies. [The Department] dispute[s]

respondents' contentions that the interrelationship of environmental impacts is region-wide and, as respondents' own submissions indicate, [it] appear[s] to have determined that the appropriate scope of comprehensive statements should be based on basins, drainage areas, and other factors.
* * *We cannot say that [the Department's] choices are arbitrary. [R]espondents' contention as to the relationship between all proposed coal-related projects in the Northern Great Plains region does not require that [the Department] prepare one comprehensive impact statement covering all before proceeding to approve specific pending applications.

Justices Marshall and Brennan concurred in part and dissented in part.

## Notes

Is a study "devoted entirely to the environment" (in the Court's language) under another statute, such as the Interior Department's study in *Kleppe* v. *Sierra Club*, a substitute for an EIS under NEPA? What about the provisions of NEPA requiring specific items, such as the irretrievable commitment of resources, and ways of mitigating impact on the environment, which NEPA demands that an EIS consider?

How much does *Kleppe* v. *Sierra Club* turn on the fact that the Interior Department both prepared a programmatic EIS on its nation-wide coal leasing and intended to write site-specific EISs for each lease with significant environmental impact? Would the Court reach a different result in a case without those features?

## Environmental Impact Statement Procedure

Once an agency determines that an EIS is required, the agency (or a consultant it hires) prepares a draft EIS, or "DEIS." The draft must be circulated to all interested parties, including other federal agencies, state and local government bodies, the private sponsor of the project (if it is federally funded or licensed), and interested environmental and other civic organizations. Each of these may comment on the DEIS, pointing out, for example, failure to adequately discuss particular impacts, alternatives, or mitigation measures (ways to reduce environment impacts). The agency may then respond to these comments. The draft, comments and responses together form the Final EIS ('FEIS"). The agency then must prepare a concise Record of Decision summarizing its proposed action.

Which agency must prepare an EIS when more than one agency is involved? And when in the process of deciding to proceed must the EIS be prepared? The next case focuses on these questions.

GREENE COUNTY PLANNING BOARD v. FEDERAL POWER COMMISSION, United States Court of Appeals, Second Circuit, 1972. 455 F.2d 412, cert. denied 409 U.S. 849.

Irving R. Kaufman, Circuit Judge:

[T]he Power Authority of the State of New York (PASNY) filed an application [with the Federal Power Commission] to construct, operate and maintain a 1,000,000 kilowatt pumped storage power project along the middle reaches of Schoharie Creek in the towns of Blenheim and Gilboa, New York, some forty miles southwest of Albany.

[T]he Commission granted the license [, but] prohibited construction of the transmission lines until further Commission approval was given to "plans for preservation and enhancement of the environment as it may be affected by the transmission lines' design and location." * * *

PASNY applied for construction authorization of the [transmission lines and submitted an EIS to the Commission in accordance with a Commission regulation which] required each applicant for a license for a "major project" to file its own detailed statement of environmental impact developing fully the five factors listed in section 102(2)(C) of NEPA. [Petitioners, opponents of the power plant, moved before the FPC to require the Commission] to file its own impact statement pursuant to NEPA. [They then moved to vacate the license of the project,] alleging that the Commission did not comply with * * * the mandates of NEPA. * * *

The parties * * * are in vigorous disagreement over when the Commission must make its impact statement. The Commission argues that PASNY's statement, reviewed as to form by the Commission and circulated by it, suffices for the purposes of Section 102(2)(C) and that the Commission is not required to make its *own* statement until it files its final decision. Petitioners argue that the Commission must issue its statement prior to any formal hearings. PASNY, perhaps recognizing that the Commission's position is untenable, but nevertheless anxious to expedite the proceedings, proposes a third course of action. It urges that the Commission can draft its statement on the basis of the hearings, but to be circulated by it for comment before its final decision. It is clear to us that petitioners offer the correct interpretation.

> * * As long as six years ago, this Court remanded a case to the Commission because, in granting a license for the construction of a similar pumped storage power project at Storm King Mountain on the Hudson River, it had failed to weigh the factors of "the conservation of natural resources, the maintenance of natural beauty, and the preservation of historic sites." *Scenic Hudson Preservation Conference* v. *Federal Power Commission* [Chapter 1, *supra*]. But NEPA, which was a response to the urgent need for a similar approach in all federal agencies, went far beyond the requirement that the agency merely consider environmental factors and include those factors in the record subject to review by the courts. * * * We view [NEPA] as * * * a mandate to consider environmental values "at every distinctive and

comprehensive stage of the [agency's] process." The primary and nondelegable responsibility for fulfilling that function lies with the Commission. * * *

The * * * Commission has abdicated a significant part of its responsibility by substituting the statement of PASNY for its own. The Commission appears to be content to collate the comments of other federal agencies, its own staff and the intervenors and once again to act as an umpire.[a] The danger of this procedure, and one obvious shortcoming, is the potential, if not likelihood, that the applicant's statement will be based upon self-serving assumptions. In fact, PASNY's statement begins: "Neither the construction nor the operation of the transmission line will have any significant adverse impact on the environment." But, the line, if constructed as proposed, will cut a swath approximately 35 miles long and 150 feet wide across the face of Greene and Schoharie Counties.

[I]ntervenors generally have limited resources, both in terms of money and technical expertise, and thus may not be able to provide an effective analysis of environmental factors. It was in part for this reason that Congress has compelled agencies to seek the aid of all available expertise and formulate their own position early in the review process. The Commission argues, however, that written testimony of its staff demonstrates that the Commission has not left the applicant and the intervenors to develop the record. It insists that its staff has undertaken field research in an effort to investigate alternatives proposed by PASNY and also any additional feasible alternatives. It is clear to us that this testimony cannot replace a single coherent and comprehensive environmental analysis, which is itself subject to scrutiny during the agency review processes. If this course of action we approve were not followed, alternatives might be lost as the applicant's statement tended to produce a *status quo* syndrome. [W]e deem it essential that the Commission's staff should prepare a detailed statement before the Presiding Examiner issues his initial decision. Moreover, the intervenors must have a reasonable opportunity to comment on the statement. But, since the statement may well go to waste unless it is subject to the full scrutiny of the hearing process, we also believe that the intervenors must be given the opportunity to cross-examine both PASNY and Commission witnesses in light of the statement. [As the CEQ points out,] "Often individuals and groups can contribute data and insights beyond the expertise of the Agency involved." We leave to the Commission to determine the most efficient procedure for meeting this mandate.

---

[a] Recall the *Scenic Hudson* decision, Chapter 1: the Commission may not be "an umpire blandly calling balls and strikes."

Notes

Does this decision leave the applicant powerless to affect the preparation of the EIS? What steps can it take to insure that the EIS accurately reflects the data that led the applicant to select the site in the first place?

In *"SCRAP II" (Aberdeen & Rockfish R.R.* v. *Students Challenging Regulatory Agency Procedures* [*SCRAP*]), 422 U.S. 289, 95 S. Ct. 2336, 45 L.Ed.2d 191 (1975), dealing with the higher Interstate Commerce Commission-approved freight rates for scrap metal as against new metal (See *"SCRAP I,"* Chapter 1; *National Association of Recycling Industries* v. *ICC,* Chapter 9), the Supreme Court upheld the Interstate Commerce Commission's granting of an increase in railroad freight rates prior to completing its final EIS. (The Commission's draft EIS had been prepared.) The plaintiffs objected on environmental grounds to increases for scrap metal. The Court (White, J.) held:

> Where an agency initiates federal action by publishing a proposal and then holding hearings on the proposal, [NEPA] would appear to require an impact statement to be included in the proposal and to be considered at the hearing. Here, however, until the October 4, 1972, report [approving the rate increase], the ICC had made no proposal, recommendation or report. The only proposal was the proposed new rates filed by the railroads. Thus, the earliest time at which the statute required a statement was the time of the ICC's report of October 4, 1972[.]
>
> The action taken here was a decision--entirely nonfinal with respect to particular rates--not to declare unlawful a *percentage increase* which on its face applied equally to virgin and some recyclable materials and which on its face limited the increase permitted on other recyclables. As in most general revenue proceedings, the "action" was taken in response to the railroads' claim of a financial crisis; and the inquiry * * * was primarily into the question whether such a crisis--usually thought to entitle the railroads to the general increase--existed, leaving *primarily* to more appropriate future proceedings the task of answering challenges to rates on individual commodities or categories thereof. The point is that it is the latter question--usually involved in a general revenue proceeding only to a limited extent--which may raise the most serious environmental issues. The former question--the entitlement of the railroads to some kind of a general rate increase--raises few environmental issues and none which is claimed in this case to have been inadequately addressed in the impact statement. * * * Thus even if NEPA * * * were read to require the ICC to address comprehensively the underlying rate structure at least once before approval of a facially

> neutral general rate increase, no purpose could have been served by ordering it to thoroughly explore the question in the confined and inappropriate context of a railroad proposal for a general rate increase when it was already doing so in a more appropriate proceeding.[a]

Justice Douglas alone dissented.

Does it matter that the railroads' rate increases automatically take effect unless suspended by the ICC, in contrast to an application for a permit to build a power plant where the applicant can't proceed until permission is granted?

In practice, federal licensing agencies such as the Nuclear Regulatory Commission (noted earlier) and the Federal Energy Regulatory Commission (successor to the Federal Power Commission) continue to require a final EIS before their hearings commence, as *Calvert Cliffs* and *Greene County* dictate. The CEQ regulations now so require. See 40 CFR §§ 1500.5(a), 1501.1(a), 1502. The EIS process must be completed before an agency proceeds with a project of its own, like a highway or prison. In rulemaking, the draft EIS must accompanying the proposed rule and the final EIS must be prepared before the rule is adopted.

In *Natural Resources Defense Council* v. *Callaway,* Chapter 7, Part B, the court set aside the Army Corps of Engineers permit allowing the Navy to deposit dredge spoil in an area of Long Island Sound where it was likely to injure fishing and shellfishing areas both because the permit contravened Clear Water Act § 404 and because the EIS was found wanting. Reread the first two pages of the decision before looking at the court's decision as to which agency need prepare the EIS.

NATURAL RESOURCES DEFENSE COUNCIL, INC. v. CALLAWAY, United States Court of Appeals, Second Circuit, 1975. 524 F.2d 79.

Mansfield, Circuit Judge:

* * *The plaintiffs' next contention concerns the authorship of the EIS, which was prepared by the Navy. Section 102(2)(C) of NEPA requires that an EIS be prepared "by the responsible official" for the federal project in question. Plaintiffs argue that the Corps of Engineers through its power to grant or deny permits, 33 U.S.C. §§ 403 and 1344, controlled the environmental decisions connected with the project, including the dredging, designation of disposal site, and dumping of the spoil, whereas the Navy was a mere permit applicant, and that the Corps was therefore the federal agency primarily responsible for the project and for the preparation of the EIS.

If this were a project initiated by a state or a private party the Corps might indeed have been required to prepare the EIS. Our decisions in *Conservation*

---

[a] A separate ICC proceeding dealt specifically with the environmental effects of freight rate disparities, such as the rates for scrap metal.

*Society of Southern Vermont, Inc.* v. *Secretary of Transportation,* 508 F.2d [927 (1974),[a] and *Greene County Planning Board* v. *FPC, [infra,]* * * * clearly hold that a federal agency cannot abdicate its responsibility independently to evaluate federal actions proposed to it by other, non-federal entities. * * *

When two or more cooperating federal agencies are the only entities involved in a proposed project, however, the situation is quite different. Federal participation in the preparation of the EIS is assured. The only issue is which, as between federal agencies, should be treated as the "lead" agency responsible for its preparation. The Council on Environmental Quality ("CEQ") has issued Guidelines which allow for the designation of a "lead" agency to prepare the EIS on all aspects of a federal project involving more than one federal agency. The agencies themselves are to designate the "lead" agency, taking into account

> the time sequence in which the agencies become involved, the magnitude of their respective involvement, and their relative expertise with respect to the project's environmental effects.

The district court concluded on the basis of these guidelines that the Navy's preparation of the EIS was not improper. We agree.

Although the Corps, by recommending the New London dump site and implying that it would not issue a permit to the Navy unless that site was designated, became rather heavily involved in the project, other evidence demonstrates that the project nevertheless remains essentially a Navy one. The dredging is being done for the benefit of the Navy, at the Navy's expense, and to fulfill a governmental responsibility entrusted to the Navy. Furthermore, since the Navy conceived of the project, it was the first federal agency involved. Thus, while the Corps is a participant to the extent of issuing permits, the Navy is active in all aspects of the project. It, not the Corps, was responsible for drawing up and letting contracts for the work and seeing that the work was properly performed. All of these factors point to the Navy as the responsible agency. Furthermore, only the Navy has continuing responsibility to see that the dredged channel remains at the proper depth and in good repair.

* * * Appellants' further argument that the Navy's partial delegation of its duty as the "responsible official" to a consultant to prepare the EIS violated our decisions in *Conservation Society of Southern Vermont, Inc.* v. *Secretary of Transportation, supra,* and *Greene County Planning Board* v. *FPC, supra,* misconstrues our holdings in those cases. Rather than hire its own personnel to

[a] This decision was vacated by the Supreme Court, 423 U.S. 809 (1975), because of an amendment to NEPA authorizing state agencies to prepare an EIS for a federal action funded under a program of grants to states provided the state agency is one of statewide jurisdiction, such as a highway department, and is responsible for the project. The federal agency retains final responsibility for the adequacy of the EIS. 42 U.S.C.A. § 4332(D).

prepare the impact statement, the Navy in this case contracted out the work to an independent consultant.

We agree with the district court that this procedure is acceptable in these circumstances and is not prohibited by the decisions relied upon by plaintiffs. The evil sought to be avoided by the holdings in *Conservation Society* and *Greene County* is the preparation of the EIS by a party, usually a state agency, with an individual "axe to grind," i.e., an interest in seeing the project accepted and completed in a specific manner as proposed. Authorship by such a biased party might prevent the fair and impartial evaluation of a project envisioned by NEPA. Here no problem of self-interest on the part of the author exists. As the Navy's hiree, the independent consultant has no interest but the Navy's to serve and is fully responsible to the Navy for any shortcomings in the EIS. Therefore, we see no difference for NEPA purposes between this procedure and preparation of the EIS by Navy personnel. In both cases the preparers are guided exclusively by the interests of the Navy and the dictates of the NEPA process. * * *

(Now reread the remainder of the opinion printed in Chapter 7.) Note the discussion as to whether the Army Corps had the supplemental information before making its decision, and whether the EIS process had been short circuited.)

B. ALTERNATIVES

Note that agencies must consider alternatives both in an EIS and in the more general mandate of § 102(E) that federal agencies "study, develop and describe appropriate alternatives to recommended courses of action in any proposal which involves unresolved conflicts concerning alternative uses of available resources." That provision applies whether or not an EIS is required. See the *Strycker's Bay* case, Part C of this chapter.

NATURAL RESOURCES DEFENSE COUNCIL v. MORTON, United States Court of Appeals, D.C. Circuit, 1972. 458 F.2d 827.

Leventhal, Circuit Judge:

This appeal raises a question as to the scope of the requirement of the National Environmental Policy Act (NEPA) that environmental impact statements contain a discussion of alternatives. Before us is the [EIS] filed * * * by the Department of Interior with respect to its proposal under * * * the Outer Continental Shelf Lands Act, for the oil and gas general lease sale, of leases to some 80 tracts of submerged lands, primarily off eastern Louisiana [, consisting of] almost 380,000 acres, about 10% of the offshore acreage presently under Federal lease.

[T]hree conservation groups brought this action * * * to enjoin the proposed sale. [The EIS] is not challenged on the ground of failure to disclose the problems of environmental impact of the proposed sale. On the contrary, these problems are set forth in considerable range and detail.

[The District] Court found that the Statement failed to provide the "detailed statement" required by NEPA of environmental impact and alternatives. * * *

We think the Secretary's Statement erred in stating that the alternative of elimination of oil import quotas was entirely outside its cognizance. Assuming, as the Statement puts it, that this alternative "involves complex factors and concepts, including national security, which are beyond the scope of this statement," it does not follow that the Statement should not present the environmental effects of that alternative. While the consideration of pertinent alternatives requires a weighing of numerous matters, such as economics, foreign relations, national security, the fact remains that, as to the ingredient of possible adverse environmental impact, it is the essence and thrust of NEPA that the pertinent Statement serve to gather in one place a discussion of the relative environmental impact of alternatives.

The Government also contends that the only "alternatives" required for discussion under NEPA are those which can be adopted and put into effect by the official or agency issuing the statement. [I]t stresses that the objective of the Secretary's action was to carry out the directive in the President's clean energy message of June 4, 1971 [advocating offshore oil leasing].

While we agree with so much of the government's presentation as rests on the assumption that the alternatives required for discussion are those reasonably available, we do not agree that this requires a limitation to measures the agency or official can adopt. This approach would be particularly inapposite for the lease sale of offshore oil lands hastened by Secretary Morton in response to the directive which President Nixon set forth in his message to Congress on the Supply of Energy and Clean Air, as part of an overall program of development to provide an accommodation of the energy requirements of our country with the growing recognition of the necessity to protect the environment.

When the proposed action is an integral part of a coordinated plan to deal with a broad problem, the range of alternatives that must be evaluated is broadened. While the Department of the Interior does not have the authority to eliminate or reduce oil import quotas, such action is within the purview of both Congress and the President, to whom the impact statement goes. The impact statement is not only for the exposition of the thinking of the agency, but also for the guidance of these ultimate decision-makers, and must provide them with the environmental effects of both the proposal and the alternatives, for their consideration along with the various other elements of the public interest. * * *

The need for continuing review of environmental impact of alternatives under NEPA cannot be put to one side on the ground of past determinations by Congress or the President. We are aware that the 1953 Outer Continental Shelf Lands Act contains a finding of an urgent need for OCS development and authorization of leasing. Similarly we are aware that the oil import quota program was instituted by the President on a mandatory basis in 1959 * * * and that the President's authority, based on national security considerations, is contained in legislation derived from * * * 19 U.S.C. § 1862. But [a]s to both programs Congress contemplated continuing review. The OCS leasing was specifically made subject to executive authority to withdraw unleased lands from disposition from time to time. Import controls were from the outset dependent on continuing Presidential findings as to the nature and duration of controls deemed necessary. * * *

What NEPA infused into the decision-making process in 1969 was a directive as to environmental impact statements that was meant to implement the Congressional objectives of Government coordination, a comprehensive approach to environmental management, and a determination to face problems of pollution "while they are still of manageable proportions and while alternative solutions are still available" rather than persist in environmental decision-making wherein "policy is established by default and inaction" and environmental decisions "continue to be made in small but steady increments" that perpetuate the mistakes of the past without being dealt with until "they reach crisis proportions."

* * * We think there is merit to the Government's position insofar as it contends that no additional discussion was requisite for such "alternatives" as the development of oil shale, desulfurization of coal, coal liquefaction and gasification, tar sands and geothermal resources since [t]he Statement sets forth that their impact on the energy supply will not likely be felt until after 1980, and will be dependent on environmental safeguards and technological developments. Since the Statement also sets forth that the agency's proposal was put forward to meet a near-term requirement, imposed by an energy shortfall projected for the mid-1970's, the possibility of the environmental impact of long-term solutions requires no additional discussion at this juncture. * * * [T]he requirement in NEPA of discussion as to reasonable alternatives does not require "crystal ball" inquiry. Mere administrative difficulty does not interpose such flexibility into the requirements of NEPA as to undercut the duty of compliance "to the fullest extent possible." But if this requirement is not rubber, neither is it iron. The statute must be construed in the light of reason if it is not to demand what is, fairly speaking, not meaningfully possible, given the obvious, that the resources of energy and research--and time--available to meet the Nation's needs are not infinite.

Still different considerations are presented by the "alternatives" of increasing nuclear energy development, listed in the Statement, and the possibilities * * * of federal legislation or administrative action freeing current offshore and state-controlled offshore production from state market demand prorationing, or changing the Federal Power Commission's natural gas pricing policies.

The mere fact that an alternative requires legislative implementation does not automatically establish it as beyond the domain of what is required for discussion, particularly since NEPA was intended to provide a basis for consideration and choice by the decisionmakers in the legislative as well as the executive branch. But the need for an overhaul of basic legislation certainly bears on the requirements of the Act. We do not suppose Congress intended an agency to devote itself to extended discussion of the environmental impact of alternatives so remote from reality as to depend on, say, the repeal of the antitrust laws.

In the last analysis, the requirement as to alternatives is subject to a construction of reasonableness[.] NEPA was not meant to require detailed discussion of the environmental effects of "alternatives" put forward in comments when these effects cannot be readily ascertained and the alternatives are deemed only remote and speculative possibilities, in view of basic changes required in statutes and policies of other agencies--making them available, if at all, only after protracted debate and litigation not meaningfully compatible with the time-frame of the needs to which the underlying proposal is addressed.

Notes

Note that the EIS in *NRDC* v. *Morton* was invalidated not for failing to discuss the environmental impacts of the project but for inadequately dealing with alternatives which those impacts made it necessary to describe.

The CEQ, as discussed in the note following *Hanly* v. *Kleindienst,* is the agency with responsibility for coordinating environmental policy and informing the President.

Some courts take the view that where no EIS need be prepared, an agency need only consider alternatives that are within its jurisdiction to employ. See *City of New York v. Department of Transportation*, 715 F.2d 732 (2d Cir.1983), cert. denied 465 U.S. 1055 (U.S. Department of Transportation need not consider alternative of shipping nuclear waste by sea when adopting rule for road shipment that was held not to require an EIS).

## C. IS NEPA SUBSTANTIVE?

STRYCKER'S BAY NEIGHBORHOOD COUNCIL, INC. v. KARLEN, Supreme Court of the United States, 1980. 444 U.S. 223, 100 S. Ct. 497, 62 L.Ed.2d 433.

Per Curiam.

At the center of this dispute is the site of a proposed low-income housing project to be constructed on Manhattan's Upper West Side. In 1962, the New York City Planning Commission (Commission), acting in conjunction with the United States Department of Housing and Urban Development (HUD), began formulating a plan for the renewal of 20 square blocks known as the "West Side Urban Renewal Area" (WSURA)[.] As originally written, the plan called for a mix of 70% middle-income housing and 30% low-income housing and designated the site at issue here as the location of one of the middle-income projects. In 1969, after substantial progress toward completion of the plan, local agencies in New York determined that the number of low-income units proposed for WSURA would be insufficient to satisfy an increased need for such units. In response to this shortage the Commission amended the plan to designate the site as the future location of a high-rise building containing 160 units of low-income housing. HUD approved this amendment in December 1972.

Meanwhile [plaintiffs] sued in the United States District Court for the Southern District of New York to enjoin the Commission and HUD from constructing low-income housing on the site. The present respondents, Roland N. Karlen [et al.] intervened as plaintiffs, while petitioner Strycker's Bay Neighborhood Council, Inc., intervened as a defendant.

The District Court entered judgment in favor of petitioners [HUD et al.]. It concluded, inter alia, that petitioners had not violated [NEPA].

While the Court of Appeals agreed with the District Court that HUD was not required to prepare a full-scale [EIS,] it held that HUD had not complied with § 102(2)(E), which requires an agency to "study, develop, and describe appropriate alternatives[,"] [and] remanded the case, requiring HUD to prepare a "statement of possible alternatives, the consequences thereof and the facts and reasons for and against. . . ."

On remand, HUD prepared a lengthy report * * * assert[ing] that, "while the choice of Site 30 for development as a 100 percent low-income project has raised questions about the potential social environmental impacts involved, the problems associated with the impact on social fabric and community structures are not considered so serious as to require that this component be rated as unacceptable." The * * * report incorporated a study wherein the [City Planning] Commission evaluated nine alternative locations for the project and found none of them acceptable. [HUD] credited the Commission's conclusion that any relocation of the units would entail an unacceptable delay of two years or more. According to HUD, "[m]easured against the environmental costs associated with the minimum two-year delay, the benefits seem insufficient to justify a mandated substitution of sites."

[After] the District Court again entered judgment in favor of petitioners * * * the Second Circuit vacated and remanded again[.] [T]he Court of Appeals looked to "[t]he provisions of NEPA" for "the substantive standards necessary to review the merits of agency decisions. . . ." The Court of Appeals conceded that HUD had "given 'consideration' to alternatives" to redesignating the site. Nevertheless, the court believed that "'consideration' is not an end in itself." Concentrating on HUD's finding that development of an alternative location would entail an unacceptable delay, the appellate court held that such delay could not be "an overriding factor" in HUD's decision to proceed with the development. According to the court, when HUD considers such projects, "environmental factors, such as crowding low-income housing into a concentrated area, should be given determinative weight." The Court of Appeals therefore remanded the case to the District Court, instructing HUD to attack the shortage of low-income housing in a manner that would avoid the "concentration" of such housing on Site 30.

In *Vermont Yankee Nuclear Power Corp.* v. *Natural Resources Defense Council, Inc.*, 435 U.S. 519, 98 S. Ct. 1197, 55 L.Ed.2d 460 (1978), we stated that NEPA, while establishing "significant substantive goals for the Nation," imposes upon agencies duties that are "essentially procedural."[a] As we stressed in that case,

---

[a] *Vermont Yankee*, discussed in Chapter 11, Part C, held as to NEPA that the Act did not require the Atomic Energy Commission -- predecessor to the Nuclear Regulatory Commission -- to substantively

NEPA was designed "to insure a fully informed and well-considered decision," but not necessarily "a decision the judges of the Court of Appeals or of this Court would have reached had they been members of the decisionmaking unit of the agency." Vermont Yankee cuts sharply against the Court of Appeals' conclusion that an agency, in selecting a course of action, must elevate environmental concerns over other appropriate considerations. On the contrary, once an agency has made a decision subject to NEPA's procedural requirements, the only role for a court is to insure that the agency has considered the environmental consequences; it cannot "interject itself within the area of discretion of the executive as to the choice of the action to be taken." * * *

In the present case there is no doubt that HUD considered the environmental consequences of its decision to redesignate the proposed site for low-income housing. NEPA requires no more. [T]he judgment of the Court of Appeals is therefore reversed.

Justice Marshall, dissenting.

The issue raised by these cases is far more difficult than the per curiam opinion suggests. The Court of Appeals held that [HUD] had acted arbitrarily in concluding that prevention of a delay in the construction process justified the selection of a housing site which could produce adverse social environmental effects, including racial and economic concentration. Today the majority responds that "once an agency has made a decision subject to NEPA's procedural requirements, the only role for a court is to insure that the agency has considered the environmental consequences," and that in this case "there is no doubt that HUD considered the environmental consequences of its decision to redesignate the proposed site for low-income housing. NEPA requires no more." The majority finds support for this conclusion in the closing paragraph of our decision in Vermont Yankee[.]

Vermont Yankee does not stand for the broad proposition that the majority advances today. The relevant passage in that opinion was meant to be only a "further observation of some relevance to this case." * * * That "observation" was a response to this Court's perception that the Court of Appeals in that case was attempting "under the guise of judicial review of agency action" to assert its own policy judgment as to the desirability of developing nuclear energy as an energy source for this Nation, a judgment which is properly left to Congress. * * * The Court of Appeals had remanded the case to the agency because of "a single alleged oversight on a peripheral issue, urged by parties who never fully cooperated or indeed raised the issue below." It was in this context that the Court remarked the "NEPA does set forth significant substantive goals for the Nation, ,but its mandate to the agencies is *essentially* procedural." Ibid. (emphasis supplied). Accordingly, "[a]dministrative decisions should be set aside in this context, *as in every other,*

---

reconsider the licensing of nuclear generating stations because of risks discussed in a report of the Advisory Committee on Reactor Safeguards, an agency within the Commission.

only for substantial procedural or *substantive* reasons as mandated by statute," ibid. (emphasis supplied). Thus Vermont Yankee does not stand for the proposition that a court reviewing agency action under NEPA is limited solely to the factual issue of whether the agency "considered" environmental consequences. The agency's decision must still be set aside if it is "arbitrary, capricious, an abuse of discretion, or otherwise not in accordance with law," 5 U.S.C. § 706(2)(A), and the reviewing court must still insure that the agency "has taken a 'hard look' at environmental consequences." * * *

In the present case, the Court of Appeals did not "substitute its judgment for that of the agency as to the environmental consequences of its actions," for HUD in its Special Environmental Clearance Report acknowledged the adverse environmental consequences of its proposed action. As the Court of Appeals observed, the resulting high concentration of low-income housing would hardly further racial and economic integration. The report also discusses two alternatives, Sites 9 and 41, both of which are the appropriate size for the project and require "only minimal" amounts of relocation and clearance. Concerning Site 9 the report explicitly concludes that "[f]rom the standpoint of social environmental impact this location would be superior to Site 30 for the development of low-rent public housing." The sole reason for rejecting the environmentally superior site was the fact that if the location were shifted to Site 9, there would be a projected delay of two years in the construction of the housing.

The issue before the Court of Appeals, therefore, was whether HUD was free under NEPA to reject an alternative acknowledged to be environmentally preferable solely on the ground that any change in sites would cause delay. This was hardly a "peripheral issue" in the case. Whether NEPA, which sets forth "significant substantive goals," Vermont Yankee, permits a projected two-year time difference to be controlling over environmental superiority is by no means clear. Resolution of the issue, however, is certainly within the normal scope of review of agency action to determine if it is arbitrary, capricious, or an abuse of discretion. The question whether HUD can make delay the paramount concern over environmental superiority is essentially a restatement of the question whether HUD in considering the environmental consequences of its proposed action gave those consequences a "hard look," which is exactly the proper question for the reviewing court to ask. * * *

I do not subscribe to the Court's apparent suggestion that Vermont Yankee limits the reviewing court to the essentially mindless task of determining whether an agency "considered" environmental factors even if that agency may have effectively decided to ignore those factors in reaching its conclusion. Indeed, I cannot believe that the Court would adhere to that position in a different factual setting. Our cases establish that the arbitrary or capricious standard prescribes a "searching and careful" judicial inquiry designed to ensure that the agency has not exercised its discretion in an unreasonable manner. *Citizens To Preserve Overton Park, Inc.* v. *Volpe.* Believing that today's summary reversal represents a departure from that principle, I respectfully dissent.

Notes

*Strycker's Bay* could, as the dissent suggests, easily have been limited to its peculiar factual context--the great delay in a needed housing development, and the use of the NEPA process as a neighborhood tug-of-war between proponents of low-income and of middle-income buildings. But the Court has not so limited it. See *Methow Valley, infra.*

Did the majority accurately rely on the holding in *Vermont Yankee,* or is Justice Marshall in fact correct when he says that case "does not stand for the broad proposition that the majority advances"?

Is it "mindless," as Justice Marshall's acerb dissent states, for a court to determine whether the agency in fact considered the environmental impact of its actions? Does this turn on how one defines "consider"?

Did the Court adhere to the hard look doctrine of *Overton Park,* Ch. 1, *supra*? Should the delay that HUD's developing a more acceptable alternative might cause outweigh the mandate of NEPA?

NEPA also requires environmental impact statements to consider methods of mitigating environmental harm. Here, too, the Supreme Court has ruled NEPA has no substantive mandate. In *Robertson* v. *Methow Valley Citizens Council*, 490 U.S. 332, 109 S.Ct. 1835, 104 L.Ed.2d 351 (1989), the Court ruled a federal agency need not adopt mitigation measures to reduce environmental harm -- in that case, air quality and deer herd protection in weighing a ski resort in a national forest administered by the United States Department of Agriculture -- as long as it discusses these measures.

D. JUDICIAL REVIEW

Although NEPA contains no explicit provision for judicial review, the federal courts have consistently viewed failure to comply with the Act as reviewable under the Administrative Procedure Act, 5 U.S.C.A. § 701. This means plaintiffs must show standing as in *Sierra Club v. Morton* (Chapter 1). NEPA has no citizen-suit provision.

Must the plaintiff's alleged injury be environmental in nature? What if the injury is economic? Either class of injury seems sufficient. *Shiffler v. Schlesinger*, 548 F.2d 96 (3d Cir. 1979).

Will a court preliminarily enjoin a project upon a showing that an EIS was not prepared, or is inadequate, or must the plaintiff prove irreparable injury as well? Similarly, after trial, is a plaintiff who proves that an adequate EIS should have been prepared entitled to have a project enjoined on that ground alone, or must the court balance the equities before issuing an injunction? See *State of New York* v. *Nuclear Regulatory Commission*, 550 F.2d 745 (2d Cir. 1977), holding the ordinary rules, requiring irreparable injury prior to a preliminary injunction and, by extension, balancing the equities prior to a permanent one, apply. In that case, brought to enjoin federally permitted air shipments of plutonium through New York in the absence of an EIS, the plaintiff proved an EIS was needed and ultimately obtained a declaratory judgment to that effect. But the Court of Appeals upheld the denial of a preliminary injunction based on the trial court's finding of no irreparable injury.

But see *Scherr* v. *Volpe*, 466 F.2d 1027, 1034 (7th Cir. 1972), upholding a preliminary injunction based on failure to prepare an EIS for a highway-widening project: "If these agencies were permitted to avoid their responsibilities under the Act until an individual citizen, who possesses vastly inferior resources, could demonstrate environmental harm, reconsideration at that time by the responsible federal agency would indeed be a hollow gesture."

## E. STATE ENVIRONMENTAL QUALITY ACTS

FRIENDS OF MAMMOTH v. MONO COUNTY, Supreme Court of California, 1972. 8 Cal. 3d 247, 104 Cal.Rptr. 761, 502 P.2d 1949.

Mosk, J.

[International Recreation, Ltd. (International) applied to the county planning commission for a permit to build a condominium development of six buildings, each of six to eight stories, with parking and recreational facilities, in a mountainous and sparsely populated county.]

Mammoth Lakes, the section of Mono County immediately involved in this action, consists of some 2,100 acres of land surrounded by the Inyo National Forest. Plaintiffs assert that acute water and sewage problems will be created if International is permitted to construct its proposed condominium complex [, as well as] diminution of open space in general. * * *

The principal legal question that arises is whether the [Environmental Quality Act] applies to private activities for which a permit or other similar entitlement is required. * * *

California's Environmental Quality Act of 1970 [EQA] requires various state and local governmental entities to submit environmental impact reports before undertaking specified activity. These reports compel state and local agencies to consider the possible adverse consequences to the environment of the proposed activity and to record such impact in writing.

Under section 21100, the reports are required of "state agencies, boards and commissions[."]

Section 21151, the specific provision involved in the case at hand, states:

["L]ocal governmental agencies shall make an environmental impact report on any project they intend to carry out which may have a significant effect on the environment and shall submit it to the appropriate local planning agency[."]

Only if [that] provision covers the issuance of a permit does the mandate of the act govern here. This determination necessarily turns on whether the term "project" as used in section 21151 includes private activity for which a government permit is necessary.

We begin our inquiry by noting that nowhere in the act is "project" defined. [W]e must rely on a cardinal principle of statutory construction: that absent "a single meaning of the statute apparent on its face, we are required to give it an interpretation based upon the legislative intent with which it was passed." * * *

The clearest manifestation of this intent can be found in section 21000, subdivision (g), which provides: "It is the intent of the Legislature that all agencies of the state government which *regulate* activities of private individuals, corporations, and public agencies which are found to affect the quality of the environment, shall *regulate* such activities so that major consideration is given to preventing environmental damage." It is significant that *regulate* is the verb employed in this subdivision. Its use demonstrates that the concern of the Legislature was not limited solely to activities which the government performs in a proprietary capacity. Instead the Legislature apparently desired to ensure that governmental entities in their *regulatory* function would determine that private individuals were not forsaking ecological cognizance in pursuit of economic advantage. One of the most common means by which a government agency regulates private activity is through the granting or denial of a permit.

* * * Other provisions in the EQA likewise support the conclusion that the Legislature intended to include the permit-issuing process as a governmental activity for which an environmental impact report is required. For example, section 21000, subdivision (e), states: "*Every citizen* has a responsibility to contribute to the preservation and enhancement of the environment." Such responsibility may never be exercised if the EQA is to apply only to activities in which the government is directly engaged. "Every citizen" is an unmistakable reference to private individuals as distinguished from government officials.

[W]e conclude that the Legislature intended the EQA to be interpreted in such manner as to afford the fullest possible protection to the environment within the reasonable scope of the statutory language. We also conclude that to achieve that maximum protection the Legislature necessarily intended to include within the operation of the act, private activities for which a government permit or other entitlement for use is necessary. * * *

## Notes

Is a city's plan to annex a small adjacent unincorporated area with an eye to permitting a shopping mall the sort of action requiring environmental assessment under a state environmental policy act? See *City of Bellevue* v. *King County Boundary Review Bd.*, 90 Wash. 2d 856, 586 P.2d 470 (1978):

Even a cursory reading of the record suggests that the fate of the Evergreen East project--at least to the extent of the pace and scale of the project, and the requirements and restrictions placed upon the developers by the responsible municipality--may be bound up with whether Redmond's annexation goes through, or the land remains in King County's jurisdiction, or even becomes annexed to Bellevue. It is clear that the Evergreen East project itself will have massive environmental impact, and any decision which will affect that development must necessarily involve consideration, to the extent possible, of the nature of the effect that such decision will have.

We express no opinion as to whether an assessment of environmental factors which includes discussion of this possibility must result in a decision to prepare a full EIS. Not every annexation proposal automatically requires filing of an EIS.

It is possible that the board may properly find that the impact on the project will be minor no matter what annexation decision is made. Nevertheless, the board was required at least to consider, as fully as possible, this and all other environmental factors involved in this annexation before approving it. The board did not meet its responsibilities; it failed to make an adequately based threshold determination.

H.O.M.E.S. v. NEW YORK STATE URBAN DEVELOPMENT CORP., Supreme Court of New York, Appellate Division, Fourth Department, 1979. 69 A.D.2d 222, 418 N.Y.S.2d 827.

Witmer, J.

[The Urban Development Corp. (UDC), a state agency, contracted with Syracuse University to construct a domed sports stadium seating 50,000 people, to be built largely with State funds.]

[T]he Syracuse-Onondaga County Planning Agency wrote a letter to the University, with copies to the City Planning Commission and the County Planning Board, expressing its concern for the "increased traffic flows and the need for parking" to avoid massive traffic congestion in the city and immediate neighborhood of the stadium, and it suggested that a plan approved by "key governmental agencies" should be developed, including adequate vehicular access and parking[.]

[T]he City Planning Commission held a special meeting for a formal detailed presentation of the domed stadium proposal. It was openly recognized that no plan to handle traffic had been devised. Fire Chief Hanlon spoke critically of the project, foreseeing traffic congestion, even riots, and no excess or emergency vehicles. A witness from the Department of Transportation foresaw "a horrendous problem" with parking and said, "We're just not going to be able to get through."

The new facility, he stated, has 15 exits whereas [the existing] Stadium has only 6; and nearly twice as many people will pour out, twice as fast, into streets which cannot accommodate the present traffic.

[Petitioners contend the] UDC erred in determining that an environmental impact statement was not required[.]

In enacting [the State Environmental Quality Review Act] the New York State Legislature declared a State policy to promote efforts which will prevent or eliminate damage to the environment and enhance human and community resources[.] Environment is defined in the statute as "the physical conditions which will be affected by a proposed action, including land, air, * * * noise, * * * and existing community or neighborhood character"[.] The New York State [regulations] specified as important considerations for the need of an EIS, a substantial adverse change in existing air quality or noise levels, encouraging or attracting of a large number of people to a place or places for more than a few days, compared to the number of people who would come to such place absent such action, the impairment of the character or quality of existing community or neighborhood character, and the creation of a hazard to human health and safety.* * *

Like the proverbial ostrich, respondents have incredibly put out of sight and mind a clear environmental problem. [T]he stadium is a major project[.] It is estimated to attract from five to ten times as many patrons per year as did Archbold Stadium. The record shows that the traffic and parking problems have heretofore been serious on days when the stadium was used. With the new stadium, they will be much worse in the absence of comprehensive plans and actions to avoid them. Without such, not only will the residents in the area have extreme difficulty entering and leaving their homes and enjoying the use thereof but, more importantly, even fire fighting equipment and other emergency vehicles will be unable to get through to serve the public.

Whether the UDC properly issued its negative declaration that the project will have no significant impact on the environment and hence there is no need for an EIS depends upon whether it made a thorough investigation of the problems involved and reasonably exercised its discretion.

The record shows that UDC did not meet the legal requirements in arriving at its determination that the planned domed facility had no environmental significance on the area. Clearly UDC failed to take a "hard look" at the problems and adverse potential effects of the project on traffic stoppage, parking, air pollution or noise level damage. * * * In Alice-In-Wonderland manner, respondents separated and put aside the realities of the traffic and parking problems from the totality of this project. [T]he record is clear that UDC was fully aware of the traffic and parking problems in the area, and its determination that the construction and use of the domed facility will not significantly affect the environment is directly contrary to the facts; and its action in issuing the negative declaration was arbitrary and capricious.

Notes

Under the New York statute actions require an impact statement as long as they "may have a significant effect on the environment." N.Y. Envtl. Conserv. Law § 8-0109. Note that this is a broader test than NEPA itself employs.

Some state environmental review acts have been found to have substantive mandates. In *Town of Henrietta* v. *Department of Environmental Conservation,* 76 A.D.2d 215, 430 N.Y.S.2d 440 (4th Dep't 1980), the Department (DEC) approved water quality and water supply permits for a shopping center under the New York environmental review statute subject to conditions mitigating its impact on a nearby wetland and limiting parking spaces to reduce its effect on air quality. The court held:

> Petitioners seek in this proceeding to annul the conditions imposed upon the approvals granted by the DEC, contending the SEQRA[a] does not authorize DEC to attach conditions to a permit or approval where such conditions have no relevance to the permit or approval sought. * * *
>
> The EIS, the heart of SEQRA, clearly is meant to be more than simple disclosure statement as petitioners would construe it. Rather, it is to be viewed as an environmental "alarm bell" whose purpose is to alert responsible public officials to environmental changes before they have reached ecological points of no return[.]
>
> * * * A reasonable interpretation of the New York statute indicates that the Legislature intended an EIS under SEQRA to have a * * * broad scope. SEQRA requires an EIS to set forth "any adverse environmental effects which cannot be avoided should the proposal be implemented" and defines "environment" very broadly to include, inter alia, "land, air, water, minerals, flora, fauna, [and] noise." The statute cannot be construed as merely procedural or informational since it states that all approving agencies involved in an action must actually consider the EIS and formulate its decision on the basis of all the adverse environmental impacts disclosed therein. Since SEQRA requires an approving agency to act affirmatively upon the adverse environmental impacts revealed in an EIS an EIS filed pursuant to SEQRA must also be recognized as not a mere disclosure statement but rather as an aid in an agency's decision-making process to evaluate and balance the competing factors.

---

[a] The State Environmental Quality Review Act, discussed in *H.O.M.E.S., supra.*

* * * In view of what we deem to be a clear legislative mandate that the EIS be given a broad construction, it follows that it applies to the entire project and is not limited to the specific pending permit applications. [A]n agency in approving an action must make a written finding that it has imposed whatever conditions are necessary to minimize or avoid all adverse environmental impacts revealed in the EIS.

We caution, however, that SEQRA must be construed in the light of reason. Any limitations or conditions imposed accordingly must be governed by a "reasonableness test" if they are to survive judicial review * * *.

As we view it, condition 10, leaving [a portion of the area adjacent to the wetland] undeveloped, is pivotal in its scope and is intended to mitigate the development's impact on wildlife habitat. The EIS specifically concluded that the mall would result in a total elimination of wildlife species on the portion of the site proposed for development.

* * * The effect of the proposed mall on conservation (condition 17) is a relevant concern under SEQRA. The statute itself explicitly states that an EIS must set forth "effects of the proposed action on the use and conservation of energy resources, where applicable and significant." By imposing condition 17, the DEC has not improperly interjected itself into the exclusive domain of the State Energy Commissioner, relative to the State Energy Conservation Construction Code, as petitioners claim. Condition 17 does not attempt to enforce that Code. Rather, it represents an attempt by the DEC to fulfill its obligations under SEQRA to analyze the project's effect on "the use and conservation of energy resources where applicable and significant" and to insure that fulfills the objectives of the state's energy policy.
Condition 12 allows the exact number of parking spaces envisioned by the petitioners for the project in its own [draft] EIS. Additionally, the number of parking spaces at the mall is integrally related to site-generated traffic volume, which is, in turn, directly related to air quality, definitely a valid concern for DEC under SEQRA. * * *

The courts in several other states, including California, have likewise held their environmental review statutes to be substantive.

About half the states have enacted environmental impact legislation modeled on NEPA. Some, like New York's and California's, apply to all actions by state and municipal agencies. Some states' statutes only apply to particular state agencies, such as departments of transportation.

New York's courts have adopted a narrow view of standing to judicially review SEQRA decisions. They require a plaintiff to assert environmental, as opposed to economic, injury (or threatened injury), and the injury must be different from that suffered by the public generally. *Society of Plastics Industry, Inc. v. County of Suffolk*, 77 N.Y.2d 761, 570 N.Y.S.2d 778, 573 N.E.2d 1034 (1991).

# 11. ELECTRIC GENERATION

## A. SITING OF POWER PLANTS

Discussion of power plant siting begins with the salient decision in *Scenic Hudson Preservation Conference v. Federal Power Commission*, reprinted in Chapter 1. There the focus was on the scope of judicial review of administrative proceedings--in this case, the granting of a license by the Federal Power Commission (now the Federal Energy Regulatory Commission) to a private electric utility, Consolidated Edison, to build a pumped-storage hydroelectric plant at New York's Storm King Mountain. This chapter looks at the same case from the perspective of the Federal Power Act and the agency's licensing authority over hydroelectric plants.

SCENIC HUDSON PRESERVATION CONFERENCE v. FEDERAL POWER COMMISSION, United States Court of Appeals, Second Circuit, 1965. 354 F.2d 608. Cert. denied, 384 U.S. 941 (1966).

[Recall the decision as it appears in Chapter 1.

In a footnote, the court recounted the reasons for passage of the Federal Power Act:]

The Supreme Court has noted that:

> The movement toward the enactment of the Act in 1920 may be said to have taken its keynote from President [Theodore] Roosevelt's veto of a bill which would have turned over to private interests important power sites on the Rainy River. *Federal Power Comm. v. Union Electric Co.*, 381 U.S. 90, 98-99 n.11, 85 Sup. Ct. 1253, 1258 (1965).

President Roosevelt's veto message read:

> We are now at the beginning of great development in water power. Its use through electrical transmission is entering more and more largely into every element of the daily life of the people. Already the evils of monopoly are becoming manifest; already the experience of the past shows the necessity of caution in making unrestricted grants of this great power.

See also President Roosevelt's letter appointing the Inland Waterways Commission (1908), which reads in part:

> Works designed to control our waterways have thus far usually been undertaken for a single purpose, such as the improvement of navigation, the development of power, the irrigation of arid lands, the protection of lowlands from floods, or to supply water for domestic and manufacturing purposes. While the rights of the people to these and similar uses of water must be respected, the time has come for merging local projects and uses of the inland waters in a comprehensive plan designed for the benefit of the entire country. Such a plan should consider and include all the uses to which streams may be put, and should bring together and coordinate the points of view of all users of waters.* * * [The plans of the Commission should be formulated] in the light of the widest knowledge of the country and the people, and from the most diverse points of view.

## Notes

You should also reread the note in Chapter 1 following *Scenic Hudson* outlining the subsequent litigation.

The 1971 decision, known as *Scenic Hudson II*, confirmed the FPC's decision to permit the plant. The issue of its impact on the fishery, an added starter at the original proceedings, now became the main question. This was in large part due to concern over the cumulative effect of Storm King, the existing Con Edison nuclear plants downriver at Indian Point, and a couple of power plans operated by other utilities. Nuclear and fossil-fueled power plants use water in their boilers and, in the case of nuclear plants, to cool the reactor. This water must be drawn off the river, which can kill fish by impingement--being impaled on the intake screens--as well as by entrainment--being caught up in the cooling system itself.

Cooling towers, which recycle the water and vastly reduce the river water needed to cool a nuclear plant, are an effective but costly solution. The State of New York, the Natural Resources Defense Council and others contended the federal permits for the Indian Point plants should require cooling towers. After lengthy litigation before the EPA, in which the applicant's water-quality permit was opposed on those grounds, the parties agreed to the comprehensive settlement referred to in Chapter 1. Plans for Storm King were abandoned, as were the cooling towers. And the utilities agreed to build fish hatcheries, stock the Hudson to replace fish taken at their plants, and take steps to reduce the water used during spawning season.

Like all settlements, this left unanswered the underlying legal issues. When will the EPA, or the Nuclear Regulatory Commission, require cooling towers for a nuclear plant? Are fish hatcheries and stocking adequate alternatives where fish are killed? Who should bear the cost of damage to a resource on which livelihoods depend?

In *Chemehuevi Tribe of Indians v. Federal Power Commission*, 420 U.S. 395, 95 S. Ct. 1066, 43 L.Ed. 2d 279 (1975), suit was brought by several tribes of Indians and environmental groups to require the Federal Power Commission (FPC) to recognize as under its licensing jurisdiction thermal-electric power generating plants (fueled by coal, oil or gas) that draw cooling water from navigable streams. The plaintiffs wanted the FPC to require ten public utility companies in the Southwest to obtain licenses for six fossil-fueled steam plants they were building along the Colorado River and its tributaries. The plants were to be part of a projected vast electric power complex designed to transmit power in interstate commerce to cities as far as 600 miles from the plants.

Section 4(e) of the Federal Power Act, 16 U.S.C.A. § 797(e), authorizes the FPC (now the Federal Energy Regulatory Commission) to issue permits for "project works necessary or convenient * * * for the development, transmission, and utilization of power across, along, from, or in any of the streams or other bodies of water over which Congress has jurisdiction * * * or for the purpose of utilizing the surplus water or water power from any Government dam * * * " The plaintiffs argued that the steam plants are all "project works" (defined in the Act, 16 USCA § 761(11) & (12), to include power plants), that water is an indispensable part of the generation of electricity since it is used to condense the steam that turns the turbines, and that all the plants used "surplus water" to develop power. Since this literal reading of the statute is not at variance with the Act's purpose, plaintiffs argued, steam plants should be included under the FPC's jurisdiction.

The Supreme Court, however, examining the Act's legislative history and the FPC's consistent interpretation of the Act since 1920, held Congress intended only hydroelectric power generating plants to be subject to the FPC's licensing requirements. When the 1920 Act was reenacted in 1935 as Part I of the Federal Power Act, the Court noted, Congress chose not to expand the FPC's jurisdiction to include steam plants.

The Court recognized that steam plants effectively appropriate the power potential of public waters for private interests, but found the express language of the Act limited the FPC's jurisdiction nonetheless:

> The complainants finally argue that even though it may have been proper 50 years ago to construe the Commission's licensing jurisdiction as limited to hydroelectric projects, such a construction does great violence to the policies central to the Federal Power Act in the light of modern conditions. Because the cooling water used by the six plants involved in this case will be evaporated rather than returned to the river system, those plants will withdraw permanently up to 250,000 acre feet of water annually from the Colorado River system--more water than was used by all the steam plants in the United States in 1920. Unless such uses are regulated by subjecting

them to the licensing jurisdiction of the Commission, the complainants argue, private power interests will succeed in appropriating the power potential in public waters, the very evil the Federal Water Power Act was designed to eliminate.

Whatever the merits of the complainants' argument as a matter of policy, it is properly addressed to Congress, not to the courts. The legislative history of the Federal Water Power Act conclusively demonstrates that in 1920 Congress intended to provide for the orderly development of the power potential of the Nation's waterways only through the licensing of hydroelectric projects. And in 1935, when the Act was re-enacted as Part I of the Federal Power Act, Congress chose not to expand the licensing authority of the Commission [.]

Moreover, several times in recent years the Commission has sought an expansion of its licensing jurisdiction to include thermal-electric power generating plants, but Congress has failed to approve any of these proposals.

It may well be that the "obvious" distinction, recognized by Congress in 1920, in 1935, and in subsequent years of inaction * * * between utilization of water resources by a hydroelectric project and a thermal-electric power plant is no longer viable. But until Congress changes the licensing provisions of Part I of the Federal Power Act, it is our duty to apply the statute as it was written and has been construed for the past 54 years.

## Siting Legislation

Since 1920, hydroelectric generating plants, including dams and pumped storage plants, have required licenses from the FPC (now the Federal Energy Regulatory Commission) under the Federal Power Act, 16 U.S.C.A. §§ 791a-828c. The Commission considers siting as well as design. Similarly, since 1954 nuclear plants must be federally licensed as to design, construction and radiation safety under the Atomic Energy Act, 42 U.S.C.A. §§ 2011-2282.

The states, however, share jurisdiction as to siting and environmental impacts other than radiation. See *Northern States Power Co. v. Minnesota*, 447 F.2d 1143 (8th Cir. 1971), aff'd 405 U.S. 1035, 92 S. Ct. 1307, 31 L.Ed.2d 576. And in the case of both hydroelectric and nuclear plants the state must certify under Clean Water Act § 401 that the plant will meet its water-quality standards. See *DeRham v. Diamond* and *Public Utility District of Jefferson County v. Washington*, Chapter 7, Part C. All major electric generating plants require water--hydro plants to turn their turbines, other to make steam and, in the case of nuclear plants, to cool their reactors.

It is only since the 1970s that fossil-fueled generating plants, in which coal, oil or gas heat the steam which turns the turbine, have been subjected to comprehensive licensing schemes. Mainly as a result of the protracted litigation surrounding such projects as Storm King Mountain in New York (See Chapter 1 and Note *supra*) and the uncertainty and economic and political costs encountered by utility companies whenever plans for a new plant were introduced, most states have enacted power plant siting laws. See, *e.g.*, Ohio Rev. Stat. §§ 469.300-469-570; N.Y. Pub. Service Law §§ 160-172.

Under state siting laws, decisions are made by the public utility commission or an interagency siting board and are judicially reviewable by a proceeding that precludes all other court challenges. The statute provides for relatively concise hearings concentrating on the main issues. Localities are divested of power to require other permits or licenses for plants approved by the siting. In New York, an application fee of $150,000 is imposed which is available to opponents of the proposed plant, including municipalities and conservation and consumer groups.

Of course, federal environmental statutes must be satisfied by any new power plants. Coastal zoning commissions like California's have the power to forbid location of electric power plants in areas that would interfere with the coastal act's objectives. See *California's Energy Commission: Illusions of a One-Stop Power Plant Siting Agency*, 24 U.C.L.A. L. Rev. 1313 (1977). So it is clear that no matter how carefully constructed a state's siting legislation, utilities will never have total "one-stop shopping" for plant location. The complex interweaving of state and federal laws instead creates a groundwork for the balancing of important competing societal interests, such as energy needs, environmental safeguards and the protection of fishing and other economic activities.

## B. ELECTRIC RATES AND DEMAND

Electric rates require the approval of a public service or public utility commission in every state. As with gas, telephone, and other utility companies, their inherent monopoly within their service area has mandated state control of their charges to avoid excessive or unjust rates for basic services. As long as the company is guaranteed a fair return on its property the regulation of its rates has long been held a valid exercise of the police power. See *Smyth v. Ames*, 169 U.S. 466, 18 S. Ct. 418, 42 L.Ed. 819 (1898) (railroad freight rates).

Weinberg, *Power Plant Siting in New York: High Tension Issue*, 25 N.Y. Law School L. Rev. 569 (1980), discussing the protracted litigation surrounding the Storm King plant at Cornwall, New York, notes:

> If, like Sisyphus, the electric utilities seem to be perpetually engaged in frustrating endeavor, the explanation lies with the economic structure of the industry. Electric rates, which in New York require the approval of the Public Service Commission (PSC), are largely, and were until quite recently almost entirely, based on the declining-block rate structure system. This system, conceived in

the early part of the century to foster increased demand for electricity, encourages the use of large amounts of electricity by reducing a consumer's per-unit costs as consumption increases. In an era when most homes had only a few electric appliances and others were without electricity entirely, the declining-block rate system made sense. By the 1960s, however, demand for electricity had reached levels close to the limit of many companies' ability to produce it. Con Edison, supplying power to a large metropolitan area which contains a great number of air-conditioned buildings, was particularly hard-pressed during the summer months. Consequently, the company was confronted with a continuing need to expand its generating capacity--especially by the construction of peak-power units such as the proposed Cornwall plant--and to replace obsolete, air polluting, coal-fired facilities.

Less costly and more conservation-oriented solutions to this dilemma existed. The declining-block rate structure was not etched in stone, and has since been substantially modified to reduce unnecessary demand for power. Furthermore, electric companies can offer price incentives for power used during off-peak hours in order to lower demand during peak hours to distribute the cost more fairly--a device used in telephone and transportation pricing for decades. Offering incentives for consumers to iron, do laundry and operate dishwashers before or after periods of peak use will reduce the need for plants such as Cornwall, which are designed to furnish power for those peak hours. These devices are now being belatedly employed. A decade ago, their use would have reduced the need for some of the costly power plants which, together with the oil price squeeze, led to the enormous electric rate increases of the early seventies.

NEW YORK STATE COUNCIL OF RETAIL MERCHANTS, INC. v. PUBLIC SERVICE COMMISSION, New York Court of Appeals, 1978. 45 N.Y.2d 661, 412 N.Y.S.2d 358, 384 N.E.2d 1282.

Jones, J.

* * * On August 8, 1975 Long Island Lighting Company (LILCO) filed an application with the Public Service Commission for a general rate increase. [T]he commission had [earlier] issued an order stating that the "rapidly increasing cost of fuel both make it urgent, in the interest of energy conservation and the efficient use of resources, that the structure of energy prices reflect, to the greatest extent feasible, the variations in the incremental costs of service because of differences in the time of consumption, as well as in all other cost-influencing factors" [--"marginal costs." The Commission found] "that marginal costs do provide a reasonable basis for electric rate structures." The Commission added, however: "This finding does not

mean that rate structures must in *all* cases embody marginal cost pricing, or that rate structures in *any* case should be based exclusively on such principles. But it does mean that marginal costs are an important tool for consideration in all rate cases, and that failures to take these principles into account should be justified."

* * * LILCO, having been directed by the Commission to file a rate based on marginal costs, with the benefit of suggestions made by Commission staff, calculated the company's marginal costs and then placed those costs into three rating periods [based on use]. [T]he following periods were identified:

Period 1 (off-peak period, lowest demand): Midnight to 7 A.M.; all days, all year;

Period 2 (peak period, greatest demand): 10 A.M. to 10 P.M. weekdays and Saturdays, June 1 to September 30; and

Period 3 (intermediate or "shoulder" period): all remaining times.

The company then selected the group of its consumers to which new rates based on quantity and time-of-day consumption would be applied in the first phase of eventual across-the-board application. It chose its [175] largest commercial and industrial consumers.

[T]he Commission's determination in approving LILCO's proposal must be upheld if there exists a rational, though not necessarily cost-related, predicate for the Commission's action. We find that there is a rational basis both for the determination that introduction of the newly designed rate structure should proceed on a step-by-step basis rather than across the board at the outset, and for the conclusion that the first step classification proposed by LILCO was reasonable in the circumstances.

[T]here was warrant for the Commission's determination to implement time-of-day rates in progressive steps rather than to apply the new rates to all customers at one time. [Likewise,] there was a rational basis for approval of the group of consumers selected by LILCO for first stage application of the new rate structure. * * * LILCO had at its own expense placed the type of sophisticated meters required by such a rate with its largest use commercial and industrial class of customers for the purpose of collecting load data. Not only could it be found that it was appropriate to use the large use consumers because their high kilowatt hour usage would result in a much lower metering cost per kilowatt hour, thus producing a minimal customer burden relative to what it would be for other customers on LILCO's system; additionally, meters were already in place for these consumers, thereby postponing "the enormous cost that a widescale mandatory metering program would entail." Necessary consumer education can most efficiently be undertaken with a relatively small group of informed, sophisticated consumers. The group selected was making substantial payments to LILCO and thus had a real potential for usage responsiveness; its large consumption of energy offered both opportunity and inducement to take effective action, perhaps even at some initial cost to the consumers, to shift more load to off-peak periods. There was warrant for the hope that some significant decrease in the use of inefficient generating facilities might be realized * * * .

* * * There was uncontroverted evidence that production costs increased in times of peak demand when it became necessary to put the less efficient, more costly generating facilities on the line. * * * Even in the absence of proof that each of the affected consumers had an elasticity of demand in consequence of which it could respond to price signals, it cannot be concluded that the new rate structure will not produce significant changes in consumption patterns, whether by way of shifts from peak period consumption to consumption in off-peak or shoulder periods or by way of reduced consumption of energy in consequence of the installation of more efficient electricity using equipment or the redesign of present equipment to achieve the same end. It will only be after the new rates have been in operation that the practical effect of the carrot and the club can reliably be measured. * * *

Additionally the real test on this approach will come when time-of-day pricing is applied across the board, not alone to the small segment of consumers to which the new rate structure is initially applied in first stage implementation, but to all of LILCO's customers. [The] rate proposal represents a rational and reasonable step in the direction pointed by the Commission toward time-of-day pricing for electricity and * * * finds substantial support in this record. * * *

## Deregulation

Since the 1990s some states have ended the traditional monopoly enjoyed by electric utilities within their service area and begun to allow other electric suppliers to compete for customers. This idea flows from the success in lowering telephone rates by permitting competition. Are there other concerns with regard to electricity that ought to be taken into account? Producing electric power (unlike providing telephone service) has significant environmental impacts--air and water pollution, nuclear concerns, and the like. Will fostering competition among power producers tempt some to cut corners in terms of environmental protection? If power produced in more environmentally benign ways is more costly, how can the states encourage customers to use it in preference to cheaper power produced at greater cost to air and water quality?

Does the federal government, which historically left electric utility regulation to the states, have a role to play in this drama?

## The Public Utility Regulatory Policies Act

In an effort to encourage state public utility commissions to adopt conservation-oriented rate structures, in 1978 Congress adopted the Public Utility Regulatory Policies Act (PURPA), 16 U.S.C.A. §§ 2601-2645. The Act requires state commissions to consider conservation-oriented federal standards, including (1) allowing the declining-block electric rate system, under which cost decreases as use increases, only where the utility can show its costs actually decrease with volume, and (2) time-of-day and seasonal rate differentials such as those adopted by New York in *Council of Retail Merchants*.

States must furnish the Federal Energy Regulatory Commission with reasons for *not* adopting the Act's standards. And no utility purchasing power for resale to consumers from a federal agency, such as the Tennessee Valley Authority, may contract to prevent implementation of the standards designed to protect consumers from cut-offs of power without adequate notice. The Act's most significant single provision requires utilities to purchase power generated by a consumer's own windmill, solar cell or other generator at the market price, and to sell power to these customers when they need it. This is aimed at curtailing the practice of some utilities of refusing to supply self-generating customers when their windmill or dam is inoperable, and refusing to buy excess power produced by these customers.

Does PURPA exceed the power of Congress under the Commerce Clause and interfere with the states' attributes of sovereignty in contravention of the Tenth Amendment? See *Federal Energy Regulatory Comm'n v. Mississippi*, 456 U.S. 742, 102 S. Ct. 2126, 72 L.Ed. 2d 532 (1982), in which the Court upheld the Act, noting the federal government could have preempted the field entirely. Four justices dissented.

## Costs of Unbuilt Power Plants

Public utility commissions allow electric utilities to earn a reasonable profit based on their total assets, or "rate base." Should the rate base include power plants under construction? Generally, it does not. This means utilities have to borrow the extensive funds needed to build power plants, adding the interest they must pay to their costs of operations.

What if a power plant, like the proposed hydro plant at Storm King Mountain, never gets completed? Utilities are generally allowed to recover from ratepayers (consumers) "prudent investment" expenses in such cases. Whatever costs are found by regulatory commissions not to be reasonable and prudent must be absorbed by the company's shareholders.

## Regulating Promotional Advertising

Electric utilities often include with their monthly bills an insert containing some energy-related message for the customer. State public utility commissions have the authority to regulate, to a certain extent, the content of these inserts. The limits on this kind of regulation, however, have been clearly set by the Supreme Court.

In *Consolidated Edison Co. v. Public Service Comm'n*, 447 U.S. 530, 100 S. Ct. 2326, 65 L.Ed.2d 319 (1980), the Supreme Court struck down a regulation by New York's commission which forbade utilities from including inserts that discussed "controversial issues of public policy." Con Edison had been inserting messages promoting nuclear energy as a means of achieving American independence from foreign oil. The Court was unpersuaded by the Commission's contention that the bill inserts constituted a substantial intrusion into the customer's privacy which should be regulated vigorously. It said instead that any restriction on the company's right to discuss matters of public policy must meet the test for an encroachment on First Amendment freedoms--the restriction must be narrowly drawn to attain a compelling state goal, or must be a valid time, place or manner regulation, or within the narrow category of permissible subject-matter regulations (such as restrictions of speech on military bases or on public transportation). Since none of the tests were satisfied by the Commission's prohibition, based clearly on the content of the utility's message, it could not stand.

Advertising by public utilities is governed by a different standard. In *Central Hudson Gas & Elec. Corp. v. Public Service Comm'n*, 447 U.S. 557, 100 S. Ct. 2343, 65 L.Ed.2d 341 (1980), the Commission barred electric utilities from promoting the use of electricity in their advertisements. The regulation was designed to stem consumer demand for electricity during the energy crisis of the 1970s.

The Court held advertising, as commercial speech, can only be restricted by statutes that are carefully designed to achieve a substantial state interest, and drawn as narrowly as possible to accomplish that goal. The Court agreed that energy conservation is a substantial state interest, but held the regulation unconstitutional because it swept too broadly and only indirectly furthered that goal. For example, the ban outlawed advertisements for products such as heat pumps which would in fact foster energy conservation.

What more effective means may a state employ to accomplish the end sought by New York?

## C. NUCLEAR POWER

### 1. Federal Regulation

VERMONT YANKEE NUCLEAR POWER CORP. v. NATURAL RESOURCES DEFENSE COUNCIL, INC., Supreme Court of the United States, 1978. 435 U.S. 519, 98 S. Ct. 1197, 55 L.Ed. 2d 460.

Justice Rehnquist delivered the opinion of the Court.

* * * Under the Atomic Energy Act of 1954, * * * 42 U.S.C. § 2011 [--2282], the Atomic Energy Commission[2] was given broad regulatory authority over the development of nuclear energy. Under the terms of the Act, a utility seeking to construct and operate a nuclear power plant must obtain a separate permit or license at both the construction and the operation stage of the project. In order to obtain the construction permit, the utility must file a preliminary safety analysis report [and] an environmental report. This application then undergoes exhaustive review by the Commission's staff and by the Advisory Committee on Reactor Safeguards (ACRS),

---

[2] The licensing and regulatory functions of the Atomic Energy Commission (AEC) were transferred to the Nuclear Regulatory Commission (NRC) * * * by the Energy Reorganization Act of 1974. Hereinafter both the AEC and NRC will be referred to as the Commission.

a group of distinguished experts in the field of atomic energy. Both groups submit to the Commission their own evaluations, which then become part of the record of the utility's application.[3] The Commission staff also undertakes the review required by NEPA and prepares a draft environmental impact statement, which after being circulated for comment, is revised and becomes a final environmental impact statement. Thereupon a three-member Atomic Safety and Licensing Board conducts a public adjudicatory hearing, and reaches a decision[4] which can be appealed to the Atomic Safety and Licensing Appeal Board, and * * *, in the Commission's discretion, to the Commission itself. * * * The final agency decision may be appealed to the courts of appeals. * * * The same sort of process occurs when the utility applies for a license to operate the plant, except that a hearing need only be held in contested cases and may be limited to the matters in controversy.[5]

These cases arise from two separate decisions of the Court of Appeals for the District of Columbia Circuit. In the first, the court remanded a decision of the Commission to grant a license to petitioner, Vermont Yankee Nuclear Power Corp., to operate a nuclear power plant.* * * In the second, the court remanded a decision of that same agency to grant a permit to petitioner, Consumers Power Co., to construct two pressurized water nuclear reactors to generate electricity and steam.* * *

In December 1967, * * * the Commission granted petitioner Vermont Yankee a permit to build a nuclear power plant in Vernon, Vt. * * * Thereafter, Vermont Yankee applied for an operating license. Respondent Natural Resources Defense Council (NRDC) objected to the granting of a license, however, and therefore a hearing on the application commenced[.] Excluded from consideration at the hearings, over NRDC's objection, was the issue of the environmental effects of operations to reprocess fuel or dispose of wastes resulting from the reprocessing operations.[6] This ruling was affirmed by the Appeal Board[.]

In November 1972, however, the Commission, making specific references to the Appeal Board's decision with respect to the Vermont Yankee license, instituted

---

[3] ACRS is required to review each construction permit application for the purpose of informing the Commission of the "hazards of proposed or existing reactor facilities and the adequacy of proposed reactor safety standards."

[4] The Licensing Board issues a permit if it concludes that there is reasonable assurance that the proposed plant can be constructed and operated without undue risk and that environmental cost-benefit balance favors the issuance of a permit.

[5] When a license application is contested, the Licensing Board must find reasonable assurance that the plant can be operated without undue risk and will not be inimical to the common defense and security or to the health and safety of the public. The Licensing Board's decision is subject to review similar to that afforded the Board's decision with respect to a construction permit.

[6] The nuclear fission which takes place in light-water nuclear reactors apparently converts its principal fuel, uranium, into plutonium, which is itself highly radioactive but can be used as reactor fuel if separated from the remaining uranium and radioactive waste products. Fuel reprocessing refers to the process necessary to recapture usable plutonium. Waste disposal, at the present state of technological development, refers to the storage of the very long-lived and highly radioactive waste products until they detoxify sufficiently that they no longer present an environmental hazard. There are presently no physical or chemical steps which render this waste less toxic, other than simply the passage of time.

rulemaking proceedings "that would specifically deal with the question of consideration of environmental effects associated with the uranium fuel cycle in the individual cost-benefit analysis for light water cooled nuclear power reactors." * * * The Commission [proposed to give] specified numerical values for the environmental impact of this part of the fuel cycle, which values would then be incorporated into a table, along with the other relevant factors, to determine the overall cost-benefit balance for each operating license.

Much of the controversy in this case revolves around the procedures used in the rulemaking hearing[.] [T]he Commission indicated that while discovery or cross-examination would not be utilized, the Environmental Survey would be available to the public before the hearing along with the extensive background documents cited therein. All participants would be given a reasonable opportunity to present their position[.] Written and, time permitting, oral statements would be received and incorporated into the record.

* * * In April 1974, the Commission issued [the proposed] rule[.] Respondents appealed * * * to the Court of Appeals for the District of Columbia Circuit.

In January 1969, petitioner Consumers Power Co. applied for a permit to construct two nuclear reactors in Midland, Mich. * * * Saginaw [, a citizen group,] intervened and opposed the application. Hearings were then held on numerous radiological-health and safety issues. Thereafter, the Commission's staff issued a draft environmental impact statement. Saginaw submitted 119 environmental contentions[.] The staff revised the statement and issued a final environmental statement in March 1972. Further hearings were then conducted[.] [T]he Appeal Board ultimately affirmed the Licensing Board's grant of a construction permit and the Commission declined to further review the matter.

[O]n November 6, 1973, more than a year after the record had been closed in the *Consumers Power* case, and while that case was pending before the Court of Appeals, the Commission ruled in another case that while its statutory power to compel conservation was not clear, it did not follow that all evidence of energy conservation issues should therefore be barred at the threshold. Saginaw then moved the Commission to * * * reopen the *Consumers Power* proceedings.

[T]he Commission declined to reopen the proceedings. The Commission first ruled it was required to consider only energy conservation alternatives which were "'reasonably available,'" would in their aggregate effect curtail demand for electricity to a level at which the proposed facility would not be needed, and were susceptible of a reasonable degree of proof. * * * It then determined, after a thorough examination of the record, that not all of Saginaw's contentions met these threshold tests. * * *

It further determined that the Board had been willing at all times to take evidence on the other contentions. Saginaw had simply failed to present any such evidence. The Commission further criticized Saginaw for its total disregard of even those minimal procedural formalities necessary to give the Board some idea of exactly what was at issue. The Commission emphasized that "[p]articularly in these circumstances, Saginaw's complaint that it was not granted a hearing on alleged energy conservation issues comes with ill grace." * * * And in response to Saginaw's contention that regardless of whether it properly raised the issues, the Licensing Board must consider all environmental issues, the Commission basically agreed, as did the Board itself, but further reasoned that the Board must have some workable procedural rules and these rules in this setting must take into account that energy conservation is a novel and evolving concept. NEPA "does not require a `crystal ball' inquiry." *Natural Resources Defense Council v. Morton*, [Chapter 10, Part A]. * * * As we gain experience on a case-by-case basis and hopefully, feasible energy conservation techniques emerge, the applicant, staff, and licensing boards will have obligations to develop an adequate record on these issues in appropriate cases, whether or not they are raised by intervenors.

However, at this emergent stage of energy conservation principles, intervenors also have their responsibilities. They must state clear and reasonably specific energy conservation contentions in a time fashion. Beyond that, they have a burden of coming forward with some affirmative showing if they wish to have these novel contentions explored further.

* * * Respondents then challenged the granting of the construction permit in the Court of Appeals for the District of Columbia Circuit.

With respect to the challenge of Vermont Yankee's license, the court [of appeals] first ruled that in the absence of effective rulemaking proceedings, the Commission must deal with the environmental impact of fuel reprocessing and disposal in individual licensing proceedings. * * * The court then examined the rulemaking proceedings and, despite the fact that it appeared that the agency employed all the procedures required by [the Administrative Procedure Act,] and more, the court determined the proceedings to be inadequate and overturned the rule. Accordingly, the Commission's determination with respect to Vermont Yankee's license was also remanded for further proceedings. * * *

With respect to the permit to Consumers Power, the court first held that the environmental impact statement * * * was fatally defective for failure to examine energy conservation as an alternative to a plant of this size. * * *

Petitioner Vermont Yankee first argues that the Commission may grant a license to operate a nuclear reactor without any consideration of waste disposal and fuel reprocessing.

Vermont Yankee will produce annually well over 100 pounds of radioactive wastes, some of which will be highly toxic. The Commission itself, in a pamphlet published by its information office, clearly recognizes that these wastes "pose the most severe potential health hazard...." Many of these substances must be isolated for anywhere from 600 to hundreds of thousands of years. It is hard to argue that these wastes do not constitute "adverse environmental effects which cannot be avoided should the proposal be implemented," or that by operating nuclear power plants we are not making "irreversible and irretrievable commitments of resources." [NEPA.]

For these reasons we hold that the Commission acted well within its statutory authority when it considered the back end of the fuel cycle in individual licensing proceedings.

We next turn to the invalidation of the fuel cycle rule [, which] the Court of Appeals struck down * * * because of the perceived inadequacies of the procedures employed in the rulemaking proceedings. * * *

The court below uncritically assumed that the additional procedures will automatically result in a more adequate record because it will give interested parties more of an opportunity to participate in and contribute to the proceedings. But informal rulemaking need not be based solely on the transcript of a hearing held before an agency. Indeed, the agency need not even hold a formal hearing. See [Administrative Procedure Act §4,] 5 U.S.C. § 553(c) * * * .

* * * Respondent NRDC also argues that the fact that the Commission's inquiry was undertaken in the context of NEPA somehow permits a court to require procedures beyond those specified in § 4 of the APA when investigating factual issues through rulemaking. The Court of Appeals was apparently also of this view, indicating that agencies may be required to "develop new procedures to accomplish the innovative task of implementing NEPA through rulemaking." * * *

But we search in vain for something in NEPA which would mandate such a result. [J]ust two Terms ago, we emphasized that the only procedural requirements imposed by NEPA are those stated in the plain language of the Act. *Kleppe v. Sierra Club[.]*

In short, nothing in the APA, NEPA, the circumstances of this case, the nature of the issues being considered, past agency practice, or the statutory mandate under which the Commission operates permitted the court to review and overturn the rulemaking proceeding on the basis of the procedural devices employed (or not employed) by the Commission so long as the Commission employed at least the statutory *minima*, a matter about which there is no doubt in this case.

There remains, of course, the question of whether the challenged rule finds sufficient justification in the administrative proceedings that it should be upheld by the reviewing court. * * * We accordingly remand so that the Court of Appeals may review the rule as the Administrative Procedure Act provides. * * * The court should * * * not stray beyond the judicial province to explore the procedural format or to impose upon the agency its own notion of which procedures are "best" or most likely to further some vague, undefined public good.

We now turn to the Court of Appeals' holding "that rejection of energy conservation on the basis of the `threshold test' was capricious and arbitrary," * * * and again conclude the court was wrong.

The Court of Appeals ruled that the Commission's "threshold test" for the presentation of energy conservation contentions was inconsistent with NEPA's basic mandate to the Commission. * * * The Commission, the court reasoned, is something more than an umpire who sits back and resolves adversary contentions at the hearing stage. * * * And when an intervenor's comments "bring `sufficient attention to the issue to stimulate the Commission's consideration of it,' " the

Commission must "undertake its own preliminary investigation of the proffered alternative sufficient to reach a rational judgment whether it is worthy of detailed consideration in the EIS. Moreover, the Commission must explain the basis for each conclusion that further consideration of a suggested alternative is unwarranted." * * *

While the court's rationale is not entirely unappealing as an abstract proposition, as applied to this case we think it basically misconceives not only the scope of the agency's statutory responsibility, but also the nature of the administrative process, the thrust of the agency's decision, and the type of issues the intervenors were trying to raise.

There is little doubt that under the Atomic Energy Act * * *, state public utility commissions or similar bodies are empowered to make the initial decisions regarding the need for power. 42 U.S.C. § 2021(k). The Commission's prime area of concern in the licensing context, on the other hand, is national security, public health, and safety. And it is clear that the need * * * for the power was thoroughly explored in the hearings. * * *

NEPA, of course, has altered slightly the statutory balance, requiring "a detailed statement by the responsible official on....alternatives to the proposed action." But, [t]o make an impact statement something more than an exercise in frivolous boilerplate, the concept of alternatives must be bound by some notion of feasibility. * * * *National Resources Defense Council v. Morton[.]* Common sense also teaches us that the "detailed statement of alternatives" cannot be found wanting simply because the agency failed to include every alternative device and thought conceivable by the mind of man.

With these principles in mind we now turn to the notion of "energy conservation," an alternative the omission of which was thought by the Court of Appeals to have been "forcefully pointed out by Saginaw in its comments on the draft EIS." [I]t is largely the events of recent years that have emphasized not only the need but also a large variety of alternatives for energy conservation. Prior to the drastic oil shortages incurred by the United States in 1973, there was little serious thought in most Government circles of energy conservation alternatives.

We think these facts amply demonstrate that the concept of "alternatives" is an evolving one, requiring the agency to explore more or fewer alternatives as they become better known and understood. This was well understood by the Commission, which, unlike the Court of Appeals, recognized that the Licensing Board's decision had to be judged by the information then available to it. And judged in that light we have little doubt the Board's actions were well within the proper bounds of its statutory authority. Not only did the record before the agency give every indication that the project was actually needed, but also there was nothing before the Board to indicate to the contrary.

[W]hile it is true that NEPA places upon an agency the obligation to consider every significant aspect of the environmental impact of a proposed action, it is still incumbent upon intervenors who wish to participate to structure their participation so that it is meaningful, so that it alerts the agency to the intervenors' position and contentions. This is especially true when the intervenors are requesting the agency to embark upon an exploration of uncharted territory, as was the question of energy conservation in the late 1960s and early 1970s.

In fact, here the agency continually invited further clarification of Saginaw's contentions. Even without such clarification it indicated a willingness to receive evidence on the matters. But not only did Saginaw decline to further focus its contentions, it virtually declined to participate[.]

Finally, we turn to the Court of Appeals' holding that the Licensing Board should have returned the [Advisory Committee on Reactor Safety (ACRS)] report to ACRS for further elaboration, understandable to a layman, of the reference to other problems.

The Court of Appeals reasoned that since one function of the report was "that all concerned may be apprised of the safety or possible hazard of the facilities," the report must be in terms understandable to a layman and replete with cross-references to previous report in which the "other problems" are detailed [, or else] the entire agency action * * * must be nullified.

Again, the Court of Appeals has unjustifiably intruded into the administrative process. The ACRS report served an important function. But the legislative history shows that the function of publication was subsidiary to its main function, that of providing technical advice from a body of experts uniquely qualified to provide assistance. * * * The basic information to be conveyed to the public is not necessarily a full technical exposition of every facet of nuclear energy, but rather the ACRS's position, and reasons therefor, with respect to the safety of a proposed nuclear reactor.

[W]e find absolutely nothing in the relevant statutes to justify what the court did here. The Commission very well might be able to remand a report for clarification, but there is nothing to support a court's ordering the Commission to take that step or to support a court's requiring the ACRS to give a short explanation, understandable to a layman, of each generic safety concern.

All this leads us to make one further observation of some relevance to this case. To say that the Court of Appeals' final reason for remanding is insubstantial at best is a gross understatement. Consumers Power first applied in 1969 for a construction permit--not even an operating license, just a construction permit. The proposed plant underwent an incredibly extensive review. The reports filed and reviewed literally fill books. The proceedings took years, and the actual hearings themselves over two weeks. To then nullify that effort seven years later because one report refers to other problems, which problems admittedly have been discussed at length in other reports available to the public, borders on the Kafkaesque. Nuclear energy may some day be a cheap, safe source of power, or it may not. But Congress has made a choice to at least try nuclear energy, establishing a reasonable review process in which courts are to play only a limited role. The fundamental policy questions appropriately resolved in Congress and in the state legislatures are not subject to re-examination in the federal courts under the guise of judicial review of agency action. Time may prove wrong the decision to develop nuclear energy, but it is Congress or the States within their appropriate agencies which must eventually make that judgment. In the meantime courts should perform their appointed function. * * * And a single alleged oversight on a peripheral issue, urged by parties who never fully cooperated or indeed raised the issue below, must not be made the basis for overturning a decision properly made after an otherwise exhaustive proceeding.

Reversed and remanded.

## Notes

Does *Vermont Yankee* erode the hard look doctrine of *Overton Park,* Chapter 1, in its obeisance to the administrative agency's broad discretion? It was the same Court of Appeals for the District of Columbia Circuit which held in *Ethyl Corp. v. EPA,* Chapter 1, that "[r]egulators such as the Administrator must be accorded flexibility . . ." which the Supreme Court in *Vermont Yankee* found exceeded its "appointed function" by second-guessing the NRC. But in *Ethyl Corp.* the Court of Appeals spoke of "a flexibility that recognizes the special judicial interest in favor of protection of the health and welfare of the people, even in areas where certainty does not exist." Did the Court in *Vermont Yankee* accord the NRC that sort of flexibility where judicial concern for protection of health might lead to overturning the NRC's decision?

How much is *Vermont Yankee* explained by the failure of the intervenors in Consumers Power to adequately raise their environmental concerns at the agency level?

Note also that *Vermont Yankee* rejected the utilities' contention that nuclear waste issues need not be dealt with in proceedings to license individual plants. There, as in the rest of its decision, the Court upheld the agency's determination. Would the case have been decided differently had the NRC not so ruled, giving room for the conclusion that the agency was unconcerned about the nuclear waste problem?

Does *Vermont Yankee* represent a shift away from the Court of Appeals' decision in *Calvert Cliffs,* Chapter 10, Part A? Or are the two cases in harmony, in melody if not in tone?

In the wake of *Vermont Yankee* the controversial NRC rule was remanded to the Court of Appeals for consideration on its merits. The Court of Appeals again overturned it and the Supreme Court again unanimously reversed, upholding the rule. *Baltimore Gas and Electric Co. v. Natural Resources Defense Council, Inc.*, 462 U.S. 87, 103 S. Ct. 2246, 76 L.Ed.2d 437 (1983). Nuclear waste became the subject of federal legislation, described after the following note.

## Emergency Response Plans

The Three Mile Island incident in 1979, in which a nuclear plant in Pennsylvania suffered a near-meltdown--an occurrence the industry had described as virtually impossible--prompted a major overhaul of the Act's requirements for power plants. Each nuclear facility must prepare an emergency response plan for approval by the Federal Emergency Management Agency (FEMA) and the NRC, including already-licensed plants. This proved a means of challenging new plants, such as the proposed Shoreham power station on Long Island. Such plans must show how the authorities will rapidly move residents from a ten-mile radius of the plant to safer quarters. But what if state and local authorities refuse to certify that residents can be safely moved? May the utility itself submit a plan, using its own employees, or is this a usurpation of the state's police power by a private company? See *Cuomo v. Long Island Lighting Co.*, 127 A.D.2d 626, 511 N.Y.S.2d 867 (2d Dept. 1987), reversed as request for advisory opinion 71 N.Y.2d 349, 520 N.E.2d 546, 525 N.Y.S.2d 828 (holding such a private plan invalid). More conventional evacuation plans, with state and municipal authorities cooperating, have been upheld. See *Commonwealth of Massachusetts v. United States Nuclear Regulatory Comm'n*, 878 F.2d 1516 (1st Cir. 1989) (plan upheld even though FEMA had found it inadequate; NRC is not bound by FEMA's determination).

## Transporting and Disposing of Nuclear Materials

The risks of nuclear power are not limited to those of the reactor. Both nuclear fuel and the nuclear waste generated by reactors pose hazards in shipment and in storage. Congress has imposed strict safeguards on air shipment of plutonium and similar nuclear materials, following a suit to enjoin such shipments into New York's Kennedy Airport. *State of New York v. Nuclear Regulatory Comm'n*, 550 F.2d 745 (2d Cir. 1977). Although the plaintiff's attempt to enjoin such shipments until the Commission prepared an EIS was unsuccessful, the suit focused Congressional attention on the risks and led to legislation restricting the civil air transportation of nuclear fuels until a container safer than those then in use is developed. See 49 U.S.C.A. § 1807.

The shipment of spent nuclear fuel rods by truck to storage sites also imposes hazards of collision, especially in crowded areas. As municipalities wrote local laws in the late 1970s restricting highway transportation of nuclear waste and other radioactive materials, the United States Department of Transportation, fearing a patchwork of local obstacles to this traffic, in 1981 exercised its authority to preempt local laws under the Hazardous Materials Transportation Act, 49 U.S.C.A. §§ 1801-1819. In *City of New York v. United States Dep't of Transportation,* 539 F.Supp. 1237 (S.D.N.Y. 1982) the court enjoined the federal regulations, as applied to transporting spent nuclear fuel through densely populated areas, pending the agency preparing an EIS examining alternatives.

This judgment was reversed, 715 F.2d 732 (2d Cir. 1983), cert. den., 465 U.S. 1055. The Court of Appeals held a "worst-case" accident was unlikely and therefore need not be considered in an EIS. Nor, it concluded, does the Hazardous Materials Transportation Act mandate the safest mode of shipment in all cases, as long as "acceptable levels" of safety are maintained.

What alternatives would be safer than highway transport? Air? Barge? Avoiding densely populated areas by road is difficult in some areas, and impossible in shipping spent fuel from Long Island to storage sites elsewhere in the country.

The storage of these materials is fraught with similar risks. At present only three storage sites are licensed by the NRC. That agency continues its search for a permanent site and for safer means of permanent disposal of spent fuel, liquid waste and other radioactive refuse. Can the NRC's ultimate selection of a site be imposed on an unwilling state or municipality?

The failure of the NRC to resolve the storage issue led California to halt nuclear power plant construction pending its resolution. See *Pacific Gas & Electric Co. v. State Energy Comm'n* in Subpart 2 of this Chapter.

States' attempts to bar the importation of nuclear waste for disposal have, following *City of Philadelphia v. New Jersey* (Chapter 9, Part A), been overturned as discrimination against interstate commerce and as preempted by the Hazardous Materials Transportation Act. See *Washington State Building Council v. Spellman*, 518 F. Supp. 928 (E.D. Wash. 1981), aff'd 684 F.2d 627; *People of State of Illinois v. General Electric Co.*, 683 F.2d 206 (7th Cir. 1982).

## The Nuclear Waste Policy Act

In 1982 Congress attempted to put the nuclear waste problem to bed. The Nuclear Waste Policy Act, 42 U.S.C.A. §§ 10101-10226, empowers the President to select a site for a repository of high-level nuclear waste. (A separate statute deals with less radioactive low-level waste, discussed further on.) The Secretary of Energy was to recommend at least five suitable sites, after consulting with the governors of those states. The President was then to submit two of the recommended sites to Congress, which could approve them, subject to a state veto that Congress could override. It should be noted, however, that the Supreme Court has held that such Congressional overrides of executive decisions by federal agencies are unconstitutional violations of the separation of powers. *Immigration & Naturalization Service v. Chadha*, 462 U.S. 919, 103 S. Ct. 2764, 77 L.Ed.2d 317 (1983). In any event, in 1986 the Secretary of Energy recommended Yucca Mountain, Nevada as the first high-level site.

Congress promptly amended the Act to select that site and bar the state from objecting. Nevada has attempted to challenge these provisions. See *Nevada v. Watkins*, 914 F.2d 1545 (9th Cir. 1990), cert. denied 499 U.S. 906 (state lacks standing to challenge Department of Energy's access to Yucca Mountain land adminstered by Bureau of Land Management since no showing that state owns or uses adjacent lands). A 1997 report by the Department of Energy indicates that there may be water seepage into the area where the nuclear waste is to be stored. How should this issue be dealt with?

Should the states have a veto? Should Congress, or the federal government generally if Congress cannot, be able to trump the state's veto?

## Low-Level Nuclear Waste

Low-level waste, consisting of clothing, film, and the like, is governed by the Low-Level Radioactive Waste Policy Act. 42 U.S.C.A. §§ 2021b-2021j. This statute places the burden of siting squarely on the states, encouraging them to join regional compacts to dispose of low-level waste, as most have now done. A state not joining a compact must dispose of waste generated within its borders. Stringent penalties apply to states failing to take either course. Such states by 1993 were to automatically take title to, and legal liability for, all such waste generated in that state. Is this constitutionally permissible under the Tenth Amendment?

The Supreme Court ruled this provision unconstitutional in *New York v. United States*, 505 U.S. 144, 112 S.Ct. 2408, 120 L.Ed.2d 120 (1992), holding the Tenth Amendment, which reserves to the states all powers not conferred on Congress in Article I of the Constitution, bars Congress from "requir[ing] the States to govern according to Congress' instructions." The Court (O'Connor, J.) held:

> The take title provision offers state governments a "choice" of either accepting ownership of waste or regulating according to the instructions of Congress. [The Government does] not claim that the Constitution would authorize Congress to impose either option as a freestanding requirement. On one hand, the Constitution would not permit Congress simply to transfer radioactive waste from generators to state governments. Such a * * * transfer, standing alone, would in principle be no different than a congressionally compelled subsidy from state governments to radioactive waste producers. The same is true of the provision requiring the States to become liable for the generators' damages. Standing alone, this provision would be indistinguishable from an Act of Congress directing the States to assume the liabilities of certain state residents. Either type of federal action would "commandeer" state governments into the service of federal regulatory purposes, and would for this reason be inconsistent with the Constitution's division of authority between federal and state governments. On the other hand, the second alternative held out to state governments--regulating pursuant to Congress' direction--would, standing alone, present a simple command to state governments to implement legislation enacted by Congress. As we have seen, the Constitution does not empower Congress to subject state governments to this type of instruction.

Because an instruction to state governments to take title to waste, standing alone, would be beyond the authority of Congress, and because a direct order to regulate, standing alone, would also be beyond the authority of Congress, it follows that Congress lacks the power to offer the States a choice between the two. Unlike the first two sets of incentives, the take title incentive does not represent the conditional exercise of any congressional power enumerated in the Constitution. * * * A choice between two [unconstitutional] regulatory techniques is no choice at all. Either way, "the Act commandeers the legislative processes of the States by directly compelling them to enact and enforce a federal regulatory program," *Hodel* [see Chapter 3, subd. H], an outcome that has never been understood to lie within the authority conferred upon Congress by the Constitution.

[The Government] emphasize[s] the latitude given to the States to implement Congress' plan. The Act enables the States to regulate pursuant to Congress' instructions in any number of different ways. States may avoid taking title by contracting with sited regional compacts, by building a disposal site alone or as part of a compact, or by permitting private parties to build a disposal site. States that host sites may employ a wide range of designs and disposal methods, subject only to broad federal regulatory limits. This line of reasoning, however, only underscores the critical alternative a State lacks. A State may not decline to administer the federal program. No matter which path the State chooses, it must follow the direction of Congress.

The take title provision appears to be unique. No other federal statute has been cited which offers a state government no option other than that of implementing legislation enacted by Congress. Whether one views the take title provision as lying outside Congress' enumerated powers, or as infringing upon the core of state sovereignty reserved by the Tenth Amendment, the provision is inconsistent with the federal structure of our Government established by the Constitution. * * * No matter how powerful the federal interest involved, the Constitution simply does not give Congress the authority to require the States to regulate. The Constitution instead gives Congress the authority to regulate matters directly and to pre-empt contrary state regulation. Where a federal interest is sufficiently strong to cause Congress to legislate, it must do so directly; it may not conscript state governments as its [agents].

Respondents [the United States and its officials] note that the Act embodies a bargain among the sited and unsited States, a compromise to which New York was a willing participant and from which New York has reaped much benefit. Respondents then [ask]:

How can a federal statute be found an unconstitutional infringement of State sovereignty when state officials consented to the statute's enactment?

The answer follows from an understanding of the fundamental purpose served by our Government's federal structure. The Constitution does not protect the sovereignty of States for the benefit of the States or state governments as abstract political entities, or even for the benefit of the public officials governing the States. To the contrary, the Constitution divides authority between federal and state governments for the protection of individuals. State sovereignty is not just an end in itself: "Rather, federalism secures to citizens the liberties that derive from the diffusion of sovereign power." *Coleman v. Thompson,* 501 U.S. 722, 759, 111 S.Ct. 2546, 2570, 115 L.Ed.2d 640 (1991) (Blackmun, J., dissenting) at 2781. [The] constitutional authority of Congress cannot be expanded by the "consent" of the governmental unit whose domain is thereby narrowed, whether that unit is the Executive Branch or the States.

State officials thus cannot consent to the enlargement of the powers of Congress beyond those enumerated in the Constitution. Indeed, the facts of this case raise the possibility that powerful incentives might lead both federal and state officials to view departures from the federal structure to be in their personal interests. Most citizens recognize the need for radioactive waste disposal sites, but few want sites near their homes. As a result, while it would be well within the authority of either federal or state officials to choose where the disposal sites will be, it is likely to be in the political interest of each individual official to avoid being held accountable to the voters for the choice of location. If a federal official is faced with the alternatives of choosing a location or directing the States to do it, the official may well prefer the latter, as a means of shifting responsibility for the eventual decision. If a state official is faced with the same set of alternatives--choosing a location or having Congress direct the choice of a location--the state official may also prefer the latter, as it may permit the avoidance of personal responsibility. The interests of public officials thus may not coincide with the Constitution's intergovernmental allocation of authority. Where state officials purport to submit to the direction of Congress in this manner, federalism is hardly being advanced.

Justices White, Blackmun and Stevens dissented.

Note: Liability for Nuclear Disasters

The prospect of a nuclear accident has in recent years left the realm of science-fiction and, with Three Mile Island and other incidents, become cause for serious concern. The tort liability of reactors in nuclear power plants is governed by the Price-Anderson Act, 42 U.S.C.A. § 2210, enacted in 1957 when nuclear power was in its infancy. Now that it has reached adolescence, does the Act's coverage still fit?

Under Price-Anderson, nuclear power plants are strictly liable for accidents, up to a $560 million limit. Financial responsibility is shared by the reactor owners ($315 million), insurance ($140 million) and the government ($105 million). Above the limits, the utilities are absolved from liability under the Act--a scheme upheld by the Supreme Court in *Duke Power Co. v. Carolina Environmental Study Group*, 438 U.S. 59, 98 S. Ct. 2620, 57 L.Ed. 2d 595 (1978), as against the claim that the $560 million limit was not rationally related to the potential losses. The Court (Burger, Ch. J.) held:

> Assuming, *arguendo*, that the $560 million fund would not insure full recovery in all conceivable circumstances--and the hard truth is that no one can ever know--it does not by any means follow that the liability limitation is therefore irrational and violative of due process. The legislative history clearly indicates that the $560 million figure was not arrived at on the supposition that it alone would necessarily be sufficient to guarantee full compensation in the event of a nuclear incident. Instead, it was conceived of as a "starting point" or a working hypothesis. The reasonableness of the statute's assumed ceiling on liability was predicated on two corollary considerations--expert appraisals of the exceedingly small risk of a nuclear incident involving claims in excess of $560 million, and the recognition that in the event of such an incident, Congress would likely enact extraordinary relief provisions to provide additional relief, in accord with prior practice [, as with floods, earthquakes and the like].
>
> [W]hatever ceiling figure is selected will, of necessity, be arbitrary in the sense that any choice of a figure based on imponderables like those at issue here can always be so characterized. This is not, however, the kind of arbitrariness which flaws otherwise constitutional action. * * *
>
> The remaining due process objection to the liability-limitation provision is that it fails to provide those injured by a nuclear accident with a satisfactory *quid pro quo* for the common law rights of recovery which the Act abrogates. Initially, it is not at all clear that the Due Process Clause in fact requires that a legislatively enacted compensation scheme either duplicate the recovery at common law or provide a reasonable substitute

> remedy.[7] However, we need not resolve this question here since the Price-Anderson Act does, in our view, provide a reasonably just substitute for the common-law or state tort law remedies it replaces. * * *
>
> We view the congressional *assurance* of a $560 million fund for recovery, accompanied by an express statutory commitment, to "take whatever action is deemed necessary and appropriate to protect the public from the consequences of" a nuclear accident, 42 U.S.C. § 2210(e), to be a fair and reasonable substitute for the uncertain recovery of damages of this magnitude from a utility or component manufacturer, whose resources might well be exhausted at an early stage. The record in this case raises serious questions about the ability of a utility or component manufacturer to satisfy a judgment approaching $560 million--the amount guaranteed under the Price-Anderson Act.

In *Jaffee v. United States*, 592 F.2d 712 (3d Cir. 1979), cert. denied, 441 U.S. 961, soldiers ordered to stand in a field during an atomic blast in New Mexico in 1953 brought a class action for subsequent illnesses. The court held that the Government's sovereign immunity under *Feres v. United States*, discussed in the *Agent Orange* case, Chapter 8, Part C, barred recovery by armed services personnel from the Government or its officials for injuries incurred while on duty. The plaintiffs were, however, entitled to an injunction directing the Government to warn members of their class regarding the medical risks of the radiation to which their military duty had exposed them.

2. State and Local Controls

PACIFIC GAS AND ELECTRIC CO. v. STATE ENERGY RESOURCES CONSERVATION AND DEVELOPMENT COMMISSION, Supreme Court of the United States, 1983. 461 U.S. 190, 103 S.Ct. 1713, 75 L.Ed.2d 752.

White, J.

* * * This case emerges from the intersection of the federal government's efforts to ensure that nuclear power is safe with the exercise of the historic state authority over the generation and sale of electricity. At issue is whether Cal.Pub.Res. Code §§ 25524.1(b) and 25524.2, which condition the construction of nuclear plants on findings by the State Energy Resources Conservation and Development Commission that adequate storage facilities and means of disposal are available for nuclear waste, are preempted by the Atomic Energy Act[.]

A nuclear reactor must be periodically refueled and the "spent fuel" removed. This spent fuel is intensely radioactive and must be carefully stored. The general practice is to store the fuel in a water-filled pool at the reactor site. For

---

[7] Our cases have clearly established that "[a] person has no property, no vested interest, in any rule of the common law." Second Employers' Liability Cases, 223 U.S. 1, 50 (1912), quoting *Munn v. Illinois*, 94 U.S. 113, 134 (1877). * * *

many years, it was assumed that this fuel would be reprocessed; accordingly, the storage pools were designed as short-term holding facilities with limited storage capacities. As expectations for reprocessing remained unfulfilled, the spent fuel accumulated in the storage pools, creating the risk that nuclear reactors would have to be shut down. This could occur if there were insufficient room in the pool to store spent fuel and also if there were not enough space to hold the entire fuel core when certain inspections or emergencies required unloading of the reactor. In recent years, the problem has taken on special urgency. Some 8,000 metric tons of spent nuclear fuel have already accumulated, and it is projected that by the year 2000 there will be some 72,000 metric tons of spent fuel. Government studies indicate that a number of reactors could be forced to shut down in the near future due to the inability to store spent fuel.

[In addition,] permanent disposal is needed because the wastes will remain radioactive for thousands of years. * * * Problems of how and where to store nuclear wastes has engendered considerable scientific, political, and public debate There are both safety and economic aspects to the nuclear waste issue: first, if not properly stored, nuclear wastes might leak and endanger both the environment and human health; second, the lack of a long-term disposal option increases the risk that the insufficiency of interim storage space for spent fuel will lead to reactor-shutdowns, rendering nuclear energy an unpredictable and uneconomical adventure.

The California laws at issue here are responses to these concerns. In 1974, California adopted Cal.Pub.Res.Code §§ 25000-25986. The Act requires that a utility seeking to build in California any electric power generating plant, including a nuclear power plant, must apply for certification to the State Energy Resources and Conservation Commission (Energy Commission).

* * * Section 25524.1(b) provides that before additional nuclear plants may be built, the Energy Commission must determine on a case-by-case basis that there will be "adequate capacity" for storage of a plant's spent fuel rods "at the time such nuclear facility requires such . . . storage."

* * * Section 25524.2 deals with the long-term solution to nuclear wastes. This section imposes a moratorium on the certification of new nuclear plants until the Energy Commission "finds that there has been developed and that the United States through its authorized agency has approved and there exists a demonstrated technology or means for the disposal of high-level nuclear waste."

[Petitioners contend] the two sections * * * are invalid under the Supremacy Clause because they are preempted by the Atomic Energy Act. The District Court [so] held[.] The Court of Appeals [reversed, holding] the nuclear moratorium provisions of § 25524.2 were not preempted because of §§ 271 and 274(k) of the Atomic Energy Act, [which allow] states to regulate nuclear power plants "for purposes other than protection against radiation hazards." The court held that § 25524.2 was not designed to provide protection against radiation hazards, but was adopted because "uncertainties in the nuclear fuel cycle make nuclear power an uneconomical and uncertain source of energy."

[T]he Atomic Energy Act * * * does not at any point expressly require the States to construct or authorize nuclear power plants or prohibit the States from deciding * * * not to permit the construction of any further reactors. Instead, petitioners argue that the Act is intended to preserve the federal government as the sole regulator of all matters nuclear, and that § 25524.2 falls within the scope of this impliedly preempted field. But as we view the issue, Congress * * * intended that the federal government should regulate the radiological safety aspects involved in the construction and operation of a nuclear plant, but that the States retain their traditional responsibility in the field of regulating electrical utilities for determining questions of need, reliability, cost and other related state concerns.

Need for new power facilities, their economic feasibility, and rates and services, are areas that have been characteristically governed by the States.

* * * As we noted in *Vermont Yankee Nuclear Power Corp. v. NRDC*, "There is little doubt that under the Atomic Energy Act of 1954, state public utility commissions or similar bodies are empowered to make the initial decision regarding the need for power."

* * * The [Atomic Energy] Act provide[s] for licensing of private construction, ownership, and operation of commercial nuclear power reactors. * * *

The Commission, however, was not given authority over the generation of electricity itself, or over the economic question whether a particular plant should be built. [And] [i]t is almost inconceivable that Congress would have left a regulatory vacuum; the only reasonable inference is that Congress intended the states to continue to make these judgment. Any doubt that rate making and plant-need questions were to remain in state hands was removed by § 271, which provided:

> Nothing in this chapter shall be construed to affect the authority or regulations of any Federal, State or local agency with respect to the generation, sale, or transmission of electric power produced through the use of nuclear facilities licensed by the Commission . . .

[T]hus from the passage of the Atomic Energy Act in 1954 * * * to the present day, Congress has preserved the dual regulation of nuclear-powered electricity generation: the federal government maintains complete control of the safety and "nuclear" aspects of energy generation; the states exercise their traditional authority over the need for additional generating capacity, the type of generating facilities to be licensed, land use, rate-making, and the like.

* * * But deciding how § 25524.2 is to be construed and classified is a more difficult proposition. * * * Respondents * * * argue * * * that although safety regulation of nuclear plants by States is forbidden, a state may completely prohibit new construction until its safety concerns are satisfied by the federal government. We reject this line of reasoning. State safety regulation is not preempted only when it conflicts with federal law. Rather, the federal government has occupied the entire field of nuclear safety concerns, except the limited powers expressly ceded to the states. When the federal government completely occupies a given field or an

identifiable portion of it, as it has done here, the test of preemption is whether "the matter on which the state asserts the right to act is in any way regulated by the federal government," *Rice v. Santa Fe Elevator Corp.* 331 U.S. [218], at 236, 67 S.Ct. [1146] at 1155 [, 91 L.Ed. 1447 (1947)]. A state moratorium on nuclear construction grounded in safety concerns falls squarely within the prohibited field. Moreover, a state judgment that nuclear power is not safe enough to be further developed would conflict directly with the countervailing judgment of the NRC that nuclear construction may proceed notwithstanding extant uncertainties as to waste disposal.

* * * That being the case, it is necessary to determine whether there is a non-safety rationale for § 25524.2. California has maintained, and the Court of Appeals agreed, that § 25524.2 was aimed at economic problems, not radiation hazards. The California Assembly Committee On Resources, Land Use, and Energy, which proposed a package of bills including § 25524.2, reported that the waste disposal problem was "largely economic or the result of poor planning, *not* safety related" (emphasis in original). The Committee explained that the lack of a federally approved method of waste disposal created a "clog" in the nuclear fuel cycle. Storage space was limited while more nuclear wastes were continuously produced. Without a permanent means of disposal, the nuclear waste problem could become critical leading to unpredictably high costs to contain the problem or, worse, shutdowns in reactors.* * *

The Court of Appeals adopted this reading of § 25524.2 * * *.

Once a technology is selected and demonstrated, the utilities and the California Public Utilities Commission would be able to estimate costs; such cost estimates cannot be made until the federal government has settled upon the method of long-term waste disposal. * * *Therefore, we accept California's avowed economic purpose as the rationale for enacting § 25524.2. Accordingly, the statute lies outside the occupied field of nuclear safety regulation.

Petitioners' second major argument concerns federal regulation aimed at the nuclear waste disposal problem itself. It is contended that § 25524.2 conflicts with federal regulation of nuclear waste disposal, with the NRC's decision that it is permissible to continue to license reactors, notwithstanding uncertainty surrounding the waste disposal problem, and with Congress' recent passage of legislation directed at that problem. * * *

The NRC [has] concluded that, given the progress toward the development of disposal facilities and the availability of interim storage, it could continue to license new reactors. The NRC's imprimatur, however, indicates only that it is safe to proceed with such plants, not that it is economically wise to do so.

[While] the Nuclear Waste Policy Act of 1982 may convince state authorities that there is now a sufficient federal commitment to fuel storage and waste disposal that licensing of nuclear reactors may resume, and, indeed, this seems to be one of the purposes of the Act, it does not appear that Congress intended to make that decision for the states through this legislation.

[I]t is certainly possible to interpret the Act as directed at solving the nuclear waste disposal problem for existing reactors without necessarily encouraging or requiring that future plant construction be undertaken. * * *

Congress has left sufficient authority in the states to allow the development of nuclear power to be slowed or even stopped for economic reasons. * * *

Affirmed.

Justice Blackmun, with whom Justice Stevens joins, concurring in part and concurring in the judgment.

I join the Court's opinion, except to the extent it suggests that a State may not prohibit the construction of nuclear power plants if the State is motivated by concerns about the safety of such plants. * * *

Congress has occupied not the broad field of "nuclear safety concerns," but only the narrower area of how a nuclear plant should be constructed and operated to protect against radiation hazards. States traditionally have possessed the authority to choose which technologies to rely on in meeting their energy needs. Nothing in the Atomic Energy Act limits this authority, [so that] a ban on construction of nuclear power plants would be valid even if its authors were motivated by fear of a core meltdown or other nuclear catastrophe. * * *

## The Silkwood Case

The issue of state jurisdiction to impose liability for nuclear mishaps surfaced again in the *Silkwood* litigation.

In *Silkwood v. Kerr-McGee Corp.*, 464 U.S. 238, 104 S.Ct. 615, 78 L.Ed.2d 443 (1984), the plaintiff sought compensatory and punitive damage under Oklahoma law for nuclear contamination of the person, apartment and belongings of the decedent, Karen Silkwood, a workplace safety activist employed by a nuclear materials processor. The Tenth Circuit Court of Appeals, reversing a jury verdict of $10.5 million, ruled (a) her injuries resulted from her employment so the plaintiff was limited to a workers' compensation claim, and (b) punitive damages under state law amounted to state regulation of radiation and were preempted by the Atomic Energy Act. The Supreme Court reversed, 5-4, on the preemption claim, holding punitive damages not barred by the federal law. The Court ruled "there is no indication that Congress even seriously considered precluding the use of such remedies," especially since it failed to provide a federal tort remedy. Further, the existence of the Price-Anderson Act, limiting liability for major nuclear accidents, "indicates that Congress assumed that persons injured by nuclear accidents were free to utilize existing state tort law remedies." Nor, it held, do punitive damages conflict with the federal regulatory scheme.

On remand, the Court of Appeals again vacated the punitive damages, holding the jury should have been limited to considering only the property damage in setting the punitive damages but had improperly considered the personal injuries as well. 769 F.2d 1451, cert. denied 476 U.S. 1104. The suit was settled thereafter for $1.38 million. The settlement leaves unresolved not only the question whether, as the plaintiff claimed, the contamination was not in the course of employment, but also the standard of liability -- the plaintiff had argued for strict liability.

## 12. INTERNATIONAL ENVIRONMENTAL LAW

### A. BASIC PRINCIPLES

We have already seen the international dimensions of environmental law, in connection with wildlife protection, for example. In the past decade international agreements to safeguard the environment have become of major importance, raising fascinating and complex issues.

In 1972 international environmental law was a fledgling field with less than three dozen multilateral agreements.[a] Today international environmental law is arguably setting the pace for cooperation in the international community in the development of international law. There are nearly nine hundred international legal instruments that are either primarily directed to international environmental issues or contain important provisions on them. This proliferation of legal instruments is likely to continue. * * *

Before 1900 there were few multilateral or bilateral agreements concerning international environmental issues. Relevant international agreements were based on unrestrained national sovereignty over natural resources and focused primarily on boundary waters, navigation, and fishing rights along shared waterways, particularly the Rhine River and other European waterways. They did not address pollution or other ecological issues. The dramatic exception to this pattern emerged in 1909 in the United States-United Kingdom Boundary Waters Treaty, which provided in Article IV that water "shall not be polluted on either side [of the United States-Canadian border] to the injury of health or property on the other."

In the early 1900s, countries began to conclude agreements to protect commercially valuable species. These agreements include the 1902 Convention for the Protection of Birds Useful to Agriculture, the 1916 Convention for the Protection of Migratory Birds in the United States and Canada, and the Treaty for the Preservation and Protection of Fur Seals signed in 1911. Only one convention focused on wildlife more generally: the 1900 London Convention for the Protection of Wild Animals, Birds and Fish in Africa.

By the 1930s and 1940s, states recognized the importance of conserving natural resources and negotiated several agreements to protect fauna and flora generally. These include the 1933 London Convention on Preservation of Fauna and Flora in Their Natural State (focused primarily on Africa), and the 1940 Washington Convention on Nature Protection and Wild Life Preservation (focused on the Western Hemisphere). During this period, states also concluded the well known International Convention for the Regulation of Whaling, as well as other conventions concerned with ocean fisheries and birds.

---

[a] Edith Brown Weiss, *International Environmental Law: Contemporary Issues and the Emergence of a New World Order*, 81 GEO. L. J. 675 (1993). Copyright 1993. Reprinted with the permission of the publisher, Georgetown University and the *Georgetown Law Journal*, © 1993.

In the first half of this century there was little development and application of customary international norms to environmental issues. The classic Trail Smelter Arbitration between Canada and the United States, which affirmed Canada's responsibility for the damage from copper smelter fumes that transgressed the border into the state of Washington, was the notable exception. The language of the Arbitral Tribunal has been cited widely as confirming the principle that a state is responsible for environmental damage to foreign countries caused by activities within its borders, even though in this case Canada's liability for the damage was determined in the compromise establishing the Tribunal. One of the most important aspects of the Arbitration is the Tribunal's decision that if there is a threat of serious continuing harm, the state must cease the harmful conduct (which implies that damages would not be sufficient). The Tribunal required the parties to effectuate a monitoring regime to ensure that further damaging pollution did not occur. Because the Trail Smelter Arbitration is a rare example of international environmental adjudication in this early period, it has acquired an unusually important place in the jurisprudence of international environmental law.

During the 1950s and early 1960s, the international community was concerned with nuclear damage from civilian use (a by-product of the Atoms for Peace Proposal) and marine pollution from oil. Thus, countries negotiated agreements governing international liability for nuclear damage and required measures to prevent oil pollution at sea.

In the 1960s, environmental issues began to emerge within countries. Rachel Carson published her famous book *Silent Spring*,[2] and comparable books were published in European countries. In the United States, this new environmental awareness led to the adoption of the first major piece of federal environmental legislation, the National Environmental Policy Act of 1969, which initiated the environmental impact statement. In 1971 the U.S. Council on Environmental Quality and the U.S. Environmental Protection Agency were formed.

Internationally, during the 1960s, multilateral international environmental agreements increased significantly. Conventions were negotiated relating to interventions in case of oil pollution casualties, to civil liability for oil pollution damage, and to oil pollution control in the North Sea. The African Convention on the Conservation of Nature and Natural Resources was concluded in 1968.

Modern international environmental law dates to approximately 1972 when countries gathered for the United Nations Stockholm Conference on the Human Environment, and the United Nations Environment Program (UNEP) was established. Many important legal developments took place in the period surrounding the Conference, including negotiation of the Convention on International Trade in Endangered Species, the London Ocean Dumping Convention, the World Heritage Convention, and the first of the UNEP regional

---

[2] Rachel Carson, SILENT SPRING (1963).

seas conventions. Since then, there has been a rapid rise in international legal instruments concerned with the environment, to the point that we are concerned today with developing new means for coordinating the negotiation and implementation of related agreements, in particular their administrative, monitoring, and financial provisions.

Since 1970, hundreds of international environmental instruments have been concluded. Including bilateral and multilateral instruments (binding and nonbinding), there are close to nine hundred international legal instruments that have one or more significant provisions addressing the environment. * * *

The scope of international agreements has expanded significantly since 1972: from transboundary pollution agreements to global pollution agreements; from control of direct emissions into lakes to comprehensive river basin system regimes; from preservation of certain species to conservation of ecosystems; from agreements that take effect only at national borders to ones that restrain resource use and control activities within national borders, such as for world heritage's, wetlands, and biologically diverse areas. The duties of the parties to these agreements have also become more comprehensive: from undertaking research and monitoring to preventing pollution and reducing certain pollutants to specified levels. Notably, there is no example in which the provisions of earlier conventions have been weakened; rather, they have been strengthened or their scope has been expanded.

The international community is increasingly aware that it is important not only to monitor and research environmental risks, but also to reduce them. Thus states have moved from international agreements that mainly address research, information exchange, and monitoring to agreements that require reductions in pollutant emissions and changes in control technology. The Protocol on Sulphur Dioxide to the Untied Nations Economic Commission for Europe (U.N.-ECE) Convention on Long Range Transboundary Air Pollution calls for a thirty percent reduction in national annual sulphur emissions or their transboundary fluxes by 1993, and the Montreal Protocol on Substances That Deplete the Ozone Layer, including the 1990 Adjustments and Amendments, requires that chloroflurocarbons and halons, except for essential uses, be phased out by the year 2000.[b] The emphasis on preventing pollution is likely to continue as we appreciate that the capacity of our environment to absorb the byproducts of production and consumption is limited.* * *

Most of these agreements were considered impossible ten years ago; some were thought impossible only months before they were concluded. The provisions in the new agreements are generally more stringent and detailed than in previous ones, the range of subject matter broader, and the provisions for implementation and adjustment more sophisticated. This history is encouraging because it suggests that the international community's learning curve as reflected in international environmental law is surprisingly steep. This should give us hope

---

[b] See Subsection D.

that we may be able, with some success, to address the immense challenges of global environmental change and to meet the urgent need for environmentally sustainable development. * * *

As environmental consciousness expands, the practice of nations alters to comply with the new norms, which makes it easier to contend that an "international custom, as evidence of a general practice accepted as law," has emerged.[c]

There is a quartet of cases that quite usefully establishes some of the strengths, and also the weakness, of customary international law. The *Corfu Channel* case is authority for the proposition that if a nation knows that harmful effects may occur to other nations from facts within its ken and fails to disclose them, it will be liable to the nation that suffers damage.[7] In other words, every state has a duty not to knowingly allow its territory to be used for acts contrary to the rights of other states. While that principle ought not to be overworked, it is capable of wide application.

One can conceivably imagine the principle being applied to a nation that allowed the unlimited manufacture and use of chlorofluorocarbons, to the detriment of the ozone layer, even though the nation was not a party to either the Vienna Convention or the Montreal Protocol. It is not necessary to extrapolate from the principles of customary international law very far, if at all, to fit them into some of the circumstances that might arise in relation to pollution of the atmosphere.

The *Trail Smelter* arbitration, which dealt with transboundary air pollution, also has potential application to ozone and climate change.[8] To the extent that the case establishes a principle of good neighborliness, it may be applied to global environmental problems. The principle would be that no state has the right to use its territory in such a manner as to cause injury to the atmosphere by emissions when serious consequences are involved and the injury to the atmosphere is demonstrated by clear and convincing evidence. Indeed, the principle established by the case may go further than this and is certainly capable of extension.

The *Lake Lanoux* arbitration turned on the interpretation of a particular treaty, but it may establish that principle that a state has the duty to give notice when its actions may impair the environmental enjoyment of another state. A nation is not entitled to ignore the interests of another.[10] That principle can have

---

[c] Geoffrey Palmer, *New Ways to Make International Environmental Law,* 86 AM. J INT'L L. 259 (1992). Copyright 1991. Reprinted by permission from 86 AJIL 259 (1992), © The American Society of International Law.

[7] Corfu Channel (UK v. Alb.), 1949 ICJ REP. 4 (Judgment of Apr. 9). One would have supposed that the principle applied to the Chernobyl accident, but the timidity of nations with nuclear installations of their own appears to have made them leery of bringing claims.

[8] Trail Smelter (U.S. v. Can.), 3 R. INT'L ARB. AWARDS 1905 (1938 & 1941).

[10] Lake Lanoux Arbitration, 12 INT'L ARB. AWARDS 281, 315-16 (1957)***.

clear and obvious application to situations involving ozone depletion and climate change.

The *Nuclear Tests* cases, brought by Australia and New Zealand in the International Court of Justice, do not establish much, regrettably, because the Court ducked the issue.[11] Nonetheless, some legal inferences can be drawn from the decision. The burden of the complaint was that the nations were entitled to be free from the hazardous increased radiation due to fallout from the Mururoa atmosphere testing atoll. Because France ceased atmospheric testing while the case was before the Court, the judges found it unnecessary to address the issue, attributing "legal effect" to France's public undertaking to halt the testing. Press statements do not often have legal effect at international law, but this one did. The case can be used to argue that there are circumstances in which government declarations can be binding, a prospect pregnant with possibilities.* * *

But, even on the most optimistic view, customary international law can hardly be said to have sufficient scope or content to prevent damage and provide sufficient sanctions to be directed against the perpetrators of the damage when it occurs. Above all, customary international law is not a regulatory system and cannot be turned into one. Yet a regulatory system is required. It should have defined standards, monitoring, exchange of information and some prohibitions.* * *

The precautionary principle is now an important instrument for providing guidance to states and the international community in the development of international environmental law and policy in the face of scientific uncertainty, and was unanimously endorsed by the Rio Declaration.[d] The emergence of the principle reflects a shift away from the traditional approach which calls on parties to international environmental treaties, to adopt decisions which are based upon "scientific findings" or methods, or are "in the light of knowledge available at the time." Lack of full scientific certainty previously might have meant no action. * * *

The first treaty to use the term was the 1985 Vienna Convention, which was mindful of the "precautionary measures" which had already been taken at the national and international levels. By 1987 the Montreal Protocol had noted the "precautionary measures" to control emission from certain chlorofluorocarbons (CFCs) at the national and international levels and by 1990, the amendments to the Montreal Protocol provided that the parties were "determined to protect the ozone layer by taking precautionary measures to control equitably total global emissions of substances that deplete it." For the first time in a treaty, precautionary measures were expressly stated to be one of the reasons for adopting international measures.

The precautionary approach has now been used in relation to a range of environmental issues. In 1987, the Ministerial Declaration of the Second North

---

[11] Nuclear Test (Austl. v. Fr.; NZ v. Fr.), Interim Protection, 1973 ICJ REP. 99 and 135 (Orders of June 22); 1974 ICJ REP. 253 and 257 (judgments of Dec. 20).

[d] Philippe Sands, The *"Greening" of International Law: Emerging Principles and Rules*, 1 IND. J. GLOBAL LEGAL STUD. 293 (1994). 

Sea Conference accepted that "in order to protect the North Sea from possibly damaging effects of the most dangerous substances, a precautionary approach is necessary." In March 1990, at the Third North Sea Conference, the Ministers pledged to continue to apply the precautionary principle. The 1990 Bergen Ministerial Declaration on Sustainable Development in the ECE Region was the first international act to state the principle as one of general application which was linked to sustainable development. The Declaration stated that:

> In order to achieve sustainable development, policies must be based on the precautionary principle. Environmental measures must anticipate, attack and prevent the causes of environmental degradation. Where there are threats of serious or irreversible damage, lack of full scientific certainty should not be used as a reason for postponing measures to prevent environmental degradation.

Since then at least seven international treaties, two of which are of global application on environmental matters of broad concern, have adopted the precautionary principle or its underlying rationale. The 1992 Biodiversity Convention notes that "where there is a threat of significant reduction or loss of biological diversity, lack of full scientific certainty should not be used as a reason for postponing measures to avoid or minimize such a threat," and the 1992 Climate Change Convention states that:

> [Parties] should take precautionary measures to anticipate, prevent or minimize the causes of climate change and mitigate its adverse effects. Where there are threats of serious or irreversible damage, lack of full scientific certainty should not be used as a reason for postponing such measures, taking into account that policies and measures to deal with climate change should be cost effective so as to ensure global benefits at the lowest possible cost.

* * * What does the principle mean, and what status does it have in international law? * * * At the most general level, it has been understood to mean that States will agree to act carefully and with foresight when making decisions which concern activities that may have an adverse impact on the environment. A more generally accepted view is that the principle requires activities and substances which may be harmful to the environment to be regulated, and possibly prohibited, even if no conclusive or overwhelming evidence is available as to the harm or likely harm they may cause to the environment. As the Bergen Ministerial Declaration put it, "lack of full scientific certainty should not be used as a reason for postponing measures to prevent environmental degradation."

A more fundamental change would be adopted by an interpretation of the precautionary principle which would shift the burden of proof away from those who are opposing certain activities on environmental grounds and onto those who are carrying out the activities which are the subject of possible regulation. This interpretation would require polluters, and polluting states, to establish that their activities and the discharge of certain substances would not adversely or significantly affect the environment before they were granted the right to release the potentially polluting substances or carry out the proposed activity. This interpretation may also require international regulatory action, as a matter of law, where the scientific evidence suggests that lack of action may result in irreversible harm to the environment. * * *

## B. BIODIVERSITY

The term "biodiversity" is used by scientists to refer to the variety of plant and animal life on earth or in a particular ecosystem. Some areas of the globe have greater biodiversity -- more plant and animal species -- than others.[a] For example, food crop species are not uniformly distributed over the planet but are concentrated in the tropics and some of the subtropics. These areas of high food crop concentration are known as "natural diversity centers" or Vavilov Centers, after the Russian geneticist who was one of the first to attempt a systematic collection of seeds from these regions. * * * Because the glaciers of the last glacial period did not reach the equator, and our present-day major natural diversity centers lie outside the Arctic zone, experts assume that the diversity centers have never been covered with ice and have evolved uninterrupted as complex biotic centers. Other climate factors such as rain and sun patterns in equatorial regions also provide excellent growing conditions.

Vavilov theorized it was in these places of high plant genetic diversity that agriculture originated. * * *

* * * The nine major natural diversity centers are Ethiopia, the Mediterranean area, Asia Minor, Central Asia, India-Burma, China, Siam, Malaysia-Java, Mexico-Guatemala, and Peru-Ecuador-Bolivia.

[A]ny comprehensive long-term agricultural policy will need to include goals beyond those of increasing crop yields. A good policy must incorporate soil improvement and pest control, as well as population control initiatives and consumption habit reforms in order to establish more balanced and sustainable agricultural resource use. This is particularly true of policies aimed at alleviating the problem of widespread hunger within the rapidly expanding world population. The eventual tripling in human population, as projected by many demographers, would simply be incompatible with the preservation of needed natural diversity.

The World Watch Institute states that "[p]robably the most immediate threat to human welfare posed by the loss of biological diversity arises from the shrinkage of the plant gene pools available to agricultural scientists and farmers."

---

[a] June Starr & Kenneth C. Hardy, *Not by Seeds Alone: The Biodiversity Treaty and the Role for Native Agriculture*, 12 STAN. ENVTL. L.J. 85. 

The dramatic loss of plant genetic diversity means that modern farming stands to lose the fundamental building blocks needed to produce the crops of tomorrow. The ability to breed crops with higher yields and greater resistance to insects and disease will be threatened by the loss of plant genetic diversity.

For thousands of years, plant breeding has been a dynamic process as farmers saved their best seeds from each harvest to plant the next year, and local domesticated strains interbred with wild varieties growing nearby. Local farmers selected the best plants to withstand local diseases, parasites, and drought. Although this appears to be a simple method of farming by today's technologically advanced standards, traditional methods remain practical: parasites were unable to establish themselves as frequently. Damage from pests and disease is mitigated to a great extent because most pests and plant diseases are effective only against a particular genetic variety of a crop. Intercropping within the same field creates natural barriers to parasitic hosts. Also, local farmers may grow plants near other crops that may repel certain insects. Of course some parasites continue to exist, like the swarms of locusts that devour all the crops within the area in which they alight. But the effects of parasites are limited and regional. Therefore, when a crop has a broad genetic base with many existing varieties, the risk of widespread crop failure is reduced.

The tendency of modern farming is to grow genetically uniform hybrid crops over large areas of land, a practice known as monocropping. For example, 72% of the United States potato crop is comprised of only four varieties. Even more striking, only ten major food crops provide most of the world's food. Compared to fifty years ago, there are now fewer crop types and less diversity within each crop type. As a result, the risk of widespread crop failure is proportionately greater because large scale monocropping is genetically more vulnerable to insects and disease-causing organisms.

For example, many scientists believe that the underlying cause of the great Irish potato famine of the mid-nineteenth century was a narrow genetic base for the potato, resulting in most of the crop being susceptible to the fungus. *Phytophtthora infestans*. More recent crop failures include human intervention, like the widespread use of corn having T-cytoplasm making it susceptible to corn blight, which destroyed one-fifth of the U.S. corn crop in 1970.

When an insect or disease afflicts a particular crop, the modern farmer counters the risk of crop failure by contacting seed breeders, who then search for a resistant gene and breed it into the crop. But breeding for resistance after the fact is an ongoing task, because insects and disease-causing organisms generally adapt to the plant's genetic defenses within five to fifteen years. New genes must continually be found to combat the renewed attacks of insects and disease.

As the genetic pool from which to draw shrinks, the search for new genes becomes more arduous. The chance of breeding higher yield crops decreases, the risk of crop failure increases, and the prices of agricultural products rise. As gene pools become extinct, modern agriculture is put at risk, and famine and starvation of many populations becomes a distinct threat. * * * Loss of ecosystems is recognized as a major threat not merely to our quality of life, but to human survival itself. A major component of this threat to our survival is the effect that the loss of genetic variety among plant species will have on modern agriculture. The background gene pool for all of the foods produced by modern agriculture is comprised of landraces (traditional farmer plant varieties) and cultivars (modern cousins of landraces). When modern crops are threatened by drought, pests, fungi, and other destructive forces, biologists and plant breeders look to cultivars and ancient landraces for genetic material in order to build up crop resistance to such threats. But this biological arsenal is being rapidly depleted. Most landraces are found in tropical and subtropical zones outside the temperate climates of Europe and North America. Many of these landraces have been, or are being, extinguished because of economic development, pollution, and population increase, and because farmers in the developing world are turning to modern hybrids instead of relying upon their traditional methods of open pollination and genetic selection. Furthermore, the increasing rate of extinction of wild plant species (uncultivated plants related to landraces) results in the irreversible loss of genetic resources that may someday be of immense value to agriculture, biology, medicine, and industry.

*In situ* preservation of plant genetic diversity is the best guarantee of adequate genetic material for modern farming. *Ex situ* preservation and market mechanisms, while complimentary to *in situ* efforts, are not adequate given the great number and variety of plant species. *In situ* preservation also allows crop varieties and wild landraces to evolve over time. *In situ* preservation can best be accomplished by encouraging traditional farming communities to grow local crops. This entails supporting native agriculture at the grass roots level, providing scientific and cultural assessments of plant genetic diversity, and being sensitive to local level farming techniques and cultural practices.

Traditionally, scientists have been able to roam the globe collecting samples of plant and other materials in the spirit of "free scientific inquiry," and for the benefit of the scientific and world community. Plant research for modern farming has taken place against this backdrop. Until recently, biologists and others freely operated under this regime; much of their research, however, has been channeled toward commercial agricultural activity, neglecting the villages and regions from which the samples were collected.

Developing countries are now challenging this free flow regime for several reasons. First, almost all modern food crops originated in developing nations of the southern hemisphere whose plant genetic resources were used in the development of the modern crop variety. These nations in turn buy modern crop varieties from companies located in technologically advanced countries in the northern hemisphere. Many developing countries consider this practice fundamentally unfair. They claim they are in effect buying back what they freely gave up. But this is a simplified argument that neglects the costs of the money and labor expended in research and development; few of the seeds and cultivars collected actually prove useful. Second, developed countries use patents and licenses derived from intellectual property rights to restrict access to their developed plant varieties. Developing countries want reimbursement for their input since no such protection exists for raw plant genetic material.

The phrase *ex situ* generally means "off site" or "off location." *Ex situ* preservation refers to the effort to preserve plant life outside of its original area of growth using plant repositories, botanical gardens, seed banks, and "grow outs." Since the age of discovery, sailors, travelers, adventurers, and government officials have collected plants, seeds and bulbs from around the world and transported them to their home countries.

[But] available technology limits what seed banks may preserve. Seeds that respond well only under particular weather and soil conditions may be difficult to store. For example, many types of seeds must be grown out frequently, and cannot be stored for more than three to five years. [And] plant evolution does not occur in seed banks. Plants possess their valuable genetic characteristics today because they evolved over the centuries, naturally and through cultivation, but this process is halted when the seeds are not allowed to grow. Fourth, funding to maintain seed banks has been consistently inadequate. Finally, even if such funding were available at adequate levels, it would be very risky for the success of modern farming and the world's food supply to depend on an artificial setting that may fall victim to accidents, misuse or political pressures.

The Preamble to the Biodiversity Convention recognizes that "*in situ* conservation of ecosystems and natural habitats and the maintenance and recovery of viable populations of species in their natural surroundings," is crucial to maintaining biological diversity. This emphasis on maintaining food stocks in their natural settings is a relatively new approach by the United Nations and developed countries to preserving biological diversity. *Ex situ* methods may assure the availability of a number of gene sources, but the risks of *ex situ* maintenance include high costs, underfunding, electrical failure, political manipulation, and the threat of regional conflicts. * * * Article 8 calls for Contracting Parties (i.e., signatories) to determine areas where biological diversity is especially important and needs to be protected, and to establish guidelines to manage these protected areas. * * *

Some authors have criticized attempts to maintain traditional agro-economic systems in developing countries, stating that they are socially and economically impractical. Even if *in situ* conservation was possible, they argue, setting aside protected areas would relegate some farmers to a state of poverty, because traditional varieties often do not produce the high yields and substantial income that hybrid crops do. Lastly, plant breeding companies do not trust traditional farmers to continue to provide "cheap" access to seeds and cultivars.

It is true that the technological advancements which accompany development programs are daunting. These criticisms of *in situ* conservation are important, but *ex situ* conservation efforts alone are inadequate. Seeds, cultivars, and ancient landraces grown *in situ* must be actively preserved as a "safety net" because of faulty cold storage facilities, shifts in governmental funding priorities, crop failures or other catastrophes. A narrow genetic base may be the most expedient and practical way for plant breeding companies to obtain uniform high-yielding seeds. But this method ignores long-term crop evolution. According to one expert, "[t]here is nothing biologically unsound about breeding for high yields *** [but] it is unthinkable not to preserve and maintain the ready reserves for genetic diversity that still exist in native agriculture for future plant breeding needs."

Even if *ex situ* sources were not vulnerable to financial, political and natural disasters, evolutionary growth is not possible without *in situ* preservation. *Ex situ* gene banks can only accommodate a limited supply of plant germplasm representing only a fraction of the huge variety of wild species. The evolution of traditional varieties in the wild offers many advantages: they often survive better than modern hybrids in adverse conditions, and do not need the technical and chemical support of modern hybrids. * * *

## Notes

How should futures conventions on biodiversity deal with these issues? Should the laws relating to patents be amended to permit the patenting of seeds? If a native plant has important medicinal or other value, how should the revenue derived from it be divided? Is the native country entitled to a share? Would it be under present law?

In some countries, such as Costa Rica, pharmaceutical manufacturers are buying or leasing rain forest, agreeing to preserve it in exchange for a major share of any earnings from drugs they develop from plants located there. Is this a fair approach? Population increases compel farmers in less developed countries to destroy rainforest in order to use the land for agriculture or fuel. How can this process be reduced, or its impacts reduced?

One important mechanism consists of debt-for-nature swaps. Institutions buy the debt of less developed countries (LDCs), at a discount. In exchange, the LDC agrees to maintain the rain forest or other environmentally valuable resources intact. Why is this solution encountering resistance at times?

## C. GLOBAL WARMING

If global warming were to occur in the future as projected by the computer models of climate, major disruptions would take place in many aspects of our environment.[a] Sea level rise and changes in the patterns of rainfall and temperature in land might lead to massive destruction of many kinds of ecosystems. Many species would become threatened or endangered. Legally protected natural areas would be threatened by inundation or would become inappropriate habitats for the organisms they were meant to protect. Fresh water

---

[a] DANIEL B. BOTKIN, *Global Warming: What It Is, What Is Controversial About It, and What We Might Do in Response to It.* 9 UCLA JOURNAL OF ENVIRONMENTAL LAW & POLICY 119 (1991).

would become an even scarcer resource than it is today, while salt water would intrude inland. Coastal wetlands, caught between the rising sea and housing developments, could become even rarer than they are today.

Increases in the need for water in agriculture and urban use would conflict with the maintenance of natural areas. Effects would not be limited to natural ecosystems, but would affect agriculture, commercial forestry and fisheries, as well as outdoor recreation. Urban and suburban settlements and industrial complexes would be affected. Settlements near the ocean shore might be undercut or flooded as the sea level rises, raising questions or responsibility and liability. * * *

Global warming refers to a variety of complex climatic changes that would accompany a rapid increase in the ecoconcentration of certain gases in the atmosphere known as greenhouse gases. These gases are: water vapor, carbon dioxide, methane, nitrous oxide, and CFCs (chloro-fluoro-carbons). * * * These gases are small molecules that are transparent to visible light, but opaque to some longer wavelengths known as infrared radiation (also sometimes called informally "heat radiation"). * * *

The analogy of the greenhouse is helpful in understanding the effect of greenhouse gases on the Earth's atmospheric temperature. The glass of a greenhouse is transparent to visible light and opaque to infrared light. Therefore, much of the incoming visible light from the sun passes through the glass and warms the interior surfaces. The surfaces in the greenhouse radiate in the infrared, which the glass then absorbs. The glass becomes warmer and radiates in the infrared both up into the air outside the greenhouse and back down into the greenhouse. The energy reradiated warms the interior of the greenhouse. Greenhouse gases in the Earth's atmosphere have the same effect as the glass in a greenhouse. The gases allow visible light to reach and heat the surface, and absorb and reradiate the infrared energy emitted from the Earth's surface. Another reason that a greenhouse is warmer than the outside is that the walls and roof prevent convective loss of heat. * * *

Scientists generally agree that the concentration of greenhouse gases in the atmosphere is increasing[, due] primarily to human activities. The increase in carbon dioxide is attributed to burning of fossil fuels and to land clearing, especially of forests and soils, especially when these occur in tropical areas that are among the world's largest remaining storehouses of organic matter. CFCs are manufactured gases. Their buildup in the atmosphere is the result of industrial and residential use of these gases, primarily in refrigeration and as propellants in spray cans. * * *

The controversies about global warming have to do with how the biosphere as a whole will respond to an increase in the concentration of greenhouse gases and how these increases will change the entire temperature and precipitation characteristics of the biosphere.

Once crucial controversy has to do with the effect of global warming on water vapor. If the Earth's surface were to warm, the rate of water evaporation would increase. Lakes, rivers, and oceans would evaporate more water, as would forests, grasslands and farms. There would be more water vapor in the atmosphere than at present. The controversy is whether this additional evaporated water would increase or decrease the Earth's average atmospheric temperature. If the water remained as vapor, it would act as additional greenhouse gas and lead to a further warming of the Earth. * * *

Rapid climate change would lead to changes in vegetation over wide areas. For example, rapid changes in temperature and rainfall would favor shorter-lived grasses as forests would decline over large areas. Vegetation can affect the atmosphere in four ways that can in turn affect weather and climate. Changes in vegetation affect how much light is reflected, how much water is evaporated from the surface, how fast winds flow at the surface, and how much carbon is removed annually from the atmosphere. If global warming occurs, changes in vegetation might cause positive or negative feedbacks, further increasing or compensating for the greenhouse effect. How these changes would in turn affect climate is not well understood.

[I]f global warming were to occur, a variety of consequences would follow. It would lead to increases in temperatures that would be especially pronounced in mid-latitudes. Drier soil conditions would affect agriculture, forests, grasslands, and agricultural and urban water demand. An increase in the variability of climate could cause increases in severe droughts on one hand and increases in episodes of severe storms and flooding on the other. A rise in sea level resulting from the melting of polar ice and thermal expansion of water would affect coastal resources including fisheries, wetlands, and human habitation along coasts. Changes in climate could threaten endangered species and raise new concerns about national laws and international agreements affecting biological conservation. * * *

Computer aided projections suggest that global warming may have surprisingly rapid and severe effects on forests of mid and high latitudes, with some forests projected to change within the next decade or two. If global warming were to occur as projected by global circulation models, forests in many areas would undergo rapid and severe changes, beginning with a die-back of existing species, followed, where conditions were appropriate, by an influx of species from drier and warmer habitats. If this were to happen there would be major impacts on all uses and benefits of the forests. Such effects could become noticeable by the turn of the century. * * *

Global warming would lead to an increase in the rate of sea level rise for two reasons. First, as the oceans warm, their waters would expand. Second, as the air temperature rises, glaciers would melt, increasing the amount of water in the oceans. Estimates of the potential rise in the sea level vary widely, but reasonable range is the one reported by EPA to be between a 0.5 to 2 meters (roughly 2 to 7 feet) sea level rise by year 2100. The sea level rise would affect both natural and developed areas. According to the analysis by the EPA, a one meter rise would inundate between 25 to 80% of the United States' coastal wetlands and between 40 and 73% could be lost, as could 5,000 to 10,000 square miles of unprotected shoreland. It has been estimated that a rise in sea level of one-half meter could inundate one-third of coastal wetlands in the United States. Remaining wetlands would suffer changes in salinity. Widespread reduction in existing wetlands could lead to declines in waterfowl, with effects on sport hunting and on the conservation of endangered species.

Before human settlement and global warming, a sea level rise would have occurred slowly enough to allow species of wetland vegetation to become established in new inland marshes. The speed with which global warming induced sea level rise might occur might overwhelm natural migration rates of coastal vegetation. In addition, today, the area inland is typically covered with the concrete or is drained, filled, and subject to other intense land uses. For example, in California, approximately 90% of coastal wetlands have been destroyed by development and other human activities. The remaining 10% lies generally between the ocean and highly developed areas. With a rapid rise in sea level, many of these wetlands now protected under Section 404 of the Clean Water Act of 1997[b] would be inundated. * * *

Global warming would lead to an increase in water demand and a decrease in available water. * * * [P]rojections* * * suggest that rising temperatures will increase water evaporation from forests, grasslands, and cropland to such an extent that the water lost from soils would exceed the amount added from additional rainfall. As a results, much of the land will become drier. The effects of a drier climate will be felt in commercial as well as agricultural and urban water use. Surface runoff would decrease, leading to a decline in stream and river flow and a decline in lake levels. This could lead to more frequent episodes of river water levels too low for transport of goods by boats as occurred recently on the Mississippi River. Conflicts over water resources for agricultural and urban use would be especially acute. * * *

The EPA forecasts dire consequences for crops if global warming occurs. For example, in California, crop yields could be reduced by 20 to 40%, depending on crop type and location. Corn production is estimated to decrease between 14 and 31%; tomatoes between 5 and 15%. In the warmer parts of the southeast of the United States, agricultural yields might decline by as much as 91% and between 10 and 57% of the farmland might be taken out of production. * * *

Present projections of impacts suggest that global warming would have severe effects that might become evident soon after the turn of the century. * * *

There are two dangers which lawmakers must avoid: the first is paying too little attention to the possibility of global warming; the second is treating the concern with global warming as a fad and developing superficial responses in the interest of political expediency rather than from a basis in careful consideration of the impacts. * * *

---

[b] See Chapter 7(B).

If we want to attempt to slow global warming, then we need to begin to consider our options at once. * * * For example, [l]egislation should * * * be directed at reducing the net atmospheric concentration of greenhouse gases. Such legislation could include programs in energy conservation, use of alternative energy, and prudent, large scale tree planting. Additional legal responses are needed to arrange for and lighten the effects of global warming. For example, modification is needed of laws concerning protection of natural areas and conservation of biological diversity. We need to allow for adjustment of habitats including park and reserve boundaries and provide migration corridors. Land use and development regulations should be reconsidered, especially in areas at high risk of change during global warming, such as coastal areas. Legislation will also be needed to deal with increasing demands for a decreasing supply of water. The key question for implementing any of the legal responses is the timing. What work should begin now before clear evidence that global warming is upon us? The potential impacts of global warming seem severe enough to warrant immediate, careful consideration of the possible legal responses. * * *

## Notes

The 1992 Climate Change Convention, adopted at the Rio Environmental Conference, provides:

* * * 2. (a) Each of [the] Parties shall adopt national policies and take corresponding measures on the mitigation of climate change, by limiting its anthropogenic [*i.e.*, created by humankind] emissions of greenhouse gases and protecting and enhancing its greenhouse gas sinks and reservoirs. These policies and measures will demonstrate that developed countries are taking the lead in modifying longer-term trends in anthropogenic emissions consistent with the objective of the Convention, recognizing that the return by the end of the present decade to earlier levels of anthropogenic emissions of carbon dioxide and other greenhouse gases not controlled by the Montreal Protocol [on the ozone layer (see Part D)] would contribute to such modifications and taking into account the differences in these Parties' starting points and approaches, economic structures and resource bases, the need to maintain strong and sustainable economic growth, available technologies and other individual circumstances, as well as the need for equitable and appropriate contributions by each of these Parties to the global effort regarding that objective. * * *

(d) The Conference of the Parties shall, at its first session, review the adequacy of subparagraphs (a) and (b) above.[a] Such review shall be carried out in the light of the best available scientific information and assessment on climate change and its impacts, as well as relevant technical, social and economic information. Based on this review, the Conference of the Parties shall take

---

[a] Subparagraph (b) requires countries to submit detailed information.

appropriate action, which may include the adoption of amendments to the commitments in subparagraphs (a) and (b) above. * * *

3. The developed country Parties * * * shall provide new and additional financial resources to meet the agreed full costs incurred by developing country Parties in complying with their obligations * * *. They shall also provide such financial resources, including for the transfer of technology, needed by the developing country Parties to meet the agreed full incremental costs of implementing [such] measures. * * *

Notes

The 1997 Kyoto Agreement implementing this Convention calls for significant reductions in carbon dioxide emissions from the 1990 levels - - 8% by the European Union by 2010, 7% by the United States, and 6% by Japan. However, the United States Senate failed to ratify this treaty, and the George W. Bush administration has essentially disavowed it. Nonetheless, Kyoto is to take effect among the countries that signed it, including Europe, Russia, and Japan, now that countries producing 55% of carbon emissions have approved it, which occurred with Russia's approval in November 2004.

Should these reductions take into account deforestation, or credit countries with forests (which absorb carbon dioxide)? What long-range solutions to the global warming problem should be implemented? How does this bear on the clean air and energy-use concerns voiced earlier in this book?

## D. STRATOSPHERIC OZONE DEPLETION

A diffuse layer of ozone in the upper reaches of our atmosphere has shielded life on the planet from ultraviolet radiation for millions of years.[a] A seemingly unrelated event in 1928 was the development of chlorofluorocarbons (CFCs) by Dupont chemists. These extremely stable and consequently long-lived substances were hailed as technological triumphs. [F]or almost fifty years after the discovery of CFCs, the community was ignorant of the threat CFCs posed and, as a consequence, focused only upon the benefits they accorded. CFCs came to be used in a multitude of ways, and amount and types of CFCs utilized grew dramatically, first after the World War and again in the late 1960s.

In 1974 however, two scientists postulated that these stable substances, for the most part, ultimately reached the stratosphere; that once there, they finally became exposed to the ultraviolet radiation from which they had been shielded by the ozone layer; that this highly energetic radiation broke down the CFC molecule, releasing chlorine atoms; and that such chlorine atoms then served as catalysts in reactions which broke down ozone molecules. It was estimated that each chlorine atom released could destroy 100,000 ozone molecules, ultimately

[a] David D. Caron, *Protection of the Stratospheric Ozone Layer and the Structure of International Environmental Law Making*. 14 HASTINGS INT'L & COMP. L. REV. 755 (1991). Copyright 1991.

depleting the ozone layer and exposing the planet to increased harmful ultraviolet radiation. * * *

Public debate regarding regulation initially focused upon the use of CFCs as propellants in aerosols, a use that clearly resulted in release of CFCs into the atmosphere. Not without difficulty, a number of states, including the United States, Canada, and Sweden, moved toward national bans on such aerosols. These efforts at unilateral action added new characteristics to the debate. [T]he concern arose in U.S. governmental circles that these unilateral efforts might be counterproductive in that the actions of a few states took pressure off other states to do likewise. In other words, there was a free rider problem. * * *

Even as the national debates proceeded, the groundwork for an international approach was laid[, resulting in] the Vienna Conference in March 1985, which ultimately adopted a framework convention. * * *

Even as work proceeded in anticipation of a second meeting to adopt a protocol, two important trends were occurring. First a British research group in May 1985 announced that huge losses in Antarctic ozone had occurred in the springs of 1982, 1983, and 1984. By late summer 1985 American satellite measurements, free of certain previous interpretational errors, confirmed the British findings.

[Second,] the major producers of CFCs had come to believe that environmentally safe substitutes for CFCs existed, and that it was for each of them in their individual interest to be the first to develop and offer such substitutes. Although it was thought that such substitutes would be several times more expensive than CFCs, it was also thought that there would be a market for them in a world that called for limits on the use of CFCs. Simultaneously, numerous large users of CFCs moved to eliminate their reliance on such substances.

For these reasons, the Montreal meeting was quite different from the one held only two years earlier in Vienna in that virtually all of the interested parties were now in agreement that some amount of phased reductions was appropriate. Thus, even though the final report of the international study of the Antarctic hole was not yet released, a Protocol to the Vienna Convention calling for a fifty percent reduction in the production and consumption of specified CFCs over an approximately ten year period was adopted in Montreal in September, 1987.

[P]lanning for adjustment and amendment [of the Montreal Protocol] began almost immediately. * * * Of particular importance at this time, although less publicly dramatic than the Antarctic ozone hole, was the release of a study by the U.S. Environmental Protection Agency asserting that even assuming one hundred percent global participation in the Protocol, the presence of chlorine in the stratosphere would, by the year 2075, increase by a factor of three. * * *

By the opening of the London Meeting in June 1990, the negotiating parties were in agreement not merely on accelerating the phased reductions, but on phasing out entirely the substances specified by the Montreal Protocol [by] the end of the year 2000[.]

## Notes

This agreement has been effectively implemented. Production, use and trade in CFCs as aerosol propellants has been mostly halted, and CFCs and related products in air conditioning and refrigeration are likewise being phased out.

Should the industrialized countries furnish financial assistance to developing countries in eliminating CFCs, carbon dioxide emissions and other harmful substances? Should reductions apply equally to industrialized and developing countries? Which have a greater responsibility to curb these emissions?

TABLE OF CASES

# TABLE OF AUTHORITIES

# INDEX

Made in the USA
Las Vegas, NV
19 January 2022